EATING DISORDERS AND OBESITY

EATING DISORDERS AND OBESITY

A Comprehensive Handbook

Edited by
KELLY D. BROWNELL
CHRISTOPHER G. FAIRBURN

Foreword by **Paul E. Garfinkel**

THE GUILFORD PRESS
New York   London

Library of Congress Cataloging-in-Publication Data
Eating disorders and obesity : a comprehensive handbook /
    edited by Kelly D. Brownell, Christopher G. Fairburn.
        p. cm.
    Includes bibliographical references and index.
    ISBN 0-89862-850-4
    1. Eating disorders.   2. Obesity.   I. Brownell, Kelly D.
II. Fairburn, Christopher G.
    [DNLM: 1. Eating Disorders. 2. Obesity. 3. Body Weight.
WM 175 E14618 1995]
RC552.E18E2825 1995
616.85'26—dc20
DNLM/DLC
for Library of Congress   94-45037
                                                              CIP

To my parents, Arnold and Margaret,
my wife, Mary Jo,
and my children, Matthew, Kevin, and Kristy

K.D.B.

To my parents, Ernest and Margaret,
my wife, Susan,
and my children, Guy and Sarah

C.G.F.

FOREWORD

The relationship of eating and weight regulation to emotional and physical well being has fascinated scientific thinking for centuries. In almost every culture and religion, attitudes and customs to the emaciated or the obese are discernible, as are rituals and taboos regarding foods, many of which have been thought to have specific relationships to cognitive, affective, or behavioral functions. Interest in these subjects has peaked in the last 20 years as obesity and the eating disorders, anorexia nervosa and bulimia nervosa, have assumed an increased importance in the clinical arena. One-third of the American people are now obese, up from 25% just 15 years ago. Serious forms of the eating disorders affect 2% of the female population, and more mild variants are probably five times as common. Morbidity and mortality associated with these states is considerable. More scholars and clinicians have been devoting their attention and energies to these disorders, their causes, interventions, and strategies for prevention; and more scholarly and sophisticated publications have been appearing in recent years, but there has been no attempt to bring them all together in one comprehensive book.

This volume is welcome and has been long overdue. It is devoted to a comprehensive and current review of all aspects of obesity and the eating disorders—including the interface of these with factors affecting weight regulation. Drs. Kelly Brownell and Christopher Fairburn have solicited chapters from the major leaders in the fields of psychiatry, psychology, metabolism, physiology, nutrition, pharmacology, and surgery and have compiled a remarkable set of chapters covering every major area of contemporary concern. It sets a very high standard, one which I hope will be maintained in future editions of this important volume.

More and more in recent years, people have come to accept a multidimensional framework for understanding and approaching obesity and the eating disorders. These views reflect the complexity and variety of factors involved in the pathogenesis, course, and comorbidities of these disorders. However, these theories do not permit a view that "anything goes." More and more, the field has demanded and been backed by solid empirical findings. The contributors to this volume have reflected this high standard toward empiricism in their comments here.

The Preface to this volume reviews the purpose and rationale for a comprehensive textbook at this time—as such it sets the stage. Section I on the regulation of eating and weight naturally covers such factors as genetic influences and physiological, psychological, and energy related factors. It also covers specific subjects such as pregnancy, cigarette smoking, and age, each as they relate to weight regulation. Section II focuses on the importance of dieting in our world today; social and cultural influences and their relation to body image and the eating disorders are covered in some detail, as is the entire controversy over dieting itself. Section III highlights the issue of measurement and covers everything from assessments of body energy stores to food intake, energy expenditure, and measures of psychopathology. Sections IV through VII cover all aspects of the eating disorders including history, clinical features, theories of pathogenesis and complications, as well as detailed views on approaches to treatments. Sections VIII and IX cover obesity in a similar fashion.

This book contains the most current information on all aspects of eating disorders and obesity so that professionals with clinical or research questions in this area will have the critical information at hand in one volume. Students will find this invaluable.

However, there is a further benefit from this volume. By treating these disorders in such a clear, eclectic, and scientific fashion, this volume will continue to help reduce the stigma associated with these disorders. Many in our society take a moralistic stance to the obese and those with an eating disorder. They blame and criticize the sufferers for their illness. Or our society blames those closest to them, and here we have the Casablanca syndrome, where we round up the usual suspects. It is considered to be entirely the mother's fault or the family's fault. Or our society is embarrassed by those with eating disorders and obesity and sends them off to hidden-away places. Alternatively, we as a society can accept with compassion the obese and those with anorexia and bulimia nervosa as we do those with any other type of pain and anguish, with an effort to better understand and help them.

This volume presents a remarkable array of up-to-date information combining the latest scientific knowledge with humanistic concern. Both the editors and contributors have done their parts in producing an excellent, useful, and valuable book.

PAUL E. GARFINKEL
Toronto, Ontario

PREFACE

TOWARD INTEGRATING TWO FIELDS

This book has two goals. The first is to strengthen connections between the eating disorders and obesity fields. For many years we have been concerned at their separation—separate books, journals, conferences, and experts. Few individuals, either clinicians or researchers, straddle both fields. Yet, as we will discuss, eating disorders and obesity are intimately related. It is our hope that by bringing together in one volume a concise account of knowledge in the two fields, we will foster their integration.

The second goal is to provide those who work in the two fields a useful and unusual resource—a book that contains authoritative accounts by acknowledged world experts on all the main topics of relevance to eating disorders and obesity. Hence the distinctive form and content of the book, as discussed below.

The regrettable separation of the eating disorders and obesity fields is due in part to their history (see Chapters 25, 26, and 66). The fields have different emphases, with the obesity field being dominated by medical perspectives and concerns about physiology and health risk, and the eating disorders field having stronger roots in psychology, psychiatry, and the social sciences. As a consequence, people working in these fields often have different training and interests, approach issues such as treatment in a different way, and interact far less than is ideal. Yet there are many issues of relevance that are common to the two areas. Several examples illustrate this point.

First, the basic physiology of hunger and satiety has been studied in great detail (see Section I), but most often in the context of regulatory behavior, physiological psychology, and obesity. Despite the obvious importance of these factors to food intake and weight regulation, relatively little attention has been paid to these matters as they relate to eating disorders. It is possible, for instance, that disruption in the physiological processes governing satiety may contribute to binge eating and that the act of binge eating may itself affect normal satiety signals (see Chapter 43).

A second example is body image. Again, considerable work has been done on body image, but in this case in connection with eating disorders (see Chapter 64). The topic is also of great importance to the obesity field but has remained relatively ignored there. Among the questions to be answered are the following: (1) What is the nature of the core body image disturbance in obesity, if indeed there is one? (2) Does body image disturbance precede or result from weight gain? (3) Does the age at which weight gain occurs affect body image? (4) Do some obese people lose weight and keep it off yet still have a body image disturbance?

A third area of common ground is the issue of binge eating. Binge eating, the cardinal feature of bulimia nervosa, and present in some patients with anorexia nervosa, is now recognized to be a problem in up to one-quarter of those seeking treatment for obesity (see Chapter 78). It has become increasingly clear that obese persons who binge eat are an important subgroup of the obese population. They show distinct clinical features and possibly a worse response to treatment for obesity (see Chapters 78 and 94).

Another link between the two areas is etiological in nature. There is evidence that vulnerability to obesity, through either personal or family history, is a specific risk factor for the development of bulimia nervosa (see Chapter 35). There is also evidence that the presence of such a history predicts poor outcome in the long term. How vulnerability to obesity increases the risk of developing bulimia nervosa is a key research question.

An issue that threatens to divide the two fields is dieting. For the eating disorders, dieting is a common behavioral precursor and a prominent clinical feature (see Chapters 16, 27, and 35), while for obesity, dieting is the potential solution to a massive public health problem (see Chapters 67, 71, and 99). A division between the fields has become evident in the past several years, with articles and books calling for a moratorium on dieting and claiming that it is never effective and does more harm than good (see Chapter 17). The resolution depends on an open and lively debate that is possible only if interaction occurs across the disciplines.

FORM AND CONTENT OF THE BOOK

The word "comprehensive" appears in the subtitle of this book for good reason—the second of our two goals was to create a text that covers all the major issues in the eating disorders and obesity fields. A good therapist would tell us that we set ourselves an unreasonable task and were doomed to disappointment. Yet we believed this goal was worth aspiring to, and we hope that to a large extent it has been realized.

We were also committed to producing an authoritative book. With this in mind, once we had settled on its content, we approached the leading expert on each topic and, with few exceptions, each agreed enthusiastically to contribute. These experts were issued this challenge: to provide a succinct yet comprehensive account of his/her area, highlighting what is known and not known.

Somewhat unusually, the authors were asked not to include references. This was to free them to provide a clear synthesis of information without having to provide a lengthy exposition of specific studies. However, each chapter is accompanied by a section titled "Further Reading," in which up to 10 key sources are listed and annotated so readers can seek additional information if they wish.

The book is divided into nine sections. Sections I, II, and III contain 22 chapters on topics that cut across the eating disorders and obesity fields. A reader progressing from the beginning to the end of the book will be grounded first in issues of fundamental importance across fields and only then will encounter information specific to the two fields. We are firm in our conviction that these 22 chapters provide essential information, and that by drawing from basic science, professionals are in the best position to develop approaches for treatment and prevention.

Section I is on "Regulation of Eating and Weight." Processes of energy intake and expenditure, peripheral and central control of eating and weight, and genetic influences on shape and weight are discussed. The influence of pregnancy, aging, weight cycling, and cigarette smoking on eating and weight are examples of the overriding issues covered in this section.

Where Section I provides basic biological science, the focus of Section II on "Dieting and Body Image," is on the basic social science perspective. It is well known that social variables are associated with risk for developing both obesity and eating disorders. These chapters examine that risk, discuss mechanisms by which the risk leads to disorders in some individuals, and consider the individual–environment interaction as a key variable that crosses fields.

Section III, on "Measurement," includes chapters that discuss research and clinical methods for assessing body composition, energy intake, energy expenditure, physical activity, and eating disorder psychopathology. Again, these topics are relevant to both fields.

In Sections IV–VII, attention turns to the eating disorders. Section IV is on "Classification, Clinical Characteristics, and History," and Section V deals with "Epidemiology, Etiology, and Course." Chapters in Section IV focus on the history and clinical features of the eating disorders and their relationships to other conditions. In Section V, chapters focus on genetic, social, and family variables; descriptive epidemiology; and the clinical course of eating disorders.

Sections VI and VII cover the "Physiological and Medical Aspects" and "Treatment" of eating disorders. Basic physiology, medical complications, and medical management are discussed in Section VI. In Section VII, the array of treatment approaches that have been used is the focus, along with the settings in which they have been applied. As with many disorders, treatments ranging from psychoanalysis to pharmacotherapy are used for eating disorders. These are reviewed critically, so the reader is in a position to see each in the context of supporting research and clinical management.

The final two sections of the book, Sections VIII and IX, cover obesity. Section VIII, on the "Scope, Consequences, and Physiology of Obesity," contains 16 chapters on the definition, prevalence, medical and psychosocial effects, and key issues in understanding obesity, from molecular biology to binge eating. In keeping with our philosophy that fundamental issues and basic science hold the key to developing treatment, this section precedes the section on treatment.

Section IX highlights the complexity of treating and preventing obesity. No longer are obesity experts complacent in naming one approach as the "treatment of choice." Integration of knowledge in exercise physiology, nutrition, psychology, and medicine is a clear mandate for the field. The chapters in Section IX provide an excellent review of the many areas relevant to treatment.

A FINAL NOTE

We vowed to make this book timely. This was a challenge, given the large number of contributors, but we established and met an aggressive schedule, due mainly to the dedicated efforts of our colleagues. We recognize that the eating disorders and obesity fields are changing rapidly and that up-to-date information is essential to good clinical work, teaching, training, and research. Even as the ink dries on this volume, we are thinking ahead to a second edition. Thus, readers are encouraged to contact us with ideas for improving this book.

We hope that in bringing together the material in this volume we have produced a useful and comprehensive text. By ensuring that the chapters are brief yet authoritative, our hope is that the reader can, in short order, be exposed to state-of-the-art information on the great majority of topics in the two areas.

We are grateful for the dedicated efforts of the people who worked with us to make this book possible. The chapter authors, with schedules as complex as ours, were kind in sharing their time and knowledge. In addition, thanks are due to Melissa Napolitano and Jennifer Hoffman of Yale and Jacqui Carter of Oxford, for their help with the editing process. C.G.F. also wishes to acknowledge the personal support of the Wellcome Trust.

We hope readers are as stimulated by reading this book as we were by editing it.

KELLY D. BROWNELL
Yale University

CHRISTOPHER G. FAIRBURN
University of Oxford

CONTRIBUTORS

Suzanne Abraham, PhD, Department of Obstetrics and Gynaecology, University of Sydney, Australia

W. Stewart Agras, MD, Department of Psychiatry and Behavioral Sciences, Stanford University School of Medicine, Stanford, California

Ann L. Albright, PhD, Department of Nutrition, University of California, Davis, California

Arnold E. Andersen, MD, Department of Psychiatry, University of Iowa School of Medicine, Iowa City, Iowa

Reubin Andres, MD, Gerontology Research Center, National Institute on Aging, Baltimore, Maryland

Richard L. Atkinson, MD, Departments of Medicine and Nutritional Sciences, University of Wisconsin, Madison, Wisconsin

Hinrich Bents, PhD, Christoph Dornier Center for Clinical Psychology, Tibusstr, Munster, Germany

Pierre J. V. Beumont, MSc, MPhil, FRCP(E), FRACP, FRANZCP, FRCPsych, Department of Psychiatry, University of Sydney; Department of Psychiatry, Royal Prince Alfred Hospital; Anorexia and Bulimia Nervosa Unit, Lynton Hospital, Sydney, Australia

Per Björntorp, MD, PhD, Department of Heart and Lung Diseases, Sahlgren's Hospital, University of Göteborg, Sweden

George L. Blackburn, MD, PhD, Nutrition/Metabolism Laboratory, Department of Surgery, New England Deaconess Hospital, Harvard Medical School, Boston, Massachusetts

Steven N. Blair, PED, Division of Epidemiology and Clinical Applications, Cooper Institute for Aerobics Research, Dallas, Texas

John E. Blundell, PhD, Department of Psychology, University of Leeds, United Kingdom

Claude Bouchard, PhD, Physical Activity Sciences Laboratory, Laval University, Québec, Canada

Kelly D. Brownell, PhD, Departments of Psychology and Epidemiology and Public Health, Yale Center for Eating and Weight Disorders, Yale University, New Haven, Connecticut

Rachel Bryant-Waugh, BSc, MSc, DPhil, Department of Psychological Medicine, Great Ormond Hospital for Children, London, United Kingdom

Peter J. Cooper, DPhil, Department of Psychology, University of Reading, United Kingdom

Zafra Cooper, DPhil, DipPsych, Oxford University Department of Psychiatry, Warneford Hospital, Oxford, United Kindgom

Alberto Cormillot, MD, Clinica Cormillot, Buenos Aires, Argentina

Christopher Dare, MD, Department of Psychotherapy, Institute of Psychiatry, University of London; Bethlem Royal and Maudsley Hospital, London, United Kingdom

William H. Dietz, MD, PhD, Division of Gastroenterology and Nutrition, New England Medical Center, Tufts University School of Medicine, Boston, Massachusetts

Adam Drewnowski, PhD, Human Nutrition Program, School of Public Health, University of Michigan, Ann Arbor, Michigan

Johanna Dywer, DSc, RD, Frances Stern Nutrition Center, New England Medical Center Hospitals, Tufts University School of Medicine, Boston, Massachusetts

Ivan Eisler, PhD, Section of Psychotherapy, Department of Psychiatry, Institute of Psychiatry, University of London; Bethlem Royal and Maudsley Hospital, London, United Kingdom

Leonard H. Epstein, PhD, Department of Psychology, State University of New York at Buffalo, Buffalo, New York

Christopher G. Fairburn, DM, FRCPsych, Oxford University Department of Psychiatry, Warneford Hospital, Oxford, United Kingdom

Manfred M. Fichter, MD, Department of Psychiatry, University of Munich; Klinik Roseneck affiliated with the Medical Faculty of the Ludwig-Maximilians, University of Munich, Germany

John P. Foreyt, PhD, Nutrition Research Clinic, Baylor College of Medicine, Houston, Texas

Gary D. Foster, MS, Weight and Eating Disorders Program, Department of Psychiatry, University of Pennsylvania School of Medicine, Philadelphia, Pennsylvania

Paul E. Garfinkel, MD, FRCP(C), Clarke Institute of Psychiatry; University of Toronto, Ontario, Canada

David M. Garner, PhD, Neurobehavioral Associates, Okemos, Michigan

John S. Garrow, MD, PhD, FRCP, The Dial House, Herts, England

James Gibbs, MD, Bourne Laboratory, Cornell University Medical Center, White Plains, New York

David S. Goldbloom, MD, FRCP(C), General Psychiatry Division, Clarke Institute of Psychiatry; University of Toronto, Ontario, Canada

M.R.C. Greenwood, PhD, Office of Science and Technology Policy, The White House, Washington, DC

Katherine A. Halmi, MD, Cornell University Medical College; Eating Disorders Program, New York Hospital-Westchester Division, White Plains, New York

C. Peter Herman, PhD, Department of Psychology, University of Toronto, Ontario, Canada

David B. Herzog, MD, Eating Disorders Unit, Massachusetts General Hospital, Harvard Medical School, Boston, Massachusetts

Stanley Heshka, MD, Obesity Research Center, St. Luke's–Roosevelt Hospital Center, Columbia University College of Physicians and Surgeons, New York

Steven B. Heymsfield, MD, Obesity Research Center, St. Luke's–Roosevelt Hospital Center, Columbia University College of Physicians and Surgeons, New York

Jules Hirsch, MD, Laboratory of Human Metabolism and Behavior, The Rockefeller University, New York

Hans W. Hoek, MD PhD, Department of Psychiatry, University Hospital, Utrecht, The Netherlands

Edward S. Horton, MD, Joslin Diabetes Center, Boston, Massachusetts

L. K. George Hsu, MD, Eating Disorders Program, New England Medical Center; Department of Psychiatry, Tufts University School of Medicine, Boston, Massachusetts

Robert W. Jeffery, PhD, Division of Epidemiology, School of Public Health, University of Minnesota, Minneapolis, Minnesota

Craig Johnson, PhD, Eating Disorders Program, Laureate Psychiatric Clinic and Hospital; University of Tulsa, Oklahoma

Allan S. Kaplan, MD, MSc, FRCP(C), Eating Disorder Day Centre, The Toronto Hospital, Toronto General Division, Ontario, Canada

Walter H. Kaye, MD, University of Pittsburgh School of Medicine, Department of Psychiatry, Western Psychiatric Institute and Clinic, Pittsburgh, Pennsylvania

Richard E. Keesey, PhD, Department of Psychology, University of Wisconsin, Madison, Wisconsin

Sidney H. Kennedy, MD, FRCP(C), Psychosomatic Medicine and Programme for Eating Disorders, The Toronto Hospital; University of Toronto, Ontario, Canada

Robert C. Klesges, PhD, The Universities Prevention Center, Department of Psychology, University of Memphis, Tennessee

John G. Kral, MD, PhD, Department of Surgery, State University of New York Health Science Center, Brooklyn, New York

Shiriki K. Kumanyika, PhD, Center for Biostatistics and Epidemiology, Pennsylvania State University College of Medicine, Hershey, Pennsylvania

J. Hubert Lacey, MD, MPhil, FRCPsych, Division of General Psychiatry, St. George's Hospital Medical School, London, United Kingdom

Bryan Lask, MB, BS, FRCPsych, MPhil, Department of Psychological Medicine, Great Ormond Street Children's Hospital, London, United Kingdom

Rudolph L. Leibel, MD, Laboratory of Human Metabolism and Behavior, The Rockefeller University, New York

Sarah F. Leibowitz, PhD, The Rockefeller University, New York

Derek Llewellyn-Jones, MD, Department of Obstetrics and Gynaecology, University of Sydney, Australia

Timothy G. Lohman, PhD, Department of Exercise and Sport Sciences, University of Arizona, Tucson, Arizona

JoAnn E. Manson, MD, DrPH, Division of Preventive Medicine and the Channing Laboratory, Department of Medicine, Harvard Medical School and Brigham and Women's Hospital, Boston, Massachusetts

Marsha D. Marcus, PhD, Departments of Psychology and Psychiatry, Eating Disorders Clinic, Western Psychiatric Institute and Clinics, University of Pittsburgh, Pennsylvania

G. Alan Marlatt, PhD, Addictive Behaviors Research Center, Department of Psychology, University of Washington, Seattle, Washington

James E. Mitchell, MD, University of Minnesota, Department of Psychiatry, Minneapolis, Minnesota

Barbara J. Moore, PhD, Division of Nutrition Research Coordination, National Institute of Diabetes and Digestive and Kidney Diseases, National Institutes of Health, Bethesda, Maryland

Marion P. Olmsted, PhD, CPsych, Ambulatory Care for Eating Disorders, The Toronto Hospital, Ontario, Canada

Robert L. Palmer, FRCPsych, Department of Psychiatry, University of Leicester, Leicester General Hospital, Leicester, United Kingdom

Brenda Parry-Jones, BA, DAA, Department of Child and Adolescent Psychiatry, University of Glasgow, Royal Hospital for Sick Children, Yorkhill, Glasgow, United Kingdom

William Ll. Parry-Jones, MA, MD, FRCP, FRCPsych, Department of Child and Adolescent Psychiatry, University of Glasgow, Royal Hospital for Sick Children, Yorkhill, Glasgow, United Kingdom

Michael G. Perri, PhD, Department of Clinical and Health Psychology, University of Florida, Gainesville, Florida

Robert C. Peveler, DPhil, MRCPsych, Department of Psychiatry, University of Southampton, Royal South Hants Hospital, Southampton, United Kingdom

Karl M. Pirke, MD, Center for Psychobiology and Psychosomatic Research, Department of Psychoendocrinology, University of Trier, Germany

F. Xavier Pi-Sunyer, MD, Obesity Research Center, St. Luke's–Roosevelt Hospital Center, Department of Medicine, Columbia University College of Physicians and Surgeons, New York

Eric T. Poehlman, PhD, Geriatrics Service, Baltimore VA Medical Center, University of Maryland, Baltimore, Maryland

Janet Polivy, PhD, Department of Psychology, Erindale College, University of Toronto, Mississauga, Ontario, Canada

Eric Ravussin, PhD, Clinical Diabetes and Nutrition Section, National Institute of Diabetes and Digestive and Kidney Diseases, National Institutes of Health, Phoenix, Arizona

Judith Rodin, PhD, Office of the President, University of Pennsylvania, Philadelphia, Pennsylvania

Barbara J. Rolls, PhD, Program in Biobehavioral Health, Pennsylvania State University, University Park, Pennsylvania

James C. Rosen, PhD, Department of Psychology, University of Vermont, Burlington, Vermont

Wim H. M. Saris, MD, Department of Human Biology, University of Limburg, Maastricht, The Netherlands

Joseph A. Silverman, MD, Columbia University, College of Physicians and Surgeons, New York

Gerard P. Smith, MD, Bourne Laboratory, Cornell University Medical Center, White Plains, New York

Jeffery Sobal, PhD, MPH, Division of Nutritional Sciences, Cornell University, Ithaca, New York

Alan Stein, MRCPsych, Section of Child and Adolescent Psychiatry, University of Oxford, Park Hospital for Children, Oxford, United Kingdom

Hans Christoph Steinhausen, MD, Department of Child and Adolescent Psychiatry, University of Zürich, Switzerland

Judith S. Stern, ScD, Departments of Nutrition and Internal Medicine, University of California, Davis, California

Ruth H. Striegel-Moore, PhD, Department of Psychology, Wesleyan University, Middletown, Connecticut

Sachiko T. St. Jeor, PhD, RD, Nutrition Education and Research Program, University of Nevada School of Medicine, Reno, Nevada

Michael Strober, PhD, Eating Disorders Program, Neuropsychiatric Institute and Hospital, School of Medicine, University of California, Los Angeles, California

Albert J. Stunkard, MD, Weight and Eating Disorders Program, Department of Psychiatry, University of Pennsylvania School of Medicine, Philadelphia, Pennsylvania

Stephen W. Touyz, BSc (Hons), PhD, Department of Medical Psychology, Westmead Hospital; Department of Psychiatry, University of Sydney; Dieting Disorders Centre, University of Sydney, Australia

Brunna Tuschen, PhD, Department of Psychology, Philipps University Marburg, Germany

Walter Vandereycken, MD, PhD, Department of Psychiatry, University of Leuven, Belgium

Kelly Bemis Vitousek, PhD, Department of Psychology, University of Hawaii, Honolulu, Hawaii

Thomas A. Wadden, PhD, Weight and Eating Disorders Program, Department of Psychiatry, University of Pennsylvania School of Medicine, Philadelphia, Pennsylvania

B. Timothy Walsh, MD, College of Physicians and Surgeons, Columbia University; Eating Disorders Research Unit, New York State Psychiatric Institute, New York

Roland L. Weinsier, MD, DrPH, Department of Nutrition Sciences, University of Alabama at Birmingham, Alabama

Denise E. Wilfley, PhD, Yale Center for Eating and Weight Disorders, Department of Psychology, Yale University, New Haven, Connecticut

Walter Willett, MD, DrPH, Departments of Nutrition and Epidemiology, Harvard School of Public Health; The Channing Laboratory, Department of Medicine, Harvard Medical School, Brigham and Women's Hospital, Boston, Massachusetts

David F. Williamson, PhD, MS, Division of Nutrition, National Center for Chronic Disease Prevention and Health Promotion, Centers for Disease Control and Prevention, Atlanta, Georgia

Jack H. Wilmore, PhD, Department of Kinesiology and Health Education, University of Texas at Austin, Texas

G. Terence Wilson, PhD, Graduate School of Applied and Professional Psychology, Rutgers University, Piscataway, New Jersey

Rena R. Wing, PhD, Obesity and Nutrition Research Clinic, Departments of Psychology, Psychiatry and Epidemiology, Western Psychiatric Institute and Clinics, University of Pittsburgh, Pennsylvania

Barbara J. Wingate, MD, Department of Psychiatry, University of Pennsylvania School of Medicine, Philadelphia, Pennsylvania

Stephen A. Wonderlich, PhD, Department of Neuroscience, University of North Dakota Medical School, Fargo, North Dakota

Susan C. Wooley, PhD, Eating Disorders Center, Psychiatry Department, University of Cincinnati, College of Medicine, Cincinnati, Ohio

Joel Yager, MD, Neuropsychiatric Institute and Hospital, University of California Los Angeles, California

CONTENTS

V EPIDEMIOLOGY, ETIOLOGY, AND COURSE OF EATING DISORDERS

VI PHYSIOLOGICAL AND MEDICAL ASPECTS OF EATING DISORDERS

IX ASSESSMENT AND TREATMENT OF OBESITY

EATING DISORDERS AND OBESITY

· I ·
REGULATION OF EATING
AND WEIGHT

• 1 •

CENTRAL PHYSIOLOGICAL DETERMINANTS OF EATING BEHAVIOR AND WEIGHT

Sarah F. Leibowitz

In modern society, nutritional and appetite disorders occur in epidemic proportions and are serious health hazards. Obesity and diabetes affect over 30% of our population, while eating disorders, such as anorexia nervosa and bulimia nervosa, occur in a growing number of adolescents and young adults. Disturbed eating patterns are a primary symptom of numerous psychiatric disorders, and loss of appetite and cachexia, during illness or in the elderly, preclude proper medical treatment for restoring good health or preserving life. Increased understanding of the systems of the body and brain, related to energy and nutrient balance, may help us to treat and ultimately prevent these common disorders.

INTEGRATION OF DIVERSE SIGNALS

In recent years, researchers in neurobiology have used an integrative, interdisciplinary approach to obtain information about the multiple determinants of eating behavior, energy balance, and body weight (see Chapter 3). These include such diverse signals as (1) simple nutrients in the blood, including glucose, fatty acids, or amino acids; (2) classical neurotransmitter molecules for rapid, short-term communication; (3) larger neuropeptides for slower, more long-term action; and (4) hormones for both neuromodulatory and metabolic processes. These signals derive from different peripheral organs, in particular, the adrenals, liver, pancreas, and gastrointestinal tract, and also from different areas of the central nervous system, from the hindbrain to the forebrain. Moreover, they are dynamic in nature, shifting across the daily cycle, developmental stages, the female estrous cycle, and seasonal periods.

Systems in the Body

In the periphery, a variety of substances are believed to be involved, in both animals and humans, in the complex process of integrating physiological and behavioral systems geared toward energy and nutrient homeostasis (see Chapter 2). From the gastrointestinal tract, cholecystokinin and other peptides are released after a meal to coordinate several aspects of digestion, absorption, and metabolism and to transmit information to the brain, via the vagus nerve, that signals meal termination and satiety. The pancreatic peptide hormone insulin has also been linked to satiety in addition to the metabolism and utilization of food. The adrenal steroids corticosterone (in the rat) and cortisol (in humans) have different actions mediated by mineralocorticoid receptors, which increase the ingestion and metabolism of fat, and by glucocorticoid receptors, which predominantly influence carbohydrate intake and its metabolism. This glucoregulatory action occurs when the body's carbohydrate stores are low, for example, at the start of the natural feeding cycle, and thus blood steroid levels are particularly high in order to mobilize and convert calories to glucose. The gonadal steroids, for example, estrogen, also introduce a major behavioral and metabolic signal at critical times of the estrous cycle and around puberty, when the body's nutrient stores must be enhanced for reproduction.

Systems in the Brain

In addition to hormones, the process of integrating metabolic information from the periphery with neurochemical signals in the central nervous system requires the involvement and specialized functions of multiple brain areas. These areas include the lower brainstem, in particular the dorsal vagal complex, which relays and integrates neural information between peripheral autonomic–endocrine organs and several forebrain structures: (1) the pons–midbrain and the thalamus, which interpret this information in relation to the sensory properties of foods; (2) the hypothalamus, which, through its extensive vascularity and connections with the pituitary and hindbrain, remains closely linked to circulating nutrients, hormones, and neural signals; and (3) forebrain structures, such as the nucleus accumbens, amygdala, and frontal cortex, which perform higher-order functions to integrate incoming information with various cognitive factors pertaining to the rewarding and aversive aspects of food.

The role of the hypothalamus in relating hormones and metabolism to behavior has received considerable attention and will be the focus of this review. A number of neurochemical and neuroendocrine systems have been identified in this structure that are believed to be involved in controlling appetite for carbohydrate, fat, and protein. They also modulate metabolism and contribute to the body's nutrient stores and, ultimately, weight gain. These systems will be described and evaluated with respect to their possible contribution to normal physiological functions and to the development or maintenance of clinical eating and body weight disorders.

NUTRIENT BALANCE

Maintenance of Carbohydrate Balance

Maintenance of carbohydrate stores involves the coordinated effort of several brain neurochemicals and hormones. These substances translate metabolic signals, reflecting decreased carbohydrate stores and intracellular glucose utilization, into neural signals for promoting carbohydrate intake and metabolism. They include the amino acid gamma-aminobutyric acid, the amine norepinephrine, the peptide neuropeptide Y, and the glucocorticoid actions of corticosterone. Their primary site of action is in the medial region of the hypothalamus—in particular, the paraventricular nucleus. The neurotransmitters and glucocorticoid receptors are known to exist at this site, and their local administration stimulates eating behavior (specifically, carbohydrate ingestion), causes an increase in the utilization of carbohydrate to promote fat storage, and reduces sympathetic activity to conserve energy.

The activity of these neurochemicals and their receptors peaks sharply at specific times, for example, during the initial hours of the natural eating cycle and when the body's glycogen stores and blood glucose levels are particularly low. At this time, carbohydrate is strongly preferred by animals and humans, perhaps since it is most efficient in replenishing glucose stores in a hungry animal. Simultaneously, a natural rise occurs in circulating levels of corticosterone, whose main function is to enhance the body's carbohydrate stores. This rise initiates a positive feedback loop, which involves a stimulatory effect of this steroid, via glucocorticoid receptors, on the synthesis and release of the neurochemicals in the hypothalamus and, in turn, a stimulatory action of these neurochemicals themselves on adrenal release of corticosterone. Brain substances involved in turning off this positive feedback loop include serotonin, its amino acid tryptophan, and cholecystokinin, which are released by a carbohydrate-rich meal. In addition to suppressing carbohydrate ingestion, these neurochemicals stimulate metabolic rate and sympathetic activity and reduce body weight gain.

Evidence suggests that disturbances in the endogenous activity of these neurochemicals and steroids contribute to the development or maintenance of abnormal patterns of eating and body weight gain. For example, when pharmacologically or surgically deprived of their natural neurotransmitter or steroid, animals fail to exhibit normal carbohydrate feeding, both in the initial hours of the active feeding cycle or in response to the physiological challenge of food deprivation. Conversely, with excessive hypothalamic infusions of norepinephrine, neuropeptide Y, or corticosterone, animals respond by overeating carbohydrate, which leads to an increase in fat deposition and body weight gain. In fact, animals that are genetically obese or who spontaneously overeat palatable, energy-rich diets have excessive levels of circulating corticosterone, hypothalamic norepinephrine, and neuropeptide Y. These disturbances may be consequent to deficiencies in insulin sensitivity and, thus, glucose homeostasis.

Maintenance of Fat Balance

A specific set of substances in the hypothalamus controls the ingestion and deposition of fat. They include the peptide galanin, the opioid peptides, and the mineralocorticoid actions of corticosterone. These substances act within the medial hypothalamus to potentiate fat intake and are more abundant in animals with a strong natural preference for fat and, consequently, higher body weight. In contrast to those controlling carbohydrate balance, these systems involved in fat balance exhibit greater activity during the middle to late hours of the natural feeding cycle. During this time, appetite for fat naturally rises; peptide synthesis is increased; and circulating corticosterone, remaining at low basal levels, binds specifically to mineralocorticoid receptors that enhance the deposition as well as ingestion of fat. The catecholamine dopamine appears to be one neurochemical involved in turning off these anabolic signals. Its hypothalamic action is reflected in the inhibitory effect, on fat intake and body weight, produced by amphetamine, which releases dopamine, and by phenylpropanolamine, a structurally similar, over-the-counter diet product. The opposite effect, in contrast, is commonly seen with neuroleptic drugs that antagonize dopamine receptors.

Maintenance of Protein Balance

In rats and humans, appetite for protein, similar to that for fat, increases gradually over the course of the active feeding cycle, perhaps to enhance nutrient stores in preparation for an inactive period of little eating. The finding that the opioid peptides potentiate protein and fat intake suggests that these neurochemicals may assist in balancing the intake and perhaps storage of these two nutrients. Another peptide, growth hormone-releasing factor, may also function in the medial hypothalamus to coordinate behavioral and physiological functions related to protein balance. In addition to stimulating the release of growth hormone, which promotes protein synthesis and growth, this peptide, acting in part through opioid systems, potentiates the ingestion of food, specifically protein.

Developmental Patterns and Gender Differences

In animals and humans, appetite before puberty is characterized by a stronger prefer-ence for carbohydrate in females and for protein in males. This preference for carbo-hydrate in females may be attributed to a natural, prepubertal surge in hypothalamic levels of neuropeptide Y in association with increased adrenal activity. The appetite for protein in males, in contrast, occurs in response to a rise in growth hormone-releasing factor. After puberty, this pattern dramatically shifts in both males and females, with a sharp increase in appetite for fat. This growing preference for fat-rich diets, associated with a rise in fat deposition and body weight gain, develops along with a sharp increase in hypothalamic levels of galanin and the opioids, induced by a rise in gonadal steroid levels. This pattern, the result of the actions of estrogen, is observed earlier and more dramatically in female subjects, who require fat stores for reproduction.

CLINICAL STUDIES OF EATING AND BODY WEIGHT DISORDERS

The ultimate goal of studies in animals is to determine whether the same neurochemical and hormone systems also function in humans and whether disturbances in these systems contribute to the development or maintenance of nutritional and body weight disorders. Remarkable similarities between humans and lower mammals are found in their responses to various pharmacological agents that affect eating and body weight and in their diurnal rhythms and gender differences in nutrient selection. Moreover, the drugs most commonly used today in the management of obesity, anorexia nervosa, and bulimia nervosa have their primary effect in modulating the balance between the monoamines, norepinephrine, serotonin, and dopamine.

There is some evidence to suggest that disturbances in brain neurochemical systems, together with neuroendocrine processes, may contribute to the development of abnor-mal patterns of eating and body weight gain in humans. For example, recent clinical studies have revealed altered levels of the amines and neuropeptides in the cere-brospinal fluid of patients with anorexia nervosa or bulimia and with common eating problems, such as food cravings, seasonal appetite disturbances, and stress-related eat-ing. The contribution of neuroendocrine disturbances is demonstrated by the reciprocal changes in fat balance observed in Cushing's and Addison's diseases, consequent to abnormal cortisol levels, and by the hyperphagia and increased weight gain in diabetics, caused possibly by insufficient insulin-mediated control of hypothalamic peptide synthesis. Understanding the dramatic rise in fat intake and fat deposition that occurs in women at puberty, and its relationship to estrogen-stimulated production of hypothalamic peptides, may help in identifying therapies for eating disorders that frequently develop around this time.

These findings, in animals and humans, are now generating considerable excitement; the hope is that compounds affecting these brain neurochemical and neuroendocrine systems, in conjunction with nutritional and behavioral strategies, will have real therapeutic value in a range of eating and body weight disorders and also for psychiatric disorders that have a strong nutritional component.

ACKNOWLEDGMENTS

Research conducted in my laboratory that is described in this chapter was supported by Grant No. MH43422 from the National Institute of Mental Health.

FURTHER READING

Bray, G. A. (1991). Treatment for obesity: A nutrient balance/nutrient partition approach. *Nutrition Reviews, 49*, 33–45. Broad overview of brain systems controlling nutrient balance.

Gibbs, J., & Smith, G. P. (1992). Peripheral signals for satiety in animals and humans. In G. H. Anderson & S. H. Kennedy (Eds.), *The biology of feast and famine* (pp. 61–72). New York: Academic Press. Review focused on cholecystokinin.

Hoebel, B. G., Leibowitz, S. F., & Hernandez, L. (1992). Neurochemistry of anorexia and bulimia. In G. H. Anderson & S. H. Kennedy (Eds.), *The biology of feast and famine* (pp. 21–45). New York: Academic Press. Review of brain neurochemical processes related to eating disorders.

Kaye, W. H. (1992). Neurotransmitter abnormalities in anorexia nervosa and bulimia nervosa. In G. H. Anderson & S. H. Kennedy (Eds.), *The biology of feast and famine* (pp. 105–134). New York: Academic Press. Review of neurochemical disturbances in eating disorders.

Leibowitz, S. F. (1988). Hypothalamic paraventricular nucleus: Interaction between α2-noradrenergic system and circulating hormones and nutrients in relation to energy balance. *Neuroscience and Biobehavioral Review, 12*, 101–109. Review focused on norepinephrine.

Leibowitz, S. F. (1991). Brain neuropeptide Y: An integrator of endocrine, metabolic and behavioral processes. *Brain Research Bulletin, 27*, 333–337. A review focused on neuropeptide Y.

Leibowitz, S. F. (1991). Brain neurochemical systems controlling appetite and body weight gain. In N. J. Rothwell & M. J. Stock (Eds.), *Obesity and cachexia* (pp. 33–48). New York: Wiley. A comprehensive summary of evidence supporting a role for brain neurochemical systems in the control of eating behavior and body weight.

Leibowitz, S. F. (1991). Hypothalamic galanin in relation to feeding behavior and endocrine systems. In T. Hokfelt & T. Bartfai (Eds.), *Galanin: A new multifunctional peptide in the neuro-endocrine system* (pp. 393–406). New York: Macmillan. A review focused on galanin.

Leibowitz, S. F. (1992). Neurochemical–neuroendocrine systems in the brain controlling macronutrient intake and metabolism. *Trends in Neuroscience, 15*, 491–497. A brief review of brain neurochemical systems controlling appetite for nutrients.

Woods, S. C., & Gibbs, J. (1989). The regulation of food intake by peptides. *Annals of the New York Academy of Sciences, 575*, 236–243. A review on insulin.

• 2 •

PERIPHERAL PHYSIOLOGICAL DETERMINANTS OF EATING AND BODY WEIGHT

GERARD P. SMITH
JAMES GIBBS

A complete measurement of food intake over time is obtained by measuring the size and number of meals. Thus the functional unit of analysis of food intake is the meal. Investigation of the peripheral physiological controls of meal number and size has revealed distinct signals and mechanisms for the initiation, maintenance, and termination of a meal.

INITIATION OF EATING

Only one physiological control of the initiation of eating has been identified in the rat. This is a decline of blood glucose of about 12% that occurs approximately 5 minutes prior to the initiation of a spontaneous meal under ordinary laboratory conditions. Because the fall in blood glucose levels is not sufficient to produce a significant decrease in the metabolic utilization of glucose in any tissue, it is the pattern of the decline and rise of blood glucose levels that is the adequate stimulus for the initiation of eating. The mechanisms that produce or sense this pattern of glucose-level change are unknown, and it is not clear if this signal is present in humans.

This pattern of glucose-level change is probably a weak signal for initiating a meal in comparison with psychosocial and environmental stimuli, particularly those that have been learned and are part of the daily routine in a specific ecological niche.

MAINTENANCE AND TERMINATION OF EATING

Positive and Negative Feedback Processes

Once begun, eating is maintained for a period of time and then stops. How long eating is maintained depends on the interaction of two opposing physiological processes—a positive feedback process and a negative feedback process (Figure 2.1). The positive-feedback process stimulates the central network that controls eating; the negative feed-back process inhibits this network. Eating continues despite brief pauses as long as the

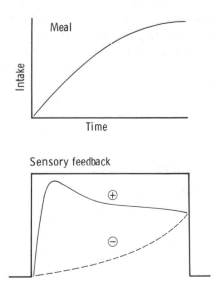

FIGURE 2.1. Upper panel shows the cumulative intake curve of a representative meal. Lower panel shows the initiation, maintenance, and termination of eating (solid line, square wave) and the underlying positive ($\oplus$, solid line) and negative ($\ominus$, dotted line) feedback processes that determine the maintenance and termination of eating. The shapes of the lines denoting the feedback processes are schematic. From Smith et al. (1990, p. 65). Copyright 1990 by John Wiley & Sons, Inc. Reprinted by permission.

potency of the positive feedback to the central network exceeds the potency of the negative feedback. Eating stops when the potency of negative feedback stimuli equals or exceeds the potency of the positive feedback stimuli (Figure 2.1). Although there is compelling evidence for the interaction of these opposing feedback processes in animals and humans, our ignorance is nearly total concerning the central mechanisms used by the brain to measure and compare the potencies of the two feedback processes.

These feedback processes are initiated by the mechanical and chemical stimuli of the ingested food. The unconditioned potency of these stimuli is determined by their quantitative aspects, for example, concentration or strength, spatial distribution in relevant receptor fields, and duration of action. But given the rapid learning about the satiating and hedonic consequences of foods that is the mechanism for conditioned preferences, aversions, and satiation, it is clear that after one or more experiences, the potency of food stimuli is determined by prior experience. Thus peripheral physiological controls rarely act in a simple stimulus–response mode—they are modulated by prior experience.

Sites and Mechanisms of Positive Feedback

The mouth and nose are the principal sites of positive feedback. The intimate contact of mechanical and particularly chemical stimuli with receptors in the mucosa of these regions means that the orosensory effects of food stimuli are mediated to the brain by afferent fibers of primary olfactory, gustatory, and somatosensory neurons of cranial nerves 1, 5, 7, 9, and 10. But identification of peripheral afferent paths does not reveal either the mechanisms of transduction at specific peripheral receptors or the synaptic mechanisms in the central terminations of these afferent fibers.

We do know, however, that central dopaminergic and opioid mechanisms, probably in the limbic system of the forebrain, are necessary for the normal processing of this positive feedback stimulation, because specific antagonists of these neuromodulators decrease the potency of orosensory positive feedback (see Chapter 1). There is also suggestive evidence for positive feedback stimulation from food stimuli acting in the stomach and postabsorptively, perhaps in the liver.

Sites and Mechanisms of Negative Feedback

Food stimuli activate the negative feedback process by acting in the mouth, the stomach, and the small intestine. The negative feedback process is most potent when these sites are activated sequentially by ingested food. This implies that there is synergistic interaction between food stimuli acting at these sites, and, indeed, temporal and spatial summation has been clearly demonstrated in the rat and probably occurs in humans.

Despite the demonstration of the importance of the mouth and the stomach for activating the negative feedback process, no mechanism has been identified for transducing the stimuli or for mediating the effect of receptor stimulation of these sites on the brain. For example, afferent fibers of the vagus nerve have frequently been asserted to mediate the inhibitory effects of gastric distension on food intake. But recent experiments have failed to support this assertion. It is possible that peptides released by gastric stimuli, such as gastrin-releasing peptide, are involved in mediating negative feedback from the stomach, but this is not proven.

We know more about the small intestine. Chemical stimuli of ingested food are more potent here than are mechanical stimuli. Chemical stimuli activate vagal afferent fibers directly. They also work indirectly through the release of cholecystokinin from mucosal cells in the upper small intestine and glucagon from the pancreas; these peptides then stimulate vagal afferent fibers.

The satiating effect of cholecystokinin released from the small intestine has now been well documented in a variety of animals and is probably also a physiological function of the peptide in humans. The kinds of evidence required to prove the satiating effect of endogenous cholecystokinin provide a case study of how formidable a task it is to evaluate a candidate peptide as a peripheral physiological control of food intake.

Note that the negative feedback process is activated only by preabsorptive stimuli. This comes as a surprise to many of us who were taught that the initiation and size of meals were controlled directly by postabsorptive metabolic depletion and repletion. But recent work locates these controls as preabsorptive rather than as postabsorptive. It is true, of course, that acute blockade of energy metabolism by specific antagonists of carbohydrate and fatty acid utilization initiate eating and can increase meal size, but there is no evidence that these metabolic perturbations occur under the usual conditions in which rodents and humans eat meals.

ANALYSIS OF A CHANGE IN MEAL SIZE

Given the fact that once eating begins, the duration of eating and the size of a meal are determined by the central integration of the afferent information (conditioned and unconditioned) generated by food stimuli acting from the tip of the tongue to the end of the small intestine, it is clear that any observation of some genetic, neural, physiological, pharmacological, or psychological stimulus that increases or decreases meal size is descriptive. Any change in meal size requires analysis to determine whether it results from a change in the positive feedback process, a change in the negative feedback process, or a reciprocal change in both feedback processes. This can now be done in experimental animals where surgical procedures and experimental control of the delivery of food stimuli to different parts of the gut can analyze changes in the mechanisms of the positive feedback process separately from the mechanisms of the negative feedback process. Development of reliable and sensitive markers of the feedback processes in humans is essential to progress in this area.

The peripheral controls of meal size are embedded in the large and complicated system that controls energy balance. It is not known how this integration is achieved, but a central action of insulin has been proposed as an important mechanism for coordinating intake and body weight.

SUMMARY

A complex network of peripheral and central factors govern eating and body weight. Work thus far has helped identify the agents and sites of action. The next generation of research should bring important advances in understanding the integration of these factors.

ACKNOWLEDGMENTS

We thank Jane Magnetti for processing the manuscript. The work of G. P. S. is supported by a Research Scientist Award (No. MH00149) from the National Institute of Mental Health.

FURTHER READING

Booth, D. A. (1985). Food-conditioned eating preferences and aversions with interoceptive elements: Conditioned appetites and satieties. In N. S. Braveman & P. Bronstein (Eds.), *Experimental assessments and clinical applications of conditioned food aversions* (pp. 22–41). New York: New York Academy of Sciences. A review of the role of experience in forming food preferences and aversions to foods.

Campfield, L. A., & Smith, F. J. (1990). Systemic factors in the control of food intake. In E. M. Stricker (Ed.), *Handbook of behavioral neurobiology: Vol. 10. Neurobiology of food and fluid intake* (pp. 183–206). New York: Plenum Press. A presentation of evidence that the pattern of premeal circulating glucose represents a physiological mechanism of meal initiation.

Gibbs, J., & Smith, G. P. (1992). Peripheral signals for satiety in animals and humans. In G. H. Anderson & S. H. Kennedy (Eds.), *The biology of feast and famine* (pp. 61–72). New York: Academic Press. A review of the roles of cholecsytokinin, pancreatic glucagon, and bombesin-like peptides in producing meal termination.

Kraly, F. S., Carty, W. J., & Smith, G. P. (1978). Effect of pregastric food stimuli on meal size and intermeal interval in the rat. *Physiology and Behavior, 20,* 779–784. Study showing that the contact of food with the pregastric surface of the gastrointestinal tract can terminate the meal, although the size of the meal is abnormally enlarged.

Kraly, F. S., & Gibbs, J. (1980). Vagotomy fails to block the satiating effect of food in the stomach. *Physiology and Behavior, 24,* 1007–1010. Study demonstrating that the contact of food with the pregastric and gastric surfaces of the gastrointestinal tract result in a meal of normal size, even when the subdiaphragmatic vagus has been severed.

Sclafani, A. (1991). The hedonics of sugar and starch. In R. C. Bolles (Ed.), *The hedonics of taste* (pp. 59–87). Hillsdale, NJ: Erlbaum. Summary of the ingestive and postingestive influences on the palatability of carbohydrates.

Smith, G. P. & Gibbs, J. (1992). The development and proof of the cholecystokinin hypothesis of satiety. In C. T. Dourish, S. J. Cooper, S. D. Iversen, & L. L. Iversen (Eds.), *Multiple cholecystokinin receptors in the CNS* (pp. 166–182). Oxford: Oxford University Press. Evidence for the physiological role of endogenous cholecystokinin in producing satiation.

Smith, G. P., Greenberg, D., Corp, E., & Gibbs, J. (1990). Afferent information in the control of eating. In G. A. Bray, D. Ricquier, & B. M. Spiegelman (Eds.), *Obesity: Towards a molecular approach* (pp. 63–79). New York: Wiley–Liss. Short review describing the importance of food-elicited afferent information from the various regions of the gastrointestinal tract in supplying postitive and negative signals influencing meal size.

Woods, S. C., Porte, D. Jr., Strubbe, J. H., & Steffens, A. B. (1986). The relationships among body fat, feeding, and insulin. In R. C. Ritter, S. Ritter, & C. D. Barnes (Eds.), *Feeding behavior: Neural and humoral controls* (pp. 315–327). New York: Academic Press. Evidence supporting the role of insulin as a key signal regulating body weight.

• 3 •

THE PSYCHOBIOLOGICAL APPROACH TO APPETITE AND WEIGHT CONTROL

JOHN E. BLUNDELL

A PSYCHOBIOLOGICAL SYSTEM

The power of a systems approach is that it allows the simultaneous evaluation of a number of factors that influence the expression of appetite and the control of body weight. The approach permits an assessment of the *relative* strength of each factor rather than concentrating on one domain only. Research is certainly needed on the specific mechanisms that control particular aspects of our physiology, biochemistry, and behavior that are related to eating and weight control. Also required is a conceptualization of how these mechanisms act cohesively to influence the physiology, conscious sensations, and actions of people functioning as individuals. This can be provided by the psychobiological system.

The essence of the view proposed here is the intention to understand the control of appetite and body weight (and disorders of these phenomena) as the products of a network of interactions among elements forming part of a psychobiological system. A simplified model of the system is set out in Figure 3.1.

This conceptualization draws attention to the interrelationships between particular domains of influence, including the external environment (cultural and physical), the behavioral act of eating (quantitative and qualitative dimensions); the processes of ingestion and assimilation of foods, the storage and utilization of energy; the brain mechanisms implicated in the control system; and the mediating subjective states such as intentions, attributions, and cognitions.

Principles of the System: Regulation and Adaptation

What factors give rise to appetite disturbance, and does this affect weight gain, weight maintenance, weight stability, or weight loss? To answer this question, it seems necessary to ask about the role of appetite in body weight control. Does the modulation of appetite have anything to do with fluctuations in body weight?

On the basis of evidence accumulated during studies on the energy expenditure of obese subjects, it has been concluded that obese subjects, in general, do not show a reduced energy expenditure. This means that the energy expenditure of obese subjects

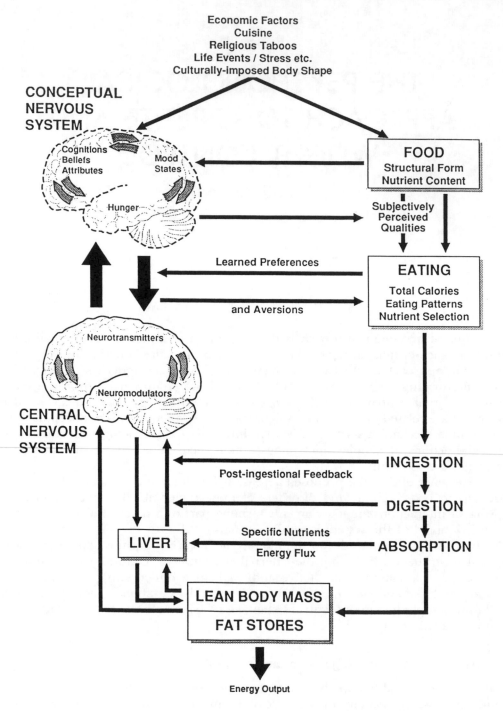

FIGURE 3.1. Conceptualization of certain significant aspects of the biopsychological system underlying the control of feeding behavior.

is consistent with the amount of their fat and lean body tissue. Since total body cell mass is higher in obese than in lean people, the total energy expenditure of obese people is higher, and therefore their energy intake must be higher if they are to be in energy balance. Accordingly, obese people (in general) eat more energy-rich foods than do lean people (although the form of this energy is also important). This argument has taken away one of the impediments to an understanding of appetite and weight by undermining the belief that obese people are uniformly small eaters (have low energy intakes). These low recorded energy intakes are now recognized as arising from a methodological weakness of techniques of recording habitual food intake.

Even though the quantitative expression of appetite is related to variations in body weight, this relationship does not disclose how appetite is itself modulated. The expression of appetite (in the form of motivation to eat, eating patterns, cravings, preferences, etc.) can be seen as an important output of the psychobiological system, and one product of this output will be changes in body weight. What principles govern the way in which the psychobiological system guides the expression of appetite? A consideration of anthropological, epidemiological, and experimental evidence suggests that it is easier for human beings to gain weight than to reduce weight. This finding implies that the control of appetite (by the psychobiological system) is asymmetrical rather than symmetrical. Figure 3.2 illustrates a simple conceptualization of how this asymmetry arises.

The extension of Claude Bernard's principle of homeostasis to include behavior is often referred to as the behavioral regulation of internal states. Logic demands that behavior (eating) is controlled in accordance with biological states of need. This control constitutes a form of biological regulation. However, the expression of behavior is also subject to environmental demands, and behavior is adapted in the face of particular

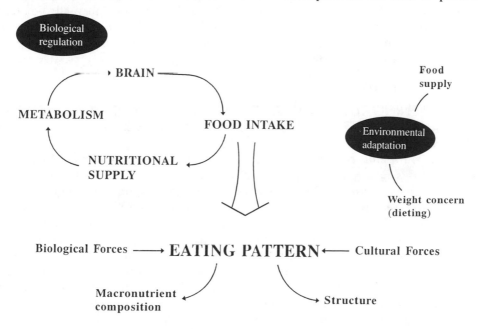

FIGURE 3.2. Schematic diagram illustrating that the pattern of eating behavior arises from an interaction between biological regulation and environmental adaptation. Eating is a product of both biology and culture.

circumstances. In the case of human appetite, consideration should be given to the conscious and deliberate control over eating behavior. Human beings can decide to alter their own behavior (in this case, eating) in order to meet particular objectives; for example, a display of moral conviction (political hunger strike) or a demonstration of esthetic achievement (e.g., dieting). In both of these examples eating is curtailed, with an ensuing interruption or depletion of the nutrition supply.

Regulatory mechanisms will tend to oppose this undersupply and generate a drive to eat. In many parts of the world environmental adaptation also means adjusting to a food supply characterized by an abundance of palatable, energy-dense (mainly high-fat) foods or by a large proportion of fatty items. Exposure to these types of diets usually gives rise to an overconsumption of energy. Since this does not appear to be biologically driven (by a need state) or consciously intended, this phenomenon has been referred to as passive overconsumption. This type of consumption, in turn, in an interaction with genetic vulnerability, leads to an increase in fat deposition. A good example of such an interaction is the change in dietary habits and levels of obesity occurring in the Pacific islands of Polynesia and Micronesia. This obesity appears largely to be due to the high energy density of the types of foods these people consume, and since fat is the most energy-dense nutrient, fat contributes most to overall energy density and therefore to the phenomenon of passive overconsumption.

This passive overconsumption that leads to the accumulation of body fat does not appear to generate any biological drive to undereat. Obese people do not appear to get any help from their adipose tissue to reduce their appetites. Hence the operation of the regulatory system is not symmetrical. Two principles may be deduced. First, biological processes exert a strong defense against undereating, which serves to protect the body from an energy (nutritional) deficit. Therefore undereating must normally be an active and deliberate process. Second, biological defenses against overconsumption are weak or inadequate. This means that overeating may occur despite the best efforts of people to prevent it. In contrast to undereating (dieting), overeating can be a passive process.

PARTITIONING THE NETWORK OF THE PSYCHOBIOLOGICAL SYSTEM: NUTRITION AND THE APPETITE CASCADE

How does the appetite control system operate to reflect these processes? One way to think about this issue is to consider how eating behavior is held in place by the interaction between the characteristics of food and the biological responses to ingestion. These biological responses are often thought of as "satiety signals." Several characteristics of ingested food must be monitored, including taste (intensity and hedonic aspects), volume and weight, energy density, osmolarity, and the proportion of macronutrients. Biological responses generated include oral afferent stimulation, stomach distension, rate of gastric emptying, release of hormones such as cholecystokinin and insulin, triggering of digestive enzymes (and cofactors), and plasma profiles of glucose, amino acids, and other metabolites (see Chapters 1 and 2). The organization of this activity can be conceptualized in the form of a cascade (Figure 3.3, lower portion).

Two features are worth considering. First is the distinction between satiation and satiety. Satiation refers to the processes that bring a period of eating to an end; these processes influence the size of meals and snacks. Satiety refers to the inhibition of hunger and further eating that arises as a consequence of food ingestion. These two

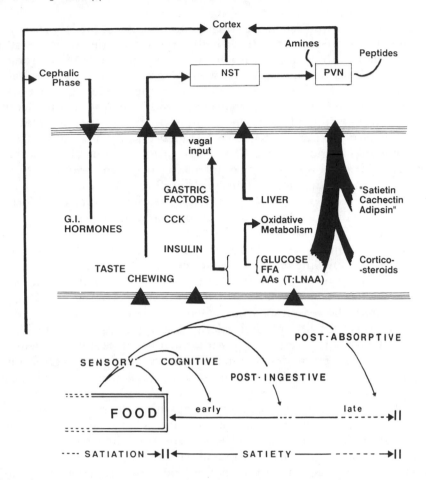

FIGURE 3.3. Diagram showing the expression of appetite as the relationship between three levels of operations: behavior, peripheral physiology and metabolites, and brain activity. PVN, paraventricular nucleus; NST, nucleus of the tractus solitarius; CCK, cholecystokinin; AA, amino acids; FFA, free fatty acids; T:LNAA, tryptophan:large neutral amino acids.

kinds of processes therefore control events occurring during meals and between meals. Second is the potency of the mediating processes of the cascade and particularly the relative strength of postabsorptive mechanisms. It is clearly the properties of food (and the act of ingesting it) that trigger the initiation of the overlapping physiological responses. The amount (quantity) and nature (quality) of the food will determine the intensity and time course of the biological processes generated. This situation reflects the idea of the different satiating power of different types of food.

One important issue in assessing the role of the nutrient composition of food on appetite is the relative balance between preabsorptive and postabsorptive satiety signals. Different nutrients affect these domains with different potencies. For example, carbohydrates appear to generate strong but short-lived postabsorptive signals that may be reflected in plasma glucose profiles. In turn this profile will control the rate of the utilization of glucose or the access of glucose to glucoreceptor or glucosensitive cells in the liver or brain. The rapid digestion of carbohydrates means that this postabsorptive phase of satiety will occur quite soon after ingestion. Because of the low energy density of many carbohydrate foods, it is likely that a high-carbohydrate diet will generate strong satiation (which will limit the energy consumed in meals) and a relatively strong satiety, the duration and intensity of which will vary with the nature of the carbohydrate itself.

Dietary fat appears to have a different effect on the mediating processes of the satiety cascade. There is good evidence from animal and human studies that certain oils infused into the intestine inhibit hunger and eating. This effect depends, at least in part, on the release of cholecystokinin (CCK), since the satiety effect can be antagonized by the CCK-A-type antagonist lorglumide (see Chapter 2). Infusions of oil also slow the rate of gastric emptying. This effect may prolong or intensify satiety. However, these actions are not generated by oils infused intravenously. Therefore the strong effect of fat in generating satiety signals appears to occur through preabsorptive action. These physiological effects may be the basis for the often-encountered feeling of fullness produced by the consumption of high-fat foods.

This pattern of events creates a paradox. On the one hand, there is the potent preabsorptive satiety and feeling of fullness generated by fat; on the other hand, there is the repeated demonstration of overconsumption of high-fat foods in the short and medium term. What is the explanation for the existence of fat-induced satiety and high-fat hyperphagia? The reason seems to depend on the features of high-fat foods— their extremely high palatability and their energy density. It appears that, although fat does generate a strong satiety response (preabsorptive)—this is not sufficient to overcome the facilitation of ingestion due to taste and density. Therefore, a large amount of high-fat energy can be consumed before the satiety signals provide feedback and influence eating behavior.

This case study of the action of dietary fat on appetite illustrates the strength of the psychobiological approach. Various components of the system must be researched and defined, but an appreciation of several different aspects of the system—nutrient composition, mechanisms mediating the sensations of palatability, relative actions of pre- and postabsorptive satiety signals—can indicate how various processes contribute jointly to a measured outcome.

INTERRELATED LEVELS IN THE SYSTEM

The biological responses generated by food ingestion form part of a feedback circuit that influences the pattern of eating being displayed. This circuit can be seen as a network with three levels, which are displayed in simplified form in Figure 3.3. The network includes the level of psychological events (hunger, perception, cravings, and hedonic sensations) and behavioral operations (meals, snacks, energy, and macronutrient intakes); the level of peripheral physiology and metabolic events; and the level of neurotransmitter and metabolic interactions in the brain. The expression of appetite reflects the synchronous operation of events and processes in the three levels. Neural events trigger and guide behavior, but each act of behavior involves a response in the peripheral physiological system; in turn, these physiological events are translated into brain neurochemical activity. This brain activity represents the strength of motivation and the willingness to refrain from feeding.

Even before food touches the mouth, physiological signals are generated by the sight and smell of food (see Chapter 2). These events constitute the cephalic phase of appetite. Cephalic-phase responses are generated in many parts of the gastrointestinal tract; their function is to anticipate the ingestion of food. During and immediately after eating, afferent information provides the major control over appetite. It has been noted that "afferent information from ingested food acting in the mouth provides primarily positive feedback for eating; that from the stomach and small intestine primarily negative feedback" (Smith, Greenberg, Corp, & Gibbs, 1990, p. 63). Initially, the brain is informed about the amount of food ingested and its nutrient content via afferent input. During the postingestive (preabsorptive) and postabsorptive phases of satiety the brain is informed about all aspects of the physiological and metabolic states resulting from food consumption.

Traditional views of the neural control of appetite have been based on opposed hunger and satiety centers in the hypothalamus. These concepts are now out of date. It may be useful to recognize distinct roles for the hindbrain (particularly the nucleus of the solitary tract and the closely associated area postrema) and the forebrain and to consider separate processes of registration, transcription, and integration. Changes in the gastrointestinal tract resulting from food consumption are registered in the hindbrain. This information is transcribed onto neurotransmitter pathways (amines and associated peptides) and projected to hypothalamic and limbic zones where integration with neuroendocrine and metabolic activity is organized. Information arriving from the periphery via neural pathways is complemented by qualitatively different types of information that can be detected in blood and cerebrospinal fluid. A large number of neurotransmitters, neuromodulators, pathways, and receptors are implicated in the central processing of information relevant to appetite (see Chapter 1). The profile of this activity reflects the flux of physiological and biochemical transactions in the periphery and represents the pattern of behavioral events and associated motivational states.

IMPLICATIONS OF THE SYSTEMS APPROACH

Viewed in this way, the psychobiological system permits an understanding of the interrelationships among behavioral events that comprise eating, peripheral physiology and metabolism, and central neurochemical processes. The system also provides the possibility of thinking about the way in which conscious motivations and cravings may emerge from the timing and organization of actions within the system.

Recognizing the holistic nature of the psychobiological system also has clinical implications. In a healthy, well-functioning appetite system, it can be assumed that the three levels operate harmoniously and are well integrated. However, it has been argued that dieting is a form of behavioral control that desynchronizes the appetite system. During the development of eating disorders, the bingeing, vomiting, and other drastic procedures lead to an erratic delivery of nutrients with aberrant triggering of physiological responses. This means that the processes of the satiety cascade will be severely disorganized. This disorganization will lead to a desynchronization between behavior and physiology and between physiological processes and neurotransmitter activity. Therefore the harmonious interplay of levels of functioning (Figure 3.3), which is responsible for the orderly expression of appetite, will be undermined. This corruption of the processes of the biopsychological system is likely to confer an enduring legacy that will have to be dealt with through treatment.

FURTHER READING

Blundell, J. E. (1991). Pharmacological approaches to appetite suppression. *Trends in Pharmacological Sciences, 12,* 147–157. Detailed account of the integration of biological mechanisms influencing food intake.

Blundell, J. E. (1991). The biology of appetite. *Clinics in Applied Nutrition, 1,* 21–31. Overall review of the operation of the psychobiological system.

Blundell, J. E., & Hill, A. J. (1986). Biopsychological interactions underlying the study and treatment of obesity. In M. J. Christie & P. G. Mellett (Eds.), *The psychosomatic approach: Contemporary practice of whole person care* (pp. 115–138). Chichester: Wiley. Description of some specific interactions among nutrition, physiology, and behavior.

Eaton, S. B., & Konner, M. (1985). Paleolithic nutrition: A consideration of its nature and current implications. *New England Journal of Medicine, 312,* 283–289. Fascinating account of the evolutionary and anthropological background of current eating habits.

Prentice, A. M., Black, A. E., Murgatroyd, P. R., Goldberg, G. R., & Coward, W. A. (1989). Metabolism or appetite: Questions of energy balance with particular reference to obesity. *Journal of Human Nutrition and Dietetics, 2,* 95–104. Coherent description of the evidence concerning appetite control in the light of energy balance.

Ravussin, E., & Swinburn, B. A. (1992). Pathophysiology of obesity. *Lancet, 340,* 404–408. Closely argued account of the role of macronutrient (particularly fat) balance in the control of body weight.

Smith, G. P., Greenberg, D., Corp, E., & Gibbs, J. (1990). Afferent information in the control of eating. In G. A. Bray (Ed.), *Obesity: Toward a molecular approach* (pp. 63–79). New York: Liss.

VanItallie, T. B., & Vanderweele, D. A. (1981). The phenomenon of satiety. In P. Björntorp, M. Cairella, & A. N. Howard (Eds.), *Recent advances in obesity research III* (pp. 278–289). London: Libbey. Classical and comprehensive description of the physiological mechanisms underlying a frequently misunderstood phenomenon.

• 4 •

GENETIC INFLUENCES ON BODY WEIGHT AND SHAPE

Claude Bouchard

With recent advances in human genetics and molecular biology, scientists involved in the study of types of human obesity have become more optimistic about the possibility of identifying the genes associated with the predisposition to these diseases. There are good reasons to believe that this new enthusiasm is justified. Our growing understanding of the human genome, the high degree of homology between humans and common laboratory mammal models for a large number of genes and chromosomal regions, and the availability of a variety of technologies and tools to study and manipulate DNA in the laboratory are among the reasons for hope. The genes associated with an increased susceptibility to gain weight and become obese will eventually be identified and characterized. However, the difficulties to be overcome along this path should not be underestimated.

GENETICS, BODY MASS, AND BODY FAT

Most studies have used the body mass index (BMI) as the phenotype of interest. In a report published by the Carnegie Institute of Washington in 1923, C. B. Davenport described the first comprehensive attempt to understand the role of inheritance in human body mass for stature. One of his findings was that normal-weight parents will sometimes have offspring who become obese as adults, yet he also observed that obese parents frequently have normal-weight adult descendants. His study demonstrated quite convincingly that BMI values were more similar among family members than among unrelated persons. Seventy years later, we know more about the familial aggregation of obesity, but the progress has not been breathtaking.

Heritability Levels

Heritability has been considered in a large number of twin, adoption, and family studies. The level of heritability is simply the fraction of the population variation in a trait (e.g., BMI) that can be explained by genetic transmission. Heritability level estimates depend on how the study is conducted and on the kinds of relatives upon which they are based.

For instance, studies conducted with identical twins and fraternal twins, or with identical twins reared apart, have yielded the highest heritability levels, with values clustering around 70% of the variation in BMI.

In contrast, adoption studies have generated the lowest heritability estimates (about 30% and less). Family studies have generally yielded levels of heritability intermediate between the twin and adoption studies. A few investigations have included all or most of these kinds of relatives in the same analysis. The application of analytical techniques developed to use all the information and maximum likelihood procedures in these studies has led to the conclusion that the true heritability estimate for BMI in large sample sizes is between 25% and 40%. Recent surveys undertaken in Sweden and the United States with the collaboration of severely obese and morbidly obese subjects, together with information obtained about their parents, siblings, and spouses, suggest that the genetic contribution to obesity may indeed be about 25% to 40% of the individual differences in BMI.

The Single-Gene Hypothesis

In several studies based on familial data, it has been reported that a single major gene for high body mass was segregating from parents to their children. However, results of three studies did not show support for Mendelian transmission unless age and/or gender variations in the major gene were taken into account. From this small body of data, the trend seems to be for a major recessive gene that accounts for about 20% to 25% of the variance, but with age-associated effects, with a gene frequency of about 0.2. One can therefore estimate that the homozygotes for the putative recessive gene may be represented in about 5% of the population. These results must be viewed with great caution, as they are based only on the unmeasured genotype approach, and the responsible genes have not been identified.

The Risk of Becoming Obese

The results of a number of studies have shown that obese children frequently have obese parents. Thus, in about 30% of cases, both parents of obese children are obese, with a range in frequency of about 5% to 45%. About 25% to 35% of cases of obese children occur in families with normal-weight parents despite the fact that the risk of becoming obese is higher if a child has obese parents.

It is commonly observed that severely or morbidly obese persons are on the average about 10 BMI units heavier than their parents, brothers, and sisters. These obese subjects are also clearly much heavier than their obese relatives of the previous generation. Moreover the prevalence of obesity is increasing from generation to generation in almost all populations that have been studied thus far.

GENETICS AND NUTRIENT PARTITIONING

Nutrient partitioning can be defined in terms of the pattern of deposition of the ingested energy in the form of fat (lipid) or lean (protein) tissue. In adult humans, the prime metabolic fate of the ingested energy is to sustain ATP synthesis for the maintenance of cells, tissues, and a variety of essential functions. Most dietary energy is used to meet these needs, particularly in mature individuals. By some estimates, 95% to 99% of food energy is used for maintenance in the broad sense.

When basic maintenance needs have been met, any excess dietary energy can be used to support the metabolic processes leading to protein synthesis or fat deposition. Thus nutrient partitioning becomes an even more important metabolic property when the nutrients ingested are in excess of maintenance needs. Animal husbandry has shown that nutrient partitioning can be altered by a variety of factors, including diet, variations in energy expenditure, and genetics.

A nutrient-partitioning phenotype resulting in greater protein deposition should result in a decrease in the energy efficiency of energy storage in comparison with a profile favoring lipid accretion. These considerations are of considerable importance in understanding the etiology of excess body fat in humans. A nutrient-partitioning profile favoring lipid accretion over protein deposition is likely to contribute to a chronic state of positive energy balance for two main reasons. The first is the higher energy efficiency of energy storage in the form of lipid deposition. Second, when nutrient partitioning favors lipid accretion, fat-free mass is likely to contribute a progressively decreasing proportion of total body mass. In turn, the resting metabolic rate will not increase at the same rate as body mass, thus setting the stage for a state of chronic positive energy balance.

Experiments on animals have shown there are strain differences in nutrient partitioning, an indication that genes are important determinants of the phenotype. The genetic epidemiology of the nutrient-partitioning phenotype has not been considered to any extent in humans. Only one report has dealt with the heritability of nutrient partitioning and is based on data from the Quebec Family Study. A total transmission effect of about 50% was found, with a genetic transmission of approximately 20% after adjustment for the proper concomitants.

GENETICS, FAT DISTRIBUTION, AND PHYSIQUE

Fat distribution is of considerable clinical importance (see Chapter 79). There is a small body of knowledge on fat distribution, shape, and physique suggesting that genetic variation may be of great importance for some phenotypes.

The heritability of subcutaneous fat distribution after adjustment for total body fat attains 30% to 50% of the phenotype variance. Such is the case for the amount of fat on the trunk and abdominal area or for the amount of lower-body fat (both assessed from skinfolds or CT scans), adjusted statistically for age, gender, and total body fat. At this time, no heritability estimate has been reported for the amount of abdominal visceral fat, the most atherogenic fat depot of the human body. Only two studies have dealt with the issue of a major gene effect on indicators of regional fat distribution. In both, it was concluded that a major gene effect was detectable and that it accounted for about 40% of the phenotype variance. In addition, these studies showed that a multifactorial component was contributing another 10% to 20% of the subcutaneous fat distribution.

Family studies, twin studies, and adoption data reveal that some of the individual differences in physique are inherited. For instance, in a series of reports based on the Heath and Carter somatotype components, we have shown that the heritability levels were quite low for the endomorphic and ectomorphic components but clearly higher for the mesomorphic component.

RESPONSE TO EXPERIMENTAL OVERFEEDING

In some individuals prone to excessive accumulation of fat, losing weight represents a continuous battle. Yet there are others who seem relatively protected against such a menace. To examine whether such differences could be accounted for by genetic factors, differences in the sensitivity of individuals to gain fat when chronically exposed to a positive energy balance and the dependence or independence of such differences on the genotype were considered. An affirmative answer to both questions would suggest a significant genotype–environment interaction. The results of a complex experiment suggest that such an effect does exist for total body fat and fat topography.

We studied 12 pairs of male identical twins who consumed a caloric surplus of 1,000 kilocalories per day, 6 days per week, for 100 days. Significant increases in body weight and fat mass were observed after the overfeeding. There were considerable interindividual differences in the adaptation to excess calories and the observed variation was not randomly distributed, as indicated by the significant within-pair resemblance in response. For instance, there was at least three times more variance in response between pairs than within pairs for gains in body weight and fat mass. These data demonstrate that some individuals are more at risk than others to gain fat (high responders) when surplus energy intake is set at the same level for everyone and when all subjects are confined to a sedentary life-style. The within-identical-twin-pair response to the standardized caloric surplus suggests that the amount of fat stored is probably influenced by the genotype. However, the intrapair resemblance in the amount of weight or fat mass gained reached only about 0.50, as shown by the intraclass coefficients computed with the changes in these phenotypes from overfeeding. In other words, nongenetic factors were responsible for the intrapair variation in body mass and body fat gains.

The results also suggested that the within-pair resemblance for fat gains in specific fat depots was even higher than for the total amount of body mass or body fat gained. For instance, there was about six to seven times more variation between pairs of twins than within pairs for the amount of fat gained on the trunk or the abdominal or abdominal visceral area, after adjustment for the amount of fat mass gained.

THE COMPLEXITY OF HUMAN OBESITY

Excessive body fat content is a complex multifactorial trait evolving under the interactive influences of dozens of affectors from the social, behavioral, physiological, metabolic, cellular, and molecular domains. Segregation of the genes is not easily detected in familial or pedigree studies, and whatever the influence of the genotype on the etiology, it is generally attenuated or exacerbated by nongenetic factors.

Efforts to understand the genetic basis of such traits can be successful only if they are based on an appropriate conceptual framework, adequate phenotype and intermediate phenotype measurements, proper samples of unrelated persons and nuclear families or extended pedigrees, and extensive candidate gene typing and other molecular markers. In this context, the distinction between "necessary" genes and "susceptibility" genes is particularly relevant. For instance, in the case of obesity, there are several examples of necessary loci resulting in excess body mass or body fat for height; that is, carriers of the deficient alleles have the disease (e.g., Prader–Willi cases). However, cases such as these represent only a small fraction of the obese population.

In contrast, a susceptibility gene is defined as one that increases susceptibility or risk for the disease but is not necessary for disease expression. An allele at a susceptibility gene may make it more likely that the carrier will become affected, but the presence of that allele is not sufficient by itself to explain the occurrence of the disease. It merely lowers the threshold for a person to develop the disease.

In addition, it is likely that body fat content is also modulated over the lifetime of a person by a variety of gene–environment interaction effects. These effects result from the fact that sensitivity to environmental agents or conditions or life-style differences vary from individual to individual because of genetic individuality. Among the factors of interest here are dietary fat, energy intake, level of habitual physical activity, smoking, and alcohol intake. Moreover, even though data are lacking on the topic, it is obvious that gene–gene interaction effects need to be considered. However, little research bearing directly on this topic has been reported so far.

From the research currently available, a good number of genes seem to have the capacity to cause obesity or increase the likelihood of becoming obese when they are altered or dysfunctional in mammals. Even though the investigation of molecular markers of obesity has barely begun, already identified are about 20 genes, loci, or chromosomal regions that appear to play a role in determining the obesity phenotypes. They are located on about a dozen different chromosomes. Many additional genes will surely be identified such that the panel of human obesity genes, based on association, linkage, or animal models, will grow and become quite large. This may reflect how most human obesity cases come about. In other words, the susceptibility genotypes may result from allelic variations at a good number of genes.

Association and linkage genetic studies are now more frequently reported. Based on the current understanding of the pathophysiology of human obesity, we expect that the candidate gene approach will yield useful association and linkage results. Moreover, with the advent of a comprehensive human genetic linkage map, linkage studies with a large number of markers covering most of the chromosomal length of the human genome are likely to be helpful in the identification of putative obesity genes or chromosomal regions. Recent progress in animal genetics, transfection systems, transgenic animal models, recombinant DNA technologies applied to positional cloning, and methods of identifying loci that contribute to quantitative traits have given a new impetus to this field. The stage is now set for major advances in the understanding of the genetic and molecular basis of complex diseases such as human obesity.

FURTHER READING

Borecki, I. B., Bonney, G. E., Rice, T., Bouchard, C., & Rao, D. C. (1993). Influence of genotype-dependent effects of covariates on the outcome of segregation analysis of the body mass index. *American Journal of Human Genetics, 53,* 676–687. Provides an overview of the evidence for the role of genes in human obesity and its major determinants.

Bouchard, C., Després, J. P., & Mauriège, P. (1993). Genetic and nongenetic determinants of regional fat distribution. *Endocrine Reviews, 14,* 72–93. A summary of the literature on the causes of variation in fat topography.

Bouchard, C., Tremblay, A., Després, J. P., Nadeau, A., Lupien, P. J., Thériault, G., Dussault, J., Moorjani, S., Pineault, S., & Fournier, G. (1990). The response to long-term overfeeding in identical twins. *New England Journal of Medicine, 322,* 1477–1482. A paper describing the resemblance in twins in the changes in body composition and fat distribution with chronic exposure to overfeeding.

Friedman, J. M., Leibel, R. L., & Bahary, N. (1991). Molecular mapping of obesity genes. *Mammalian Genome, 1*, 130–144. An overview of the rodent model of obesity and of the positional cloning strategy to identify genes determining obesity.

Greenberg, D. A. (1993). Linkage analysis of "necessary" disease loci versus "susceptibility" loci. *American Journal of Human Genetics, 52*, 135–143. A paper defining the concepts of association and linkage and their usefulness in the identification of genes with major or minor effects.

Reed, D. R., Bradley, E. C., & Price, R. A. (1993). Obesity in families of extremely obese women. *Obesity Research, 1*, 167–172. Familial aggregation for severe obesity and risk of obesity, with parental phenotypes.

Rice, T., Borecki, I. B., Bouchard, C., & Rao, D. C. (1993). Segregation analysis of fat mass and other body composition measures derived from underwater weighing. *American Journal of Human Genetics, 52*, 967–973. Segregation analysis of specific body composition phenotypes derived from underwater weighing.

Rice, T., Borecki, I. B., Bouchard, C., & Rao, D. C. (1993). Segregation analysis of body mass index in an unselected French-Canadian sample: The Québec Family Study. *Obesity Research, 1*, 288–294. Segregation analysis for BMI and comparisons with previous studies.

• 5 •

ENERGY INTAKE
AND BODY WEIGHT

ANN L. ALBRIGHT
JUDITH S. STERN

The relationship of energy intake and body weight is summarized by the following equation:

$$Energy_{in} - Energy_{out} = Energy_{stored}$$

Excessive energy intake or reduced energy output results in energy storage and weight gain. A reduction in intake or an increase in expenditure results in reduced energy storage and weight loss. This simple equation is deceptive in that food choice, energy intake, energy storage, and body weight are influenced by a number of factors, including the pattern of eating and the type and combination of macronutrients (Figure 5.1). Consider, for example, a Thanksgiving meal where social, emotional, environmental, and hedonic factors can lead to overeating even when an individual acknowledges she/he is "full."

IS ENERGY INTAKE OUT OF CONTROL?

It is counterintuitive to believe that food intake is controlled in the face of an epidemic of obesity in the United States. Despite the U.S. government's declaration that fewer citizens will be obese by the year 2000, adults *gained* an average of 10 pounds between National Health and Nutrition Examination Survey (NHANES) II and NHANES III surveys (a period spanning approximately 11 years, from 1980 to 1991). The average nonoverweight man consumes about 1 million kilocalories each year, and a change of only 3% in energy intake or output will result in a weight gain of almost 10 pounds per year. Therefore, precise regulation of energy balance is needed for weight stability.

FOOD INTAKE AND OBESITY

Increased body weight is frequently attributed to increased food intake, but the issue of whether obese individuals eat more than normal-weight individuals is complex, and answers have varied depending on how food intake was measured. In genetically obese

27

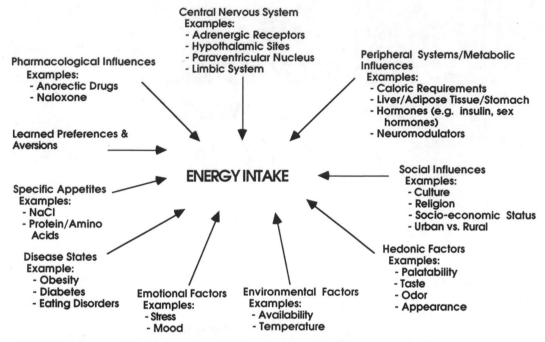

FIGURE 5.1. Some of the factors that influence energy intake and subsequent body weight.

rats, increased energy intake beginning at weaning is associated with rapid weight gain. As weight gain slows, food intake of these rats is comparable to that of nonobese littermates even though the obese rats outweigh the lean rats by 100%.

Excessive food consumption is not a primary cause of obesity in all cases. Obese rats pair fed with lean rats gain less weight but still weigh more than lean rats and are still obese. In humans, not all studies find relationships between daily energy intake and adiposity or body weight, but there are limitations in the methods used to assess food intake and the energy content of the food. In one study, caloric labeling was more accurate for nationally advertised foods than for regionally distributed foods (mean percentage over label per item was +2.2% vs. +25.2%, respectively).

Reports of caloric intake vary with the method and the type of subject (see Chapter 19). In one study of normal and overweight women, information was presented from 1- and 3-day food records and from clinic dietary and research diet histories. For normal-weight women, all methods revealed a daily energy intake within a few kilocalories (1,964–2,201 kilocalories). Obese women averaged 1,591 kilocalories in 3-day records and 2,829 kilocalories in research dietary histories. More precise results are obtained using stable isotopes or studying people housed in metabolic wards.

Fat, Carbohydrate, and Protein

Energy intake is only one consideration in body weight change. Epidemiologic data reveal that consumption of high-fat foods and concentrated sweets independently predict increases in body weight. Conversely, eating a diet comprising foods low in fat and sugar is associated with maintenance of lower weight in formerly obese women. These data are supported by work in experimental animals. When fed fat and sugar together, rats gain more body fat than when fed fat and sugar separately. Sugar and fat fed in combination increase plasma insulin levels and the activity of lipoprotein lipase, an enzyme necessary for storage of circulating fat in adipose tissue.

The case linking dietary fat and obesity in humans is not definitive, but available evidence suggests cause and effect. In some studies, obese individuals derive a greater proportion of energy intake from fat; obese women have a higher percentage of energy intake from fat than do obese men. Fat intake may be increased by weight cycling (see Chapter 11). Studies in which individuals are purposely overfed show that weight gain is more rapid on a high-fat diet than on an equivacaloric high-carbohydrate diet (Figure 5.2) Fat overfeeding produces a greater positive fat balance than does carbohydrate overfeeding, especially in obese subjects.

The Importance of Meal Patterns

Laboratory rats that eat their daily food in large meals ("meal feeding") gain more weight and become fatter than animals that eat the same amount and type of food in many small meals ("nibbling"). Meal feeding is associated with increased energy efficiency in animals. In humans, such data are suggestive but not definitive.

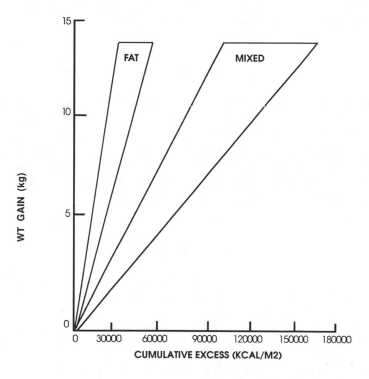

FIGURE 5.2. Weight gained by overfeeding a mixed diet for 7 months versus fat for 3 months. From Danfort (1985, pp. 1136). Copyright 1985 by *American Journal of Clinical Nutrition*. Adapted by permission of the American Society for Clinical Nutrition.

Energy Restriction, Dietary Fat, and Body Weight

In rats fed a modest energy-restricted diet, those with a 45% fat restriction had significantly greater weight loss and reduction in adiposity than did 12% fat-restricted rats. This finding suggests that body composition is not normalized by a moderate reduction of energy intake unless fat is reduced. Body composition varies with the type of fat (saturated fatty acids promote greater fat gain than do polyunsaturated fatty acids), genetic background, within-strain differences, gender, and age.

The overconsumption of fat has been attributed to its sensory qualities. It is possible, but unlikely, that dietary fat may be overconsumed because it is less satiating than other nutrients. However, fat stimulates the release of cholecystokinin, which might lead to early satiety.

Insight into specific effects of fat on food intake and body weight may come from studies of metabolism. Fat is not metabolized as rapidly after meals as are carbohydrate and protein. Changes in carbohydrate and protein oxidation rates may compensate for fluctuations in their intake. Fat intake does not cause comparably rapid changes in its oxidation rate, which would result in increased fat storage.

Scientific debate continues about the effects of macronutrients on satiety. Some high-carbohydrate foods may exert a restraining effect on appetite. When subjects eat freely from a selection of high-carbohydrate foods, energy intake is suppressed. However, people may eat to maintain a critical level of carbohydrate in the diet, so when carbohydrate content is low, food intake may increase to achieve some regulated level of carbohydrate intake. There are differential effects of glucose (insulinogenic) versus fructose (noninsulinogenic) preloads on subsequent meal size.

CONCLUSION

It has been argued that diet composition is not a major factor in weight gain but is central to the maintenance of lost weight. The degree of negative energy balance is a major determinant of the amount and rate of weight loss. With weight loss, energy requirements and perhaps fat oxidation are reduced. To prevent fat storage and a subsequent increase in body weight, fat oxidation may be increased (e.g., via exercise) or fat intake reduced. These observations support the notion that the combination of a reduced-fat diet and regular exercise is the key to weight maintenance.

FURTHER READING

Beaudoin, R., & Mayer, J. (1953). Food intake of obese and nonobese women. *Journal of the American Dietetic Association, 29,* 29–33. One of the original studies investigating food selection patterns of obese and nonobese women.

Blundell, J. E., Green, S., & Burley, V. (1994). Carbohydrates and human appetite. *American Journal of Clincial Nutrition, 59,* 728S–734S. Thorough review of factors that exert influence on hunger and appetite.

Centers for Disease Control. (1994). Health objectives for the nation: Daily dietary fat and total food-energy intakes—Third National Health and Nutrition Examination Survey, Phase 1, 1988–1991. *Morbidity and Mortality Weekly Report, 43,* 116–125. Presentation of selected results from NHANES III, including body weight, food-energy, and fat intakes in the United States.

Danforth, E. Jr. (1985). Diet and obesity. *American Journal of Clinical Nutrition, 41,* 1132–1145. Discussion of the effect of fat content in the diet and body weight gain.

Flatt, J. P. (1988). Importance of nutrient balance in body weight regulation. *Diabetes/Metabolism Reviews, 4,* 571–581. Discussion of the relative contributions of fat oxidation and carbohydrate oxidation to body weight regulation.

Hill, J. O., Drougas, H., & Peters, J. C. (1993). Obesity treatment: Can diet composition play a role? *Annals of Internal Medicine, 119,* 694–697. Proposes that diet composition has a greater impact during the maintenance of reduced body weight than during weight reduction.

Miller, W. C. (1990). Diet composition, energy intake, and nutritional status in relation to obesity in men and women. *Medicine and Science in Sports and Exercise, 23,* 280–284. Supports the idea that diet composition may play a more important role in the development of obesity than does total energy intake.

Thomas, P. R., & Stern, J. S. (1994). *Weighing the options: Criteria for evaluating weight-management programs.* Washington DC: National Academy of Sciences Press. This book provides information on demographic trends in body weight and food intake in the United States. It examines how client demographics and characterics—including their health status, knowledge of weight-loss issues, and attitudes toward weight and body image—affect which programs clients choose, how successful they are likely to be with their choices, and what this information means for outcome measurements.

• 6 •

ENERGY EXPENDITURE AND BODY WEIGHT

Eric Ravussin

Obesity results from a chronic excess of energy intake relative to energy expenditure. Some researchers have hypothesized that energy imbalance is a result of inherited metabolic characteristics, whereas others believe it is caused by poor health habits, that is, by "gluttony and sloth."

A consistent observation is that human obesity is a familial disorder (see Chapter 4). Since family members share not only genes but also diet, cultural background, and many aspects of life-style, other methods are needed to divide this familial trait into its genetic and environmental components. Studies of twins and adoptees have provided evidence for an important genetic basis for obesity (see Chapter 4). Data from studies on over-feeding in monozygotic twins show that weight gain for a given energy excess depends mostly on genotype. Studies of twins reared apart or together indicate that approximately 70% of the variance in adult body mass index is related to genetic variability, whereas the remaining 30% is mostly attributable to the effect of "nonshared environment" unique to the individual.

The large impact of genetics on body weight is certainly apparent in the relatively uniform environment of industrialized countries where fatty food is plentiful and labor-saving devices are common. The increased prevalence of obesity that accompanied industrialization and urbanization, in migrating populations and after World War II, emphasizes, however, the importance of the environment as an influence on body weight. It is safe to say that the prevalence of obesity *in populations* is largely determined by the environment, whereas obesity *in individuals* in a given environment is largely determined by their genetic responses to that environment. Whether genetic factors influence body weight by acting on energy expenditure or on food intake (or both) is not known. Since food intake assessment under laboratory conditions is precise but does not reflect everyday life, and since the accuracy and precision of food intake measurements under free-living conditions are poor, scientists have concentrated on the energy expenditure side of the energy balance equation.

RELEVANCE OF THE COMPONENTS OF ENERGY EXPENDITURE TO OBESITY

Technology advances have made possible the use of indirect calorimetry (respiratory chambers) to measure metabolic rates of individuals over periods of hours or days. In

such chambers all components of sedentary energy expenditure can be measured—
sleeping metabolic rate, the energy cost of arousal, the thermic effect of food, and the
energy cost of spontaneous physical activity (Figure 6.1).

Resting Metabolic Rate

The resting metabolic rate (RMR) is the energy expended by a person who is fasting and
at rest in the morning under comfortable ambient conditions. The RMR includes the
cost of maintaining the integrated system of the body and the homeothermic temperature at rest. In most sedentary adults, RMR accounts for approximately 60% to 70% of
the daily energy expenditure. The strong relationship between RMR and body size has
been known for many years and has led to the development of equations still widely used
to predict RMR for each sex from height and weight. The heavier the individual, the
greater the *absolute* RMR and, indeed, total energy expenditure. Although RMR correlates best with fat-free body mass, it is also, to a lesser extent, independently influenced
by fat mass, age, and sex. Together, fat-free mass, fat mass, age, and sex explain
approximately 80% to 85% of the variance in RMR. As shown in sibling and twin studies,
some of the interindividual variability in RMR is likely to be genetically determined (see
Chapter 4).

The activity of the sympathetic nervous system and resting skeletal muscle metabolism are also determinants of RMR. Whether the level of physical activity or physical
fitness is a determinant of RMR remains controversial. The variability in adjusted
metabolic rate is related to the variability in body temperature. Body temperature might,
therefore, be a marker of a high or low *relative* metabolic rate.

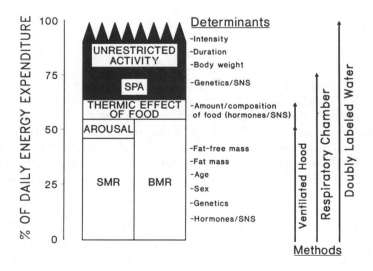

FIGURE 6.1. Components of daily energy expenditure in humans and methods of measurement.
Daily energy expenditure can be divided into three major components: the basal metabolic rate
(BMR) (sleeping metabolic rate [SMR] + energy cost of arousal), which represents 50% to 70% of
daily expenditure; the thermic effect of food, which represents approximately 10% of energy
expenditure; and the energy cost of physical activity (spontaneous physical activity [SPA] +
unrestricted/voluntary physical activity), which represents 20% to 40% of daily energy expenditure. SNS, sympathetic nervous system.

Thermogenesis

Thermogenesis is the increase in RMR in response to stimuli such as food intake, cold or heat exposure, psychological influences such as fear or stress, or the administration of drugs or hormones that mimic the physiological response to such stimuli. The thermic effect of food (the major form of thermogenesis) accounts for approximately 10% of daily energy expenditure.

Opinions differ about whether a decreased thermic effect of food is present in obese individuals or is involved in the etiology of obesity. In reviewing published studies comparing the thermic effect of food in lean and obese subjects, in 28 studies a lower thermic effect of food was present in the obese, whereas in 17 no difference between groups was apparent.

The thermic effect of food is the most difficult and the least reproducible component of energy expenditure to assess because it is influenced by many factors, such as test meal size and composition; palatability of the food; technique used for measurements; time and duration of measurements; and the subject's genetic background, age, physical fitness, and sensitivity to insulin. All these factors might explain the inconsistency and variability of the results when the thermic effect of food is measured. Recent studies in postobese subjects and in lean subjects during artificial abdominal insulation with blankets have shown that the reduced thermic effect of food in the obese is likely to be a secondary feature to the obese state. Prospective studies have not identified a low thermic effect of food as a predisposing factor for body weight gain. In summary, it can be safely stated that any decrease in the thermic effect of food amounts to only a small number of calories and that a minimal weight gain (and thus increased RMR) would be sufficient to offset this decreased energy expenditure.

Physical Activity

The most variable component of daily energy expenditure is that expended during physical activity, which may account for a significant number of calories in very active people. However, sedentary adult individuals exhibit a range of physical activity that still represents about 20% to 30% of the total calorie expenditure. Reduced physical activity as a cause of obesity is an obvious and attractive hypothesis that is supported by the secular increase in obesity paralleling the increase in sedentary life styles (see Chapter 84). However, until the recent introduction of the doubly labeled water method to measure energy expenditure in free-living conditions (see Chapter 20), there has been no satisfactory method by which to assess the impact of physical activity on daily energy expenditure.

Figure 6.1 presents the methods used to assess the different components of daily energy expenditure and to differentiate unrestricted from spontaneous physical activity by combining measurements of energy expenditure using doubly labeled water and indirect calorimetry (respiratory chamber or ventilated hood). Significant differences between individuals with respect to spontaneous physical activity (the name given to small, "fidgeting-type" movements) have been reported. A low level of spontaneous physical activity was also shown to be a risk factor for body weight gain. Clearly the total energy expenditure from physical activity under free-living conditions is much greater than spontaneous physical activity and also varies widely among individuals. The energy cost of weight-bearing activities is proportional to body weight and therefore is higher in obese individuals, although obesity is generally associated with lower activity levels. The net energy expenditure related to physical activity is therefore similar or lower in obese people than in lean people. Recent studies in which the doubly labeled water method was used have shown that the level of physical activity decreases with both increasing age and increasing adiposity.

Total Energy Expenditure

Total energy expenditure is usually assessed under sedentary conditions in a respiratory chamber by indirect calorimetry or, more recently, under free-living conditions by the doubly labeled water technique.

Indirect calorimetry provides measurements of energy expenditure and fuel mix derived from oxygen consumption, carbon dioxide production, and nitrogen excretion. During the past two decades this method has been used in respiratory chambers around the world. All the studies in respiratory chambers have shown that 24-hour energy expenditure is directly proportional to body fat-free mass or body weight (Figure 6.2).

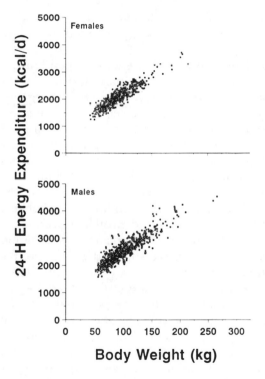

FIGURE 6.2. Relation between 24-hour energy expenditure and body weight in female and male subjects. Upper panel: 591 measurements of 24-hour energy expenditure in woman with a mean age of 33 ± 12 years (range 18–85 years), body weight of 90 ± 27 kilograms (range 41–320 kilograms), and percentage body fat of 43% ± 9% (range 10%–62%). The mean 24-hour energy expenditure was 2,065 ± 387 kilocalories per day (range 1,251–4,381 kilocalories per day). Lower panel: 967 measurements of 24-hour energy expenditure in men with a mean age of 31 ± 10 years (range 18–81 years), body weight of 95 ± 30 kilograms (range 51–266 kilograms), and percentage body fat of 30% ± 11% (range 3%–62%). The mean 24-hour energy expenditure was 2,462 ± 447 kilocalories per day (range 1,584–4,530 kilocalories per day).

The major disadvantage of this technique is the confinement of the subjects to a small room.

Measuring energy expenditure in unconfined subjects has obvious advantages, but the original methods for estimating this type of energy expenditure, such as factorial methods and measured energy intake, often result in poor agreement with respiratory chamber measurements. The doubly labeled water technique was first used in human subjects in 1982. It is a form of "indirect indirect calorimetry" based on the differential elimination of deuterium (^{2}H) and ^{18}O (taken as a drink of water enriched with ^{2}H$_2$^{18}O) from body water after a loading dose of these two isotopes. Since ^{18}O exits the body as water and CO_2, and deuterium exits the body only as water, the difference between the two elimination rates is proportional to CO_2 production and, therefore, to energy expenditure.

The greatest advantage of the doubly labeled water method is that it provides an integrated measure of total carbon dioxide production over periods of 5 to 20 days and yet requires only periodic sampling of urine for measurements of deuterium and ^{18}O enrichment. Subjects can be studied in the free-living state and are not limited in activity by wearing cumbersome monitors. The method is totally noninvasive, can be used in pregnant women, infants, children, and adults as well as in elderly subjects and has now been validated repeatedly in humans. Recent studies using the doubly labeled water method have shown that total daily energy expenditure is mostly related to body weight.

Two points emerge from the studies of energy expenditure. Consistently one finds that the larger the body size (greater fat-free mass and fat mass) the higher the *absolute* metabolic rates (sedentary and free-living RMR). Thus energy intake studies that show no correlations or negative correlations between energy intake and body weight are confounded by underreporting in the obese. The second point is that the lowest 24-hour energy expenditures are in very lean women and are of the order of 1,250 to 1,300 kilocalories per day (Figure 6.2). Therefore energy intakes of less than this range will produce an energy deficit and weight loss in any individual.

Recently the pioneering work of Flatt has redirected the research in energy metabolism. Flatt noted that under normal conditions, carbohydrate, protein, and alcohol are not converted to fat. Glycogen and protein stores are closely controlled, and increasing the intake of nonfat nutrients stimulates the oxidation rates proportionally. Thus a chronic imbalance between intake and oxidation of nonfat nutrients cannot lead to obesity. On the other hand, fat stores are not controlled, and the capacity for expansion is enormous. Because an increase in fat intake does not stimulate fat oxidation, a positive fat balance results that has the potential to become chronic. Obesity is therefore due to a long-standing positive fat balance that may simply be due to a high fat diet and/or an impaired capacity for fat oxidation. The use of the fat-balance equation instead of the energy-balance equation adds another option for the treatment of obesity, that of changing the quality of the diet (i.e., lowering the fat content).

METABOLIC PREDICTORS OF BODY WEIGHT GAIN

In prospective studies conducted in Native American Pima subjects, four metabolic parameters that are known to have a familial component have been found to predict weight gain. These are (1) a low *relative* RMR (adjusted for differences in fat-free mass, fat mass, age, and sex), (2) a low level of spontaneous physical activity, (3) a high 24-hour respiratory quotient, and (4) high insulin sensitivity.

Cross-sectional studies show that all four parameters correlate with body size: RMR versus fat-free mass; energy cost of spontaneous physical activity versus weight; 24-hour respiratory quotient versus body fat; and insulin sensitivity versus weight. When these parameters are adjusted for differences in body size, the initial value predicts the rate of change in body weight over the subsequent years: RMR adjusted for differences in fat-free mass, fat mass, age, and sex; 24-hour respiratory quotient adjusted for fat mass; and insulin sensitivity adjusted for weight. After weight gain the original deviation from the value predicted on the basis of population (e.g., low *relative* RMR, high 24-hour respiratory quotient, and high insulin sensitivity) tends to diminish, suggesting a progressively decreasing physiological drive for further body weight gain. Thus the high RMR, high energy cost of spontaneous physical activity, low respiratory quotient, and low insulin sensitivity seen in obese people may act to limit additional weight gain. The relationships of these metabolic factors with body weight changes are relatively weak, indicating that other factors are also involved, such as total food intake, the composition of the diet, and the level of physical activity. However, it is important to realize that, even if weak, the impact of the four metabolic factors considered here is of similar magnitude to that reported for socioeconomic and life-style factors.

In conclusion, interindividual variations in resting metabolic rate, spontaneous physical activity, the relative rates of carbohydrate-to-fat oxidation, and the degree of insulin sensitivity seem to be closely involved in energy balance and in determining body weight in some individuals. In view of the known familial nature of these parameters, it seems likely that they contribute to the inherited tendency to obesity.

FURTHER READING

Flatt, J. P. (1993). Dietary fat, carbohydrate balance and weight maintenance. *Annals of the New York Academy of Sciences, 683*, 122–140. Fat balance versus energy balance.

Garrow, J. S. (1978). *Energy balance and obesity in man* (2nd ed.). Amsterdam: Elsevier. The most comprehensive book on energy balance.

Ravussin, E., & Swinburn, B. A. (1992). Effect of caloric restriction and weight loss on energy expenditure. In T. A. Wadden & T. B. VanItallie (Eds.), *Treatment of the seriously obese patient* (pp. 162–189). New York: Guilford Press. Pros and cons of "metabolic adaptation" during weight loss.

Ravussin, E., & Swinburn, B. A. (1992). Pathophysiology of obesity. *Lancet, 340*, 404–408. Metabolic risk factors for body weight gain.

Ravussin, E., & Swinburn, B. A. (1993). Energy metabolism. In A. J. Stunkard & T. A. Wadden (Eds.), *Obesity: Theory and therapy* (2nd ed., pp. 97–123). New York: Raven Press. Recent review of the literature dealing with energy metabolism and obesity.

Schoeller, D. A., & Field, C. R. (1991). Human energy metabolism: What have we learned from the doubly labeled water method? *Annual Review of Nutrition, 11*, 355–373. Review of the literature concerning the doubly labeled method.

• 7 •
EFFECT OF ENERGY IMBALANCE ON ENERGY STORES AND BODY WEIGHT

John S. Garrow

It is obvious that if energy intake is greater (or less) than energy output, then the energy stores of the body must increase (or decrease). If the energy stores change, body weight will usually change in the same direction, but the relationship between weight change and energy storage is not simple, and there are special circumstances in which they can (for a short time) move in opposite directions. This causes confusion in the patient, who concludes that the diet (or other treatment) does not work, because the observed weight change is not of the desired magnitude or may even be in the wrong direction.

Table 7.1 sets out the approximate contributions of water, protein, fat, glycogen, and mineral to body weight and to energy stores in a normal adult male and in an obese adult male. The largest component of body weight is water, which makes no contribution to energy stores. The largest component of energy stores is fat, which contributes about 17% of body weight in a normal man. Even in the case of an obese man, who has double the normal fat stores, fat contributes only about 28% of body weight. Thus, by altering the proportion of fat to water in the body, the relationship of weight to energy storage can be markedly changed.

The components shown in Table 7.1 are not free to change independently of each other. It is convenient to think of a normal adult as having two components: fat and fat-free mass (see Chapter 8). In Table 7.1, the fat component is 12 kilograms and the fat-free mass the remainder, 58 kilograms. However, when in the obese adult the fat mass increases from 12 kilograms to 24 kilograms, the fat-free mass also increases by 4 kilograms by the addition of 3 kilograms of water and 1 kilograms of protein. It has been shown among adults of similar height that the excess weight in obese individuals compared with lean individuals consists of 75% fat and 25% fat-free mass. Table 7.2 shows that the energy stored in this excess weight is 7,000 kilocalories per kilogram. Thus we would expect that during periods of energy imbalance, weight should change by 1 kilogram for every 7,000 kilocalories of energy excess or deficit. This expectation is upheld by observation in the second and subsequent weeks of weight loss during moderate energy restriction. However, somewhat different rules apply during the first week of moderate energy restriction, during starvation, and during prolonged overfeeding. These exceptions will be discussed below.

TABLE 7.1. Contribution of Main Components of the Body to Weight and Energy Stores in a Typical Adult Male and in an Obese Adult Male

	Typical adult male		Obese adult male	
Component	Weight (kg)	Energy (Mcal)	Weight (kg)	Energy (Mcal)
Water	42	0	45	0
Protein	12	48	13	52
Fat	12	108	24	216
Glycogen	0.5	2	0.5	2
Mineral and other	3.50	0	3.50	0
Total	70	158	86	270

Note. Values are approximate.

Early Weight Loss during Moderate Energy Restriction

Figure 7.1 shows the cumulative weight loss in a large series of obese women who were fed a diet supplying 800 kilocalories per day for 3 weeks in a metabolic ward. Their energy intake and output were carefully monitored, and during the second and third week of the study, the weight loss conformed to the rule that 1 kilograms of weight lost signifies a decrease of 7,000 kilocalories in energy stores. However, during the first week, weight loss was less predictable and (in general) more rapid than this rule predicts.

Several factors probably explain the initial rapid and irregular phase of weight loss. The most important is that at the beginning of a period of energy restriction, the energy deficit is met by sacrificing glycogen rather than adipose tissue. Glycogen binds three times its weight of water, so when 1 kilogram of glycogen/water is used, the energy yield is only 1,000 kilocalories, rather than the 7,000 kilocalories derived from a similar weight of adipose tissue. Another factor that helps to explain the rapid-weight-loss phase is that the diet supplied on the metabolic ward had relatively low concentrations of sodium and dietary fiber. Thus, patients who had been eating a high-fiber or high sodium diet before admission would experience a decrease in bowel contents, or in extracellular water, on switching to the metabolic ward diet.

In some patients there was paradoxical weight gain during the first week on a diet supplying 800 kilocalories per day. This weight gain certainly did not signify an increase

TABLE 7.2. Energy Value of 1 Kilogram of Adipose Tissue Consisting of 750 Grams of Fat and 250 Grams of Fat-Free Tissue

Component	Weight (g)	Energy (kcal)
Fat	750	6,750
Fat-free tissue[a]	250	250
Total	1,000	7,000

[a]Fat-free tissue may be regarded either as 25% protein +75% water or as 25% glycogen + 75% water. In either case the energy value is 1,000 kilocalories per kilogram.

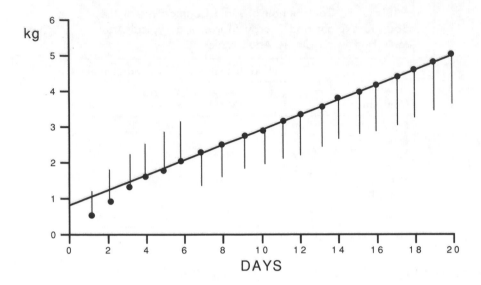

FIGURE 7.1. Mean cumulative weight loss among 108 obese women on a diet of 800 kilocalories per day for 3 weeks (bars show 1 SD)

in energy stores, since measured energy output was never less than 1,400 kilocalories per day. The explanation is probably that patients had become either dehydrated or extremely glycogen depleted by the use of diuretics, purgatives, or starvation immediately before admission to the metabolic ward. Restoration of a normal level of water or glycogen would cause a weight gain that was greater than the weight loss associated with a decrease in energy stores. By the end of the first week, weight loss began to obey the prediction of 1 kilogram per 7,000 kilocalories of energy deficit.

WEIGHT LOSS DURING TOTAL STARVATION

Twenty years ago, total starvation was advocated as a treatment for obesity, because weight loss was rapid (approximately 3 kilograms per week over a period of 6 to 12 weeks) and apparently well tolerated. The treatment was abandoned because some patients unexpectedly died; at autopsy they were found to have degenerative changes in heart muscle. It is obvious that if the patient was losing 3 kilograms/week of tissue that had an energy value of 7,000 kilocalories per kilogram, the average energy deficit would be 3,000 kilocalories per day, which is impossible, since few starving patients have an energy output as high as 3,000 kilocalories per day.

The explanation is that during total starvation, the composition of weight lost is approximately 50% fat and 50% fat-free mass. This ratio is shown by the loss of about 15 grams of nitrogen per kilograms of weight lost. The energy value of this mixture of fat and lean tissue is 5,000 kilocalories per kilogram, so a loss of 3 kilograms/week of this material during total starvation implies an average daily energy expenditure of 2,140 kilocalories per day, which is a plausible value.

WEIGHT CHANGE DURING OVERFEEDING

It is much more difficult to predict the weight that will be gained during overfeeding than the weight that will be lost during underfeeding, for several reasons. First, it is more difficult to obtain volunteers for long-term overfeeding than for long-term underfeeding experiments, since far more people wish to lose weight than gain it. With short-term studies it is difficult to predict weight change due to the effect of changes in glycogen stores, which were discussed above. Second, during overfeeding energy expenditure increases by two mechanisms: The thermic effect of feeding is greater with a greater energy intake, and resting metabolic rate increases as body weight increases. Therefore, a given increase in energy intake causes a positive energy balance of ever-decreasing magnitude. Finally, and most mysterious, there is "adaptive thermogenesis": an increase in energy expenditure that occurs under conditions of overfeeding by processes that are not fully understood but that include alterations in the metabolism of both catecholamines and thyroid hormones.

Examples of weight gain during prolonged experimental overfeeding are provided by the Vermont study. Normal volunteers were fed about 7,000 kilocalories per day for 6 months and gained about 18 kilograms each. Unfortunately, their energy balance was not accurately measured, since the prime objective of the study was to see whether insulin insensitivity was induced in normal people by experimental obesity (it was). If we assume that the positive energy balance was at least 3,000 kilocalories per day for 180 days, the total excess intake was 540 megacalories, which, if stored as adipose tissue, would have caused a weight gain of 77 kilograms, but the observed weight gain was only about 18 kilograms. On this evidence only, $^{18}/_{77}$, or 23%, of the excess was accounted for by energy storage, so the remaining 77% was somehow lost.

Shorter-term but better controlled experiments with smaller weight gains were reported by Webb and Annis. They overfed volunteers by 1,000 kilocalories per day for 30 days and observed an average weight gain of 2.4 kilograms, which is about 56% of that predicted had all the excess been stored as adipose tissue. Some subjects in this experiment described themselves as "easy gainers" and others as "hard gainers," but there was no difference between these groups in the amount of weight gained for the same excess energy intake. Indeed, in reviews of metabolic responses to overfeeding it is now concluded that although adaptive thermogenesis exists, it is certainly not able to dispose of substantial increases in energy intake, and most of the extra energy output can be explained by changes in metabolic rate that are a consequence of the changes in body composition.

FURTHER READING

Forbes, G. B., & Drenick, E. J. (1979). Loss of body nitrogen on fasting. *American Journal of Clinical Nutrition, 32,* 1570–1574. An excellent review of the time span and composition of the diet and the obesity of subjects on the protein content of weight loss.

Garrow, J. S. (1988). *Obesity and related diseases.* London: Churchill-Livingstone. Monograph on the etiology, effects, and treatment of obesity and the diseases to which obese people have a higher susceptibility than normal. Contains a large series of measurements of fat-free mass by density, water, and postassium in obese and lean subjects.

Norgan, N. G. (1990). Thermogenesis above maintenance in humans. *Proceedings of the Nutrition Society, 49,* 217–226. Review of the effects of overfeeding in human subjects on body composition and energy expenditure.

Webb, P., & Annis, J. F. (1983). Adaptation to overeating in lean and overweight men and women. *Human Nutrition: Clinical Nutrition, 37C,* 117–131. Experimental test of the view that some people are "easy gainers" or "hard gainers" when overfed. Results showed no difference in energy efficiency.

· 8 ·

BODY COMPOSITION

Jack H. Wilmore

Western culture has become increasingly focused on issues of body weight. Part of this interest is driven by the imposed cultural standard of extreme leanness as an index of beauty and success in women (see Chapter 15). While more subtle, for men there is a similar drive for leanness and muscularity that is associated with the need to be attractive and popular (see Chapter 31). Added to this is the common knowledge that excessive weight is associated with increased risk for a growing number of diseases and disabilities. But is weight really the problem?

BODY WEIGHT VERSUS BODY COMPOSITION

It is important to distinguish between body weight and body composition. Body weight is simply the mass of the body, obtained by weighing a person on a scale. Body composition represents the chemical or anatomical composition of the body as is illustrated in Figure 8.1. For most people, fat is the major component of concern. In the chemical model, fat is a distinct entity, whereas in the anatomical model, fat is the major component of the adipose tissue. Adipose tissue is composed of a cellular matrix of connective tissue in which are embedded fat cells or adipocytes, which are filled with triglycerides. Small droplets of triglycerides are also stored in almost all of the body's cells.

It is impossible to measure each of the chemical or anatomical components in living humans. This problem has led to a simplified two-component model of body composition. One of the original models, proposed by Albert R. Behnke in the 1940s, divided the body into lean body mass and the fat body mass. Lean body mass was defined as the fat-free mass plus essential fat, with the essential fat being that necessary for survival. While intuitively correct, the model is problematic from a measurement perspective, since no measurement technique is able to differentiate essential from nonessential fat. Thus the two-component model of Josef Brožek, which simply divides the body into its fat and fat-free masses, has become the most commonly accepted model.

Most recently, techniques have become available to measure the mineral and water components, and these techniques have been incorporated into multicomponent models of body composition. However, for the purposes of this chapter, the Brozek model, defining the body by its fat and fat-free components, will be used.

From this discussion, it is obvious that our cultural obsession with weight must be reevaluated. It has been clearly demonstrated that an individual may be overweight by standard weight tables based on height and frame size and yet have normal or

Body Composition Models

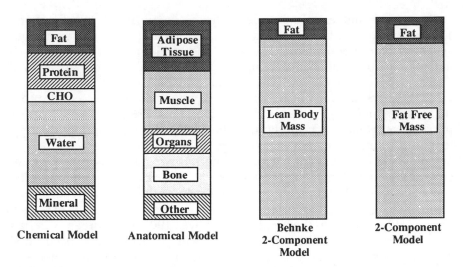

FIGURE 8.1. Illustration of the chemical, anatomical, and two-component models of body composition. From Wilmore (1992, p. 82). Copyright 1992 by Lea & Febiger. Reprinted by permission.

below-normal levels of body fat. Athletes typically fall into this category. Likewise, a person can be of normal weight, or even underweight, and yet carry too much body fat.

Since both appearance and health risk are associated with above-normal levels of body fat, it is important to refocus our concern on relative body fat, that is that percentage of the total body weight which is fat. Obesity, which refers to abnormally high relative body fat, is defined as exceeding 35% body fat in women and 25% body fat in men. Borderline obesity is defined as relative fat values of 30% to 35% in women and 20% to 25% in men. These relative fat values for categorizing the degree of obesity have been arbitrarily determined but are generally accepted within the scientific and clinical community. Specific techniques for measuring relative body fat are discussed in detail in Chapter 18.

REGULATION OF BODY COMPOSITION AND BODY FAT DISTRIBUTION

How is body composition regulated? While this process is not totally understood, genetic factors play a dominant role (see Chapter 4), and there is increasing evidence that both the endocrine system and the sympathetic nervous system play major roles (see Chapters 1 and 2).

There are few differences in body composition between boys and girls until puberty. At this point, boys experience an accelerated growth of their fat-free mass, primarily skeletal muscle, while girls experience an accelerated growth of their fat mass, primarily in the subcutaneous fat stores. The boys' increase in fat-free mass is associated with a marked increase in the production and release of androgens, primarily testosterone, while the girls' increase in fat mass is related to the increased production and release of estrogens.

The hormonal and enzymatic milieu dictates patterns of fat distribution. The pattern of fat in the hips, buttocks, and thighs of girls and women is due largely to the high concentration of lipoprotein lipase (LPL) and low lipolytic activity in these regions. Boys and men pattern fat primarily in the trunk and abdominal areas. While most women seem to feel cursed by this preferential distribution of fat to the hips, buttocks, and thighs, these specific fat stores appear to be important for successful reproductive function in sustaining pregnancy and lactation. Further, the female pattern of fat distribution places women at a substantially lower health risk than does the upper body fat distribution found in males (see Chapter 79).

A strong genetic component interacts with this sexual dimorphism. This interaction has been well established in a series of studies by Claude Bouchard and his colleagues at Laval University in Quebec, Canada (see Chapter 4). Periods of overfeeding of identical monozygotic twins (1,000 kilocalories above maintenance levels, 6 out of every 7 days), led to a threefold variation in the weight gained over 100 days between twin pairs, while there were relatively small differences within twin pairs. These extreme differences might be explained by differences in the hormonal and sympathetic nervous system responses to the overfeeding stimulus, responses that probably control the wastage component of metabolism (futile cycles are one example).

Most likely, factors involved in the regulation of food intake play the predominant role in the long-term regulation of body composition. These factors are complex and have been discussed in other chapters (see Chapters 1–5).

ALTERATIONS IN BODY COMPOSITION BY DIETING AND EXERCISE

Body composition is altered by both diet and exercise intervention. With very-low-calorie diets (VLCDs), there is a major loss in fat-free mass. In several studies, as much as 60% of the weight loss during the first few weeks of VLCD came from the fat-free mass, primarily water and protein. Over an extended period of time, the rate of loss of fat-free mass is reduced, while that of the fat mass is increased. Reducing the caloric deficit by allowing the individual to consume more calories will reduce the extent of fat-free mass loss. With obese patients, however, some loss of fat-free mass should be expected. The fat-free mass increases with weight gain primarily to provide the additional support needed to transport the increased fat mass, so this additional fat-free mass is no longer needed when fat is lost.

Physical activity also plays a major role in the regulation of body composition. Weight gains, largely of fat, have been associated with periods of reduced activity in both animals and humans. Increasing physical activity reduces body fat stores and maintains, or even increases, the fat-free mass. Longitudinal aging studies have demonstrated that those who stay physically active have smaller losses of fat-free mass and smaller gains in fat mass. Most recently, researchers have realized the importance of maintaining the fat-free mass, as decreases in resting metabolic rate with aging have been tightly coupled to concomitant decreases in fat-free mass. This suggests that resistance-type exercise training, or general physical activity that overloads the skeletal muscles, might be important for long-term weight and body fat regulation.

FURTHER READING

Behnke, A. R., & Wilmore, J. H. (1974). *Evaluation and regulation of body build and composition*. Englewood Cliffs, NJ: Prentice-Hall. An excellent historical perspective of body composition and its regulation.

Björntorp, P., Smith, U., & Lönnroth, P. (Eds.). (1988). *Health implications of regional obesity* (*Acta Medica Scandinavica* Symposium Series No. 4). Stockholm: Almqvist & Wiksell International. An outstanding summary of the health risks associated with different patterns of fat distribution.

Bouchard, C., Tremblay, A., Despres, J. P., Nadeau, A., Lupien, P. J., Theriault, G., Dussault, J., Moorjani, S., Pinault, S., & Fournier, G. (1990). The response to long-term overfeeding in identical twins. *New England Journal of Medicine, 322*, 1477–1482. A classic study of the variation in weight gain with overfeeding across twin pairs.

Brownell, K. D., Rodin, J., & Wilmore, J. H. (Eds.). *Eating, body weight and performance in athletes: Disorders of modern society*. Philadelphia: Lea & Febiger. A current review of body composition issues as they relate to disordered eating, with a focus on athletic populations.

Brožek, J., Grande, F., Anderson, J. T., & Keys, A. (1963). Densitometric analysis of body composition: Revision of some quantitative assumptions. *New York Academy of Science, 110* (Part I), 113–140. Addresses the issue of the composition of the density of the fat-free mass and has presented the classic Brožek et al. equation for estimating relative body fat.

Lohman, T. G. (1992). *Advances in body composition assessment*. Champaign, IL: Human Kinetics. A current review of body composition assessment procedures across the age span.

VanItallie, T. B. (1985). Health implications of overweight and obesity in the United States. *Annals of Internal Medicine, 103*, 938–988. A comprehensive summary of the health risks associated with overweight and obesity.

Wilmore, J. H. (1992) Body weight and body composition. In K.D. Brownell, J. Rodin, & J. H. Wilmore (Eds.), *Eating, body weight and performance in athletes: Disorders of modern society* (pp. 77–93). Philadelphia: Lea & Febiger. A review of the principles of body composition assessment and their application to weight loss and gain.

Wilmore, J. H., & Costill, D. L. (1994). *Physiology of sport and exercise*. Champaign, IL: Human Kinetics. An updated account of the role of physical activity in weight regulation.

A SET-POINT MODEL OF BODY WEIGHT REGULATION

Richard E. Keesey

HOMEOSTASIS—STABILITY OF THE *MILIEU INTÉRIEUR*

More than a century ago, the French physician and physiologist Claude Bernard described in wonder the stability of our *milieu intérieur,* under even the extremes of our natural environment. Bernard correctly attributed this internal stability to the exquisite capacity of the body to monitor its internal state and to make adjustments to compensate for any perturbation of that stability. Walter Cannon, an American investigator, introduced the term "homeostasis" to characterize this condition of internal stability. He and others contributed greatly to our understanding of the specific mechanisms responsible for maintaining body core temperature, body fluid volume and osmolarity, blood pH, and many other factors, all within tight tolerances.

SET POINTS AND SYSTEMS ENGINEERING

Both Bernard and Cannon emphasized the crucial role of feedback in homeostasis, whereby the signal generated by a deviation from the preferred internal state initiates the responses necessary to counter the perturbing influence and restore the normal condition. The system they conceptualized for physiological regulation thus closely resembles the set-point models developed by systems engineers for regulating components of the physical environment at specified levels. In systems engineering, the set point is an independent, adjustable signal against which a feedback signal from the controlled system can be compared. It thus "sets" the value of the variable the control system maintains. Not surprisingly, set-point models have had a profound influence on both theory and research in regulatory physiology. Certainly, only a brief examination of the literature on body temperature regulation is needed to appreciate the extent to which research in this area has been influenced by the set-point concept.

Body Energy Set Points

Body energy (or body weight, which can serve as a convenient index of body energy) exhibits features consistent with its being regulated by a set-point mechanism. In support of this concept is the relative weight stability of individuals and, more importantly, evidence for mechanisms that actively resist changes in weight. For example, compensatory adjustments both in energy intake and its rate of expenditure are seen following weight perturbations. If body weight is caused to decline from the normally maintained level, coordinated adjustments both in food intake and whole-body metabolism occur that favor restoration of the lost weight. Food, if available, is ingested in larger amounts. Concurrently, the rate at which the body expends energy is adjusted downward. In addition, the strength of the tendencies toward increased intake and reduced expenditure diminishes, the closer a person comes to fully regaining the lost weight. A balance of energy intake and expenditure is then realized when weight is restored to its former level.

Coordinated countervailing intake and expenditure adjustments are also seen when body weight is elevated from the normally maintained level. Intake is sharply curtailed under such circumstances, while rates of energy expenditure are sharply increased. The resulting imbalance of intake and expenditure, which in this case favors the loss of body energy, again persists until body weight is restored to its apparent set point.

The Body Weight Set Point and Energy Expenditure

Although energy expenditure is adaptively increased or reduced when body weight is perturbed, daily energy expenditure stands in a specific relationship to body mass when an individual is in energy balance at the normally maintained body weight. An examination of the relationship between daily energy expenditure and maintained body weight provides the basis for interpreting the considerable natural variation between individuals in the body weight each typically maintains.

Kleiber, a noted animal nutritionist, demonstrated that the daily resting energy expenditure (kilocalories per day) of mammals of all sizes is accurately predicted by raising the body weight (BW_{kg}) each maintains to the 0.75 power and multiplying the obtained value by a constant (kilocalories per day $= k\,BW_{kg}^{0.75}$). If one solves for k (i.e., $k =$ kilocalories per day $\div BW_{kg}^{0.75}$) using the daily expenditure data Kleiber reported from 4 mammals—a 410-gram guinea pig expending 35.1 kilocalories per day, a 3-kilogram cat expending 152 kilocalories per day, a 57.2-kilogram woman expending 1,368 kilocalories per day, and a 600-kilogram cow expending 7,877 kilocalories per day—values of 68.5, 66.7, 65.8, and 65.0 are obtained, with a mean of 66.5.

In a similar vein, we have found that different-sized members of the same species appear to conform to this interspecies relationship between body size and daily resting energy expenditure. In Figure 9. 1 the observed 24-hour energy expenditure of 70 male rats of the same age, but ranging in body weight from 340 grams to 430 grams, is expressed relative to the body weight each maintains raised to the 0.75 power. The value of k (66.5) obtained by Kleiber from the interspecies comparisons is indicated by the slashed horizontal line. As expected, the mean value of k obtained from all 70 rats (kilocalories per day $\div BW_{kg}^{0.75} = 65.3$) closely approximates the interspecies value. Of particular interest, however, is the observation (see Figure 9.1) that the value of k obtained for individual rats, regardless of the body mass each maintained, likewise conformed well to this expected value. Evidently, just as different-sized species metabolize at a rate normal for their tissue mass, so too do different-sized members of the same species.

To appreciate the significance of the preceding observation, it must be recognized that the daily energy expenditure of any individual rat will conform to the expected value of k only so long as its body weight remains at the particular level it typically maintains. Note in Figure 9.1 what happened to the energy expenditure of a rat that

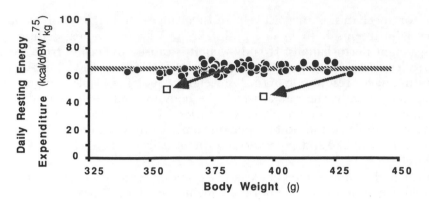

FIGURE 9.1. Daily resting energy expenditure (kilocalories per day) expressed per body weight to the 0.75 power of individual male rats of the same strain and age. The body weights of the largest rat and another of average weight were reduced by 8% and 6.5%, respectively. The arrows indicate, for each rat, the changes in daily resting energy expenditure associated with this displacement from the normally maintained body weight. Based on unpublished observations of Hirvonen and Keesey.

normally maintained a body weight of 380 grams when its caloric intake was restricted and its weight declined. The adjustment in energy expenditure which, as discussed earlier, serves to stabilize body energy at a particular level, occurs as predicted, so this rat's daily energy expenditure rate at a body weight of 355 grams is markedly lower than that of rats that spontaneously maintain this exact weight. Evidently this particular rat's daily energy needs are at the expected level (i.e., kilocalories per day $\div$ $BW_{kg}^{0.75}$ = 66) only when its body weight is at the higher level it normally maintains, one that we might thus characterize as its set point. Likewise the daily energy expenditure of any rat depicted in this figure will be at the expected level when, and only when, that rat is at a particular body weight. At any other body weight, its daily energy needs will be either greater or less than the value predicted from the Kleiber equation. We can thus define the body weight set point of each rat as that particular body weight at which its daily energy expenditure conforms to the value predicted from the basic body mass-energy expenditure relationship to which mammals of all sizes and species apparently conform.

IMPLICATIONS FOR OBESITY

Extending this line of argument a step further, consider not a rat of average weight but rather the heaviest of those depicted in Figure 9.1. If a definition of obesity is used that is based on the deviation from the standard or average weight for age and sex, this rat would certainly qualify as overweight or obese. Yet it can be seen to metabolize energy at a daily rate normal and appropriate for its body size. However, when this rat was placed on a diet causing its weight to decline to the average for rats of this age, its daily energy expenditure declined to a level substantially below the normal. Thus, being "overweight" appears to be as natural for this rat as being of average weight is for the majority.

The implication of the preceding observation is that obesity, rather than stemming from a regulatory dysfunction, may instead represent a condition of regulation at an elevated set point. The possibility that the status of many genuinely obese individuals is one of unperturbed regulation at an elevated set point can be tested. Were obese individuals to (1) show rates of daily energy expenditure normal and appropriate to their larger body mass and (2) display adjustments in daily energy expenditure appropriate to maintaining their obesity when it was perturbed, they would certainly display the characteristics of regulation at an elevated set point. It is worth noting in this regard that rats maintained on a high-fat diet long enough to produce a hyperplastic form of obesity do show both daily energy expenditure rates normal for their increased body size and a decided metabolic resistance to weight loss. Genetically obese (Zucker) rats likewise display a strong metabolic resistance even to modest weight reductions. Since similar reports are found in the literature on human obesity, the proposition that obesity in a significant number of cases may represent a condition of normal energy regulation at an elevated set point clearly deserves consideration.

SET-POINT ANALYSIS OF BODY WEIGHT: FEATURES, LIMITATIONS, AND MISCONCEPTIONS

The utility of the set-point concept can at times be limited by the difficulty in translating the formally defined features of control models from systems engineering into physiological systems. Our understanding of the physiological systems may at times be too limited to identify the physiological counterpart of each component of the engineer's set-point system. Recall, for example, that it is by altering the "independent and *adjustable*" set-point signal that one changes the value of the variable the control system regulates. Yet the level at which this regulated variable is held would change as well if the gain of the feedback signal were to change. Ordinarily, it would be a simple matter for the systems engineer to determine whether it was an alteration in the set-point or feedback signal alteration that caused a shift in the regulated variable. But, as critics properly point out, our understanding of the system for body energy regulation is still too limited to permit one to distinguish between these two possibilities or even to know whether body energy regulation can be achieved without a set-point signal simply by modulating the gain of the feedback signal. All that presently can be said with certainty is that the regulation of body energy gives the appearance of being under the control of a set-point mechanism.

On the other hand some criticisms of set-point approaches to body energy regulation are without a sound basis. One is the contention that changes in the body weight of an adult weaken or refute arguments for its set-point regulation. Supporters of such a view ignore the fact that an adjustable set point is a feature basic to the design of control systems. Clearly changes in the level of a physiological variable are in no way inconsistent with its set-point regulation. Rather, if the new level is itself appropriately defended by responses that oppose threats to its maintenance, the change may be said to be regulated by an alteration in set point.

Many physiological systems certainly behave as though the set point is subject to regular and/or intermittent adjustment. Regular and physiologically defended shifts in body core temperature are seen daily, seasonally (in hibernators), and during the menstrual cycle. Sepsis-induced elevations in core temperature (fever) are likewise widely accepted as being caused by an alteration in set point. Likewise a variety of pharmacological agents, hormones, central nervous lesions, and toxins induce acute, or even chronic, shifts in the level of maintained body weight. In each case the energy intake and expenditure adjustments that first bring about the shift in body weight, and that then serve to maintain weight at the new level, clearly suggest a change in the system set point. Thus, rather than refuting a set-point interpretation, weight changes in the adult may provide supporting evidence for the set-point regulation of body weight and energy.

In a more general way, set-point models can assist investigators both in formulating systematic approaches to the study of the complex mechanisms of energy homeostasis and in identifying the features and elements such a system most probably uses to achieve this condition. Certainly a systems approach to the analysis of body energy regulation provides a framework for conceptualizing the sorts of physiological and metabolic adjustments needed to achieve the weight stability people typically display. Finally, a better understanding of the control system for energy regulation may in time lead to methods of resetting the systems of obese individuals whose condition results from having an elevated regulatory set point.

FURTHER READING

Cabanac, M. (1991). Open-loop methods to study the ponderostat. In M. I. Friedman, M. G. Tordoff, & M. R. Kare (Eds.), *Appetite and nutrition.* New York: Marcel Dekker. A thorough discussion of key issues and arguments related to the application of the set-point concept to physiological systems for regulation, with a focus on body weight.

Cabanac, M., Duclaux, R., & Spector, N. H. (1971). Sensory feedbacks in regulation of body weight: Is there a ponderstat? *Nature, 229,* 125–127. An early report by Cabanac, a prominent and long-time advocate of the set-point concept in body weight regulation.

Cannon, W. B. (1939). *The wisdom of the body.* New York: W.W. Norton. A classic in the area of physiological regulation by the person responsible for making "homeostasis" a household term.

Keesey, R. E. (1988). The relation between energy expenditure and the body weight set-point: Its significance to obesity. In G. D. Burrows, P. J. V. Beumont, & R. C. Casper (Eds.), *Handbook of eating disorders: Part 2. Obesity* (pp. 87–102). Amsterdam: Elsevier. A consideration of the special relationship between daily resting energy expenditure and the set point for regulated body weight.

Keesey, R. E. (1993). Physiological regulation of body energy: Implications for obesity. In A. J. Stunkard & T. A. Wadden (Eds.), *Obesity: Theory and therapy* (pp. 77–96). New York: Raven Press. A view of obesity as a natural condition of body energy regulation at an elevated set point.

Keesey, R. E., & Powley, T. L. (1986). The regulation of body weight. *Annual Review of Psychology, 37,* 109–133. A homeostatic perspective on body weight based on parallels between the systems regulating blood pressure and body energy.

Mrosovsky, N. (1990). *Rheostasis: The physiology of change.* New York: Oxford University Press. A contemporary account of physiological regulation emphasizing the role of "feedforward" mechanisms both in promoting programmed change of the interior environment and in anticipating threats to its stability.

Mrosovsky, N., & Powley, T. L. (1977). Set-points for body weight and fat. *Behavioral Biology, 20,* 205–223. A defense of the use of the set-point concept in body energy regulation.

Powley, T. L., & Keesey, R. E. (1970). Relationship of body weight to the lateral hypothalamic feeding syndrome. *Journal of Comparative and Physiological Psychology, 68,* 541–544. An early application of the set-point concept to the regulation of body weight.

Wirtshafter, D., & Davis, J. D. (1977). Set-points, settling points, and the control of body weight. *Physiology and Behavior, 19,* 75–78. A critique of the application of set-point models to body weight regulation.

• 10 •

PREGNANCY AND WEIGHT GAIN

BARBARA J. MOORE
M. R. C. GREENWOOD

During the first half of the 20th century, restriction of weight gain during pregnancy was common obstetrical practice. According to Hytten and Leitch, the origin of this practice was the observation made during the latter half of the 19th century that food restriction effectively retarded intrauterine growth of the fetus, thus reducing head circumference. This was considered desirable because it facilitated delivery and reduced complications and mortality associated with childbirth. Because of the prevalence of rickets and consequent pelvic malformations, complications associated with childbirth was the leading cause of death among adult women of childbearing age.

During the 1950s, the wisdom of restricting weight gain was seriously challenged on the grounds that women were no longer dying in great numbers during the perinatal period. At the same time, data suggested that low birth weight in neonates was strongly associated with increased infant morbidity and mortality. Furthermore, the smaller head circumference of low-birth-weight babies raised the possibility of suboptimal brain development. The removal of pregnancy weight gain restrictions has been advocated since then.

In the 1990s it is still not unusual for women to believe they should restrict their weight gain to only 15 or 20 pounds during pregnancy, even though less restrictive weight gain recommendations were formalized in 1990 by the Institute of Medicine (IOM). These new guidelines take into account the prepregnancy body weight or, more specifically, the body mass index (BMI) of the mother. The BMI is calculated as body weight in kilograms per height in meters^2. Women considered underweight (BMI below 19.8) are counseled to gain the most weight during pregnancy: 28 to 40 pounds. Normal-weight women (BMI 19.8–26.0) should gain 25 to 35 pounds; overweight women (BMI >26.0–29.0) should gain 15 to 25 pounds; and obese women (BMI >29.0) should gain a minimum of 15 pounds, but not much more. For women carrying twins, the recommended weight gain is 35 to 45 pounds.

OBESITY AND PREGNANCY

. . . 40–50 per cent of severely obese women who come to our Obesity Unit state that their excessive weight was initiated by previous pregnancies."
—OHLIN AND ROSSNER (1990)

The IOM recommendations have been greeted in some quarters with concern that they will predispose some women to obesity. Others in the field, especially researchers familiar with data on weight gain during pregnancy, have commented that the medical guidelines are finally "catching up with women's behavior." This latter view is important because unnecessary stress and feelings of guilt were common among women whose weight gain exceeded the restrictive guidelines in the past.

Today there remains a concern that weight gained during pregnancy is related to weight retained postpartum. Some researchers have postulated that repeated pregnancies may represent a form of weight cycling that results in the development of obesity. It is common for patients to report no weight problem until the birth of a child or, in some cases, a first male child. Despite these widespread anecdotal reports, whether pregnancy predisposes women to obesity remains unclear.

Animal studies show that pregnancy is associated with the deposition of body fat and that this fat is deposited in specific regions. It is presumed that the gestational deposition of fat around the hips, buttocks, and thighs in women corresponds to the fat deposition known to occur in many species of animals during pregnancy. These fat stores have been referred to as "lactational stores," because the increased food intake that is both recommended and observed in lactating women (and in animals) is sufficient to meet only 60% of the energy demands of lactation. Hence the mobilization of internal energy, or triglycerides stored in adipose tissue, is necessary. Fat deposition during pregnancy and subsequent fat mobilization during lactation have been well documented in animals and is presumed to occur in humans.

Despite this presumption, there is a paucity of data documenting the actual changes in body-fat content that occur during pregnancy and the postpartum period in humans. This lack of data is attributable to the difficulty of measuring body composition in humans during pregnancy and lactation, when dramatic fluid shifts and increases in the hydration of lean body mass violate the basic assumptions upon which the techniques of assessing body composition are based (see Chapter 18). For this reason clinicians and researchers have relied on measurements of body weight to assess the impact of reproduction on the development of obesity. Yet body weight changes may not be a suitable proxy for body fat changes.

EFFECTS OF PREGNANCY ON BODY WEIGHT

In 1993, Lederman reviewed the literature published during the previous decade on weight changes related to pregnancy and parity in well-nourished women in developed countries. Extrapolation to women in underdeveloped countries, where food restriction and negative energy balance may be common, is probably not appropriate. Lederman asked whether weight increases permanently as a result of pregnancy and discussed the determinants of postpartum weight retention. She estimated the postpartum weight retained in association with pregnancy to be less than 1.5 kilograms (3 pounds) and concluded that factors other than pregnancy are likely to explain the majority of weight gain attributed to reproduction in humans. Her analysis of cross-sectional studies showed that increased body weight associated with aging explains most instances of increased weight observed with parity.

As Lederman points out, a major methodological problem in most studies is the use of self-report for estimations of prepregnancy body weight. There are data suggesting that self-reported values for prepregnancy body weight tend to be inaccurate and consistently low. Furthermore, underestimation of prepregnancy body weight tends to be greater in overweight women. Therefore the use of data based on self-report leads to an overestimation of both weight gained during pregnancy and weight retained postpartum, and the magnitude of this error tends to be larger in overweight women.

A study in 1994 by Smith et al. corrected problems in earlier studies by measuring weights on 2,788 women followed prospectively. Over the 5-year study, primiparous women gained 2 to 3 kilograms more than did nulliparous subjects, while weight change did not differ between nulliparous and multiparous subjects (even though the multiparous women had pregnancies during the study). The primiparous women had the greatest increases in waist–hip ratio, independent of weight gain, and black women had greater weight changes than did white women in each parity group. This study suggests moderate, persistent weight gains in all groups, with slightly more in women after a first pregnancy.

IDENTIFICATION OF A SUBPOPULATION VULNERABLE TO WEIGHT RETENTION

Despite the shortcomings of using body weight as a proxy for body fat, several studies suggest there may be a subpopulation of women at high risk for developing obesity postpartum. One is a study by Ohlin and Rossner of 2,295 women, 96% of whom were Swedish citizens; the remainder were from "miscellaneous, mainly Nordic, countries." Weight retention was examined in 1,423 women studied at 1 year postpartum.

The average retained weight gain was 1.5 ± 3.6 kilograms (mean $\pm$ SD) over the study period. The range of weight changes observed was -12.3 to 26.5 kilograms. This study included no nonpregnant age-matched controls to allow evaluation of the effects of aging on weight gain during the 21-month study period, but the authors estimated such age-related weight gain to be 0.18 kilograms, based on evaluations of cross-sectional data in a similar population. In addition, body weight prior to pregnancy was not measured but was based on self-report, necessitating a further adjustment of 0.80 kilograms to account for the probable underestimation of prepregnancy body weight. The authors concluded that the difference of 0.53 kilograms ($1.51 - [0.80 + 0.18] = 0.53$) is the "true" average weight retention 1 year postpartum. The authors note that this is a modest gain but that 14% of the women were heavier by at least 5 kilograms at 1 year postpartum, which is in agreement with other studies. These women experienced significant weight gain, suggesting that a subpopulation of women may be predisposed to significant postpartum weight retention.

Weight gain following pregnancy is certainly not inexorable, even in overweight women. Some women lose weight, and others remain stable or gain modest amounts. But there is a significant proportion of women in whom marked weight retention is observed, and their weight gain is correlated with larger weight gains during pregnancy. An important study in this regard is that of Parker and Abrams, who examined the effects of race on postpartum weight retention.

These workers studied data collected on 990 black and 1,129 white women who participated in the 1988 National Maternal and Infant Health Survey. Although these women began pregnancy with normal weight for height, black mothers were twice as likely to retain at least 20 pounds postpartum than were white mothers. This difference remained when the results were controlled for socioeconomic status. High prenatal weight gain was associated with an increased risk of weight retention for both black and white mothers, but the risk for black mothers was double that of white mothers. The data cited earlier by Smith et al. support these findings.

TO GAIN OR NOT TO GAIN

Before we allow the concept of rigid calorie restriction for pregnant women once more to rear its ugly head, we should remember that placing pregnant women on restricted diets not only restricted fetal growth but also created enormous stress between women and their obstetrical caregivers. . . .

—B. ABRAMS

The concern that excessive pregnancy weight gain increases the risk of obesity, especially among black women, must be balanced by an equal concern about the fact that black women, *on average,* gain less weight during pregnancy than do white women, and the incidence of low-birth-weight infants born to black mothers is correspondingly larger. Hence health care professionals should be encouraging the majority of black women to gain more weight during pregnancy while keeping a watchful eye for those in whom weight gain may be excessive.

To consider this clinical balancing act in light of the IOM recommendations, Keppel and Taffel studied postpartum body weight, taking into account prepregnancy BMI and the IOM-recommended weight gain. Their analysis confirmed that a higher proportion of black women do not achieve pregnancy weight gains consistent with the IOM recommendations. Furthermore, black women were more likely to report being told to gain less than the amount recommended (22 to 27 pounds) than were their white counterparts with comparable BMIs. Nonetheless, a significant proportion (30%) of the black women retained more than 14 pounds postpartum. This proportion was twice as large as that of white women who retained the same amount of weight.

This study is important because it shows clearly the association between weight gain advice and actual weight gain. Health care professionals can successfully encourage women to gain a specific amount of weight during pregnancy to support optimal pregnancy outcome. The study results also point out the critical need for black women to receive advice about how to lose weight following delivery.

The analyses of Lederman and other researchers raises the distinct possibility that the predisposition of some black women to excessive postpartum weight retention is not rooted in biological antecedents. Further research is needed to examine that possibility and to see whether race is a proxy for other individual, social, cultural, economic, and environmental factors that promote postpartum weight retention. The identification of these factors will be necessary if postdelivery weight reduction is to be successful.

DOES LACTATION PROMOTE POSTPARTUM FAT LOSS?

The energy costs of breast-feeding in humans has been estimated to be approximately 800 kilocalories/day. Lactation should promote fat loss, especially in depots associated with reproduction (i.e., hips, thighs, and buttocks), if energy expenditure is not decreased and/or food intake does not increase sufficiently to meet energy needs. Numerous animal studies show that fat mobilization and reduced body fat content occur during lactation.

Because of serious methodological difficulties in examining this question in humans, the effect of lactation on body composition is still not clear. For clinicians and health care providers, prudent advice is to recommend breast-feeding on the grounds that it provides optimal nutrition for the infant and may promote fat mobilization in the mother. Because of fluid retention and increased hydration of lean body mass during lactation, body weight may not decrease, as an increase in body water content may more than offset any decrease in body fat. Hence the changes in body composition during lactation should remain an active area of research.

FURTHER READING

Hytten, F. E., & Leitch, I. (1971) *The physiology of human pregnancy*. Oxford: Blackwell Scientific. An informative and well-written book on this subject. The original edition, published in 1951, includes interesting chapters that are not included in subsequent editions.

Institute of Medicine, Subcommittee on Nutritional Status and Weight Gain during Pregnancy. (1990). *Nutrition during pregnancy*. Washington, DC: National Academy Press. The source of current weight gain recommendations.

Keppel, K. G., & Taffel, S. M. (1993). Pregnancy-related weight gain and retention: Implications of the 1990 Institute of Medicine Guidelines. *American Journal of Public Health, 83,* 1100–1103. A study showing pregnancy outcome and weight retained by groups gaining amounts of weight recommended by IOM.

Lederman, S. A. (1993). The effect of pregnancy weight gain on later obesity. *Obstetrics and Gynecology 82,* 148–155. A review suggesting that weight retention attributed to pregnancy may largely be associated with aging.

Ohlin A., & Rossner, S. (1990). Maternal body weight development after pregnancy. *International Journal of Obesity, 14,* 159–173. A study showing that postpartum weight retention is modest on average but that a proportion of women appear vulnerable to significant weight gain.

Parker, J. D., & Abrams, B. (1993). Differences in postpartum weight retention between black and white mothers. *Obstetrics and Gynecology, 81,* 768–774. A study suggesting that a greater proportion of black women may be vulnerable to postpartum weight retention than are white women of comparable prepregnancy BMI.

Smith, D. E., Lewis, C. E., Caveny, J. L., Perkins, L. L., Burke, G. L., & Bild, D. E. (1994). Longitudinal changes in adiposity associated with pregnancy: The CARDIA Study. *Journal of the American Medical Association, 271,* 1747–1751. Prospective study of 2,788 women, in which the finding was a 2- to 3-kilograms greater weight gain in primiparous than in nulliparous women over a 5-year period, suggesting modest but persistent weight gains associated with pregnancy.

EFFECTS OF WEIGHT CYCLING ON METABOLISM, HEALTH, AND PSYCHOLOGICAL FACTORS

KELLY D. BROWNELL

The term "weight cycling" and its colloquial counterpart "yo-yo dieting" were born in the mid-1980s. Less than a decade has elapsed since the first studies on the topic were published, yet few topics in the eating disorders and obesity fields have generated more debate. Presumably because dieting is relevant to the lives of so many people, the media has seized on the topic and has bombarded the public with decidedly mixed messages.

The uncertainty in the popular press reflects differences of opinion among scientists. There is abundant evidence showing an association of body weight variability with morbidity and mortality, yet the studies have limitations. Some scientists are impressed with the associations, others with the limitations. Hence several editorials in the literature have urged a cautious approach, adding that more research must take place before final conclusions can be drawn.

There has also been considerable debate about whether weight cycling contributes to obesity by prompting metabolic changes that impede weight loss and promote regain over successive diets. Again, there are editorials suggesting that available evidence argues against this conclusion. Yet in a survey of obesity experts conducted by Bray and colleagues, genetics, physical activity, weight cycling, and depression were listed as the key causes of obesity.

The resolution of this debate has important implications. The rate of dieting in industrialized countries is very high, exemplified by 50% of American women dieting at any one time. Public health recommendations about dieting practices are at issue because the health and well-being of so many people might be affected.

DEFINITION AND PREVALENCE

No consistent definition of weight cycling has emerged from work in the field. In animal studies, cycling is a categorical variable, and cycles have been defined by their length, magnitude or rate of weight loss, and other factors. It is more often the case in human studies that weight variability is defined as a continuous variable expressed as variability in weight across repeated measurements. The standard deviation, coefficient of variation, and time-dependent slope around a regression line have been used. As discussed by Williamson in Chapter 72, and by Wing in the articles listed under "Further Reading" in this chapter, there are limitations to each method. Ultimately, the definition may change depending on the particular outcome under study (e.g., metabolism vs. mortality).

When a definition of weight cycling becomes clear, many key questions await inquiry; for example: How many cycles are necessary to trigger a given outcome? Are the rate and magnitude of weight change relevant? Is the composition of the diet during weight loss and regain phases important?

The extent of weight variability in the population can only be estimated. Subjects' weights in most studies are recorded only every 1 or 2 years, while studies with more frequent subject weights do not have representative samples of the population. Over the first 14 years of the Framingham Study, the standard deviation of body mass was 5.7% for men and 6.7% for women. Men in the Multiple Risk Factor Intervention Trial (MRFIT) had an average standard deviation in weight of 2.9 kilograms over the 6- to 7-year trial. In a 6.5-year longitudinal study of blood pressure in middle-aged adults, the sum of all weight losses and gains, respectively, from annual measurements was 10.3 kilograms and 10.5 kilograms for men and 14.1 kilograms and 12.4 kilograms for women. The total gain for men represented 12% of initial body weight and for women represented 21%.

More work is necessary to define the natural history of weight change. From what little is known, it appears that weights are more variable in women than in men. Whether this finding can be explained by biological variables, such as menstrual shifts in fluid, or by behavioral factors, such as dieting, is not known.

ASSOCIATION WITH WEIGHT CHANGE AND METABOLISM

The weight-cycling field began with a metabolic hypothesis: that cycles of loss and regain would be perceived as a threat to energy stores and therefore would produce adaptive changes to inhibit weight loss and promote regain. Results of one early study with animals and another with humans supported this hypothesis.

Many studies were done in the late 1980s and early 1990s to test this initial hypothesis. Some supported the hypothesis, but more did not. The results of studies on specific metabolic outcomes such as body composition and metabolic rate have also been mixed, with more studies showing no associations with weight cycling.

These mixed findings have led to different conclusions by experts in the field. One position is that the lack of consistent findings is reason to abandon the hypothesis, while another is that the metabolic adaptation may indeed occur in some organisms under a set of circumstances yet to be defined. The latter position is consistent with clinical reports from many overweight people who report more difficulty losing weight with successive diets. This phenomenon might be due to poorer compliance over time (as suggested by the results of one study); age-related changes in metabolic variables; or, as suggested by the original hypothesis, the body's defensive reaction to the threat of repeated dieting.

It is not possible to resolve this question in the absence of much more research. Existing animal studies vary widely in methods, with differences in the sex of the animals, age, strain, level of obesity, and many other important variables. Without a concerted effort to define a model that could then be used across studies, it is inevitable that the inconsistency will persist.

ASSOCIATION WITH MORBIDITY AND MORTALITY

The Epidemiology of Weight Variability and Health

Seven epidemiologic studies have been published on weight variability and health. In the two smallest studies, no association of weight variability with morbidity and mortality was found. In one larger study, the Harvard Alumni study, weight cycling *per se* was not examined. Instead, it was found that individuals who lost or gained weight over the course of the study had increased mortality, and that these individuals reported greater total lifetime weight loss. The results of the remaining studies have shown strong associations between weight variability and negative health outcomes. Two of these studies will be discussed here.

Lissner et al. studied 3,130 subjects in the Framingham Heart Study. The coefficient of variation of weight was calculated from weights measured every 2 years for the first 14 years of the study plus recalled weight at age 25. Only health outcomes occurring at least 4 years after the last measured weight were counted, to decrease bias from the possibility that antecedent disease might influence weight variability. Both all-cause and coronary heart disease (CHD) mortality were increased significantly in both men and women with high levels of weight variability. Morbidity from CHD was also increased.

Blair et al. used data from the MRFIT study to examine weight variability and health in 10,594 men at high risk for CHD. During the 6- to 7-year trial, 6 to 7 weights were available for the subjects who received usual care, and 18 to 21 weights were available for subjects who received intensive life-style intervention. Increased weight variability was associated with 50% to 60% increases in mortality from all causes, CHD, and cardiovascular disease (CVD). In subjects who had undergone at least one complete weight cycle, there was a 55% increase in all-cause mortality, compared with subjects with stable weights.

Possible Mechanisms

Several mechanisms have been proposed to explain the link between weight variability and health. These mechanisms include changes in cardiovascular risk factors, body composition, body fat distribution, preference for dietary fat, and the stress of dieting itself. While the cardiovascular risk factors are the most obvious candidates, several studies have not shown relationships between weight variability (based on self-reported weight history) and variables such as blood pressure and cholesterol levels. Several animal studies suggest that weight cycling may increase the preference for dietary fat. The other mechanisms have not been tested.

Limitations in Existing Research

Methodological shortcomings temper the confidence one might otherwise have in what appears to be a robust phenomenon. Two criticisms are most prominent in critiques of the literature. The first is that existing studies assess weight variability, not weight loss produced specifically by dieting. Existing studies were not designed to study weight cycling, so data on whether weight change is produced by dieting simply do not exist. In several studies, however, strong correlations between self-reports of dieting and weight fluctuation have been found.

The second key issue involves how weight cycling is measured and expressed.

Standard indices of variability (e.g., standard deviation) can yield similar scores for individuals with much different patterns of weight change. Individuals who lose consistently, gain consistently, or alternate between losing and gaining might appear similar with some measures of variability. Innovation in statistical methods will be necessary to resolve these problems, but in at least one study (the MRFIT study described above) it was found that cycles of loss and gain were specifically associated with risk.

WEIGHT CYCLING AND PSYCHOLOGICAL OUTCOMES

Dieting is often accompanied by hopes of changed health and appearance, and weight regain may lead to despair, but relatively little is known about the psychological correlates of weight cycling. This is an issue of great potential importance, because whether or not health and metabolism are affected, weight cycling might be a key public health issue if an impact on psychological and social functioning is found.

The object of one study of this issue was to compare the prevalence of psychopathological conditions in obese and nonobese individuals. No differences existed, but individuals with a history of weight cycling showed more signs of pathological conditions than those without such a history, independent of weight. Another study showed lower life satisfaction to be related to weight cycling in females but not in males. A study of distance runners found weight cycling to be associated with disturbed eating practices, and a large-scale study found that binge eaters were more likely than non-binge-eaters to have a history of weight cycling. Other studies have not shown associations between weight cycling and psychological variables. This is clearly an area in need of further study.

CONCLUSIONS

The field is in desperate need of more research on weight cycling. The stakes are high because (1) so many people are affected, and (2) research to date suggests significant relationships between weight variability and important health outcomes. The issue of metabolic changes with weight cycling has not been resolved, and little research has focused on its possible psychological effects.

FURTHER READING

Blair, S. N., Shaten, J., Brownell, K. D., Collins, G., & Lissner, L. (1993). Body weight fluctuation, all-cause mortality, and cause-specific mortality in the Multiple Risk Factor Intervention Trial. *Annals of Internal Medicine, 119,* 749–757. Well-designed epidemiologic study, using data from the MRFIT study, linking increased weight variability to the risk of cardiovascular disease and all-cause mortality.

Bouchard, C. (1991). Is weight fluctuation a risk factor? *New England Journal of Medicine, 324,* 1887–1888. Editorial accompanying the paper by Lissner et al. (1991) that points to methodological limitations in exiting studies and concludes that the issue of weight cycling and mortality should be studied in more detail.

Bray, G. A., York, B., & DeLany, J. (1992). A survey of the opinions of obesity experts on the causes and treatment of obesity. *American Journal of Clinical Nutrition, 55,* 151S–154S. A survey of obesity experts attending a scientific meeting; these experts considered weight cycling a key cause of obesity, just behind genetics and physical inactivity.

Brownell, K. D., Greenwood, M. R. C, Stellar, E., & Shrager, E. E. (1986). The effects of repeated cycles of weight loss and regain in rats. *Physiology and Behavior, 38*, 459–464. Early study with animals suggesting that repeated cycles of weight loss and regain were associated with a reduced rate of weight loss and an increased rate of regain over successive diets.

Brownell, K. D., & Rodin, J. (1994). Medical, metabolic, and psychological effects of weight cycling. *Archives of Internal Medicine, 154*, 1325–1330. Review of the literature on weight cycling, integrating both animal and human studies, with special focus on animal work pertaining to metabolic issues and epidemiologic work linking weight variability to mortality.

Lissner, L., Odell, P. M., D'Agostino, R. B., Stokes, J., Kreger, B. E., Belanger, A. J., & Brownell, K. D. (1991). Variability of body weight and health outcomes in the Framingham population. *New England Journal of Medicine, 324*, 1839–1844. Large, well-controlled epidemiologic study using the Framingham cohort, which showed that risk for all-cause and cardiovascular mortality as much as doubled in individuals with high body weight variability.

Reed, G. W., & Hill, J. O. (1993). Weight cycling: A review of the animal literature. *Obesity Research, 1*, 392–402. Review of animal studies suggesting no consistent effects of weight cycling on metabolic variables.

Rossner, S. (1989). Weight cycling: A new risk factor. *Journal of Internal Medicine, 226*, 209–211. Emphasis on the importance of weight cycling as a possible risk factor and to pregnancy as a possible form of weight cycling.

Wing, R. R. (1992). Weight cycling in humans: A review of the literature. *Annals of Behavioral Medicine, 14*, 113–119. Review and critical analysis of the weight-cycling literature concluding that the metabolic effects suggested by early studies were not supported by later research, that the possible health risks need further exploration, and that methodological issues in defining and expressing weight cycling must be resolved.

Wing, R. R. (1993). Weight cycling: the public concern and the scientific data. *Obesity Research, 1*, 390–391. Editorial stating that media messages about the dangers of weight cycling are drawn from incomplete evidence and that additional study is necessary before recommendations can be made to the general public.

• 12 •

CIGARETTE SMOKING AND BODY WEIGHT

Robert C. Klesges

There is increasing interest in the relationships between smoking and body weight. The fear of postcessation weight gain is a major barrier to smoking cessation and is believed to be a precipitant of smoking relapse, particularly in women (who are more weight conscious). The issues regarding smoking and body weight can be summarized in three major areas: (1) How much weight gain occurs following smoking cessation? (2) What are the determinants of postcessation weight gain? and (3) What can be done to reduce postcessation weight gain? In this review, each of the issues will be addressed separately.

SMOKING CESSATION AND WEIGHT GAIN

A pervasive, but completely unfounded, myth in smoking cessation is the "one-third statistic"; that is, one-third of smokers lose weight following smoking cessation, one-third stay the same, and one-third gain weight. This statistic offered real hope—two-thirds of people who quit smoking will either not change or, better yet, lose weight! Unfortunately, this statistic is wrong. Most empirical studies report that the vast majority of individuals gain weight following smoking cessation (80% to 85%), with the remainder staying the same.

Several early reviews, in which a large number of studies mostly conducted in the 1970s and 1980s were summarized, provided reassuring news regarding the magnitude of the weight gain following smoking cessation. The conclusion in several studies was that the average weight gain was minimal—about 4½ to 7 pounds more than a nonsmoker would gain in a comparable period. However, problems with self-reports of height, weight, and smoking status; a preponderance of smokers who smoked lightly; and the use of point-prevalence assessments of smoking status created a need for more definitive studies.

More recent studies, using superior methodologies, have documented that the average weight gain is much higher than these earlier estimates. Average weight gains of more than 10 pounds are extremely common. Additionally, certain groups of people appear to be at higher risk for postcessation weight gain. Women, African Americans, heavy smokers, and normal-weight smokers are all at higher risk for postcessation weight gain. In general, however, while the vast majority of smokers will not gain medically significant weight following smoking cessation, some (15% to 20%) will gain more than 30 pounds.

While an average increase of 10 pounds may be reassuring for some individuals, many, particularly weight-conscious women, view this weight gain as esthetically unacceptable. As discussed below, much of the concern related to postcessation weight gain relates to cosmetic appearance and not health issues. A 10-pound weight gain might not even be noticed in some men, but a 5-pound weight gain could be devastating to some women.

Future research in this area should focus on a careful assessment of who is at most risk for postcessation weight gain. An eventual goal would be to construct a risk profile for weight gain, so that a smoker could assess, with a reasonable degree of accuracy, how much weight gain he/she can expect once he/she quits.

CAUSES OF POSTCESSATION WEIGHT GAIN

While a large number of studies have been conducted on the determinants of postcessation weight gain, there is surprisingly little consistency regarding the causes. For weight to change, some component of energy balance (i.e., energy intake, physical activity, or some form of metabolic rate) needs to change.

In some studies, large increases in dietary intake following smoking cessation are reported, while in other studies, no (or only short-term) differences in intake are found. When changes in intake are observed, they typically involve fat or sugar consumption.

The data on physical activity and its role in smoking cessation is one of the few areas in which research results are clear—no differences in physical activity are observed. Occasionally, a study will contain a report of an increase in physical activity following smoking cessation, but in no study has a decrease in physical activity ever been reported that would be consistent with weight gain.

Metabolic rate has three major components: (1) resting energy expenditure, which accounts for the majority of kilocalories burned in a day; (2) the thermic effect of food, or the kilocalories burned to digest and store food; and (3) the thermic effect of exercise, that is, the kilocalories expended as a result of physical activity. Regarding resting energy expenditure, in most, but not all, studies acute increases in metabolic rate following smoking are found. Both the obese (relative to normal-weight individuals) and those who smoke heavily (relative to lighter smokers) are likely to have a blunted (or smaller rise in) metabolic response. To date, the bulk of the evidence suggests that smoking does not produce a heightened thermic effect of food but may produce a heightened thermic effect of exercise.

Taken in total, the bulk of the evidence suggests that smoking increases the metabolic rate, although there appear to be important differences among individuals. Future research should focus on a careful determination of smoking's role in energy balance.

PREVENTING POSTCESSATION WEIGHT GAIN

Given that many smokers indicate they continue to smoke to control weight, the development of effective treatments for postcessation weight gain appears fairly straightforward.

Since successful multicomponent programs exist for weight control, one would simply combine these strategies with the known multicomponent programs for smoking cessation. Unfortunately, when, in recent investigations, weight-control interventions were added to the smoking cessation programs, two results were typically observed: (1) The programs were unsuccessful in reducing postcessation weight gain; and (2) the programs were unsuccessful in enhancing smoking cessation. If anything, subjects who take part in the weight-control program do worse than those who do not. There are many possible reasons, but the most likely is that subjects are overwhelmed with all the strategies they must learn to both quit smoking *and* eliminate postcessation weight gain.

Recent work has focused on pharmacologic adjuncts to smoking cessation that will at least temporarily reduce postcessation weight gain. Subjects can first deal with issues related to smoking cessation without having to expend great effort to reduce postcessation weight gain. Once nonsmoking is mastered, the subjects can focus on modifying diet and exercise to reduce weight gain (which is likely to occur once they stop taking the drug). Several studies are ongoing in this area. Recently, work has been completed with fenfluramine, fluoxetine, and the over-the-counter product phenylpropanolamine (PPA). Additionally, nicotine gum, when used consistently, has been shown to reduce postcessation weight gain.

Since many subjects may be overwhelmed by trying to reduce weight and quit smoking simultaneously, priority should be given to the development of nonpharmacological approaches to help the weight-conscious smoker quit smoking without significant weight gain. Because at least part of the weight gain following cessation seems to be due to metabolic effects, one thing is certain—if there is no alteration in dietary intake and/or physical activity, some weight gain will occur. Simple strategies for reducing postcessation weight gain might be employed. For example, focusing only on fat intake is a much simpler strategy than modifying the entire diet. Additionally, recent work by Epstein and colleagues suggests that focusing on reducing sedentary activities may be easier, more rewarding, and more successful than focusing on increasing aerobic activities. These and other simple strategies should be tested and evaluated in the future.

ACKNOWLEDGMENTS

This study was supported by two grants (Nos. HL45057 and HL46352) awarded by the National Heart, Lung, and Blood Institute. Support was also received from a Centers of Excellence grant awarded to the Department of Psychology, University of Memphis, by the state of Tennessee.

FURTHER READING

Klesges, R. C., Meyers, A. W., Klesges, L. M., & LaVasque, M. (1989). Smoking, body weight, and their effects on smoking behavior: A comprehensive review of the literature. *Psychological Bulletin, 106,* 204–230. A succinct, but somewhat dated, comprehensive review. A description of over 70 studies on the relationship between smoking and body weight (cross-sectional and longitudinal) is presented in tabular form.

Klesges, R. C., & Shumaker, S. A. (Eds.) (1992). Proceedings of the National Working Conference on Smoking and Body Weight. *Health Psychology, 11,* ii–66. This monograph was a special supplement to *Health Psychology* and was based on the Memphis State University/National Heart, Lung, and Blood Institute Conference on Smoking and Body Weight. More than 50 national experts on smoking, obesity, and smoking/body weight research contributed to this monograph. It is the most comprehensive and thorough review to date.

U.S. Department of Health and Human Services. (1990). *The health benefits of smoking cessation: A report of the Surgeon General* (DHHS Publication No. [CDC] 90–8416). Washington, DC: U.S. Government Printing Office. An attempt, in this comprehensive review to evaluate, among other things, the health risks of smoking relative to the potential health risks of excessive weight gain following smoking cessation.

• 13 •

BODY WEIGHT AND AGE

Reubin Andres

Many cross-sectional studies of body weight and age show that the mean weights of men and women increase from the early adult years to middle age and then decline in old age. Weights tend to be highest at about age 60 in men and age 70 in women. Within these *average* trends however, there is great diversity. Some individuals gain a great deal more than average; others show no increase or even a decline in the earlier adult years. Furthermore, not all elderly lose weight; some are stable, others gain. Data are much more extensive from developed countries than from developing societies.

The mechanisms underlying these trends are diverse and not entirely understood. Weight gain in the earlier years of adult life is generally conceded to be due to a decrease in overall energy expenditure without a concomitant decrease in energy intake. A progressive decline in lean body mass over the adult years (perhaps modifiable if not entirely preventable by physical activity) also leads to a decline in resting energy requirements. The mechanisms underlying the tendency to lose weight in the last decades of life (70s, 80s, and 90s) are complex and include the increasing prevalence of significant illness, the use of medications that influence appetite, problems with dentition and swallowing, digestive disorders, economic factors, lack of socialization at meals, difficulties in shopping, and perhaps neural and endocrine changes associated with the processes of aging.

It is commonly averred that excessive weight is the major health problem in the younger adult years but that loss of weight is a hazard in the elderly. Thus body weight on the one hand may be a causative health problem on its own or, on the other hand, an indication of the presence of serious health concerns.

RECOMMENDED BODY WEIGHT AND AGE

One of the unresolved controversies of the past 10 years concerns the age specificity of weight recommendations. The dominant weight-for-height tables over the past 50 years have been those issued at intervals (1940–1941, 1959, 1983) by the Metropolitan Life Insurance Company. The recommended weights have changed with each issuance, but only to a relatively minor degree.

The structure of the three sets of tables has been uniform: a table for each sex, with heights graduated in inches and a range of weights for each of three "body frames." While the specific statistical principles underlying the construction of the tables were not provided, the values were based upon the experience of a group of major insurance companies with mortality follow-up data on very large numbers of "insured lives"; people whose heights and weights were assessed at entry and who passed individual health evaluations were granted policies without penalties for significant illness. Even though data were available for individuals aged 20 and 29 and 60 to 69 years, the most recent tables (1983) are said to be applicable to men and women from ages 25 to 59 years only. In other words, recommendations for persons above age 60 are not provided and, also important, there is no adjustment for age. The clear implication of these tables is that "best" weight is the same for all adults, at least from age 25 to 59 years.

Independent Analysis of Actuarial Data

Fortunately actuarial data were provided in detailed tables for both sexes and for the age decades 20 to 29 through 60 to 69 *(Build Study 1979)*. A reanalysis of the data in these tables shows very clearly that (1) the relationship of body mass index (BMI) (in kilograms weight per meter^2 height) to mortality forms a U-shaped curve at all ages in both sexes, with lowest mortality in an intermediate BMI zone; and (2) the nadirs of the BMI–mortality curves increase strikingly with increasing age in both sexes.

An age-specific set of recommendations was constructed and presented at a National Institutes of Health (NIH) Consensus Development Conference in 1985 (Table 13.1). No sex differences in the best BMIs were found in this analysis. Thus Table 13.1 is more complex than the 1983 Metropolitan tables because of the inclusion of recommendations for five separate age decades of life, but this complexity is counterbalanced by having a "unisex" table and also by deleting recommendations for three frame sizes, since no measurement of frame had been made in the Build Study. For the Metropolitan tables, body weights were evidently divided into three frame sizes purely by sweet reasonableness, not by data analysis.

Update on Other Weight Recommendations

The Consensus Development Conference did not accept our proposed table in 1985, nor did the Expert Panel clearly recommend the use of the Metropolitan 1959 or the updated 1983 tables. Since then, however, there have been several developments. In 1989 a publication by the Committee on Diet and Health of the National Research Council (NRC) presented an age-specific table that was, in essence, a minor modification of our recommendations (Table 13.2). In 1990, the latest update, a joint publication under the imprimatur of the U.S. Departments of Agriculture (USDA) and Health and Human Services (USHHS), became available *(Dietary Guidelines for Americans)*. The age adjustment was condensed into only two age groups, 19 to 34 years and 35 years and older (Table 13.2). The reversal of the recommendations of the Consensus Development Conference by the NRC and the USDA and USHHS, however, has by no means settled the controversy. An exchange of letters to the editor of the *American Journal of Clinical Nutrition* condemning and defending these later recommendations has kept the issue alive.

OTHER STUDIES OF BEST BODY WEIGHT IN MIDDLE AND OLD AGE

A large number of studies on other populations have now been reported. There have been two major study designs. In the simpler design, subjects were enrolled at specified ages, heights and weights were obtained at entry, and mortality was to be monitored over

TABLE 13.1. Comparison of Weight-for-Height Recommendations of the Metropolitan 1983 Tables with the Age-Specific Recommendations of the Gerontology Research Center

Height (ft–in)	Metropolitan 1983 weights (lb) for ages 25–59[a]		Gerontology Research Center weight range (lb) for men and women by age (years)[b]				
	Men	Women	25	35	45	55	65
4–10	. . .	100–131	84–111	92–119	99–127	107–135	115–142
4–11	. . .	101–134	87–115	95–123	103–131	111–139	119–147
5–0	. . .	103–137	90–119	98–127	106–135	114–143	123–152
5–1	123–145	105–140	93–123	101–131	110–140	118–148	127–157
5–2	125–148	108–144	96–127	105–136	113–144	122–153	131–163
5–3	127–151	111–148	99–131	108–140	117–149	126–158	135–168
5–4	129–155	114–152	102–135	112–145	121–154	130–163	140–173
5–5	131–159	117–156	106–140	115–149	125–159	134–168	144–179
5–6	133–163	120–160	109–144	119–154	129–164	138–174	148–184
5–7	135–167	123–164	112–148	122–159	133–169	143–179	153–190
5–8	137–171	126–167	116–153	126–163	137–174	147–184	158–196
5–9	139–175	129–170	119–157	130–168	141–179	151–190	162–201
5–10	141–179	132–173	122–162	134–173	145–184	156–195	167–207
5–11	144–183	135–176	126–167	137–178	149–190	160–201	172–213
6–0	147–187	. . .	129–171	141–183	153–195	165–207	177–219
6–1	150–192	. . .	133–176	145–188	157–200	169–213	182–225
6–2	153–197	. . .	137–181	149–194	162–206	174–219	187–232
6–3	157–202	. . .	141–186	153–199	166–212	179–225	192–238

Note. Heights and weights are without shoes and clothes.
[a]The weight range is from the lower weight for the small frame to the upper weight for the large frame.
[b]Data are from Andres (1985).

TABLE 13.2. Recommended Ranges of Body Mass Index

NRC[a]		DGA[b]	
Age (years)	BMI	Age (years)	BMI
19–24	19–24	19–34	19–25
25–34	20–25		
35–44	21–26	35+	21–27
45–54	22–27		
55–64	23–28		
>65	24–29		

[a]Published in *Diet and Health* (National Research Council, 1989, p 564).
[b]Published in *Dietary Guidelines for Americans* (U.S. Congress, 1990).

a period of years. The BMI range with the lowest resultant mortality could then be assigned as the recommended BMI for specific age groups. A number of criticisms have been directed at these studies, the major one being that two confounding variables might influence both body weight and mortality: (1) Cigarette smokers weigh less and die earlier than nonsmokers, and (2) undetected illness might have the same effects—low body weights and high mortality. The published studies of diverse populations vary widely in their comprehensiveness in dealing with these serious potential defects.

Effects of Cigarette Smoking

In some reports, including those of actuarial studies, smoking was not included as a factor. In others, smoking was taken into account either by analyzing the data from smokers and nonsmokers separately (stratification), by simply deleting the smokers from the analysis, or by "adjusting" for cigarette smoking in multiple logistic models. It is remarkable that this theoretically important confounding factor actually has very little effect on the end results; the BMIs at the nadirs of the U-shaped curves are nearly identical for smokers and nonsmokers.

Effects of Illness

Two techniques have been used by epidemiologists to take into account the potentially important confounding influence of subjects who are ill. When subjects first enter into a study, they are clinically evaluated; subjects in whom significant illness is detected are deleted from the study population. There are no agreed-upon "rules of exclusion" for this kind of effort. Thus one finds great diversity among population studies in the comprehensiveness of the screening exam and in the exclusionary criteria. In free-living populations, however, as with cigarette smoking, there is surprisingly little effect of "clinical cleanup" on the derived BMI-mortality U-shaped curves. Perhaps the percentage of lethal illnesses in a group of free-living volunteers is simply too low to have a significant effect on the shape of the resultant curves. It is also conceivable that not all significant illnesses cause weight loss. Some may result in weight gain due, for example, to reduced activity accompanying illness or to edema.

    The second technique used to minimize the effects of illness is to create a period of "temporal separation" between the initial enrollment examination and the start of the follow-up period. Thus, as an example, it has been assumed in some studies that if an undetected but lethal illness is present at enrollment and the enrollment weight has already been influenced by this illness (say, e.g., metastatic cancer), it is highly likely death will occur in a short period of time. Thus subjects who die, of whatever cause, in the first 2, 3, or 5 years of enrollment are simply dropped from the study, since these are the subjects who might already have had their enrollment weights influenced by an illness. The 2- to 5-year span, then, is the period of temporal separation—the period of time before the follow-up clock is started. Combining the techniques of careful clinical evaluation and temporal separation offers high confidence that illness will not be a significant confounding influence.

IMPLICATIONS OF AGE-SPECIFIC WEIGHT RECOMMENDATIONS

If the recommended body weights are higher for older than for younger individuals, the implication seems clear that some weight gain should be permitted (or even recommended) as individuals age. For example, an increase in BMI of 1 kilogram per meter^2 per decade of life (the NRC value in Table 13.2) would be equivalent to 7 pounds per decade for a man of average height and to 6 pounds per decade for the average women.

As a further test of this conclusion, the question can be asked: What is the mortality experience in populations with respect to *change* in body weight as time passes? The published literature of such studies is complex, confusing, and controversial. Several papers were presented at a 1993 NIH Technology Assessment Conference and subsequently published in a supplement of the *Annals of Internal Medicine* titled "Methods for Voluntary Weight Loss and Control." The overall impact of these studies is that, taken at face value, those individuals who lose weight (even in small amounts) and those who gain a considerable amount of weight while passing through the adult years of life have high rates of mortality; those who either maintain their weight or, better, gain small amounts of weight, show the lowest mortality. Thus these results confirm those weight tables that show age-specific increases at higher ages.

FURTHER READING

Andres R. (1985). Mortality and obesity: The rationale for age-specific height–weight tables. In R. Andres, E. L. Bierman, & W. R. Hazzard (Eds.), *Principles of geriatric medicine* (pp. 311–318). New York: McGraw-Hill. An independent analysis of the actuarial data published in the *Build Study 1979*.

Andres R., Muller, D. C., & Sorkin, J. D. (1993). Long-term effects of change in body weight on all-cause mortality. *Annals of Internal Medicine, 119*, 737–43. A summary of the methodology and results of studies of 11 diverse populations in the United States and Europe.

Build Study 1979. (1980). Chicago: Society of Actuaries and Association of Life Insurance Medical Directors of America. Comprehensive tabular data on the experience of the insurance industry that provided the basis for the construction of the 1983 Metropolitan tables.

Manson, J. E., Stampfer, M. J., Hennekens, C. H., & Willett, W. C. (1987). Body weight and longevity. A reassessment. *Journal of the American Medical Association, 257*, 353–358. A critique of potential confounding variables in population studies.

Metropolitan Life Insurance Company. (1983). 1983 Metropolitan Height and Weight Tables. *Statistical Bulletin of the Metropolitan Life Insurance Company, 64* (January–June), 2. The most recent tables summarizing the data published in the *Build Study 1979*.

National Research Council, Committee on Diet and Health. (1989). *Diet and health: Implications for reducing chronic disease risk* (pp. 563–565). Washington, DC: National Academy Press. Chapter 21, "Obesity and Eating Disorders," presents a table of desirable BMIs in relation to age, with specific ranges of BMI from ages 19 to 24 years through 65+ years.

U.S. Congress, Senate Committee on Appropriations, Subcommittee on Agriculture, Rural Development, and Related Agencies. (1990). *Dietary guidelines for Americans.* Washington, DC: U.S. Government Printing Office. Weight-for-height tables with a single age adjustment for adults younger and older than age 35. These tables have the imprimatur of the U.S. Departments of Agriculture and of Health and Human Services.

Willett, W. C., Stampfer, M., Manson, J., & Van Itallie, T. (1991). New weight guidelines for Americans: Justified or injudicious? [Letter] *American Journal of Clinical Nutrition, 53,* 1102–1103. Criticisms of the recommendations in *Dietary guidelines for Americans.* Responses to this letter appeared in subsequent letters to the *American Journal of Clinical Nutrition* (1991, *54,* 171–174; and 1992, *55,* 481–483).

· II ·
DIETING AND BODY IMAGE

• 14 •

SOCIAL INFLUENCES ON BODY WEIGHT

Jeffery Sobal

People in different societies and filling different roles within a society vary in their body weights. Just as you are what you eat, you are what you weigh. Stunkard noted that social factors may be the most important influence on the prevalence of obesity today (see Chapter 10). Understanding how different types of social factors are involved in weight is important in dealing with obesity and eating disorders.

Fatness and thinness are the outcome of biological, psychological, and social processes that occur within relationships and social institutions. While weight is determined by the balance between energy intake and expenditure, this balance is a product of immediate, proximate, and ultimate influences. Eating and activity are the immediate behavioral influences on weight, with food habits and exercise patterns determining caloric intake and activity levels. Proximate influences on weight include personal factors that shape diet and activity, which can be seen as personal attributes such as motivations and skills as well as cognitive factors such as knowledge and attitudes. Interpersonal relationships, roles, and norms shape the operation of personal factors. Ultimate influences on weight include the sociocultural structures and processes that control the overall environment within which behaviors, personal factors, and relationships operate. Sociocultural factors include cultural values, economic resources, and social institutions within which other factors function.

LEVELS OF SOCIAL INFLUENCES

Social influences on weight operate at several levels: families, organizations, communities, and societies. Each level includes different factors that influence weight.

Families provide food systems, structured activities, and social values about appropriate weight of family members. Weight patterns in families tend to be consistent, but this tendency is more than simple genetics, because unrelated family members are influenced by family processes. Family dynamics, such as the adaptability and cohesion of the family system, have important influences on eating disorders among specific members of the family.

Organizations in society, such as work sites or schools, provide an important context within which weight-related behaviors are enacted. These organizations make varying demands on individuals for energy expenditure and provide constraints on and opportunities for eating. Organizations also provide a climate that may support or repress changes in behaviors and weight levels.

Communities provide a context within which people live their lives. Local community food systems serve as "foodsheds" (a concept similar to "watersheds"), which can be conducive to higher or lower body weights by offering calories, fat, and eating opportunities. Communities also offer varying work and recreational opportunities and access that play key roles in energy expenditure. Most important, communities have shared interests and values that may encourage people to be overweight or underweight by the variations in the social support they provide for being thinner or fatter.

Societies, at a higher level of analysis, provide macrolevel food systems, energy expenditure demands and opportunities, and social values that shape the weight of their citizens. Societal practices and policies concerning agriculture, food, transportation, recreation, and other areas of society are key influences on weight. Values about eating, activity, and appropriate body shape are transmitted by mass media and oral traditions within societies and are reinforced in everyday social interactions that express social norms about weight and apply sanctions against people who deviate from accepted weight standards.

CULTURAL AND HISTORICAL INFLUENCES

Culture is the system of categories, rules, and values that governs structures, processes, and ideals in a society. Culture is probably the most powerful determinant of body weight because it sets the context for eating and activity and also assigns moral and social meanings to weight. People in traditional cultures experience a continuing risk of insufficiency in their food systems; hence fatness is a sign of health and wealth even though the luxury of becoming obese is rare. By contrast, the food systems of industrialized cultures offer ample amounts of a wide variety of energy-dense foods, making it easy for most people to gain weight and difficult to lose weight. Slimness has become increasingly valued as a cultural ideal by members of industrialized societies, and consequently fatness is rejected and stigmatized.

Weight patterns are not constant within societies, with historical variations in the influences on body weight. Most people in past eras desired, but were not able to attain, body weights higher than those valued today. During the 20th century, the ideals of beauty for women, and to a lesser extent for men, have increasingly emphasized slimness. Solid historical epidemiological data about body weight is not available for the first half of the 20th century, but in recent decades in the United States the average body weight of the population has been increasing (see Chapter 68). At the same time, societal ideals have increasingly valued slimness. The increasing discrepancy between actual versus desired body weights has led to "normative discontent" with weight among women and has promoted efforts to lose weight (see Chapters 15 to 17).

Social Variables Influencing Weight

In industrialized societies, social epidemiologists find that fatness varies in relationship to many social roles, including gender (women are fatter), life course position (fatness increases until people become elderly, then declines; see Chapter 13), ethnicity (African American women in the United States are fatter; see Chapter 76), socioeconomic status (lower socioeconomic status women are fatter), marriage (married men are fatter), parenthood (more parous women are fatter), and residence (people living in rural areas and some geographic regions are fatter). These intertwined weight patterns can be understood through the use of social science perspectives on how social values, roles, and behaviors operate to influence body weight.

Gender roles provide socially defined expectations and concerns about body weight. Women are judged more by their appearance than are men (see Chapter 15), and this has led to greater concern about thinness among women, especially younger women. Most efforts to lose weight and maintain weight loss are motivated more by appearance than by health, particularly for women. Younger men tend to desire to gain weight to appear big and strong; their weight-change efforts are motivated more by the desire to look good than to be healthy. The emphasis on slimness for women has resulted in frequent dieting by most women and the development of the eating disorders of anorexia nervosa and bulimia in a small proportion of women (see Chapter 16).

Progression through the life course is associated with a rising concern with weight that begins in childhood and continues throughout adulthood, with an eventual decline in the concern about appearance and the growth of interest in health. Young children typically pay little attention to their weight, but as they become socialized into adult roles they internalize weight expectations associated with the roles they adopt. Thus young girls often become interested in thinness even before they enter school; boys develop concerns about strength and weight gain later. The entry into adolescence heightens the concern with appearance that is associated with dating and mating. There is less concern with appearance after marriage, and the approach of later adulthood brings health concerns to the fore. Elderly individuals are concerned about excess and insufficient weight because of their health implications.

"Ethnicity" is the cultural identity of individuals within a larger society, and it is an important influence on body weight (see Chapter 76). Just as different cultures value higher or lower weights, different ethnic groups within a culture value being heavier or lighter. These values may be linked to ethnic dietary patterns or to exercise behaviors. As individuals and groups become acculturated into another society, they tend to lose their past ethnic behaviors and their body weights tend to become more similar to those of the people of their new society. In the United States, African American ethnic groups have tended to have higher body weights, especially women; other ethnic groups show varying patterns. Native Americans and Pacific Islanders becoming acculturated into Western society frequently become obese.

Socioeconomic status (SES) stratifies people by income, education, occupation, and family background. Among women, there is a clear inverse relationship between socio-economic status and weight, with upper-SES women being thinner than their lower-SES counterparts. Among men, there are mixed patterns of SES and weight. The relationship between SES and weight operates in a bidirectional manner; SES influences weight through the availability of resources, patterns of life style, and availability of knowledge. Conversely, weight influences SES through prejudice and discrimination against obese people, preventing their access to important social positions needed for social mobility to attain higher SES.

Marriage is one of the most important social roles in the lives of many individuals. Heavier people (especially women) have a more difficult time attracting desirable marital partners. People tend to gain weight when they marry, and couples tend to change weight together in a pattern of marital synchrony. Married men are generally heavier than those who are not married. Overall, entering marriage is more difficult for heavier people, and the marital role is associated with greater body weight.

Parenthood is a role associated with greater concern about one's children and less concern about oneself. While biological factors certainly play a role in the association between parity and weight for women, the social expectations and demands of the parental role are a powerful influence upon body weight. The cultural image of mothers as large people who provide for others parallels the pattern for women to gain weight as they have children and to add additional weight with each child.

Weight varies in relation to geographic locations. Rural people are generally heavier than those in metropolitan areas. Individuals in particular regions also vary in body weight. These patterns are associated with other demographic variables, such as the geographic differential among occupations, but are also a product of regional traditions in values about weight and regional differences in dietary patterns and levels of activity.

CONCLUSION

The social sciences offer perspectives about the various influences on body weight that are not available from biomedical models. Social science theories can be used to frame the issue of body weight and generate explanations that provide insights into body weight variations. These theories range from the cultural—how modernization may change a group's values concerning weight; to the social—the social roles and weight expectations of a group; to the psychological—changes in a group's attitudes and patterns concerning weight.

Body weight is clearly part of a social context. An awareness of the social elements that influence body weight and the operation of the social context permits a better understanding of the weight of individuals, the weight patterns of populations, and the changes in both over time. The social influences on body weight need to be assessed and considered in interventions to modify weight and maintain weight changes.

FURTHER READING

Brown, P. J. (1993). Cultural perspectives on the etiology and treatment of obesity. In A. J. Stunkard & T. A. Wadden (Eds.), *Obesity: Theory and therapy* (pp. 163–178). New York: Raven Press. Provides an extensive discussion of obesity and culture.

Garner, D. M., & Garfinkel, P. E. (1980). Cultural expectations of thinness in women. *Psychological Reports, 47,* 483–491. A classic paper giving evidence for a historical increase in the values that emphasize slimness in the ideal body shape for U.S. women.

Kallen, D. K., & Sussman, M. B. (Eds.). (1984). *Obesity and the family.* New York: Haworth Press. A collection of papers in which family issues in obesity are discussed.

Parham, E. S. (1993). Nutrition education research in weight management among adults. *Journal of Nutrition Education, 25,* 258–268. Reviews social psychological influences and educational issues in obesity.

Rodin, J. L., Silberstein, L., & Streigel-Moore, R. (1984). Women and weight: A normative discontent. In T. B. Sonderegger (Ed.), *Psychology and gender: Nebraska Symposium on Motivation* (pp. 267–307). Lincoln: University of Nebraska Press. Discussion of the social pressures to be slim and of gender roles.

Sobal, J. (1991). Obesity and socioeconomic status: A framework for examining relationships between physical and social variables. *Medical Anthropology, 13,* 231–247. Presentation of a framework for examining social variables and weight.

Sobal, J., Rauschenbach, B., & Frongillo, E. (1992). Marital status, fatness, and obesity. *Social Science and Medicine, 35,* 915–923. An investigation revealing that married men, but not women, tend to be overweight.

Sobal, J., & Stunkard, A. J. (1989). Socioeconomic status and obesity: A review of the literature. *Psychological Bulletin, 105,* 260–275. Extensive review and discussion of SES and obesity.

Stunkard, A. J. (1975). From explanation to action in psychosomatic medicine: The case of obesity. *Psychosomatic Medicine, 37,* 195–236. Description of psychosocial factors involved in obesity.

Stunkard, A. J. (1980). The social environment and the control of obesity. In A. J. Stunkard (Ed.), *Obesity* (pp. 438–462). Philadelphia: W. B. Saunders. Examination of the importance of the social contexts of obesity and how they may be involved in weight control efforts.

• 15 •

CULTURAL INFLUENCES ON EATING DISORDERS

Denise E. Wilfley
Judith Rodin

In Western culture, thinness in women has come to symbolize competence, success, control, and sexual attractiveness, while obesity represents laziness, self-indulgence, and a lack of willpower. Fashion images of the "waif look" in the 1990s are the most recent expression of what has become an obsession with thinness. Top fashion models who portray this look are often 5'7" and taller, yet weigh barely over 100 pounds. Given these current unrealistic societal ideals, many adolescent girls and women experience discontent with their weight and shape; nevertheless, only a small percentage develop full-blown eating disorders. We will discuss how the current sociocultural milieu places young girls and women at increased risk for the development of eating disorders and explore additional factors that may potentiate this risk.

CULTURAL ATTITUDES

Epidemiologic studies indicate that the prevalence of anorexia nervosa (AN) has increased over the past 20 years, particularly among women between the ages of 15 and 25 years (see Chapter 36). In the case of bulimia nervosa (BN), we lack sufficient research data to examine the epidemiological trends in its occurrence. Some data do suggest that the increase in AN is related to the strong emphasis contemporary society places on an unrealistically thin appearance. In fact, scientists have postulated that eating disorders are a culture-bound syndrome that cannot be understood apart from its specific cultural context. According to this view, it is the cultural meanings of thinness and eating (associated with contemporary Western orientations toward the female body) that encourage the development of eating disorders like AN and BN, although genetic, psychological, and familial factors place certain individuals at greater risk. Scientists who support this view predict that eating disorders will increase in prevalence in rapidly industrializing non-Western societies, especially among the elite class, who are the most likely to assimilate the Western values of female slenderness as an expression of attractiveness and social prestige.

In fact, there is considerable evidence that AN occurs predominantly in industrialized, developed countries and appears to be uncommon outside the Western world and in less affluent Western countries. In support of these data, recent findings indicate that when immigrants move from less industrialized countries to more industrialized countries (e.g., Arab college students to London), they are more likely to develop eating disorders. To explain these findings, DiNicola offers a comprehensive model of AN as a culture-reactive syndrome that includes viewing AN as both a culture-bound syndrome (CBS) and a culture-change syndrome (CCS). AN is viewed as a CBS because most cases of AN occur in Western, technologically advanced, industrialized countries. However, infrequent cases of AN do appear where there is rapid socioeconomic change or when individuals move from one culture to another. To account for "orphan AN cases," an additional cultural hypothesis of AN has been advanced—as a CCS.

Although eating disorders are also found in males (see Chapter 31), the disproportionate ratio of female to male sufferers (approximately 10:1) is substantially greater than for any other common psychiatric disorder. Thus female gender is considered a risk factor for eating disorders. Central to explaining this striking gender difference and to understanding the nature of eating disorders is the present cultural context.

SOCIETY'S MANDATE FOR WOMEN TO SEEK UNNATURAL BEAUTY IDEALS

Society has long dictated ways for women to alter their bodies to achieve "unnatural" beauty ideals. What a society considers as signifying physical beauty varies across time and cultures. Women, much more so than men, have consistently tried to change their bodies to conform to a specific era's image of beauty. For example, in the 12th and 13th centuries, Chinese women bound their feet tightly, which was considered the *sine qua non* of both beauty and sexuality and was a permanent display of high status, since these women were unable to perform manual labor. Yet women with bound feet were crippled to the point of being unable to walk normally and often had to crawl or be carried. And in the 19th century, attaining the beautiful female body required wearing a corset, a practice that increased the likelihood of indigestion, constipation, and general weakness. Early in the 20th century, women bound their breasts with foundation garments to flatten their chests. Women's bodies have always been perceived as unfinished, in need of refining and realignment to make them conform to cultural standards of beauty.

Being thin and physically fit is the contemporary ideal of female attractiveness. In recent decades Western cultures have experienced a marked trend toward an increasingly thin beauty ideal for women. Today's aesthetic ideal is a lean, physically fit body. And our contemporary society is able to go to unprecedented lengths with new technology and cosmetics to achieve the ideal body. To attain this ideal, women have increased their dieting and exercise behavior. In the United States billions of dollars are spent by consumers who are in pursuit of the perfect body. Money is spent on diet programs, exercise paraphernalia, cosmetics, fashionable clothing, and various forms of cosmetic surgery (e.g., breast implants, liposuction, eye lifts) in order to "look good." In this technologically driven society, it seems as if the goal of looking good is possible for anyone who just works hard enough, exercises long enough, and restricts her/his food intake enough.

The ideal body has symbolic connotations as well: success, self-control, and acceptance. And the mass media have been unrelenting in portraying this image to all women. Such far-reaching exposure creates a reverberating impact. The media expose everyone to a single "right" look, and the beauty industry promises that anyone can achieve this appearance if she/he buys enough, from makeup to cosmetic surgery. Today, not only is how we look extremely important, but we have come to accept homogeneous images of beauty. Women have become casualties of technology—their looks are fabricated and their bodies objectified.

Brownell and others have noted that this search for the perfect body is driven by two beliefs. First is that the body is infinitely malleable and that with the right diet, exercise program, and personal effort, an individual can achieve the aesthetic ideal. Second, once the ideal is achieved, there will be considerable rewards, such as career advancement, wealth, happiness, and interpersonal attraction.

The contemporary beauty ideal of "thinness equals attractiveness" prescribes a body weight that for most women is unrealistically low because of biological and genetic factors. In fact, the body cannot be shaped at will. Genetic factors play a substantial role in limiting one's ability to change body weight and body shape (see Chapter 4).

This mismatch between cultural pressures and biological realities leads to the critical question of how much control a person actually has over weight and shape. A healthy woman of normal weight has 22% to 25% body fat, yet our current aesthetic ideal is based on actresses and models who have only 10% to 15% body fat. According to a recent study, the majority of *Playboy* centerfolds and Miss America contestants were 15% or more below their expected weight. Moreover, many top fashion models also meet the weight criteria for AN (15% or more below their expected weight).

The exercise and weight loss needed to pursue the aesthetic ideal are far in excess of what is necessary (or recommended) for healthy living. For example, Miss America contestants work out an average of 14 hours per week, with some exercising as many as 35 hours per week. Although the current societal ideal is unrealistic and unattainable for most women, those who do not meet the ideal are often judged to be self-indulgent and lacking in willpower.

Attractiveness, Body Image, and Self-Worth

Culturally bound and consensually validated definitions of what is desirable and attractive play an important role in the development of body image. Because of the high value Western society places upon appearance, self-worth is enhanced for those who are judged attractive and is challenged for those who are deemed unattractive. Attractiveness relates to self-acceptance for both men and women, but attractiveness and body attitudes are a more salient component of self-concept for women than for men. By adolescence, girls are more concerned with their looks than are boys, and they also perceive themselves to be less attractive than boys do. Girls who perceive themselves to be less attractive have lower self-esteem scores than do girls who are more satisfied with their appearance. Men and women also have fundamentally different concepts of the body; men view their bodies as functional and active, whereas women tend to view their bodies as aesthetic and decorative.

ETHNICITY, SOCIAL CLASS, AND EATING DISORDERS

Dieting, weight and shape concerns, and eating disorders occur most frequently among white, middle- to upper-class females (see Chapter 36). However, studies have recently revealed a broader social class distribution and documented eating disturbance among non-Caucasian individuals and culturally diverse ethnic groups. Eating disorder traits, including binge eating, excessive restraint, fear of fatness, and dissatisfaction with body image, have been shown to be related to non-Caucasian individuals' degree of Westernization and assimilation into the Caucasian culture. Moreover, preliminary studies suggest that recurrent binge eating is as common among black women as it is among white women and also suggest that research on binge eating disorder clearly needs to include women of color.

Certain subcultures intensify the sociocultural pressures toward thinness. Eating disorders are most common among those populations most invested in dieting to achieve slimness. These disorders occur more frequently among people in certain occupations (e.g., modeling), certain sports (e.g., ballet and wrestling), and certain subcultures (e.g., homosexual men) in which concerns about shape and weight are heightened.

Certain biologic, familial, and personality factors increase the risk of the development of eating disorders. Even in Western culture, with its unrealistic standards of beauty, only a small subset of women actually develop eating disorders. Women with eating disorders, in comparison with those without eating disorders, aspire to be thinner, report more weight and shape dissatisfaction, and attribute greater importance to weight and shape as central to their identity. More studies are needed to clearly identify which putative risk factors place women at increased risk above and beyond cultural factors.

SUMMARY

Western, technologically advanced cultures are particularly likely to promote the thin beauty ideal and to reinforce cultural beliefs about the importance of weight control. The increased frequency of dieting, eating, and body shape concerns among females in Western culture has led some writers to speak of a phenomenon of "normative discontent" regarding body shape. Both AN and BN occur most frequently in Caucasian females of the middle to upper social classes in Western cultures.

Recent research, however, suggests that as non-Caucasian groups and developing, non-Western cultures embrace the values of the dominant, Western culture, they too are experiencing an increase in eating-related problems and eating disorders. Data suggest that special populations with heightened weight/shape demands, such as certain athletes and models, may be particularly susceptible to AN and BN because of the increased pressures to conform to a certain ideal body weight/shape. Even more common in the general population are subthreshold problems characterized by binge eating, dieting, and body dissatisfaction.

FURTHER READING

Brownell, K. D. (1991). Dieting and the search for the perfect body: Where physiology and culture collide. *Behavior Therapy, 22,* 1–12. The first paper to clearly articulate how Western culture's beauty ideal and the biological limitations to achieving this aesthetic ideal collide.

Brownell, K. D., Rodin, J., & Wilmore, J. H. (Eds.). (1992). *Eating, body weight, and performance in athletes.* Philadelphia: Lea & Febiger. The first comprehensive reference guide for identifying and treating athletes who struggle with eating, weight, and shape concerns.

DiNicola, V. F. (1990). Anorexia multiforme: Self-starvation in historical and cultural context. Part I: Self-starvation as a historical chameleon; Part II: Anorexia nervosa as a culture-reactive syndrome. *Transcultural Psychiatric Research Review, 27,* 165–197; 245–286. In a historical, scholarly, and scientific manner, DiNicola argues that there is a necessary connection between AN and culture. He provides a comprehensive model of AN as both a culture-bound syndrome and a culture-change syndrome.

Rodin, J. (1992). *Body traps.* New York: William Morrow. A book that explores how psychological and sociocultural factors interrelate to create "body traps." The clinical vignettes used to depict the struggles that women experience with their weight and shape are illuminating for both lay individuals and professionals.

Rodin, J. (1993). Cultural and psychosocial determinants of weight concerns. *Annals of Internal Medicine, 119,* 643–645. A coherent synthesis of the sociocultural and psychological determinants that underlie Western culture's extreme emphasis on weight and appearance.

Rodin, J., Silberstein, L., & Striegel-Moore, R. (1985). Women and weight: A normative discontent. In T.B. Sonderegger (Ed.), *Psychology and gender: Nebraska Symposium on Motivation* (pp. 267–307). Lincoln: University of Nebraska Press. A classic paper that identifies and labels the phenomenon, among women, of "normative discontent" with their body weight and shape.

Striegel-Moore, R. H., Silberstein, L. R., & Rodin, J. (1986). Toward an understanding of risk factors for bulimia. *American Psychologist, 41,* 246–263. A seminal paper that postulates risk factors for bulimia based on the current state of the science.

Wiseman, C. V., Gray, J. J., Mosimann, J. E., & Ahrens, A. H. (1992). Cultural expectations of thinness: An update. *International Journal of Eating Disorders, 11,* 85–89. This paper replicates and updates the study by Garner et al. (1980; Cultural expectations of thinness is women. *Psychological Reports, 47,* 483–491) that documented a large discrepancy between "the ideal" image of the female body and the average body size of women.

· 16 ·

DIETING AND ITS RELATION TO EATING DISORDERS

JANET POLIVY
C. PETER HERMAN

Concern about the putative negative health consequences of obesity, along with recent changes in the roles and expectations for women have led to a derogation of a fat or even curvaceous body shape and an idealization of a slim physique. As discussed in Chapter 15, a preoccupation with achieving or maintaining a thin body has become prevalent among young women. This desire for thinness has spawned a proliferation of weight loss techniques, books, programs, and aids, as well as chronic caloric restriction or dieting to promote weight loss. This concern with weight loss is evident even among preteenage females. Since the 1970s, dieting has become prescriptively normative and statistically normal among young women in Western society. Women tend to see themselves as being too fat and perceive dieting to be the solution to the "problem" of overweight.

THE MEANING OF DIETING

What does it mean for so many people to be dieting in order to lose weight? Dieting entails replacing internally regulated (hunger-driven) eating with planned, cognitively determined, diet-approved eating, or dietary restraint. The restrained eater must ignore internal signals of hunger (and satiety) to adhere to a calorically reduced eating plan that will presumably lead to weight loss. Unfortunately, ignoring internal hunger signals often results in the disruption of normal caloric regulation, especially when dieting becomes chronic.

Restrained Eating

The eating behavior of chronic dieters (or restrained eaters, as they are often referred to in the literature and will be referred to here) has repeatedly been shown to differ in important respects from the eating behavior of nondieters, or unrestrained eaters. When confronted with situations in which they have consumed a food high in calories that breaks their diet's caloric allowance, chronic dieters do not compensate by minimizing further eating, as nondieters do after eating a large amount. Instead, dieters appear to become disinhibited; after being preloaded with fattening food, they eat *more* than similarly treated nondieters or than dieters who have not contravened their diets. In fact, regardless of whether the initial food eaten was actually highly caloric, as long as dieters *believe* that it was, they tend to overeat subsequently when offered attractive food.

This tendency of chronically restrained eaters to eat more rather than less following a "fattening" preload has been called "counterregulation." Of course, it is not the case that the more fattening food one feeds a dieter, the more she eats subsequently in a positive feedback loop. Even a dieter will be unable to continue eating (or overeating) after an extremely large, calorically dense preload. In general, however, dieters are only weakly responsive to internal regulatory signals of hunger and satiety; instead, they regulate their intake cognitively and tend to overeat whenever they believe that their restrictive diets have been breached.

Chronically restrained eaters are susceptible to a variety of other disruptions of their diets. For example, dieters who feel intoxicated (by alcohol) overeat. Likewise, dieters who are emotionally distressed or dysphoric tend to eat more than calm dieters or distressed nondieters. Even watching an amusing film clip can stimulate overeating in dieters. Dietary restraint thus seems to be fragile and easily disrupted. Not surprisingly, chronically restrained eaters do not appear to be particularly successful at losing much weight, though their weights certainly do fluctuate more than those of nondieters.

Comparisons of dieters' and nondieters' behaviors and attributes unrelated to eating reveal differences as well. Dieters are more distractible when performing a task, although they actually perform better than nondieters do if there are no competing cues or distractions. Dieters' thinking and memory also seem to differ from those of nondieters. Dieters tend to categorize foods as either guilt inducing or acceptable (and eat accordingly). They also remember more eating- and weight-related information about a stranger and are slower than nondieters on the Stroop color-word naming test when food and weight words are presented. They have also been shown to be more irrational on Ellis's irrational thoughts measure.

At the emotional level, restrained eaters have been shown to be more responsive or labile than unrestrained eaters, with more extreme reactions to both positive- and negative-valence emotional events or cues. Restrained eaters also have lower self-esteem than do unrestrained nondieters and tend to report being more anxious and neurotic. Finally, restrained eaters appear to be more suggestible than are unrestrained eaters. Dieters seem to be insecure and uncertain of themselves and their internal state; as a consequence, they are more vulnerable to social or environmental influences.

It is not clear whether these characteristics of restrained eaters precede their dieting endeavors, are caused by them, or simply accompany dieting. Longitudinal studies of children not yet exposed to dieting are needed.

DIETING AND EATING DISORDERS

Dieting has been implicated as a triggering factor in eating disorders (see Chapter 35). Both anorexia nervosa and bulimia nervosa often seem to begin with an apparently normal attempt to diet to lose weight. In young women predisposed to psychological disorders (i.e., those who have underlying ego deficits such as a lack of self-worth, interpersonal distrust, maturity fears, and a sense of ineffectiveness), dieting seems to exacerbate their psychological deficiencies and may precipitate an eating disorder. The link between dieting and the development of an eating disorder in a susceptible individual is so widely recognized that eating disorders have been referred to in some recent papers as "dieting disorders."

Many of the characteristics of dieters that we have delineated above also apply, usually in a more extreme form, to patients exhibiting eating disorders. For example, bulimia nervosa patients alternately restrict their intake and overeat, just as dieters do. In fact, the triggers for overeating in both dieters and bulimics are often quite similar: emotional events, perceived diet breaking, or disinhibitors such as alcohol. Anorexia nervosa patients are more successful at maintaining their diets and losing weight than are most normal dieters, but they begin similarly, by restricting their intake. However, the anorexic appears to lose control of the process, as her ever-decreasing weight goals force her to restrict her intake more and more.

Restrained eaters and eating-disorder patients also resemble each other psychologically to some extent. Both exhibit personality traits of low self-esteem, body image dissatisfaction, lack of internal sensitivity or awareness, increased compliance, and heightened emotionality. Their thinking patterns also show similar distortions, including irrationality, dichotomous categorization of foods as good versus bad, and a heightened cognitive focus on food and body shape.

Many of the similarities between dieters and eating-disorder patients relate to attributes connected to food, eating, or body weight concerns. In particular, the parallels in thinking center on thoughts about and reactions to food and body shape. Obviously dieters and eating-disorder patients share a concern about their weight, eating, and appearance. It is not surprising then that both display this concern through the differential processing and retention of such charged material, as well as an intense preoccupation with weight loss and dissatisfaction with their bodies. The dichotomous thinking of dieters, though, appears to be confined to food and eating, while that of eating-disorder patients seems to extend to all areas of their lives.

Similarly, some of the shared personality characteristics may well relate to the dieting activity common to both groups. Insensitivity to internal cues is a quality that dieting is likely to promote. If one has to eat less than usual in order to lose weight, it is necessary to ignore hunger. Over time ignoring hunger may well progress to an insensitivity to internal cues of many sorts, with a correspondingly greater reliance on external/environmental cues, a characteristic of both dieters and eating-disorder patients.

Low self-esteem may precede dieting in both groups and may be a factor that prompts dieting as a means of self-improvement. Low self-esteem may also stem from repeated unsuccessful dieting attempts. The lower self-esteem of dieters is not equivalent, however, to the sense of worthlessness or ineffectiveness that characterizes eating-disorder patients. It seems more likely that the ego deficits of eating disorders precede the eating pathology and are an underlying cause of eating disorders rather than a reaction to stringent dieting.

There are other important differences between normal restrained eaters and eating-disorder patients. Eating-disorder patients show a constellation of ego deficits not found in dieters. Maturity fears, interpersonal distrust, clinical depression, substance abuse, and familial and relationship problems characterize eating-disorder patients but not normal dieters. It is thus important to recognize that dieting is a trigger and precondition for eating disorders in susceptible individuals only (see Chapter 17). In those with a basically healthy personality, dieting either creates or reflects characteristics different from those observed in nondieters, but these differences only rarely progress to the level of pathology observed in eating disorders. Dieting leads to bingeing but not necessarily to bulimia if there is no predisposition to pathology. In those with preexisting deficits, dieting may direct the pathology into an eating disorder, but dieters differ from eating-disorder patients in as many respects as they resemble them.

In conclusion, dieting is associated with attributes that distinguish its practitioners from normal nondieters. It also serves as a precondition for more pathological reactions in some individuals, culminating in eating disorders. Finally, it reflects an attitude of self-rejection, an overconcern with body shape and appearance, and the pursuit of what is probably a chimerical ideal of thinness.

FURTHER READING

Brownell, K. D. (1991). Dieting and the search for the perfect body: Where physiology and culture collide. *Behavior Therapy, 22,* 1–12. An integrative examination of the effects of dieting and the socially sanctioned pursuit of thinness.

Bruch, H. (1973). *Obesity, anorexia, and the person within.* New York: Basic Books. The classic discussion of obesity, the quest for thinness, and eating disorders by the *éminence grise* of this field.

Fairburn, C. G., & Wilson, G. T. (Eds.). (1993). *Binge eating: Nature, assessment, and treatment.* New York: Guilford Press. A recent volume presenting theorizing by a variety of experts on binge eating and its etiology, nature, and treatment.

Garner, D. M., Olmstead, M. P., Polivy, J., & Garfinkel, P.E. (1984). Comparison between weight-preoccupied women and anorexia nervosa. *Psychosomatic Medicine, 46,* 255–266. A study investigating and documenting the similarities and differences between highly weight-conscious dieters and anorexia nervosa patients.

Garner, D. M., Garfinkel, P. E., Rockert, W., & Olmstead, M.P. (1987). A prospective study of eating disturbances in the ballet. *Psychotherapy and Psychosomatics, 48,* 170–175. A longitudinal prospective study of predictors of eating disorders in adolescent ballet students, showing that dieting and body dissatisfaction are the best predictors of who will develop an eating disorder (latest in a series of such studies by this expert group of researchers).

Polivy, J., & Herman, C. P. (1985). Dieting and bingeing: A causal analysis. *American Psychologist, 40,* 193–201. An examination of the literature on dieting and eating disorders in which the authors conclude that dieting triggers or promotes eating disorders, especially binge eating.

Polivy, J., & Herman, C. P. (1987). The diagnosis and treatment of normal eating. *Journal of Consulting and Clinical Psychology, 55,* 635–644. A review of the literature on dieting and eating disorders indicating the degree to which cultural influences promote dieting and eating disorders.

Streigel-Moore, R. H., Silberstein, L. R., & Rodin, J. (1986). Toward an understanding of risk factors for bulimia. *American Psychologist, 41,* 246–263. A review of the cultural pressures on women to be thin, undertaken to answer, regarding bulimia, why women, which women, and why now. Sociocultural, developmental, psychological, and biological factors are examined.

Tuschl, R. J. (1990). From dietary restraint to binge eating: Some theoretical considerations. *Appetite, 14,* 105–109. (Invited responses follow, pp. 110–229.) An analysis of how dieting may relate to binge eating, with a series of responses from other experts in the field.

Wooley, O. W., & Wooley, S. C. (1982). The Beverly Hills Eating Disorder: The mass marketing of anorexia nervosa. *International Journal of Eating Disorders, 1,* 258–269. An analysis of how a particular diet promotes pathological eating and encourages the development of anorexia nervosa.

· 17 ·

THE CONTROVERSY OVER DIETING

G. Terence Wilson

For decades dieting was the thing to do. The assumption that dieting would lead to the twin advantages of better health and improved looks was held as a self-evident truth. More recently, however, dieting has been denounced. Researchers have increasingly questioned the effects of dieting, charging that it is ineffective at best and damaging to health at worst. Some critics have asserted that dieting is more likely to make people gain rather than lose weight, make them sicker rather than healthier, and make them unhappier rather than happier. These allegations have been the rationale behind such extreme recommendations as the call for a moratorium on weight loss programs. In a related fashion, dieting has been indicted as an element of societal oppression in some feminist critiques of contemporary culture and weight regulation.

Often lost in the ideological zeal and emotional arguments that increasingly accompany discussion of the pros and cons of dieting is a clear understanding of what precisely it is that is said to be good or bad. From a scientific perspective it is unhelpful to ask whether or not dieting helps or harms people. The more useful question is, what are the effects of what form of dieting (namely, self-imposed change in food intake), in whom, and for what purpose?

DIETING AND VOLUNTARY WEIGHT LOSS IN OBESE PERSONS

Scientifically based weight control programs have long eschewed "fad diets" as quick and easy solutions to losing weight. Often these diets are of dubious nutritional value if not downright hazardous to health. Modern behavioral weight control treatments emphasize change in nutrition as one of several components of a comprehensive program aimed at life-style modification, including increased physical activity (see Chapter 85). The goal is a balanced but flexible diet that emphasizes reduced intake of saturated fat and increased intake of complex carbohydrates. Overall caloric intake is restricted to one degree or another. Some programs include a very-low-calorie diet (VLCD) as an interim stage in the overall program.

Comprehensive weight control programs that combine dietary modification with increased exercise and other life-style changes are effective in producing significant weight loss in people with mild to moderate obesity. This weight loss is successfully maintained by roughly two-thirds of patients in the short-term, although long-term 5-year follow-ups reveal that almost all patients revert to their baseline weights. Extreme critics of dietary interventions have branded these sophisticated, multicomponent weight control programs as harmful to health, devastating to psychological well-being, and iatrogenic in initiating disordered or binge eating.

Effects on Weight and Health

A pattern of recurrent weight gains and losses has been identified as weight cycling, or what is more popularly known as "yo-yo dieting." The putative negative effects of weight cycling are alleged to include reduction in lean body mass relative to body fat; enhanced metabolic efficiency, making future weight loss even more difficult or even leading to still greater obesity; and increased risk of cardiovascular disease (see Chapter 11). Whether the gradual weight loss produced by state-of-the-art behavioral treatment programs, followed by gradual regain often extending over a period of a year or more, is an example of yo-yo dieting is questionable. It would appear to be markedly different from the rapid loss of relatively large amounts of weight that have been studied in animal models of weight cycling. Furthermore, the data on the negative effects of weight cycling are mixed at best. Some researchers have concluded that there is no consistent evidence linking weight cycling to changes in metabolism or body composition, whereas others acknowledge the inconsistent findings in the literature but contend these effects may occur in some people under some conditions.

The evidence on health outcomes in people, despite inconsistencies, does suggest that weight variability has a negative impact on all-cause mortality, and particularly on cardiovascular mortality (see Chapter 11). However, drawing causal inferences from existing studies linking variability in weight to health outcomes is fraught with difficulties. One problem is determining whether the cycles of weight loss reported were voluntary or not. The possibility that these instances of weight loss reflected an existing illness is difficult to discount. Given these findings, it is farfetched to argue that it is not obesity per se that is linked to increased morbidity and mortality but associated dieting-induced weight cycling. In a study of the longevity of Harvard alumni, researchers found that variability in weight predicted early mortality. The data also clearly showed that the more obese the alumni, the higher their risk of mortality from all causes and from coronary heart disease.

Psychological Effects

Behavioral weight control programs have consistently resulted in favorable short-term psychological effects, including significant reductions in depression, enhanced self-esteem, and improved interpersonal functioning. Critics have asserted that subsequent relapse, the experience of most patients who lose weight, can have severely negative psychological consequences. Although anecdotal accounts to this effect abound, controlled studies of the psychological sequelae of treatment-induced weight loss followed by relapse are lacking.

Effects on Binge Eating

It has been suggested that the dietary treatment of obesity may also contribute to the development of binge eating. This hypothesis has been directly tested in two studies. The first assessed the frequency of binge eating episodes during a combined VLCD and behavioral weight-loss program. Once the low-calorie formula diet ended and patients were reintroduced to food, 30% of those who had been identified as nonbinge eaters prior to treatment reported binge-eating episodes. Treatment did not increase binge eating in those patients identified as binge eaters, however. In fact, 39% of these patients ceased binge eating as a result of treatment. These preliminary data indicate that strict dieting may trigger binge eating in some obese patients. The second study showed that a standard VLCD program reduced the frequency and size of binge eating episodes in obese binge eaters. Also relevant in this context are the findings of a 10-year study of behavioral treatment of obese children that showed higher than expected rates of bulimia nervosa, underscoring the importance of assessment of disordered eating in treatment programs for obesity.

DIETING AND VOLUNTARY WEIGHT LOSS
IN NORMAL-WEIGHT PERSONS

Persons of normal weight show reactions to dieting that differ markedly from those seen in overweight persons. The negative effects of extreme dieting were shown by Keys and colleagues' study of young men on a semistarvation diet that resulted in the loss of roughly 25% of their body weight. Extreme negative emotional reactions were common. More conventional, self-initiated dieting is also associated with adverse psychological effects in young women of normal weight. Cross-sectional studies of adolescent girls have indicated that, independent of the effect of body weight itself, dietary restraint is correlated with feelings of failure, lowered self-esteem, and depressive symptoms. Dieting has also been shown to predict stress; however, stress does not predict dieting.

DOES DIETING CAUSE EATING DISORDERS?

Dieting as a Risk Factor

Dieting is clearly linked to the development of anorexia nervosa and bulimia nervosa in young women (see Chapter 16). Clinical descriptions consistently indicate that patients with bulimia nervosa almost always report that their binge eating began when they were on a diet (see Chapter 35). Eating disorders are most common in the specific groups that are most involved in dieting and weight loss—predominantly white, middle- to upper-class women. An overall correlation appears to exist between cultural pressure to be thin and prevalence of eating disorders, both across and within different ethnic groups (see Chapter 15). Eating disorders also occur more frequently among persons involved in occupations and sports that require low body weight (see Chapter 34).

Results of two prospective studies have linked dieting to the development of eating disorders. One study consisted of a representative sample of 15-year-old schoolgirls in London. Compared with nondieters, dieters were significantly at risk for developing an eating disorder within 1 year. Only a small proportion of the girls who were dieting at the beginning of the study (21%) subsequently were diagnosed as having an eating disorder, but dieters were eight times more likely than nondieters to develop an eating disorder. The second prospective study was an analysis of more than a 1,000 female twins located through the Virginia Twin Registry. Self-reported weight fluctuation (maximum–minimum weight) and current dieting status predicted the diagnosis of bulimia nervosa during an interview conducted 1 to 3 years later.

Dieting may not be a risk factor for obese patients who binge eat, what has been called binge eating disorder (see Chapters 78 and 94). Patients with this disorder engage in recurrent binge eating but do not meet the diagnostic criteria for bulimia nervosa because no compensatory behavior (e.g., purging) or comparable attitudinal disturbance exists. Obese binge eaters report less dietary restraint than bulimia nervosa patients. Moreover, a large percentage of obese binge eaters report that their binge eating preceded dieting, whereas dieting almost always antedates binge eating in bulimia nervosa patients. These findings, taken in conjunction with the data indicating that even severe dieting does not exacerbate existing binge eating in obese patients, suggest that dieting has quite different effects in obese and normal-weight individuals.

Dieting Alone Does Not Cause Eating Disorders

Some investigators consider dieting to be a necessary but not sufficient cause of eating disorders. Others question whether dieting is simply an antecedent with no causal significance. The available data do not provide a definitive answer to this question. In linking dieting to the development of disordered eating and eating disorders, it is important to be aware of the different types of dieting and dieters. Dieters may vary both in the pattern and the content of their daily eating behavior. A subgroup of restrained eaters who appear to have achieved stable, long-term weights that are lower than their previous weights have been called "successful dieters" or "weight suppressors." They differ functionally from other restrained eaters in that they do not show counterregulation in the laboratory. It has been suggested that some forms of dietary restraint are more likely to disrupt eating habits than others and that the more chaotic the everyday eating behavior, the higher the risk of developing an eating disorder.

Most adolescent and young adult women in the United States diet. Yet the lifetime prevalence for bulimia nervosa in women is estimated to be 1.5% to 2%. Some other factors must interact with dieting to cause eating disorders. These risk factors may range from genetic predisposition and biological vulnerability, through personality and individual psychopathological factors, to familial influences. We do not know the nature of these risk factors or their psychopathological mechanisms.

MECHANISMS LINKING DIETING TO BULIMIA NERVOSA

Dieting has various biological, cognitive, and affective consequences that may predispose persons to binge eating. Among its biological effects, short-term dieting in normal subjects produces an increase in the prolactin response to the administration of L-tryptophan, which investigators have interpreted as evidence of reduced serotonin (5-hydroxytryptamine, 5-HT) levels in the brain. Patients with eating disorders have been found to have low levels of 5-hydroxyindoleactic acid, a 5-HT metabolite, in their cerebrospinal fluid, suggesting reduced brain serotonin levels.

At the cognitive level, unrealistically rigid standards of dietary restraint, coupled with a sense of deprivation, leave the dieter vulnerable to loss of control after perceived or actual transgression of the diet. A lapse leads to an "all-or-nothing" cognitive reaction. In this phenomenon, called the "abstinence violation effect," the person attributes the lapse to a complete inability to maintain control, abandons all attempts to regulate food intake, and overeats. This mechanism has been advanced to explain counterregulation, but direct empirical support is lacking.

Dieting can be associated with different conditioning processes that may predispose a person to binge eating. First, it may increase the appeal of "forbidden" or "binge" foods (typically those high in fat and sugar) directly by nutritional preference conditioning. Second, terminating meals because of a self-imposed limit rather than satiation, combined with variability in intake (skipping meals), can extinguish conditioned satiety responses and lead to increasingly larger meal sizes (see Chapter 16). Finally, dieting may cause stress or make the dieter more vulnerable to its effects. Stress is a precipitant of binge eating.

CONCLUSION

"Fad" diets that offer quick-fix options for weight control are often unhealthy and should be proscribed. The moderate and nutritionally sound dieting that is part of state-of-the-art behavioral treatment programs is effective in the short term in producing significant weight loss, reducing other health risk factors, and enhancing psychological well-being. In the long term these programs have thus far not been shown to be effective in controlling weight, and their health effects remain to be determined.

It is important that the nutritional components of comprehensive weight-control programs offer flexible and nutritionally sound food choices in order to avoid the rigid dietary restraint that has been linked to binge eating. This may be particularly important in dietary interventions in young children.

Dieting in normal-weight individuals is associated with adverse psychological sequelae and cannot be recommended. Dieting is a risk factor for the onset of eating disorders. Instead of rigid dieting, people should focus on flexible and healthy eating habits, increased exercise, and acceptance of biologically determined body weight and shape.

FURTHER READING

Brownell, K. D. (1994). *The LEARN program for weight control.* Dallas: American Health. A comprehensive, state-of-the-art treatment manual for obesity.

Brownell, K. D., & Rodin, J. (in press). Medical, metabolic, and psychological effects of weight cycling. *Archives of Internal Medicine.* A balanced review of animal and human studies of weight cycling.

Cowan, P. J., Anderson, I. M., & Fairburn, C. G. (1992). Neurochemical effects of dieting: Relevance to changes in eating and affective disorders. In G. H. Anderson & S. H. Kennedy (Eds.), *The biology of feast and famine.* New York: Academic Press. A study of dieting's effects on neurotransmitters.

Epstein, L. H., Valoski, A., Wing, R. R., & McCurley, J. (1994). Ten year outcomes of behavioral family-based treatment for childhood obesity. *Health Psychology, 13,* 573–583. A summary of successful treatment studies of childhood obesity.

Garner, D. M., & Wooley, S. C. (1991). Confronting the failure of behavioral and dietary treatments for obesity. *Clinical Psychology Review, 11,* 729–780. A critique of dietary and behavioral treatments of obesity.

Hsu, L. K. G. (1990). *Eating disorders*. New York: Guilford Press. A thorough review of the association between dieting and eating disorders.

Rosen, J. C., Tacy, B., & Howell, D. (1990). Life stress, psychological symptoms and weight reducing behavior in adolescent girls: A prospective analysis. *International Journal of Eating Disorders, 9:* 17–26. An analysis of the relationship between dieting and stress.

Smoller, J. W., Wadden, T. A., & Stunkard, A. J. (1987). Dieting and depression: A critical review. *Journal of Psychosomatic Research, 31,* 429–440. A summary of the psychological effects of treatment-induced weight loss.

Tuschl, R. J., Laessle, R. G., Platte, P., & Pirke, K. M. (1990). Differences in food-choice frequencies between restrained and unrestrained eaters. *Appetite, 14,* 9–13. An analysis of the link between dieting and binge eating.

Wadden, T. A., & Bartlett, S. J. (1992). Very-low-calorie diets: An overview and appraisal. In T. A. Wadden & T. B. VanItallie (Eds.), *Treatment of the seriously obese patient* (pp. 44–79). New York: Guilford Press. A detailed review of low-calorie diets and their role in behavioral treatment programs.

Wing, R. R. (1992). Weight cycling in humans: A review of the literature. *Annals of Behavioral Medicine, 14,* 113–119. A critical analysis of the effects of weight cycling in people.

· III ·
MEASUREMENT

• 18 •

MEASUREMENT OF BODY ENERGY STORES

Timothy G. Lohman

The purpose of this chapter is to provide a brief review of the major laboratory and field methods of assessing energy stores in the human body. These methods can be used to measure energy stores in the human body more directly than using measures of height and weight. A consideration of various body composition methodologies as well as prediction equations and their application to different populations are covered. A brief review of various methods of assessing fat distribution is also presented.

A fat content above 25% for males and 32% for females is generally considered as the cut point for mild obesity (see Chapter 8). Body fatness between 10% and 20% for males and 17% and 25% for females is considered optimal. A fat content below 5% for males and 14% for females is not recommended for optimal health.

TRADITIONAL LABORATORY METHODS

Three major laboratory methods have, until recently, been accepted as reference procedures for estimating human body composition. All three methods are based on the assumption that the composition of the fat-free body is relatively constant. This assumption applies reasonably well in the healthy adult population. Each of these methods—underwater weighing, hydrometry, and potassium-40 whole-body counting—has advantages and limitations leading to a prediction error of ±2% to 4% body fatness for the individual (Table 18.1). Most investigators have found that body density, estimated by underwater weighing, and total body water content, estimated by isotope dilution, provides values for percent body fat with lower prediction errors than are obtained using the whole-body potassium method. Definitive proof of these findings, however, must await the development of a reference method with an error of estimation of 1%. At present we have no such reference method.

Since the density of the fat-free body varies from individual to individual because of variations in the water, protein, and mineral content of the body, the widely used Siri equation (% fat = $495/D - 450$) may not be applicable to all people. Thus a person with a body density (D) of 1.050 grams per cubic centimeter and a predicted body fat content of 21.4% (Siri equation) may actually have 18.0% body fat if, for example, the density of the

TABLE 18.1. Percent-Fat Prediction Errors of Three Laboratory Methods

Method	Prediction error in percent fat	Variation in fat-free body composition[a]
Underwater weighing	2.5%	Density 1.10 ± 0.006 g/cc
Total body water	2.5%	Water 73.8 ± 2.0%
Whole-body potassium	3.5%	K 2.66 ± 0.11 g/kg

[a]The actual variability in the composition of the fat-free body is not well-established and varies with investigation, population and methodology. The standard deviations given are therefore only estimates from several studies.

fat-free body was 1.09 grams per cubic centimeter instead of 1.10 grams per cubic centimeter. This lower density of the fat-free body is found in subjects who have a lower body mineral content and higher body water content than the reference values indicate. Similarly, by using total body water content to estimate body fat content (F = fraction of body weight as fat), the formula below can be used:

$$F = 1 - w/w'$$

where w is the measurement of total body water in liters and w' is the proportion of water in the fat-free body (assumed to be 0.73 ± 0.01). If the subject is somewhat dehydrated during the body composition measurement procedure, yielding, for instance, a value of 71% water in the fat-freee mass (FFM), then the estimated percent fat on that day of measurement will be 17.3%, as compared with 15.0% at 73% water in the FFM measured on another day.

A subject may have a greater muscle content than the mean of the population, leading to a higher whole-body potassium content of the FFM, for example, 2.74 grams per kilograms rather than the assumed 2.66 grams per kilogam. In such a case, using the 2.66 grams per kilogram constant would lead to a higher estimate of FFM mass, and therefore an underestimation of the percent of body fat.

FIELD METHODS OF ASSESSING BODY COMPOSITION

The most widely used field method of estimating body fatness is through the use of height and weight tables or body mass index (BMI; weight in kilograms per meter^2 height) (see Chapter 67). Nomograms have been developed to convert BMI to percentage fat, but a large prediction error of 5% is characteristic of this method. Body mass indices of 27.3 for women and 27.8 for men, equated to the 85th percentile for national norms, have been defined as measures of overweight.

Overweight is distinguished from obesity because individuals may carry more muscle and bone than normal for their height and may not be overfat. In other definitions of overweight, using the height and weight charts, a subject's weight is compared with a reference weight, and the percentage above the reference weight is calculated. A better definition of obesity is based on an estimation of the fat content of the body using a field method such as skinfold measurement or bioelectric impedance (BIA) rather than height and weight. The prediction error of percent fat from skinfold measurements or BIA is usually lower than that from height and weight (Table 2). Because of the large prediction errors of BMI, skinfold measurement and BIA are becoming more popular methods in both clinical and research settings.

TABLE 18.2. Percent Fat Prediction Errors
from Three Field Methods

Method	Prediction error, % fat[a]
BMI	5.0
Skinfolds	3.2 to 4.0
BIA	3.0 to 4.0

[a]Prediction errors are based on standard errors of
estimates from several studies in the literature.

The recommended method for estimating body fat content by skinfold, is to measure two to five sites on the extremities and trunk, using the caliper and an equation for a
specific population from which the formula was developed. Because formulas and
populations have been widely studied and cross-validated (tested in other samples of the
same population), this approach is widely used in the fields of clinical nutrition, exercise
science, and human biology. It is essential to use a set of standardized skinfold measurements for the optimum use of this approach.

In the relatively new method of estimating body composition of BIA, a small current
of 50 kilohertz is run through the body and the resistance is measured. This method is
highly reliable, easy to administer, and comparable to the skinfold procedure in its
validity. Again, selection of the proper equation and population is essential; also, accuracy may be affected if BIA is measured in subjects after they exercise or are dehydrated.

NEW METHODOLOGIES

Recently three new methodologies—dual energy X-ray absorptiometry (DXA), total
body electrical conductivity (TOBEC), and near-infrared interactance (NIR)—have been
developed to estimate body composition. The DXA and TOBEC validation studies show
that both methods can be used to estimate body fatness with errors comparable to those
based on body water content and body density by underwater weighing. Because we do
not yet have a reference method that is ideal, we cannot determine the actual error in
these new, promising methods because of errors inherent in our criterion methods.

The development of DXA is especially promising because it can be used to estimate
bone mineral density as well as body fatness. Recent evidence indicates it can be used to
estimate regional (arm, leg, trunk) as well as total composition. Furthermore, it is
possible to use DXA to define an area in the abdominal trunk that includes subcutaneous
and visceral fat; its validation against computed tomography (CT) also shows much
promise.

The third method, NIR, is the least valid of the three methods. The original
research on this method relied on the results of spectral analysis of the interactance
signal in the infrared region of the spectrum for five skinfold sites and found good
predictability, compared with that of body fat determinations using the total body water
method. In more recent research, however, a simplified commercial version of the more
expensive original instrument was used, along with a prediction formula based on height
and weight and one fat measurement over the biceps area. In general, studies show only
a slight improvement in prediction when NIR is used in preference to height and weight
alone.

Multicomponent Models

Multicomponent models, namely, measuring several components of the body in the same subjects, has been used to obtain more accurate estimates of body fatness than are yielded by the two-component model with its assumptions of constant fat-free body composition. With the development of DXA to estimate bone mineral density, the estimation of water (w), mineral (m), and fat (f) content is now possible in body composition studies. Using the formula where D_b is the body density determined from underwater weighing,

$$\% \text{ fat} = \left(\frac{2.74\%}{D_b} - 0.714w + 1.146m - 2.0503 \right) 100$$

this multicomponent approach allows for the estimation of body composition in children, the elderly, athletes, and other populations for whom the two-component model does not apply. Several other multicomponent approaches have recently been developed.

POPULATION-SPECIFIC CONSIDERATIONS

Measurement of body composition in different populations varying in age, ethnic group, gender, and athletic status is an important consideration when formulas developed for one population do not always apply to another. In using skinfold and BIA equations, it is particularly important to be certain that the equation has been cross-validated in several samples of the population under consideration. The use of the wrong equation can lead to an overestimation or underestimation of body fat content. This is particularly true in obese subjects when formulas developed for nonobese populations are sometimes applied to subjects with higher fat levels.

MEASUREMENT OF FAT DISTRIBUTION

Because of the association of fat distribution with diabetes and coronary heart disease, it is important to assess not only total fatness but also regional fatness and fat topography (see Chapter 79). Several approaches to fat distribution have been used, with the waist-to-hip circumference ratio being selected most often in large epidemiologic studies. Waist circumference can also be used by itself as an indicator of abdominal obesity. Another approach to fat distribution is the ratio of subscapular-to-triceps skin fold.

More recently it has been hypothesized that visceral fat, more so than subcutaneous abdominal fat, is associated with increased risk for chronic diseases (see Chapter 79). Direct measures of visceral fat can only be obtained by CT and magnetic resonance imagery (MRI). Further validation studies of DXA, as a measure of regional body composition as compared with CT and MRI, will help resolve this critical question. A final point that needs evaluation is the combination of DXA and truncal skinfold measurements, which may serve as an indirect index of visceral fatness and may provide a more practical approach than CT or MRI analysis.

SUMMARY

In this chapter various methods of assessing energy stores in the body were reviewed. The major laboratory body composition methods—underwater weighing, total body water content, and body potassium level—are especially applicable to the adult population and are mainly limited in their prediction accuracy by the assumptions of the two-component model, especially in children and the elderly. The multicomponent model, in which several components of the body are estimated, has been used to better estimate body fatness in the elderly, children, and various ethnic groups, for whom the constancy of fat-free body composition does not apply. Recent research with new methodologies offers the potential of estimating regional body composition as well as total body fatness, thereby elucidating the role of fat distribution as a separate risk factor for chronic disease and discerning the best way to assess fat distribution from among the multitude of approaches now in use.

FURTHER READING

Forbes, G. B. (1987). *Human body composition.* New York: Springer-Verlag. A comprehensive account of many biological problems in the field of human body composition.

Lohman, T. G. (1992). Advances in body composition assessment. *Current Issues in Exercise Sciences Series,* Monograph No. 3. Champaign, IL: Human Kinetics. Presents recent issues and controversies in the field.

Lohman, T. G., Roche, A. F., & Martorell, R. (Eds.). (1988). *Anthropometric standardization reference manual.* Champaign, IL: Human Kinetics. A reference manual for anthropometry and a collection of articles featuring various scientific perspectives on the field of body composition

Lukaski, H. C. (1987). Methods for assessment of human body composition: Traditional and new. *American Journal of Clinical Nutrition, 46,* 437–456. A review of the theory and validation of all the major body composition methods.

• 19 •

MEASUREMENT OF FOOD INTAKE

Sachiko T. St. Jeor

The measurement of food intake and understanding its associations with ingestive behaviors are critical to defining the etiology, diagnosis, and treatment of the eating disorders and obesity. Complex interactions of physiological cues, psychological status, behavioral factors, and environmental opportunities, however, make food intake highly variable and difficult to characterize accurately. Thus, after years of work, problems still exist in the assessment of food intake and the delineation of eating patterns, dietary preferences, and problem intake behaviors. Yet there are methods for use in research and clinical settings that are helpful in assessing food intake.

CURRENT METHODS OF MEASURING FOOD INTAKE

Five basic methods of dietary assessment have proven useful in recording and quantitating energy and nutrient intake. Diet histories, prospective food records for varying lengths of time, repeated 24-hour dietary recalls with trained interviewers, food frequency questionnaires, and various food lists have been used. Major limitations start with the high cost of administration and tedious, time-consuming analyses and extend to the reliability/validity of interpretations, extrapolations to implying usual or habitual intake, and generalizability to other groups or individuals. Distinct differences are apparent in the application of these methods for research or clinical purposes.

Data Collection

Standardized formats for data collection have been developed, but these formats vary according to each method used. Since self-reports of intake are most commonly used, an important variable is introduced in the form of the recording bias of the subject. How the subject is instructed to provide data on actual food intake and whether these data are collected retrospectively by recall or prospectively by records are also key factors. Further, the accuracy with which portions of food are estimated or weighed, how food preparation procedures are described, and the specificity with which the food is characterized are all factors that affect the accuracy of assessment.

Validation of what is actually eaten is almost impossible, and the issues of relative accuracy or calibration are now being addressed. Correlations between different methods have been made, generally by comparisons with food records, which are thought to reflect the variability in individual intake more accurately than recall methods. Although the exact number of days needed is still questioned, a period of 7 days is recommended for the assessment of individual intake, since the variation between weekday and weekend intake is included and day-to-day variation can be captured, as is particularly important in working with patients who exhibit abnormal eating behaviors. However, both 3-day and 4-day records are still commonly used, when cost is a consideration, and do provide useful data.

Long-term studies have shown that the number of days of food-intake monitoring needed to bring accuracy to within 10% of usual intake varies among individuals and also within individuals for different nutrients. Long-term studies have demonstrated that 3 days was the mean length of time required to estimate the true average intake for energy (kilocalories), whereas to estimate the average intake of vitamin A, which is concentrated in some foods, 41 days were necessary. An estimate of total energy intake is important in assessing the variability of other nutrients. Four days of food-intake monitoring insure that 95% of the observed values of calorie-adjusted total fat intake lie within 20% of the true mean and within 40% when not calorie adjusted. Furthermore, although increasing the number of days of monitoring better reflects an individual's true or usual intake, other studies have shown that random day-to-day variations in dietary patterns occur and account for 37% of the variance in an individual's intake. Thus at least three recalls representing nonconsecutive days are recommended to assess the intake pattern of an individual.

In general, the energy-adjusted coefficients that correlate nutrient intake, assessed by food-frequency questionnaires (FFQ) and food records kept by different populations for varying lengths of time, are in the range of $r = .40-.70$. Correlations between the FFQ and the 4-day diet record (FDDR) in the Women's Health Trial were lower for energy ($r = .30$), fat ($r = .29$) and fat as percent energy ($r = .40$). However, when comparisons of responsiveness to intervention were compared at a 1-year interval, the FDDR was only slightly more sensitive than the FFQ to changes made by participants, and a fat-related diet habits questionnaire was most responsive. These data suggest that shorter, inexpensive measures can be as useful as multiple-day diet records, especially when specific nutrients or foods are targeted for evaluation, as is the case with various food lists.

The major recognized sources of error in data collection include bias by the respondent (recalls), the recorder (records), the interviewer (recalls), the interpreter, or the reviewer (records). In addition, the process of collecting dietary data itself may affect eating patterns and introduce respondent bias. Studies have shown that obese subjects tend to underreport food intake and that estimated quantities may account for substantial errors in self-reported intake. Errors introduced by the interviewer, on the other hand, include behavioral factors, such as the manner of asking questions and the style of probing. An interviewer's nonverbal body language or mannerisms may be limiting in that they may distract a subject or suggest what answers would be preferred. This is of particular importance in evaluating problematic eating behaviors.

Data Analyses

Data analysis has been complicated by the numerous foods available, estimations of food portions, and descriptions of how the food is prepared and eaten. The method of choice must first focus on the food(s), food component, or nutrient under study. Dietary intake is most often defined in terms of nutrient composition and its contribution to nutritional adequacy. Data bases and computer software programs for quantitating these self-reports have greatly facilitated the assessment of nutrient intake for both research and clinical applications that differ in their need for specificity, accuracy, and practical applications.

Although there are a number of sources of information, the publications and programs of the U.S. Department of Agriculture (USDA) provide the most comprehensive and up-to-date information. The USDA Nutrient Data Base for Standard Reference is available in two versions (full and abbreviated). The full version contains all 32 nutrients, whereas the abbreviated one contains 20 of the most used nutrients. This information is available on diskettes, but interface programs must be developed by users.

Two well-established analysis systems for researchers provide this interface and programming for data analyses: (1) the Minnesota Nutrition Data System (NDS), available from the Nutrition Coordinating Center, Division of Epidemiology, School of Public Health, Suite 300, 1300 South Second Street, Minneapolis, MN; and (2) the Food Intake Analysis System, available from the University of Texas Health Science Center, Houston, School of Public Health. Both these contractors also provide support for data entry and analyses of food frequencies, recalls, and records and recipes. Less expensive, practical computerized data bases and interactive programs are available for personal computers and are also widely used. These include the Food Processor (Esha Research, P.O. Box 13028, Salem, OR 97309) and Nutritionist IV (N-Squared Computing, First DataBank Division, The Hearst Corporation, 1111 Bayhill Drive, San Bruno, CA 94066). Finally, for quick, ready reference, three popular handbooks containing nutrient information in common portions or household units are recommended: (1) *Food Values of Portions Commonly Used* (Pennington, 1994, Philadelphia: Lippincott); (2) *Nutritive Value of Foods,* Home and Garden Bulletin No. 72 (USDA, 1991); and (3) *Food Finder* (Hands, 1990, Esha Research, P. O. Box 13028, Salem, OR 97309).

Application of Food-Intake Measurements to Eating Disorders and Obesity

There currently is no one accepted format or data collection instrument that has been widely accepted and used in research or clinical settings specific for eating disorders. Rather, in specialty clinics food diaries have been adapted by adding common behavioral questions to the diary. Examples of such questions include situational descriptions focusing on general as well as problematic eating (such as bingeing) and include location; social situations accompanying eating; hunger ratings; and feelings before, during, or after the targeted event, along with the time, quantity, and duration. Some diaries focus on the problem behavior (bingeing, purging) alone, while others focus on the behavior in relation to the total diet. The interpretation of these records then becomes highly individualized and more suitable for use in clinical settings.

Assessment of food intake in the clinical setting focuses on the individual. In this context, the emphasis is on understanding the psychological, physiological, behavioral, and environmental factors influencing eating. Interviews, along with self-report questionnaires and/or food-intake records kept prospectively, have proven to be useful, but longer-term food records (4 to 7 days) or multiple recalls (3 random days) are needed to more accurately characterize an individual's intake. Food-group checklists, computerized self-assessments, and calorie counters have been used but are not generally suitable for research purposes; also, important individual behaviors are often not picked up in such procedures. Furthermore, quantitative scales that assess a subject's perceived food amounts, feelings, cognitions, and times, as well as expanded record forms that allow for extensive descriptions of events associated with eating (i.e., amount, time, duration, place, feelings/mood, with whom, behaviors, speed of eating, perceived hunger, activities, and effort) have been used, especially in the clinical setting. Subjects' reports and the clinician's interpretations play a key role in these assessments. It is important to impress on the individual the necessity of being truthful and of admitting to binges, the use of laxatives, the induction of vomiting, and other relevant behaviors, since these data aid in determining treatment.

Test meals have been used in the laboratory setting to assess episodes of binge eating. In one study, subjects were told that its purpose was to learn about the food preferences of overweight people (not binge eating) and were asked for their food preferences. The subjects were challenged with a yogurt shake and multiple-item meals containing their preferred foods, including the foods eaten during binges, which were served in a private room in an outpatient clinic. Subjects rated their hunger, desire to binge, and a variety of other factors and were given instructions either to eat as they normally would or to consume as much as they could. Measures included total meal duration and the amount of each food consumed. The energy values and nutrient composition of the diet were calculated both from manufacturers' data and the use of the Nutritionist III software program. This study demonstrated it was possible, in a laboratory setting, to detect differences in the amounts and types of food chosen by subjects with and without binge eating disorder (BED).

CONCLUSIONS

The etiology of obesity, anorexia nervosa, bulimia, and binge eating involves a departure from "normal" eating patterns and food intake. The regulation of caloric intake and body weight is a related problem. Information regarding normal as well as abnormal eating patterns and food-intake selections in susceptible individuals would provide critical information for prevention and treatment. To develop optimal methods will require interdisciplinary collaboration with improved technological and methodological advances focusing on the comprehensive assessment of specific and overall food intake; the role of the total diet; and the impact on weight, weight changes, long-term nutrition status, and health.

FURTHER READING

Agras, W. S. (1987). The eating disorders: Assessment. *Eating disorders.* Management of obesity, bulimia, and anorexia nervosa. New York: Pergamon Press. Presents self-monitoring forms and daily food records to be used by patients with eating disorders.

Basiotis, P. P., Welsh, S. O., Cronin, F. J., Kelsay, L., & Mertz, W. (1987). Number of days of food intake records required to estimate individual and group nutrient intakes with defined confidence. *Journal of Nutrition, 117,* 1638–1641. Addresses usual food intake and day-to-day variability using the analyses of food-intake records collected over 1 year and analyzed for energy content and 18 nutrients.

Buzzard, I. M., & Willett, W. C. (Eds). (1994). First International Conference on Dietary Assessment Methods: Assessing diets to improve world health. *American Journal of Clinical Nutrition, 59,* 143S–306S. Proceedings of a conference held in St. Paul, MN, in which gaps in dietary intake methodology, guideliness for selecting appropriate assessment methods, and research priorities to stimulate interdisciplinary approaches are presented.

Dwyer, J. T. (1994). Dietary assessment. In M. E. Shils, J. A. Olson, & M. Shike (Eds.), *Modern nutrition in health and disease* (pp. 842–860). Philadelphia: Lea & Febiger. Good summary and review of dietary assessment methods, along with their strengths, limitations, and applications.

Kristal, A. R., Beresford, S. A., & Lazovich, D. (1994). Assessing change in diet-intervention research. *American Journal of Clinical Nutrition, 59*(Suppl.), 185S–189S. Introduces "responsiveness," or the index of an instrument's sensitivity in measuring change by pre-intervention and postintervention intake, bias, and type of intervention, along with concepts applicable to improving food-intake assessment relative to eating disorders.

Smith, J. L. (Ed.). (1992). *Nutrient databank directory* (8th ed.). Delaware: University of Delaware. A directory that is a compilation of questionnaire responses. Features contents, costs, contact person, and other data for available nutrient data banks.

St. Jeor, S. T., Guthrie, H. A., & Jones, M. B. (1983). Variability in nutrient intake in a 28-day period. *Journal of the American Dietetic Association, 83*, 155–162. Outlines relationships between food records of 3, 4, and 7 days compared with 28 days, and addresses the variability of energy intake and seven selected nutrients by weeks and day of the week.

Tarasuk, V., & Beaton, G. H. (1991). The nature and individuality of within-subject variation in energy intake. *American Journal of Clinical Nutrition, 54*, 464–470. Discussion of within-subject variation among 29 adults participating in the Beltsville One-Year Dietary Intake Study, in which environmental and biological determinants, as well as methodological errors, are inherent in the estimation of energy intake are noted.

Willett, W. (1990). *Nutritional epidemiology*. New York: Oxford University Press. A comprehensive book addressing all aspects of dietary intake methodology. Epidemiological issues regarding the relationships between diet and long-term health and disease are put into perspective.

Yanovski, S. Z. (1993). Binge eating disorder: Current knowledge and future directions. *Obesity Research, 4*, 306–318. Description of ingestive behaviors and nutrient intake studied in the laboratory, by 7-day diet diaries and 24-hour recalls in obese binge eaters.

• 20 •

MEASUREMENT OF ENERGY EXPENDITURE

Eric T. Poehlman
Edward S. Horton

THE COMPONENTS OF ENERGY EXPENDITURE

Changes in body energy content occur through changes in the balance between daily energy intake and energy expenditure. Energy intake is episodic in nature, derived primarily from the carbohydrates, proteins, and fats in foods consumed. The total daily energy expenditure is relatively constant and, for theoretical and analytical purposes, can be divided into several components (see Chapter 6).

The Resting Metabolic Rate

The resting metabolic rate (RMR) represents the largest portion of daily energy expenditure (60% to 75%) and is a measurement of the energy expended for the maintenance of normal body functions and homeostasis. These processes include resting cardiovascular and pulmonary functions, the energy consumed by the central nervous system, cellular homeostasis, and other biochemical reactions involved in the maintenance of resting metabolism.

The RMR is primarily related to the magnitude of the fat-free mass in the body and is also influenced by age, gender, body composition, and genetic factors. For example, it is well known that the RMR decreases with advancing age (2% to 3% per decade), and this fall is primarily attributed to the loss of fat-free mass. Males tend to have a higher RMR than females because of their greater body size. The dependency of the RMR on body composition must be considered when individuals of different age, sex, and physical activity status are compared. Other processes, such as sympathetic nervous system activity, thyroid hormone activity, and sodium–potassium pump activity, have been shown to contribute to the variation in the RMR.

The Thermic Effect of Meals

The thermic effect of meals (TEM) is the increase in energy expenditure associated with food ingestion (see Chapter 6). The TEM represents approximately 10% of the daily

105

energy expenditure and includes the energy costs of food absorption, metabolism, and storage. The magnitude of the TEM depends on several factors, including the caloric content and the composition of the meal, as well as the antecedent diet of the individual. Following meal ingestion, energy expenditure increases for 4 to 8 hours, its magnitude and duration depending on the quantity and type of macronutrient ingested (i.e., protein, fat, or carbohydrate).

The TEM has been divided into subcomponents: obligatory and facultative thermogenesis. The obligatory component of the TEM is the energy cost associated with the absorption and transport of nutrients and the synthesis and storage of protein, fat, and carbohydrate. The "excess" energy expended above the obligatory thermogenesis is the facultative thermogenesis and is thought to be partially mediated by sympathetic nervous system activity.

The TEM has also been shown to decrease with advancing age and may be associated with the development of insulin resistance. It is presently unclear how exercise training influences the TEM, although there is clearly some interaction between physical exercise and TEM. There is presently no evidence that gender influences postprandial thermogenesis.

The Thermic Effect of Physical Activity

The most variable component of the daily energy expenditure is the thermic effect of physical activity. This component includes the energy expended above the resting metabolic rate and the thermic effect of feeding and includes the energy expended through voluntary exercise and the energy devoted to involuntary activity such as shivering, fidgeting, and postural control. In sedentary individuals, the thermic effect of activity may comprise as little as 100 kilocalories per day; in highly active individuals it may approach 3,000 kilocalories per day. Thus physical activity represents a significant factor governing the daily energy expenditure in humans because it is extremely variable and is subject to voluntary control. Physical activity tends to decrease with advancing age; this decrease in physical activity may be associated with a loss of fat-free mass and an increase in adiposity. Males in general tend to have a greater caloric expenditure associated with physical activity than females, due partially to the greater energy cost of moving a larger body mass.

The RMR, TEM, and physical activity are only partially distinct entities, because they often overlap during the course of a normal day. Although there are daily variations in energy balance, putting individuals in a slight energy deficit or surplus, it is clear that the maintenance of a stable body weight depends on the tight coupling of energy intake and energy expenditure over long periods of time. It is presently unclear which psychological and/or physiological factors influence the coupling of energy intake with energy expenditure to maintain energy balance.

METHODS OF MEASUREMENT

Many methods of measuring energy expenditure have become available over the years, and they vary in complexity, cost, and accuracy. It is important to gain an appreciation of the differences in the methods and of their applications in laboratory and other settings. We will briefly describe the techniques that have been used to measure total daily energy expenditure and its components.

The Resting Metabolic Rate and Thermic Effect of a Meal

The most widely used methods for measuring the energy expenditure involve indirect calorimetry. Direct calorimetry (the measurement of heat loss from a subject) has been used to measure energy expenditure, but the high cost and complicated engineering of this method have discouraged investigators from using this approach.

The term "indirect" refers to the estimation of energy production by measuring oxygen consumption and carbon dioxide production rather than by directly measuring heat transfer. This method requires that a steady state of carbon dioxide production and respiratory exchange be reached and that subjects have a normal acid–base balance. To determine the RMR, measurements are usually taken with the subject in a supine or semireclined position after a 10 to 12 hour fast. Depending on the equipment, the subject typically breathes through a mouthpiece, face mask, or ventilated hood or is placed in a room calorimeter in which expired gases are collected. Typical RMR values range from 0.7 kilocalories per minute to 1.6 kilocalories per minute, depending on the subject's body size, body composition, level of physical training, and gender. The room where the measurements are conducted is usually darkened and quiet, and the volunteer remains undisturbed during the measurement process. The measurement of RMR typically lasts 30 minutes to 1 hour, whereas postprandial measurements frequently take 3 to 8 hours. These measurements are generally easily reproducible (with a coefficient of variation of less than 5%).

Several methods have been used to measure oxygen consumption and carbon dioxide production at rest. Generally, an "open circuit" method is used in which both ends of the system are open to atmospheric pressure and the subject's inspired air and expired air are kept separate by means of a three-way respiratory valve or nonrebreathing mask. The expired gases are usually collected in a Douglas bag or Tissot respirometer for the measurement of oxygen and carbon dioxide content. Hyperventilation may occur in subjects who are not well adapted to a mouthpiece and may result in inappropriately high levels of oxygen consumption and carbon dioxide production. When a mask is used, it is frequently difficult to obtain an airtight seal around the subject's nose and mouth.

To circumvent some of these problems, ventilated hoods have been developed in which the subject is fitted with a transparent hood equipped with a snugly fitting collar. Fresh air is drawn into the hood via an intake port, and expired air is drawn out of the hood by a motorized fan. The flow rate is measured by a pneumotachograph, and aliquots of the outflowing air are analyzed for oxygen consumption and carbon dioxide production after temperature and water vapor content have been adjusted. Oxygen consumption and carbon dioxide production are calculated from the differences in their concentrations in the inflowing and outflowing air and the flow rate. Ventilated hoods are excellent for both short- and long-term measurements but are less useful in measuring the energy expenditure of physical activity; in the latter case the subject may find the hood uncomfortable, and there is a problem with the dissipation of perspiration and water vapor.

Physical Activity

The measurement of the energy expenditure resulting from physical activity has traditionally presented several methodological challenges. Indirect calorimetry (using a mouthpiece or face mask) has been used to assess oxygen consumption and carbon dioxide production. This method generally yields reliable and accurate measurements of the energy cost of physical activity in a laboratory setting but give no information about the energy cost of physical activity under free-living conditions because of the stationary nature of the equipment. Portable respirometers employ a face mask with valves that direct expired air through collection tubes to a respirometer carried on the subject's back. The respirometer contains a flowmeter and a sampling device that collects an aliquot of expired gases for analysis at a later time. There are drawbacks to this method: first, there is an inherent delay in obtaining results, and second; the rate of energy expended during the period of work performance is integrated over the entire period of gas collection.

In an attempt to avoid some of the problems associated with the measurement of free-living physical activity, several less complicated (and less accurate) methods have been devised. These methods employ physiological measurements, observation, and records of physical activity, as well as activity diaries or recall. Heart-rate recording, used to measure energy expenditure, is based on the correlation between heart rate and oxygen consumption during moderate to heavy exercise. The correlation, however, is much poorer at lower levels of physical activity, and a subject's heart rate may be altered by such events as anxiety or a change in posture without significant changes in oxygen consumption.

It is possible to estimate energy expenditure over relatively long periods of time by measuring energy intake and changes in body composition. However, there are errors inherent in attempting an accurate determination of energy intake over several days, weeks or months, as well as in the methods available for determination of body composition.

Time-motion studies have also been used to estimate the energy expenditure of physical activity in real-life situations. In time and motion studies, detailed records of physical activity are kept by an observer, and energy expenditure is estimated from the duration and intensity of the work performed. The major problem with this method is the marked individual variations in the energy costs of doing a particular task.

Physical activity diaries and physical activity recall instruments have been used to quantify the energy costs of different activities over a representative period of time. Record keeping is often inaccurate and may interfere with the subject's normal activities. Furthermore, the subject's recall of physical activity depends on his/her memory, which may not always be reliable. Measuring motion by devices such as a pedometer or an accelerometer may provide an index of physical activity (i.e., counts) but does not quantitate energy expenditure. In summary, the measurement of free-living physical activity continues to be the most significant challenge in the field of energy metabolism.

Daily Energy Expenditure

In recent years large respiration chambers have been built in laboratories. Such a chamber operates on the same principal as the ventilated hood system: It is essentially a large, airtight room in which temperature and humidity are controlled. Fresh air is drawn into the chamber and allowed to mix. Simultaneously, air is drawn from the chamber, and the flow rate is measured and analyzed continuously for oxygen and carbon dioxide content. The size of the room affords the subject sufficient mobility to sleep, eat, exercise, and perform normal daily routines, making detailed measurements of energy expenditure possible over a period of several hours or several days. Room calorimeters are probably the best method currently available for conducting short-term studies (several days) of energy expenditure in humans when the object is to measure RMR, the thermic effect of a meal, and the energy expenditure of physical activity. Physical activity level is quantified by a radar system that is activated by movement of the subject within the chamber. As with other movement devices, the radar system does not quantitate the intensity of activity. It is also highly likely, however, that free-living physical activity is blunted in the room calorimeter because of its confining nature. Thus room calorimeters do not offer the best model for examining adaptations in free-living physical activity. However, although room calorimeters are moderately expensive to construct, they provide reliable information on daily energy expenditure and substrate oxidation.

The doubly labeled water technique offers promise as a method to determine energy requirements in free-living populations and in subjects in whom traditional measures of energy expenditure, using indirect calorimetry, have proven inpractical and difficult (e.g., for infants and critically ill patients).

The basis of this technique is that after a bolus dose of two stable isotopes of water (^2H_2O and $H_2^{18}O$), ^2H_2O is lost from the body in water alone, whereas $H_2^{18}O$ is lost not only in water but also as $C^{18}O_2$ via the carbonic anhydrase system. The difference in the two turnover rates is therefore related to the carbon dioxide production rate, and with a knowledge of the fuel mixture oxidized (from the composition of the diet), energy expenditure can be calculated.

The main advantages of the doubly labeled water technique are (1) it measures total daily energy expenditure, which includes an integrated measure of resting metabolic rate, the thermic response to feeding, and the energy expenditure of physical activity; (2) it permits an unbiased measurement of free-living energy expenditure; and (3) measurements are conducted over extended periods of time (1 to 3 weeks). Thus energy values derived from the doubly labeled water method are representative of the typical daily energy expenditure and therefore the daily energy needs of free-living adults. Furthermore, this technique provides an excellent estimate of free-living physical activity. Daily free-living physical activity is calculated from the difference between the total daily energy expenditure and the combined energy expenditures of the RMR and the thermic effect of meals. Thus the application of doubly labeled water provides the most realistic estimate in free-living subjects of the average daily energy expenditure associated with physical activity.

A limitation of the doubly labeled water technique is that it cannot be used to identify the individual components of energy expenditure. Another disadvantage is its expense and limited availability. Consequently the technique does not lend itself to epidemiological studies or studies of large groups of subjects. However, this technique is now being used to examine energy requirements of persons in a variety of healthy and diseased states. With the use of the doubly labeled water method, the measurement of daily energy expenditure becomes a proxy measure of daily energy requirements.

The labeled bicarbonate method has recently won favor as a technique to measure energy expenditure over shorter periods of time (several days) than those covered by the doubly labeled water method. When labeled bicarbonate is infused at a constant rate, it reaches a rapid equilibrium with the body's CO_2 pool. The extent of the isotopic dilution depends on the rate of CO_2 production, provided there is no isotopic exchange or fixation. Thus variations in the dilution of isotope reflect variations in CO_2 production and hence energy expenditure. Because the method assesses CO_2 production rather than oxygen consumption, it requires assumptions about the respiratory quotient similar to those required by the doubly labeled water method.

In the final analysis, cost and the specific research questions generated should direct the selection of methods to measure energy expenditure. Questions of substrate oxidation and its impact on the regulation of energy balance, for example, are most applicable to the techniques of indirect calorimetry using room calorimeters and ventilated hood systems. On the other hand, more reliable information on the adaptations of free-living subjects to environmental perturbations over long periods of time is provided by the use of the doubly labeled water method combined with indirect calorimetry systems.

FURTHER READING

Dauncey, M. J. (1990). Activity and energy expenditure. *Canadian Journal of Physiological Pharmacology, 68,* 17–27. The important role of variations in physical activity as a significant factor in modifying daily energy needs is primary focus of this review.

Horton, E. S. (1984). Appropriate methodology for assessing physical activity under laboratory conditions in studies of energy balance in adults. In E. Pollitt & P. Amante (Eds.), *Energy intake and activity* (pp. 115–129). New York: Liss. This earlier publication systematically outlined the current methodology of assessing energy expenditure, including the relevant weaknesses and strengths of each technique.

Murgatroyd, P. R., Shetty, P. S., & Prentic, A. M. (1993). Techniques for the measurement of human energy expenditure: A practical guide. *International Journal of Obesity, 17,* 549–568. A user's guide to the weaknesses and strengths associated with field and laboratory tools to measure daily energy expenditure and its components.

Poehlman, E. T. (1992). Energy expenditure and requirements in aging humans. *Journal of Nutrition, 122,* 2057–2065. The use of doubly labeled water as a methodological tool to estimate daily energy requirements is highlighted in this paper.

Poehlman, E. T. (1993). Regulation of energy expenditure in aging humans. *Journal of the American Geriatric Society, 41,* 552–559. This paper highlights the effects of aging on total daily energy expenditure and its components.

Tremblay, A., Despres, J. P., & Bouchard, C. (1985). The effect of exercise training on energy balance and adipose tissue morphology and metabolism. *Sports Medicine, 2,* 223–233. This comprehensive review outlines the impact of endurance training on body composition, energy expenditure, and adipose tissue biochemistry.

• 21 •

MEASUREMENT OF PHYSICAL ACTIVITY

Steven N. Blair

Physical inactivity is a major public health problem in industrialized societies. Approximately 250,000 deaths per year from cardiovascular disease, diabetes, and colon cancer can be attributed to the sedentary life-styles of adults in the United States alone. In addition, decades of inactivity leading to low levels of physical fitness are an important cause of functional limitations and loss of independence in older individuals. Other benefits of regular physical activity include an enhanced sense of well-being, weight control, and improvements in clinical measures such as blood lipid levels and blood pressure. The importance of physical inactivity as a public health problem is demonstrated by recent physical activity initiatives from such groups as the American Heart Association, Centers for Disease Control and Prevention, National Institutes of Health, Office of Disease Prevention and Health Promotion of the U.S. Public Health Service, and American College of Sports Medicine.

Physical activity has both acute and chronic effects on body functions such as thermoregulation, hormonal balance, immune response, and muscle function. The potential impact of activity on so many variables underscores the importance of measuring physical activity in most clinical and epidemiological studies and in clinical practice, whether or not activity is an area of primary interest.

ISSUES IN PHYSICAL ACTIVITY ASSESSMENT

Most health behaviors, including physical activity, are difficult to assess. Research on physical activity has been hampered by the lack of well-standardized and validated methods, so better approaches are needed. Although existing techniques are somewhat imprecise, various assessment methods do provide reasonable estimates of type and amount of activity that are accurate enough to use in classifying individuals into broad categories.

Validation Standards

One major problem in assessing physical activity is the lack of a feasible and accepted validation standard. Thus we are never quite certain of the "truth" against which estimates of activity can be compared. Objective measurements of energy expenditure, such as direct or indirect calorimetry, are intrusive and produce major alterations, and therefore bias, in habitual activity patterns. A more recent objective measure of physical activity, the doubly labeled water technique, shows promise for validation studies (see Chapters 6 and 20). Its high cost, approximately $1,000 per test, makes it infeasible for large clinical trials or epidemiological studies and renders it only marginally feasible for smaller validation studies.

Several indirect measures have been used as markers for physical activity or as validation standards. One measure, physical fitness, has the advantage of being objective, but low-intensity activities may not be adequately assessed by this approach. Genetic influences on physical fitness and on the fitness response to exercise also are potential problems. Direct observation and recording of activity by a trained observer may be intrusive and also is not entirely objective. Some have used energy-intake estimates derived from dietary assessment as a marker for physical activity, but energy intake in free-living individuals is probably as difficult to measure accurately as is activity. In summary, habitual physical activity is difficult to measure precisely, but reliable and valid methods of estimating activity patterns are available.

PHYSICAL ACTIVITY ASSESSMENT METHODS

Two types of physical activity assessment approaches are recommended for use in clinical and epidemiological studies: questionnaires and electronic or mechanical body-movement sensors.

Questionnaires

Voluntary physical activity is a continuous variable and can be expressed as a measure of energy expenditure. For some studies or applications, an estimate of energy expenditure may be the appropriate measure of physical activity to use. In other situations it may be desirable to quantify participation in specific activities, and sometimes it may be sufficient to group individuals into broad activity categories. Thus the type of questionnaire selected should match the specific needs of a study. The following sections contain brief descriptions of recommended questionnaire approaches for each of these purposes.

Estimating Energy Expenditure

The intensity of activity (rate of energy expenditure) and the time spent in the activity are the prerequisites for estimating energy expenditure. The ratio of activity—metabolic rate/resting metabolic rate (metabolic equivalents, or METs)—is useful in estimating the rate of energy expenditure. The energy expenditure at rest (1 MET) is equivalent to 3.5 milliliters of oxygen utilization in metabolic processes per kilogram of body weight per minute, which translates to 1 kilocalorie per kilogram of body weight per hour. Thus energy expenditure rates can be estimated by classifying the activity by its MET value and multiplying by the time spent in the activity and by body weight. For example, walking at 3 miles per hour triples the resting energy expenditure (3 METs). Therefore, walking at 3 miles per hour for 30 minutes equals a total energy expenditure of 120 kilocalories for an 80-kilogram person (80 [resting energy expenditure of 1 kilocalorie per kilogram per hour] × 3 [METs] × 0.5 [30 minutes]).

Total energy expenditure per day can be estimated by using a structured interview or questionnaire to elicit the types of activity in which the individual participates and the amount of time spent in each category. To facilitate obtaining these data, we typically ask individuals to report the amount of time spent in various categories of activity intensity. For example, participants may be queried about the amount of time spent in sleep and quiet rest (1 MET) and in moderate (3.0–4.9 METs), hard (5.0–6.9 METs), and very hard (≥7.0 METs) activities over the course of the day. Time spent in light activities (1.1–2.9 METs) can be obtained by subtraction. Multiplying the MET value for a category by the number of hours spent in activities included in that category will yield an estimate of energy expended, and summing the products of all activity categories will give the kilocalories expended per kilogram of body weight per day. We typically have used this approach as a 7-day physical activity recall, but the method also may be applied to data derived for a typical day. Further details on this method can be found in my article on the 7-day physical activity recall.

Participation in Specific Activities

It may sometimes be useful to record a subject's participation in specific physical activities. For example, if an intervention emphasizes walking, specific questions about the duration, frequency, and speed of walking are asked. In other circumstances it may be important to document participation in certain sports or other exercises. Examples of questions we have used in our epidemiological studies are shown in Table 21.1. The scoring of these questions may simply be based on a list of the activities in which an individual or a group participates and the frequency of participation, or the scores may be used to estimate energy expenditure in the listed activities.

Assignment to Broad Activity Categories

We have occasionally used simple single questions to classify individuals into broad activity categories. Some of these questions are as follows:

1. "How many times a week do you engage in sufficient activity to cause sweating and a noticeable increase in your heart rate and respiration?"
2. "Compared to others of your same age and sex, how physically active do you consider yourself to be? Take into account all your physical activities, including those performed on the job and in home and yard work, sports and exercise, and other leisure-time activities." Response categories for this question lie along a 5- or 7-point scale, ranging from "very sedentary" to "very active."
3. "How much exercise do you feel you get?" Response categories are "As much as needed" or "Less than needed."

For population-based studies, these simple questions suffice to place individuals into broad activity categories. Results of several epidemiological studies show differences in morbidity and mortality across categories, as determined by questions such as those mentioned in this section. These simple questions are probably not accurate enough for individual use in intervention programs.

TABLE 21.1. Physical Activity Questionnaire

1. Please think about sitting activities such as the following: eating, reading, desk work, watching television, listening to the radio, sitting in a car (not as the driver).
   a. On average, how many hours did you spend during each of the last 5 weekdays doing these activities or others like them?

   _____ hours
   b. Last Saturday and Sunday, on average, how many hours did you spend doing these sitting activities or others like them?

   _____ hours

During the last 3 months, which of the following moderate or vigorous activities did you perform *regularly*? (Please circle YES for all that apply and NO if you do not perform the activity; provide an estimate of the amount of activity for all marked YES. Be as complete as possible.)

2. Walking
   NO   YES   How many sessions per week?   _____
   How many miles (or fractions of a mile) per session?   _____
   Average duration per session (in minutes)   _____
   What is your usual pace of walking? Circle ONE only.
   Casual or strolling (less than 2 miles per hour)
   Average or normal (2 to 3 miles per hour)
   Fairly brisk (3 to 4 miles per hour)
   Brisk or striding (4 miles per hour or faster)
3. Stair climbing
   NO   YES   How many flights of stairs do you climb *up* each day?   _____
   (1 flight = 10 steps)
4. Jogging or running
   NO   YES   How many sessions per week?   _____
   How many miles (or fractions of a mile) per session?   _____
5. Treadmill
   NO   YES   How many sessions per week?   _____
   Average duration per session (in minutes)   _____
   Speed? ___ (mph) Grade? ___ (%)
6. Bicycling
   NO   YES   How many sessions per week?   _____
   How many miles per session?   _____
   Average duration per session (in minutes)   _____
7. Swimming laps
   NO   YES   How many sessions per week?   _____
   How many miles per session?   _____
   (880 yards = 0.5 miles)
   Average duration per session (in minutes)?   _____
8. Aerobic dance/calisthenics/floor exercise
   NO   YES   How many sessions per week?   _____
   Average duration per session (in minutes)   _____
9. Moderate sports (e.g., leisure volleyball, golf [not riding in a golf cart], social dancing, doubles tennis)
   NO   YES   How many sessions per week?   _____
   Average duration per session (in minutes)?   _____
10. Vigorous racquet sports (e.g., racquetball, singles tennis)
    NO   YES   How many sessions per week?   _____
    Average duration per session (in minutes)?   _____
11. Other vigorous sports or exercise involving running (e.g., basketball, soccer)
    NO   YES   Please specify: _____
    How many sessions per week?   _____
    Average duration per session (in minutes)?   _____

12. Other activities
    NO   YES   Please specify: _____
                        How many sessions per week?   _____
                        Average duration per session (in minutes)?   _____
13. Weight training (machines, free weights)
    NO   YES   How many sessions per week?   _____
                        Average duration per session (in minutes)?   _____
14. Household activities (sweeping, vacuuming, washing clothes, scrubbing floors)
    NO   YES   How many hours per week?   _____
15. Lawn work and gardening
    NO   YES   How many hours per week?   _____

Electronic or Mechanical Monitoring

Several investigators and clinicians report success with monitors designed to detect body movement. The simplest and oldest of these is the pedometer. We have had some success in using pedometers as step counters in intervention programs. Participants wear the pedometers for several days to establish the average number of steps taken over the course of a day. Pedometers offer an easy way for individuals to self-monitor and thus be able to set realistic goals. The intervention encourages the participant to gradually increase the number of steps taken daily by integrating more physical activity into routine activities at home and work—for example, doing more walking and stair climbing. Standard behavioral techniques such as goal setting and behavioral contracting are also used (see Chapter 84).

Newer motion sensors use more sensitive and sophisticated motion detection systems, such as accelerometers, and can detect movement in more than one plane, in contrast to pedometers, which measure movement in only one plane. One of the new sensors, the TriTrac, detects movement in all three planes (available from Hemokinetics, Inc., Professional Products Division, 5930 Seminole Center Court, Madison, WI 53711). The advantages of instruments such as the TriTrac are that they are unobtrusive, relatively inexpensive, and provide objective data on physical activity. Motion sensors are especially useful in working with children, since it is difficult to elicit reliable and valid responses from them using self-report questionnaires.

SUMMARY

Physical activity is an important health behavior, and it influences or is influenced by other health behaviors and interventions. Therefore, assessment of physical activity is necessary in many clinical and epidemiological studies and programs. Physical activity is similar to other health behaviors in that it is difficult to measure accurately. Several useful techniques are available, however. Questionnaires that elicit self-reports of activity participation provide estimates of total energy expenditure and participation in specific activities or serve to group individuals into broad activity categories. Electronic or mechanical devices that detect body movement also may be used, especially in clinical intervention programs.

FURTHER READING

Ainsworth, B. E., Haskell, W. L., Leon, A. S., Jacobs, D. R. Jr., Montoye, H. J., Sallis, J. F., & Paffenbarger, R. S. Jr. (1993). Compendium of physical activities: Classification of energy costs of human physical activities. *Medicine and Science in Sports and Exercise, 25,* 71–80. This report provides a five-digit coding scheme in which physical activities are classified by purpose of activity (e.g., sports), specific type, and rate of energy expenditure.

Ainsworth, B. E., Jacobs, D. R. Jr., & Leon, A. S. (1993). Validity and reliability of self-reported physical activity status: The Lipid Research Clinics questionnaire. *Medicine and Science in Sports and Exercise, 25,* 92–98. The LRC questionnaire has a high reliability and low-to-moderate validity.

Blair, S. N., Haskell, W. L., Ho, P., Paffenbarger, R. S. Jr., Vranizan, K. M., Farquhar, J. W., & Wood, P. D. (1985). Assessment of habitual physical activity by a seven-day recall in a community survey and controlled experiments. *American Journal of Epidemiology, 122,* 794–804. The 7-day physical activity recall interview yields estimates of total daily energy expenditure.

Haskell, W. L., Yee, M. C., Evans, A., & Irby, P. J. (1993). Simultaneous measurement of heart rate and body motion to quantitate physical activity. *Medicine and Science in Sports and Exercise, 25,* 109–115. Recordings of both heart rate and body movement over the course of the day give a more accurate estimate of total physical activity than either measure used separately.

Jacobs, D. R. Jr., Ainsworth, B. E., Hartman, T. J., & Leon, A. E. (1993). A simultaneous evaluation of 10 commonly used physical activity questionnaires. *Medicine and Science in Sports and Exercise, 25,* 81–91. This study provides an evaluation of 10 widely used questionnaires.

Paffenbarger, R. S. Jr., Blair, S. N., Lee, I-M., & Hyde, R. T. (1993). Measurement of physical activity to assess health effects in free-living populations. *Medicine and Science in Sports and Exercise, 25,* 60–70. The use of physical activity questionnaires in survey research is discussed, and a comprehensive example questionnaire is included in the paper.

Sallis, J. F., Buono, M. J., Roby, J. J., Micale, F. G., & Nelson, J. A. (1993). Seven-day recall and other physical activity self-reports in children and adolescents. *Medicine and Science in Sports and Exercise, 25,* 99–108. These authors review the use of physical activity questionnaires in young populations, and issues regarding their applications are discussed.

• 22 •

MEASUREMENT OF EATING DISORDER PSYCHOPATHOLOGY

David M. Garner

EATING DISORDER PSYCHOPATHOLOGY

The general clinical features and psychopathology associated with anorexia nervosa and bulimia nervosa are well documented and widely accepted (see Chapters 23, 27, and 28). Less is known about psychopathology associated with the binge eating disorder and other eating disorders that fall outside the boundary defined by anorexia and bulimia nervosa (see Chapters 24 and 78). Recent descriptive refinements, along with advances in the areas of diagnosis, pathogenesis, and treatment, have resulted in tremendous improvements in the technology of assessment. While there is no universally accepted assessment protocol for eating disorders, there is a consensus on the value of a multitrait and multimethod approach to assessment. This consensus is based on the conceptualization of eating disorders as multidetermined and heterogeneous.

The targets for the assessment of eating-disorder patients can be divided into two main areas. Included in the first are the specific psychopathology and behavioral patterns that define the core features of the disorders. Symptoms such as binge eating, extreme weight control behaviors, and stereotypic attitudes toward weight or body shape fall into this category. The second area includes psychopathology not necessarily specific to eating-disorder patients but that has particular theoretical or clinical relevance. Examples include psychological features such as low self-esteem, perfectionism, fears of psychobiological maturity, poor impulse control, and reactions to sexual abuse. There are also more general associated features, such as depression, anxiety, and poor social functioning, that are important aspects of the psychopathology.

Body Weight History

Although body weight is not "psychopathology" per se, it is obviously a fundamental aspect of eating disorders. Determining the patient's current body weight and weight history provides essential diagnostic information. This information serves as a basis for exploring the central psychopathology of eating disorders (the meaning that body weight and shape has for the patient). Since amenorrhea is required for anorexia nervosa, the patient's menstrual history should be determined within the context of her weight history.

Binge Eating

Binge eating is a key symptom in bulimia nervosa and binge eating disorder. It occurs in about 50% of patients with anorexia nervosa. Thus determining the presence or absence of binge eating is critical to diagnosis and treatment planning. In DSM-IV, binge eating is defined as having two main characteristics: (1) consumption of a large amount of food relative to the circumstances, and (2) the experience of loss of control (see Chapter 78). Despite the definitional requirements, research has indicated that a significant minority of eating-disorder patients describe binges involving relatively small amounts of food. Moreover, in some cases there is no real loss of control. Thus until there is agreement on the significance of the size of binge episodes, it is recommended that assessments follow the system proposed in the Eating Disorder Examination (below) for dividing episodes of overeating into four types based on the amount of food eaten (large or small) and loss of control (present or absent). It is also important to determine the age of onset, frequency, and duration of binge eating episodes. Likewise, the circumstances surrounding binge episodes (settings, times of day, social context, thoughts and emotions) should be ascertained.

Extreme Weight-Losing Behaviors

The intensity of the dieting efforts and the types of weight-losing behaviors employed may reflect a psychopathologic condition. A dieting history should pinpoint when dieting first began and its course over time. Information should be gathered regarding extreme weight control behaviors, including self-induced vomiting, laxative and diuretic abuse, use of diet pills or other drugs to control appetite, use of emetics, chewing and spitting food out before swallowing, prolonged fasting, and excessive exercise. Diabetic patients may manipulate their insulin levels, and patients taking thyroid replacement hormone may alter their dosages to control body weight. Establishing the frequency (as well as the number of symptom-free days) of vomiting, laxative abuse, and other extreme weight control behaviors is essential in determining the severity of the disorder and the need for medical consultation.

Psychopathology Related to Weight or Body Shape

Psychopathology related to weight or shape has been described in various ways over the years; it has been characterized as a drive for thinness, a fear of fatness, shape and weight dissatisfaction, body size misperception, body image disturbance, and fears associated with physical maturity. Dissatisfaction with overall body shape and disparagement directed toward specific bodily regions are common in patients with eating disorders and should be foci of assessment. Some patients overestimate their body size. Although research has shown that such an overestimation is not unique to eating-disorder patients, it may have clinical importance, particularly for emaciated patients. A critical psychopathological feature of anorexia and bulimia nervosa is that patients must be more than merely dissatisfied with their body; they must rely on weight or shape as the predominant or even the sole criterion for judging their self-worth. This feature has recently been made mandatory for a diagnosis of the two main eating disorders, according to DSM-IV. Patients with anorexia nervosa often deny the seriousness of a current low weight, at the same time expressing an intense fear of gaining weight.

General Psychopathology Relevant to Eating Disorders

Eating-disorder patients have been described as suffering from feelings of ineffectiveness, low self-esteem, lack of autonomy, obsessiveness, interpersonal sensitivity, introversion, poor relationship skills, social anxiety, dependence, perfectionism, fears of psychobiological maturity, poor impulse control, external locus of control, conflict avoidance, developmental pathology, failure in separation–individuation, vulnerability to substance abuse, interoceptive deficits, and idiosyncratic or dysfunctional thinking patterns. A complete psychological assessment should include these areas as well as an evaluation of the patient's stable personality features, overall psychological distress, depression, anxiety, family functioning, history of sexual abuse, and social and vocational adaptation, all of which may be relevant to the development and maintenance of these syndromes.

Psychopathology Secondary to Starvation

It may not be apparent from the patient's initial assessment whether psychological distress, cognitive impairment, and behavioral symptoms signal a fundamental emotional disturbance or are secondary elaborations resulting from weight loss and chaotic dietary patterns. Symptoms such as poor concentration, lability of mood, depressive features, obsessional thinking, irritability, difficulties with decision making, impulsivity, and social withdrawal have been identified in normal subjects undergoing semistarvation (see Chapter 16). Thus these symptoms may reflect secondary effects of weight suppression rather than primary psychopathology.

ASSESSMENT METHODS

Various approaches to information gathering have been developed for eating disorders, including clinical interviews, self-report measures, self-monitoring, direct behavioral observation, symptom checklists, clinical rating scales, the Stroop color-naming task, and standardized test meals. The most commonly used methods are semistructured clinical interviews, self-monitoring, and self-report measures. The most well formulated of these methods, along with their respective strengths and weaknesses, will be described briefly. Other measures and methods are covered by the reviews noted in the "Further Reading" list at the end of this chapter.

Clinical Interviews

Clinical interviews have been the primary method for gathering information on eating disorders. The development of standardized, semistructured clinical interviews designed to evaluate the psychopathology of eating disorders represents a major advancement in the field. Five such interviews have been described in sufficient detail to warrant their use (see Wilson, in "Further Reading"). The Eating Disorder Examination (EDE) is the most well validated and has generated a large body of research. It is an investigator-based semistructured interview for assessing psychopathology specific to eating disorders and is the current interview method of choice. Responses are organized in four subscales (restraint, eating concern, shape concern and weight concern). The EDE can be used to arrive at a diagnosis; it has proven sensitive to treatment effects; and it defines different forms of overeating based on the amount of food eaten (large versus small) and the presence or absence of loss of control. The EDE is the current "gold standard" for assessing the specific symptoms of eating disorders and should be used whenever practical. It has the advantages of allowing a fine-grained appraisal of the specific psychopathology of eating disorders, and it permits the investigator to clarify the meaning behind a patient's responses to questions. In one study in which the EDE was compared with a parallel self-report measure, the interview was found to be more accurate than the self-monitoring measure in identifying ambiguous symptoms such as binge eating. The disadvantages of the interview include the fact that it takes an hour or more to administer, it requires a trained interviewer, and it is not suitable when anonymity or group administration is required.

Self-Monitoring

Self-monitoring requires patients to record in diaries their food intake, extreme weight control behaviors, and thoughts or feelings. Self-monitoring is a valuable assessment tool and probably yields more accurate information regarding eating behaviors and eating disorder symptoms than methods requiring retrospective reports or generalizations about behavior. Its disadvantages are that it may be unacceptable to certain patients, and it may influence the frequency of the very behaviors being monitored.

Self-Report Measures

Various self-report instruments have been introduced to measure eating disorder symptoms. The two most widely used in clinical and research settings are the Eating Attitudes Test (EAT) and the Eating Disorder Inventory (EDI). The EAT is a widely used, standardized, self-report measure of eating disorder symptoms. A factor analysis of the original 40-item version resulted in a brief, 26-item measure of global eating disorder symptoms. The EDI is a standardized, multiscale instrument with a much broader focus and the ability to provide a psychological profile that may be useful in clinical situations. It comprises three subscales (the drive for thinness, bulimia, and body dissatisfaction) that tap into attitudes and behaviors concerning eating, weight, and shape, plus five subscales that assess more general psychological traits or organizing constructs clinically relevant to eating disorders (ineffectiveness, perfection, interpersonal distrust, interoceptive awareness, and maturity fears). The EDI-2 adds three new subscales to the original instrument (asceticism, impulse regulation, and social insecurity). The EAT and EDI have good psychometric properties and are sensitive to the effects of treatment.

The bulimia test (BULIT-R) is a 28-item, multiple-choice, self-report measure based on the DSM-III-R criteria for bulimia nervosa. It has generated considerable research and is a reliable psychometric measure of the severity of bulimia nervosa.

Self-report measures have the advantage of being relatively economical, brief, easily administered, and objectively scored. They are not susceptible to bias from interviewer-subject interactions and can be administered anonymously. The major disadvantage of self-report measures is that they are less accurate than interview methods, particularly when ambiguous behaviors such as binge eating are being assessed. Self-reports should be supplemented by symptom frequency data derived from an interview or a symptom checklist.

The different methods for assessing psychopathology in eating disorders have different aims, strengths, and weaknesses. The strategy adopted should be guided by the aims of the assessment and, whenever possible, convergent methods should be employed.

FURTHER READING

Fairburn, C. G., & Belgin, S. J. (1994). The assessment of eating disorders: Interview or self-report questionnaire. *International Journal of Eating Disorders, 16,* 363–370. A detailed comparison of an investigator-based interview and a self-report measure based on that interview. The comparison showed that both measures give similar results when unambiguous behavior is being assessed but that the interview is favored when more complex behavior is being assessed.

Fairburn, C. G., & Cooper, Z. (1993). The Eating Disorder Examination (12th ed.). In C. G. Fairburn & G. T. Wilson (Eds.), *Binge eating: Nature, assessment, and treatment* (pp. 317–360). New York: Guilford Press. The primary reference for the EDE.

Foreyt, J. P., & McGavin, J. K. (1988). Anorexia nervosa and bulimia. In E. J. Mash & L. G. Terdal (Eds.), *Behavioral assessment of childhood disorders* (2nd ed., pp. 776–805). New York: Guilford Press. An excellent review of assessment methods.

Garner, D. M. (1991). *Eating disorder inventory—2 professional manual.* Odessa, FL: Psychological Assessment Resources. A comprehensive reference source for the EDI.

Garner, D. M., Olmsted, M. P., Bohr, Y., & Garfinkel, P. E. (1982). The eating attitudes test: Psychometric features and clinical correlates. *Psychological Medicine, 12,* 871–878. The primary reference for the EAT.

Rosen, J. C., & Srebnik, D. (1991). The assessment of eating disorders. In P. McReynolds, J. C. Rosen, & G. Chelune (Eds.), *Advances in psycholgical assessment.* New York: Plenum Press. An excellent review of assessment methods for eating disorders.

Thelen, M. H., Farmer, J., Wonderlich, S., & Smith, M. (1991). A revision of the bulimia test: The BULIT-R. *Psychological Assessment: A Journal of Consulting and Clinical Psychology, 3,* 119–124. The primary reference for the development and validation of the BULIT-R.

Williamson, D. A. (1990). *Assessment of eating disorders: Obesity, anorexia and bulimia nervosa.* New York: Pergamon Press. Another excellent overview of assessment methods.

Wilson, G. T. (1993). Assessment of binge eating. In C. G. Fairburn & G. T. Wilson (Eds.), *Binge eating: Nature, assessment, and treatment* (pp. 227–249). New York: Guilford Press. An excellent review outlining the advantages and disadvantages of major assessment methods as they relate specifically to binge eating behavior.

· IV ·
CLASSIFICATION, CLINICAL CHARACTERISTICS, AND HISTORY OF EATING DISORDERS

CLASSIFICATION AND DIAGNOSIS OF EATING DISORDERS

Paul E. Garfinkel

The diagnostic consideration of the eating disorders anorexia nervosa and bulimia nervosa has received more attention in the past two decades than previously, as clinicians have become aware of the frequency of these disorders and the difficulties associated with their treatment. The classification of anorexia nervosa has passed through several phases. In this century, these phases have progressed from the view that the disorder was either entirely a form of pituitary disease or a nonspecific variant of many other psychiatric disorders to the more current view that it is a specific syndrome with core clinical features that distinguish it from other states. In the late 1970s, recognition of the frequency of the symptom of bulimia gave rise to an awareness both of its frequency among people with anorexia nervosa syndrome and of a large group of people who had many of the features of anorexia nervosa, but had not reached such low body weights. Since then, the group with bulimia nervosa, has been the subject of much study, and the classification of the syndrome has been refined.

In this chapter the current view of the core clinical features of these syndromes will be reviewed, and the viewpoint that anorexia nervosa and bulimia nervosa represent distinct syndromes will be contrasted with the various nonspecific classifications.

CRITERIA FOR DIAGNOSING ANOREXIA NERVOSA

Various methods of defining anorexia nervosa have been suggested. Some have been concentrated on psychopathology alone; however, these criteria have often lacked reliability in their application. Since 1969, a variety of operational criteria have been developed that emphasize signs and symptoms and usually include characteristic psychopathology and behavior, as well as disturbed endocrine function. In 1970, Russell suggested three criteria for the diagnosis of anorexia nervosa: (1) behavior that is designed to produce marked weight loss; (2) the characteristic psychopathology of a morbid fear of becoming fat; and (3) evidence of an endocrine disorder, amenorrhea in females, and loss of sexual potency and sexual interest in males. While others have suggested other diagnostic criteria since, they generally involve aspects of Russell's original criteria. The most recent evolution, in DSM-IV, is displayed in Table 23.1. For comparison, the ICD-10 criteria are shown in Table 23.2. These criteria are discussed in greater detail below.

TABLE 23.1. DSM-IV Diagnostic Criteria for Anorexia Nervosa

A. Refusal to maintain body weight at or above a minimally normal weight for age and height (e.g., weight loss leading to maintenance of body weight less than 85% of that expected, or failure to make expected weight gain during period of growth, leading to body weight less than 85% of that expected).

B. Intense fear of gaining weight or becoming fat, even though underweight.

C. Disturbance in the way in which one's body weight or shape is experienced, undue influence of body weight or shape on self-evaluation, or denial of the seriousness of the current low body weight.

D. In postmenarchal females, amenorrhea, i.e., the absence of at least three consecutive menstrual cycles. (A woman is considered to have amenorrhea if her periods occur only following hormone, e.g., estrogen, administration).

Specify type:

Restricting Type: during the current episode of Anorexia Nervosa, the person has not regularly engaged in binge-eating or purging behavior (i.e., self-induced vomiting or the misuse of laxatives, diuretics, or enemas)

Binge-Eating/Purging Type: during the current episode of Anorexia Nervosa, the person has regularly engaged in binge-eating or purging behavior (i.e., self-induced vomiting or the misuse of laxatives, diuretics, or enemas)

Note. From American Psychiatric Association (1994). *Diagnostic and Statistical Manual of Mental Disorders* (4th ed., pp. 544–545). Washington, DC: Author. Copyright 1994 by the American Psychiatric Association. Reprinted by permission.

TABLE 23.2. DSM-IV Diagnostic Criteria for Bulimia Nervosa

A. Recurrent episodes of binge eating. An episode of binge eating is characterized by both of the following:

(1) eating, in a discrete period of time (e.g., within any 2-hour period), an amount of food that is definitely larger than most people would eat during a similar period of time and under similar circumstances

(2) a sense of lack of control over eating during the episode (e.g., a feeling that one cannot stop eating or control what or how much one is eating)

B. Recurrent inappropriate compensatory behavior in order to prevent weight gain, such as self-induced vomiting; misuse of laxatives, diuretics, enemas, or other medications; fasting; or excessive exercise.

C. The binge eating and inappropriate compensatory behaviors both occur, on average, at least twice a week for 3 months.

D. Self-evaluation is unduly influenced by body shape and weight.

E. The disturbance does not occur exclusively during episodes of Anorexia Nervosa.

Specify type:

Purging Type: during the current episode of Bulimia Nervosa, the person has regularly engaged in self-induced vomiting or the misuse of laxatives, diuretics, or enemas

Nonpurging Type: during the current episode of Bulimia Nervosa, the person has used other inappropriate compensatory behaviors, such as fasting or excessive exercise, but has not regularly engaged in self-induced vomiting or the misuse of laxatives, diuretics, or enemas

Note. From American Psychiatric Association (1994). *Diagnostic and Statistical Manual of Mental Disorders* (4th ed., pp. 549–550). Washington, DC: Author. Copyright 1994 by the American Psychiatric Association. Reprinted by permission.

Behavior That Is Designed to Produce Marked Weight Loss

There has been general agreement that a drive for thinness is necessary for the diagnosis. Different investigators have described this criterion in somewhat differing terms: "the relentless pursuit of thinness" (Bruch); "the pursuit of thinness" (Theander); "the deliberate wish to be slim" (Selvini-Palazzoli); or "the pursuit of thinness as a pleasure in itself" (Ziegler & Sours). In the recent DSM-IV criteria, a degree of precision has been added by the description "the refusal to maintain body weight over a minimal normal weight for age and height" and by the inclusion of both weight loss and a failure to make expected weight; the latter accounts for younger patients who would be expected to continue growing.

While there has been agreement on the presence of the drive for thinness and the need for weight loss, the amount of weight loss that is necessary for the diagnosis has varied. This is not surprising, since there have been no studies to determine when the symptoms of starvation actually supervene or when physiological consequences are first evident.

Psychopathology Characterized by a Morbid Fear of Becoming Fat

This criterion in Russell's classification corresponds with criteria B and C in DSM-IV—it involves both the intense fear of becoming fat and the regulation of self-esteem to an excessive degree by concerns with weight and shape. This relates to attitudes and feelings the person has about her body or particular body parts. The presence of this core psychopathology has been demonstrated in empirical studies using self-report instruments and structured interviews. And this feature helps to distinguish anorexia nervosa from other psychiatric syndromes.

The earlier DSM-III criteria described this feature in terms of "body image disturbance." Many studies of body image in patients with anorexia nervosa have focused on a narrow definition that is related to visual self-perception. Data here show that many people with anorexia nervosa do not overestimate their sizes and that overestimation is not unique to those with the disorder. Given these data, it was appropriate to change this criterion to focus on the attitudinal and affective dimensions of body image. Also, it is important to refer to the denial of the serious consequences of the weight loss by patients with anorexia nervosa, a phenomenon frequently observed in people with this condition and one that, although poorly understood, was noted over 100 years ago. By emphasizing the disturbance in a person's way of experiencing body weight or shape in terms of (1) reference to extremes of self-evaluation and (2) denial, overlap with the general population can be reduced.

Evidence of an Endocrine Disorder, Amenorrhea in Females, and Loss of Sexual Potency and Interest in Males

There is no doubt that amenorrhea is a common feature in cases of anorexia nervosa and that, in part, it is based on the loss of body weight and fat. But the presence of amenorrhea is incompletely understood, and it can occur in a significant minority of women with anorexia nervosa before there is any real weight loss.

There is value in retaining the criterion for amenorrhea since it is seen so regularly in patients with anorexia nervosa and since it emphasizes the hypothalamic dysfunction that occurs in this syndrome. While there has often been some question about whether the inclusion of amenorrhea as a diagnostic criterion affects the definition of a case, recent evidence suggests that a significant proportion of women with "subthreshold" anorexia nervosa do not meet the criteria for the diagnosis because they have not missed three consecutive menstrual cycles.

Binge Eating/Purging and Restricting Subtypes of Anorexia Nervosa

A number of studies have documented important and reliable differences between anorexic patients who are periodically bulimic and those who are consistent dietary restricters. The bulimic anorexics differ in a number of parameters; they generally weighed more before the illness and more often had been obese; they also come from families in which obesity is more common. They are the individuals who are much more likely to induce vomiting and misuse laxatives in their attempts to control their weight. They are also an impulsive group. This trait is evident not only in their eating behavior but in other areas as well: bulimic anorexics frequently have problems with alcohol or street drugs; they may also steal and, compared with restricters, they more frequently attempt self-mutilation and suicide. An impulsive cognitive style has also been demonstrated in this group. The bulimic group of anorexics also differ in personality characteristics: they are frequently borderline narcissistic or antisocial, a group that discharges impulse through action, in contrast to the far more inhibited restricters. Because of these important differences between the two anorexia nervosa groups, the DSM-IV classification of anorexia nervosa recognizes two subtypes, differentiated by the presence or absence of binge eating. However, a minority of anorexics who purge but do not binge will be classified here as belonging to the binge eating/purging subtype, since they are similar to those who binge.

CRITERIA FOR BULIMIA NERVOSA

When Russell first proposed diagnostic criteria for bulimia nervosa he suggested three components: (1) powerful and intractable urges to overeat; (2) avoidance of the fattening effects of food by inducing vomiting, abusing purgatives, or both; and (3) a morbid fear of becoming fat. These criteria, which are discussed in greater detail below, have undergone various modifications (the most recent in DSM-IV are listed in Table 23.3; Table 23.4 shows the ICD-10 criteria. The earlier DSM-III criteria did not include a reference to shape and weight concerns or a frequency criterion. These modifications have made the diagnosis much more restrictive.

Powerful and Intractable Urges to Overeat

This component corresponds to DSM-IV criteria A, B, and D. While there is now a consensus on the need for the presence of binge eating as a diagnostic criterion for bulimia nervosa, it has been more difficult to reach agreement on the definition of what constitutes a binge and of what the minimum binge frequency should be for the syndrome. With regard to the former, some have focused on the quantity of food eaten, others on the subjective state, and still others on the need for discrete episodes of overeating or a rapid rate of eating. While this last component was part of the DSM-III and DSM-III-R criteria, it was removed from DSM-IV, since many patients report a slow

TABLE 23.3. ICD-10 Diagnostic Criteria For Anorexia Nervosa

For a definite diagnosis, all of the following are required:

(a) Body weight is maintained at least 15% below that expected (either lost or never achieved), or Quetelet's body-mass index is 17.5 or less. Prepubertal patients may show failure to make the expected weight gain during the period of growth.

(b) The weight loss is self-induced by avoidance of "fattening foods." One or more of the following may also be present: self-induced vomiting; self-induced purging; excessive exercise; use of appetite suppressants and/or diuretics.

(c) There is body-image distortion in the form of a specific psychopathology whereby a dread of fatness persists as an intrusive, overvalued idea and the patient imposes a low weight threshold on himself or herself.

(d) A widespread endocrine disorder involving the hypothalamic–pituitary–gonadal axis is manifest in women as amenorrhoea and in men as a loss of sexual interest and potency. (An apparent exception is the persistence of vaginal bleeds in anorexic women who are receiving replacement hormonal therapy, most commonly taken as a contraceptive pill.) There may also be elevated levels of growth hormone, raised levels of cortisol, changes in the peripheral metabolism of the thyroid hormone, and abnormalities of insulin secretion.

(e) If onset is prepubertal, the sequence of pubertal events is delayed or even arrested (growth ceases; in girls the breasts do not develop and there is a primary amenorrhoea; and in boys the genitals remain juvenile). With recovery, puberty is often completed normally, but the menarche is late.

Atypical Anorexia Nervosa: This term should be used for those individuals in whom one or more of the key features of anorexia nervosa, such as amenorrhoea or significant weight loss, is absent, but who otherwise present a fairly typical clinical picture. Such people are usually encountered in psychiatric liaison services in general hospitals or in primary care. Patients who have all the key symptoms but to only a mild degree may also be best described by this term. This term should not be used for eating disorders that resemble anorexia nervosa but that are due to known physical illness.

Note. From World Health Organization (1992). *The ICD-10 Classification of Mental and Behavioral Disorders: Clinical Descriptions and Diagnostic Guidelines* (pp. 176–181). Geneva: Author. Copyright 1992 by the World Health Organization. Reprinted by permission.

or moderate rate of eating, and it is difficult to determine the speed of such eating reliably.

Appropriately, the other three components do need to be specified in determining the presence of a binge. With regard to quantity, some have recommended that if the amount of food eaten is greater than the patient feels is allowed, then it is a binge. This definition, however, can lead to the rather strange situation of some patients "bingeing" on two cookies. A much more appropriate approach is to define excessive quantity by objective standards. What is most relevant is that the person is eating more than is normal, given what other people eat, and the time and social circumstances of the person's last meal. This approach to defining the excessive quantity permits its objective definition and also takes into account the great individual variation in food consumption that has been documented in patients with bulimia nervosa.

Binge eating episodes are also characterized by a subjective sense of loss of control; that is, the person senses that he/she cannot prevent the occurrence of the binge or terminate it once it has started. A variety of dysphoric mood states precede the binge and precipitate it; the binge itself has the immediate effect of reducing the unpleasant mood, but this respite is then followed by physical discomfort and the fear of gaining weight.

The final criterion of the binge—the eating must occur in a discrete period of time—refers to a definite, time-limited period that is not necessarily limited to a single

TABLE 23.4. ICD-10 Diagnostic Criteria for Bulimia Nervosa

For a definite diagnosis, all of the following are required:

(a) There is a persistent preoccupation with eating, and an irresistible craving for food; the patient succumbs to episodes of overeating in which large amounts of food are consumed in short periods of time.

(b) The patient attempts to counteract the "fattening" effects of food by one or more of the following: self-induced vomiting; purgative abuse; alternating periods of starvation; use of drugs such as appetite suppressants, thyroid preparations, or diuretics. When bulimia occurs in diabetic patients they may choose to neglect their insulin treatment.

(c) The psychopathology consists of a morbid dread of fatness, and the patient sets herself or himself a sharply defined weight threshold, well below the premorbid weight that constitutes the optimum or healthy weight in the opinion of the physician. There is often, but not always, a history of an earlier episode of anorexia nervosa, the interval between the two disorders ranging from a few months to several years. This earlier episode may have been fully expressed, or may have assumed a minor cryptic form with a moderate loss of weight and/or a transient phase of amenorrhoea.

Atypical Bulimia Nervosa: This term should be used for those individuals in whom one or more of the key features listed for bulimia nervosa is absent but who otherwise present a fairly typical clinical picture. Most commonly this applies to people with normal or even excessive weight but with typical periods of overeating followed by vomiting or purging. Partial syndromes together with depressive symptoms are also not uncommon, but if the depressive symptoms justify a separate diagnosis of a depressive disorder, two diagnoses should be made.

Note. From World Health Organization (1992). *The ICD-10 Classification of Mental and Behavioral Disorders: Clinical Descriptions and Diagnostic Guidelines* (pp. 176–181). Geneva: Author. Copyright 1992 by the World Health Organization. Reprinted by permission.

setting. It is included to remove continual snacking, or "grazing," from qualifying as a binge.

Far less clear is the frequency of binge eating necessary for the diagnosis of the syndrome. In DSM-III-R, a minimum of twice per week was specified, and this frequency does have a significant impact on the definition of a case. The value of setting a minimum frequency is to exclude the binge eater who is infrequently bulimic and who does not display the full syndrome. However, the problem here is the arbitrary nature of setting the frequency at twice per week. When investigators tried to study this issue by relating the frequency of binge eating to coexisting psychopathology or clinical outcome, the results have been mixed. While having a minimum frequency for binge episodes is necessary, further research must be conducted to determine the most appropriate cut-off point.

Avoidance of the Fattening Effects of Food by Inducing Vomiting, Abusing Purgatives, or Both

This stratagem corresponds with criterion C in DSM-IV and refers to the presence of purging behavior in Russell's classification and of purging or other means of controlling weight in DSM-III-R.

There are good reasons to include purging behaviors as a diagnostic criterion: (1) The presence of vomiting and laxative abuse is often an indication of the intensity of a person's concern with weight and shape; (2) while dieting and vigorous exercise are not considered especially unusual, self-induced vomiting or laxative misuse is thought to be pathological behavior in our society; (3) purging behaviors are discrete and easily defined and quantified, thus obviating some of the problems associated with defining a binge; (4) evidence suggests that purging bulimics differ from nonpurging binge eaters in terms of psychopathology; and (5) a final argument in favor of narrowing the diagnosis of bulimia nervosa to those who purge relates to prediction of course. The serious physiological complications of this disorder are often directly related to the various pathological weight control methods.

The arguments above emphasize the value of a separate classification for those people with bulimia nervosa who induce vomiting or misuse laxatives. However, such a classification raises two concerns:

1. What about binge eaters who do not purge? There is some evidence that this group has less severe psychopathologies than do purging bulimics. Nonpurging bulimics tend to have less body image disturbance and less anxiety concerning eating relative to purging bulimics. There is also evidence that nonpurging bulimics binge less often and are less likely to engage in impulsive self-harming behaviors. They tend to be obese and to attend commercial weight control clinics for obesity. In the DSM-IV classification, the bulimia nervosa group is subdivided into purging and nonpurging types. The distinction between bulimia nervosa and binge eating disorder is discussed in Chapters 24 and 78.

2. What about binge eaters who engage in weight control behavior other than vomiting or laxative misuse? As noted above, dieting and exercise are considered to be much more normal by our society. But many bulimic diabetics do not use their prescribed insulin so as to control weight; other bulimics take thyroxine, diuretics, or amphetamines. At the present time, research data have not clearly differentiated between bulimics who purge with vomiting or laxatives and those who compensate for bingeing by other behaviors. The authors of DSM-IV, however, feel it would be helpful to subdivide the bulimia nervosa syndrome into two groups, as shown in Table 23.2, if only to help in data collection and in furthering understanding.

A Morbid Fear of Becoming Fat

This fear of becoming fat corresponds to criterion D in DSM-IV; the earlier DSM-III criteria for bulimia did not include such concerns with shape and weight. The advantages of this criterion include the following: (1) It covers what many view to be the central psychopathology in bulimia nervosa, the morbid fear of becoming fat or of body fat, and it is this fear that leads to behaviors to control body weight; this characteristic distinguishes bulimia nervosa from binge eating, which may occur independently of such weight concerns; (2) it makes the diagnosis much more restrictive; (3) inclusion of shape and weight concerns draws the syndrome closer to its related disorder, anorexia nervosa. Shared psychopathologies have been noted in empirical studies of the two syndromes, except for the distinguishing features previously described as characteristic of bulimics.

A significant body of empirical research provides data that suggest that while concerns with weight and shape are common in the general female population, they differ in women with bulimia nervosa by virtue of their intensity; for patients with anorexia nervosa, the difference lies in the central role of these concerns in governing a person's sense of self-esteem. While there is some overlap with the normal female population, false positives are minimized when criteria A through D are required for the diagnosis. The presence of this last criterion, however, eliminates the diagnosis of bulimia nervosa in people who binge and vomit without these weight and shape concerns.

OTHER VIEWS OF THE CLASSIFICATION OF THE EATING DISORDERS

The foregoing discussion focused on the diagnostic criteria for anorexia nervosa and bulimia nervosa, with the view that these are distinct psychiatric syndromes with characteristic features that distinguish them from other disorders and are reliable over time. However, there have been other points of view—including whether anorexia nervosa and bulimia nervosa are variants of other illnesses, or whether anorexia nervosa represents a nonspecific syndrome that may appear in many emotional disorders.

Eating Disorders as Variants of Other Illnesses

While the earliest writers, such as Gull, Gilles de la Tourette, and Déjérine and Gauckler, considered anorexia nervosa a distinct disorder, others considered it a variant of affective disorder, schizophrenia, obsessional disorder, and hysteria.

Depression

Clinically, eating disorders and depression may be difficult to distinguish from one another because of their shared signs and symptoms, familial tendencies, natural history, similar neuroendocrine abnormalities, and responses to medications. These similarities have caused some to suggest that eating disorders are variants of affective illness. However, close examination suggests these arguments are not strong and that while there is an association between these disorders—in terms of risk and course—there are also features that distinguish between them.

It is known that a depressed mood is frequently seen in patients with anorexia nervosa and bulimia nervosa; vegetative features of a major depression are common among such patients (40%). However, depressive syndromes are common in people with a variety of illnesses, and it is also known that starvation itself may produce cognitive, affective, and social changes resembling major depression. More compelling are the familial and natural history data. An increased risk of depression in first-degree relatives of both anorexia nervosa and bulimia nervosa patients has regularly been reported, and the Toronto group found a sixfold increase in the frequency of affective disorder among women treated for anorexia nervosa 4 to 8 years earlier.

Others have inferred links between bulimia nervosa and affective disorder based on their shared neurohumoral abnormalities or responses to medications. However, the actual degree of similarity of the neuroendocrine parameters is unclear. And while both bulimia nervosa and depressive patients respond to short-term tricyclic or other antidepressant medications, one cannot infer a common syndrome, because the mechanisms producing the same responses may differ.

In both circumstances, self-esteem is reduced; in patients with eating disorders, the loss of self-esteem is specifically linked to the fear of fatness, to body weight, and to loss of control over eating; whereas with primary depression the sense of worthlessness is more generalized. The familial risk data and the data on the course of anorexia nervosa suggest an association, but the other linking data are not strong.

Schizophrenia

In 1913 Dubois first described anorexia nervosa in an adolescent girl with signs of schizophrenia. Since that time several writers have reported their belief that anorexia nervosa is a variant of schizophrenia. Some features of schizophrenia may seem to be present in patients with anorexia nervosa. Volitional defects seen in patients with schizophrenia may also seem to be present in patients with anorexia nervosa because of the latter's general negativism, indecisiveness, and social withdrawal. The anorexia nervosa patient's body-image distortion may reach delusional proportions and resemble psychotic perceptions and delusions. However, the fundamental schizophrenic disturbances in affect, thought processes, and volition are not found in anorexia nervosa patients. Results of several studies have shown no increased risk for schizophrenia in anorexic patients or in their families.

Obsessional Disorder

Many patients with anorexia nervosa display obsessional symptomatology, leading some to conclude it is a form of obsessive–compulsive neurosis. The obsessional symptomatology can be magnified by the severe starvation state. Although some anorexia nervosa patients have obsessional character traits, these traits do not signify an obsessive–compulsive disorder. Many of the anorexic patient's obsessional-like symptoms are not viewed by her as ego-alien, as are true symptoms of an obsessive–compulsive disorder. Only the anorexic patient's preoccupation with food is seen as ego-alien, while her preoccupation with weight, body shape, and drive for thinness are not.

Hysteria (Conversion Disorder)

Several times in the last 100 years, investigators believed that anorexia nervosa was a hysterical symptom. Lasègue termed this disorder "anoréxie hystérique" after observing hysterical symptoms in a patient with anorexia nervosa. Gilles de la Tourette considered anorexia nervosa to be a manifestation of hysteria and different from what he termed "anorexie gastrique," which was due to gastrointestinal symptoms. Both Janet and Dally believed there was a subgroup of patients with anorexia nervosa who also had hysteria. Hysterical personality disorder, somatization disorder, and conversion disorder have all been linked to hysterical phenomena, but anorexia nervosa does not clearly resemble any of these.

Anorexia Nervosa as a Nonspecific Symptom

Thirty-five years ago, Bliss and Branch introduced the concept that anorexia nervosa was a nonspecific symptom that occurred in many emotional disorders that presented with significant weight loss and that it was virtually impossible to distinguish it from other forms of emaciation. Anorexia nervosa then became an umbrella diagnosis that encompassed illnesses such as schizophrenia, depression, conversion disorder, and other emotional states in which there was significant weight loss. Bliss and Branch stated: "Anorexia nervosa is a symptom found at times in almost all psychiatric categories." This view is not accepted today. Most investigators view anorexia nervosa as distinct from other causes of weight loss. The distinguishing features center around the fundamental drive for thinness and associated behaviors as described above.

FURTHER READING

Fairburn, C. G., & Garner, D. M. (1988). Diagnostic criteria for anorexia nervosa and bulimia nervosa: The importance of attitude to shape and weight. In D. M. Garner & P. E. Garfinkel (Eds.), *Diagnostic issues in anorexia nervosa and bulimia nervosa* (pp. 36–65) New York: Brunnel/Mazel. A review highlighting the importance of this feature.

Garfinkel, P. E. (1992). Evidence in support of attitudes to shape and weight as a diagnostic criterion of bulimia nervosa. *International Journal of Eating Disorders, 11,* 321–325. A review of the research on the attitudinal disturbance in bulimia nervosa.

Garfinkel, P. E., Garner, D. M., Kaplan, A. S., et al. (1983). Emotional disorders that cause weight loss. *Canadian Medical Association Journal, 129,* 939–945. A discussion of the differential diagnosis of anorexia nervosa.

Garfinkel, P. E., Goldbloom, D. S., Olmsted, M. P., et al. (1992). Body dissatisfaction in bulimia nervosa: Relationship to weight and shape concerns and psychological functioning. *International Journal of Eating Disorders, 11,* 151–161. An empirical study of the affective dimension of body image.

Garfinkel, P. E., Moldofsky, H., Garner, D. M. (1980). The heterogeneity of anorexia nervosa: Bulimia as a distinct subgroup. *Archives of General Psychiatry, 37,* 1036–1040. An early case series differentiating subtypes of anorexia nervosa.

Garner, D. M., Shafer, C. L., & Rosen, L. W. (1992). Diagnostic issues in eating disorders. In S. R. Hooper, G. W. Hynd, & R. E. Mattison (Eds.), *Assessment and diagnosis of child and adolescent psychiatric disorders: Current issues and procedures.* Hillsdale, NJ: Erlbaum. A review of the essential diagnostic features of eating disorders.

• 24 •

ATYPICAL EATING DISORDERS

Christopher G. Fairburn
B. Timothy Walsh

What is an eating disorder? Perhaps surprisingly, there have been few attempts to address this seemingly fundamental question. Rather the term "eating disorder" is equated with two specific syndromes: anorexia nervosa, which was characterized in the late 19th century, and bulimia nervosa, which was described as recently as 1979. The problem with equating eating disorders with anorexia nervosa and bulimia nervosa is that at least one-third of those presenting for the treatment of an "eating disorder" have neither of these conditions.

We suggest that an eating disorder be defined as a persistent disturbance of eating or eating-related behavior that results in the altered consumption or absorption of food and that significantly impairs physical health or psychosocial functioning. This disturbance should not be secondary to any recognized general medical disorder or any other psychiatric disorder. Clearly anorexia nervosa and bulimia nervosa fulfill this definition. The term "atypical eating disorders" may be used to denote the remaining disorders—in other words, those conditions that meet the definition of an eating disorder but not the criteria for either anorexia nervosa or bulimia nervosa.

Both the 10th edition of the *International Classification of Diseases* (ICD-10) and the fourth edition of the American Psychiatric Association's *Diagnostic and Statistical Manual of Mental Disorders* (DSM-IV) recognize the existence of atypical eating disorders. In ICD-10 six different codes are allocated to them (see Table 24.1). In DSM-IV they are placed together within the single residual category of eating disorder not otherwise specified (EDNOS) (see Table 24.2).

CLINICAL FEATURES

There is barely any literature on atypical eating disorders. There have been no descriptive studies of the atypical eating disorders as a whole, the available accounts being mainly clinical reports. However, it seems that they may be meaningfully divided into two broad groups: those resembling anorexia nervosa or bulimia nervosa but not quite meeting their diagnostic criteria, and those with a qualitatively different clinical picture. In the case of the former, the patients have a disturbance that is very similar to the index disorder but fails to meet its criteria either because one of the essential diagnostic features is missing (sometimes the term "partial syndrome" is used) or because

TABLE 24.1. Atypical Eating Disorders in ICD-10

F50.1 Atypical Anorexia Nervosa
This term should be used for those individuals in whom one or more of the key features of anorexia nervosa (F50.0), such as amenorrhoea or significant weight loss, is absent but who otherwise present a fairly typical clinical picture. Patients who have all the key symptoms but to only a mild degree may also be best described by this term.

F50.3 Atypical Bulimia Nervosa
This term should be used for those individuals in whom one or more of the key features listed for bulimia nervosa (F50.2) is absent, but who otherwise present a fairly typical clinical picture. Most commonly this applies to people with normal or even excessive weight but with typical periods of overeating followed by vomiting or purging. Partial syndromes together with depressive symptoms are also not uncommon. Includes normal weight bulimia.

F50.4 Overeating Associated with Other Psychological Disturbances
Overeating that has led to obesity as a reaction to distressing events should be coded here. Includes psychogenic overeating.

F50.5 Vomiting Associated with Other Psychological Disturbances
Apart from the self-induced vomiting of bulimia nervosa, repeated vomiting may occur in dissociative disorders (F44.-), hypochondriacal disorder (F45.2), when vomiting may be one of several bodily symptoms, and in pregnancy, when emotional factors may contribute to recurrent nausea and vomiting. Includes psychogenic hyperemesis gravidarum and psychogenic vomiting.

F50.8 Other Eating Disorders
Includes pica of nonorganic origin in adults and psychogenic loss of appetite.

F50.9 Eating Disorder, Unspecified

Note. Adapted from World Health Organization (1992). *ICD-10 Classification of Mental and Behavioral Disorders: Clinical Descriptions and Diagnostic Guidelines* (pp. 176–181). Geneva: Author. Copyright 1992 by the World Health Organization. Reprinted by permission.

the disorder is not severe enough to meet the specified threshold (a "subthreshold disorder").[1] For example, an individual with all the features of anorexia nervosa other than amenorrhea would be considered to have a partial syndrome. Another example are those individuals who have all the features of bulimia nervosa except that their overeating does not meet the definition of a "binge" (see Chapter 22). Examples of subthreshold disorders include those otherwise typical cases of anorexia nervosa in which body weight is not sufficiently low and those disorders resembling bulimia nervosa in which the frequency of binge eating is not sufficiently high.

Atypical eating disorders less closely resembling anorexia nervosa or bulimia nervosa have been the subject of very little attention. A variety of such problems are encountered. One example comprises those chronic dieters who constantly monitor their weight to prevent even minor increases. Such people often lead restricted lives, since they are unable to eat normally. They are prone to react adversely to natural increases in weight; for example, those associated with pregnancy. Indeed, pregnancy can precipitate a frank

[1]The expression "subclinical eating disorder" is sometimes used in this context. This use is not appropriate, since the term "subclinical" has a different meaning within medicine, in that it refers to a disorder that is not yet accompanied by symptoms.

TABLE 24.2. Atypical Eating Disorders in DSM-IV

307.50 Eating Disorder Not Otherwise Specified
The Eating Disorder Not Otherwise Specified category is for disorders of eating that do not meet the criteria for any specific Eating Disorder. Examples include

1. For females, all of the criteria for Anorexia Nervosa are met except that the individual has regular menses.
2. All of the criteria for Anorexia Nervosa are met except that, despite significant weight loss, the individual's current weight is in the normal range.
3. All of the criteria for Bulimia Nervosa are met except that the binge eating and inappropriate compensatory mechanisms occur at a frequency of less than twice a week or for a duration of less than 3 months.
4. The regular use of inappropriate compensatory behavior by an individual of normal body weight after eating small amounts of food (e.g., self-induced vomiting after the consumption of two cookies).
5. Repeatedly chewing and spitting out, but not swallowing, large amounts of food.
6. Binge eating disorder: recurrent episodes of binge eating in the absence of the regular use of inappropriate compensatory behaviors characteristic of Bulimia Nervosa.

Note. From American Psychiatric Association (1994). *Diagnostic and Statistical Manual of Mental Disorders* (4th ed., p. 550). Washington, DC: Author. Copyright 1994 by the American Psychiatric Association. Reprinted by permission.

(i.e., typical) eating disorder. Another group has recently received particular attention and consists of those with binge eating disorder.

BINGE EATING DISORDER

The term "binge eating disorder" has been coined by American investigators to denote those individuals who have recurrent binges in the absence of the extreme compensatory weight control behaviors seen in people with bulimia nervosa. Such people are thought to constitute about one-fifth of those who present for the treatment of obesity (see Chapter 78). They are also encountered in community-based studies of binge eating, where the association with obesity is much less marked. Research on binge eating disorder is still at an early stage, but it seems the disorder has some features in common with bulimia nervosa although there are noteworthy differences too. In common are the bulimic episodes themselves, which resemble those seen in cases of bulimia nervosa except that they often last longer and have a less clear beginning and end. Also shared is a high level of general psychiatric symptoms. The differences include the overall eating pattern, which in people with binge eating disorder is not characterized by strict attempts to diet as in those with bulimia nervosa but rather by a more general tendency to overeat. Another differentiating feature is the relative absence (by definition) of extreme weight control measures such as self-induced vomiting and the misuse of laxatives and diuretics. Binge eating disorder seems to affect a somewhat older age group than bulimia nervosa; there is also evidence that the sex ratio may be less uneven, with proportionately more male patients. Exactly how binge eating disorder and bulimia nervosa are related is at present unclear.

Binge eating disorder is not an officially recognized eating disorder: Rather, it is one example within the EDNOS category of DSM-IV. A set of diagnostic criteria has been provided to aid further study (see Table 24.3). There is no equivalent disorder in ICD-10.

TABLE 24.3. DSM-IV Research Criteria for Binge Eating Disorder

A. Recurrent episodes of binge eating. An episode of binge eating is characterized by both of the following:

    (1) eating, in a discrete period of time (e.g., within any 2-hour period), an amount of food that is definitely larger than most people would eat in a similar period of time under similar circumstances; and

    (2) a sense of lack of control over eating during the episode (e.g., a feeling that one cannot stop eating or control what or how much one is eating).

B. The binge-eating episodes are associated with three (or more) of the following:

    (1) eating much more rapidly than normal

    (2) eating until feeling uncomfortably full

    (3) eating large amounts of food when not feeling physically hungry

    (4) eating alone because of being embarrassed by how much one is eating

    (5) feeling disgusted with oneself, depressed or very guilty after overeating

C. Marked distress regarding binge eating is present.

D. The binge eating occurs, on average, at least 2 days a week for 6 months.
Note: The method of determining frequency differs from that used for Bulimia Nervosa; future research should address whether the preferred method of setting a frequency threshold is counting the number of days on which binges occur or counting the number of episodes of binge eating.

E. The binge eating is not associated with the regular use of inappropriate compensatory behaviors (e.g. purging, fasting, excessive exercise) and does not occur exclusively during the course of Anorexia Nervosa or Bulimia Nervosa.

Note. From American Psychiatric Association (1994). *Diagnostic and Statistical Manual of Mental Disorders* (4th ed., p. 731). Washington, DC: Author. Copyright 1994 by the American Psychiatric Association. Reprinted by permission.

SECONDARY DISTURBANCES OF EATING

Disturbances of eating also occur in association with other disorders. Anorexia and hypophagia are seen in many people with physical disorders as well as in depression and dementia. Food refusal in the form of a hunger strike sometimes occurs in the context of severe personality disturbance. Hyperphagia is characteristic of certain organic disorders that include hypothalamic tumors and the Kleine–Levin and Prader–Willi syndromes. It is also seen in some cases of depression, mania, and dementia. Anxiety about eating with others may be an expression of social phobia, and repeated spontaneous vomiting may also be anxiety related. According to the definition of eating disorders given above, these disturbances of eating are not "eating disorders" as such, since they are secondary either to general medical disorders or to other psychiatric conditions. This perspective is consistent with that of DSM-IV. However, ICD-10 diverges from DSM-IV in this respect in allowing eating disturbances associated with other conditions to be classified in the eating disorders section (F50), where they can receive the code F50.4, F50.5, or F50.8 (see Table 24.1).

CONCLUSIONS

Attention to the atypical eating disorders is long overdue. These atypical conditions constitute a sizeable proportion of the morbidity associated with eating disorders, and they can be difficult to treat. Descriptive and analytic studies, suitably designed, would help characterize these disorders, and treatment studies would clarify their prognoses and responses to specific interventions. There is a strong case for encouraging investigators to study broad, rather than narrow, samples of those with eating disorders (contrary to the usual practice), since in this way alternative methods of classifying these disorders could be devised and put to the test. It must be emphasized, however, that classificatory schemes are likely to vary depending on the purpose they are intended to serve. A nosological system that segregates individuals in the community on the basis of their natural course may differ significantly from a system that groups clinic patients on the basis of their response to different treatments. And a system based on familial associations might well differ yet again.

As was emphasized in this chapter, there is a complementary relationship between the definitions of the "typical" and the "atypical" eating disorders. Thus changes in the criteria for anorexia nervosa and bulimia nervosa may affect the definition of atypical eating disorders. If, for example, bulimia nervosa were to be redefined so that it included only those individuals who practice self-induced vomiting or the misuse of laxatives or diuretics (i.e., the purging type of bulimia nervosa in DSM-IV; see Chapter 23), cases of individuals who are now classified as having non-purging bulimia nervosa would be moved into the atypical group. Conversely, we believe that attempts to define and characterize the atypical eating disorders are likely to clarify and improve the classification of the typical eating disorders.

ACKNOWLEDGMENTS

C. G. F. is supported by a Wellcome Trust Senior Lectureship (13123). B. T. W. is supported in part by Grant Nos. MH-38355, MH-42206, and MH-49886 from the National Institutes of Health.

FURTHER READING

Bunnell, D. W., Shenker, I. R., Nussbaum, M. P., Jacobson, M. S., & Cooper, P. J. (1990). Subclinical versus formal eating disorders: Differentiating psychological features. *International Journal of Eating Disorders, 9*, 357–362. A study of referrals to a pediatric eating disorder clinic in which almost half of the patients were found to have atypical eating disorders.

Devlin, M. J., Walsh, B. T., Spitzer, R. L., & Hasin, D. (1992). Is there another binge eating disorder? A review of the literature on overeating in the absence of bulimia. *International Journal of Eating Disorders, 11*, 333–340. A review of the literature regarding overeating as of the early 1990s.

Fairburn, C. G., Welch, S. L., & Hay, P. J. (1993). The classification of recurrent overeating: The "binge eating disorder" proposal. *International Journal of Eating Disorders, 13*, 155–159. A discussion of some of the problems with the binge eating disorder proposal.

Herzog, D. B., Hopkins, J. D., & Burns, C. D. (1993). A follow-up study of 33 subdiagnostic eating disordered women. *International Journal of Eating Disorders, 14*, 261–267. A study of the course of atypical eating disorders in which considerable movement between typical and atypical eating disorders and high levels of continuing morbidity were revealed.

Mitchell, J. E., Pyle, R. L., Hatsukami, D., & Eckert, E. D. (1986). What are atypical eating disorders? *Psychosomatics, 27*, 21–28. A description of 25 cases.

Spitzer, R. L., Devlin, M. J., Walsh, B. T., Hasin, D., Wing, R. R., Marcus, M. D., Stunkard, A., Wadden, T. A., Yanovski, S., Agras, W. S., Mitchell, J., & Nonas, C. (1992). Binge eating disorder: A multisite field trial for the diagnostic criteria. *International Journal of Eating Disorders, 11,* 191–203. See comment or reference below.

Spitzer, R. L., Yanovski, S., Wadden, T., Wing, R., Marcus, M. D., Stunkard, A., Devlin, M., Mitchell, J., Hasin, D., & Horne, R. L. (1993). Binge eating disorder: Its further validation in a multisite study. *International Journal of Eating Disorders, 13,* 137–153. These two articles by Spitzer and colleagues represent the first formal attempts to define and validate binge eating disorder.

Williamson, D. A., Gleaves, D. H., & Savin, S. S. (1992). Empirical classification of eating disorder not otherwise specified: Support for DSM-IV changes. *Journal of Psychopathology and Behavioral Assessment, 14,* 201–216. An attempt to identify subgroups within Eating Disorders Not Otherwise Specified using cluster analytic methods.

Yanovski, S. Z. (1993). Binge eating disorder: Current knowledge and future directions. *Obesity Research, 1,* 306–324. A clear and useful summary of recent work on binge eating disorder.

• 25 •

HISTORY OF ANOREXIA NERVOSA

Joseph A. Silverman

In this chapter an attempt will be made to describe a few of the more important events in the history of anorexia nervosa. The data are taken from the English, French, and American literature of the past three centuries.

Accounts describing cases of self-starvation have been circulated since biblical times. Most of these tales, while interesting, are of questionable value as medical reports, being a curious melange of truth, hyperbole, religiosity, and, occasionally, fraud.

THE 17TH CENTURY

In 1689, a textbook of medicine was published in London, entitled *Phthisiologia, seu Exercitationes de Phthisi*. Its author was Richard Morton, a fellow of the College of Physicians. In this volume, translated into English 5 years later and subtitled *A Treatise of Consumptions,* Morton outlined in painstaking detail the many disease processes that cause wasting of body tissue. All the material was based on his own clinical observations.

Morton is best known today as the author of the first medical account of anorexia nervosa, a condition that he referred to as "nervous consumption," caused "by sadness and anxious cares." He described two patients, one an 18-year-old girl who developed amenorrhea from "a multitude of cares and passions of her mind." His second patient was a 16-year-old boy who "fell gradually into a total want of appetite, occasioned by his studying too hard and the passions of his mind." In each case, Morton had ruled out physical illness as the cause of the weight loss. He specifically stated (in case 2), "And therefore I judg'd this consumption to be nervous, and to have its seat in the whole habit of the body, and to arise from the system of nerves being distemper'd."

In both cases, his use of the term "nervous consumption" was based on diagnosis by exclusion.

THE 18TH CENTURY

Seventy-five years would pass before another important account of self-starvation appeared. In 1764, Robert Whytt, professor of the Theory of Medicine at the University of Edinburgh published a book entitled *Observations on the Nature, Causes, and Cures of those Disorders which have been commonly called Nervous, Hypochondriac or Hysteric to which are prefixed some Remarks on the Sympathy of the Nerves.*

In his text, Whytt wrote a description of "a nervous atrophy" and presented a case study, with the following comments:

> A marasmus, or sensible wasting of the body, not attended with sweatings, any consider-
> able increase of the excretions by urine or stool, a quick pulse, or feverish heat, may
> deserve the name of nervous: . . . But this kind of atrophy, tho' not, perhaps, owing to
> any fault in the spirits, or even in the brain or nervous system in general, may yet deserve
> the name of nervous, as it seems, frequently, to proceed from an unnatural or morbid
> state of the nerves, of the stomach, and intestines. . . . Further, the watching or want of
> refreshing rest, and low spirits or melancholy, which generally accompany this disease,
> may contribute to prevent the proper nutrition of the body.

Whytt's patient was a 14-year-old boy who was "observed to be low-spirited and thoughtful, to lose his appetite and have a bad digestion." No constitutional illness could be detected. Whytt therefore concluded, "Since, with all my attention, I neither could discover the cause of the patient's first complaints, nor of the sudden and contrary turn which they took afterwards; I shall not pretend to reason on his case; but I thought it deserved to be mentioned, as a good instance of a nervous atrophy."

It should be noted that Whytt was the first to describe the bradycardia that accompanies starvation.

THE 19TH CENTURY

Almost 100 years would elapse before another truly significant account of eating disorders appeared in print. When it did, in 1860, it failed to receive the attention it deserved, despite its importance. It was quickly forgotten and did not appear again for more than another century. This paper, perhaps the seminal report of the 19th century, was written by Dr. Louis-Victor Marcé of Paris, and was entitled, "Note sur une Forme de Délire Hypochondiaque Consécutive aux Dyspepsies et Caractérisée Principalement par le Refus d'Aliments."

Marcé wrote as follows:

> Amongst the numerous and varied forms of dyspepsia, there are some which should es-
> pecially attract the attention of psycopathists, on account of the peculiar mental condition
> thereby determined.
>
> We see, for instance, young girls, who at the period of puberty, and after a precocious
> physical development, become subject to inappetancy carried to the utmost limits. Whatever
> the duration of their abstinence, they experience a distaste for food, which the most pressing
> want is unable to overcome. . . . Deeply impressed, whether by the absence of appetite or by
> the uneasiness caused by digestion, these patients arrive at a delirious conviction that they
> cannot or ought not to eat. In one word, the gastric nervous disorder becomes cerebro-
> nervous.

He further commented:

> I would venture to say that the first physicians who attended the patients misunderstood the
> true signification of this obstinate refusal of food: far from seeing in it a delirious idea of a
> hypochondriacal nature, they occupied themselves solely with the state of the stomach, and
> prescribed, as a matter of course, bitters, tonics, iron, exercise, [and] hydrotherapeutics with a
> view to stimulate the activity of the digestive functions. However apparently excellent these

measures may be, they always proved insufficient when the malady was in the advanced stage. It is then no longer the stomach that demands attention . . . it is the delirious idea which constitutes henceforth the point of departure, and in which lies the essence of the malady; the patients are no longer dyspeptics—they are insane.

The next important event in the history of eating disorders occurred on August 8, 1868, during the "Address in Medicine" delivered before the British Medical Association. The speaker, Dr. William W. Gull of Guy's Hospital, described the general state of medicine and the progress made in science and philosophy. In his lengthy report, Gull stated:

At present our diagnosis is mostly one of inference, from our knowledge of the liability of the several organs to particular lesions; thus we avoid the error of supposing the presence of mesenteric disease in young women emaciated to the last degree through hysteric apepsia, by our knowledge of the latter affliction, and by the absence of tubercular disease elsewhere.

This brief statement, seemingly unrelated to anything else in Gull's oration, deeply embedded and difficult to find, went unnoted for at least the next 5 years.

In April of 1873, Charles Lasègue of Paris published a manuscript entitled "De l'Anoréxie Hystérique," in which he described eight patients aged between 18 and 32 years. In his report he emphasized the emotional etiology of the illness. Lasègue conveyed a sense of the spirit and feelings of these patients, the nuances of their disturbed relationships, and the subtleties of their intrapsychic turmoil. He considered the illness to be "a hysteria linked to hypochondriasis."

He wrote as follows:

A young girl, between 15 and 20 years of age, suffers from some emotion which she avows or conceals. Generally it relates to some real or imaginary project, to a violence done to some sympathy, or to some more or less conscient desire.

He cautioned his readers to realize the gravity of the situation:

Woe to the physician who, misunderstanding the peril, treats as a fancy without object or duration, an obstinacy which he hopes to vanquish by medicines, friendly advice, or by the still more defective resource, intimidation. With hysterical subjects, a first medical fault is never reparable. Ever on the watch for judgements concerning themselves, especially such as are approved by the family, they never pardon. At this initial period, the only prudent course is to observe, to keep silent, and to remember that when voluntary inanition dates from several weeks, it has become a pathological condition, having a long course to run.

Six months after Lasègue's report, Gull presented a paper entitled "Anorexia Nervosa (Apepsia Hysterica, Anorexia Hysterica)" to the Clinical Society of London. His report emphasized the clinical findings of starvation in three patients. Gull did not concern himself, as did Lasègue, with the illness's emotional aspects. He underscored the occurrence of amenorrhea, constipation, loss of appetite, decreased vital signs, and emaciation. Gull's therapy was simple:

The treatment required is obviously that which is fitted for persons of unsound mind. The patients should be fed at regular intervals, and surrounded by persons who would have moral control over them; relations and friends being generally the worst attendants.

Gull believed the illness to be due to a "morbid mental state," which he later called a "perversion of the ego."

THE 20TH CENTURY

During the 20th century, a major breakthrough occurred that led to a revolution in our understanding of anorexia nervosa. It came from the pen of Dr. Hilde Bruch, of Baylor University, Texas, who was, in her lifetime, considered the doyenne of the investigators of anorexia nervosa. A prodigious worker and prolific writer, she delved into the psyche of anorexic patients in an attempt to find common threads in their emotional pathologies. She discovered that the following three areas of disordered function could be recognized:

1. ". . . a disturbance of delusional proportions in the body image and body concept. Cachexia is regarded with unconcern, and is defended as normal and right, and as the only possible security against the dreaded fate of being fat. The true anorexic is identified with her skeleton-like appearance, denies its abnormality, and actively maintains it."

2. ". . . a disturbance in the accuracy of the perception or cognitive interpretation of stimuli arising in the body, with failure to recognize signs of nutritional need as the most pronounced deficiency. Awareness of hunger in the ordinary sense seems to be absent. The patient's sullen comment, 'I do not need to eat,' probably expresses what she feels and experiences most of the time."

3. ". . . a paralyzing sense of ineffectiveness which pervades all thinking and activities. They experience themselves as acting only in response to demands coming from other people in situations, and not as doing things because they want to."

Thus it was not until the end of the 20th century that we had some insight into the true psychopathology of these patients. For the preceding 300 years, this poorly understood illness had been ascribed variously to "a nervous consumption" (Morton); "a nervous atrophy" (Whytt); "a hypochondriacal delirium" (Marcé); "a hysteria linked to hypochrondriasis" (Lasègue); and "a perversion of the ego" (Gull).

FURTHER READING

Bliss, E. L., & Branch, C. H. H. (1960). *Anorexia nervosa: Its history, psychology and biology*. New York: Paul B. Hoeber. This is an early classic.

Skrabanek, P. (1983). Notes toward the history of anorexia nervosa. *Janus, 70*, 109–128. A later and definitive history.

Vandereycken, W., & van Deth, R. (1994). *From fasting saints to anorexic girls: The history of self-starvation*. London: Athlone Press. A new authoritative history of self-starvation and anorexia nervosa.

• 26 •

HISTORY OF BULIMIA AND BULIMIA NERVOSA

BRENDA PARRY-JONES
WILLIAM LL. PARRY-JONES

The syndrome of bulimia nervosa was defined by Russell only in 1979. The term "bulimia," however, can be traced in western European sources for over 2,000 years with remarkable consistency of meaning, namely, a state of pathological voracity, culminating in the ingestion of an excessive quantity of food.

ETYMOLOGY

Derived from the Greek *bous,* "ox," and *limos,* "hunger," many variants were generated from the medieval Latin *bulimus* and *bolismus* and the middle French *bolisme.* Literally translated as "ox-hunger," "bulimia" carried the dual connotation of having an appetite as large as that of an ox or the ability to consume an ox. Manuscripts and printed works from the 14th to the 20th century demonstrate widespread usage of the term "bulimia" and of variant terms such as "cynorexia," "canine appetite," and "morbid hunger." The earliest English-language usage, *bolismus,* dates from 1398. "Canine appetite," essentially a vulgar, colloquial form, implied a primitive, doglike appetite, often relieved by vomiting. In 1892, *Tuke's Dictionary of Psychological Medicine* claimed that bulimia and canine appetite were the same condition.

SOURCES

The approach to constructing a historical profile of bulimia has to be wide-ranging. Sources are sporadic and heterogeneous, covering, in variable depth, a period of two millennia. They include classical texts; treatises by medieval physicians; scholastic writings; theological works; sensational accounts of oddities; and, more predictably, medical dictionaries, nosologies, case histories, and early publications on eating pathology. Although discursive literature about bulimia as a remarkable form of hyperorexia is available, actual case descriptions, unlike the frequent historical accounts of fasting, are limited.

CHRONOLOGICAL PROFILE

Antiquity

The *Anabasis* of Zenophon (c. 428–354 B.C.) refers to a condition of faintness and physical collapse that occurred among Greek expeditionary forces wintering in Asia Minor. Advised that they suffered from bulimia and that food intake would be restorative, Xenophon distributed provisions and mobility recommended. This presentation of bulimia, as a state of extreme hunger, weakness, and faintness, persisted in classical sources until the 4th century A.D. Galen (c. 129–199 A.D.), elaborating on this theme, defined bulimic symptoms as food craving, collapse, paleness, cold extremities, stomach oppression, and weak pulse. Similarly, the Greek-derived Syriac *Book of Medicines* (c. 200–500 A.D.) attributed *bolimos* and "lust of the dog" to stomach faintness from cold, weakness, or emptiness. The contemporaneous Jewish Talmud described *boolmot*, a ravenous, life-threatening condition involving impaired judgement about food intake and decreased alertness, for which honey and sweet foods were administered. Despite the tradition of induced emesis between banquet courses by surfeited Roman patricians, reported graphically by Petronius in the first century A.D., most early references to bulimia describe a physiological response to prolonged food deprivation in the context of cold, faintness, and exhaustion, rather than disinhibited consumption. An exception can be found in the 5th-century writings of Aurelianus, who discussed, in the context of chronic diseases, "morbid hunger" and "phagedaena." He defined the former as a disease of the gullet characterized by a ravenous appetite, the absence of mastication, and vomiting; and he described the emaciated sufferers as having swollen faces and decayed teeth, the latter affording interesting parallels with the parotid enlargement and dental caries seen in modern-day sufferers of bulimia nervosa.

The Middle Ages

During the medieval period, two opposing forces operated. On the one hand, gluttony was one of the seven deadly sins reviled by the Roman Catholic Church; on the other, the insecurity of food supplies and short life expectancy made uncontrolled consumption a reality during times of prosperity. Evidence that gross overeating was no rarity is supported by the inclusion of bulimia and "houndes appetite" among the common medical conditions discussed by Bartholomaeus Anglicus (fl. 1230–1250), who noted that these excessive eaters remained "lene and wasted," and by the incorporation of a herbal remedy, accompanied by the earliest known illustration of an indulging bulimic, in *De Arte Phisicali et Cirurgia*, (1412) by John of Arderne (see Figure 26.1). Self-induced vomiting as a penance featured in the lives of some ascetic medieval nuns, notably Catherine of Siena (d. 1380), who procured emesis using a straw. Although literary works by Boccaccio, Chaucer, and Rabelais testify to the existence of gluttons and gluttony, case descriptions of identified bulimics are rare and anecdotal before the 17th century. Three extant examples refer to the purging of a 6th-century female bulimic with intestinal worms; bulimia preceding attested miraculous fasting by a cloistered German peasant girl in Monheim, in 895; and the death, in 1494, of the Flemish painter Hans Memling, a lifelong bulimic, following the voracious ingestion of a huge pike.

16th to 19th Centuries

During this period, we have identified 36 cases of hyperphagia, 23 of which occurred in the 19th century. With the inclusion of the four medieval subjects already cited, the 40 cases examined can be broadly categorized as 25 that displayed hyperphagia in the form of gluttony, sometimes verging on monstrosity; and 15 with some features resembling bulimia nervosa (e.g., rapid ingestion, secret eating, night bingeing, vomiting, and normal body weight). Additionally there were three 19th-century reports relating to a separate, clearly differentiated group of 22 patients, whose short-lived voracity was directly attributable to head injury, brain disease, hydrocephalus, or epilepsy.

20th Century

The most striking feature in 20th-century reports is the absence of gross hyperphagia comparable with the classic 19th-century bulimic cases. Physicians such as Osler recognized bulimia as an anomaly of the sense of hunger or repletion, seen usually in patients with hysteria and neurasthenia. In the 1930s, bulimia was reported also as a symptom of emotional deprivation and poor social adaptation among maladjusted juveniles and refugees. References to episodic overeating in the context of anorexia nervosa, a feature identified in 1866 by Gull in his first anorexic patient, increased after 1900. The earliest bulimic cases approximating modern diagnostic criteria were reported in the 1930s, chiefly in German sources, becoming more frequent during the post-World War II period. By the 1960s bingeing and self-induced vomiting had become established features within some presentations of anorexia nervosa. The increased incidence of bulimia during the 1970s finally precipitated its recognition as a separate eating disorder in 1979.

CLASSIFICATION

Variations in the form and presentation of bulimia have been described historically, some striking a surprisingly modern note. Three 17th- and 18th-century texts, for example, contain comments on the life-dominating effects of continual devouring and vomiting, with emphasis on the patient's uneasiness unless he/she was "continually a-cramming" and the observation that some insatiable eaters neither vomited nor purged but digested everything. Such facts were incorporated in the earliest nosologies.

Sauvage's classification system (1771) listed seven subtypes of bulimia in which the voracity had concomitant clinical features, namely emesis, faintness, worm infestation, absence of evacuations, diarrhea with atrophy, convulsions, and overacidity. Cullen's influential classification (1780) was simpler. Under the category of false appetites, his tripartite grouping of idiopathic bulimia distinguished a gluttonous form without overt stomach disease, a syncopal manifestation necessitating recurrent feeding, and an emetic form following gross intake. Almost two-thirds of our 40 cases fall into Cullen's first subgroup; the majority of the remaining subjects had bulimia emetica, and there were few examples of the syncopal form. Cullen's classification was widely adopted, with some elaborations, including the definition of nine bulimic subtypes by Hooper (1820). Before acquiring syndromal status as bulimia nervosa, bulimia was defined in the ICD-9 (1977) simply as polyphagia, excessive eating, or hyperalimentation.

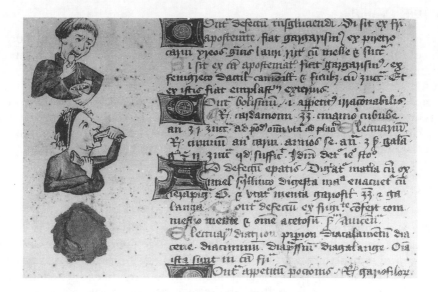

FIGURE 26.1. Remedy for bolismus, or irrational appetite, in *De Arte Phisicali et Cirurgia* of John of Arderne, 1412. The bulimic is the lower figure. From a facsimile (Cambridge University Library: Keynes F.6.18) of MS.X.118 in the Royal Library, Stockholm. Reproduced by permission of the Syndics of Cambridge University Library, UK.

CAUSATION, TREATMENT, AND OUTCOME

Bulimia was viewed originally as a somatic disorder, caused either by vicious, cold humors that produced unnatural emptiness of the stomach, animal hunger, faintness, and exhaustion; or by parasitic worms. With the eclipse of "humoral pathology," causative theories were diversified to include digestive dysfunction, stomach acidity, gastritis, defective gastric secretions, congenital structural abnormalities, brain disease, and head injury. A psychological dimension, "defection of spirits," was first noted in 1701. Thereafter the relationship of bulimia with neurotic and hysterical disorders was increasingly addressed and, by the 19th century, bulimia became widely accepted as a simple functional disorder, or dyspepsia, seen mostly in neurotic subjects. Its occurrence during convalescence and in debility following surgery or protracted childbirth was also acknowledged. By the early 20th century, its frequent manifestation in "hysterical" females gained recognition.

Early treatments focused on counteracting cold humors by warming and comforting the stomach, internally and externally. Red wine; nutritious flesh; hot spices, with stimulating aromatics to relieve flatulence and bowel discomfort; and fat, greasy foods for their aversive effect were recommended in medieval pharmocopeia. Later, anthelmintics, antiphlogistics, ice, mercury, acids, opium, testaceous powders, valerian, chloral, bromides, belladonna, antispasmodics, and purges predominated. Such polypharmacy reflected medical bewilderment about the nature of bulimia, resulting in the treatment of individual symptoms. Prompt medical intervention; dietary control; and regular exercise and special diets, including food boiled to jelly and tablets of "portable" soup, succeeded with some pre-20th-century patients.

Prognosis was variable. In many of our 40 cases, the outcome was unknown; in the remainder, outcomes included recovery, chronicity, death, and, in one instance, suicide. Some bulimics flaunted their voracity, earning their living as public exhibitionists. Mortality before the age of 40, gradual loss of intelligence, and torpid states characterized some of the grossly hyperphagic patients; and marasmus, dropsy, and hectic fever were stated causes of death. Postmortem findings remained inconclusive.

CONTINUITIES AND DISCONTINUITIES
BETWEEN BULIMIA AND BULIMIA NERVOSA

The continuities between bulimia and bulimia nervosa that are reflected in the historical cases include regular, rapid overconsumption of food; an alternation between excessive eating and abstinence or low intake; body weights ranging from low to normal, but rarely obese; neurotic traits; night bingeing; and vomiting, occasionally self-induced. There is some evidence of lowered mood, vigorous exercising, and avoidance of shared family meals. Four of the historical subjects were self-mutilators; one woman exhibited all the risk factors considered significant in the onset of self-injury, namely parental loss, serious childhood illness, physical and sexual abuse, violence, and body alienation. Additionally, the eating pattern of this subject showed identical seasonal variation over 10 years.

Discontinuities with modern bulimia nervosa comprised a wide age-range (childhood to middle age); male predominance; worm infestation and convalescence as precipitants; cravings for raw fish, meat, and offal; and a perverted appetite for nonfoods such as grass, thistles, and candles. Most significant was the absence of any evidence of self-purging, diuretic misuse, concern for body weight or shape, or fear of loss of control over eating.

OVERLAP OF SYMPTOMS WITH OTHER EATING DISORDERS

The historical findings confirm an occasional overlap of the symptoms of bulimia with those of anorexia nervosa, in terms of alternating overeating and fasting or low intake, self-induced vomiting, and overexercising. There was an overlap with pica, in terms of an excessive craving for specific foods or nonfoods; and with rumination disorder, in terms of rapid intake and poor mastication of ingestae.

CONCLUSIONS

The increasing incidence of anorexia nervosa and bulimia nervosa after World War II, widely interpreted as due to the changing sociocultural expectations of young women, is incontestable. Far less clear is the pattern of emergence of bulimia nervosa. Some symptoms show continuities with pre-20th-century bulimia, but the central facet of bulimia nervosa—the combination of certain characteristic extreme concerns about body shape and weight and the use of compensatory measures such as self-induced vomiting and laxative abuse—appears to relate exclusively to the present century and the pressures of idealized slimness. Bulimia nervosa made its debut insidiously, via anorexia nervosa. Tracing its emergence is difficult owing to the rarity of early 20th-century case material. The availability of data covering a longer time span, however, allows bulimia nervosa, the "nervous" bulimia, to fall into historical perspective as the latest version, with its own distinctive psychopathological characteristics, in a long and varied sequence of bulimic disorders.

FURTHER READING

Blachez, P. F. (1869). Boulimie. In A. Dechambre (Ed.), *Dictionnaire encyclopédique des sciences médicales* (Vol. 10, pp. 318–325). Paris: Masson et Fils. A state-of-the-art encyclopedia entry, clarifying and illustrating, with some contemporary French case descriptions, the presentation, causation, and interpretations of bulimia in the mid-19th century.

Casper, R. C. (1983). On the emergence of bulimia nervosa as a syndrome. A historical view. *International Journal of Eating Disorders, 2,* 3–16. One of the earliest investigations of the complexities surrounding the relationship of the ancient symptom of bulimia with the emergent syndrome of bulimia nervosa. The discussion is set against the wider background of the development of body shape and weight concerns in both anorexia nervosa and bulimia nervosa and the attribution of this feature to cultural and economic changes.

Habermas, T. (1989). The psychiatric history of anorexia nervosa and bulimia nervosa: Weight concerns and bulimic symptoms in early case reports. *International Journal of Eating Disorders, 8,* 259–273. A key article, providing a thought-provoking and critical appraisal, from a German angle, of the historical background to the emergence of weight concern and bulimic symptoms in 20th-century cases of anorexia nervosa and bulimia nervosa.

Habermas, T. (1992). Further evidence on early case descriptions of anorexia nervosa and bulimia nervosa. *International Journal of Eating Disorders, 11,* 351–359. An important contribution, substantiating the view that both anorexia nervosa and bulimia nervosa are historically new syndromes if the fear of becoming overweight is held to be an essential diagnostic criterion.

Parry-Jones, B. (1991). Historical terminology of eating disorders. *Psychological Medicine, 21,* 21–28. The first detailed historical and lexicographical analysis, using 14th- to 20th-century sources, of terms describing five presentations of disordered eating, including bulimia and canine appetite.

Parry-Jones, B., & Parry-Jones, W. Ll. (1991). Bulimia: an archival review of its history in psychosomatic medicine. *International Journal of Eating Disorders, 10,* 129–143. The earliest discussion of 12 bulimic cases derived from 17th- to 19th-century British and European sources, in terms of symptoms, causation, treatment, etiology, and classification, highlighting continuities and discontinuities with the modern syndrome of bulimia nervosa.

Parry-Jones, B., & Parry-Jones, W. Ll. (1993). Self-mutilation in four historical cases of bulimia. *British Journal of Psychiatry, 163,* 394–402. The first historical exploration of the suggested association between bulimia and self-mutilative behavior, based on 18th- and 19th-century case studies.

Russell, G. F. M. (1979). Bulimia nervosa: An ominous variant of anorexia nervosa. *Psychological Medicine, 9,* 429–448. The classic description and naming of the syndrome of bulimia nervosa.

Stein, D. M., & Laakso, W. (1988). Bulimia: A historical perspective. *International Journal of Eating Disorders, 7,* 201–210. An interesting review of historical references, chiefly in medical and psychological dictionaries and encyclopaedias, of the concept of bulimia over the last three centuries. The authors suggest that, despite the recent view of bulimia as a variant of anorexia nervosa, historical evidence suggests there were earlier conceptualizations of bulimia, both as a symptom and as a syndrome.

Ziolko, H. U., & Schrader, H. C. (1985). Bulimie. *Fortschritte der Neurologie und Psychiatrie, 53,* 231–258. The most extensive documentation of sources for the history of binge eating or bulimia as a symptom (380 references to Latin, English, German, and French sources, divided into pre- and post-1000 A.D.).

• 27 •

THE CLINICAL PRESENTATION OF ANOREXIA AND BULIMIA NERVOSA

Pierre J. V. Beumont

Anorexia nervosa and bulimia nervosa are characterized by an excessive concern about being fat, which leads to attempts to restrict eating. For that reason both syndromes might better be called dieting disorders rather than eating disorders. An unfortunate consequence of the current emphasis on the diagnostic distinction between these two illnesses is that the commonalities of presentation for all patients with dysfunctional dieting have been obscured. In fact, there are far more similarities than there are differences in the clinical features these patients exhibit.

ANOREXIA NERVOSA

Anorexia nervosa is a condition of self-engendered weight loss, usually seen in adolescent girls or young women, less commonly in prepubertal children, middle-aged women, or men. It has been recognised in medicine for more than 120 years but is largely confined to affluent societies that espouse Western cultural ideals. Within such communities anorexia nervosa occurs at all socioeconomic levels. The various criteria that have been proposed for its diagnosis (see Chapter 23) point to three sets of related features: (1) an intense preoccupation with weight and shape; (2) behaviors that are directed at the relentless pursuit of thinness; and (3) the physical consequences of these behaviors, such as emaciation, disturbances of endocrine function, and other nutritional abnormalities.

Psychiatric Presentation

The phenomenology of the core psychological disturbance is difficult to define. It has been termed a manifestation of hysteria, a phobia of weight gain, an obsession, or even a delusion. Perhaps it is best conceived as an overvalued idea. Patients are overwhelmed by concerns about their bodies and protest that they feel themselves to be obese even when they are actually emaciated. They are preoccupied with plans to further reduce their weight or, at the very least, to prevent any gain. They appear to be genuinely terrified at the prospect of being overweight, and some state openly that they would rather be dead than fat. Although so extreme as to be pathological, such beliefs represent only an exaggeration of the widespread concern about weight control that has been engendered in our community.

Onto this core concern are imposed other psychological symptoms, many of which are known to be common to semistarvation irrespective of the cause (see Chapter 53). These symptoms include depressed mood, irritability, social withdrawal, loss of sexual libido, preoccupation with food, obsessional ruminations and rituals, and eventually reduced alertness and concentration. The dysphoria is particularly important. It is so common that it is best considered an integral feature of the illness that does not warrant a separate diagnosis. This intimate association is not understood by many clinicians, who, confused by patients' depressed moods, sleep disturbances, and raised cortisol levels (leading to a positive result on a dexamethasone suppression test) make an inappropriate second diagnosis of a mood disorder. That diagnosis leads to the prescription of tricyclic antidepressant drugs that pose physical dangers to the anorexic patient whose cardiac function may already be compromised. The depression usually lessens during nutritional rehabilitation, and recourse to medication should be reserved for patients in whom such improvement does not occur (see Chapter 55). Similarly, severe obsessional symptoms, usually relating to eating and food but sometimes of a more general nature, are common in anorexia patients (see Chapter 28). Often, but not invariably, these symptoms also improve with weight gain.

The illness is generally associated with premorbid perfectionism, introversion, poor peer relations, and low self-esteem. Characteristically, the patient is described as having been a perfect child, always biddable and helpful, whose current obstinate refusal to eat is all the more extraordinary because of her previous compliance. In the incipient stages of the illness, as she becomes increasingly preoccupied with dieting, the patient withdraws from peer relationships, often concentrating on study or work with obsessive intensity and to the exclusion of all other interests. However, these features are not found in all patients, some of whom are more extroverted and interactive, with outgoing personality profiles.

Patients react to efforts to alter their behaviour with anger, deception, and manipulative behaviour, all inconsistent with their previous behavioral standards. With the development of chronicity, they become absorbed by their illness, dependent on family or therapists, and restricted in their activities. The serious long-term effects of regression, invalidism, and social isolation come to dominate the clinical picture.

Many patients' emotional problems arise from separation anxiety and difficulties with identity. There is sometimes a "pathogenic secret" concerning physical or sexual abuse, which results in low self-esteem and intense feelings of shame (see Chapter 40). Starving is a means of assuaging the pain and also of gaining control over the course of sexual development. Hence the patient holds onto her emaciation as a form of self-realization and identifies with her wasted body.

Although this pattern of disturbance imparts a conformity to the psychiatric presentation, the underlying psychodynamic psychopathology is varied. Each patient needs to be understood as an individual so that her basic vulnerability, the pressures that precipitated her illness, and the factors that hold her back from recovery are all recognized and appreciated (see Chapter 35).

Dieting (Restricting) and Purging Forms of Anorexia Nervosa

Anorexic behaviors, although all directed at either decreasing energy intake or increasing energy expenditure, are not uniform. Some patients employ only those restrictive behaviors commonly associated with normal dieting, such as undereating, refusal of high-energy foods, and strenuous exercise. When first seen clinically, such patients exhibit the "dieting" or "restricting" form of the illness; they differ from healthy girls mainly in the extent to which they pursue these activities and their inability to desist from them. Other patients go beyond restriction to more dangerous behaviors, such as self-induced vomiting and laxative or diuretic abuse. The presentation then is that of the "purging" form of anorexia nervosa.

Restricting Behaviors

The food choices of anorexia patients are determined by unhealthy attitudes and misconceptions acquired from dubious sources of information such as popular women's magazines. As the fads reported in these periodicals have changed over the years, so have the foods rejected by anorexia patients. Previous generations selectively avoided simple sugars and other carbohydrates (sweets and potatoes). Today, fatty foods and red meat are considered "unhealthy," and vegetarianism has become the most common dietary perversion. Great reliance is placed on energy-reduced dietary products, on foods with a high fiber content, and on supplementary vitamins.

At table, anorexia patients cut their food into minute portions, choose inappropriate utensils (a teaspoon for dessert), eat painfully slowly, add excessive condiments, adopt a bizarre sequence of dishes, drink too much (or too little) fluids, dispose of food secretly, and count calories. These behaviors result in conflict at family meals that, together with the patient's increasing anxiety related to food, lead her to avoid eating in company. She takes different meals than those of other family members and eats at different times, often very late at night and only after hours of procrastination. Patients are preoccupied with thoughts of food and become overinvolved in activities such as cooking. They may take over the responsibility of buying food and preparing the family meals, although they will eat hardly anything themselves.

Overactivity

Many anorexia nervosa patients are overactive. It is almost as characteristic a feature as the dietary restriction and is just as difficult to modify. It appears to be of two kinds of overactivity.

First, many patients overexercise quite deliberately in order to burn calories and induce weight loss. The activity may be surreptitious, such as going up and down stairs frequently on the pretext of fetching different things, or getting off public transport several stops before the actual destination and walking the rest of the way. Some patients follow the advice sometimes given to dieters: "Never sit if you can stand, never stand if you can walk, never walk if you can run." For others the activity is strenuous physical exercise, usually in the form of aerobic exercise classes, jogging, or swimming. Typically the exercise is solitary. It has a strongly obsessive character and is performed in a regular and rigid sequence. Patients experience guilt feelings if they do not do the exercise, whatever the reason. Commonly, exercise and eating are linked by "debting" behavior; that is, the patient "earns" the right to eat food with a certain number of calories by undertaking prescribed activities; conversely, she must "pay" for some self-indulgence by an extra exercise session.

The second kind of overactivity is a persistent restlessness that is typical of almost all patients once they have become emaciated. It is often associated with sleep disturbance, appears beyond voluntary control, and may be an analogue of the ceaseless overactivity seen in laboratory animals when they are deprived of food. The restlessness persists until the patient's physical condition has deteriorated to such an extent that she shows weakness and lassitude.

Purging Behaviors

In addition to food restriction, some anorexic patients use vomiting, laxatives, and diuretic abuse to further induce weight loss. This purging form of the illness is particularly malignant, since the behaviors in themselves are injurious to health. Serious physical complications usually arise in patients who maintain a persistently low weight and in whom purging behaviors are prominent (see Chapter 47).

Patients sometimes can relate the factors that lead to the onset of purging. For some, persistent food restriction eventually led to episodes of reactive hyperphagia or bulimia, and vomiting was first induced to compensate for an eating binge. Just as frequently, vomiting was used deliberately to bring about weight loss; in such cases, the patient subsequently may have allowed herself to eat in a less restricted manner, since she knew she would now be able to dispose of the food.

At first some physical maneuver is necessary to bring on retching, or Ipecac is ingested as an emetic, but patients soon learn to vomit at will. Strong cathartics or herbal laxatives are also taken, ostensibly to combat constipation but really to induce diarrhea. Although patients believe the diarrhea will prevent them from absorbing calories, the weight loss produced is simply the result of dehydration. Oral diuretics have a similar effect.

Compared with "restricting-only" patients, purging anorexics are more likely to have other problems with impulse control and substance abuse.

Physical Consequences

The extent of undernutrition may be gauged by reference to the body mass index (BMI = weight in kilograms per height in meters^2; normal range is 20 to 25 for adults). Because current diagnostic criteria (DSM and ICD) include subjects with a BMI of 17.5 or even higher, some patients may be considered thin rather than emaciated. Others, however, have lost 50% or more of normal body weight (BMI 10 or less). Fortunately, the effects of starvation depend on the kind of dietary deficiency from which it arises, and the nutritional disturbance seen in an anorexia nervosa patient is usually more benign than that found in a victim of protein-calorie malnutrition or famine with an equivalent weight loss. In anorexia nervosa patients malnutrition, as opposed to undernutrition, is often relatively mild and manifested only in signs such as the overgrowth of lanugo hair, alopecia, and follicular keratosis (dry, scaly skin). However, some patients do show more serious evidence of vitamin deficiency and significant protein depletion.

In the early phase of the illness, the anorexic patient chooses a diet low in energy-dense foods but relatively high in protein and other essential nutrients. This type of diet, together with the characteristically high level of activity, exerts a nitrogen-sparing effect so that the initial weight reduction is due mainly to loss of fat. Normally the body's immediate energy requirements are met by glucose, and glucose is the only form of energy the brain can metabolize. With severe weight loss, the glucose stored in glycogen deposits in the liver is soon exhausted and fat reserves are mobilized, leading to the formation of ketone bodies. These ketone bodies account for the sweet smell of acetone on the breath of emaciated patients. As the body accommodates to the state of semistarvation, gluconeogenesis is stimulated and protein tissue is broken down. These processes lead to protein depletion, water loss from the intracellular compartment, electrolyte imbalance, and metabolic complications.

The medical complications of anorexia nervosa are discussed in Chapter 47. They are varied and often serious, accounting for the high prevalence of physical morbidity and the alarming mortality rate among anorexia nervosa patients (see Chapter 41). Many of the most characteristic complications (i.e., altered thyroid metabolism and anovular infertility with amenorrhea) may best be considered as physiological adaptations to the state of starvation and do not require treatment. More serious physical complications, which may require specific intervention, are usually found in patients with a chronic illness who are severely emaciated, abuse laxatives, and induce vomiting. These complications often go unnoticed before the anorexia nervosa patient is admitted to a hospital and may be exposed only when initial refeeding upsets the patient's precarious equilibrium; this scenario is particularly true of the physical problems that result from an electrolyte imbalance associated with purging behaviours. Or, like osteoporosis and the stunting of growth, these complications may develop insidiously during the course of a chronic illness.

Although it is almost invariable, the prominence assigned to the symptom of amenorrhea in the various sets of diagnostic criteria is unwarranted. It is merely one aspect of the widespread endocrine dysfunction found in anorexia patients. The menstrual disorder often precedes severe weight loss and may persist for months after weight restoration. Ultrasound studies confirm ovarian regression. Depressed sexual libido and low testosterone levels are the equivalent symptoms and signs in male patients.

BULIMIA NERVOSA

Bulimia nervosa is a variant of anorexia nervosa, with which it shares many clinical and demographic features. An essential diagnostic distinction is that bulimia nervosa patients maintain an apparently normal weight. Unlike anorexia nervosa, bulimia nervosa has come to medical attention only in recent years, but it is probably even more common (see Chapter 36). It is most closely related to the purging form of anorexia nervosa, although it is not usually as serious a condition because the associated undernutrition is less severe.

Bulimia nervosa often arises from a preexisting anorexic illness. Even when this is not the case, the development of the disturbance is essentially similar to that of anorexia nervosa and originates from a background of long-continued attempts to restrain eating. The persistent dietary restriction is eventually interrupted by episodes of reactive hyperphagia (binge eating, or bulimia) and compensatory behaviors that usually include vomiting and laxative abuse. By these means the patient maintains an apparently stable weight within the normal range despite overeating. The behavioral disturbance becomes the focus of intense guilt feelings. Nevertheless the bulimic episodes often serve to reduce tension, making them even more difficult to relinquish.

The clinical picture of bulimia nervosa is distinctive. The restricted eating comes first, motivated by the supreme importance the patient attributes to being slender, the essential feature of the psychopathology. All bulimia nervosa patients attempt to control their weight by dieting and abstaining from high-energy foods, at least in the early stage of their illness. They are constantly preoccupied with thoughts of food as a reaction to their long-continued restricted eating practices. The pattern of eating that develops is one of alternation between fasting or extreme dieting on the one hand and episodes of gorging on the other. Self-induced vomiting and laxative abuse usually occur after the gorging behavior has been established. Some patients recall their delight at discovering that they could eat as much as they craved without gaining weight.

Initially, patients are secretive about their bulimic episodes, so that overeating and vomiting may occur for years without other family members becoming aware of them. Other patients leave such obvious signs of their disturbed behavior (stacks of empty food containers in the kitchen or plastic bags filled with vomitus under the bed) that one may only conclude they wished to be discovered, perhaps to declare the level of their distress.

Bulimic episodes are frequently planned, and foods are stored to be consumed at a time when the patient will be able to gorge without interruption. Binge foods are selected because they are easy to swallow and regurgitate. Typically they are the fatty, sweet, high-energy foods that patients deny themselves at other times. Some patients may take as much as 30 times the recommended daily allowance of calories in one binge, but usually the amount of food ingested is more moderate. It is important, however, for the clinician to ascertain that the amount of food eaten in an alleged binge is in fact excessive. Much confusion is caused by anorexia nervosa patients or restricted eaters who label any break in their dieting or any meal in which they eat more than they would have liked as an episode of binge eating (a "subjective" binge). A useful strategy for the clinician is to refer to "gorging" rather than to "bingeing," as the former term seems to elicit a more accurate response.

People with bulimia nervosa have a tendency to eat rapidly during a binge, stuffing in a large amount of food within minutes. Chronic patients, however, will binge eat at a slower rate, particularly if there is little risk of discovery. Others report "picking" behavior, taking in small quantities at a time (i.e., a teaspoon of ice-cream, a small piece of cake, or a portion of cheese) but continuing this "picking" for hours until they have ingested thousands of calories.

Bulimic episodes may be precipitated by many different factors: anxiety, tension or boredom; being reminded about food; drinking alcohol or smoking cannabis; being anxious about a date; or being tired from working hard. Only rarely do patients admit that hunger led them to binge, even though they may have fasted for 24 hours before an episode of gorging.

Patients with bulimia nervosa may attempt to resist the urge to eat by taking appetite suppressants or other stimulants. They may also avoid situations in which they are likely to be exposed to food or will find it difficult to exert rigid control over their eating, such as going out to dinner with friends or to a party. This avoidance behavior adds to the problems they already have with social relations and helps establish a vicious cycle of increasing binge eating, purging, and social withdrawal.

Many bulimia nervosa patients have problems with activity, either exercising frenetically after each binge in an attempt to compensate for the overindulgence or else going through phases of eating in a restricted, "healthy" way and exercising regularly, alternating with phases of bingeing and complete inactivity.

Some patients chew food and then spit it out (regurgitation), but most induce vomiting; at first they need to activate the gag reflex by inserting a finger down the throat but later learn to vomit at will by contracting the thoracic and abdominal muscles.

Others use the emetic Ipecac, take massive amounts of purgatives to bring on diarrhea, or abuse diuretics to lose fluid. They feel disgusted with themselves for having overeaten but are relieved by the purging behavior, are no longer uncomfortable because of abdominal distension, and are gratified to feel that they will not gain weight as a result of the binge.

Mood disturbances are so common in bulimia nervosa patients that it has been suggested the condition is a form of depressive illness (see Chapter 28). However, careful analysis of the history usually reveals that the eating disturbance preceded the depression, and the patient herself usually relates her unhappiness to her eating problems. The mental state is characterized by feelings of anxiety and tension, helplessness, failure, and self-deprecatory thoughts. Some patients report past sexual and physical abuse; these experiences contribute to their low self-esteem and self-loathing (see Chapter 40). Self-mutilation is common, as are thoughts of suicide and some patients try to kill themselves after binge eating. On the other hand, because the bulimic episodes and the consequent purgation often have an anxiety-relieving effect, other patients admit they resort to binge eating at times when they are experiencing difficulty in coping with stress.

A significant proportion of bulimia nervosa patients have preexisting personality difficulties, a history of disturbed interpersonal relations, and difficulties in impulse control and substance abuse. In these premorbid features they tend to differ from anorexia nervosa patients, particularly those with the restrictive form of that illness, who are usually more reserved, introverted, inhibited, and obsessional.

The medical complications of bulimia nervosa are described in Chapter 48.

ATYPICAL EATING DISORDERS

About a third or more of patients considered for treatment at eating disorder clinics do not fulfill the diagnostic criteria of either anorexia or bulimia nervosa and are classified as atypical (see Chapter 24). They include partial cases of anorexia nervosa who severely restrict their eating but who are not thin enough and of bulimia nervosa (relatively infrequent binge episodes or binge eating without associated purgation), obese patients with a markedly disturbed pattern of eating resembling that of bulimia nervosa but without the compensatory weight-losing behaviors (sometimes assigned to a category known as "binge eating disorder"; see Chapters 24 and 78), and cases of food refusal and undernutrition secondary to hypochondriasis, abnormal illness behavior, or psychotic ideation. Although very varied, the clinical features these cases present bear many resemblances to the more clearly defined syndromes that have been described in this chapter.

FURTHER READING

Abraham, S. F., & Beumont, P. J. V. (1982). How patients describe bulimia or binge eating. *Psychological Medicine, 12,* 625–635. An objective description of how bulimic patients describe their own disorder, in the context of a detailed clinical examination.

Al-Alami, M., Beumont, P. J. V., & Touyz, S. (1987). The further development of the concept of anorexia nervosa. In P. J. V. Beumont, G. D. Burrows, & R. Casper (Eds.), *The handbook of eating disorders: Part 1. Anorexia and bulimia nervosa* (pp. 117–141). Amsterdam: Elsevier/North-

Holland. The authors review the various clinical features of anorexia nervosa on which attention has been focused for the last century and longer.

Beumont, P. J. V., Al-Alami, M., & Touyz, S. (1987). Evolution of the concept of anorexia nervosa. In P. J. V. Beumont, G. D. Burrows, & R. Casper (Eds.), *The handbook of eating disorders: Part 1. Anorexia and bulimia nervosa* (pp. 105–116). Amsterdam: Elsevier/North-Holland.

Beumont, P. J. V., Arthur, B., Russell, J. D., & Touyz, S. W. (1994). Excessive physical activity in dieting disorder patients: Proposals for a supervised exercise programme. *International Journal of Eating Disorders, 15,* 21–36. Overactivity is frequently overlooked as a major feature of the clinical presentation of dieting disorders. In this the authors examine the phenomenon from a clinical viewpoint.

Beumont, P. J. V., George, G. C. W., & Smart, D. E. (1976). "Dieters" and "vomiters and purgers" in anorexia nervosa. *Psychological Medicine, 6,* 617–622. The separation between restrictive and purging forms of anorexia nervosa antedates the description of bulimia. The purging variety of anorexia is indeed an ominous variant of the illness, with distinct clinical features.

Cooper, P. J., & Fairburn, C. G. (1993). Confusion over the core psychopathology of bulimia nervosa. *International Journal of Eating Disorders, 13,* 4, 385–389. By means of an empirical study the authors focus on the core psychopathology of bulimia nervosa.

Russell, G. F. M. (1979). Bulimia nervosa: An ominous variant of anorexia nervosa. *Psychological Medicine, 9,* 429–448. This seminal paper established the intimate relationship that exists between bulimia and anorexia nervosa, particularly the purging form of the latter illness.

Touyz, S. W., Beumont, P. J. V., Collins, J. K., McCabe, M., & Jupp, J. (1984). Body shape perception and its disturbance in anorexia nervosa. *British Journal of Psychiatry, 144,* 167–171. Rather than being evidence of a core disturbance of perception, the apparent body image distortion reported in anorexia nervosa patients relates to affective changes and to a mis-conception of what constitutes normality. An interesting aspect of the paper is the support it gives to the study of Cooper and Fairburn (1993), although it derives from a completely different set of data.

Turner, M. S., & Shapiro, C. M. (1992). The biochemistry of anorexia nervosa. *International Journal of Eating Disorders, 12,* 2, 179–193. A recent review of the metabolic disturbance that occurs in anorexia nervosa patients.

Vandereycken, W., & van Deth, R. (1990). A tribute to Lasègue's description of anorexia nervosa (1873), with completion of its English translation. *British Journal of Psychiatry, 157,* 902–908. The anorexia nervosa patients who were described in France and in England between 1850 and 1870 more closely resemble the anorexia patients we see today than the schizophrenia patients described by Kraepelin at the turn of the century resemble the psychotic patients of today. The authors give a succinct summary of Lasègue's masterly description of the illness.

· 28 ·

EATING DISORDERS AND THEIR RELATIONSHIP TO MOOD AND ANXIETY DISORDERS

PETER J. COOPER

People with eating disorders also frequently have symptoms of depression. Thus studies of patients with anorexia nervosa have revealed high rates of lowered mood, feelings of hopelessness, guilt, worthlessness, and irritability, as well as concentration impairment and sleep disturbance. Suicidal thoughts are also often present and, indeed, suicide is one of the most common causes of death among those who die of the disorder. Studies of patients with bulimia nervosa have similarly shown depressive symptoms to be common. The diagnostic and clinical significance of these symptoms is not entirely clear. In the case of anorexia nervosa the depressive symptoms might be largely secondary to the profound weight loss. This view is supported by the fact that depressive symptoms arise in laboratory-induced starvation states, as well as by the finding that the mood of patients with anorexia nervosa tends to lift in response to weight gain. The depressive symptoms of bulimia nervosa might also be secondary to the eating disorder, in this case arising as a consequence of the distress caused by the loss of control over eating, the pervasive adverse impact of these patients' disturbed eating habits and extreme concerns about their body shape and weight, and shame and guilt over their secrecy and deceit. Two lines of clinical evidence support this view. First, the marked mood swings these patients experience closely track their degree of control over their eating. Second, an improvement in eating habits, brought about by therapeutic measures aimed solely at patients' disturbed eating, incidentally leads to a significant improvement in mood. If this account of the origins of the disturbances in mood in people with eating disorders were correct and complete, the depressive symptoms present in such people would not be of etiological importance and would be unlikely to have significant prognostic implications.

Patients with eating disorders also commonly display a number of anxiety symptoms. Thus patients with anorexia nervosa often show marked psychic and autonomic anxiety when presented with food, and they frequently exhibit a range of obsessional and compulsive symptoms. Similarly, it is common for patients with bulimia nervosa to report experiencing profound anxiety in social situations where they are presented with food or feel their body is exposed or under scrutiny. As with the depressive symptoms, these anxiety symptoms may all be secondary to the primary eating disorder; the fact that they tend to improve or disappear as a consequence of improvement in the eating disorder supports this view. Again, if this account were a complete explanation, the anxiety symptoms in people with eating disorders would not have etiological implications and would be of limited, if any, prognostic significance.

There is another, rather different view of these same symptoms in people with eating disorders. According to this account, these affective symptoms are features of separate psychiatric disorders that coexist with the eating disorder. This possibility raises three important scientific and clinical questions:

1. Does the rate of depressive and anxiety disorders in people with eating disorders (i.e., comorbidity) in fact exceed that expected by a chance association of these independent disorders?
2. If the comorbidity rate is higher than expected, how is this phenomenon to be explained?
3. What is the importance of comorbidity for the etiology, treatment, and prognosis of the eating disorder?

Each of these questions will be addressed in relation to depressive and anxiety disorders. However, it is first necessary to discuss certain problems in interpreting the findings of the research to date.

PROBLEMS IN INTERPRETING THE COMORBIDITY DATA

The information available on the rate of depressive and anxiety disorders in people with eating disorders all comes from studies of patients seeking treatment. This situation raises a number of problems. To determine whether the frequency of an observed association between two disorders exceeds that expected by chance, it is necessary to know the base rate for both disorders. These base rates can be obtained only from representative community samples, and their product (the chance rate of co-occurrence) can be meaningfully compared with the observed comorbidity rate only in a sample of cases drawn from a similarly representative epidemiological sample. There are two principal reasons comorbidity rates derived from patient samples will not stand in for rates derived from the community. First, the biases that are likely to operate in determining which cases in a given sample are referred for treatment make clinic data difficult to interpret. Second, unless all the people in a population whose symptoms satisfy a particular diagnosis are referred to a clinic (which is, of course, most improbable), comorbidity estimates derived from that clinic's data will inevitably be higher than the true rate (the so-called Berkson effect). This overestimation occurs because the chance of a person with two disorders being referred for treatment equals the combined likelihood of referral for each disorder separately.

Since there are no community-based studies of comorbidity among people with eating disorders, and since the problems inherent in interpreting data from clinic samples are substantial, the published research findings must be interpreted with considerable caution.

DEPRESSIVE DISORDERS

Rates

A number of studies of depressive disorder among patients with eating disorders have been conducted. In some, standardized psychiatric assessments have been used, and operational diagnostic criteria have been applied. The reported rates of depressive disorders vary markedly between studies, probably reflecting referral biases. However, in all studies a high rate has been found, and, averaging across studies, it appears that about half the people with eating disorders who are seen in clinics have a lifetime history of major depressive disorder. This rate is substantially higher than that found in nonpsychiatric controls. Studies that have examined the rate of depressive disorder among patients with the different subtypes of eating disorder have generally revealed a particular association with bulimic symptomatology. Thus in one German study, 15% of the group with restricting anorexia nervosa had such a history, compared with 46% of both those with the bulimic subtype of anorexia nervosa and those with bulimia nervosa. Other studies have produced broadly similar findings, except that in some the rate of depressive disorder has been found to be particularly high among those with the bulimic variant of anorexia nervosa.

Reasons

In studies where the temporal relationship between the eating disorder and the depressive disorder has been determined, in only a small minority of cases has the mood disturbance been found to precede the eating disorder. Furthermore, where patients in remission and patients in the acute phase of the disorder are compared, the latter show markedly higher rates of depressive disorder. Both these findings point strongly to the depressive disorder being a consequence of the primary eating disorder.

The family history data cast further light on the relationship between eating disorders and depressive disorders. Several studies of the lifetime prevalence of psychiatric disorders among the first-degree relatives of patients with eating disorders have revealed a higher than normal rate of major depressive disorder, especially among the mothers of patients. In some studies this association has been found only when the patient with the index eating disorder has concomitant depression, but this is not a consistent finding. Despite this raised rate of depressive disorder among relatives of patients with eating disorders, in the only study in which cross-prevalence has been established, no corresponding increase was found in the rate of eating disorders among the first-degree relatives of patients with depressive disorder. This finding suggests that the two disorders do not share a common pathogenesis and that the transmission of the two disorders is not fundamentally related.

Significance

There is scant support for the argument that eating disorders are a form of depressive disorder. The depressive symptoms that commonly occur in patients with eating disorders, and that frequently collectively meet the criteria for a diagnosis of major depressive disorder, mostly appear to arise as a secondary consequence of the eating disorder. This conclusion is supported by several lines of evidence. First, the depressive disorder rarely predates the onset of the eating disorder. Second, depressive disorder is not equally likely to occur across all types of eating disorder but instead is particularly prevalent in the bulimic variants where patients are invariably distressed by their lack of control over their eating and over the secondary adverse effects of the eating disorder. Third, depressive symptoms and depressive disorders are much more prevalent in the acute phase of eating disorders than in periods of remission. Fourth, the pattern of depressive symptoms in patients with eating disorders is quite different from the pattern in patients with major depressive disorder. Finally, while the higher rate of depressive disorder among the relatives of patients with eating disorders suggests the familial transmission of a vulnerability to mood disorders, the absence of a higher rate of eating disorders among the relatives of patients with depressive disorder runs counter to the claim of a common pathogenesis.

Clinically the presence of a major depressive disorder in patients with eating disorders does not generally carry prognostic significance. In clinical trials evaluating psychological treatments or the use of antidepressant medication, a current or past history of depressive disorder has not been found to be related to outcome. Despite this general finding, in a small minority of patients, where the depressive disorder does appear to be independent of the eating disorder, it may be necessary first to effect an improvement in mood before it is possible to treat the eating disorder.

ANXIETY AND OBSESSIVE–COMPULSIVE DISORDERS

Rates

As noted, a wide range of anxiety symptoms is common among patients with eating disorders. However only certain anxiety disorders appear to arise in these patients. Agoraphobia, simple phobias, and panic disorder appear to be no more common in patients with eating disorders than in nonpsychiatric controls. However, social phobia is common among eating disorder patients: In one American study it has been found to occur in one-fifth of patients with anorexia nervosa, ten times more frequently than among the controls; and in a German study of patients with bulimia nervosa, half the cases were found to fulfill the criteria for social phobia. A number of studies have also revealed a high rate of obsessive–compulsive disorder among patients with eating disorders. Thus in the American study of comorbidity referred to above, a lifetime rate of 16% was found, a value four times greater than among controls; and the German study mentioned revealed a similar high rate. The rate of obsessive–compulsive disorder appears to be roughly the same for all subtypes of eating disorders.

Reasons

The high rate of anxiety symptoms in patients with eating disorders is not surprising. The central features of the eating disorders are a fear of eating certain foods, a fear of social situations involving eating, and a fear of having one's body exposed to scrutiny. The anxiety symptoms that are essentially expressions of these fears are clearly not indicative of independent anxiety disorders. Indeed, the general improvement in mental state and the marked improvement in social functioning produced by the normalization of body weight and eating habits strongly supports the argument that these anxiety symptoms arise as a direct result of the primary eating disorder.

The basis of the association with obsessive–compulsive disorder is less clear. One possibility that has not received serious consideration is that the association is actually between depression and obsessive–compulsive symptomatology. It is well established that obsessional and compulsive symptoms are exacerbated by depression. It is therefore possible that these symptoms in patients with an eating disorder are secondary to their low mood rather than linked directly to their eating disorder. Unfortunately no study has been done to examine the rate of obsessional and compulsive symptoms and disorders in patients with eating disorders in terms of the presence of significant depression. Another possibility is that the obsessional and compulsive symptoms may be a consequence of the dieting and the resulting starvation state. This possibility is plausible, since it is known that obsessional symptoms, like depressive ones, arise as a consequence of dieting and starvation. This view of these symptoms as secondary phenomena gains support from the fact that in none of the studies conducted to date has it been found that the a raised rate of obsessive–compulsive disorder predated the onset of the eating disorder.

The argument that eating disorders may be a form of obsessive–compulsive disorder is being taken seriously in the literature, but the evidence is not compelling. Although the rate of obsessive–compulsive disorder does appear to be raised among patients with eating disorders, in fact the disorder occurs in a minority of patients and could therefore account for only a small proportion of cases. Furthermore, the two disorders run a very different course. Also, the response of patients with eating disorders to antidepressant medication used successfully to treat obsessive–compulsive disorder is generally poor (see Chapter 55). However, two findings do suggest there may be a relationship between these two classes of disorder. First, it has been found that patients with a diagnosis of obsessive–compulsive disorder exhibit a raised rate of disturbed eating habits and abnormal attitudes toward weight and shape, and possibly of frank eating disorders as well. Second, results of one study of the mothers of patients with anorexia nervosa showed that the lifetime prevalence of obsessive–compulsive disorder was higher than that of controls. These findings require replication. The rate of eating disorders among the mothers of patients with obsessive–compulsive disorder also remains to be established. Nevertheless these findings raise the possibility that patients with either disorder share some as yet undetermined vulnerability to both.

Significance

Although the anxiety symptoms and disorders present in people with eating disorders have not been studied in as much detail as these patients' depressive symptoms and disorders, their significance appears to be the same. There is no evidence that anxiety symptoms and disorders are important etiologically or prognostically. For a small minority of those with anorexia nervosa whose acute anxiety hinders progress in refeeding, some authorities advocate the judicious short-term use of anxiolytics. However, there are no grounds for using such medication in patients with bulimia nervosa.

CONCLUSION

The rate of depressive and anxiety disorders in patients with eating disorders has consistently been found to be high. However, without comorbidity data derived from community samples, the significance of such raised comorbidity rates is uncertain. In any event, a careful examination of the pattern of symptoms associated with the mental state of patients with eating disorders, the timing of the onset of comorbid disorders, the cross-prevalence of disorders in the family members of those with eating disorders and those with depressive and anxiety disorders, and the response to various treatments of patients who have or do not have a comorbid diagnosis point strongly to the conclusion that the depressive and anxiety symptoms and disorders in patients with eating disorders are generally secondary to the core disturbance in eating habits and ideation. Given that studies of clinic populations inevitably overestimate the significance of comorbidity, it is most improbable this general conclusion will require revision once the necessary community studies have been conducted.

FURTHER READING

Cooper, P. J., & Fairburn, C. G. (1986). The depressive symptoms of bulimia nervosa. *British Journal of Psychiatry, 148,* 268–274. A statistical comparison of the mental-state profiles of a group of patients with bulimia nervosa and a group of patients with major depressive disorder.

Halmi, K., Eckert, E., Marchi, P., Sampugnaro, V., Apple, R., & Cohen, J. (1991). Comorbidity of psychiatric diagnoses in anorexia nervosa. *Archives of General Psychiatry, 48,* 712–718. An examination of comorbidity in a follow-up study of a large sample of patients who had suffered from anorexia nervosa. The mental-state histories of first-degree relatives were also examined.

Hsu, L. K. G., Kaye, W., & Weltzin, T. (1993). Are eating disorders related to obsessive compulsive disorders? *International Journal of Eating Disorders, 14,* 305–318. A review of six lines of evidence supporting the idea that eating disorders may be related to obsessive–compulsive disorder.

Laessle, R. G., Kittl, S., Fichter, M. M., Wittchen, H., & Pirke, K. M. (1987). Major affective disorder in anorexia nervosa and bulimia: A descriptive study. *British Journal of Psychiatry, 151,* 785–789. An examination of the rate and timing of depressive and anxiety disorders in patients with restricting anorexia nervosa, bulimic anorexia nervosa, and bulimia nervosa.

Steere, J., Butler, G., & Cooper, P. J. (1990). The anxiety symptoms of bulimia nervosa. *International Journal of Eating Disorders, 9,* 293–301. A statistical comparison of the mental-state profiles of a group of patients with bulimia nervosa and a group of patients with generalized anxiety disorder.

Strober, M., Lampert, C., Morrell, W., Burroughs, J., & Jacobs, C. (1990). A controlled family study of anorexia nervosa: Evidence of familial aggregation and lack of shared transmission with affective disorder. *International Journal of Eating Disorders, 9,* 239–253. A study of the lifetime prevalence rates of eating disorders and affective disorders in the first-degree relatives of patients with anorexia nervosa and in two control groups.

Swift, W. J., Andrew, D., & Barklage, N. E. (1986). The relationship between affective disorder and eating disorders: A review of the literature. *American Journal of Psychiatry, 143,* 290–299. A review of six lines of enquiry into the relationship between affective disorder and eating disorder.

• 29 •

EATING DISORDERS AND ADDICTIVE DISORDERS

G. Terence Wilson

The binge eating that is a prominent feature of many eating disorders shares many similarities with alcohol and drug abuse. People with binge eating and alcohol or drug problems report strong urges, or "cravings," to consume the substance. Both groups experience a sense of loss of control over their consummatory behavior. Both report using the substance to regulate their emotional state and cope with stress. Both become preoccupied with the substance and make repeated attempts to stop. Both may deny the gravity of their problem or seek to keep it secret, and both may suffer negative psychological and social consequences as a result of their behavior. Many patients experience both eating and alcohol or drug problems, sometimes simultaneously. As a result of these similarities, binge eating and eating disorders have been viewed as a form of chemical dependency or addiction.

The addiction model of binge eating and eating disorders is exemplified by the 12-Step approach of Overeaters Anonymous, modeled as it is after Alcoholics Anonymous. Among the assumptions of this approach are the following: that some individuals are biologically vulnerable to certain foods (e.g., sugar) that can cause chemical dependence; that treatment is predicated on abstaining from these toxic foods (chemicals); that the eating disorder is a progressive illness that can never be eliminated but only managed as a lifelong problem; and that since they are essentially different expressions of the same underlying problem, the treatment of binge eating and eating disorders should not differ fundamentally from that of alcohol or drug dependence.

The similarities between binge eating and alcohol and drug abuse seem obvious, but they are superficial and may obscure what are fundamentally important differences.

DIFFERENCES BETWEEN EATING DISORDERS AND ADDICTIVE DISORDERS

It is widely accepted that the defining characteristics of chemical dependency or addiction are tolerance, physical dependence and withdrawal, craving, and loss of control over use of the substance.

None of these features define the nature of binge eating in cases of bulimia nervosa. Consider the notion of craving. If defined as an "irresistible desire," as in the disease theory of alcoholism that informs the 12-Step model of eating disorders, the concept is unsupported. There is no evidence that people with eating disorders experience craving as a direct biochemical result of consuming a particular "toxic" nutrient. In one study, bulimia nervosa patients and controls consumed a 500-milliliter drink containing either 1,200 kilocalories of carbohydrates or an inactive placebo mixture with few calories. The results showed little carbohydrate-specific effect on subjective responses in either group. What effects there were tended to be negative and inconsistent with the notion that binge eating is mediated by carbohydrate craving. Ratings of mood were not improved by the consumption of the carbohydrate drink. In fact, the rating for "good mood" was lower in the patients following carbohydrate consumption. Measures of prolactin, growth hormone, and cortisol levels failed to indicate any carbohydrate-mediated stimulation in either group.

Other well-controlled studies show that patients with bulimia nervosa do not "crave" sugar or even preferentially consume simple carbohydrates during binge eating. When the binge eating and other eating episodes of bulimia nervosa patients and that of normal controls are studied directly in the laboratory, macronutrient selection is found to be similar for both groups. The most striking difference between the binge meals of bulimic patients and the "normal" meals of controls is the amount of food consumed, not its macronutrient composition. This suggests that the essential appetitive abnormality of bulimia nervosa is in the control of amount of food consumed, not in the craving for a specific macronutrient. The same holds true for obese binge eaters.

The concept of loss of control is the defining feature of the classical disease theory of alcoholism. The notion was that the ingestion of alcohol triggers an uncontrollable biochemical reaction to continue drinking that overrides all reason or choice. Alcoholics cannot stop drinking even though they recognize its destructive consequences. Hence the phrase, "One drink away from a drunk." Binge eaters often speak of being "one bite away from a binge."

Experimental research, however, has failed to support this commonly held assumption. In alcohol dependence it is clear that self-regulation of alcohol consumption is critically influenced by a range of social learning processes, including operative reinforcement contingencies and the person's expectations regarding its effects. Although the severity of physical dependence might interact with psychosocial contingencies in regulating drinking, ingestion of more alcohol alone does not necessarily trigger uncontrollable drinking. Although sparse, the data indicate that bulimia nervosa patients do not always necessarily lose control and binge despite violating their dietary restraint by ingesting a high-sugar/high-fat food, especially if they know they cannot purge.

One failing of the addiction model is that it does not discriminate among the different eating disorders and even obesity, which is not a psychiatric disorder at all. It is clear that obese binge eaters differ from normal-weight bulimia nervosa patients in several important respects (see Chapter 78). For example, the former do not report the same dietary restrictions outside of binges, and many appear to have begun binge eating prior to dieting. In bulimia nervosa patients, dieting virtually always precedes binge eating (see Chapter 35). Thus the binge eating of obese patients seems to more closely resemble the type of unstructured and uncontrolled consumption exhibited by substance abusers, and the choice of obese patients would be a more logical choice than bulimia nervosa patients in exploring putative common mechanisms.

The addiction model of eating disorders is an instance of the seemingly endless extension of the addiction concept to explain any form of habitual behavior, including work, sex, and watching television. For example, the behavior of restricting anorexics, who do not binge, is explained away by saying that they are "addicted" to starvation. The paradox of how a person can be simultaneously addicted to both the use and the nonuse of a substance—as in the case of the bulimic anorexic—underscores how the concept of addiction is debased in a variety of superficial and misleading tropes.

THERAPEUTIC IMPLICATIONS OF THE ADDICTION MODEL

The critical analysis of the addiction model of eating disorders is not simply a matter of semantics. This type of thinking has significant implications for the treatment of large numbers of people. The addiction model prescribes unremitting dietary restraint, featuring absolute avoidance of particular foods (e.g., sugar), highly structured eating patterns, a sense of powerlessness, and reinforcement of a dichotomous thinking pattern. These prescriptions conflict with much of what is now known about the development, maintenance, and modification of binge eating in cases of bulimia nervosa. Those who have attempted to make the 12-Step approach more compatible with the empirical evidence on eating disorders have sought to redefine such core principles as abstinence from particular foods, recasting it as abstention from activities such as binge eating and overexercising; and affirmation of powerlessness, newly interpreting it as the acceptance of body weight and shape. These attempts simply erode the distinctiveness of the 12-Step approach without adding substantively to existing data-based models. More generic features of 12-Step groups, such as social support, are undoubtedly valuable but not unique to this approach.

In contrast to the addiction model, cognitive-behavioral therapy is designed to reduce dietary restraint, attenuate abnormal attitudes about the importance of body weight and shape, and alter all-or-nothing thinking concerning eating and personal control (see Chapters 57 and 60). Whereas most bulimia nervosa patients complain they have no control over their eating and that they eat too much, the data show they actually eat too little aside from their binge eating episodes. Both the physiological sequelae of caloric deprivation and the psychological costs of self-denial must be remedied by the establishment of regular, nutritionally balanced meals and the introduction of previously avoided foods into a more flexible diet.

Aside from anecdotal testimony, there is no evidence to support the effectiveness of 12-Step treatment approach for binge eating. Unlike the 12-Step approach, cognitive-behavioral therapy has been extensively evaluated in controlled clinical trials (see Chapter 60). The findings are robust. This therapy produces broad and lasting reductions in binge eating and the other hallmark symptoms of bulimia nervosa. Initial results similarly indicate that cognitive-behavioral therapy is effective in treating binge eating in the obese. The consistent success of methods derived from a model so at odds with the addiction approach must call into question the fundamental premises of the latter.

Another implication of the addiction model embodied in many 12-Step programs is that treatment must focus directly on the restructuring of eating habits. Psychological therapy is not encouraged other than to address related personal issues. This dismissal of the role of psychological therapy is refuted by the documented success of interpersonal psychotherapy (see Chapter 60). In interpersonal psychotherapy there is no focus whatsoever on the patient's eating habits or weight, only on past and present interpersonal issues in the person's life. Yet interpersonal psychotherapy has been shown to be as effective as cognitive-behavioral therapy in reducing binge eating in normal-weight bulimia nervosa patients.

DO EATING DISORDERS AND SUBSTANCE ABUSE DISORDERS CO-OCCUR?

Eating disorders may not be a form of psychoactive substance abuse, but the two disorders have been closely linked in the literature.

Substance Abuse in Individuals with Eating Disorders

Studies of patients with either anorexia nervosa or bulimia consistently reveal significantly higher rates of past and present substance abuse than would be expected in the general population. However, evidence of an association between binge eating and substance abuse in obese patients is mixed at best, raising the question of which specific features of eating disorders are linked with substance abuse. For example, it has been found that the symptoms of body image concerns and dietary restraint are more strongly associated with alcohol abuse than with binge eating in female high school students.

The comorbidity between the two disorders might simply reflect Berkson's bias, namely, the increased tendency for patients with more than one problem to find their way into treatment. There is evidence that only a minority of individuals with an eating disorder enter treatment, and it is plausible that those with additional disorders are more likely to seek treatment and are therefore more likely to be represented in clinical samples. The only way to establish an inherent association between the two disorders is to study representative community samples. Two studies of this kind have yielded mixed results. An analysis of the comorbidity of alcoholism and other psychiatric disorders using Epidemiological Catchment Area data revealed no association between alcohol abuse and anorexia nervosa. The prevalence of bulimia nervosa was not assessed. A second study, of over 2,000 female twins from the Virginia population-based twin register, showed a significant lifetime association between bulimia nervosa and alcoholism.

Even if it is assumed that an association exists between eating disorders and substance abuse, there is the question of whether this association is a specific one. Rates of substance abuse tend to be elevated for patients with psychiatric disorders in general, indicating that patients with psychological problems are more likely to abuse alcohol or drugs. Moreover, there are data showing that the comorbidity of anxiety and mood disorders with anorexia nervosa and bulimia nervosa is higher than that of substance abuse disorder and eating disorders (see Chapter 28).

Eating Disorders in Individuals with Substance Abuse

If eating disorders and substance abuse do covary, there should be a complementary higher prevalence of eating disorders in people with substance abuse disorders. This is precisely what has been found in studies of clinical samples of alcoholics. The largest such study, from Japan, comprised a sample of 3,592 patients (336 women). Fully 11% of the women, but only 0.2% of men, were diagnosed as having had an eating disorder. The prevalence in women under 30 years of age was 72%, roughly 24 times the prevalence in the general Japanese population. Bulimia nervosa was the most common problem. Since all the studies to date have used patient samples, it is unknown whether this comorbidity is confined to this subgroup of substance abusers. Also, it is unclear whether this association is specific. It may be that the rate of eating disorders is comparable in other psychiatric disorders, such as anxiety disorders.

Three other findings from studies of substance abusers are important. One is that eating disorders appear to go largely undetected by treatment staff. A second is that eating disorders seem to precede the development of substance abuse, leading some investigators to conclude that an eating disorder is a risk factor for alcohol dependence. This temporal pattern is difficult to interpret, however, because the age of onset of eating disorders is typically younger than that of alcohol abuse. Nevertheless a consistent finding in different countries is that alcohol-dependent patients with an eating disorder are younger than those without an eating disorder. This finding suggests that eating disorders may significantly influence the course of alcohol abuse and dependence.

Family Studies

Research has typically shown higher than expected rates of alcohol and drug problems in family members of patients with anorexia and bulimia nervosa. However, this association appears to be nonspecific, because the prevalence of alcohol problems in the families of patients with eating disorders seems to be no higher than in families of patients with other psychiatric disorders, such as anxiety. Furthermore, the family studies done to date have included as probands eating-disorder patients seeking treatment. Studies of representative individuals drawn from the community are needed.

MECHANISMS LINKING EATING DISORDERS AND SUBSTANCE ABUSE

Several mechanisms have been proposed to explain the putative relationship between the two sets of disorders. One is that of a common genetic/biological diathesis, although the nature of such a vulnerability has yet to be specified. Another explanation of why an eating disorder might contribute to the development of an alcohol problem is the reciprocal reinforcement hypothesis. In animals, food deprivation reliably increases the self-administration of alcohol, and there is evidence of a change in the central reward mechanisms, in addition to specific effects on operant behavior. Humans, too, may increase their drug intake when deprived of food. Both anorexic patients who are binge eaters and bulimia nervosa patients significantly restrict their caloric intake between binges. This self-imposed dietary restriction might have two major effects: first, it might increase the reward value of highly palatable, high-fat "binge" foods and prompt binge eating; and second, it might increase the reward value of alternative reinforcers such as psychoactive substances, thereby leading to their abuse.

Several testable predictions follow from the latter hypothesis. One is that obese binge eaters who do not show the extreme dietary restraint that characterizes anorexia and bulimia nervosa would be less likely to engage in complementary substance abuse. A problem with this analysis is that it does not explain why it is predominantly the bulimic and not the restrictor anorexia nervosa patients who abuse alcohol or drugs. Both groups of patients severely restrict food intake, but only one turns to alternative consummatory reinforcers. Hence something more than dietary restriction is required to explain comorbid substance abuse. In addition, since nonbulimic restrained eaters often restrict their food intake as much as bulimia nervosa patients do, they should abuse other substances as much as binge eaters do. Another prediction is that in successfully treated bulimia nervosa patients, the elimination of binge eating and significantly reduced dietary restraint should preempt substance abuse. The broad-based and lasting effects of successful treatment, showing no symptom substitution, are consistent with this view.

A third hypothesis is that both binge eating and substance abuse are different expressions of an underlying impulse-control disorder. This hypothesis, in contrast to the reciprocal reinforcement view, predicts that the rates of substance abuse should be as high in obese binge eaters as in bulimia nervosa patients. Obese binge eaters are characterized by high levels of emotional, or "impulsive," eating. It also predicts that the removal of the eating problem should increase the probability of substance abuse. The absence of any documented symptom substitution in successfully treated bulimia nervosa patients is inconsistent with this hypothesis.

FURTHER READING

Fairburn, C. G., Agras, W. S., & Wilson, G. T. (1992). The research on the treatment of bulimia nervosa: Practical and theoretical implications. In G. H. Anderson & S. H. Kennedy (Eds.), *The biology of feast and famine: Relevance to eating disorders* (pp. 317–340). New York: Academic Press. A comprehensive review of the research on the treatment of bulimia nervosa.

Fingarette, H. (1988). *Heavy drinking: The myth of alcoholism as a disease.* Berkeley: University of California Press. A critical analysis of the disease theory of alcoholism.

Higuchi, S., Suzuki, K., Yamada, K., Parish, K., & Kono, H. (1993). Alcoholics with eating disorders: Prevalence and clinical course. *British Journal of Psychiatry, 162,* 403–406. The largest study of the prevalence of eating disorders in alcoholic patients.

Kassett, J. A., Elliot, M. P. H., Gershon, S., Maxwell, M. E., Guroff, J. J., Kazuba, D. M., Smith, A. L., Brandt, H. A., & Jimerson, D. C. (1989). Psychiatric disorders in the first-degree relatives of probands with bulimia nervosa. *American Journal of Psychiatry, 146,* 1468–1471. A study of psychiatric disorders in the relatives of patients with bulimia nervosa.

Kendler, K. S., MacLean, C., Neale, M., Kessler, R., Heath, A., & Eaves, L. (1991). The genetic epidemiology of bulimia nervosa. *American Journal of Psychiatry, 148,* 1627–1637. A study of the genetic epidemiology of bulimia nervosa.

Krahn, D. D. (1991). The relationship of eating disorders and substance abuse. *Journal of Substance Abuse, 3,* 239–254. A review of the mechanisms that might explain the association between eating disorders and addictive disorders

Turner, M. St J., Foggo, M., Bennie, J., Carroll, S., Dick, H., & Goodwin, G. M. (1991). Psychological, hormonal and biochemical changes following carbohydrate bingeing: A placebo controlled study in bulimia nervosa and matched controls. *Psychological Medicine, 21,* 123–133. An experimental study of the "carbohydrate-craving" hypothesis.

Walsh, B. T. (1993). Binge eating in bulimia nervosa. In C. G. Fairburn & G. T. Wilson (Eds.), *Binge eating: Nature, assessment and treatment* (pp. 37–49). New York: Guilford Press. A review of laboratory studies of the eating behavior of patients with bulimia nervosa.

Wilson, G. T. (1993). Binge eating and addictive disorders. In C. G. Fairburn & G. T. Wilson (Eds.), *Binge eating: Nature, assessment and treatment* (pp. 97–120). New York: Guilford Press. A critical review of the literature on the association between eating disorders and addictive disorders.

Yanovski, S. Z. (1993). Binge eating disorder: Current knowledge and future directions. *Obesity Research, 1,* 306–324. A comprehensive review of the literature on binge-eating disorder.

· 30 ·

PERSONALITY AND EATING DISORDERS

Stephen A. Wonderlich

For many years, personality constructs have been considered important factors in the development and maintenance of eating disorders. Although empirical research on the relationship of personality and eating disorders has been methodologically limited, some themes or tentative conclusions are emerging. After commenting briefly on conceptual and methodological issues regarding the study of personality and eating disorders, I will summarize the empirical literature addressing personality traits and disorders in anorexic and bulimic subjects, examine the clinical relevance of personality variables for the eating disorders, and finally comment briefly on the treatment of personality disorders in eating disordered individuals.

CONCEPTUAL AND METHODOLOGICAL ISSUES

The conceptual relationship between personality and the eating disorders is very complex. Personality disturbance may be considered a predisposing factor, a complication or scar, a pathoplastic influence, or a distinct entity that is unrelated to the eating disturbance. Unfortunately, the absence of prospective studies has largely left the nature of this relationship unclear. Furthermore, methodological issues such as the effects of starvation or mood-related states on personality assessment, age-inappropriate measures of personality in adolescence, a general reliance on small clinical samples, and continued controversy over the best means of assessing personality (self-report vs. structured interview vs. outside informant) further complicate these studies and limit the strength of the conclusions that can be drawn from this literature.

PERSONALITY AND ANOREXIA NERVOSA

Traits

Clinical reports, psychometric studies, and family informant studies converge to depict the premorbid personality of the restricting anorexic as obsessional, socially inhibited, compliant, and emotionally restrained. However, obsessionality, introversion, and dependency may be significantly exacerbated by starvation states, a finding that potentially confounds the relationship of enduring personality variables with the acute effects of weight loss. Consequently, a recent finding that the personalities of *long-term recovered* anorexics were characterized by elevated levels of restraint, risk avoidance, and conformity provides relatively strong support for the idea that these personality factors are fundamentally related to anorexia nervosa. Yet even these findings may be contaminated by the long-term "scarring" effects of anorexia nervosa and do not necessarily have etiologic significance.

The convergence of these studies has led some to suggest that constitutionally determined temperament factors have a significant role in the development of anorexia nervosa. Strober has applied Cloninger's psychobiological model of personality in an organismically focused developmental model of anorexia. He suggests that the restricting anorexic typically displays the following configuration of personality traits, all of which are suggested to be quite heritable: low novelty seeking, high harm avoidance, and high reward dependance. There has been modest support for the application of this model to anorexia nervosa, but Cloninger's model has been criticized on both methodological and conceptual grounds. Interestingly, he has recently developed a new personality model with a fourth temperament dimension (i.e., persistence) and three character dimensions (i.e., self-directedness, cooperativeness, and self-transcendence). In particular, these new concepts of persistence and self-directedness seem relevant to the clinical presentation of anorexia nervosa, and future studies of the application of Cloninger's model to anorexia nervosa should examine this new, more comprehensive model of personality.

In spite of these prototypic personality features of the anorexic, variability in personality functioning among anorexics is also considerable. An early study identified three personality types among anorexics: (1) a mildly obsessional style without severe personality disturbance; (2) a more severely neurotic, socially avoidant type; and (3) a more seriously impaired type with greater impulsivity, dysphoria, and low frustration tolerance. Perhaps the most important subtype distinction has been the separation of bulimic anorexia nervosa from the restricting form. While bulimic anorexics appear to share compliant perfectionism with restrictors, they tend to be more impulsive, emotionally distraught, extraverted, and sexually active.

Personality Disorders

The DSM-IV personality disorder criteria continue to be a source of debate regarding issues such as categorical versus dimensional assessment, the actual number of personality disorders, and inadequate diagnostic reliability. Also, self-report measures of personality disorders are generally thought to be overly sensitive and produce high rates of false-positive diagnoses.

In spite of these and other methodological difficulties already mentioned, the study of personality disorders in patients with anorexia nervosa generally parallels the trait findings. When assessed postmorbidly, 23% to 80% of anorexic patients receive a personality disorder diagnosis. Again consistent with personality trait studies, bulimic anorexics tend to display more pervasive personality disturbance, with a greater likelihood of receiving a cluster B (dramatic–erratic) personality diagnosis, than restrictors, who tend to receive cluster C (anxious–fearful) diagnoses. Cluster A (odd–eccentric) personality disorder diagnoses are rare for anorexia nervosa, unless the assessment relies on self-report measures, in which case such diagnoses are occasionally made.

PERSONALITY AND BULIMIA NERVOSA

Traits

Although bulimic individuals are frequently considered to be of "normal" weight, they actually may be maintaining a weight below their genetically influenced ideal weight. Consequently, as with anorexics, the effects of starvation-related states may influence personality. Nonetheless certain findings have emerged from the study of personality traits in symptomatic bulimics. A variety of personality measures have been employed and converge to depict the typical bulimic individual as impulsive, interpersonally sensitive, and low in self-esteem. Studies using the Minnesota Multiphasic Personality Inventory (MMPI) repeatedly produce a personality profile associated with poor impulse control, chronic depression, acting-out behavior, and low frustration tolerance. However, MMPI studies have also revealed substantial variability in personality functioning, with a considerable minority of subjects scoring within normal limits on all scales and others producing results indicative of much more anxiety, rumination, and social withdrawal.

A recent study, which attempted to control statistically for state effects, examined the hypothesis that bulimia nervosa is associated with excessive impulsivity. Although bulimics appeared more rebellious than controls or anorexics, they did not display predicted elevations in impulsivity or novelty seeking. And although bulimic individuals exhibit impulsive behaviors, this trait may not translate into heightened impulsivity as defined by these measures. Clearly, further studies are needed to clarify the relation between the trait of impulsivity and bulimia.

Personality Disorders

Estimates of the prevalence of diagnoses of personality disorder in samples of bulimic patients have ranged from 21% to 77%, most often occurring in the dramatic–erratic cluster (cluster B) of DSM-IV. As with anorexia nervosa, variability within the bulimic category remains evident, with some studies reporting high rates of other personality disorders, such as avoidant or obsessive–compulsive.

The relationship of all eating-disorder subtypes, but particularly bulimia nervosa, to borderline personality disorder (BPD) has been a source of considerable debate and disparate findings. Rates of BPD in sample populations of bulimics have ranged from 2% to 47% and appear substantially influenced by subject and instrumentation variability across studies, as well as by conceptual disagreement about the diagnostic status of BPD. Some argue that BPD is rare in bulimic patients and that depression is often misdiagnosed as BPD. Others suggest that bulimia is conceptually confounded with BPD and that bulimic symptoms may mimic BPD. In support of this idea are data indicating a decrease in BPD with short-term, symptom-focused interventions, a change that should not occur if BPD was independent of the effect of acute symptoms.

At present it appears that some acutely symptomatic bulimic individuals show an unstable "phenocopy" of BPD that is highly state related and resolves with treatment. Others display a more prototypic BPD, and their bulimic symptoms are part of a larger pattern of chronic behavioral and emotional dysregulation.

CONCURRENT PERSONALITY DISTURBANCE AND
EATING DISORDER SYMPTOMS: CLINICAL IMPLICATIONS

Clinical Features

Generally, eating disordered individuals with comorbid personality disorders or low-level ego functions do not differ from those without personality disturbances in their weight histories or bingeing, although there is some evidence that personality disorder is associated with a longer duration of illness and elevated rates of purging. The presence of a personality disorder in eating disordered individuals, particularly BPD, has been related to a consistent set of concurrent problems, such as increased affective disturbance, suicidal and parasuicidal gestures, family dysfunction, and the likelihood of being hospitalized. Most of these associated problems do not appear related to the severity of eating-related symptoms, but they do show a strong relationship to depression.

Course

There have been very few follow-up studies to examine the influence of personality on the course of eating disorders. There is some evidence that at 1-year follow-up, personality disorder is associated with a slower recovery and with the likelihood of still meeting the diagnostic criteria for bulimia nervosa. Results of studies in which ego functioning was examined indicate that borderline-level functioning predicts poor outcome for eating symptoms at 1 year but not at 2 years. Three- and 5-year follow-up data also indicate that borderline personality disorder is associated with poor outcome in eating-related symptomatology.

Treatment Response

A small series of studies has examined the influence of personality on the response to explicit treatment protocols for bulimia nervosa. Equivalent studies of anorexic patients have not been conducted. Generally results of these studies indicate that the presence of personality disorders, particularly in cluster B (dramatic–erratic), in patients with bulimia nervosa inhibits their engagement in psychotherapeutic treatment (i.e., cognitive behavior therapy) and reduces the effectiveness of such interventions. Interestingly, while one study indicated that the presence of a high cluster B personality disturbance in bulimics predicted a favorable response to desipramine, another found the opposite relationship.

TREATING PATIENTS WITH EATING DISORDERS
AND CONCURRENT PERSONALITY DISORDERS

Although there is evidence that treatments for eating disorders may influence the symptoms of personality disorder, there is also evidence that a subgroup of eating disordered patients display more enduring personality disorders that are associated with a poor prognosis for the eating disorder. Clinical speculation has been that the treatment of the eating disordered patient who also has a severe personality disorder should include interventions that address the pervasive interpersonal disturbances that characterize this subgroup. However, in no formal treatment outcome studies have the traditional treatment of eating disorders been integrated with interventions deliberately targeting symptoms of personality disorder. In one uncontrolled study, the results indicated that bulimic patients who had a concurrent personality disorder responded more completely when treatment sessions were more frequent.

The frequent co-occurrence of personality disorders and eating disorders clearly indicates that treatment protocols that address such comorbidity need to be developed. Several recent approaches to the treatment of personality disorders, along with traditional techniques, should be carefully considered in the development of such protocols. For example, recent interpersonally oriented models of personality disorders (such as that devised by Benjamin) provide new approaches to treating relationship disturbances, ranging from the marked instability of the dramatic–erratic disorders to the chronic submission and passivity often seen in the anxious–fearful personality disorders. Also, new cognitive models of the personality disorders (e.g., those of Beck and Linehan) provide highly structured treatment techniques for addressing cognitive vulnerabilities that are specific to each personality disorder. Linehan's dialectical behavior therapy, particularly her emphasis on dialectical reasoning, may be effective in treating the frequently encountered all-or-nothing thinking styles posited as characterizing both borderline disturbances and the eating disorders. Furthermore, psychodynamic models (e.g., those of Kernberg and Adler) have emphasized the significance of the therapeutic relationship in the treatment of personality disorders, an issue that should be carefully considered in the treatment of patients with these disorders. Finally, symptom-focused pharmacotherapy continues to be potentially beneficial in the management of the extreme affective or cognitive reactions frequently encountered in individuals with personality disorders.

FURTHER READING

Beck, A. T., Freeman, A., & Associates. (1990). *Cognitive therapy of personality disorders*. New York: Guilford Press. An excellent introduction to specific cognitive treatment strategies for each DSM-III-R personality disorder.

Benjamin, L. S. (1993). *Interpersonal diagnosis and treatment of personality disorders*. New York: Guilford Press. Provides a clinically useful application of Benjamin's Structural Analysis of Social Behavior to the DSM-III-R personality disorders.

Dennis, A. B., & Sansone, R. A. (1990). The clinical stages of treatment for the eating disorder patient with borderline personality. In C. Johnson (Ed.), *Psychodynamic treatment for anorexia and bulimia nervosa* (pp. 128–164). New York: Guilford Press. Integrates psychodynamic and cognitive treatment techniques in a very practical approach to treating the eating disordered individual who has a concurrent borderline personality disorder.

Garfinkel, P. E., & Gallop, R. (1992). Eating disorders and borderline personality disorder. In D. Silver & M. Rosenbluth (Eds.), *Handbook of borderline disorders* (pp. 579–598). Madison, CT: International Universities Press. In addition to an overview of the empirical literature regarding eating disorders and personality disorders, Garfinkel and Gallop provide a brief and succinct outline of inpatient and outpatient issues in the treatment of such individuals.

Linehan, M. M. (1993). *Cognitive-behavioral treatment of borderline personality disorder*. New York: Guilford Press. Provides a detailed overview of dialectical behavior therapy, which has recently been shown to effectively reduce suicidal and parasuicidal behavior in borderline individuals.

Strober, M. (1991). Disorders of the self in anorexia nervosa: An organismic–developmental paradigm. In C. Johnson (Ed.), *Psychodynamic treatment of anorexia nervosa and bulimia nervosa* (pp. 354–373). New York: Guilford Press. An original and thoughtful integration of theories regarding temperament, adolescent development, and psychoanalytically informed self psychology.

Swift, W. J., & Wonderlich, S. A. (1988). Personality factors and disorders in eating disorders: Traits, disorders, and structures. In D.M. Garner & P.E. Garfinkel (Eds.), *Diagnostic issues in anorexia nervosa and bulimia nervosa* (pp. 112–164). New York: Brunner/Mazel. Provides the first comprehensive overview of personality traits and disorders in the eating disorders, as well as a psychodynamically informed approach to treatment.

Vitousek, K., & Manke, F. (1994). Personality variables and diagnoses in anorexia nervosa and bulimia nervosa. *Journal of Abnormal Psychology, 103,* 137–148. The most recent and comprehensive overview of the relationship of both personality traits and disorders in anorexia and bulimia nervosa.

Wonderlich, S. (1992). Relationship of family and personality factors in bulimia. In J. H. Crowther, D. L. Tannenbaum, S.E. Hobfoll, & M.A.P. Stephens (Eds.), *The etiology of bulimia nervosa: The individual and familial context* (pp. 103–126). Washington, DC: Hemisphere Publishing. Examines how personality and family variables may interact as risk factors for bulimia nervosa.

Wonderlich, S. A., & Mitchell, J. E. (1992). Eating disorders and personality disorders. In J. Yager, H. E. Gwirtsman, & C. K. Edelstein (Eds.), *Special problems in managing eating disorders* (pp. 51–86). Washington, DC: American Psychiatric Press. A comprehensive overview of the relationship of personality disorders and eating disorders, as well as the clinical relevance of this relationship.

• 31 •

EATING DISORDERS IN MALES

Arnold E. Andersen

Eating disorders present an example of a disorder in which there is a much lower prevalence in males than in females. Among the few examples of differential prevalence in the opposite direction are pedophilia and perhaps antisocial personality disorder. Despite being mentioned among the first case presentations in the English language 300 years ago, males with eating disorders have been relatively ignored, neglected, dismissed because of statistical infrequency, or legislated out of existence by theoretical dogma. There is a need to improve our recognition of eating disorders in males and to provide more adequate treatment. In addition, the category of males with eating disorders presents intellectual challenges regarding the etiology and mechanism for this gender-divergent abnormality of human motivated behavior.

FACTS, WORKING PROBABILITIES, AND UNCERTAINTIES

The basic body of information concerning males with eating disorders will be presented in three overlapping but relatively distinct categories: fairly well-established facts based on sound scientific studies; reasonable approximations to fact based on clinical experience; and areas of frank uncertainty. Since we do not know how much we do not know, the "facts" of one generation may turn out, with later, newer methods of research, to be less secure than we had hoped. It is possible and useful to divide the available information into these three roughly hewn categories.

Generally Accepted Facts Based on Scientific Studies

Epidemiology

Males with eating disorders have been reported since 1689. Recent community-based epidemiological studies have established a ratio of one male case to ten females, a ratio comparable to that reported by large, clinic-based studies. Some would put the proportion at 5% of cases or as high as 15%.

There is clearly less general sociocultural reinforcement for slimness and dieting for males than for females, with only 10% as many articles and advertisements promoting dieting in magazines read by young males as compared with those read by young females. Beginning as early as lower elementary school, boys are less likely than young girls to consider themselves overweight or in need of dieting. Adult males tend to describe themselves as overweight only at weights 15% higher, in relation to ideal body weight, than the weight at which females believe they are overweight. Women feel thin, generally, only when below 90% of ideal body weight, whereas men rate themselves as thin until they are as high as 105% of an ideal body weight.

Males are about equally divided between those who wish to increase weight and those who wish to decrease weight; whereas in women, the desire for weight loss predominates. While men are about as equally concerned with shape as with weight, women are predominantly concerned with weight.

In both men and women the desire to lose weight tends to be concentrated among specific subgroups. Males who wrestle, for example, correspond roughly to women who undertake ballet training; both groups show a disproportionate increase in eating disorders, seven to ten times normal. The desire to lose weight is more common in males with a homosexual orientation, but in these men it is still less than in heterosexual females. While the average frequency of homosexual orientation in males with eating disorders is approximately 21%, homosexual males still represent a distinct minority of cases.

Males who develop eating disorders are more likely to have experienced actual, medically defined, premorbid obesity than have females. The general principle holds that most women who diet *feel* fat, while slightly more than half of the males who diet *are* medically obese to some degree. Interestingly, in young preadolescents with eating disorders, the sex ratio of cases appears to be approximately equal (see Chapter 32).

Natural History and Diagnosis

Males who develop eating disorders can be generally divided into three groups: those in whom the onset was preadolescent, those in whom it was adolescent or young adult, and those in whom it was adult. Dieting in males is often related to participation in sports, past obesity, gender identity conflicts, and the avoidance of feared medical illness.

The diagnostic criteria for males with anorexia are similar to those for females (see Chapter 23), requiring self-induced starvation and a morbid fear of fatness/relentless pursuit of thinness, but different in the specific reproductive hormone abnormality involved. Males with anorexia nervosa are characterized by lower testosterone levels, causing decreased sexual drive and performance, with changes occurring in a gradual manner rather than the more abrupt changes seen in females in the form of sudden cessation of menses. The diagnosis of bulimia is gender independent. All in all, doctors are less likely to think of making a diagnosis of eating disorders in males than females.

Treatment

The basic principles of treatment of males and females with eating disorders are similar: restoring normal weight, interrupting abnormal behaviors such as binge and purge activity, treating comorbid conditions, persuading patients to think differently about the value of weight loss or shape change; and preparing them for reintegration into their respective sociocultural groups after treatment. Males with eating disorders commonly have much the same comorbid conditions as do females, especially mood disorders, personality disorders, and some medical conditions such as osteoporosis, even though the last occurs less frequently in males than in females. The conditions requiring hospitalization are independent of gender.

The restoration of a healthy weight in males is associated with an increased testosterone level in 80% to 90% of cases, but in 10% to 20% cases, males remain with features of testicular abnormality.

Males with eating disorders are usually relieved and grateful to work with clinicians who appreciate their concerns. Anorexia nervosa is especially more ego alien to males than to females. Even girls and women with eating disorders, who themselves have experienced social isolation because of their illness, tend to stigmatize males with eating disorders. Males with eating disorders often feel lonely and do not feel they are a part of therapeutic groups consisting mainly of women.

Outcome

Being male is not by itself an adverse prognostic factor. Men can do well in treatment, and often do, especially with experienced treatment teams employing multidimensional approaches.

Generally Accepted Facts with Less Rigorous Evidence

Epidemiology

There is a rough correlation between the decreased incidence of cases of anorexia nervosa in males and the decreased sociocultural reinforcement for slimming men receive. Case reports suggest an increased probability of males with eating disorders being HIV positive compared with females with eating disorders. The two genders appear to have experienced similar proportional increases in the incidence of eating disorders up until the mid-1980s, although the absolute rate is much lower. It is possible that about that time the distressed cachetic appearance of the first males with AIDS decreased the value of slimness in men.

Testosterone may provide some protective effect against the development of eating disorders. The testosterone-guided developmental pattern in males, reinforced by sociocultural norms, has tended to emphasize, as the predominant body goal, a mesomorphic and athletic appearance, a body size and shape that are incompatible with severe starvation. The typical age of onset for both genders is adolescence.

Natural History and Diagnosis

Hippocrates suggested that males may not tolerate weight loss as well as females. Bingeing and vomiting appear to be somewhat more frequent in males with eating disorders than in females with the same disorders. Males appear to undergo puberty with less distress than do females in regard to the acquisition of secondary sexual characteristics and sexual functioning. The trends of society in the last 50 years to become more sexualized and less institutionalized in normative social behaviors, as well as the lower age of puberty, may have affected boys less than girls.

Males with eating disorders are more likely to have alcohol-related comorbid conditions and obsessional features, but females have an increased likelihood of mood disorders.

Binge eating disorder (see Chapters 24 and 78) may go unrecognized in males because an overeating male is less likely to provoke attention than an overeating female. Males score lower in the drive for thinness on the Eating Disorder Inventory, confirming an overall less severe drive for thinness than in females.

Treatment

It appears helpful to have, whenever possible, more than one male with an eating disorder in a treatment program. They seem to do better in separate groups of males only, at least for some of their treatment. It also appears useful to explore individual aspects of the etiology of eating disorders in males rather than to assume they follow a pattern similar to those in females. The more ill the individual, the less influence gender has on treatment. The more normal the weight and the more normal the behaviors of males, the more gender-related features of treatment come into play.

As males improve in weight, manifestations of increased testosterone levels are commonly seen, such as flirting, masturbation, and comments of a sexual nature. Males are more likely to ask for weight training as part of their treatment program.

Outcome

As with females, males have a worse prognosis when they come into treatment with severe, long-established low weight; marked comorbid features; pronounced binge–purge behavior; an unsupportive family; and the lack of a follow-up treatment facility.

Uncertain, Unknown, or Conflicting Information

Epidemiology

The predisposing and precipitating factors specific for eating disorders in males are not known. Whether cases in males are increasing is frequently asked, but no reliable data exist. The sex ratio among subtypes of anorexia and bulimia nervosa is not known. The co-occurrence of eating disorders among male twins has been described infrequently, probably due to the less likely occurrence of both twinship and eating disorders in males.

It has been speculated that compulsive athleticism is an indirect manifestation of anorexia nervosa in males. The issue of whether or not insulin-dependent diabetes mellitus increases the risk of an eating disorder in males, has never been researched.

Natural History and Diagnosis

It has been suggested, but never proven, that testicular abnormalities predispose males to eating disorders. Whether specific family functioning styles are related to the onset of eating disorder illness has never been investigated. While the course of the illness appears roughly similar in most males, point-by-point comparisons of the stages of development of the illness have not been studied.

The exact type and frequency of comorbid conditions in males with eating disorders have not been established. The mechanisms of the medical conditions of osteopenia/osteoporosis in males have not been investigated, but they are probably related to factors other than estrogen deficit. Integral to understanding the etiology of eating disorders is more extensive and reliable knowledge of the regulation of eating behavior in males.

Treatment

The effectiveness of specific treatments for bulimia nervosa in males has never been tested. Also, the specific psychodynamic features of males with eating disorders have not been well investigated.

The crucial question of whether the gender of the therapist is important in treatment has not been raised with respect to males. The role, if any, of testosterone in decreasing abdominal fat deposition in males during the refeeding process has never been studied but represents a logical area of interest. Sonogram studies of testicular size during the starvation and refeeding processes, comparable to those demonstrating ovarian change, have never been undertaken.

No studies of the ideal method of refeeding males with anorexia nervosa have been done. Whether their lipid pattern during the restoration of healthy weight is similar to or different from that of females remains unknown.

Outcome

While short-term studies suggest that outcome in males and females is comparable, long-term studies are lacking. The percentage of male patients with eating disorders who die earlier than expected is not known. Specific scales for assessing multi-dimensional outcome in males have not yet been developed. It cannot be assumed that the measures used to follow up the progress of females are applicable to males.

The children of former eating-disordered males have never been studied. The adverse effects in the children might include increased interuterine and neonatal mortality as well as an increased incidence of eating disorders among adolescent children of males with eating disorders.

The feasibility of primary and secondary prevention of eating disorders in males has not been studied (see Chapter 51). It is possible that the recent legal guidelines that limit the amount of weight loss allowed for high school wrestlers may decrease the incidence of eating disorders.

CONCLUSIONS

There are many similarities in the natural history, diagnosis , treatment, and outcome between males and females with eating disorders—enough similarities to allow the clinician to feel confident in identifying cases and undertaking the essentials of treatment. It is clear, however, that the experience of maleness in our society, from conception on, is very different from that of femaleness. These differences include the effect of a steady state of gonadotropin levels compared with a cyclical gonadotropin influence in females, the percent of body fat during normal development, the biopsychosocial experience of puberty, the genomically influenced typical body shape and percentage of lean muscle mass, and possibly the way some precursor amino acids for neurotransmitter synthesis are differentially metabolized in the brain.

In addition, the sociocultural environment differs from birth on between the sexes in regard to differential reinforcements for dieting and weight loss. Men and women perceive fatness differently, value different ideals of shape, and change in their valuation of slimness if they experience a gay or lesbian sexual orientation.

The more ill the individual, the less difference gender makes in treatment. The closer a patient's body weight approaches normal, the greater the relevance of gender in preparing the patient for living at a normal weight in society and in the social subgroup from which the patient comes.

Among the most intriguing and unexplained aspects of eating disorders in males are the relative influences of sociocultural and biomedical factors in the etiology and maintenance of the particular disorder. While the overarching general features of natural history and diagnosis in males with eating disorders may be similar, gender-specific differences may be relevant to the etiology and optimal treatment of the disorders.

FURTHER READING

Andersen, A. E. (1990). Diagnosis and treatment of males with eating disorders. In A. E. Andersen (Ed.), *Males with eating disorders* (pp. 133–162). New York: Brunner/Mazel. A recently edited book, bringing together the experience of 20 authors on various aspects of males with eating disorders, including history, sociocultural studies, psychological functioning, clinical studies, treatment and outcome, and an integrative paradigm.

Drewnowski, A., & Yee, D. K. (1987). Men and body image: Are males satisfied with their body weight? *Psychosomatic Medicine, 49,* 626–634. A careful look at male attitudes toward body weight and shape, a fundamental factor in understanding the gender-divergent onset and prevalence of eating disorders.

Fichter, M. M., & Dasher, C. (1987). Symptomatology, psychosexual development and gender identity in 42 anorexic males. *Psychological Medicine, 17,* 409–418. A major contribution from the broad German experience, including clinical symptomatology, sexuality, and developmental issues.

Hsu, L. K. G. (1989). The gender gap in eating disorders: Why are the eating disorders more common among women? *Clinical Psychology Review, 9,* 393–407. An integrative and broadly based analysis of the gender gap in eating disorders.

Mitchell, J. E., & Goff, G. (1984). Bulimia in male patients. *Psychosomatics, 12,* 909–912. An early report on bulimia nervosa in males, including initial treatment outcomes.

Opplinger, R. A., Landry, G. L., Foster, S. W., & Lambercht, A. C. (1993). Bulimic behaviors among interscholastic wrestlers: A statewide survey. *Pediatrics, 91,* 826–831. A detailed study of the behaviors and attitudes of a group of young males especially vulnerable to eating disorders.

Parry-Jones B. (1992) A bulimic ruminator? The case of Dr. Samuel Johnson. *Psychological Medicine, 22,* 851–862. An historical analysis of the eating pathology of Samuel Johnson. More than just a single case report, it offers an examination of eating disorders through history as well as diagnostic criteria and comorbid conditions.

Steiger, H. (1989) Anorexia nervosa and bulimia in males: Lessons from a low risk population. *Canadian Journal of Psychiatry, 34,* 419–424. The infrequent, although not rare, occurrence of eating disorders in males presents a number of intellectual and clinical lessons, as discussed in this paper.

Tridon, P., Crombez, Y., Marchand, P., Prot, F., & Vadailhet, C. (1983). L'anoréxie mentale du garçon. *Acta Paedopsychiatrica, 49,* 311–319. An example of detailed clinical work by these French clinical scholars concerning the issue of males with anorexia nervosa in a non-English-speaking culture.

Vandereycken, W., & Van den Broucke, S. (1984). Anorexia nervosa in males: A comparative study of 107 cases reported in the literature (1970–1980.) *Acta Psychiatrica Scandinavica, 70,* 447–454. A thoughtful analysis of anorexia nervosa in 107 males reported in the literature.

• 32 •

CHILDHOOD-ONSET EATING DISORDERS

Rachel Bryant-Waugh
Bryan Lask

"Childhood-onset eating disorders" refers to eating disorders with an onset before the age of 14. The term "early onset" is also sometimes used, but this usage has lead to confusion, since some authors refer to onset in adolescence (i.e., up to 18 years) as "early" to differentiate it from onset in adulthood. We prefer the term "childhood-onset" and make a plea for its consistent use for individuals between the ages of 7 and 13 years (7 is the youngest age of presentation for patients with anorexia nervosa in our experience; and 13, which is just before the first peak in incidence, generally placed at about 14 to 16 years). Childhood-onset eating disorders are sometimes further grouped according to developmental markers; for example, prepubertal, pubertal, or pre-menarchal onset.

Childhood-onset eating disorders can be clearly distinguished from the feeding problems of infants and eating problems such as food fads and selective eating. Their distinctive feature is an excessive concern with the control of body weight and shape, accompanied by grossly inadequate or chaotic food intake.

The eating disorder most common in childhood is anorexia nervosa, a discussion of which forms the main part of this chapter. The full syndrome of bulimia nervosa is rarely seen in clinics in patients under the age of 14. Other forms of eating disturbance in children in this age range are food avoidance emotional disorder and pervasive refusal syndrome (discussed later in the chapter).

ANOREXIA NERVOSA

Diagnostic Issues

Despite evidence to the contrary, there is still some dispute as to whether "true" anorexia nervosa occurs in childhood. This uncertainty may arise partly from the difficulties in applying the currently accepted diagnostic criteria for anorexia nervosa. For example, criterion D of the DSM-IV is "the absence of at least three consecutive menstrual cycles." Clearly, in girls below the age of 14, it is often inappropriate to consider absence of menses as pathological, as they may not yet have started menstruating. Further, it is difficult to ascertain whether menstruation might "otherwise have occurred" in girls below the age of 14. Also, it is difficult to calculate accurately the expected weight of children who have been failing to grow, since expected weight is determined on the basis of height and age.

Fortunately, the ICD-10 acknowledges the existence of prepubertal anorexia nervosa and the diagnostic criteria make due allowance for it (see Chapter 23). However, these criteria still do not take into consideration children who are some years away from their growth spurt and pubertal development. Certainly our own clinical experience and research evidence leaves us in no doubt that childhood-onset anorexia nervosa does occur and that it is a potentially serious illness with a rather poor prognosis.

Epidemiology

Children with anorexia nervosa come from a range of social and cultural backgrounds. It is perhaps worth mentioning that anorexia nervosa in children is not a new phenomenon; there have been case reports and descriptions of children with anorexia nervosa throughout the published history of the disorder.

The incidence of childhood-onset anorexia nervosa is not known. Certainly it seems lower than in late adolescence and early adult life. However, referrals to our clinic have gradually increased over the years, with the last 5 years or so seeing a dramatic rise in numbers. While part of this increase may be accounted for by a greater awareness of eating disorders in general and of our specialist service for children in particular, our impression is that anorexia nervosa is truly becoming more common in this age group.

A common finding in studies of children with anorexia nervosa is the relatively high percentage of boys with the disorder. In adults with anorexia nervosa, men are thought to account for 5% to 10% of cases, whereas in children, boys have been reported to represent between 20% and 25% of clinical referrals. It is not yet possible to state whether there is a true age-related difference in the gender ratio or whether these younger boys are simply more likely to come to medical attention. The limited epidemiological data specifically concerning younger individuals does suggest that the gender ratio may indeed be different, but this tentative finding needs further study.

Clinical Features

Common presenting features of childhood-onset anorexia include weight loss, determined food avoidance, preoccupation with weight and calories, dread of fatness, overexercising, and self-induced vomiting. Obsessional behavior, including extreme conscientiousness about schoolwork, and depression are also common. When initially seen in the clinic, a number of children have physical symptoms such as nausea, abdominal pain, feeling full, or being unable to swallow. Rarely is any physical cause found for these features other than poor nutrition.

Premorbidly, these children are often conscientious, hardworking, pleasant, and are "no problem." Early feeding problems and childhood obesity do not generally feature in their histories, and very few have had any previous psychiatric disorder.

Although weight loss is not an essential diagnostic feature of anorexia nervosa in this age group, all the children we have seen have indeed lost significant amounts of weight. Weight loss in children can be rapid and dramatic, and many are referred in an emaciated state. Accompanying dehydration is not uncommon and is potentially dangerous. Other physical changes include the development of lanugo hair, hypotension, bradycardia, and poor peripheral circulation, while ultrasound examinations show hepatic steatosis (fatty deposits in the liver) and uterine and ovarian regression to an infantile state.

Determined food avoidance is invariably present although sometimes heavily disguised. Children often manage to conceal their food avoidance, either by taking meals separately from the family or by pretending to eat while furtively disposing of their food. A preoccupation with weight and calories is universal. The children are extremely concerned about their weight and energy intake and often seem able to control their weight to a very fine degree. An interesting difference occurs between the sexes. Girls tend to say they want to be thin for aesthetic reasons, whereas boys often give health and fitness as their explanation for controlling their food intake. The dread of fatness is often concealed or denied, although it frequently emerges during treatment.

Exercising is a popular means of achieving weight control for children. Athletic activities such as running and swimming are commonly used as a socially acceptable means of controlling weight. When restrictions are placed on such activities, children frequently resort to climbing stairs and press-ups. It is not uncommon for some children to do several hundred press-ups daily.

Self-induced vomiting and abuse of laxatives and diuretics are less common than some of the other features, but they nonetheless occur in a significant minority of children. Almost invariably these activities are carried out secretively, and their incidence may therefore be underestimated. A number of children develop hypokalaemia, and others suffer esophageal bleeding from repeated vomiting. We know of one child aged 11 who died of repeated esophageal bleeds.

Prognosis

The prognosis in this age group is less than satisfactory. Only about two-thirds make a full recovery, with the remainder experiencing persistent difficulties. Persistent amenorrhea occurs in about 30% of these children. The long-term risks for delayed growth, infertility, and osteoporosis, among other complications, are uncertain, and further research is required.

The illness can be conceptualized as having three stages. The first stage is characterized by the predominance of the eating problems. In the second stage there is a gradual improvement in nutritional intake and the start of a phase of intense negativism, manifested by sullenness, rudeness, assertiveness, and oppositional behavior. The third stage consists of more appropriate eating and more socially acceptable ways of expressing feelings. Children who successfully pass from the second to the third stage seem to have the best chance of recovery.

BULIMIA NERVOSA

There are no satisfactory epidemiological data regarding the incidence of bulimia nervosa in children under the age of 14 years. The number of referrals of children in this age group to our clinic has always been low. During the past few years, fewer than 5% of children seen have had bulimia nervosa, and these children have all been 12 or 13 years old.

The clinical features are the same as those found in the older age group, namely, repeated bouts of overeating, a feeling of lack of control during these episodes, an excessive concern with the control of body weight, and the use of extreme measures to mitigate the effects of overeating, such as self-induced vomiting (see Chapter 27). In addition, the children are usually rather sad, or even depressed, and have a poor self-image.

FOOD-AVOIDANCE EMOTIONAL DISORDER

This eating disorder appears to be restricted to childhood. A number of children do not fully meet the criteria for anorexia nervosa, yet determined food avoidance is a prominent symptom among them. There is often a previous history of food restriction and, usually, associated symptoms of emotional disturbance such as phobias, obsessional behavior, refusal to attend school, or depression. The food avoidance is more marked than would normally be the case with emotional disorders and is often of the same intensity as is seen in anorexia nervosa patients. The distorted body image and the fear of gaining weight are absent. It may be that the disorder is a "partial syndrome" of anorexia nervosa (see Chapter 24) with a better prognosis, or it might be considered as intermediate between anorexia nervosa and emotional disorder of childhood.

PERVASIVE REFUSAL SYNDROME

This is a life-threatening condition that consists of a profound and pervasive refusal to eat, drink, walk, talk, or engage in any form of self-care. Usually a child with pervasive refusal shows the characteristic features of anorexia nervosa, but as treatment is initiated, the child rapidly manifests an increasing number of avoidant behaviors. Typically the child adopts a fetal position and quietly moans or remains totally mute, except when attempts are made to feed or in some other way care for her/him. Such efforts are met with either terror or anger, along with intense avoidance. There is no evidence of organic disease. The multiplicity and severity of childrens' symptoms do not fit comfortably into any formal diagnostic category. Our experience of this disorder leads us to believe that these children have often been sexually abused and threatened with extreme violence should they tell anyone. Thus it might eventually be conceptualized as a posttraumatic stress disorder.

TREATMENT

Given the potential seriousness of childhood-onset eating disorders, a rapidly initiated intensive and comprehensive treatment program is indicated.

The essential components of such a program include the following: providing information and education for the child, the parents, and other family members; ensuring that adults are in charge of issues concerning the child's health and safety; making a decision about the need for hospitalization; the calculation of a target weight range; and drawing up clear plans for refeeding.

In most instances, family therapy or parental counseling forms the mainstay of therapeutic input (see Chapter 56). Other useful treatments include individual therapy (psychodynamic or cognitive—see Chapters 57, 58, 60, and 61) and group therapy.

Medication is required in a minority of cases and usually takes the form of anti-depressants for children with a concurrent depressive disorder (see Chapter 55).

CONCLUSIONS

It is clear that anorexia nervosa, and other eating disorders do occur in children and that anorexia nervosa in childhood is a particularly serious illness with only a moderate prognosis. The core behavioral, psychological, and physical features seem to be similar to those in adults, although the clinical features vary and there is no typical pattern of presentation or course. Because of the lower levels of total body fat in children, they tend to become more severely emaciated than do adults. In consequence, children may suffer the physical and psychological effects of starvation rather more rapidly than adults. Given the severity of anorexia nervosa and its poor prognosis in childhood, treatment should always be both intensive and comprehensive.

FURTHER READING

Gowers, S. G., Crisp, A. H., Joughin, N., & Bhat, A. (1991). Pre-menarcheal anorexia nervosa. *Journal of Child Psychology and Psychiatry, 32,* 515–524. A comparative study of pre- and postpubertal AN.

Higgs, J., Goodyer, I., & Birch, J. (1989). Anorexia nervosa and food avoidance emotional disorder. *Archives of Diseases in Childhood, 64,* 346–351. An important article that highlights the variability in types of eating disturbance in childhood.

Jacobs, B., & Isaacs, S. (1986). Pre-pubertal anorexia nervosa: A retrospective controlled study. *Journal of Child Psychology and Psychiatry, 27,* 237–250. A retrospective case-note study of prepubertal anorexia nervosa.

Lask, B. (1992). The management of anorexia nervosa of early onset. In P. Cooper & A. Stein (Eds.), *Feeding problems and eating disorders in children and adolescents* (pp. 113–122). London: Harwood Academic Press. A clear description of a comprehensive approach to the management of eating disorders in children.

Lask, B., Britten, C., Kroll, L., Magagna, J., & Tranter, M. (1991). Pervasive refusal in children. *Archives of Diseases in Childhood, 66,* 866–869. The first paper to describe an extreme and pervasive form of refusal in childhood, which often first appears to be anorexia nervosa.

Lask, B., & Bryant-Waugh, R. (1992). Early onset anorexia nervosa and related eating disorders. *Journal of Child Psychology and Psychiatry, 33,* 281–300. The most recent review of research findings related to childhood-onset anorexia nervosa.

Lask, B., & Bryant-Waugh, R. (1993). *Childhood-onset anorexia nervosa and related eating disorders.* Hove, UK: Erlbaum. A detailed overview of eating disorders in children, with an emphasis on their clinical management.

Russell, G. F. M. (1992). Anorexia nervosa of early onset and its impact on puberty. In P. Cooper & A. Stein (Eds.), *Feeding problems and eating disorders in children and adolescents* (pp. 85–112). London: Harwood Academic. The biology and psychopathology of anorexia nervosa in younger patients.

• 33 •

EATING DISORDERS
AND CHILDREARING

Alan Stein

There is now good evidence that psychiatric disorders among parents have the potential to interfere with their childrearing capacities and hence the development of their children. Eating disorders are an important source of psychiatric morbidity among women of childbearing age. They are of particular concern for at least two reasons. First, the core symptoms are extremely pervasive and disruptive of daily living and thus may conflict with sensitive parenting. These symptoms include a preoccupation with body shape, weight, and food, as well as extreme behaviors both to limit food intake and to compensate for overeating. Second, parents with eating disorders commonly have difficulties in their interpersonal relationships, which may well extend to their relationships with their children.

Infancy and adolescence are likely to be the times when children are particularly vulnerable. Parents spend much time during the first months and years feeding their young infants, and feeding is one of the ways in which much communication occurs between parents and their children. The attitudes, preoccupations, and behaviors that people with eating disorders manifest may interfere with their ability to sit patiently feeding their infants, while responding appropriately to their hunger needs and cues. Adolescence is a time when children become increasingly aware of societal pressures and also develop an increasing interest in body shape and attractiveness. At this stage, parental attitudes toward their own body shape and weight and their own behavior with respect to eating may affect the child in two ways. First, children model themselves after their parents; and second, parents may influence adolescent children directly through their attitudes toward their children's weight, shape, and eating habits.

Given all these issues, it is surprising that little research has been conducted to examine the childrearing of parents with eating disorders. Most of the reports to date have consisted of case reports and case series, although recently a controlled study was conducted of infants of mothers with eating disorders, and in a few studies the effects of disordered eating in mothers (*not* cases of eating disorders) on their adolescent daughters were examined. The case reports and series have all raised some concerns that children of such patients may be at risk of adverse sequelae. Most of the work has concentrated exclusively on mothers with eating disorders, with little reference to fathers. In some reports it is suggested that mothers are overconcerned with their children's weight and that they then try to slim the children down. In other reports, excessive parental concerns are noted about feeding and the disruption of general parenting functions. There have been two reports that children's growth might be affected by parental eating disorders. Most notably, in a Scandinavian follow-up study of a group of mothers with a history of anorexia nervosa, it was reported that 17% of their infants failed to thrive in the year following childbirth. However, this study should be considered with great caution because the investigators relied largely on maternal reports and a loose definition of "failure to thrive." Also, the study was retrospective, with the children's ages at the time of follow-up being from 1 to 38 years.

One controlled, cross-sectional study of the 1-year-old children of mothers with eating disorders has recently been completed. The index group consisted of mothers with full cases of eating disorder and mothers with subthreshold cases. Mothers and infants were observed during both mealtimes and play. The main findings were that, when compared with controls, the index mothers were more intrusive with their infants during both mealtimes and playtimes and expressed more negative emotion (critical and derogatory remarks) during mealtimes but not during play. The most common precipitant of such negative emotion was the mothers' concern that their infants were making a "mess." There were, however, no differences between the groups in their positive expressed emotion. There was more conflict between index infants and their mothers during mealtimes; and the index mothers were more reluctant to allow their infants to attempt to feed themselves, compared with controls. Furthermore, the index infants tended to weigh less than the control infants, and infant weight was found to be independently and inversely related to both the amount of conflict during mealtimes and the extent of the mother's concern about her own body shape.

The object of three other studies was to consider if mothers' attitudes and behaviors regarding food were a factor in determining whether or not their daughters would have disordered eating. Investigators in two American studies have relied on self-report measures in groups of middle-class mothers and adolescent daughters. In the first study, mothers of daughters with disordered eating (assessed by the Eating Disorder Inventory) were compared with controls. This comparison showed that mothers whose daughters' eating was disordered were more eating disordered themselves. Furthermore, mothers of girls with disordered eating thought that their daughters should lose more weight than the mothers of girls who were not eating disordered; the former also thought their daughters were less attractive than the girls judged themselves. A second study, however, did not confirm these findings, while in a third, very small UK study of 10-year-old girls and their mothers it was found that mothers' and daughters' dietary restraint scores were correlated but that their eating attitudes (as measured by the Eating Attitudes Test) were not. The issues therefore remain as yet unresolved.

From the limited number of studies conducted to date, it is possible to deduce three broad groups of mechanisms by which parents with eating disorders may influence childrearing and hence their children's development. First, parents' disturbed attitudes concerning eating, body shape, and weight, may have direct effects on the child: For example, the parent's dread of fatness may cause them to underfeed their children; and their overconcern with shape, weight, and food intake may lead them into conflict with their children during meals as well as to being critical of their adolescent children's eating habits, body shape, and appearance. Second, a parents' eating disorders may interfere with their general parenting functions; for example, parents' preoccupation with body shape, weight, and food may impair their concentration and interfere with their responsiveness to their children's needs. Third, parents' disordered eating behavior may act as a poor role model for their children. Last, parents' eating disorders may be associated with interpersonal difficulties common in people with such disorders, and research has shown that discordant marital and family relationships have their own adverse effects on children.

One further issue is whether the effects of a parent's eating disorder on childrearing and a child's development are specific, that is, whether the disturbances are in the same domain (that of eating and weight) and whether the disturbances are tied to the specific cognitions and behaviors of eating disorders. From the evidence above it seems there are both specific and nonspecific effects, although clearly more research is required to clarify this issue.

Finally, with respect to clinical implications, only limited guidelines can be proposed on the basis of the available literature. At the outset it is important that the quality of the interactions between parents with eating disorders and their children be carefully and clinically assessed, as should the children's growth and nutritional status. As part of the assessment of parent–child interaction it is helpful to observe mealtimes (sensitively) in the home, if possible. If difficulties are noted in a family with young children, support might be directed to the parents by helping them to recognize the children's hunger and satiety cues and to prepare and pace their children's meals. Furthermore, parents should be encouraged, through support and education, to allow their infants to experiment with and learn about self-feeding at the appropriate age, so that the children are no longer always fed by the parents, a practice that, if pursued inappropriately, may lead to conflict. If older children are involved, help might take the form of working with parents to lessen the attention and criticism direct at their children's body weight and shape. The parents should also be encouraged to widen the focus of their interaction with their children. It should, however, be emphasized that children of parents with eating disorders are not invariably adversely affected: Some parents manage well, and their children develop with no apparent problems.

FURTHER READING

Brinch, M., Isager, T., & Tolstrup, K. (1988). Anorexia nervosa and motherhood: Reproduction pattern and mothering behavior of 50 women. *Acta Psychiatrica Scandinavica, 77,* 611–617. A follow-up study of a large case series of women who have had anorexia into motherhood.

Pike, K. M., & Rodin, J. (1991). Mothers, daughters, and disordered eating. *Journal of Abnormal Psychology, 100,* 198–204. An important report examining the relationship between disordered eating in mothers and their adolescent daughters.

Rutter, M. (1989). Psychiatric disorder in parents as a risk factor for children. In D. Schaffer, I. Phillips, & N. B. Enger (Eds.), *Prevention of mental disorder, alcohol and other drug use in children and adolescents* (pp. 157–189). Rockville, MD: Office for Substance Abuse, U.S. Department of Health and Human Services. A review of the mechanisms by which parental psychiatric disorder may influence child development.

Stein, A., Woolley, H., Cooper, S. D., & Fairburn, C. G. (1994). An observational study of mothers with eating disorders and their infants. *Journal of Child Psychology and Psychiatry, 35,* 733–748. The only controlled observational study in this area to date.

• 34 •

EATING DISORDERS IN ATHLETES

Kelly D. Brownell

In both the lay press and academic publications, there is increasing interest in athletes as a group at especially high risk for eating disorders. Case studies of afflicted athletes appear often in the press, exemplified by the stories of Olympic gymnast Cathy Rigby and Mary Wazater, an exceptional distance runner who, at the age of 18 and suffering from anorexia nervosa, threw herself from a railroad bridge and became quadriplegic.

In concert with public attention to the issue has been serious concern from organizations at the highest levels of sports and sports medicine. In 1989, the U.S. National Collegiate Athletic Association (NCAA) launched an intensive educational campaign designed to alert coaches, parents, administrators, and athletes to the warning signs of eating disorders and to provide information on means for seeking help. The U.S. Olympic Committee has convened several meetings on the topic, and, under the auspices of the American College of Sports Medicine, a group of professionals has called for immediate attention to the "female athlete triad" (eating disorders, amenorrhea, and osteoporosis).

The aims in this chapter are to discuss the prevalence of eating and weight disturbances in athletes, to discuss why this group is at particular risk, and to describe current intervention and prevention programs.

PREVALENCE

Limitations in existing research permit only a broad analysis of the prevalence of eating disorders among athletes. In most studies prevailing diagnostic criteria have not been used, appropriate control groups have been rare, and athletes in a single sport (and usually only females) have been the norm. Findings have included athletes showing higher prevalence than controls, no difference, and athletes showing less risk.

In the most comprehensive study to date, 522 elite female athletes in Norway, engaged in 35 sports, were compared with 448 nonathletic control subjects. On the basis of self-report questionnaires, 22% of the athletes and 26% of the control subjects were classified as "at risk for developing eating disorders." Subsequent interviews with and clinical evaluation of those at risk indicated that the athletes underreported symptoms and that 18% of the athletes and 5% of the control subjects actually suffered from eating disorders.

It appears that eating disorders are a significant problem in some groups of athletes.

While precise prevalence estimates must await more thorough studies and the resolution of the underreporting problem, it is evident that pathological eating and weight control practices and the psychological aspects of eating disorders (e.g., preoccupation with shape and weight) are common in athletes. These problems appear more severe in females than in males and in sports where low body weight is considered important to performance (e.g., distance running) or appearance (e.g., diving, gymnastics, figure skating).

WHY ARE ATHLETES AT RISK?

Athletes are subject to considerable societal pressure regarding shape and weight, but the same is true of their nonathletic peers. If the prevalence of eating disorders is higher in athletes, the key question is whether participation in some sports causes the disturbances or whether individuals with eating problems, or with psychosocial problems that increase the risk of eating disorders, are drawn to certain sports. The necessary longitudinal studies to address this question have not been done.

It is quite possible, although impossible to defend with research, that some individuals seek out and become proficient in some sports because of personality characteristics (e.g., perfectionism) common to both athletic performance and eating disorders (see Chapter 30). "Compulsive" exercising may masquerade as dedicated physical training and be socially sanctioned, thus providing acceptance of and rewards for pathological practices.

Participation in modern athletics carries a number of pressures and responsibilities that are likely to increase the risk of eating disorders in many groups of athletes. In vulnerable individuals, the risk may become reality. Lopiano and Zotos list these pressures as:

1. *Performance pressure.* Lucrative contracts, scholarships, or approval from peers and parents may all rest on fractions of a second in a race, hundredths of a point in judges' scores, or a single shot in the last seconds of competition.
2. *Coach–athlete relationship.* Pressure experienced by coaches is transmitted to athletes, with rewards to the athlete for subservience and severe training and punishments (both physical and psychological) for failure.
3. *Value incongruence.* Athletes learn values such as blind obedience and the need to intimidate or even injure opponents, which are maladaptive in general life.
4. *Visibility of participation.* All actions can be subject to scrutiny by vast numbers of others.
5. *Time demands and social isolation.*
6. *Fatigue-related stress.* This stress may result from excessive training, performance anxiety, and increasingly demanding competition.
7. *Injury.* Injuries are common, often debilitating, threaten a key aspect of an athlete's life, and may be associated with depression and compulsive behaviors.
8. *Academic pressures.* Academic institutions are now scrutinized for demanding little of athletes beyond sports, so increasing pressure is exerted on athletes to succeed as students.
9. *Stereotyping and discrimination by race and gender.* These biases may enhance pressure and minimize social support.

INTERVENTION AND PREVENTION

Intervention

Little research exists to guide the specific treatment of eating disorders in athletes beyond what is known about the general treatment of eating disorders (see Section VII). The additional factors thought to be important for clinicians working with athletes are (1) sensitivity to the pressure to keep the disorder secret (the athlete fears severe disapproval from coaches, loss of scholarships, etc.); (2) the serious threat posed to the athlete's self-esteem if his/her participation in sports is compromised; and (3) the real or imagined damage to performance if changes in diet, training, or weight must be made.

Prevention

The weight standards imposed by coaches or self-imposed by athletes tend to be arbitrary and strict. While some athletes perform well with a low percentage of body fat, not all are able to attain low levels of fat and weight or to perform best at those levels (as low as 5% body fat in some male wrestlers and female distance runners). Deriving weight standards for an athlete from the measurement of his/her body fat, establishing goal weights for individual athletes based on their own body types and performance histories at different weights, and involving sports medicine specialists may aid in the prevention of eating disorders in athletes.

Overtraining may contribute to a number of physical problems such as fatigue and injury, which in turn may impair performance. The psychological correlates of overtraining have not been documented adequately, but they may include the pathological thinking about exercise that is characteristic of some individuals with eating disorders. Prevention of eating disorders in athletes may be possible if they and their coaches are made aware that overtraining may compromise their performance and that there are limits to the "more is better" philosophy that pervades sports.

Educating coaches, athletic administrators, parents, and athletes themselves will be necessary for prevention. Many athletes either do not recognize the serious nature of eating disorders or else are willing to accept the risk imposed by the increasingly stringent levels of training and food restriction they believe will enhance their performance. Education of this kind is taking place through national athletic governing bodies such as the NCAA and through athletic departments at isolated institutions. A more systematic effort is needed so that consistent information about the risks of eating disorders and overtraining is made more widely available to athletes and those concerned with their training and performance.

A Combined Prevention and Intervention Model

Some efforts have been made to develop a comprehensive program combining prevention and intervention. Such a program exists at the University of Texas, through the Department of Intercollegiate Athletics for Women, as described by Ryan. Figure 34.1 shows a flow chart of that program.

Athletic administrators at the University of Texas conducted an innovative program derived from this model. Over a period of 1 calendar year, 120 female athletes in seven sports had their body composition (not their weight) assessed four to six times by sports medicine specialists. Coaches were given copies of this information, but no coach was

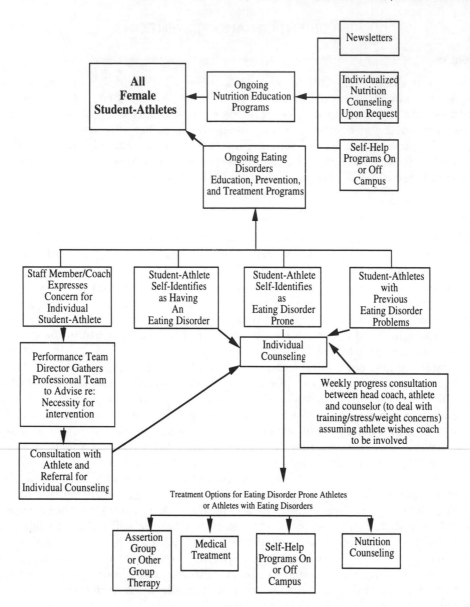

FIGURE 34.1. A comprehensive model developed by the Performance Team at the University of Texas for education, athletic policy, and counseling designed to prevent and treat eating disorders in collegiate athletes. From Ryan (1992). Copyright 1992 by Lea & Febiger. Reprinted with permission.

allowed to set goal weights, discuss an athlete's body weight or composition, or weigh athletes. Education was available to the athletes on nutrition and exercise physiology. Compared with their condition in the previous year, the athletes were leaner and more fit and reportedly were healthier and happier. These findings, while anecdotal, are promising and show a serious effort to confront a challenging problem.

What is noteworthy about the Texas program is that it begins at the same time female athletes start their participation in sports; it targets coaches, athletes, and athletic administrators; it uses multiple means for education (group education, newsletters, etc.); and it offers different options for treatment. The field would benefit from tests of this model.

SUMMARY

Important deficits exist in knowledge about the prevalence, course, prevention, and treatment of eating disorders in athletes. What is known suggests that athletes in some sports show a higher prevalence of eating disorders than do nonathletes. This higher prevalence is presumably due to the unique demands placed on modern athletes, yet whether participation in sports causes disturbed eating or individuals with disturbed eating gravitate toward certain sports has yet to be determined. Because of the growing popularity of organized sports and the increased access to sports for females, this is a subject area in need of further research on both basic and applied issues.

FURTHER READING

Brownell, K. D., Rodin, J., & Wilmore, J. H. (Eds.). (1992). *Eating, body weight, and performance in athletes: Disorders of modern society*. Philadelphia: Lea & Febiger. A comprehensive volume with sections on basic issues in eating and weight regulation, social and biological factors in the etiology and course of eating disorders in athletes, and the treatment and prevention of such disorders.

Brownell, K. D., Steen, S. N., & Wilmore, J. H. (1987). Weight regulation practices in athletes: Analysis of metabolic and health effects. *Medicine and Science in Sports and Exercise, 19,* 546–556. A review and theoretical article on eating and weight regulation issues in athletes, dealing with issues such as food efficiency, metabolism, and amenorrhea.

Garner, D. M., & Rosen, L. W. (1991). Eating disorders among athletes: Research and recommendations. *Journal of Applied Sport Science Research, 5,* 100–107. A review of the research on athletes and eating disorders and suggestions for intervention.

Lopiano, D. A., & Zotos, C. (1992). Modern athletics: The pressure to perform. In K. D. Brownell, J. Rodin, & J. H. Wilmore (Eds.), *Eating, body weight, and performance in athletes: Disorders of modern society* (pp. 275–292). Philadelphia: Lea & Febiger. A detailed description of the pressures faced by the modern athlete, with an analysis of how these pressures place athletes at risk for a number of psychosocial problems.

Ryan, R. (1992). Management of eating problems in athletic settings. In K. D. Brownell, J. Rodin, & J. H. Wilmore (Eds.), *Eating, body weight, and performance in athletes: Disorders of modern society* (pp. 344–362). Philadelphia: Lea & Febiger. An instructive chapter explaining the challenges of dealing with eating issues in athletic settings and describing a comprehensive program of education and counseling for the prevention and treatment of eating disorders in athletes.

Sundgot-Borgen, J. (1993). Prevalence of eating disorders in elite female athletes. *International Journal of Sport Nutrition, 3,* 29–40. A study of the prevalence of eating disorders across sports in elite female athletes in Norway, with a comparison of athletes and control subjects using self-report and interview measures.

Sundgot-Borgen, J. (1994). Risk and trigger factors for the development of eating disorders in female elite athletes. *Medicine and Science in Sports and Exercise, 26,* 414–419. A study of all 603 elite female athletes in Norway, with data on the factors that place athletes at risk for eating disorders and specific factors associated with the onset of such disorders.

Thompson, R. A., & Sherman, R. T. (1993). *Helping athletes with eating disorders*. Champaign, IL: Human Kinetics. A practical guide to understanding and providing counseling services to athletes with eating disorders.

Yates, A. (1991). *Compulsive exercise and the eating disorders: Toward an integrated theory of activity*. New York: Brunner/Mazel. A speculative focus on "activity disordered" individuals. Includes a review of the literature integrated with case reports.

Yeager, K. K., Agostini, R., Nattiv, A., & Drinkwater, B. (1993). The female athlete triad: Disordered eating, amenorrhea, osteoporosis. *Medicine and Science in Sports and Exercise, 25,* 775–777. A call to action, by a meeting sponsored by the American College of Sports Medicine, for research and prevention programs on three issues especially pertinent to female athletes.

· V ·
EPIDEMIOLOGY, ETIOLOGY, AND COURSE OF EATING DISORDERS

• 35 •

THE DEVELOPMENT
AND MAINTENANCE
OF EATING DISORDERS

Zafra Cooper

Anorexia nervosa and bulimia nervosa occur predominantly among young women in Western societies. Onset is usually in adolescence. While a period of dieting generally precedes the onset of both anorexia nervosa and bulimia nervosa, overeating rather than dieting occurs first in a small proportion of those with bulimia nervosa. In the majority of cases the clinical course after onset remains distinct, although about a third of those with anorexia nervosa subsequently develop nervosa nervosa. Movement from bulimia nervosa to anorexia nervosa is not common.

The etiology of anorexia nervosa and bulimia nervosa, like that of many other psychiatric disorders, is generally considered to be multifactorial. No potential etiological factor, considered in isolation, is sufficient to account for the development of disorder, nor indeed will it contribute substantially to the explanation of the variation among individuals. Whether or not disorder results and whether or not it persists are dependent on the occurrence of circumstances that activate the individual's vulnerability to particular risk factors and on the operation of protective factors. These complex interacting processes unfold over time, and it is a combination of these influences that determines whether an individual follows a path from exposure to a risk factor to the onset of disorder, and whether this disorder then becomes established or even chronic.

The process of the development and persistence of the eating disorders may be regarded as being composed of several conceptually distinct processes or stages, as illustrated in Figure 35.1. The initial stage covers the period from conception to the occurrence of what may be termed a behavioral precursor of the disorder (see the second stage, below). During this first stage the individual may be exposed to certain predisposing factors for the disorder. These factors (by definition) occur before the onset of disorder and increase the risk of its development without making it inevitable.

The second stage covers the period from the development of a behavioral precursor to the onset of frank disorder. In the majority of cases the precursor is dieting, which frequently precedes both anorexia nervosa and bulimia nervosa and is associated with a greatly increased risk of the development of one or the other of these disorders. During this stage, certain events ("precipitating factors") may occur that increase the risk of disorder by combining with dieting to lead to the onset of disorder. Dieting, although similar to a precipitating factor, differs in the important respect that it is a feature of

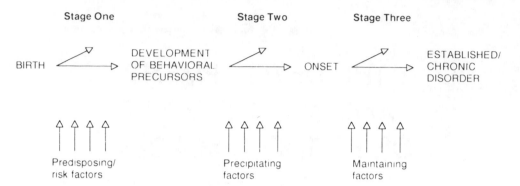

FIGURE 35.1. Stages in the development and maintenance of eating disorders.

both anorexia nervosa and bulimia nervosa once they develop. However, although it is almost invariably present, dieting is not simply the early stage of developing disorder, since in most cases it is not followed by disorder.

During the third stage, certain maintaining factors interact with protective factors to determine whether, once disorder has occurred, it is of a transient nature or whether it becomes established or even chronic.

Within this framework, providing an account of the development and maintenance of eating disorders involves describing, for both anorexia nervosa and bulimia nervosa, the combination of factors and processes that determine an individual's progression through these stages to established or chronic disorder. Clearly there may be various pathways that will lead to disorder, rather than a single one. Thus, in studies of the development of eating disorders, a combination of potential etiological factors operating together, rather than single factors in isolation, should be investigated.

STAGE ONE

The research on the etiology of eating disorders has implicated a large number of predisposing factors for the development of anorexia nervosa and, to a lesser extent, bulimia nervosa. Unfortunately much of this research has had major shortcomings. Since the research has been conducted almost entirely with clinical samples, often those attending specialist clinics, results may be distorted by selection bias. This bias is of particular concern, as there is strong research evidence that a large proportion of those with eating disorders do not come to the attention of the medical community (see Chapters 36 and 51). Most studies have had a narrow perspective, with only a limited number of putative etiological factors investigated, so little is known about the relative contribution of various factors. Few studies have included the appropriate control groups required to assess whether potential combinations of etiological factors are specific to eating disorders or whether they predispose to psychiatric disorder in general. Finally, little attention has been paid to the timing of the occurrence of supposed etiological factors, and therefore it is not always clear whether they are causes or consequences of eating disorders.

Risk Factors and the Individual

Psychological/Psychiatric Risk Factors

Many patients with anorexia nervosa and bulimia nervosa have a lifetime history of affective disorder (generally, major depressive disorder). Reported lifetime prevalence rates for major depression in patients with either disorder vary from 25% to as much as 80%. Generally the depressive disorder is concurrent with the eating disorder. Evidence that a history of depression precedes the onset of an eating disorder is more sparse. However, available findings suggest that at least a third of those with bulimia nervosa have a history of depression that precedes the onset of any eating disorder (anorexia nervosa or bulimia nervosa). While, in a recent community study of anorexia nervosa from Sweden, high rates of depressive disorder were found, there was no evidence that such disorder preceded the onset of anorexia nervosa. Thus it seems possible that a personal history of depression increases the risk of the subsequent development of bulimia nervosa rather than anorexia nervosa.

A number of possible mechanisms might account for a link between vulnerability to affective disorder and the subsequent development of an eating disorder. For example, abnormalities in serotonin (5-HT) function have been implicated in both affective disorders and eating disorders (see Chapter 45), and moderate dieting has been shown to affect 5-HT function. Alternatively, or in addition, the link between affective disorder and eating disorder might be mediated through low self-esteem encouraging individuals to diet to enhance their appearance and sense of self-control. Depressive symptoms are also common in normal-weight individuals who diet, although the exact nature of the relationship of these symptoms with dieting is not fully understood.

High levels of anxiety symptoms have been documented in both anorexia nervosa and bulimia nervosa, but there is no clear evidence that the anxiety precedes the development of either disorder. Similarly, while a high rate of obsessive–compulsive disorder among those with anorexia nervosa and bulimia nervosa has been reported in some studies, there is no evidence that it precedes the onset of the eating disorder (see Chapter 28).

Research interest in the role of personality disorder in the development of eating disorders has focused particularly on the role of obsessive–compulsive personality disorder in anorexia nervosa (see Chapters 28 and 30) and borderline personality disorder in bulimia nervosa (see Chapter 30). Data on the occurrence of personality disorder in association with eating disorders are inconsistent, but recently an excess of premorbid obsessive–compulsive personality disorder in those with anorexia nervosa (35%), compared with a control group (0.04%), has been documented. This relationship is not well understood, but perhaps such personality features lead to determined and persistent dieting.

Certain traits, such as low self-esteem and perfectionism, that are present in both anorexia nervosa and bulimia nervosa, and excessive compliance in anorexia nervosa, have been implicated as potential risk factors for subsequent disorder. It is perhaps because of these characteristics that dieting and weight loss become significant as means of enhancing the often weak sense of control these people feel they have over their lives. While these characteristics are well documented clinically, there is little systematic research evidence to support their presence prior to the onset of disorder. On the other hand, strong concerns about physical appearance and beliefs about the importance of weight and shape, while undoubtedly present at the early stages of disorder, are probably not sufficiently distinct from the disorder itself to be regarded as true risk factors.

Physical Risk Factors

Premorbid obesity has been documented in both anorexia nervosa (7% to 20%) and bulimia nervosa (18% to 40%). The most plausible explanation for this relationship seems to be that a predisposition to be overweight leads to dieting, which increases vulnerability to the development of the disorder. The common research finding that those who diet weigh relatively more than those who do not is consistent with this view. This finding suggests that a predisposition to obesity is a risk factor strictly for dieting rather than for eating disorder.

In one controlled study, a high rate (47%) of severe gastrointestinal difficulties was identified in the early feeding histories of those in whom anorexia nervosa subsequently developed. Although the exact nature of this link is unclear, the suggestion that early feeding difficulties might be a predisposing factor for anorexia nervosa has a certain plausibility. Although it was thought that diabetes mellitus might be a predisposing factor for the development of an eating disorder, subsequent careful research has not supported this view (see Chapter 49).

Despite reports of a range of neuroendocrine and metabolic disturbances in both anorexia nervosa and bulimia nervosa (see Chapters 44 and 46), the evidence to date suggests that these disturbances are secondary, rather than primary, to the disorder.

Adverse Events

Stressful life events have been implicated as predisposing factors for both anorexia nervosa and bulimia nervosa. In particular, because of the apparently high rates of childhood sexual abuse experienced by those with eating disorders (see Chapter 40), interest has focused on its role as a potential predisposing factor. While there is no evidence that demonstrates that either sexual abuse or other stressful life events are specific predisposing factors for eating disorders, rather than factors that predispose to psychiatric disorder generally, not all features that contribute to the development of disorder need be specific in their own right. They may contribute to the onset of disorder by combining with a number of other factors. Adverse life events may also play a role at a later stage in the developmental process (see Stage Two) by combining with dieting to precipitate disorder in a vulnerable individual.

Risk Factors in the Family

Family History of Psychiatric Disorder

There is growing evidence that eating disorders tend to aggregate in families (also see Chapter 37). The lifetime risk of an eating disorder among first-degree relatives of those with anorexia nervosa or bulimia nervosa is at least three times greater than for the relatives of normal controls. These findings are consistent with both genetic and environmental explanations of familial transmission. The balance of evidence from twin studies of both anorexia nervosa and bulimia nervosa indicating differential concordance rates between monozygotic and dizygotic twins seems to favor a genetic explanation. However, given possible biases in sampling and some inconsistent findings, firm conclusions cannot be drawn as yet. Genetic vulnerability may operate directly by increasing liability to anorexia nervosa or bulimia nervosa, or by predisposing to obesity or a certain type of personality that, in turn, predisposes the individual to an eating disorder.

Consistent evidence from family studies also indicates increased rates of affective disorder among first- and second-degree relatives of probands with either anorexia nervosa or bulimia nervosa. The lifetime risk for affective disorder for these relatives is three times greater than for relatives of normal control subjects. Further investigations as to whether mood disorder was present in relatives irrespective of the presence of depression in the proband with an eating disorder have produced inconsistent results, although the balance of the evidence suggests that probands with a coexisting affective disorder are more likely to have relatives with affective disorder. Since there appears to be no corresponding higher rate of eating disorders in the relatives of probands with affective disorder, it seems that eating disorders and affective disorders do not share a common family etiology. A family history of mood disorder may therefore increase a person's vulnerability to an eating disorder by predisposing that person to depression, which, in turn, may lead to disorder, as suggested above.

Several family studies have revealed high rates of alcohol abuse disorder among first-degree relatives of those with bulimia nervosa. While it is clear that these rates are significantly higher than those for the relatives of normal control subjects, few studies have investigated whether the rates are higher than those among the relatives of subjects with other psychiatric conditions. However, evidence available to date indicates that a family history of substance abuse disorder may be a specific risk factor for bulimia nervosa although the basis for such an association is unclear.

While there have been a number of reports of an increased rate of obesity in the relatives of those with eating disorders, only one controlled study of anorexia nervosa has shown that obesity was more common in these relatives than in the relatives of normal control subjects.

Family Environment and Interaction

Although specific patterns of interaction observed in the families of those with anorexia nervosa, and to a lesser extent of those with bulimia nervosa, have been thought to be pathogenic (see Chapter 38), it is unclear whether these patterns predispose toward disorder or are a consequence of it. Parental indifference and lack of care have been noted to be common, particularly in the families of those with bulimia nervosa, but not more so than in the families of depressed women in the community. Also, odd eating habits and strong concerns about appearance and weight have been described in the families of those with eating disorders. These concerns may operate environmentally, leading to the development of disorder by a process of contagion. The evidence of specific disturbances of eating in the children of mothers with eating disorders is consistent with this view (see Chapter 33).

Social and Cultural Factors

There has been increasing interest in the role that the social and cultural pressures to be thin play in leading women in Western societies to diet and thereby increase their vulnerability to the development of an eating disorder. Dissatisfaction with body shape and the desire to be thin are especially widespread among young white women in these societies, and not surprisingly this group appears to be most likely to diet, which in vulnerable individuals (see above) leads to the development of an eating disorder. It has been argued that the process of normal gender-role socialization leads women to be particularly concerned about their appearance as well as approval from others. Therefore, in a society where thinness is valued and regarded as attractive, women, and especially young women in the process of establishing their identity, are particularly vulnerable to dissatisfaction with their shape and the pursuit of thinness.

STAGE TWO

Stage Two covers the period from the development of a behavioral precursor, usually dieting, to the development of frank disorder. Some of the risk factors discussed above appear to put individuals at risk for an eating disorder by increasing the likelihood they will diet. Yet, as noted earlier, although dieting increases the risk of subsequent disorder, the majority of those who diet do not develop disorder. The crucial issue for an account of the development of eating disorders is to determine what factors combine with dieting to produce disorder. There is virtually no research evidence on this question. It is not known whether, in those who are exposed to risk factors of the kind discussed above, the development of a behavioral precursor such as dieting acts like a precipitating factor that inevitably sets them on a pathway to disorder; whether associated features must develop (e.g., cognitive distortion concerning weight and shape of the type seen in eating disorders); or whether subsequent stressful events must occur. Among the events that have been implicated as possible precipitating factors are those that are a part of normal development, such as the onset of puberty; leaving home; and the beginning of new relationships, particularly with the opposite sex; as well as a range of negative events such as the death of a close relative, illness, and adverse comments on appearance. However, the research is limited, because it is based mostly on those with eating disorder symptoms rather than those with diagnosable eating disorders, because the timing of stress has not been clearly documented, and because many of the stressors implicated have not been shown either to be specific to eating disorders or to combine in a specific way with other features to produce the disorder.

STAGE THREE

Although it is clear that some eating disorders are transient while others become established or even chronic, virtually nothing is known about the natural history of these disorders. Most studies of their course have been of people with clinically detected and treated disorders, and researchers who have investigated community samples have studied few cases over relatively short periods.

At present three views on the maintenance of eating disorders may be proposed. The cognitive view suggests that the characteristic cognitive distortions concerning the extreme importance of weight and shape make most of the other features of the disorder explicable. According to this view, these cognitive features maintain the disorder, and recovery is only possible if there is a change in these attitudes. This view constitutes the underlying rationale for the successful cognitive behavioral approach to the treatment of bulimia nervosa (see Chapter 60), and it has received some direct empirical support.

The second view suggests that it is interpersonal events that have an important influence on the course of the disorder. This view has only indirect support, derived from the finding that changes in relationships and social circumstances observed during the course of family therapy for anorexia nervosa (see Chapter 56) and interpersonal psychotherapy for bulimia nervosa (see Chapter 60) appear to have beneficial effects on the course of these two disorders. Of course these two views are not mutually exclusive, and it may well be that interpersonal events either enhance or undermine self-esteem, which in turn leads to changes in the cognitive distortions.

The third view is primarily physiologically based and applies mainly to anorexia nervosa. It is that starvation-induced changes in physiological and psychosocial functioning perpetuate the disorder. Individuals with anorexia nervosa develop a range of abnormalities that appear to be the direct result of starvation (see Chapters 44 and 53), and some of these abnormalities, it is suggested, are likely to perpetuate the disorder. For example, delayed gastric emptying may enhance the perception of fullness and thereby inhibit eating, and lowered mood is likely to increase concerns about appearance and self-worth.

CONCLUSION

Despite the growing research interest in risk factors for the development of eating disorders, little is known about how individual risk factors combine with other vulnerability and protective factors to determine whether or not an individual follows a pathway to established or chronic disorder. Understanding these processes would not only increase theoretical knowledge but would provide the information necessary to plan realistic primary prevention and early intervention programs and to improve existing treatment for eating disorders.

FURTHER READING

Fairburn, C. G., Cooper, Z., & Cooper, P. J. (1986). The clinical features and maintenance of bulimia nervosa. In K. D. Brownell & J. P. Foreyt (Eds.), *Handbook of eating disorders: Physiology, psychology, and treatment of obesity, anorexia, and bulimia.* New York: Basic Books. A detailed account of the cognitive view of the maintenance of bulimia nervosa.

Garner, D. M. (1993). Pathogenesis of anorexia nervosa. *Lancet, 341,* 1631–1635. A concise review of factors contributing to the etiology of anorexia nervosa.

Kendler, K. S., MacLean, C., Neale, M., Kessler, R., Heath, A., & Eaves, L. (1991). The genetic epidemiology of bulimia nervosa. *American Journal of Psychiatry, 148,* 1627–1637. A research report providing evidence from a large representative sample for a genetic contribution to bulimia nervosa.

Patton, G. C. (1992). Eating disorders: Antecedents, evolution and course. *Annals of Medicine, 24,* 281–285. A review of the antecedents of eating disorders, with particular emphasis on the role of dieting.

Rastam, M. (1992). Anorexia nervosa in 51 Swedish adolescents: Premorbid problems and comorbidity. *Journal of the American Academy of Child and Adolescent Psychiatry, 31,* 819–829. An excellent case control study of factors contributing to the onset of anorexia nervosa in which many of the methodological problems discussed have been surmounted.

Rathner, G. (1992). Aspects of the natural history of normal and disordered eating and some methodological considerations. In W. Herzog, H.-C. Deter, & W. Vandereycken (Eds.), *The course of eating disorders*. Berlin: Springer-Verlag. A review of the studies of the natural course of eating disorders, with particular emphasis on issues of method.

Strober, M. (1991). Family–genetic studies of anorexia nervosa and bulimia nervosa. In K. Halmi (Ed.), *The psychobiology and treatment of anorexia nervosa and bulimia nervosa*. Washington, DC: American Psychiatric Press. An excellent critical review of family studies of anorexia nervosa and bulimia nervosa.

Welch, S. L., & Fairburn, C. G. (1994). Sexual abuse and bulimia nervosa: three integrated case control comparisons. *American Journal of Psychiatry, 151*, 402–407. A research report on the role of sexual abuse in bulimia nervosa which overcomes many of the methodological problems of previous work on etiology.

Wilson, G. T. (1993). Relation of dieting and voluntary weight loss to psychological functioning and binge eating. *Annals of Internal Medicine, 119*, 727–730. A review of the findings relating to dieting and weight loss, and an excellent discussion of the role of dieting in the development and maintenance of eating disorders.

• 36 •

THE DISTRIBUTION
OF EATING DISORDERS

Hans W. Hoek

Epidemiological studies show that eating disorders are not distributed randomly among the population. Young females constitute the most vulnerable group. In clinical samples only 5% to 10% of patients with an eating disorder are males. Eating disorders seem to be "Western" illnesses: they occur predominantly in industrialized, developed countries. Any reports of eating disorders outside the Western world tend to be of an anecdotal nature. Anorexia nervosa, for instance, seems to be uncommon both in non-Western countries and in less developed Western countries. Immigrants (e.g., Arab college students in London and Greek girls in Germany) are more likely to develop an eating disorder than their peers in their country of origin. Since World War II, the Japanese health care system has been confronted with increasing numbers of patients with anorexia nervosa. This type of evidence demonstrates that sociocultural factors play an important role in the distribution of eating disorders.

People in some professions seem to be particularly at risk; fashion models and ballet dancers, for instance, seem to be at greater risk for the development of an eating disorder than many other professional groups. However, what is not known is whether "preanorectic" persons are more readily attracted to the ballet world or whether *being* a ballet dancer is the source of increased risk. In some countries eating disorders are overrepresented among the middle and upper socioeconomic classes. But this social-class bias might be connected with the structures, norms, and thresholds of the local health care system. In European countries like the Netherlands, which has a rather generous state health insurance system, class differences seem to have less impact on the presentation and recognition of eating disorders.

Anorexia nervosa and bulimia nervosa are also widely regarded as relatively "modern" disorders. But, as discussed in Chapters 25 and 26, eating disorders similar to those seen today have existed for centuries. In recent years there has been such an increase in the registered incidence of eating disorders that some people are suggesting there is an "epidemic." Epidemiological data are not confirming that there has indeed been an equivalent increase in the number of cases in the general population.

EPIDEMIOLOGICAL RESEARCH

Researchers in epidemiology study the occurrence of disorders and try to determine the factors that are associated with vulnerability to the development of particular disorders (also see Chapter 35). Epidemiological research into eating disorders is still at the stage of determining the incidence and prevalence of the disorders within populations and comparing the rates among different groups. Incidence and prevalence are the two principal measures of the distribution of a disorder. The (point-) prevalence rate is the *actual* number of cases in a population at a certain point in time. The incidence rate is defined as the number of *new* cases in the population per year. Prevalence and incidence rates of eating disorders are commonly expressed as the rate per 100,000 population (male and female persons of all ages).

Prevalence

In the epidemiological research on eating disorders, prevalence studies vastly outnumber incidence studies. Prevalence studies of eating disorders are often conducted in high-risk populations such as schoolgirls or female college students. At present a two-stage screening survey is the most widely accepted procedure for case identification in the community. The first stage involves screening a large number of individuals for suspected cases by means of a questionnaire. The second stage involves (semistructured) interviews with the persons who, based on their answers to the questionnaire, are believed to have an eating disorder. Also interviewed are a number of randomly selected persons who, according to the questionnaires, do not suffer from such a disorder, so as to confirm that they are not eating-disorder patients. The two-stage surveys, using strict diagnostic criteria, of persons making up community samples reveal much lower prevalence rates than surveys that relied exclusively on questionnaires. The average figure for the point prevalence of anorexia nervosa thus determined is 280 per 100,000 young females (i.e., 0.28%). The average point prevalence of bulimia nervosa among young females, using strict diagnostic criteria, is about 1,000 per 100,000 (i.e., 1.0%).

Incidence of Anorexia Nervosa

Because the incidence of eating disorders is relatively low, no studies have been conducted on their incidence in the general population. It is impossible to screen a large population, for instance 100,000 people, for several years. Therefore the incidence rates have been based on reports of cases in health care systems. The incidence studies of anorexia nervosa have been based on hospital records or case registers of inpatients and outpatients in mental health care facilities. Although different strategies were used in these studies, overall the results show an increase in the registered incidence of anorexia nervosa between 1930 and 1970 but no increase thereafter (see Figure 36.1). Since the 1970s the incidence of anorexia nervosa cases reported in mental health care facilities has been about 5 per 100,000 of the (total) population per year.

The incidence of anorexia nervosa has also been studied in primary care facilities. General practitioners in the Netherlands, using criteria based on DSM-III-R, have studied the incidence of eating disorders in a large representative sample of the Dutch population. Between 1985 and 1989 the incidence of anorexia nervosa cases reported for primary care facilities was 8.1 per 100,000 population per year.

It is unclear whether the increase in cases reported in health care facilities reflects an actual increase in the incidence in the community, since it might also be due to improved methods of case detection or to the wider availability of services. Studies of clinical samples will always show an underestimation of the incidence of these disorders in the

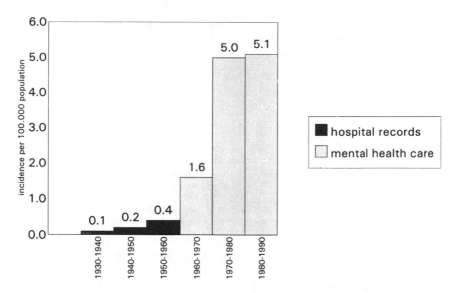

FIGURE 36.1. Registered incidence of anorexia nervosa per year (pooled data from different studies).

community, since only a minority of those with eating disorders come to medical attention.

Researchers in Rochester, Minnesota, have screened not only the records of patients with a diagnosis of anorexia nervosa, but also those of patients with amenorrhea, oligomenorrhea, starvation, weight loss, and other related diagnostic features. Between 1935 and 1984 the overall incidence of anorexia nervosa in the community of Rochester did not significantly increase. However, for 15- through 24-year-old females, a significant increase was found. The rates for older women remained relatively constant. As for the small number of males with anorexia nervosa, there was no change in incidence over time.

Incidence of Bulimia Nervosa

Since 1980, an "epidemic" of a new eating disorder, bulimia nervosa, has appeared in Western countries. Surveys using questionnaires have revealed that up to 19% of female students report bulimic symptoms.

Bulimia nervosa was distinguished as a separate disorder by Russell only in 1979 and by the American Psychiatric Association in DSM-III in 1980. Up until now the incidence of bulimia nervosa has been examined in primary care practice only, in part because most hospitals and case registers have been using the International Classification of Diseases (version 8 or 9), which does not provide a separate code for bulimia nervosa. General practitioners in the Netherlands, using DSM-III-R-based criteria, have studied the incidence of bulimia nervosa in a large representative sample of the Dutch population. They found the incidence of bulimia nervosa in primary care facilities to be 11.4 per 100,000 population per year during the period 1985 to 1989. A little over half of these patients in primary care were referred for mental health care, which yields an incidence in mental health care of 6 per 100,000 population per year.

The incidence rate of bulimia nervosa patients in primary care can serve only as minimum estimate of the true incidence rate in the community. Because of the secrecy that surrounds bulimia nervosa, the greater difficulty of detecting cases, compared with anorexia nervosa cases, and the paucity of community-based studies, the true incidence of bulimia nervosa is not known.

One-Year-Period Prevalence

One-year-period prevalence rates are useful measures for describing morbidity at different levels of health care. The 1-year-period prevalence is calculated by adding together the point prevalence and the annual incidence rate. Table 36.1 presents estimates of the 1-year-period prevalence rates per 100,000 young females at three levels of health care. Level zero represents the number of young females with an eating disorder in the community, whether or not they are receiving treatment. Level 1 consists of those patients whose primary care physicians consider as having "eating disorders." Level 2 represents patients with eating disorders who are receiving treatment from outpatient or inpatient mental health care services. The data are based on the findings of the two-stage surveys of the point prevalence of eating disorders, case register studies, and the results of the Dutch study of general practitioners' patients.

The 1-year-period prevalence rates at level zero represent the number of cases among young females in the community. The number of individuals with an eating disorder in the community who pass from level zero to level one depends on the "illness behavior" of the patient and the ability of the general practitioner to detect the eating disorder. With regard to illness behavior, we know that many patients deny or hide their eating disorder. We do not know how many people with eating disorders consult their primary care physicians for help with an eating problem or for some other reason. Results of several studies have shown that general practitioners have difficulty detecting eating disorders, particularly cases of bulimia nervosa. In countries like the Netherlands and Great Britain, the primary care physician occupies a critical position in determining who will be referred for psychiatric care: Indeed, the general practitioner can be regarded as a filter.

On the basis of the data presented in Table 36.1, it seems that over 40% (43%) of the community cases of anorexia nervosa are detected by general practitioners, and most of these patients (79%) are referred on for mental health care. In contrast, only a small proportion (11%) of the community cases of bulimia nervosa are detected, and of these only half (51%) are referred on.

TABLE 36.1. One-Year-Period Prevalence Rates per 100,000 Young Females

Level of health care	Anorexia nervosa	Bulimia nervosa
0. Community	370	1,500
1. Primary care	160	170
2. Mental health care	127	87

FURTHER READING

Fairburn, C. G., & Beglin, S. J. (1990). Studies of the epidemiology of bulimia nervosa. *American Journal of Psychiatry, 147,* 401–408. An excellent review of the prevalence of bulimia nervosa.

Goldberg, D., & Huxley, P. (1980). *Mental illness in the community: The pathway to psychiatric care.* London: Tavistock Publications. Details 1-year-period prevalence rates at different levels of morbidity for other psychiatric disorders.

Hoek, H. W. (1991). The incidence and prevalence of anorexia nervosa and bulimia nervosa in primary care. *Psychological Medicine, 21,* 455–460. The only study of the incidence of bulimia nervosa.

Hoek, H. W. (1993). Review of the epidemiological studies of eating disorders. *International Review of Psychiatry, 5,* 61–74. A recent review of epidemiological research, with a comprehensive list of references.

Hoek, H. W., & Brook, F. G. (1985). Patterns of care of anorexia nervosa. *Journal of Psychiatric Research, 19,* 155–160. Gives details of psychiatric case register studies.

Lucas, A. R., Beard, C. M., O'Fallon, W. M., & Kurland, L. T. (1991). 50-year trends in the incidence of anorexia nervosa in Rochester, Minn.: A population-based study. *American Journal of Psychiatry, 148,* 917–922. Important study of trends in the incidence of anorexia nervosa.

Russell, G. F. M. (1979). Bulimia nervosa: An ominous variant of anorexia nervosa. *Psychological Medicine, 9,* 429–448. Distinguishes bulimia nervosa as a new disorder.

Szmukler, G. I. (1985). The epidemiology of anorexia nervosa and bulimia. *Journal of Psychiatric Research, 19,* 143–153. A discussion of methodological problems in epidemiological research on eating disorders.

Vandereycken, W., & Hoek, H. W. (1992). Are eating disorders culture-bound syndromes? In K. A. Halmi (Ed.), *Psychobiology and treatment of anorexia nervosa and bulimia nervosa* (pp. 19–36). Washington, DC: American Psychiatric Press. A recent account of studies on sociocultural factors.

Williams, P., & King, M. (1987). The "epidemic" of anorexia nervosa: Another medical myth? *Lancet, i,* 205–207. The authors demonstrate that the recent increase in the incidence of anorexia nervosa may be more apparent than real.

• 37 •

FAMILY–GENETIC PERSPECTIVES ON ANOREXIA NERVOSA AND BULIMIA NERVOSA

Michael Strober

Converging evidence from family, twin, and adoption studies demonstrates the important, if not dominant, role played by genetic factors in personality formation, as well as in susceptibility to psychopathological disorders. An additional finding emerging from these very same studies concerns the strong influence of environment on the expression of personality and psychopathology phenotypes. But at odds with popular belief, the most robust of these nongenetic effects involves experiences that cause members of a family to differ in their behavior and in their liability to disorder; that is, the major contribution to familial resemblance in both normal and atypical personality development is not shared family environment but rather heredity and its interaction with life experiences—unique, or specific, to a given individual.

It is also increasingly evident that personality traits have conceptually and etiologically meaningful ties to psychopathological disorders, either predisposing to their onset, shaping the processes by which vulnerability comes to be expressed in clinical symptoms, or reflecting variable phenotypic manifestations of a common underlying liability. Observations such as these have spurred an exciting and profitable rapprochement between research efforts on personality, genetics, and psychological processes, allowing for more integrative explanatory models of complex behavioral phenomena.

Just the same, we remain distant from a definitive understanding of the fluidity and wide-ranging developmental variations in the processes underlying normal personality and maladaptation. Genetic influences on temperament and personality lay at least some of the foundation for sustained continuities in behavioral functioning, but heritability is neither fixed over the lifespan nor immutable. Much the same can be said of environmental effects and genotype–environment interactions, the relative importance of which change during the course of development. For this reason, the range of behavioral expressions of identical genetic vulnerabilities is likely to be substantial.

As cultural precepts and values also play a not unimportant role in shaping both the form and the content of psychopathological syndromes, particular clinicosomatopsychic features of illness are sometimes constituted differently in specific populations or age groups. The culture-boundness of eating disorders is, of course, self-evident (see Chapter 15). But the reframing of symptoms in terms of highly favored cultural norms provides little clarification of etiological issues. The fundamental reality is that in only a minority of young women do these culturally transacted behaviors culminate in debilitating and unrelenting cycles of starvation, binge eating, and psychological upheaval. It is because the association between maladaptivity and dieting is not widespread in the general population that the search for developmental, social, and biological risk and protective factors in the genesis of eating disorders remains scientifically defensible (see also Chapter 35).

FAMILY STUDIES

The tendency for a particular illness to cluster among relatives is the hallmark of intergenerational family transmission. This phenomenon has been demonstrated, with remarkable consistency, for all major categories of psychopathology. With regard to eating disorders, interest in the possible role of hereditary predisposition is not without historical precedent. As early as 1860, Louis Victor Marce opined that inherited psychopathologies were prominent in families of young women with anorexia nervosa, and that the rearing environment was often disturbed as well. Other, more contemporary reports can be found that also hint at the clustering of eating disorders or peculiar feeding habits in families; however, as these reports are derived without the benefit of specified diagnostic criteria, blind systematic examination of relatives, or case control subjects, their meaning is uncertain.

Recently a handful of studies have surfaced in which the researchers have attempted a more rigorous appraisal of family diagnostic patterns associated with anorexia nervosa and bulimia nervosa.

Of six published studies, in four significant evidence was found for familial aggregation, whereas in the other two the risk of eating disorders among relatives of eating disorder probands did not differ from that in relatives of controls. However, these inconsistencies are probably the result of methodological differences between studies. Both negative studies were disadvantaged by sample sizes possibly too small to make detection of familial differences possible and also by the near exclusive reliance on indirect, and therefore less precise, family diagnostic information. Overall, however, anorexia nervosa and bulimia nervosa appear to be several times more common among the biological relatives of anorexic and bulimic probands than in the general population, a finding that implicates the existence of some mechanism of transmissibility of illness within families.

TWIN STUDIES

Because separate genetic and environmental components of transmission cannot be readily inferred in the classic family study, the study of twin pairs has become an increasingly important focus of research in psychiatric genetics. A key advantage of this paradigm is that statistical analyses of differences in concordance between monozygotic (MZ) and dizygotic (DZ) twins can decompose the variance in liability to illness into independent genetic and environmental sources and give estimates of their relative magnitudes. Extensions of the twin paradigm have been used recently to elucidate the contributions made by common and unique genetic and environmental factors to syndrome comorbidities.

The author is familiar with at least six reports in which the researchers examined differential concordance for eating disorders in MZ and DZ twin pairs. Three of these reports, concerned principally with the genetics of anorexia nervosa, contain analyses apparently conducted of overlapping samples of twins recruited by advertisement and twins seeking treatment. Concordance rates are substantially greater for MZ than for DZ twins, implicating a strong etiological role for genetic factors, with heritability estimates in the range of 0.5 to 0.9. By contrast, an analysis given in one of these reports on a subset of twins ascertained as having bulimia nervosa assigns a more prominent causal role to environmental factors, with negligible genetic involvement.

Contrary to this latter finding, results of the three twin studies of bulimia nervosa give evidence of genetic factors in familial liability. However, in two of the studies, this conclusion is seriously weakened by the use of very small samples, an ascertainment strategy potentially biased toward the selection of concordant MZ twins, lack of blind diagnoses, and incomplete zygosity evaluation. These methodological inadequacies were avoided in a third study, in which personal diagnostic interviews were conducted independently with over 2,000 female twins ascertained from the Virginia population-based registry. In this series, concordance was significantly higher in MZ than in DZ twin pairs; model fitting suggested that familial resemblance for bulimia nervosa was due mainly to additive gene action, with heritability and individual-specific environmental influences each accounting for roughly 50% of the variance in liability. Rates of illness were also found to be higher in later birth cohorts, suggesting a greater likelihood of expressing bulimia in more recently born individuals. However, artifactual explanations of this phenomenon, for example, memory effects and increased self-recognition of bulimia as a treatable disorder among younger individuals, are also plausible.

OTHER FAMILIAL DISORDERS LINKED
TO ANOREXIA NERVOSA AND BULIMIA NERVOSA

In clinical samples, eating disorders are strongly associated with various other categories of psychopathological disturbance. This covariation among disorders has several potential sources, including genetic factors with behaviorally diverse expressivity, a common family environmental influence predisposing to multiple disorders, and individual–specific environmental events predisposing to multiple disorders. Accordingly, studies of the familial prevalence of psychiatric illness occurring in relation to eating disorders have been undertaken with the aim of clarifying possible causal and nosological ties.

Evidence supporting the coaggregation of various psychiatric disorders among relatives of patients with anorexia nervosa and bulimia nervosa is now available. While these studies vary appreciably in their methodological rigor, and inconsistencies in the diagnostic methods used are notable, they show, with rare exception, that the lifetime rates of certain diagnoses, mood disorders in particular, are significantly higher in relatives of patients than in relatives of control subjects. For unipolar and bipolar affective illness combined, relative risks are in the range of 2 to 3.5, indicating that affective disorders are several times more likely to develop in the biological kin of individuals with eating disorders than in people drawn at random from the general population.

Less clear is whether or not these data unambiguously support the assumption that eating disorders and mood disorders are linked to a common liability that is familially transmitted. Data relevant to this question are rather limited and contradictory. While some studies show that the increased aggregation of mood disorders in the relatives of anorexic or bulimic probands is strongly predicted by affective comorbidity in the probands, in other studies increased risk is found even among relatives of nondepressed anorexic and bulimic probands. The former observation implies independent—hence etiologically distinctive—familial transmission of these conditions, while the latter is consistent with the presence of a single, shared diathesis with variability of expression perhaps determined by unique environmental and/or genetic factors. However, in the largest of the family studies of eating disorders conducted to date, the author and his colleagues found that the cross-prevalence of eating disorders among relatives of control subjects with affective illness was zero, suggesting that the shared comorbidity of mood and eating disorders in individuals and their coaggregation in families are not likely to result from a single causal factor predisposing to both.

The possibility exists, nevertheless, of some degree of overlap in the family–genetic liability to bulimia nervosa and major depression. This overlap is suggested by a recent analysis of the sources of comorbidity in over 1,000 female twin pairs, obtained as part of the Virginia twin register study mentioned above. The best-fitting model applied to the observed lifetime comorbidity of the two diagnoses yielded a genetic correlation of 0.46, suggesting a modest sharing of predisposing genes. In other words, certain genetic factors may influence the risk of both major depression and bulimia. At the same time, the two clearly are not identical conditions, as substantial variance in the liability was found to result from genetic and environmental risk factors specific to each disorder.

Another line of inquiry gaining in importance because of its potential for supplying knowledge of etiology and pathogenesis concerns possible linkages between eating disorders and substance abuse. Clinically there is considerable support for the greater prevalence of substance use and abuse among the subgroup of eating-disorder patients with binge eating. Theoretically intriguing is the notion that this greater prevalence of abuse in the bulimic subgroup of anorexics and in those with bulimia nervosa is paralleled by analogous differences at the level of phenotypic personality structure and in the domain of family environment. Specifically, whereas restricting anorexics and their parents commonly express extremes of emotional constraint, conscientiousness, and avoidance of intense or novel experiences, the contrasting pattern of affective lability, increased sociability and stimulus seeking, coupled with family transactions marked by rancor, discord, and alienation of affection, is usually found with greater frequency in the backgrounds of patients with binge eating.

One implication of these broad generalizations is that divergent phenotypic patterns of emotionality and constraint may reflect familial temperamental traits that strongly correlate with other disinhibitory behavioral syndromes. Indeed, with respect to alcoholism, evidence from studies recently completed by me support a substantial familial link with binge eating. Specifically, relatives of patients with bulimia nervosa, as well as relatives of anorexics with binge eating, had a threefold to fourfold higher lifetime risk of substance use disorders than relatives of normal control subjects and relatives of restricting anorexics. Moreover, increased risk of substance abuse occurred even among relatives of non-substance-abusing patients, suggesting a common liability that influences the risk of both types of psychopathology.

Although further replication will be necessary to substantiate this possibility, a recent molecular genetic analysis of the D2 dopamine receptor (DRD2) gene in obese people is suggestive. The dopaminergic receptor was selected for study because of the well-established role of this aminergic system in mediating the reinforcing effects of food as well as of psychoactive substances. The prevalence of DRD2 alleles was investigated in 73 non-substance-abusing men and women. The major find of interest was that the minor allele of this gene was strongly associated with carbohydrate preference among subjects. Of course, carbohydrate preference in the obese may have little relevance to the phenomenon of binge eating. Just the same, given recent research suggesting that this minor allele may be more common among individuals with severe alcoholism, cocaine abuse, and polysubstance abuse, the intriguing possibility exists that heritable variations in functional activity of certain brain reward pathways may be one component of susceptibility to the development, and then sustained reinforcement, of a phenotypically wide range of dysregulated consummatory behaviors. Although the particular behavioral expression of this diathesis may be determined by contextual factors (e.g., a parent's emphasis on physical appearance, a person's exposure to drinking, or involvement in activities that give emphasis to weight control), a common genetic factor would explain why these behaviors covary to a high degree in individuals and within families.

SPECULATIONS ON THE NATURE AND PATHOGENIC INFLUENCE OF INHERITED DIATHESES

Because anorexia nervosa arrests the broad unfolding of self-development and pubertal biological processes, a focus on temperament and personality as heritable traits that may confer a disadvantage in negotiating developmental pressures is suggested as a new direction for theoretical and clinical understanding. Indeed, the seminal writings of Morton, Gull, and Lasègue suggest with perceptiveness and foresight that anorexia nervosa is underpinned by unusual sensitivities and extremes of personality. Clinical and empirical studies largely confirm and extend these accounts, consistently documenting in cases of anorexia nervosa the unusually common presence of emotional restraint, avoidance of novelty and intensity, anxious worry and self-doubt, compliancy, and perseverance in the face of nonreward. These traits cannot be dismissed as mere epiphenomena of starvation, as they often presage the onset of illness and remain even after long-term weight restoration. It is proposed then that the risk of anorexia nervosa is precipitated from an irreconcilable tension between heritable personality traits that bias the individual toward anxious worry, unyielding insistance on order and regularity in behavioral routines, and seeking self-validation from external rewards, and the opposing, normative pressures of adolescent development pushing toward increasing emotionality and instinctualization of behavior, adaptability to change, self-directed thought, and greater affiliation and intimacy in social ties. For the anorexic, the constructed meaning and intrapsychic experience of puberty are menacing and disquieting forces that threaten a previously well-established and reassuring sense of order and predictability, eventually prompting the urgent need for defensive adaptations that dampen emotional displays and restore rigid behavioral action patterns. It is further proposed that these phenotypic personality structures and their underlying biological substrates are continuous with the symptomaticity of anorexia nervosa itself, priming and shaping the rigidly fixed, ritualized and perseverative self-starvation and the seemingly unrelenting, obsession-like attention to body weight and shape.

Environmental influences on the unfolding of risk cannot be lightly dismissed. Inasmuch as family members often show resemblances in personality, the restricting anorexic frequently experiences an environment in which emotional restraint and rigid control of behavior are prominently expressed. And by the same token, these genotypic tendencies regularly evoke praise and admiration from teachers and peers, just as they confer extreme sensitivity on parenting styles or social interactions marked by emotional intensity, boundary intrusions, or disruptiveness. A reasonable supposition is that these gene–environment effects play an important contributory role in determining why certain individuals ultimately exhibit symptoms while others do not.

Other evidence for a correspondence between genetic, behavioral, and biological influences is provided by recent studies of functional serotonergic activity in those with anorexia nervosa (see Chapter 45). These studies indicate that neuronal serotonergic activity increases in patients well after weight is restored to normal levels. These data, however preliminary, are intriguing, given the current understanding of the role played by this neurotransmitter in restraining reward motivation for exploring novel environments, modulating feeding and sexual behavior, and regulating the sensitivity of neurobehavioral systems to stimulus events. In short, high levels of serotonergic activity in people with anorexia nervosa may play a role in its pathogenesis by shaping, in certain individuals, marked behavioral propensities toward rigidity and constraint. Complementing this idea, and of further developmental significance, is the characterization of the serotonergic system as being more responsive to stimulus perturbations in females than it is in males, possibly facilitating, at least in part, the patterning of sex-stereotypic behavioral tendencies as well as gender differences in the risk of certain pathological conditions. In sum, there is mounting logically consistent evidence of interrelationships between genetic, biological, dispositional, and socioenvironmental factors in the pathogenesis of this behavioral syndrome.

In the case of bulimia nervosa, dispositional traits such as thrill seeking and excitability, coupled with less persistence and a tendency toward more pronounced dysphoria in response to rejection or nonreward, present a contrasting pattern to that witnessed in those with restricting anorexia nervosa. It has been suggested that these personality features militate against sustained dietary restriction and thus predispose to periodic lapses in control and eventual dietary chaos. A further implication of the evidence discussed here is that heritable variations in the sensitivity of brain systems to the reward properties of feeding behavior may also exist in certain subgroups as a diathesis that facilitates the development and pathological reinforcement of extreme consummatory patterns. Considering the background of brittle family attachments and negative emotionality often associated with bulimia nervosa, the psychological effects attributed to binge eating—for example, the sense of need gratification, soothing, and temporary relief from distressful affects—may also be a necessary dynamic process that contributes to the dogged persistence of this behavior. These ideas are to be recognized as broad generalizations, since the similarity of binge eating in anorexia nervosa and bulimia nervosa may encapsulate heterogeneity across several domains of causal variables. Whether or not there are similar precursors, triggers, and maintaining factors underlying the binge eating in anorexia nervosa and bulimia nervosa is a question yet to be resolved.

CONCLUSION

This discussion highlights the potential contribution of heritable factors to the pathogenesis of eating disorders. It is implied that the search for etiologic processes must, however, retain its broad perspective, as the pathways to symptom formation are multiple and interactive. The exact manner in which genes contribute to familial aggregation of eating disorders remains speculative, but their influence on personality traits and the biological processes underlying certain components of behavior regulation offer suggestive hypotheses. Finally, it is argued that the clinical features of anorexia nervosa and bulimia nervosa are not isolated, discrete events but rather pathological exaggerations of heritable personality and biological propensies. This notion of a conceptual and empirical link between genes, personality, and symptomaticity is put forth as a plausible heuristic framework for future clinical and theoretical study.

FURTHER READING

Kendler, K. S., MacLean, C., Neale, M., Kessler, R., Heath, A., & Eaves, L. (1991). The genetic epidemiology of bulimia nervosa. *American Journal of Psychiatry, 148,* 1627–1637. This article presents results from a population-based Virginia twin registry study of the genetics of bulimia nervosa. Both genetic and environmental risk factors are identified as contributing to the liability to develop this disorder.

Strober, M. (1991). Family–genetic studies of eating disorders. *Journal of Clinical Psychiatry, 52*(10, Suppl.), 9–12. A general review of existing data pertaining to family–genetic influences on risk and vulnerability.

Strober, M. (1992). Family–genetic studies. In K. Halmi (Ed.), *Psychobiology and treatment of anorexia nervosa and bulimia nervosa* (pp. 61–76). Washington, DC: American Psychiatric Press. A detailed review and critique of family and twin studies of anorexia nervosa and bulimia nervosa.

Woodside, D. B. (1993). Genetic contributions to eating disorders. In A. S. Kaplan & P. E. Garfinkel (Eds.), *Medical issues and eating disorders: The interface* (pp. 193–211). New York: Brunner/Mazel. A review of methods in psychiatric genetics and their applications to research on eating disorders.

• 38 •

THE FAMILIES OF PATIENTS WITH AN EATING DISORDER

Walter Vandereycken

Early family theories and studies of eating disorders overemphasized the mother–child relationship, reflecting the myth that "parenting means mothering." Later the "absent father" gradually came into the picture. Then the importance of the whole family was stressed in the systems theory approach. The interaction between the parental subsystem and the children was usually analyzed in terms of communication, problem solving, boundary setting, and so on. Only in recent years have researchers started to focus on the specific educational role of parents. Eating disorder patients' siblings may be considered a "forgotten" group, and interest in married patients—their choice of partners, their marital interactions, and their offspring—is still marginal.

Most of these topics will be briefly reviewed in this chapter. The inheritance of eating disorders is discussed in Chapter 37, and the relationship between sexual abuse and eating disorders is covered in Chapter 40.

FAMILY SIZE AND BIRTH ORDER

It has been suggested that anorexia nervosa patients are, more often than expected, only children, whereas others have claimed the opposite. Systematic comparative studies of large clinical samples, however, have failed to reveal any significant relation between family size and the presence of an eating disorder. Similarly it has been suggested that anorexic patients are more often firstborns or "lastborns" than would be expected. But again, in controlled studies, no significant differences in birth order have been observed. Furthermore, follow-up studies of anorexics have shown that neither sibship position nor family size has prognostic significance. This finding does not exclude the possibility, however, that in some cases a child's occupation of a "special" position within the family may be linked to the development of an eating disorder.

SIBLINGS

In the bulk of the literature on the families of eating disorder patients, siblings occupy a strikingly marginal position. Some special attention has been paid to twins in attempts to explore possible hereditary aspects of eating disorders. Compared with those in "normal" families, siblings of eating disorder patients seem to show a somewhat greater likelihood of developing eating and weight problems themselves, as well as mental disorders, especially mood and substance abuse disorder. Nevertheless the research in this area is too fragmentary and scarce to conclude that these siblings are "sick" or "at risk." Moreover, clinicians and researchers appear to be primarily interested in the problems of sibship while overlooking the positive role brothers and sisters can play in either protecting siblings or facilitating siblings' recovery from an eating disorder. Important issues on which almost no systematic research has been done concern the patient's identification with, overattachment to, or rivalry with a sibling. These issues may pose serious difficulties, especially for twins.

FAMILY STRUCTURE AND INTERACTION

In self-report studies that reveal the "insider's perspective" on the ideational world of the family, it is suggested that bulimic patients view their families as conflicted, badly organized, noncohesive, and lacking in nurturance and caring. Anorexics perceive their families as stable, nonconflictual, cohesive, and with no lack of nurturance. Although parents in general report similar perceptions, they tend to be less extreme in their reports than their eating disordered daughters.

Observational studies, relying on the "outsider's view" of how the family interacts, seem to yield a picture that only partially corresponds to the self-report findings (the similarity is greater in bulimics than in anorexics). Compared with "normals," anorexic families show more rigidity in their family organization, have less clear interpersonal boundaries, and tend to avoid open discussions of disagreements between parents and children. As such, the anorexic family may be characterized as "consensus-sensitive," whereas the bulimic family appears more as "distance-sensitive." The latter implies stronger interpersonal boundaries, less avoidance of disagreements but a less stable family organization. Observers tend to see bulimic patients as angrily submissive to rather hostile and neglectful parents.

CHILDREARING

In the literature on the families of eating-disorder patients, the educational role of the parents and their parenting style have been neglected to a great extent. From a clinical viewpoint, the most commonly observed feature is the lack of adequate joint parental authority. This term means that the parents have problems finding a balance between adequate (i.e., rational and flexible) control of their child and the age-appropriate autonomy they give to the child. In many cases these problems appear to be related to the parents' failure to reach a basic agreement about child-rearing issues. Of course these shortcomings in conjoint parental functioning may reflect problems in the marital relationship.

The studies of parental rearing practices and attitudes have yielded a wide variety of findings that make it difficult to connect an eating disorder in adolescence with a particular pattern of parental relationship in childhood. For bulimic patients, the emerging picture seems to be relatively consistent. They recall their rearing in childhood as being characterized by a lack of care by both parents but especially by their mothers.

These mothers, however, are not perceived as overprotective. Thus a picture emerges of "neglectful parenting." Since fathers are more often seen as overprotective, their rearing practices are viewed by the patients as closer to a pattern of "affectionless control." Before attempting to explain such an experienced parenting style, one should first take some methodological problems into account (see discussion paragraph below) and second, view it in the broader perspective of family (dys)functioning as sketched in previous paragraphs.

MARRIED PATIENTS

Anorexia nervosa and bulimia nervosa are typically considered to affect adolescent girls. Nevertheless these disorders are often observed in adult women, either as a continuation of an eating disorder that originated during adolescence or as one that developed de novo during adulthood. Since many of these older patients are married or live as married, the questions arise as to what impact an eating disorder has on marital relationships and how marital relationships influence the course of an eating disorder. If a significant connection exists between the occurrence of an eating disorder and the properties of the patient's marriage, it is evident that the latter must be taken into account in treatment.

Surprisingly the marital relationships of adult eating-disorder patients have received little research attention. In fact the literature about this patient group consists almost exclusively of descriptive case reports, offering at best a variety of clinical speculations about these patients' marital characteristics. The lack of empirical data is particularly striking in view of the widely accepted role that family variables play in the development of eating disorders during adolescence. It seems reasonable to assume that the quality of these patients' marital relationships also influences the course of their eating disorders. One of the major observations emphasized in the clinical literature is that married patients and their partners often report a significant degree of dissatisfaction with their relationships. While the subjects themselves usually regard their marital problems as the result of the patient's eating problem, clinicians often assume the opposite: They conclude there is collusion, a lack of intimacy, communication deficiencies, conflict avoidance, or hidden power struggles between the two partners. Since these views are based on the clinician's subjective impression, however, they should be regarded as tentative.

In the only controlled study, in which both self-report findings and data from coded videotaped interactions were used, eating-disorder couples appeared to lack some of the "nondistressed" couples' skills of constructive communication but managed to avoid the destructive communication style of "maritally distressed" couples. The overall level of intimacy was lower than that of "normal" couples but higher than that of "maritally distressed" couples. Whereas this quantitative difference may reflect the couples' different levels of marital satisfaction, an additional qualitative discrimination might be made between eating-disorder couples and the two control groups on the basis of the former group's relatively low level of openness and intimacy. This combination of (probably interrelated) interactional problems—the lack of openness, a low level of intimacy, and deficient communication skills—may represent an important obstacle to the constructive evolution of the marriage and for recovery from the eating disorder.

DISCUSSION

Reports on the characteristics of eating-disorder families are difficult to compare because of differences in the assessment methods used (e.g., self-report measures, interview, and direct observation) and the great variation in sociocultural and demographic characteristics of the subjects. The assessment of the patients' and/or other relatives' perception of the family may also be colored by the nature of the crisis that brought the patient into treatment. Again, this assessment may be influenced by the subject's actual degree of attachment to or emotional separation from the family. Since separation–individuation is a core issue for many anorexics and bulimics, it should be taken into account when analyzing patients' family perceptions. Patients' ages and, perhaps more important, their stage in the family life cycle (e.g., the "leaving home" phase) is also relevant to the evaluation of family interactions.

An important methodological stumbling block concerns the attitude of eating-disorder patients and their families toward psychological assessment. In the acute stage, before entering into treatment, anorexic patients in particular often deny any problems. They also have a tendency to try to please clinicians and researchers, with the result that their answering patterns may be distorted in the direction of social desirability. Anorexia nervosa families of the middle and upper social classes are known for their tendency to idealize the family picture or at least to present themselves as if nothing was wrong except for the eating disorder. It is important to note that family interactions may be linked to particular communication patterns. It has been found, for example, that the levels of critical comments from parents toward bulimic offspring were significantly higher during the latter's early years than those towards anorexic offspring.

A dysfunctional family interaction, or its description by a family member, may be seen, therefore, as an expression of a more general negative atmosphere within the families of bulimic patients. However, it must also be noted that in distressed parent–child relationships, chronic negative emotions may be both a cause and a consequence of interactions that undermine parents' concerns and children's development.

These observations highlight an important point concerning the families of patients with an eating disorder, namely, that even if a disturbed family interaction pattern is found, its specificity and causal significance remain to be demonstrated. Nevertheless it is worthwhile to study family characteristics, because—even if we cannot prove they have played a special role in the development of anorexia or bulimia nervosa—they may be of great relevance to the planning of treatment, especially if a family-oriented treatment is to be used. From a transgenerational perspective, it is also important to search for repeating patterns of family interactions (such as those usually found in cases of physical and sexual abuse), since, if present, they provide a potential opportunity for preventive work, especially since it is known that eating-disorder patients sometimes have serious parenting difficulties themselves (see Chapter 33).

FURTHER READING

Hodes, M., & Le Grange, D. (1993). Expressed emotion in the investigation of eating disorders: A review. *International Journal of Eating Disorders, 13,* 279–288. Discusses an issue that is best known in studies of schizophrenic patients and might have an important prognostic meaning for anorexia nervosa and bulimia nervosa.

Van den Broucke, S., Vandereycken, W., & Vertommen, H. (1995). Marital communication in eating disorder patients: A controlled observational study. *International Journal of Eating Disorders, 17*, 1–22. The only controlled study of eating disorder patients in which both self-report and observational data on marital interaction are used.

Vandereycken, W. (in press). Parental rearing behavior and eating disorders. In C. Perris, W. A. Arrindell, & M. Eisemann (Eds.), *Parenting and psychopathology*. Chichester, UK: John Wiley. An overview of the studies on the relationship between childrearing and the occurrence of an eating disorder later in life.

Vandereycken, W., Kog, E., & Vanderlinden, J. (1989). *The family approach to eating disorders: Assessment and treatment of anorexia nervosa and bulimia.* New York and London: PMA Publishing. A detailed review and discussion of all family-related topics in eating disorders, from both a clinical and a research viewpoint.

Vandereycken, W., & Van Vreckem, E. (1992). Siblings of patients with an eating disorder. *International Journal of Eating Disorders, 12*, 273–280. A review of the research literature on family size, birth order, and eating and other disorders in siblings, as well as sibling rivalry and incest.

Wonderlich, S. (1992). Relationship of family and personality factors in bulimia. In J. H. Crowther, D. L. Tennenbaum, S. E. Hobfoll, & M. A. Parris Stephens (Eds.), *The etiology of bulimia nervosa: The individual and familial context* (pp. 103–126). Washington and Philadelphia: Hemisphere Publishing. A concise and critical review of familial processes in bulimia nervosa with special emphasis on the relationship to the patients' personality.

Woodside, D. B., & Shekter-Wolfson, L. F. (1990). Parenting by patients with anorexia nervosa and bulimia nervosa. *International Journal of Eating Disorders, 9*, 303–309. Warns that eating-disorder patients may show serious shortcomings in their own parenting.

Woodside, D. B., Shekter-Wolfson, L. F., Brandes, J. S., & Lackstrom, J. B. (1993). *Eating disorders and marriage: The couple in focus.* New York: Brunner/Mazel. The only available book on this subject, with special emphasis on clinical assessment and treatment.

• 39 •

A FEMINIST PERSPECTIVE ON THE ETIOLOGY OF EATING DISORDERS

Ruth H. Striegel-Moore

The eating disorders common among girls and women in Western or Westernized modern societies, namely anorexia nervosa and bulimia nervosa, are defined by body image disturbance, excessive weight control efforts, and, in bingeing anorexics and in bulimics, loss of control over eating. Epidemiologic studies have uncovered several important facts about these disorders (see Chapters 35 and 36). They are rarely found in non-Western societies; they are significantly more common among women than men; symptoms of eating disorders are widely prevalent among women, whereas the clinical syndromes are rare; and the prevalence of eating disorders has increased markedly during the past three decades. These observations have prompted three basic questions: Why now? Why women? and Which women in particular? An extensive feminist literature has offered answers to these three questions, which I will address in this chapter.

At its core, a feminist approach to eating disorders involves the insistence that women's attitudes toward, feelings about, and behaviors directed at influencing their bodies need to be understood within the context of Western philosophical, political, and cultural history. Symptoms of eating disorders are viewed as representing individual expressions of "dis-ease" that are rooted in the cultural construction of femininity. Anorexia nervosa and bulimia nervosa are each seen as an extreme end-point on a continuum of discontent related to weight and eating. Although feminist explanations deemphasize the role of individual characteristics (e.g., personality traits and biological variables) in the etiology of eating disorders (see Chapter 35), feminists do not minimize or negate the suffering experienced by an eating-disordered person, nor do they advocate that these disorders should go untreated.

There is a considerable diversity in feminist approaches to the etiology of eating disorders. In part this diversity reflects the evolution of feminist scholarship in general. For example, recent work shows a move away from describing women primarily as victims of an oppressive beauty norm toward more complex explorations of women's preoccupation with their bodies. The later work acknowledges female agency. Built into these later models is the recognition that women are not simply passive recipients of, but rather active respondents to, cultural demands; for example, women are seen as capable of consciously resisting, creatively subverting, or deliberately accepting such demands. The purpose of this chapter is not to do justice to the richness and diversity of these feminist efforts; rather it is to elaborate on the basic tenets of this paradigm. The question, "Why now?" will be considered first to provide the context within which the questions "Why women?" and "Which women in particular?" will be explored.

WHY NOW?

The Historical Context

Deeply rooted in Western philosophy is the view of the human body as an impediment to man's ability to achieve valued goals such as "the truth," objectivity, or self-actualization. The specific reasons for the perceived problematic nature of the body have changed over time, yet the basic stance toward the body has remained constant: The body is inferior to the mind. For example, Greek philosophers were disturbed by the unreliability of the senses, which was seen as an obstacle to man's quest for the truth. In contrast, current formulations of the body's limitations are described relative to goals such as health and achievement. Beyond this age-old juxtaposition of body and mind, to understand eating disorders requires the recognition that body and mind are gendered constructs. In Western cultures, the body is constructed as passive, untamed, in need of restraint, and feminine; the mind is seen as active, noble, cultured, and masculine.

Women's vulnerability to eating disorders further derives from the power inequity between men and women. This power differential has been shown to contribute to gender-related differences in motivation, behavior, and personality traits. For example, recent research has revealed that gender-related differences in empathy, assertiveness, and susceptibility to social influence are due primarily to differences in the social status between the sexes. An important consequence of women's inferior social status is the devaluation of characteristics associated with, or ascribed to, being female. Because power and the pressure to conform to social norms are inversely related, women experience greater social sanctions than men if they do not live up to gender-related expectations. Moreover, women encounter certain gender-specific stressful life events that contribute to the risk of developing an eating disorder. For example, women are more likely than men to experience childhood sexual abuse, an event that has been shown to be associated with psychiatric illness in adulthood. Although its role as a risk factor specific to eating disorders has been challenged, the significance of childhood sexual abuse as a general risk factor is indisputable (see Chapter 40).

Cultural Changes in the Recent Past

Several cultural factors have been implicated in the increase in incidence rates for eating disorders during the past few decades. Of these, the female beauty ideal has received the most scholarly attention. Result of several studies illustrate the contiguity between an increasingly thin female beauty ideal and a rise in the prevalence of eating disorders. Because the thin beauty ideal is biologically unattainable for most women, experiencing a discrepancy between the cultural ideal and one's biological reality is normative, and profound body image dissatisfaction is common. Moreover, our culture promotes the view of the human body as infinitely malleable and considers weight to be a matter of personal choice. Not surprisingly, then, many women engage in efforts to attain the thin ideal. These behavioral efforts, dieting and purging in particular, are thought to put women at risk for an eating disorder: Symptoms of eating disorders such as a preoccupation with food and episodic binge eating are understood to derive from the physiological and psychological consequences of dietary deprivation.

The relentless pursuit of thinness has been supported by appearance-related industries that have experienced exponential growth over the past few decades. Increasingly drastic interventions are being promoted as normal efforts to achieve thinness. One example is the extraordinary increase in the number of liposuction procedures conducted to reduce body fat. Appearance-related industries capitalize on and contribute to the growing importance of physical appearance in Western cultures' construction of personal identity: Image has become a central part of identity and is now used to convey invisible aspects of identity such as personality traits.

Several scholars have noted that in this century the shifts in the female beauty ideal toward extreme thinness have occurred during periods when women have made significant progress toward greater political or personal freedom. For example, in the United States, the flapper look was fashionable when women gained the right to vote; Twiggy came to represent the new beauty ideal of a generation of women with unprecedented access to educational opportunities. The "waif" look is now *en vogue* as women have moved beyond struggling for equal access to all educational or vocational domains and have begun to successfully integrate multiple, and potentially conflicting, social roles.

Among feminists, the meaning of the thin beauty ideal remains a matter of considerable debate. Some have proposed that our culture values thinness as a symbol of progress toward women's liberation. The thin female body is the antithesis to the ample *feminine* body, and it connotes highly valued characteristics such as independence and self-control. Women's weight-loss efforts are fueled by a "myth of transformation": beyond its promise of greater physical attractiveness, weight loss is expected to offer an escape from traditional sex-role constraints and to provide access to interpersonal and financial success.

In contrast, others have suggested that the thin ideal emerged in reaction to women's increased power, to women "taking up too much space." In this view, thinness is seen as a symbol of fragility and self-effacement. The thin ideal is thought to serve the function of controlling and containing women's social ambitions by directing women toward a beauty ideal that is attainable only through extraordinary and sustained effort, if at all. Moreover, because thinness is presented to women as a realistic possibility, failure to achieve the thin ideal renders women vulnerable to shame and self-doubt and thus undermines their sense of self-empowerment. Yet others have argued that these contradictory meanings of thinness coexist; indeed, the very appeal thinness has for women lies precisely in its multiple meanings.

Few scholars have examined whether recent concurrent changes in women's sexual behavior and the increase in eating disorders are coincidental. Specifically, during the past few decades, adolescent girls have become sexually active at increasingly younger ages, with a greater likelihood of having several sexual partners before getting married. Some girls feel ill prepared for adult sexuality and report experiencing considerable peer pressure to be sexually active. An extensive clinical literature describes the role of psychosexual development in the etiology of eating disorders, noting, for example, the fear of adult sexuality as the motivation for self-starvation. Binge eating may be the result of prolonged dieting efforts; alternatively, binge eating may develop as a means of coping with sexual anxieties. Less well understood is the influence on eating disorders of the consequences of adolescent sexual behavior, including teenage pregnancy and sexually transmitted diseases, problems that have become significantly more common during the past few decades.

It is clear that cultural factors have influenced our definitions of femininity (i.e., of the characteristics expected of and desired in women). Gender-role expectations are internalized at an early age, and gender identity forms a central aspect of overall identity. An exploration of female identity development reveals how cultural factors translate into individual vulnerability for an eating disorder.

WHY WOMEN?

Two elements of femininity as defined by Western culture are thought to contribute to women's risk for an eating disorder. These include the prescription of a "relational self" and the association between beauty and femininity.

The Relational Self

In Western culture, feminine identity is relationally defined. Women are raised to place great value on interpersonal relationships, to define themselves in terms of their relationships with others, and to develop the skills required for initiating and maintaining close relationships. As a consequence, women's self-worth is determined by the ability to engage in mutually empathic and reciprocally empowering relationships. A woman's failed effort at finding mutuality and understanding in a relationship is experienced as a fundamental challenge to her identity and evokes feelings of shame, self-doubt, and low self-esteem.

Women's relational orientation renders them vulnerable to others' opinions and behaviors, particularly during adolescence. Girls are ill prepared for the developmental tasks of adolescence, which include developing a coherent, positive sense of self; achieving autonomy; and establishing heterosexual relationships. Girls report greater identity instability, more social anxiety, and lower self-esteem than do boys. One mechanism involved in the etiology of eating disorders is stress-induced eating. Eating provides a palliative coping response to the stresses experienced because of interpersonal vulnerability.

An extensive social psychological literature gives documentation to the idea that physical attractiveness is a powerful determinant of interpersonal success. Although both women and men benefit from being attractive, beauty matters especially in the lives of women. Women's success at finding and keeping a romantic partner is influenced to a greater extent by physical attractiveness than it is for men. It makes sense that women place priority on achieving the culturally mandated beauty ideal: They are highly motivated to find social approval and to have meaningful relationships, and they realize the importance of beauty for interpersonal attraction. The emphasis on thinness and beauty underlies a second mechanism of risk. To achieve thinness, women engage in dieting and related weight control behaviors, which, in turn, contribute to the development of eating disorders.

Beauty and Femininity

Aside from the relational benefits of being attractive, concern with one's appearance and efforts to enhance and maintain one's beauty are further motivated by the fact that in popular terms feminity and beauty are inextricably linked. The importance of being attractive is conveyed to girls from an early age, and the cultural emphasis placed on attractiveness is reinforced in various contexts of socialization. Parents select (and markets provide) "gendered" clothing and toys: Products made for girls emphasize the importance of being pretty. In a recent national report of research on the status of girls in American educational institutions, it was concluded that schools continue to provide different academic and social experiences for female and male students. For example, compared with boys, girls receive more attention for their physical appearance, get less academic guidance and feedback, and are significantly more often targets of sexual harassment by peers and school staff. In the media, beauty is almost always an essential feature of female competence and achievement. Women who challenge traditional views of femininity because of their political (e.g., feminist) or sexual (e.g., lesbian) orientation are often stereotyped as unattractive.

Physically attractive women are seen by others as more feminine than less attractive women. Consistent with the current female beauty ideal, thin women are perceived as more feminine than heavier women. Efforts to improve physical appearance, including dieting to lose weight, also contribute to perceptions of femininity. Experiments have shown that women eating small meals are perceived as more feminine than women eating large meals, and that women consciously control their eating to project an image of femininity and desirability.

The benefits of pursuing beauty extend well beyond the promise of creating a favorable impression and thus of interpersonal success. Responding to challenges to their sense of self, as during developmental transitions or in response to failure experiences, women (re)affirm central aspects of their identity by pursuing beauty. For example, the use of cosmetics represents an important act in affirming female adolescent identity; dieting may serve a similar function.

In light of the powerful cultural factors described here, it is not surprising that most women experience symptoms of eating disorders. To understand which women in particular develop an eating disorder requires consideration of two questions. One, why do the clinical syndrome of anorexia nervosa and bulimia nervosa develop in only a minority of women? And two, why do eating disorders develop in these women, rather than some other form of psychopathology? These questions will now be considered briefly.

WHICH WOMEN IN PARTICULAR?

The Status of Cultural Variables as Risk Factors

The fact that only a minority of women develop an eating disorder even though most women are exposed to the cultural factors outlined here is often used by critics of the feminist paradigm as evidence that cultural factors are not central in the etiology of these disorders. In feminist etiological models it is recognized that a single-factor model cannot completely explain the etiology of eating disorders. What distinguishes feminist models from other multifactorial models is the insistence that cultural factors play a primary, rather than a moderating or mediating, role in the etiology. A woman's risk for an eating disorder derives in part from the degree of her exposure to the cultural factors described here. For example, research has shown that women in subcultures that emphasize physical appearance exhibit elevated rates of eating disorders. Risk is further determined by the degree to which a woman is exposed to mediating and moderating variables such as differences in the physiological response to dieting.

Specificity Risk Factors

Certain cultural factors are related to other forms of psychopathology as well as to eating disorders. For example, women's relational identity has been proposed as contributing to women's elevated risk for depression. The fact that certain risk factors are relevant to the etiology of several types of psychopathologies, rather than being specific to eating disorders, does not challenge the validity of the feminist approach. Feminists would argue that the failure to find specificity for certain risk factors accurately reflects these factors' contributions to multiple disorders and suggests a shared etiology.

Feminists recognize a danger in emphasizing the specificity of risk factors. In their search for specificity, researchers often place greater scientific importance on risk factors that are uniquely associated with a disorder and afford lesser significance to important but nonspecific risk factors, as has been the case of childhood sexual abuse. Feminist scholarship has been relatively uninterested in the question of differential diagnosis and has considered it of greater importance to understand and change the conditions that contribute to psychopathology in general. Such a stance is likely to meet with resistance because it challenges the very basis of current professional practice in the research and treatment of psychopathology, which involves a clear delineation of clinical syndromes.

FURTHER READING

Bordo, S. (1993). *Unbearable weight: Feminism, Western culture, and the body.* Berkeley: University of California Press. Written by a feminist philosopher, this collection of essays explores the social construction of weight, appetite, and femininity.

Brumberg, J. J. (1988). *Fasting girls.* Cambridge, MA: Harvard University Press. A social historian's account of the emergence of anorexia nervosa as a modern illness.

Chernin, K. (1981). *The obsession: Reflections on the tyranny of slenderness.* New York: Harper & Row. An exploration of the cultural meaning of thinness.

Fallon, P., Katzman, M. A., & Wooley, S. C. (Eds.). (1993). *Feminist perspectives on eating disorders.* New York: Guilford Press. This edited volume features current feminist scholarship in the research on and treatment of eating disorders.

Orbach, S. (1986). *Hunger strike: The anorectic's struggle as a metaphor of our age.* New York: W. W. Norton. A feminist analysis of anorexia nervosa.

Rodin, J., Silberstein, L. R., & Striegel Moore, R. H. (1985). Women and weight: A normative discontent. In T. B. Sonderegger (Ed.), *Nebraska symposium on motivation* (pp. 267–308). Lincoln: University of Nebraska Press. A detailed review of the psychological literature of the role that weight plays in women's lives.

Sadker, M., & Sadker, D. (1993). *Failing at fairness: How American schools cheat girls.* New York: Charles Scribner's Sons. A detailed review of studies on gender-related discrimination in the American educational system.

Striegel-Moore, R. H. (1993). Etiology of binge eating: A developmental perspective. In C. G. Fairburn & G. T. Wilson (Eds.), *Binge eating: Nature, assessment, and treatment* (pp. 144–172). New York: Guilford Press. An in-depth exploration of how an internalization of cultural factors may result in the development of a particular symptom of eating disorders, namely binge eating.

• 40 •

SEXUAL ABUSE AND EATING DISORDERS

Robert L. Palmer

It is plausible that the occurrence of abusive sexual experiences in childhood might result in later clinical eating disorders. It would be understandable if unwanted and coercive sexual experiences in earlier life impaired subsequent development in a way that increased the risk of psychological disorders such as anorexia nervosa and bulimia nervosa. This conjecture may be called the "general hypothesis." However, the idea that such experiences are noxious has particular relevance to the eating disorders because of the age and gender of the typical sufferer. Furthermore, there is a widely held view that issues of sexuality and of self-concept are especially relevant to this patient group (see Chapter 27). The proposition that there is a specific link between child sexual abuse and the eating disorders may be called the "special hypothesis."

Hypotheses of this sort have had a varied history. Freudian theory tended to promote a sophisticated skepticism concerning the literal veracity of memories about childhood sexual events. However, over the last decade or so the issue has received increasing attention. There is now evidence that sexual contact between adults and children is not uncommon. About one in ten women, and rather fewer men, can recall such events in their childhood. (The precise rates vary depending on the definitions used and the methods of enquiry.) There is also a consensus that such events may be damaging and are appropriately described as "abuse." Indeed, in some popular accounts it is even suggested that the presence of any of a wide variety of distress symptoms in adulthood should be taken as *primie facie* evidence of earlier sexual abuse. Thus has the pendulum swung. Given this range of opinion, there is a need for the careful evaluation of the evidence.

THE EVIDENCE

Before the last decade there were sporadic reports of cases in which incest or other sexual abuse preceded the development of an eating disorder. From the mid 1980s studies began to emerge in which the results of systematic enquiries were reported about the childhood sexual experiences of patients with eating disorders. These results indicated that a substantial proportion, typically about one-third of subjects, gave histories of childhood sexual experiences with adults. In some work it was suggested that there are particular links between these early experiences and the presence of bulimic symptoms or personality disorder, although the findings were not consistent. Overall, the results tended to be interpreted as supporting both the general and the special hypotheses. However, in the absence of studies with comparison groups, a skeptical view was still tenable. The interpretation of the studies and comparisons between them were hampered by differences of method and definition. Variable criteria or none at all were used to define the events being counted. Furthermore, some studies had other major flaws in method. At least two reviewers were critical of these studies and suggested that there was little solid evidence to support the increasingly prevalent belief that sexual abuse was importantly related to the eating disorders.

Another strand of research involved studies of nonmorbid groups, typically students. In these studies, self-reports of "abuse" were related to self-reports of disturbed eating attitudes and behavior. Again the results tended to show some, albeit inconsistent, positive associations. However, there were still major problems of method, and the relevance of such studies to clinical disorders was not clear. Unfortunately some large and well-designed projects examining the general hypothesis in community samples did not include the eating disorders among the conditions studied.

Most recently there have been studies in which samples of women with clinically diagnosed eating disorders were compared with those who had other psychiatric disorders or none at all. In two studies from the United Kingdom and another from the United States similar conclusions were reached. The first, in a study conducted in Leicester the rates of defined experiences reported by a series of patients with anorexia nervosa or bulimia nervosa were compared with those of a similar series of women with other psychiatric diagnoses. In general the eating-disordered subjects recalled fewer abusive events. Thus this study failed to support the special hypothesis. In the second study, carried out in the University of Michigan, similar comparison was made and similar results were obtained. In the third, a major study from Oxford, a community sample of subjects with bulimia nervosa, most of whom were not in treatment, was compared with a clinic sample of bulimic women and with two other community samples of women, one with other psychiatric disorders and one with none. The samples were carefully matched and the relevant experiences were defined. The rates reported were similar for the two bulimic groups, suggesting that abuse is not an important factor in influencing whether women with anorexia nervosa and bulimia nervosa seek treatment. The bulimic subjects reported about three times as many events of sexual abuse as the community subjects who had no psychiatric disorder. However, the rates of the bulimic women were similar to those of the community sample of women with other psychiatric diagnoses. These results support the general hypothesis.

IMPLICATIONS AND UNCERTAINTIES

The demonstration of an association between childhood sexual experiences and later eating disorders need not imply a causal relationship between the two. The association might also be explained by links with a third factor that is truly noxious. Such a factor might be another adverse childhood experience, such as neglect or other abuse or genetically determined mental illness. Alternatively, it might be that childhood sexual abuse does indeed cause a later eating disorder, but only when it is associated with other, particular factors. Further research is needed to explore such possibilities.

At present it can be stated with confidence that childhood sexual experiences with adults are neither necessary nor sufficient causes of clinical eating disorders. They are best viewed as one factor among many that may increase the risk of later disorder (see Chapter 35), probably via their effects on personality development and self-esteem. There seems to be little support for the special hypothesis, at least in relation to those with eating disorders who seek treatment at the usual age. It remains possible that a disorder diagnosed unusually early has such a special relationship to abuse. Furthermore, the evidence to date relates entirely to females; the role of abuse in influencing the risk of eating disorder in boys and young men is unknown.

Important questions concern the context of sexually abusive experiences. In a recent study in the Institute of Psychiatry in London sexual events were investigated together with measures of many other aspects of the childhood experiences of anorexic and bulimic subjects. Such an approach seems to be one way to further the work in this area. Another question concerns the role of particular events in precipitating a disorder, including sexual experiences, in late adolescence or adulthood (see Chapter 35). Clinical experience suggests that bad sexual experiences may sometimes immediately precede a disorder in an apparently significant way whether or not the individual has been the subject of childhood abuse. Furthermore, such events seem, in some cases, to resonate with earlier events, producing an enhancement of distress.

CLINICAL IMPLICATIONS

In clinical practice it is important that the issue of adverse sexual experiences in childhood, and indeed in adult life, is treated appropriately. It seems best that the matter should always be born in mind and usually broached with the patient. The clinician should carefully explore what any reported event means for the patient; such exploration may become an important focus of therapy. The discovery of past abusive experiences should be the beginning of further thought for the clinician. It should not be the occasion for premature closure around the notion that all is now explained.

FURTHER READING

Beckman, K. A., & Burns, G. L. (1990). Relation of sexual abuse and bulimia in college women. *International Journal of Eating Disorders, 9,* 487–492. An example of a nonclinical study of a sample of psychology students.

Connors, M. E., & Morse, W. (1992). Sexual abuse and eating disorders: A review. *International Journal of Eating Disorders, 13,* 1–11. A general review in which the authors reach a broadly negative conclusion.

Folsom, V., Krahn, D., Nairn, K., Gold, L., Demitrack, M. A., & Silk, K. R. (1993). The impact of sexual and physical abuse on eating disordered and psychiatric symptoms: A comparison of eating disordered and psychiatric inpatients. *International Journal of Eating Disorders, 13,* 249–257. A comparison of eating disordered and other psychiatric patients, carried out at the University of Michigan.

McClelland, L., Mynors-Wallis, L., Fahy, T., & Treasure, J. (1991). Sexual abuse, disordered personality and eating disorders. *British Journal of Psychiatry, 158* (Suppl. 10), 63–68. In this study an association was found between the presence of personality disorders and childhood sexual abuse in a series of eating disordered patients at a tertiary referral center.

Oppenheimer, R., Howells, K., Palmer, R. L., & Chaloner, D. A. (1985). Adverse sexual experiences in childhood and clinical eating disorders: A preliminary description. *Journal of Psychiatric Research, 19,* 357–361. The first study of a major series of eating disordered subjects reporting their childhood sexual experiences. An extension of this Leicester series was published in 1990: Palmer, R. L., et al., *British Journal of Psychiatry, 156,* 699–703.

Palmer, R. L., & Oppenheimer, R. (1992). Childhood sexual experiences with adults: A comparison of women with eating disorders and those with other diagnoses. *International Journal of Eating Disorders, 12,* 359–364. A report of a comparison of the Leicester series with a general psychiatric sample recruited from the same center.

Pope, H. G., & Hudson, J. I. (1992). Is childhood sexual abuse a risk factor for bulimia nervosa? *American Journal of Psychiatry, 149,* 455–463. A major review in which the authors reach negative conclusions.

Schmit, U., Tiller, J., & Treasure, J. (1993). Setting the scene for eating disorders: Childhood care, classification and course of illness. *Psychological Medicine, 23,* 663–672. This study of the childhoods of anorexic and bulimic subjects includes sexual abuse among the variety of experiences documented.

Waller, G. (1991). Sexual abuse as a factor in eating disorders. *British Journal of Psychiatry, 159,* 664–671. A study whose results suggest a particular link with bulimic symptoms.

Welch, S. L., & Fairburn, C. G. (in press). Sexual abuse and bulimia nervosa: Three integrated case control comparisons. *American Journal of Psychiatry.* The important Oxford study, which is relevant to both the general and the special hypothesis.

• 41 •

THE COURSE AND OUTCOME OF ANOREXIA NERVOSA

Hans-Christoph Steinhausen

In contrast to the outcome studies on bulimia nervosa, only recently published, outcome studies on anorexia nervosa have been published repeatedly for many decades. Follow-up reports appearing in the English and German literature for four decades, from the 1950s to the late 1980s, have been reviewed by my associates and me. A summary of these findings, including an analysis of some recent trends, is given below, together with a consideration of their implications for clinical practice and future research.

GENERAL DESCRIPTION

As can be seen from Table 41.1, there is an enormous variation in sample size, drop-out rates, and duration of follow-up among the various studies. These characteristics certainly limit the conclusions that can be drawn. Further limiting factors stem from the fact that systematic analyses of the effects of dropouts are almost entirely missing and that the majority of these investigations, including even the most recent ones from the early 1990s, are catch-up studies with some retrospective data, rather than prospective longitudinal studies.

Additional methodological shortcomings include the lack of explicit outcome criteria; incomplete information on subject characteristics; poor methods for assessing psychiatric and psychosocial status at follow-up; undue reliance on telephone interviews instead of direct examination; and the lack of multitrait, multimethod assessment approaches as well as studies of heterogeneous samples with regard to both the onset of the disease and the duration of follow-up. Perhaps the most serious weakness is that selection biases have not been systematically taken into account in the analysis of the data findings. Bias must be assumed to be present, since many reports are based on cohorts treated in specialized centers where complicated cases may be overrepresented.

FOLLOW-UP RESULTS

As the ranges in Table 41.1 show, there is extreme variation in the main features of anorexia nervosa—weight, menstruation, and eating behavior. The means indicate that

TABLE 41.1. A Summary of 68 Outcome Studies Published between 1953 and 1989 Concerning a Total of 3,104 Patients

	Mean	Range
Sample size	47	6–151
Drop-out rate (%)	13	0–77
Duration of follow-up (years)	—	<1–33
Normalization of weight (%)	59	15–92
Normalization of menstruation (%)	57	25–96
Normalization of eating behavior (%)	49	21–97
Recovered (%)	43	7–86
Improved (%)	36	1–69
Chronic disorder (%)	20	0–43
Mortality (%)	5	0–21

Note. Based on reviews by Steinhausen and Glanville (1983) and by Steinhausen, Rauss-Mason, and Seidel (1991).

in close to 60% of anorexics weight and menstruation may normalize, whereas somewhat fewer (49%) show normalized eating behavior. The distinction between recovery, improvement, and chronicity (which to a great extent is based on a popular but crude differentiation between good, fair, and poor outcome) shows that, on the average, more than 40% of anorexics recover, one-third improve, and 20% have a chronic course.

Mortality rates show the lowest variation. However, these figures represent crude, not standardized, mortality rates; in the latter, the ratio of observed to expected deaths is taken into account. In recent studies it has been found, as would be expected, that crude mortality rates rise with the length of follow-up. On the other hand, these studies, based on large samples of patients treated at specialized centers, report a somewhat better outcome than their predecessors.

The findings with respect to prognostic factors are summarized in Table 41.2. An early age of onset appears to be a favorable prognostic factor even at 20-year follow-up. However, it must be noted that this conclusion applies only to adolescent- and adult-onset cases, since the outcome of childhood-onset cases appears poor.

There is evidence that histrionic personality traits, conflict-free parent–child relationships, and a short interval between the onset of symptoms and the beginning of treatment are favorable prognostic factors. The findings with respect to the duration of inpatient treatment, the number of readmissions, anorexics' social status and educational level, and the use of overexercising and dieting as the main weight-reducing measures are not clear. In contrast, there is evidence that the following features are unfavorable prognostic factors: vomiting, bulimia, profound weight loss, chronicity, and a history of premorbid developmental or clinical abnormalities.

Besides supporting the influence of some of these prognostic factors, more recent studies have added adverse life events and certain personality characteristics to the list of unfavorable prognostic factors (see Chapter 30 for a discussion of personality and eating disorders). These personality characteristics include interpersonal distrust, deficits of self-esteem, and impulsiveness. In contrast, risk avoidance, restraint in emotional expression and initiative, and conformity to authority have been found to be associated with recovery.

TABLE 41.2. Prognostic Factors Cited in the Published Outcome Research between 1953 and 1989

	Number of Studies		
Prognostic factor	Favorable	Unfavorable	Not significant
Early age of onset	10	–	4
Hysterical personality	7	–	1
Conflict-free parent–child relationship	7	–	2
Short interval between onset of symptoms and beginning of treatment	8	–	2
Short duration of inpatient treatment/no readmissions	6	–	5
High social status and high level of education	6	–	3
Overexercising and dieting	1	–	5
Vomiting		7	1
Bulimia		8	1
High loss of weight		4	–
Chronicity		6	–
Premorbid development/clinical abnormalities		4	–

Note. Based on reviews by Steinhausen and Glanville (1983) and by Steinhausen, Rauss-Mason, and Seidel (1991).

CONCLUSIONS

A number of methodological shortcomings limit the conclusions that can be drawn from the literature on the outcome of anorexia nervosa. These shortcomings have been partly overcome by some of the more recent prospective studies. Nevertheless, a number of serious problems remain to be solved in anorexia nervosa outcome research. One of the most major problems, selection bias, may be overcome only by performing population-based studies instead of following up referrals to clinical centers. Prospective population-based outcome studies will be very difficult to perform, but they are needed to assess the influence of selection bias. In addition, the temporal relationship between anorexia and bulimia nervosa also deserves further study. Current knowledge must be considered only anecdotal. In addition, the minimum length of follow-up needs to be determined. Currently there is a convention of regarding a 4-year follow-up as sufficient. A recent 20-year follow-up study confirmed the pattern of outcome observed at 5 years, although a number of individual patients had changed considerably.

Another issue in need of further study is the interrelation between the various prognostic factors, since there may be considerable overlap among them. For instance, in addition to bulimia vomiting may explain little of the variance in outcome. A more accurate prediction of outcome in individual patients might be achieved by classifying types of patients based on more than a single characteristic rather than designating specific prognostic factors. Finally, the long-term effects of specific treatments need to be assessed. Given the considerable associated methodological problems, this is perhaps the most difficult task of all. However, results of the recent studies that reveal the positive short-term impact of treatments such as cognitive behavior therapy and family therapy may serve to stimulate this endeavor. Studies using, for example, survival analysis could show how long certain treatment effects are maintained over time.

Providing a prognosis for the individual patient remains a big problem. The variable course and the uncertain long-term effects of treatment limit the clinician's ability to predict outcome.

FURTHER READING

Herzog, W., Deter, H.-C., & Vandereycken, W. (1992). The course of eating disorders. *Long-term follow-up studies of anorexia and bulimia nervosa.* Berlin: Springer-Verlag. The most comprehensive monograph dealing with follow-up research.

Hsu, L. K. G. (1988). The outcome of anorexia nervosa: A reappraisal. *Psychological Medicine, 18,* 807–812. A brief review of outcome research including the issues of mental status, the relation of anorexia nervosa to affective disorders, and the link with bulimia nervosa.

Ratnasutiya, R. H., Eisler, J., Szmukler, G. I., & Russell, F. F. M. (1991). Anorexia nervosa: Outcome and prognostic factors after 20 years. *British Journal of Psychiatry, 158,* 495–502. An important long-term follow-up study.

Steinhausen, H.-C., & Glanville, K. (1983). Follow-up studies of anorexia nervosa—A review of research findings. *Psychological Medicine, 3,* 239–249. A detailed analysis of the English and German literature published between 1953 and 1981.

Steinhausen, H.-C., Rauss-Mason, C., & Seidel, R. (1991). Follow-up studies of anorexia nervosa: A review of four decades of outcome research. *Psychological Medicine, 21,* 447–451. An update of the previous report based on the literature of the 1980s, and a comparison with the earlier findings.

· 42 ·

OUTCOME OF BULIMIA NERVOSA

L. K. George Hsu

Apart from satisfying the clinical investigator's intellectual curiosity and the psychiatric nosologist's compulsive need to classify, a knowledge of the course and outcome of bulimia nervosa is useful to most of us who are clinicians for at least the following reasons. First, it allows us to gain a proper perspective in our treatment efforts so that, for instance, we do not confuse short-term remission with long-term cure. Second, it may allow us to define treatment goals appropriate to different stages of treatment so that, for instance, we may recommend interpersonal therapy for a patient who, having previously responded to cognitive therapy, has relapsed. Unfortunately, of course, prognostic studies of bulimia nervosa are still relatively uncommon, and therefore a clear understanding of its course and outcome is still a way off. The present review offers a synthesis of the current findings.

SHORT-TERM RETROSPECTIVE STUDIES

In at least five short-term retrospective studies patients were followed up for a year or more after treatment. The findings are summarized in Table 42.1.

These short-term retrospective studies indicate that most patients do well at 1 year after treatment—at least 75% have no bulimic symptoms. However, the retrospective design, lack of standardization in treatment procedures, reliance on indirect methods of follow-up and nonstandardized instruments, short duration of follow-up, and relatively high "untraced" (i.e., patient not available for follow-up) rate suggest that the data may be misleading.

INTERMEDIATE-TERM RETROSPECTIVE STUDIES

In at least six studies patients have been followed up for 2 or more years. Findings in these studies are summarized in Table 42.2.

Results of five of the six studies indicate that about half of the patients are in remission at the point of follow-up; about one out of six patients is bulimic; and the remainder continue to demonstrate residual, but relatively infrequent, bulimic behavior. In one British study a ninefold increase in mortality was found among bulimic patients attending a teaching hospital's Department of Psychiatry. Details of the causes of death were not provided. The mortality rate was remarkably low in the other six studies of a

TABLE 42.1. Short-Term Retrospective Studies

Author	N/n followed	Study treatment[a]	Duration of follow-up (months)	Follow-up method	Remission[b]	Diagnosable eating disorder (%)	Outcome body weight	Further treatment
1. Abraham et al. (1983)	51/43	OP, I	14–72	Interview	65(?)[d]	35(?)[d]	Normal	ND[c]
2. Fairburn (1981)	11/6	OP, I	12	ND[c]	83	17	Normal	None
3. Hsu & Holder (1986)	56/48	OP, I	12–35	Telephone	75	25	Normal	ND[c]
4. Johnson et al. (1986)	12/6	OP, I	12	ND[c]	83	17	ND[c]	ND[c]
5. Lacey (1983)	30/28	OP, I, G	Up to 24	ND[c]	100	—	Normal	11%

[a]OP, outpatient; I, individual; G, group.
[b]Percentages are based on patients successfully traced for follow-up.
[c]ND, not described.
[d](?), data not clearly described.

TABLE 42.2. Intermediate-Term Retrospective Studies

Author	N/n followed	Study treatment[a]	Duration of follow-up (months)	Follow-up method	Remission[b]	Patients with diagnosable bulimia nervosa (%)	Outcome body weight	Further treatment
1. Brotman et al. (1988)	12/12[c]	OP, I, G, M	24–60	ND[d]	58	17 (plus 25% symptomatic)	ND[d]	ND[d]
2. Collings & King (1994)	50/45	OP, I, G, M	120	Interview, telephone, physician	46	16 (plus 26% symptomatic, 2% died)	Normal	Yes for most
3. Hsu & Sobkiewicz (1989)	45/35	OP, I	48–60	Mostly telephone	47	16 (plus 16% symptomatic)	98% normal; 2% underweight	
4. Maddox et al. (1992)	43/55	DHP	24	Interview	46	17 (plus 27% symptomatic, 2% died)	No anorexia nervosa; weight range 82% to 188% average	Yes for 71%
5. Mitchell et al. (1989)	100/91	OP, G	24–60	Telephone	66	25 (plus 9% symptomatic)	92% normal; 1% underweight; 7% overweight	ND[d]
6. Patton (1988)	96	IP, OP	Mean 68	Mortality records	—	—	3 deaths SMR[e] = 9.38	—
7. Swift et al. (1987)	38/30	IP, OP(?)	24–60	Interview	13	50 (plus 37% symptomatic)	Normal	100%

[a]OP, outpatient; IP, inpatient; I, individual; G, group; M, medication; DHP, day hospital program.
[b]Percentages are based on patients successfully traced for follow-up.
[c]Includes only patients followed for at least 2 years.
[d]ND, Not described.
[e]SMR, standardized mortality ratio.

total of 288 patients: only two patients (0.7%) had died, the first in an accident and the other a suicide. However, the relatively high untraced rate in four of the studies does not allow a firm conclusion to be drawn.

The much less favorable overall outcome in the series of Swift and colleagues is puzzling. The subjects were younger and, by virtue of the fact that they were all inpatients, perhaps more severely ill. It is also possible they did not receive specific treatments targeted at their bulimic symptoms. Specific treatments appear to improve outcome, as indicated by the prospective studies I will presently review.

Taken together with the short-term retrospective studies, the overall data suggest that bulimic patients do improve with time, although there seems to be a group of patients, perhaps 20%, in which the disorder becomes entrenched; also, perhaps a subsyndromal form of the disorder remains in 30% of the patients. It is unclear at this stage whether this intermediate-outcome group engages in persistent but infrequent bulimic behavior, or whether these patients have periods of remission alternating with periods of relapse. These findings are consistent with the naturalistic data reviewed below.

PROSPECTIVE STUDIES

Four prospective treatment and follow-up studies have been published recently; their findings and those of our own unpublished study are summarized in Table 42.3. Several studies have been excluded from this review either because the number of subjects was very small or because the duration of follow-up was too brief. Two 1-year treatment studies will be discussed in this review because their findings are of value in clarifying the course of bulimic symptoms.

The question of whether the changes produced by treatment are sustained over time is only partially answered by these studies. The brief follow-up duration (no more than 1 year) limits the conclusions that can be drawn, and, except for the study by Fairburn, the fact that patients received other forms of treatment during the follow-up period also limits our ability to draw conclusions about the maintenance of change. However, investigators should bear in mind that unless psychiatric care is given in a National Health Service setting, it can be difficult to discourage patients from seeking additional treatment during the follow-up period.

It must be noted that in two other treatment studies the 1-year outcome of bulimia nervosa was found to be quite discouraging. One was a study of family therapy (see Chapter 56), and the other was a study of antidepressant drugs (see Chapter 55). Taken together, the findings of the prospective studies indicate that patients who respond to certain active psychotherapeutic treatments are likely to maintain their improvement for a 1-year period. The outcome for bulimic patients who do not respond to psychotherapy is unclear. Desipramine alone is not a very satisfactory form of maintenance treatment.

NATURALISTIC STUDIES

There has been only one satisfactory study of the course and outcome of cases in the community. In this study, 225 women who were seen for the treatment of an eating disorder were followed up for 1- to 2-year period. Among the 96 with bulimia nervosa,

TABLE 42.3. Follow-Up Findings of Prospective Studies

Author	N/Duration of follow-up	Study treatment[a]	Main findings	Relative efficacy
Agras et al. (1989)	77/6 months	1. CBT 2. CBT & ERP 3. SM 4. WL	Treatment effects maintained for all three treatments. Additional treatment during follow-up not described.	CBT (59%) statistically superior to ERP (20%) and SM (18%) in terms of maintaining abstinence.
Fairburn et al. (1993)	75/1 year	1. CBT 2. IPT 3. BT	Treatment effects of CBT and IPT maintained, not for BT. No additional treatment.	CBT superior to BT for abstinence.
Freeman et al. (1988)	92/1 year	1. CBT 2. BT 3. GRP 4. WL	Treatment effects apparently maintained. Details of outcome not provided. Additional treatment not described.	Details not provided.
Leitenberg et al. (1988)	47/6 months	1. ERPS 2. ERPM 3. CBT 4. WL	Treatment effects maintained for all three active treatments. Additional treatment not described.	ERPM and ERPS marginally better than CBT on vomiting and test meal data.
Hsu et al. (unpublished)	100/6 months	1. NC 2. CBT 3. CBT & NC 4. SGRP	Relapse rate high for patients who achieved abstinence for all three treatments. Combined = 40% CBT = 60% NC = 80% Many had additional treatments.	Numbers of abstinent subjects too low for analysis. Combined treatment tended to be better.

[a]CBT, cognitive-behavioral therapy; ERP, exposure and response prevention; SM, self-monitoring; WL, wait list; IPT, interpersonal psychotherapy; BT, behavior therapy; GRP, group therapy; ERPS, ERP in single setting; ERPM, ERP in multiple setting; NC, nutritional counseling; SGRP, support group.

86% showed a drop below full diagnostic criteria for at least 8 weeks during the 1-year interval (partial recovery), but only 56% were asymptomatic for at least 8 weeks after 1 year (full recovery). Because the study was "naturalistic," treatment was not controlled, and 79% of the bulimia nervosa patients were in treatment at 1-year follow-up. The findings of this study are remarkably consistent with those of the intermediate-term retrospective studies.

Almost nothing is known about the course of bulimia nervosa in the absence of treatment. This gap in our knowledge is important, since there is evidence that many individuals with bulimia nervosa are not receiving any form of treatment.

COMORBID DISORDERS AT OUTCOME

In very few studies have the course and outcome of comorbid disorders in bulimic patients been examined. Existing data suggest that overall psychiatric morbidity decreases with recovery and that the disorder in unrecovered patients is much more likely to have an additional Axis I or II diagnosis. A comorbid diagnosis at initial presentation does not predict a poor outcome. Long-term follow-up studies of anorexia nervosa patients has revealed that major depression may be common even among those who have recovered fully from their eating disorder, suggesting therefore that anorexia nervosa and major depression may be linked to each other in as yet unclear ways. Unfortunately, such long-term outcome data on bulimia nervosa are not available. Also, data are not available on the outcome for those bulimic patients with comorbid substance abuse.

PROGNOSTIC INDICATORS

Prognostic indicators have been examined in few studies. A shorter duration of illness, the absence of Axis II personality disturbance, and a family history of alcoholism have been found to predict good outcome in several studies. A shorter duration of illness and the absence of Axis II personality disturbance suggest a less severe form of illness, which perhaps renders it more amenable to treatment. That a family history of alcoholism predicts favorable outcome appears counterintuitive—perhaps such a history motivates patients to work harder to overcome their illness.

CONCLUSION

Currently the data suggest that the most common eating disturbance at follow-up is subsyndromal bulimia nervosa, followed by diagnosable bulimia nervosa. All the outcome data indicate that while perhaps 30% of bulimic patients have a previous history of anorexia nervosa, normal-weight bulimic patients rarely relapse into anorexia nervosa. Obesity does not appear to be common at follow-up, certainly not as common as among the general population, for which the rate is estimated to be about 25%.

In summary, the following conclusions may be drawn:

1. With cognitive behavior therapy and perhaps additional continuation treatment, about 50% of bulimia nervosa patients are asymptomatic 2 to 10 years after intake. Evidence for the efficacy of other forms of psychotherapy such as interpersonal or supportive–expressive therapy is less clear at this stage.
2. There is a group of about 20% of patients who remain persistently symptomatic.
3. The remainder (about 30%) have a course of illness characterized either by remissions and relapses or by persistent but subsyndromal bulimic behavior. It is unclear at this point whether sequential or maintenance treatment can improve the outcome in this group of patients.
4. Prognostic indicators are unclear. Patients with a less severe form of the illness may do better.
5. The mortality rate associated with this disorder is uncertain but may be higher than that expected in the general population.

Future studies should be prospective in design; involve larger numbers of patients, particularly if different treatments are to be compared; and be focused on those who have failed to respond to psychotherapy so that strategies to prevent chronicity may be devised.

FURTHER READING

Collings, S., & King, M. (1994). Ten-year follow-up of 50 patients with bulimia nervosa. *British Journal of Psychiatry, 164,* 80–87. Describes intermediate-term outcome of a consecutive series of bulimic patients and reviews current knowledge of the outcome of bulimia nervosa.

Herzog, D. B., Keller, M. B., & Lavori, P. W. (1988). Outcome in anorexia nervosa and bulimia nervosa. *Journal of Nervous and Mental Disease, 176,* 3, 131–143. A comprehensive review of 40 follow-up studies on anorexia and bulimia nervosa published between 1954 and 1986.

Herzog, D. B., Sacks, N. R., Keller, M. B., Lavori, P. W., von Ranson, K. B., & Gray, H. M. (1993). Patterns and predictors of recovery in anorexia nervosa and bulimia nervosa. *Journal of the American Academy of Child and Adolescent Psychiatry, 32,* 4, 835–842. A carefully conducted prospective naturalistic study of eating disordered patients during a 1- to 2-year period. The only prospective study of the disorder in the community to date.

Hsu, L. K. G. (1991). Outcome studies in patients with eating disorders. In S. M. Mirin, J. T. Gossett, & M. C. Grob (Eds.), *Psychiatric treatment: Advances in outcome research* (pp. 159–180). Washington, DC: American Psychiatric Press. Reviews recent outcome data for both anorexia and bulimia nervosa and discusses their implications for nosology and pathogenesis.

Patton, G. C. (1988). Mortality in eating disorders. *Psychological Medicine, 18,* 947–952. Examines the mortality rate in a large cohort of patients with bulimia nervosa.

· VI ·
PHYSIOLOGICAL AND MEDICAL ASPECTS OF EATING DISORDERS

• 43 •

HUNGER AND SATIETY IN CLINICAL EATING DISORDERS

Katherine A. Halmi

The unique abnormality of anorexia nervosa and bulimia nervosa is disturbed eating behavior. Despite this fact, the studies of eating behavior in these disorders are predominantly descriptive, with very few systematic, controlled investigations using scientific methodology.

The perception of hunger and satiety is the mechanism that integrates an individual's cognitive set (attitudes toward, and the conceptual identity of, the nutritional content of food) with her/his internal physiology (neurotransmitters, peptide hormones, metabolism affecting intake of food) to produce eating behavior. Blundell and Hill have proposed that the selection of foods involves conditioned and unconditioned responses. More specifically, they have proposed that the perceptual capacity to identify the characteristics of foods and a *mechanism* to link the biochemical consequences of ingested foods with the appearance and taste of foods are necessary to harmonize the physiological information from inside the body with the nutritional content of foods to be ingested. This mechanism is the perception of hunger and satiety. Booth has similarly proposed that the conceptual identity of a food is the result of nutritional hedonic conditioning, which is the process whereby the nutritional functions of a food are related to its sensory characteristics.

HUNGER AND SATIETY STUDIES

There are very few studies of hunger and satiety perceptions in humans. In most of the studies that have been done, hunger and satiety responses to contextual changes in food were analyzed. In their study of healthy subjects, Hill and coworkers found that the ratings of hunger and the desire to eat 2 hours after the consumption of a highly preferred food were significantly higher compared with those ratings after a less preferred food was eaten. The preferred food seemed to stimulate hunger. In all of these healthy subjects, hunger and satiety ratings were tracked in curves that were inversely proportional and similar to the ratings of the control subjects in the study by Owen and coworkers of anorexia and bulimia patients. The latter was the first study in which hunger and satiety responses in eating-disorder patients were tracked before, during, and after a meal. There were marked differences between the healthy subjects on the one hand and the anorexic and bulimic patients on the other. Most anorexic restrictors were completely full and not at all hungry throughout the entire course of the meal and showed no intersection whatsoever of their hunger and satiety curves. The anorexic bulimics often had a rapid rebound of hunger shortly after the end of the meal. These patients described themselves as being full and hungry at the same time and therefore not satiated. This study was further expanded by Sunday and Halmi to bulimics, who often reported they were hungry and not at all full through the course of a meal. Those bulimics who experienced some reduction in hunger frequently had a rebound of hunger shortly after the meal ended. All the above studies were conducted using the same liquid formula so that the proportion of nutrients could not influence the outcome of hunger and satiety perceptions. These hunger and satiety aberrations were the same immediately after treatment. If they are found to persist 6 months to 1 year after patients have maintained a normal weight and normal eating behavior, the aberrant hunger and satiety perceptions might be regarded as a marker or risk factor for anorexia and bulimia nervosa.

Using a Cabanac testing method, Garfinkel and colleagues have shown that anorexia nervosa patients have an absence of satiety aversion to sucrose, or "sweet taste." This absence of satiety aversion was stable at a 1-year follow-up and was not affected by weight gain to normal levels. This study, of course, should be replicated using food.

Results of current studies are showing that bulimic patients have increased hunger and decreased satiety responses to high-fat meals compared with low-fat, high-carbohydrate meals. These changes are not present in normal control subjects or in anorexic–restrictor patients. This observation suggests a high-carbohydrate, low-fat diet may be helpful for deterring binge eating in bulimics.

Rolls and her colleagues have shown that satiety can be specific to a particular food that has been ingested; that is, the preference for a food eaten in a meal decreases significantly more than for foods not eaten. Further, this decrease in preference is also associated with decreased consumption of that same food if it is offered again as a second course. Rolls has recently begun to examine this phenomenon, which she calls "sensory-specific satiety," in anorexic and bulimic subjects. She reports that bulimics do not show sensory-specific satiety at all and that anorexics show lower specific preference ratings following preloads; however, following cottage cheese preloads, they continue eating cottage cheese in a mixed meal. These findings imply that bulimics have different satiety and preference responses than do normal control subjects, and that anorexics' cognitive sets toward food can override changes in preference.

COGNITIVE SETS TOWARD FOODS

Cognitive sets are attitudes toward, and the conceptual identity of, the nutritional content of food. The latter concept includes taste, which is a means by which the nutritional content of food is identified.

Studies by Sunday and Halmi have demonstrated that eating-disorder patients have no deficit in the sensory perception of intensities of sweetness and fatty stimuli. However, anorexic patients show an intense dislike for high-fat stimuli, compared with bulimics and controls. Both bulimic and anorexic patients prefer sweeter stimuli than do controls. Bulimics' preferences do not change with treatment (weight restoration and cessation of bingeing and purging), suggesting that taste profiles might be an enduring characteristic. Further, these findings raise the suspicion that the pattern of sensory responsiveness to sweetness and fat during childhood and adolescence may predate changes in body weight and serve as an early psychobiological marker for eating disorders.

In studies in which attitudes toward foods have been measured, Drewnowski and Halmi, using a multidimensional scaling procedure, showed that eating-disorder patients associate calories with fat content to a greater degree than do control subjects. These researchers have also demonstrated that anorexics strongly dislike high-fat foods. Sunday and Halmi have demonstrated that restrained and unrestrained "control subjects" have different cognitive sets concerning foods and that this factor must be considered in all studies of eating behavior. They showed that perceived high amounts of calories or fat triggered stronger feelings of guilt and danger in restrained control subjects and eating-disorder patients than in unrestrained control subjects. These attitudes did not change with treatment and were found to strongly influence eating behavior.

CONCLUSION

There is accumulating evidence that the aberrant eating behavior of anorexia nervosa and bulimia nervosa patients is directly influenced by disturbances in the integrating processes of hunger and satiety perceptions. These hunger and satiety perceptions may be regarded as the result of a nutritional hedonic conditioning formed from cognitive sets and other external and internal physiological cues. All the above components can be measured and subjected to experimental perturbations for characterization. These studies are necessary because they will provide cogent information that will help in improving the treatment of individuals with eating disorders.

FURTHER READING

Blundell, J. E., & Hill, A. J. (1987). Nutrition, serotonin and appetite: Case study in the evolution of a scientific idea. *Appetite, 8,* 183–194. The rationale for Blundell's theory of eating behavior.

Booth, D. A. (1981). How should questions about satiation be asked? *Appetite, 2,* 237–244. The presentation of Booth's theory of nutritional hedonic conditioning.

Drewnowski, A., Pierce B., & Halmi, K. A. (1988). Fat aversion in eating disorders. *Appetite, 10,* 119–131. The use of the multidimensional scaling technique to assess attitudes about food in the eating-disorder patient.

Garfinkel, P. E., Moldofsky, H., Garner, D. M., et al. (1978). Body awareness in anorexia nervosa: Disturbances in body image and satiety. *Psychosomatic Medicine, 40,* 487–497. The use of the Cabanac procedure for testing satiety in patients with eating disorders.

Halmi, K. A., & Sunday, S. R. (1991). Temporal patterns of hunger and fullness ratings and related cognitions in anorexia and bulimia. *Appetite, 16,* 219–237. The use of microstructure methodology to examine many aspects of eating behavior during a meal.

Hill, A. J., Magson, L. D., & Blundell, J. E. (1984). Hunger and palatability: Tracking ratings of subjective experience before, during and after the consumption of preferred and less preferred foods. *Appetite, 5,* 361–371. The first study in which the methodology of tracking hunger and satiety perceptions was used.

Owen, W. T., Halmi, K. A., Gibbs, J., et al. (1985). Satiety responses and eating disorders. *Journal of Psychiatric Research, 19,* 279–284. The first study tracking hunger and satiety perceptions in people with eating disorders.

Rolls, B. J., Heatherington, M., Burley, V., et al. (1986). Changing hedonic responses to foods during and after a meal. In M. R. Karl & J. G. Brand (Eds.), Interaction of chemical senses and nutrition (pp. 150–175). San Diego, CA: Academic Press. A study analyzing the basis of food preferences.

Sunday, S. R., Einhorn, A., & Halmi, K. A. (1992). The relationship of perceived macronutrient and caloric content to affective cognitions about food. *American Journal of Clinical Nutrition, 55,* 362–371. A comprehensive study of preferences and attitudes toward commonly ingested foods in eating-disorder patients and control subjects.

Sunday, S. R., & Halmi, K. A. (1990). Taste and hedonics in eating disorders. *Physiology and Behavior, 48,* 587–594. An extensive study of taste preferences in patients with subtypes of anorexia nervosa and bulimia nervosa.

• 44 •

PHYSIOLOGY OF ANOREXIA NERVOSA

Christopher G. Fairburn

The physiological abnormalities seen in patients with anorexia nervosa have long been the subject of interest. Earlier in this century the disorder was mistakenly attributed to pituitary insufficiency ("functional hypopituitarism"); more recently, and again mistakenly, a primary hypothalamic disorder was suggested. It is now thought that the physiological abnormalities are secondary to the disturbances of eating and related behavior (e.g., self-induced vomiting, laxative misuse, overexercising) and that these behaviors can be best understood as the end product of a complex interplay of biopsychosocial processes (see Chapters 15 and 35).

In this chapter the physiological abnormalities found in patients with anorexia nervosa are reviewed. The medical complications are described in Chapter 47.

ENDOCRINE ABNORMALITIES

Many of the endocrine abnormalities associated with anorexia nervosa have been reproduced in studies of the physiological effects of dieting and starvation. Most of the abnormalities are reversed by the restoration of healthy eating habits and a normal weight, although there may be some delay before normal functioning returns. Cases in which there is a prepubertal or intrapubertal onset are associated with delayed pubertal development. Generally this developmental delay is reversible, although it may be permanent in severe and chronic cases. As a result there may be a failure of linear growth, impaired breast development, and amenorrhea.

The menstrual disturbance that is a required diagnostic feature for anorexia nervosa in females (see Chapter 23) frequently occurs early in the development of the disorder and may precede significant weight loss. This diagnostic feature was one of the lines of evidence used to argue for a primary disturbance of hypothalamic function. Careful history taking, however, generally reveals that the menstrual disturbance has been accompanied by a period of dietary restriction, the latter often associated with external stress and sometimes overexercising as well. Since dietary restriction, stress, and excessive exercising are all known to interfere with menstrual function, they may well account for the early amenorrhea. The delayed resumption of menstruation that sometimes follows weight gain is likely to have a similar basis.

Nevertheless, there is ample physiological evidence of hypothalamic disturbance. For example, luteinizing hormone-releasing hormone (LHRH) secretion is impaired; as a result, levels of luteinizing hormone (LH), follicle stimulating hormone (FSH), and estradiol are low. Thus the amenorrhea seen in anorexia nervosa is due to a hypogonadotropic hypogonadism. The pattern of LH release is immature, with LH levels increasing during sleep. The LH response to LHRH is reduced, but the FSH response is normal or exaggerated. These abnormalities are now thought to be secondary to the weight loss and abnormal food intake. They are generally reversible with weight gain.

Hypothalamic disturbance is also evident in the delayed thyrotropin (TSH) response to thyrotropin-releasing hormone. In addition there is reduced peripheral conversion of thyroxine (T_3) to triiodothyronine (T_3) and an increased conversion of T_4 to inactive reverse T_3. These changes are seen in other starvation states and are presumably a means of conserving energy. T_4 levels are in the low normal range, whereas T_3 levels are depressed; TSH levels are normal. Clinical evidence of hypothyroidism includes hypothermia, bradycardia, constipation, dry skin, and delayed relaxation of deep tendon reflexes.

Growth hormone (GH) levels are also often increased, another secondary effect of starvation. The response of GH to various provocation tests is impaired, suggesting disturbance at the hypothalamic level. Prolactin levels are normal.

Plasma cortisol levels are raised, and some studies have found that the normal diurnal variation is lost. In addition, there is dexamethasone nonsupression and a decreased cortisol response to insulin-induced hypoglycaemia. The elevation in cortisol levels is due in part to the increased half-life of cortisol seen in starvation and perhaps also to a relative increase in its production.

Insulin and fasting blood sugar levels are decreased or at the low range of normal. Glucose tolerance is also commonly impaired. Low carbohydrate intake is likely to be the major cause of these abnormalities.

There is a disturbance in the ability to concentrate urine, suggesting an abnormality in the secretion of arginine vasopressin (AVP). Erratic plasma levels of AVP have been reported. It has also been shown that the cerebrospinal fluid/plasma ratio of AVP is reversed. The cause of these abnormalities is not understood; however, they are reversible.

CARDIOVASCULAR ABNORMALITIES

Bradycardia and hypotension are frequently seen in patients with anorexia nervosa and other states of starvation. About a quarter of patients have a resting heart rate below 60 beats per minute, and diastolic blood pressure is often below 60. As a result dizziness is common and there may be frank syncope. Arrhythmias occur in some patients, and electrocardiographic (EKG) changes are common. These EKG changes include low voltage, sinus bradycardia, and ST segment depression. The EKG abnormalities can usually be attributed to accompanying fluid and electrolyte disturbances.

ELECTROLYTE AND METABOLIC ABNORMALITIES

Electrolyte disturbance and dehydration are found in those patients who vomit frequently or misuse large quantities of laxatives or diuretics. The exact picture varies considerably. Metabolic alkalosis, hypochloremia, hyponatremia, and hypokalemia are the most common electrolyte disturbances and may account for the tiredness and muscle weakness (and, on rare occasions, hypokalemic paralysis) experienced by some patients. The overall picture may resemble Bartter's syndrome and has been termed "pseudo Bartter's syndrome," since it is self-inflicted and usually reversible. Severe electrolyte disturbance is occasionally encountered, particularly low potassium levels, but even when it is long-standing there may be few accompanying symptoms. Hypocalcemia and hypomagnesemia are also found, and again there may be few associated symptoms. In this case it is sometimes because coexisting hypokalemia masks certain of their manifestations.

As would be expected, there is a low basal metabolic rate. Elevated levels of beta-hydroxybutyric acid and free fatty acids are found, and these, too, are a result of starvation. Hypercholesterolemia is sometimes present. This is unlikely to be dietary in origin, since the diets of patients with anorexia nervosa typically include low amounts of saturated fat and cholesterol. Beta-carotene levels are often raised, the cause again being uncertain. It may reflect increased dietary intake of carotene, although this is often denied by patients. Life-threatening hypoglycemia very occasionally occurs and may not present typically because of impaired sympathetic response. Vitamin deficiencies are uncommon. Studies of the zinc status of anorexia nervosa patients have yielded conflicting findings.

HEMATOLOGICAL ABNORMALITIES

Normocytic normochromic anemia is not unusual in anorexia nervosa patients. In addition, mild leukopenia is common, with a relative lymphocytosis. The leukopenia does not appear to increase the risk of infection. The bone marrow is often hypoplastic, with a decreased number of stem cells. The erythrocyte sedimentation rate is usually low, thereby distinguishing anorexia nervosa from many other conditions associated with weight loss.

GASTROINTESTINAL DISTURBANCES

Delayed gastric emptying and a prolonged gastrointestinal transit time are common and account for complaints of fullness after eating, bloatedness, and constipation. Acute gastric dilatation is a rare complication that can be provoked by episodes of overeating or too vigorous attempts at refeeding.

OTHER ABNORMALITIES

Electroencephalographic abnormalities are found in up to half of these patients, and, like the EKG abnormalities, they can usually be attributed to associated fluid and electrolyte disturbances. Studies using computerized tomography and magnetic resonance imaging have revealed cerebral atrophy and ventricular dilatation. This appears to be reversible and has been termed "pseudoatrophy." Functional imaging methods have yet to yield findings of note. Neurotransmitter abnormalities are discussed in Chapter 45.

Impaired temperature regulation has been observed, particularly an abnormal autonomic response to cold, with there being no increase in core temperature. The physiological basis for this abnormality is uncertain.

In longstanding cases, osteopenia and fractures are not uncommon. The severity of osteopenia appears to be positively related to the duration of the disorder and negatively related to current body weight. The pathophysiology is not understood, but estrogen deficiency and excess cortisol secretion may be responsible. The extent to which the bone loss is reversible has yet to be established.

ACKNOWLEDGMENT

I am grateful to the Wellcome Trust for their support (Senior Lectureship award 13123).

FURTHER READING

Cuellar, M. D., & Van Thiel, D. H. (1986). Gastrointestinal consequences of the eating disorders: Anorexia nervosa and bulimia. *American Journal of Gastroenterology, 81,* 1113–1124. A thorough review of gastrointestinal abnormalities.

Hagman, J. O. (1992). Brain imaging and eating disorders. In G. H. Anderson & S. H. Kennedy (Eds.), *The biology of feast and famine* (pp. 285–300). San Diego, CA: Academic Press. A review of brain imaging studies up to 1990.

Hay, P. J., Hall, A., Delahunt, J. W., Harper, G., Mitchell, A. W., & Salmond, C. (1989). Investigation of osteopaenia in anorexia nervosa. *Australian and New Zealand Journal of Psychiatry, 23,* 261–268. A study of the correlates of osteopenia.

Pomeroy, C., Mitchell, J. E., & Eckert, E. D. (1992). Risk of infection and immune function in anorexia nervosa. *International Journal of Eating Disorders, 12,* 47–55. A review of studies of the risk of infection and immune status.

Rock, C. L., & Curran-Celentano, J. (1994). Nutritional disorder of anorexia nervosa: A review. *International Journal of Eating Disorders, 15,* 187–203. A detailed review of nutritional status and treatment.

Russell, G. F. M. (1992). Anorexia nervosa of early onset and its impact on puberty. In P. J. Cooper & A. Stein (Eds.), *Feeding problems and eating disorders in children and adolescents* (pp. 85–111). Chur, Switzerland: Harwood. A review of the effects of early-onset anorexia nervosa on pubertal development.

Russell, J., & Beumont, P. J. V. (1987). The endocrinology of anorexia nervosa. In P. J. V. Beumont, G. D. Burrows, & R. C. Casper (Eds.), *Handbook of eating disorders—Part 1: Anorexia nervosa and bulimia nervosa.* Amsterdam: Elsevier. A comprehensive review of the endocrinology of anorexia nervosa.

Sharp, C. W., & Freeman, C. P. L. (1993). The medical complications of anorexia nervosa. *British Journal of Psychiatry, 162,* 452–462. A useful account of the medical complications and their physiological bases.

NEUROTRANSMITTERS AND ANOREXIA NERVOSA

WALTER H. KAYE

Anorexia nervosa is a disorder characterized by pathological feeding behavior, distortions of body image, and various forms of hypothalamic–pituitary dysfunction. While the etiology of anorexia nervosa is unknown, it has been postulated that intrinsic biological alterations, dieting, psychosocial influences, and stress are among the factors contributing to the onset of this illness (see Chapter 35). Whatever the cause, once weight loss and malnutrition occur, anorexic patients appear to enter a downward spiraling circle, with malnutrition sustaining and perpetuating the desire for more weight loss and dieting. Disturbances of brain neurotransmitter systems may contribute to a trait for developing anorexia nervosa, and the systems themselves may well be altered by malnutrition. Such cause-and-effect relationships can be teased apart by studying anorexics at various stages in their illness, while underweight and at intervals after weight restoration. The potential relationships between behavior and disturbances of brain neurotransmitters in ill and recovered subjects with anorexia nervosa will be reviewed in this chapter.

BEHAVIOR AND COMORBIDITY IN ANOREXIA NERVOSA

It is well recognized that ill anorexics have body image distortions, restricted eating, and increased physical activity. In addition, ill anorexics invariably are depressed, rigid and overcontrolled, obsessional, perfectionistic, and inhibited. It has not been clear whether such symptoms are secondary to weight loss and malnutrition, or whether these behaviors exist independently of nutritional state and might contribute to the pathogenesis of this illness.

As many as 91% of women with anorexia nervosa suffer from depressive symptoms when acutely ill, with 15% to 58% of patients continuing to exhibit some degree of depressive disturbance after weight recovery (ranging from several months to 5 years). Such data have raised a question as to whether there is some etiologic link between the two disorders. However, common behavioral accompaniments of starvation closely resemble the accessory symptoms of primary depressive disorder. Critical examination of patients' clinical phenomenology, family history, antidepressant response, biological correlates, course and outcome, and epidemiology yields *limited* support for this hypothesis (also see Chapter 28). Most important, it is debatable whether depressive symptoms explain the meaning of core symptoms of anorexia nervosa, such as body image distortion, pathological feeding behavior, perfectionism, or excessive exercise.

Elevated lifetime diagnoses (39% to 75%) of anxiety disorders are also common for anorexia nervosa patients. Unlike that for depression, the relationship of anxiety to the state of this illness has not been as well studied (see Chapter 28).

It has been suggested for more than 50 years that anorexia nervosa has some relationship to obsessive and compulsive behaviors. In this regard the inherently obsessional nature of anorexia nervosa is obvious, with obsessive calorie counting, preoccupation with the body, and incessant ruminations about food. However, it is not certain whether anorexia nervosa is a type of obsessive–compulsive disorder, whether patients with anorexia may have obsessive personalities, or whether there are other explanations (see Chapter 28). Aside from symptoms pertaining to food and body image, women with anorexia nervosa have, in fact, a high prevalence of obsessive–compulsive symptoms or disorder. It is noted in DSM-IV that compulsive behaviors, such as hand washing, may be present and may justify the additional diagnosis of obsessive–compulsive disorder. However, these symptoms may not be readily apparent, as anorexics usually deny or minimize the severity of their illness and are generally uninterested in, or resistant to, therapy. Obsessive–compulsive symptoms are second in frequency to depression in anorexia nervosa patients and a diagnosis of obsessive–compulsive disorder can be made in as many as 69% of restrictor and 44% of bulimic individuals with anorexia nervosa. Finally, anorexia nervosa and obsessive–compulsive disorder patients have similar scores on obsessive–compulsive inventories.

Similarly, more than 50 years of investigations of personality characteristics suggest that anorexics tend to be rigid, perfectionistic, and obsessional (also see Chapter 30). Obsessive behaviors have been found in patients before the onset of anorexia nervosa. Strober characterized recovered anorexic women as obsessional, with inflexible thinking, social introversion, overly compliant behavior, and limited social spontaneity. Strober suggests that these underlying traits may play a facilitatory role in the development of obsessive and compulsive symptoms during the acute illness.

I have found that people with anorexia nervosa have certain symptoms that are different from those found in patients with classic obsessive–compulsive disorder. In anorexia nervosa patients, the content of obsessive–compulsive symptoms tends to be ego syntonic and is focused on issues of symmetry and exactness, unlike that of the much wider range of symptoms of classic obsessive–compulsive disorder. However, ill anorexia nervosa patients are as impaired as patients with obsessive–compulsive disorder in terms of the intensity of the symptoms (time spent obsessing, lack of control, etc). An important aspect of these specific obsessive–compulsive symptoms is that they persist after the patient recovers from anorexia nervosa, raising the possibility that such behavior is trait related. In addition, we have found that administration of m-CPP, a relatively serotonin-specific drug, improves mood in anorexics, whereas this drug tends to make patients with obsessive–compulsive disorder more symptomatic.

Patients with anorexia nervosa invariably have a rigid, overcontrolled, perfectionistic, inhibited, and constrained temperament (also see Chapter 30). Casper, using the Multidimensional Personality Questionnaire, found that this kind of temperament in restrictor-type anorexics was independent of the state of illness. That is, restrictor-type anorexics, when underweight and 8 to 10 years after good outcome, had greater self-control, behavioral constraint, inhibition of emotionality, and conscientiousness than matched control subjects. Measured against factors devised for the Tridimensional Personality Questionnaire, anorexia nervosa patients have been found to show greater harm avoidance than controls. Our studies suggest that high levels of perfectionism and a need for symmetry and exactness persist after recovery from anorexia nervosa. Considered together, patients with anorexia nervosa at all stages of their illness, are inhibited, overcontrolled, perfectionistic, and obsessional (in terms of a need for symmetry, exactness, and correctness).

STATE-RELATED NEUROTRANSMITTER ALTERATIONS

Underweight anorexics have been found to have elevations of cerebrospinal fluid (CSF) concentrations of corticotropin-releasing hormone (CRH), neuropeptide Y (NPY), and vasopressin (AVP) and reductions of beta-endorphin and oxytocin levels. The correction of these neuropeptide disturbances by weight restoration implies that such disturbances are secondary to malnutrition and/or weight loss and not the cause. However, it is important to note that some neuropeptide alterations persist in anorexics after short-term recovery (at goal weight for 2 months or less), suggesting these disturbances are strongly entrenched and are not easily corrected by improved nutrition. Most neuropeptide disturbances are normalized after long-term weight recovery (goal weight for more than 1 year).

Alterations of neuropeptide activity (Table 45.1) are likely to contribute to several characteristic psychophysiological disturbances in acutely ill anorexics. For example, starvation-induced alterations of CRH levels contribute to hypercortisolimia. Alterations of CRH, NPY, and opioid levels may contribute to hypothalamic amenorrhea and decreased sexual activity. Elevated CRH and reduced beta-endorphin levels may contribute to dysphoric symptoms. An important consideration is that alterations of beta-endorphin, CRH, and NPY may contribute to the dissociation anorexics often display between reduced caloric intake and obsessive thoughts about food. Demitrack and colleagues have hypothesized that elevated brain oxytocin levels acting in concert with reduced brain AVP levels may impair the extinction of aversively conditioned learning in underweight anorexics. In other words, these changes might exacerbate the tendency restricting anorexics have for a perseverative preoccupation with the adverse consequences of food intake.

SEROTONIN DISTURBANCE: POSSIBLY TRAIT RELATED?

Our group has found that long-term weight-restored anorexics have elevated CSF 5-HIAA levels, the major metabolite of brain serotonin. These data are of interest because most anorexics have ingrained psychopathological traits that are consistent with a possible intrinsic disturbance of serotoninergic activity. Considerable evidence shows that brain serotoninergic pathways inhibit appetite. Thus an alteration in serotonin activity may be a trait that contributes to pathological eating behavior and weight loss.

As noted above, behaviors such as constraint, perfectionism, and a need for symmetry and exactness persist after long-term weight restoration. Results of many

TABLE 45.1. Features of Anorexia Nervosa That Might Result from Altered Neuropeptide Activity

	Underweight anorexics	Increased NPY level	Increased CRH level	Decreased beta-endorphin level	Increased AVP level	Decreased oxytocin level
Feeding	↓	↑	↓			
Motor activity	↑		↑	↓		
Blood pressure	↓	↓				
Sexual interest	↓	↓	↓			
H–P–gonadal axis	↓	↓	↓			
H–P–adrenal axis	↑	↑	↑↑	↓↓	↑	
Dysphoria	↑		↑	↓	↑	↑
Obsessive distortions	↑				↑	↑

Note. NPY, neuropeptide Y; CRH, corticotropin-releasing hormone; AVP, vasopressin; H–P, hypothalamic–pituitary; ↑, increased level; ↓, decreased level.

studies show that low levels of CSF 5-HIAA are associated with impulsive, suicidal, and aggressive behavior. Thus higher levels of CSF 5-HIAA in long-term weight-restored anorexics are significant, since these patients tend to be the opposite of impulsive and aggressive patients.

Monoamine neuronal systems, including that of serotonin, have a diffuse, widespread distribution and, it can be argued, have a threshold function for information processing separate from specific behaviors. Investigators of serotonin activity have consistently postulated that serotonin activity is inhibitory. Soubrie described the serotonin system as enabling the organism to arrange or tolerate delay before acting. Cloninger described serotonin as responsible for behavioral inhibition, specifically harm avoidance. In fact, serotonin activity is inhibitory to many behaviors, such as feeding, exploration, stimuli reactivity, aggression, and sexual activity. Moreover, several lines of evidence support the possibility that a serotonin abnormality may contribute to obsessive and anxious symptoms. In fact, medications with serotonin properties have been shown to have some efficacy in anorexia nervosa.

Taken together, it can be hypothesized that increased serotonin activity is associated with certain characteristics (such as food restriction and rigid, inhibited, anxious, or obsessional behaviors) that occur in anorexia nervosa. This hypothesis does not imply that anorexia nervosa is necessarily a disorder that is "predetermined" by biology. It may be that women in whom anorexia nervosa develops may have certain intrinsic vulnerabilities for perfectionistic, anxious, and obsessional behavior. It may take stress or psychosocial factors to exaggerate such traits into an illness. Moreover, the content of the illness may be influenced by the cultural milieu. That is, in another age such biologic vulnerabilities may have resulted in other patterns of symptoms.

CONCLUSIONS

Anorexia nervosa is a disorder of considerable morbidity and mortality, with a high rate of relapse and with no known treatment. Our ability to treat this illness has been limited, to a great extent, by a lack of understanding of its psychobiology. It is possible that the core characteristics of anorexia nervosa, such as obsessionality and pathological feeding, are related to increased serotonin activity. Once weight loss and malnutrition begin, anorexics may enter a vicious cycle in which the consequences of malnutrition perpetuate pathological behavior. Thus starvation-induced alterations of CRH, beta-endorphin, NPY, AVP, and oxytocin activity may contribute to neuroendocrine disturbances and may play a role in subsequent and more extreme behavioral and appetitive abnormalities.

The possibility that the core characteristics of anorexia nervosa are related to increased serotonin activity is important. First, this hypothesis provides a foundation on which we may design studies that might test whether certain anorexic traits (such as obsessionality, introversion, perfectionism, limited spontaneity, and overly formalistic and stereotyped behavior) correlate with serotonin activity. Second, it suggests that trials of serotonin-specific medications, which have proved successful in treating illnesses such as obsessive–compulsive disorder, may be useful. Third, the hypothesis would support other data suggesting that increased serotonin activity may be related to anxious, obsessional, or inhibited behaviors in humans.

FURTHER READING

Bastiani, A. M., Altemus, M., Pigott, T. A., Rubenstein, C., Weltzin, T. E., & Kaye, W. H. (1995). *Comparison of obsessions and compulsions in patients with anorexia nervosa and obsessive compulsive disorder*. Manuscript submitted for publication. First report describing differences in target symptoms between women with anorexia nervosa and women with obsessive–compulsive disorders.

Casper, R. C. (1990). Personality features of women with good outcome from restricting anorexia nervosa. *Psychosomatic Medicine, 52*, 156–170. The author shows that certain traits, such as a temperament toward emotional and behavioral restraint, persist after recovery from anorexia nervosa, and raises the possibility that such traits are predisposing factors.

Demitrack, M. A., Lesem, M. D., Listwak, S. J., Brandt, H. A., Jimerson, D.C., & Gold, P.W. (1990). CSF oxytocin in anorexia nervosa and bulimia nervosa: Clinical and pathophysiologic considerations. *American Journal of Psychiatry, 147*, 882–886. Describes how disturbances of these peptides may contribute to cognitive disturbances in ill eating-disorder patients.

Gold, P. W., Gwirtsman, H., Avgerinos, P. C., Nieman, L. K., Gallucci, W. T., Kaye, W. H., Jimerson, D., Ebert, M., Rittmaster, R., Loriaux, D. L., & Chrousos, G. P. (1986). Abnormal hypothalamic–pituitary–adrenal function in anorexia nervosa: Pathophysiologic mechanisms in underweight and weight-corrected patients. *New England Journal of Medicine, 314*, 1335. Documents that changes in the ACTH–cortisol axis are secondary to alterations in brain CRH secretion in patients with anorexia nervosa.

Kaye, W. H., Berrettini, W., Gwirtsman, H., & George, D. (1990). Altered cerebrospinal fluid neuropeptide Y and peptide YY immunoreactivity in anorexia and bulimia nervosa. *Archives of General Psychiatry, 47*, 548–556. Describes how alterations in these neuropeptides, which are among the most potent in their effects on feeding, may contribute to altered feeding behavior in anorexia and bulimia nervosa.

Kaye, W. H., Gwirtsman, H. E., George, D. T., & Ebert, M. H. (1991). Altered serotonin activity in anorexia nervosa after long-term weight restoration: Does elevated CSF 5-HIAA correlate with rigid and obsessive behavior? *Archives of General Psychiatry, 48*, 556–562. Describes findings indicating that anorexics may have increased brain serotonin activity after recovery, which may contribute to disturbances of feeding and an obsessive need for perfectionism and exactness.

Leibowitz, S. F., & Shor-Posner, G. (1986). Brain serotonin and eating behavior. *Appetite, 7*, 1–14. Excellent review of the contributions of brain serotonin activity to the control of feeding behavior.

Rothenberg, A. (1988). Differential diagnosis of anorexia nervosa and depressive illness: A review of 11 studies. *Comprehensive Psychiatry, 29*, 427–432. Overview showing that the diagnosis of obsessive–compulsive disorder is the second most frequent comorbid diagnosis in patients with anorexia nervosa.

Spoont, M. R. (1992). Modulatory role of serotonin in neural information processing: Implications for human psychopathology. *Psychological Bulletin, 112*(2), 330–350. Excellent theoretical overview of the role of serotonin in behavior and implications for understanding the pathophysiology of eating disorders.

Strober, M. (1991). Disorders of the self in anorexia nervosa: An organismic–developmental paradigm. In C. Johnson (Ed.), *Psychodynamic treatment of anorexia nervosa and bulimia*. New York: Guilford Press. Theoretical integration of potential psychological and biological underpinnings of anorexia nervosa.

• 46 •

PHYSIOLOGY
OF BULIMIA NERVOSA

Karl M. Pirke

Numerous published reports on the physiology of bulimia nervosa have detailed all its aspects, from metabolic changes to neurotransmitter abnormalities. Severe abnormalities reported by some investigators have not been confirmed by others. To understand these discrepancies, the interactions between eating behavior and metabolic and endocrine regulation must be considered. Therefore, in this chapter the metabolic situation of the patient with bulimia nervosa will be considered first, and its consequence for the understanding of the physiological changes will be discussed thereafter.

METABOLIC FINDINGS

Low plasma insulin levels have been reported for bulimia nervosa patients. Low C-peptide levels, low-normal glucose concentrations, increased beta-hydroxybutyric acid levels, and low triiodthyronine values have also been found in these patients. These observations support the view that the metabolic situation in bulimia nervosa patients is one of reduced caloric intake. The bulimic eating behavior is not only characterized by bingeing and purging but also by intermittent dieting and starvation. This behavior explains why these signs of malnutrition do not occur in all patients at all times.

The Hypothalamic–Pituitary–Adrenal Axis

There have been inconsistent findings in this area. One group studied the 24-hour secretion of adrenocorticotropic hormone (ACTH) and cortisol and found that, although the number of secretory episodes was not altered, the average concentration of both hormones was significantly higher in bulimic patients than in controls. The response of ACTH and cortisol to the corticotropin-releasing factor was blunted, as it is in many conditions of central hypercortisolism. In contrast, others have observed normal episodic cortisol secretion in bulimic patients with regular menstrual cycles. However, bulimic patients with amenorrhea were found to have elevated cortisol levels during the night hours. The latter group also showed decreased triiodthyronine values and elevated beta-hydroxybutyric acid levels. These additional findings indicate that patients in this subgroup are in a metabolic situation characterized by reduced caloric intake. Dexamethasone suppression test responses have been found to be pathological by most investigators. It has been shown that caloric restriction correlates with plasma cortisol levels, indicating that the abnormality of the dexamethasone test response is a consequence of temporarily reduced caloric intake.

Growth Hormone and Prolactin

An increase in the level of growth hormone (GH) during the night has been found in bulimia nervosa patients. Since anorexia nervosa and starvation due to other causes are also associated with increased GH levels, we might speculate that intermittent dieting is responsible for the GH increase. Prolactin levels increase less during the night in bulimic patients than in healthy control subjects. This difference is probably caused by reduced estrogen production in bulimics (see below).

The Hypothalamic–Pituitary–Gonadal Axis

Amenorrhea occurs in about 50% of patients with bulimia nervosa. When gonadal and gonadotropic hormone levels are measured throughout the menstrual cycle or over longer time periods, it emerges that about 50% of bulimic patients have anovulatory cycles and about 20% have luteal phase defects, as judged from the time course of estradiol and progesterone production. These findings indicate that the frequency of cycle disorders is greater in bulimic patients than would be expected from the medical history alone. The nature of the disturbance has been further evaluated by measuring episodic gonadotropin secretion at different times of the cycle. Patients with anovulatory cycles have been found to have a reduced leutinizing hormone (LH) pulse frequency when compared with healthy controls during the early follicular phase. Some, but not all, anovulatory patients showed no secretory LH episodes during the 12-hour observation period, suggesting that a hypothalamic mechanism is operating. It is unclear why some bulimic patients with normal LH secretion have anovulatory cycles. In contrast to eumenorrheic bulimic patients, anovulatory patients show significantly higher nocturnal cortisol secretion, along with elevated beta-hydroxybutyric acid and low T_3 values. Whether any of these factors is causally related to the menstrual cycle disturbance remains unclear.

Gastrointestinal and Other Peptide Hormones

Most of the studies on peptides in the cerebrospinal fluid of bulimic patients have been conducted by Kaye and his coworkers. They have found normal neuropeptide Y values but increased PYY levels after successful treatment. Since in animals it strongly stimulates feeding behavior, PYY may play a role in the development of bulimia nervosa. Since endorphins inhibit food intake we might expect that bulimic patients would show decreased central endorphin activity. Indeed, low beta-endorphin values, but normal dynorphin values, have been observed. Cholecystokinin (CCK) is of special interest in the regulation of satiety. It has been found that, in comparison with healthy volunteers, bulimic patients have reduced levels after a test meal. Thus the ability of bulimic patients to eat huge amounts of food in a short time may be partly explained by their low CCK levels, which result in low satiety.

NEUROTRANSMITTERS

Norepinephrine

Norepinephrine (NE) is the neurotransmitter of the peripheral sympathetic nervous system as well as a central nervous system neutrotransmitter. Clinical symptoms (such as bradycardia, hypotension, and hypothermia) as well as studies on NE and its metabolites in blood, cerebrospinal, and urine have clearly shown a reduced activity of the central and peripheral sympathetic nervous system in anorexia nervosa patients. Studies in bulimic patients have found similar, although less severe, alterations in NE secretion.

Methoxyhydroxyphenylglycol (MHPG) is a metabolite of central and peripheral NE. Twenty-four-hour urine excretion of MHPG is significantly lower in bulimic patients than in healthy controls. In the orthostatic challenge test, the difference between plasma NE levels in supine and standing body position is measured. The NE response has been found to be only half as high in bulimic patients as in normal control subjects. When challenged with protein-rich or carbohydrate-rich standardized test meals, bulimic patients show a significantly smaller increase in NE levels than do healthy controls. During short-term maximal ergometric challenge, NE levels reach the same maximal values as those in controls. This observation reflects the fact that the exercise-induced increase of NE levels is mainly determined by the muscular mass that is normal in patients with bulimia nervosa. In contrast to physical stress, mental stress causes a smaller NE increase in bulimic patients than in healthy controls. The reduced activity of the noradrenergic system in bulimia nervosa patients is accompanied by increased $alpha_2$-adrenoceptor capacity and increased adenylate cyclase sensitivity toward inhibiting (epinephrine) and stimulating prostaglandin E_1 influences. The $beta_2$-adrenoceptors on the lymphocytes are not altered. The receptor changes are a consequence of the reduced NE activity, since they disappear during successful treatment. Although no direct proof exists, we may speculate that the abnormalities of the noradrenergic system in bulimics are a consequence of their intermittent dieting.

Serotonin

It has been proposed that decreased activity of the central serotonin system may be a predisposing factor for the development of bulimia (see also Chapter 35). This hypothesis is based on animal experiments in which the role of serotonin in the regulation of hunger and satiety has been studied. The administration of serotonin antagonists leads to the consumption of larger meals, causing an increase in body weight. In contrast, administration of serotonin agonists leads to a decrease in food intake. Supporting this hypothesis is the observation that prolactin secretion after treatment with m-chlorophenylpiperazine (a serotonin agonist) is significantly lower in bulimic patients than in healthy controls. Since prolactin secretion is dependent on estrogens, and since oestrogen levels are low in females with bulimia nervosa, this interpretation must be regarded with caution.

There is another way to obtain information about central serotonin activity. It has been observed that the serotonin content of the brain is regulated by the uptake into the brain of the serotonin precursor tryptophan. For the six large neutral amino acids (LNAA)—leucine, isoleucine, phenylalanine, valine, tryptophan, and tyrosine—there is a common transport mechanism at the blood–brain barrier. Thus tryptophan influx into the brain is dictated by the ratio of tryptophan levels to those of the other large neutral amino acids. After a protein-rich meal, only small amounts of tryptophan enter the brain, since the ratio between the tryptophan level and those of its competitors is low. The reason for this low tryptophan ratio lies in the fact that animal protein contains little tryptophan but large amounts of tryptophan's competitors. Insulin is released after a carbohydrate meal. Insulin stimulates the influx of both glucose and the LNAA into the peripheral tissues, except for tryptophan. Thus, after a carbohydrate meal, the plasma levels of the neutral amino acids decrease, but the tryptophan concentrations remain unaltered. The tryptophan quotient therefore increases. As a result, more tryptophan is transported into the brain, and its serotonin content increases. If there is a reduction in the effectiveness of insulin, the tryptophan quotient decreases. Since lowered insulin levels are found in bulimia nervosa patients, less tryptophan may enter the brain, giving further (although only indirect) evidence for decreased central serotonergic activity in bulimic patients. Kaye and colleagues have measured the tryptophan quotient in the blood of bulimic patients during and after episodes of binge eating and observed that the binges ceased when the tryptophan quotient increased. This finding suggests that diminished serotonin activity in the brain may facilitate or even precipitate binges. Accordingly, binge eating might be regarded as form of self-medication used to combat the negative consequences of diminished serotonin activity in the brain.

FURTHER READING

Brewerton, T. D., Lydiard, R. B., Laraina, M. T., et al. (1992). CSF and β-endorphin and dynorphin in bulimia nervosa. *American Journal of Psychiatry, 149,* 1086–1090. Important report on central nervous endorphins in bulimia nervosa patients.

Geracioti, T. D., & Liddle, R. A. (1988). Impaired cholecystokinin secretion in bulimia nervosa. *New England Medicine, 319,* 683–688. First description of reduced CCK levels in bulimia nervosa patients.

Heufelder, A., Warnhoff, M., & Pirke, K. M. (1985). Platelet α_2-adrenoceptor and adenylate cyclase in patients with anorexia nervosa and bulimia. *Journal of Clinical Endocrinology and Metabolism, 61,* 1053–1060. Describes increased receptor capacity and increased sensitivity of postreceptor mechanisms in patients with eating disorders.

Jimmerson, D. C., Brandt, H. A., & Brewerton, T. D. (1988). Evidence for altered serotonin function in bulimia and anorexia nervosa: Behavioral implications. In K. M. Pirke, W. Vandereycken, & D. Ploog (Eds.), *Psychobiology of bulimia nervosa* (pp. 83–89). Berlin, Heidelberg, New York: Springer. Reviews serotonin function in eating disorders.

Kaye, W. H. (1992). Neuropeptide abnormalities. In K. A. Halmi (Ed.), *Psychobiology and treatment of anorexia nervosa and bulimia nervosa* (pp. 169–191). Washington, DC: American Psychiatric Press. Provides a summary of research on neuropeptides in eating disorders.

Levy, A. B., & Marlarkey, W. B. (1988). Growth hormone and somatomedin-C in bulimia. *Psychoneuroendocrinology, 13,* 359–362. Describes elevated GH levels in bulimics.

Pirke, K.M. (1990). The noradrenergic system in anorexia and bulimia nervosa. In H. Remschmidt & M. H. Schmidt (Eds.), *Child and youth psychiatry: European perspective* (Vol. 1, pp. 30–44). Toronto: Hogrefe & Huber Publishers. Gives an account of the reduced activity of the noradrenergic system in people with eating disorders.

Pirke, K. M., Kellner, M. B., Fried, E., Krieg, J. C., & Fichter, M. M. (1993). Satiety and cholecystokinin. *International Journal of Eating Disorders, 14*(4). Describes reduced satiety and cholecystokinin in bulimia nervosa but not anorexia nervosa.

Schweiger, U., Pirke, K. M., Laessle, R. G., & Fichter, M. M. (1992). Gonadotropin secretion in bulimia nervosa. *Journal of Clinical Endocrinology and Metabolism, 74*(5), 1122–1127. Describes the mechanism of impaired fertility in bulimic patients.

Walsh, B. T., Lo, E. S., Cooper, T., Roose, S. P., Gladis, M. Lindy, D. C., & Glassman, A. H. (1987). The dexamethasone suppression test and plasma dexamethasone levels in bulimia. *Archives of General Psychiatry, 44,* 799–800. Reports increased activity of the hypothalamic–pituitary–adrenal axis in some, but not all, bulimic patients.

• 47 •

MEDICAL COMPLICATIONS OF ANOREXIA NERVOSA

David S. Goldbloom
Sidney H. Kennedy

Since the initial modern descriptions of anorexia nervosa by Gull and Lasègue 120 years ago (see Chapter 25), there has been consistent and careful observation of the multiple somatic symptoms and sequelae of this disorder. As new measurement techniques evolve in such disparate areas as immunology and neuroimaging, new evidence emerges of its protean complications. Historically such findings have been used at times to reason backward to models of etiopathology or forward to therapeutics, usually obscuring the complexity of this multidimensional disorder and ignoring the nonspecific contribution of the effects of starvation. Nevertheless it is indisputable that no other psychiatric disorder manifests as many medical complications as does anorexia nervosa. This chapter provides an overview of these complications. The medical complications of the frequently associated disorder of bulimia nervosa are not discussed here, since these are addressed in Chapter 48.

MENSTRUAL/REPRODUCTIVE COMPLICATIONS

Primary or secondary amenorrhea is a mandatory diagnostic criterion for anorexia nervosa (see Chapter 23). Maintenance of, or reversion to, prepubertal secretory profiles of luteinizing hormone and follicle-stimulating hormone leads to a state of hypogonadotrophic hypogonadism. In males with anorexia nervosa, this state may manifest as sexual disinterest and dysfunction. In prepubertal females, it may be associated with a failure of normal breast development. The hormonal disturbance diminishes but does not eliminate the possibility of reproduction, but there is evidence of fetal risk in women with active anorexia nervosa during pregnancy. This risk has been demonstrated in a case series of pregnancies in which the babies had lower-than-average birth weights and lower scores on standard tests of neonatal status. The etiology of the endocrine dysfunction is unclear, since in a minority of cases the amenorrhea precedes significant weight loss. The treatment is weight restoration.

BONE COMPLICATIONS

Osteoporosis and stunting of growth are among the most serious and possibly irreversible consequences of anorexia nervosa. Low estrogen and elevated cortisol levels are among the mechanisms implicated in their pathogenesis. Adolescent girls are particularly at risk for osteopenia, since peak skeletal mass has often not been reached. Results of recent calcium kinetic studies suggest a reduced rate of bone formation and an increased rate of bone resorption in anorexia nervosa patients.

Fractures of the long bones, vertebrae, and sternum have been reported in anorexia nervosa patients who have had amenorrhea for as brief a period as 1 year. Although moderate levels of physical exercise appeared to mitigate against osteopenic changes in one study, further information is required on the relative importance of estrogen replacement therapy, calcium and vitamin D supplementation, and exercise in treating the bone erosion.

GASTROINTESTINAL COMPLICATIONS

Delayed gastric and whole-gut emptying times have been documented in anorexia nervosa patients and are responsible for complaints of constipation, stomach bloating, and abdominal pain. Although both subjective complaints and measured transit times improve with nutritional therapy and weight gain, there is often a role for prokinetic agents such as cisapride or domperidone during the early stages of refeeding. We typically prescribe cisapride 10 milligrams orally three times daily about 30 minutes before each meal. Frequent small meals may also be recommended if there is extreme discomfort. Although these measures facilitate physiological recovery, they do not necessarily alter the associated motivational and cognitive disturbances concerning eating.

Rarely, acute abdominal symptoms are caused by severe gastric dilation, perforation, or bleeding. These events have been reported to occur during rapid refeeding as well as following uncontrolled overeating. Uncontrolled vomiting caused by acute pancreatitis may be mistaken for self-induced vomiting. Anorexia nervosa patients may also use syrup of ipecac to induce vomiting. Emaciated patients may be particularly vulnerable to the cardiotoxic effect of the emetine contained in ipecac. The possibility of abuse of this substance should be considered in all patients with unexplained electrocardiographic abnormalities.

Both starvation and laxative abuse contribute to constipation. The use of stimulant agents containing phenolphthalein for long periods of time may cause irreversible damage to colonic innervation. In North America, Ex-lax and Correctol are the most commonly abused laxatives in this category. In most instances abrupt withdrawal of the laxatives in a medical or psychiatric unit, together with the prescription of a high-fiber diet and a bulking agent, proves effective. When excessive fluid retention occurs (which may result in a weight gain of 5 to 10 kilograms in a period of 7 to 10 days), it may be necessary to prescribe a potassium-sparing diuretic such as spironolactone for a brief time.

CARDIOVASCULAR COMPLICATIONS

Typical peripheral manifestations of anorexia nervosa include sinus bradycardia, with rates as low as 30 beats per minute, resting and orthostatic hypotension, and acrocyanosis with mottled and cold extremities. Centrally, the electrocardiograms of anorexia nervosa patients may show low voltage patterns and other wave-form disturbances that may reflect both hemodynamic and electrolyte disturbances. Imaging of the heart may reveal significant changes in architecture, including atrophy and a decrease in muscle mass and alteration in cardiac chamber size, as well as mitral valve prolapse. Presumed cardiac causes of sudden death account for some of the mortality associated with anorexia nervosa. Finally, congestive cardiac failure has been documented in the context of aggressive refeeding.

RENAL AND METABOLIC COMPLICATIONS

Dehydration is a common occurrence in persons with anorexia nervosa, particularly when vomiting and laxative or diuretic abuse are present. Chronic dehydration and hypokalemia may cause irreversible damage to renal tubules, and partial diabetes insipidus may occur secondary to abnormal vasopressin release with decreased renal concentrating capacity. Renal calculi as a consequence of chronic dehydration have also been reported. Careful monitoring of fluid balance is generally all that is required during rehydration, although patients who receive parenteral feeding are at particular risk for developing hypophosphatemia.

Symptomatic hypoglycemia is not common in anorexia nervosa patients, probably because of adaptive changes in insulin release and clearance. However, the co-occurrence of anorexia nervosa (or bulimia nervosa) and diabetes mellitus presents a serious medical problem requiring input from specialists in both diabetes and eating disorders (see Chapter 49). Despite previous reports of elevated cholesterol levels in anorexia nervosa patients, recent evidence suggests that this does not occur.

HEMATOLOGICAL COMPLICATIONS

Mild forms of anemia as well as leukopenia and thrombocytopenia are common in people with anorexia nervosa. These abnormal indices generally return to normal with refeeding and weight restoration. The anemia is usually normochronic and normocytic, although intestinal bleeding, secondary to laxative abuse, may result in iron-deficiency anemia. Despite a reduction in certain parameters of immune function, there is no evidence of increased risk of infections. Low sedimentation rates are generally found, in contrast to other pathological processes associated with weight loss.

DERMATOLOGICAL COMPLICATIONS

Several skin signs have become part of the medical folklore of anorexia nervosa. These signs include the yellowish discoloration attributed to carotene pigmentation; the appearance of fine, downy body hair (lanugo); and, in patients who induce vomiting, calluses on the dorsum of the hand (Russell's sign). None of these complications requires attention beyond routine medical treatment.

NEUROLOGICAL COMPLICATIONS

Anorexia nervosa is associated with disturbance in both central and peripheral neurological function. Centrally, at a structural level, imaging studies have documented enlargement of cerebral ventricles in persons with anorexia nervosa. While it has been argued that this finding reflects "pseudoatrophy" secondary to fluid and cortisol disturbances, and it has been shown to be reversible, its etiology and long-term outcome remain unknown. At a functional level, positron emission tomography has demonstrated glucose hypermetabolism in the caudate area. This finding is of uncertain significance. Electroencephalographic (EEG) abnormalities of various types have also been reported. Clinically these EEG findings may be manifested in impairment detected during neuropsychological evaluation and by a reduction in seizure threshold. Peripherally, generalized muscle weakness and loss of muscle mass may be present.

MORTALITY

Recent long-term follow-up studies, extending over twenty years, of anorexia nervosa patients in Scandinavia and England reveal a mortality rate of 18%, with the majority of deaths attributed to the medical complications of anorexia nervosa or bulimia nervosa. The lack of detail in these reports precludes identification of the proximate causes of death, although electrocardiogram and metabolic disturbances have been documented in a number of case reports. The high mortality rate is equal to that seen with other major psychiatric disorders such as schizophrenia and major depression. Clinicians should be particularly alert to patients with electrolyte and fluid balance disturbances, cardiac dysrhythmia, purging behavior, and advanced emaciation.

CONCLUSIONS

This brief chapter does not allow for adequate documentation of the panoply of medical complications of anorexia nervosa; ultimately, no organ system is spared. Despite the extent of these sequelae, there is no evidence that any one of them explains the origins of the illness or dictates a specific remedy. In the vast majority patients, symptoms remit with appropriate nutrition and weight restoration. Those symptoms that may be less reversible—such as osteoporotic changes—may pose a continuing threat to the individual long after the disorder has resolved. Health professionals must be vigilant regarding these complications and should ensure that patients and their families are also well informed.

FURTHER READING

Gupta, M., Gupta, A., & Habermann, H. (1987). Dermatologic signs in anorexia nervosa and bulimia nervosa. *Archives of Dermatology, 123,* 1386–1390. This is a comprehensive review of skin-related sequelae of eating disorders.

Kaplan, A. S., & Garfinkel, P. E. (Eds.). (1993). *Medical issues in the eating disorders.* New York: Brunner/Mazel. This recent text is a comprehensive review not only of the medical complications of eating disorders but also of their biological underpinnings and their relationship to medical illness.

Schocken, D., Holloway, J. D., & Powers, P. (1989). Weight loss and the heart: Effects of anorexia nervosa and starvation. *Archives of Internal Medicine, 149,* 877–881. This review article highlights the life-threatening physiological consequences of anorexia nervosa that involve the cardiovascular system.

Seeman, E., Szmukler, G., Formica, C., Tsalamandris, C., & Mestrovic, R. (1992). Osteoporosis in anorexia nervosa: The influence of peak bone density, bone loss, oral contraceptive use and exercise. *Journal of Bone and Mineral Research, 7,* 1467–1474. The authors report on the relative influences of estrogen replacement therapy and exercise on bone density in a large sample of patients with anorexia nervosa.

Sharp, C. W., & Freeman, C. P. L. (1993). The medical complications of anorexia nervosa. *British Journal of Psychiatry, 162,* 452–462. This article provides a succinct and up-to-date summary of the medical complications of anorexia nervosa.

Stacher, G., Bergmann, H., Wiesnagrotzki, S., Steiner-Mittelback, G., Kiss, A., & Abatzi, T. A. (1992). Primary anorexia nervosa: Gastric emptying and antral motor activity in 53 patients. *International Journal of Eating Disorders, 11,* 163–172. These authors examined the effects of refeeding and weight gain on gastric function in a series of emaciated patients with anorexia nervosa.

Van Dissel, J., Gerritsen, H., & Meinders, A. (1992). Severe hypophosphatemia in a patient with anorexia nervosa during oral feeding. *Mineral and Electrolyte Metabolism, 18,* 365–369. The authors emphasize the importance of phosphate evaluation during refeeding to prevent life-threatening complications.

• 48 •

MEDICAL COMPLICATIONS OF BULIMIA NERVOSA

James E. Mitchell

Bulimia nervosa can be associated with significant adverse medical sequelae. However, relative to anorexia nervosa, the medical complications of this disorder are, for the most part, relatively benign and the mortality rate appears to be surprisingly low, despite the extremes of behavior in which these patients often engage. These considerations in no way alleviate the evaluating physician from the responsibility of carefully assessing and, if necessary, monitoring certain clinical parameters in patients with active bulimia nervosa. General symptomatology will be discussed first, followed by a review of the various organ systems.

SIGNS AND SYMPTOMS

Despite the fact that patients with bulimia nervosa generally have fewer serious untoward medical complications than those with anorexia nervosa, they usually report more physical complaints when they first are seen for treatment. Not uncommonly, bulimia nervosa patients complain of fatigue, lethargy, and "feeling bloated"; at times they also report nausea, constipation, abdominal pain, and (rarely) swelling of the hands and feet, as well as tooth sensitivity and irregular menses. Results of these patients' physical examinations are generally normal, although certain telltale abnormalities may be discovered. The salivary glands may be enlarged, most often the parotid glands, which may result in a "puffy cheek" appearance. Calluses or abrasions on the dorsum of the hand may be found; the calluses result from the use of the hand to stimulate the gag reflex (originally described by Dr. Gerald Russell and referred to as "Russell's sign"). Dental enamel erosion, which is present in the majority of patients who have been vomiting for 4 years or more, is fairly pathognomonic of the disorder. Edema can be found and is particularly common in those who abuse laxatives or diuretics.

Fluid and Electrolyte Changes

Most bulimic behaviors, such as vomiting and laxative or diuretic abuse, lead to fluid loss and subsequent dehydration, which, in turn, often results in a metabolic alkalosis. Patients subsequently tend to lose large amounts of potassium in the urine and, because of the vomiting, large amounts of chloride in the emesis. Therefore, the most common

271

metabolic picture is one of metabolic alkalosis (as evidenced by an elevation in serum bicarbonate levels), hypochloremia, and/or hypokalemia. Overall, about 50% of bulimic patients have electrolyte abnormalities, detected on routine screening. Metabolic acidosis also occurs, usually in patients who are abusing laxatives, caused by the loss of bicarbonate-rich fluid in the stool. In this way it is possible to determine that some patients are surreptitiously abusing laxatives. Seldom seen are hyponatremia, hypocalcemia, hypophosphatemia, and hypomagnesemia.

Pulmonary Symptons

Isolated cases of pneumomediastinum in bulimia nervosa patients have been reported but are extremely rare and appear to occur more commonly in bulimic anorexics. Aspiration pneumonitis associated with self-induced vomiting has also been reported.

Dental Involvement

Erosion of the dental enamel, in which the lingual surface of the upper teeth is mainly affected, is essentially pathognomonic of vomiting, and most physicians who see this abnormality once can easily identify it in other cases. Another site to focus on during examination of the mouth is the amalgams (or fillings), which may end up projecting above the surface of the teeth since, unlike the surrounding enamel, they are relatively resistant to gastric acid. Studies have shown that most patients with bulimia nervosa who have been vomiting for 4 years or more will have fairly obvious evidence of enamel erosion.

Many patients with bulimia nervosa develop the habit of brushing their teeth after vomiting as a way of neutralizing the aversive residual taste. This practice, however, is unwise and actually promotes enamel loss, since the teeth are friable because of their recent exposure to the highly acidic gastric contents. It is better to encourage patients to rinse their mouths thoroughly after vomiting using, if possible, an alkaline substance such as a teaspoon of baking soda in water. Periodontal disease and an increased incidence of caries have been reported but not systematically studied.

Gastrointestinal Complications

A variety of gastrointestinal complications have been reported in bulimia nervosa patients, and several are related to specific problem behaviors. As mentioned previously, salivary gland hypotrophy, particularly involving the parotid glands, is seen relatively frequently. The pathophysiology is unclear, and the hypertrophy has been variously attributed to high carbohydrate intake or to fluid and electrolyte abnormalities. This hypertrophy has been noted to persist, at least intermittently, for several months after normalization of eating behavior. Hyperamylasemia has also been reported but should not be assumed to be salivary in origin. Radiologic fractionation studies may be useful, in that bulimia nervosa has also been associated with pancreatitis, such as cases of chronic relapsing pancreatitis that have been misdiagnosed and have not responded to standard treatment. Both esophagitis and esophageal perforation have been reported in bulimia nervosa patients, although infrequently. Mallory–Weiss tears in association with vomiting have also been described.

Gastric emptying studies, which fairly consistently have shown delays in the rate of emptying in anorexia nervosa patients, have yielded mixed results in bulimia nervosa patients, with results of some studies showing marked delay and others, normal function. Gastric dilatation, which poses the risk of gastric rupture and death, has also been found in bulimia nervosa patients and may be the most common cause of fatality. The exact pathophysiology of the gastric dilatation is unclear, but it appears that, perhaps because of pressure changes in the gut after binge eating, patients may find themselves unable to vomit. Gastric dilatation can represent a medical/surgical emergency, since decompression is necessary to prevent gastric rupture. The spilling of gastric contents into the abdominal cavity is usually fatal. The exact prevalence of acute gastric dilatation is unknown but several dozen cases have been reported.

Because of the dehydration, and also, as a result of laxative misuse, patients with bulimia nervosa commonly develop reflex constipation, which in rare cases can progress to "cathartic colon" in which the colon ceases to function adequately. Steatorrhea and protein-losing gastroenteropathy have also been reported secondary to laxative abuse. There have also been some reports of abnormal liver function.

Cardiovascular Effects

Cardiomyopathy and other types of myopathy secondary to Ipecac abuse have been reported in bulimic patients. The emetic Ipecac, when used repeatedly, is stored in muscle tissue, including cardiac muscle, which can result in problems with muscle contraction. Hypokalemic cardiomyopathy also occurs but very rarely.

Idiopathic edema may be present and is often attributable to either laxative or diuretic abuse. Orthostasis and symptomatic hypotension may be present in patients who are significantly dehydrated, again, these are particularly prevalent in those who abuse large quantities of laxatives or diuretics. Other reported conditions include EKG abnormalities and a possible increase in the prevalence of mitral valve prolapse.

Dermatologic Effects

Bulimia nervosa patients often have dry skin, a condition related to the dehydration they experience. As mentioned earlier, Russell's sign, finger calluses or abrasions on the dorsum of the hand resulting from using the hand to stimulate the gag reflex mechanically, is pathognomonic.

Neurological Signs

Abnormal results of electroencephalography (EEG) have been reported for bulimia nervosa patients, but these EEG changes appear to be secondary to fluid and electrolyte abnormalities. There seems to be no clear association between bulimia nervosa and seizure disorders. Brain scans of some patients with bulimia nervosa show evidence of mild increases in ventricular–brain ratios. These increases are usually of modest degree compared with brain scan abnormalities seen in patients with anorexia nervosa.

Endocrine/Metabolic Abnormalities

Patients with bulimia nervosa often demonstrate a variety of subtle and not-so-subtle abnormalities in various neuroendocrine and metabolic systems. Most will continue to menstruate, albeit irregularly; many demonstrate low estradiol and progesterone levels.

The issue of nonsuppression on the dexamethasone suppression test (DST) is controversial, with some authors suggesting that malabsorption of dexamethasone accounts for the abnormal DST levels, while others find elevated cortisol levels on 24-hour monitoring.

In some patients with bulimia nervosa hypoglycemia develops either after fasting or in response to binge eating and vomiting episodes. Various other neuroendocrine abnormalities have been reported, including blunting of thyroid-stimulating hormone and growth hormone (GH) in response to thyroid-releasing hormone, as well as the failure of GH to suppress in response to oral glucose administration. Elevations in beta-hydroxybutyric acid and free fatty acid levels have also been described, suggesting relative starvation despite normal body weight.

Renal Complications

Renal complications in bulimia nervosa patients are rare. Occasionally an elevation in serum blood urea nitrogen levels will be seen on routine testing in patients who are quite dehydrated, and there is a risk of kaliopenic nephropathy in those who are chronically dehydrated and hypokalemic. Reductions in the glomerular filtration rate have been reported, although they are rare.

GENERAL MEDICAL MANAGEMENT

The important medical tasks for the physician evaluating the condition of a patient with bulima nervosa are to take careful medical history and to do a physical examination and several screening laboratory tests. As part of the history, it is important to ascertain both the presence and the frequency of the various abnormal eating-related behaviors that may result in adverse medical outcomes. These behaviors include vomiting; the abuse of laxatives, diuretics, diet pills, and Ipecac; rumination; chewing and spitting out food; fasting; and excessive exercising. At a minimum, the physician should obtain vital signs, look for evidence of significant orthostatic hypotension, and obtain measurements of serum electrolyte and bicarbonate levels. Beyond these basics, the medical evaluation and monitoring should be guided by the patient's history and clinical picture. For example, a history of laxative abuse should prompt an examination of the stool for blood, and a history of Ipecac abuse should prompt a complete physical examination, obtaining on EKG and probably performing cardiac ultrasonography as well. A history of atypical symptoms with evidence of primary neurological problems should alert the clinician to the need for neuroimaging studies. The emphasis is on fitting the diagnostic evaluation to the patient's behavior, signs, and symptoms and reserving elaborate and expensive tests for those most at risk.

FURTHER READING

Altshuler, B. D., Dechow, P. C., Waller, D. A., & Hardy, B. (1990). An investigation of the oral pathologies occurring in bulimia nervosa. *International Journal of Eating Disorders, 9,* 191–199. A good introduction to the dental complications of bulimia nervosa.

Devlin, M. J., Walsh, T., & Kral, J. G.(1990). Metabolic abnormalities in bulimia nervosa. *Archives of General Psychiatry, 47,* 144–148. A good discussion of metabolism in cases of bulimia nervosa.

Kaplan, A. S., & Garfinkel, P. E. (Eds.). (1993). *Medical issues and the eating disorders.* New York: Bunner/Mazel. A recent comprehensive text on the medical issues in bulimia nervosa and anorexia nervosa.

Krieg, J. C., Lauer, C., & Pirke, K. M. (1989). Structural brain abnormalities in patients with bulimia nervosa. *Psychiatry Research, 27,* 39–48. The seminal article on structural brain abnormalities in patients with bulimia nervosa.

Mitchell, J. E., & Boutcoff, L. I. (1986). Laxative abuse complicating bulimia: Medical and treatment implications. *International Journal of Eating Disorders, 5,* 325–334. A review of the problem of laxative abuse by bulimia nervosa patients.

Mitchell, J. E., Pomeroy, C., Seppala, M., & Huber, M. (1988). Psuedo-Bartter's syndrome, diuretic abuse, idiopathic edema and eating disorders. *International Journal of Eating Disorders, 7,* 225–237. A review of the problem of diuretic abuse by bulimia nervosa patients.

Mitchell, J. E., Seim, H. C., Colon, E., & Pomeroy, C. (1987). Medical complications medical management of bulimia. *Annals of Internal Medicine, 107,* 71–77. A concise review of the medical complications of bulimia nervosa.

Pirke, K. M., Pahl, J., & Schweiger, U. (1985). Metabolic and endocrine indices of starvation in bulimia: A comparison with anorexia nervosa. *Psychiatry Research, 14,* 13–39. An important article on metabolic changes in patients with bulimia nervosa.

Pomeroy, C., & Mitchell, J. (1989). Medical complications and management of eating disorders. *Psychiatric Annals, 19,* 488–493. A concise review of medical complications and management of bulimia nervosa.

Tolstoi, L. G. (1990). Ipecac-induced toxicity in eating disorders. *International Journal of Eating Disorders, 9,* 371–375. A review of issues related to Ipecac abuse.

• 49 •

EATING DISORDERS AND DIABETES

Robert C. Peveler

The recognition of the importance of patients who have both an eating disorder and diabetes mellitus dates from the early 1970s. Interest in this special population arises from both a research perspective, in that observations on different clinical groups may inform theoretical questions about the disorders themselves, and a clinical perspective, in that patients with both disorders present particular difficulties in diagnosis and management. Most of the existing literature is concerned with eating disorder patients who have the insulin-dependent form of diabetes mellitus (IDDM), and in this chapter I will focus exclusively on this group. The chapter includes discussions of the ways in which eating disorders in such patients differ from those in nondiabetic eating disorder populations in respect to their clinical features, prevalence, diagnosis, and management.

CLINICAL FEATURES

Anorexia nervosa, bulimia nervosa and less severe forms of eating disorder have all been described in patients with diabetes. In the majority of cases, the onset of the eating disorder occurs some years after the onset of diabetes, but occasionally the order may be reversed. In most respects the clinical features of the eating disorders seen in IDDM patients resemble those of nondiabetic patients. The principal difference is that eating disorder patients with IDDM have available to them an additional means of weight control: the underuse or omission of insulin, leading to "self-induced glycosuria." This feature is common but not universal in diabetic patients with an eating disorder (found in two-thirds of patients in one study), and it is also seen in about one-third of female IDDM patients who have no eating disorder. The initial effect of this behavior on body weight is rapid, chiefly as a result of water loss.

Excessive dieting, binge eating, vomiting, the misuse of laxatives and diuretics, and self-induced glycosuria all impair glycemic control, although a minority of patients do manage to maintain satisfactory control, at least at times. Alternating periods of raised and lowered blood glucose levels may go undetected by biochemical indices such as the glycated hemoglobin test. In the short term, poor control may be manifested as recurrent symptoms of hyperglycemia (e.g., thirst or tiredness), frequent episodes of ketoacidosis (often requiring hospital admission), or hypoglycemia (leading to unconsciousness if severe). Growth retardation and pubertal delay may occur in prepubertal children. The findings of one study suggested that patients with eating disorders are at increased risk for the physical complications of diabetes (retinopathy, nephropathy, or neuropathy), but this finding requires confirmation.

PREVALENCE

Because IDDM and eating disorders are both relatively common conditions, they would be expected to co-occur by chance with reasonable frequency. There is, however, a strong clinical impression that eating disorders are overrepresented in IDDM patients. There are also some theoretical reasons to expect eating disorders to be more common in the diabetic population. First, the nonspecific stress of physical illness may increase the risk. In addition, the availability of self-induced glycosuria as a means of weight control, the experience of rapid weight fluctuations near or at the time of diagnosis, and the prescription of rigid dietary regimes are all possible etiological factors. Other factors may decrease the risk: Most patients with IDDM are aware of the health risks associated with dieting, bingeing, and vomiting; and patients with IDDM are likely to be more closely supervised both by their families and by health care professionals. These factors may increase the chance that problems will be detected early and therefore "nipped in the bud."

A number of research studies have been done to address the question of the prevalence of eating disorders in both adults and adolescents with diabetes, but many of the studies have been subject to considerable methodological limitations. First, the assessment of eating-disorder features in those with diabetes is difficult, since self-report questionnaires that are meant to measure features such as dieting are prone to confounding by the presence of diabetic dietary regimes. For example, a widely used instrument, the Eating Attitudes Test (EAT), includes items such as, "I avoid foods with sugar in them." If a patient with diabetes endorses such an item it is impossible to know whether she/he avoids sugary foods primarily for weight control or is merely following medical advice on diabetes control. Even in the nondiabetic population the efficiency of screening instruments such as the EAT is not high, and a clinical interview with the patient is required to ascertain case status. A second difficulty is that many studies have been conducted in specialist diabetes centers, in which patients with complicated diabetes, including those with eating disorders, are likely to be overrepresented. Third, since the prevalence of eating disorders in the nondiabetic population has yet to be established with precision, it is vital that any study include a well-matched nondiabetic control group, but few studies incorporate such groups.

In more recent studies, in which most of the methodological limitations have been overcome, the findings suggest that the prevalence of anorexia nervosa and bulimia nervosa is not higher than normal in those with diabetes. However, no study to date has had adequate statistical power to demonstrate conclusively that there is no increase in risk. One explanation for the perceived high prevalence is that eating disorders that do not meet full diagnostic criteria are nevertheless of considerable clinical significance in those with diabetes; also, the prevalence of these disorders in the general population is generally underestimated. Significant disturbances of eating habits and attitudes may be present in up to 10% of adolescent females, whether or not they have diabetes.

DIAGNOSIS AND MANAGEMENT

The first step in management is the successful detection of the disorder. Many patients are secretive about their behavior, and when eating disorders are first encountered clinically, it is often in an occult fashion. Poor glycemic control, repeated episodes of hypoglycemia or ketoacidosis, and weight fluctuations are important clues. The index of suspicion should obviously be highest in those patients most at risk, that is, adolescent and young adult females. The clinician should ask sensitive but direct questions about eating habits and attitudes, body weight, and methods of weight control. Screening questionnaires such as the EAT may assist in the process of detection, but a psychiatric interview is necessary to confirm the diagnosis.

Dietary counseling by a dietician or diabetes specialist nurse may be a helpful first approach, especially for patients with milder forms of eating disorder, but in most cases specialist management will be required. In all cases, close liaison between the therapist managing the eating disorder and the team managing the patient's diabetes is essential. To avoid confusion, it is desirable for one person to undertake the overall day-to-day responsibility for all aspects of the patient's medical care. When treatment is completed it is also helpful for the person treating the eating disorder to give the diabetic care team advice on continuing management so that the risk of relapse is minimized.

BULIMIA NERVOSA

Treatment for bulimia nervosa has been the subject of extensive research, particularly concerning the use of cognitive-behavioral therapy (see Chapter 60). Although most patients can be treated on an outpatient basis, the risks of impaired physical health necessitating admission are higher among those with IDDM.

The suitability of cognitive-behavioral therapy for patients with bulimia nervosa and IDDM has been assessed in only small case series. A number of difficulties have been reported. For example, engaging patients in cognitive-behavioral therapy appears to be more difficult than is usual for this type of therapy. It is possible that eating disorders in IDDM patients may be particularly intractable, since milder cases may not occur because the extra risks to health posed by diabetes may discourage their development. It is also possible that significant mood and personality disorders may be more common among diabetic patients with eating disorders than among non-diabetic patients who have eating disorders. An interesting observation is that interpersonal psychotherapy has been found to be helpful in some IDDM patients with eating disorders.

A number of modifications of the standard cognitive-behavioral protocol are required in treating IDDM eating-disorder patients. First, in addition to monitoring their own thoughts and eating habits, these patients must also monitor their insulin injections and blood glucose testing to facilitate the maintenance of adequate glycemic control while eating habits and weight control behaviors change during treatment. For this reason it is desirable that the therapist has some knowledge and experience of the management of diabetes. Second, a degree of conflict arises between the modifications to eating habits usually advocated for the management of bulimia nervosa, and the dietary advice often given for the management of diabetes. The cognitive view of bulimia nervosa is based on evidence that strict dieting predisposes individuals to the disorder, so treatment is therefore aimed at lessening the patient's wish to diet and promoting a more flexible approach to eating. By contrast, the conventional dietary management of diabetes is based on the total avoidance of foods with a high sugar content and the rigid observance of carbohydrate allowances. It may be necessary to steer a course between these two extremes.

Other approaches to the management of bulimia nervosa include group therapy; inpatient treatment; and the use of pharmacological treatments, most commonly anti-depressant drugs, especially those of the selective serotonin reuptake inhibitor group (see Chapter 65). Such treatment approaches have not been evaluated in diabetic patients, although clinical experience suggests that in some patients medication may be a useful adjunct to psychological treatment.

ANOREXIA NERVOSA

The treatment of anorexia nervosa has been subject to less systematic research than that of bulimia nervosa. Recommendations about management are therefore based largely on clinical experience. A wide range of treatments have been advocated (see Section VII). It appears that young patients are more likely to benefit from family therapy approaches, whereas older patients may respond to cognitive-behavioral interventions. Drugs appear to confer little benefit.

During the period of weight restoration it is usually necessary to accept that glycemic control will not be perfect, but severe hypoglycemia or hyperglycemia must be avoided. It is helpful for patients to monitor their insulin doses and blood glucose levels as their eating habits and weight change, and again it is desirable for the therapist to have some experience in the management of diabetes. Difficulties similar to those mentioned above regarding dietary advice also arise.

SUBTHRESHOLD CASES AND PARTIAL SYNDROMES

Unfortunately for the clinician, little is known about the optimum management of patients with these more prevalent but less severe forms of eating disorder. These disorders are considered relatively unimportant when they occur in nondiabetic patients, but when they occur in conjunction with IDDM they constitute an important clinical problem. No systematic research has been conducted on the treatment of such patients, and few recommendations can be made beyond the general principles described above.

FURTHER READING

Fairburn, C. G., Peveler, R. C., Davies, B. A., Mann, J. I., & Mayou, R. A. (1991). Eating disorders in young adults with insulin dependent diabetes: A controlled study. *British Medical Journal, 303,* 17–20. The first study of the prevalence of eating disorders in young adults with diabetes, in which thorough methods of case ascertainment and a matched nondiabetic control group were used.

Fairburn, C. G., & Steel, J. M. (1980). Anorexia nervosa in diabetes mellitus. *British Medical Journal, 280,* 1167–1168. One of the first case reports of coexisting anorexia nervosa and insulin-dependent diabetes.

Marcus, M. D., & Wing, R. R. (1990). Eating disorders and diabetes. In C. S. Holmes (Ed.), *Neuropsychological and behavioral aspects of diabetes.* New York: Springer-Verlag. A thorough review of material published on this subject up to 1990; yet to be superseded in comprehensiveness.

Peveler, R. C., Fairburn, C. G., Boller, I., & Dunger, D. (1992). Eating disorders in adolescents with insulin-dependent diabetes mellitus. *Diabetes Care, 15,* 1356–1360. An extension of the improved methods of the Fairburn et al. (1991) study to an adolescent population.

Peveler, R. C., & Fairburn, C. G. (1989). Anorexia nervosa in association with diabetes mellitus: A cognitive-behavioral approach to treatment. *Behaviour Research and Therapy, 27,* 95–99. A brief account of the treatment of a patient using cognitive-behavioral methods.

Peveler, R. C., & Fairburn, C. G. (1992). The treatment of bulimia nervosa in patients with diabetes mellitus. *International Journal of Eating Disorders, 11,* 45–53. A review of six cases illustrating the adaptation of conventional treatment approaches to bulimia nervosa patients with diabetes.

Rodin, G. M., & Daneman, D. (1992). Eating disorders and IDDM—A problematic association. *Diabetes Care, 15,* 1402–1412. A review of published work on the prevalence of eating disorders in patients with diabetes.

Steel, J. M., Young, R. J., Lloyd, G. G., & Clarke, B. F. (1987). Clinically apparent eating disorders in young diabetic women: Associations with painful neuropathy and other complications. *British Medical Journal, 294,* 859–862. A cross-sectional survey of over 200 patients with IDDM, reporting an apparently high prevalence of serious physical complications of diabetes in those with eating disorders.

Striegel-Moore, R. H., Nicholson, T. J., & Tamborlaine, W.V. (1992). Prevalence of eating disorder symptoms in preadolescent and adolescent girls with IDDM. *Diabetes Care, 15,* 1361–1368. A study done in the United States using the same methods as the Fairburn et al. (1991) study to ascertain the prevalence of eating disorders in a population of young diabetic patients.

• 50 •

SEXUAL AND REPRODUCTIVE FUNCTION IN EATING DISORDERS AND OBESITY

Suzanne Abraham
Derek Llewellyn-Jones

Studies of women aged 15 to 25 in Australia, Britain, and the United States have shown that 70% to 80% of young women want to lose weight, 55% to 70% have gone on a diet for at least 2 weeks on several occasions, 15% to 25% have had episodes of fasting, 5% to 10% have induced vomiting on several occasions, 5% to 25% have binge eaten either each week or recurrently, 6% are compulsive exercisers, and 3% to 5% have abused laxatives or diuretics.

Little is known about how these behaviors affect the women's sexuality and reproductive function. Pregnancy is perceived by many women as a challenge to their body image, control of body weight, and self-esteem. However, studies have shown that in early pregnancy concern about body image and weight declines, but in the last quarter of pregnancy these concerns increase. Most women who fast, binge eat, or induce vomiting when not pregnant experience a reduction in these behaviors during pregnancy.

With this background, in this chapter we discuss how women who have an eating disorder cope with their sexuality, and how the eating disorder affects their reproductive function.

ANOREXIA NERVOSA

Menstruation

By definition, women with active anorexia nervosa are amenorrheic and do not ovulate. During the recovery stage, menstruation and ovulation usually return when the woman has a body mass index (BMI) consistently greater than 19. Some women resume menstruation when their BMI exceeds 17. A woman whose BMI is consistently above 19, and who has not recommenced menstruating, is usually continuing to eat in a disturbed fashion.

Increasing numbers of women suffering from active anorexia nervosa are being given oral contraceptives for hormone replacement to prevent bone loss. When the woman is at a very low body weight there are no monthly withdrawal bleeds, but as she gains weight withdrawal bleeds occur. In the recovery phase it is difficult to identify when the potential for spontaneous menstruation has returned unless the hormonal treatment is withdrawn.

It is important clinically to be aware that the anovulation and amenorrhea are due to down regulation of gonadotropin-releasing hormone (GnRH) and that ovulation can be induced with GnRH analogues, even when the woman has active anorexia nervosa.

Sexuality

Before anorexia nervosa develops in them, most patients have gained a wide spectrum of sexual experience, knowledge, and attitudes; only a few have conflicts or negative feelings about their sexuality. When at a low body weight, however, most restricting anorexia nervosa patients deny their sexuality or are sexually passive. It is possible that their lowered sex hormone levels are involved in the reduced libido, which may precede the onset of amenorrhea.

On the other hand, anorexia nervosa patients who are "vomiters and purgers" are more likely to be sexually assertive (and promiscuous) than sexually passive. These women are also less likely to remain at a very low body weight.

Infertility

During the active phase of anorexia nervosa, infertility is usual, either because these women reject all sexual activity or because their hormonal deficiencies inhibit ovulation. After recovery, the fecundity of women wanting to have children is no different from that of the general population, although a significant proportion of recovered anorexia nervosa patients choose voluntary infertility.

Pregnancy

Pregnancy may occasionally occur during the active phase of anorexia nervosa if a patient's weight gain is sufficient, or it may follow hormonally induced ovulation, as discussed earlier. Women who have anorexia nervosa at the time of conception are likely to have an increase in psychological symptoms, including anxiety and depression.

The effect of the pregnancy on the eating disorder varies. In the recovery phase a woman may fear that in pregnancy she will lose control of her weight, and as a result she may prevent weight gain. Other recovered anorexia nervosa patients are relaxed about their eating behavior and control of body weight, a few even gaining "excessive" weight.

The effect of the eating disorder on the pregnancy itself also varies. Women who become pregnant when their BMI is less than 19, particularly if they have had ovulation induced, have a higher than normal frequency of spontaneous abortions and low-birth-weight babies, the latter a result of growth retardation in the last 10 weeks of pregnancy; and they are possibly more prone to giving birth to infants with birth defects.

The effect of eating disorders on the pregnancies of women who have recovered from anorexia nervosa is unclear. In one study it was found that the complications mentioned above may also occur among these women, while results of two others suggest that they do not occur in recovered women any more frequently than among those women who do not have an eating disorder. This matter requires further research.

Parenting

Parenting may be defective and inadequate in women with anorexia nervosa (see also Chapter 33). A mother with anorexia nervosa may find that her intense preoccupation with her weight and shape conflicts with her desire to nuture and feed her child. Some may choose not to breast feed, since they wish to lose the weight they gained during pregnancy. When the infant becomes a toddler, such mothers may not provide a role model for normal eating behavior if they avoid family meals and do not eat in front of others.

BULIMIA NERVOSA

Menstruation

Between 75% and 85% of women with bulimia nervosa experience secondary amenorrhea of more than 3 months duration, and for 50% to 70% of bulimia nervosa patients amenorrhea lasts for more than 12 months. As the majority of bulimic women have a BMI of more than 19, the amenorrhea is related to the weight-losing behaviors they adopt rather than to low body fat. With remission or recovery ovulation and menstruation return.

Sexuality

Women with bulimia nervosa are more sexually experienced than age-matched women in the community, although they do not start sexual intercourse at an earlier age. They associate high body weight with unattractiveness and tend to withdraw from social and sexual activity during times when their weight is high. Nearly all bulimic women have (normal) sexual desire and arousal and most are sexually active, often having had more than five sexual partners (twice the rate of age-matched women with no eating disorder). In consequence, they are more at risk for sexually transmitted diseases.

Bulimia nervosa patients are frequently sexually assertive, their sexual behavior mirroring their eating behavior. Their level of sexual activity is associated with an increased chance of pregnancy and a higher rate of induced abortion. More bulimic women than age-matched women masturbate to orgasm, have orogenital sex or anal intercourse and reach orgasm regularly.

Sexual abuse in childhood or early adolescence among women with bulimia nervosa is more common than among women in the community but no more common than among women suffering from other psychiatric conditions (see Chapter 40).

Infertility

During the course of the illness, twice as many bulimic women complain of infertility than women in the general population. With remission or recovery, over 80% of women with bulimia nervosa will achieve a pregnancy.

Pregnancy

Pregnancy is common among bulimic women. We studied 50 bulimic women for 10 or more years. At the 10-year follow-up 50% had recovered, 30% still had some evidence of an eating disorder, and 20% still had bulimia nervosa. Thirty-seven (74%) of the women became pregnant during the 10 years.

Bulimia nervosa does not adversely affect the course or outcome of pregnancy, and as the pregnancy advances the bulimic episodes usually decrease. Several reasons account for this decrease. First, many women who become pregnant are in the recovery stage. Second, in pregnancy many bulimic women are more concerned that their behavior may damage the fetus than that they may gain weight. Third, some enjoy being pregnant, since they feel that while pregnant they have no need to worry about their weight or eating behavior. Following the birth, however, the bulimic behavior may return.

The mean birth weights of the infants born to bulimic mothers do not show a greater proportion of low-birth-weight babies than that expected.

Parenting

The effect of bulimia nervosa on the mother's ability to care for her infant is unclear, since few reports have been published (see Chapter 33). They may have difficulty in establishing or persisting with breast-feeding (because of their dislike of having large breasts). Some mothers with bulimia nervosa may ignore, neglect, or punish a child who interferes with them during a bulimic episode.

OBESITY

The prevalence of obesity (BMI 30 to 39) in the fertile age group is about 8%, while morbid obesity (BMI 40+) affects fewer than 0.5% of such women.

Menstruation

With increasing obesity, particularly if the woman is morbidly obese, ovulation becomes less frequent and menstrual irregularities (especially oligomenorrhea) become more frequent.

Sexuality

There are no data showing that obesity affects a woman's sexual desire or performance.

Infertility

Less frequent ovulation reduces the chance of pregnancy. Women who are morbidly obese should reduce their weight by dieting and exercise before embarking on an *in vitro* fertilization or gamete intrafallopian transfer program, since the success rate, in terms of a healthy "take-home" baby, is lower than in women whose weight is in the normal range.

Pregnancy

Data from several hospital reports indicate that 8% to 10% of pregnant women have a prepregnancy BMI of greater than 30. Among these women, there is a threefold increase in hypertension, either pregnancy induced or chronic, and in glucose intolerance. There is an increased rate of cephalopelvic disproportion, with twice as many babies weighing over 4,000 grams, and the cesarean section rate is 1.5 times that of the overall hospital population. These women have an increased risk of postpartum hemorrhage, and the perinatal mortality rate is slightly raised.

Parenting

No increase in parenting problems has been reported among obese women compared with the rate in the general population.

COMMENT

The sexual feelings and behaviors of women who have restrictive anorexia nervosa are lessened so that they deny their sexuality or are sexually inactive. Women who have purging and vomiting anorexia nervosa or bulimia nervosa have normal or enhanced sexuality, are sexually active, and are often sexually assertive.

Women suffering from diagnosed weight-losing eating disorders have an increased chance of being infertile during the active stage of the disorder. There are women within the community who have undiagnosed eating disorders. It is likely that these women also show an increased prevalence of infertility. When seeking treatment for infertility, women may not disclose that they have an eating disorder, and the specialist may not inquire about their eating behavior. Should the matter be raised, the woman may admit that she has an eating disorder but may refuse treatment, or she may request that her condition not be disclosed to her family but also request treatment for infertility.

Because of the complications that may arise during pregnancy in women with eating disorders, as well as their increased risk of giving birth to a low-birth-weight baby, obstetricians should routinely ascertain from all patients whether they have abnormal eating behaviors, especially before offering treatment, such as ovulation induction. If an eating disorder is identified, counseling and support should be offered to help those women whose eating behavior worsens during pregnancy.

Obstetricians should also be aware of the evidence that women with eating disorders are at increased risk for postpartum depression and that their parenting may also be impaired.

Obese women are not prone to problems with their sexuality. However, obese women are more likely to be infertile, and the chance of pregnancy complications is increased, particularly those of hypertension and cephalopelvic disproportion.

FURTHER READING

Abraham, S. F., Bendit, N., Mason, C., Mitchell, H., O'Connor, N., Ward, J., Young, S., & Llewellyn-Jones, D. (1985). *Australian and New Zealand Journal of Psychiatry, 19,* 72–76. A controlled study of the psychosexual histories of women with bulimia nervosa.

Abraham, S., Mira, M., & Llewellyn-Jones, D. (1990). Should ovulation be induced in women recovering from an eating disorder who are compulsive exercisers? *Fertility and Sterility, 53,* 566–568. A study of the eating and exercise histories of women with ovulatory failure and secondary amenorrhea.

Beumont, P. J. V., Abraham, S. F., & Simson, K. G. (1981). The psychosexual histories of adolescent girls and young women with anorexia nervosa. *Psychological Medicine, ll,* 131–140. An early study of the psychosexual histories of women with anorexia nervosa.

Brinch, M., Isager, T., & Tolstrup, K. (1988). Anorexia and motherhood: Reproductional pattern and mothering behavior of 50 women. *Acta Psychiatrica Scandinavica, 77*, 98–104. A retrospective study of the pregnancies of 50 Danish women with a history of anorexia nervosa.

Fairburn, C. G., Stein, A., & Jobes, R. (1992). Eating habits and eating disorders in pregnancy. *Psychosomatic Medicine, 54*, 665–672. A prospective, population-based study of eating habits and eating disorders during pregnancy.

Fahy, T., & O'Donoghue, G. (1991). Eating disorders in pregnancy. *Psychological Medicine, 21*, 577–580. An editorial on pregnancy and parenting in women with eating disorders.

Franko, D. L., & Walton, B. F. (1993). Pregnancy and eating disorders: A review and clinical implications. *International Journal of Eating Disorders, 13*, 41–48. A recent review on pregnancy in women with eating disorders.

Lacey, J. H., & Smith, G. (1987) Bulimia nervosa: The impact of pregnancy on mother and baby. *British Journal of Psychiatry, 150*, 777–781. A study of the impact of pregnancy on women with bulimia nervosa.

Lemberg, R., & Phillips J. (1989). The impact of pregnancy on anorexia nervosa and bulimia. *International Journal of Eating Disorders, 8*, 285–295. A study of the effect of pregnancy on anorexic and bulimic symptoms.

Stewart, D., Raskin, J., Garfinkel, P. E., McDonald, O., & Robinson, G.E. (1987). Anorexia nervosa, bulimia and pregnancy. *American Journal of Obstetrics and Gynecology, 157*, 1194–1198. A study of the pregnancies of 15 women with anorexia nervosa or bulimia nervosa.

Treasure, J. L., & Russell, G. F. M. (1988). Intrauterine growth and neonatal weight gain in babies of mothers with anorexia nervosa. *British Medical Journal, 296*, 1038. A report on the pregnancies of seven women with anorexia nervosa who conceived despite low body weight and who showed poor fetal growth followed by neonatal "catch up."

· VII ·
TREATMENT OF EATING DISORDERS

• 51 •

THE PREVENTION OF EATING DISORDERS

Christopher G. Fairburn

The aim of preventive interventions in medicine is to eliminate disease-related morbidity and mortality. It is conventional to classify these interventions according to the stage in the evolution of the disorder at which they are directed. The interventions may be focused on the processes involved in the development of the disorder, in which case the goal is to prevent the onset of new cases (i.e., to reduce the incidence of the disorder). This is termed "primary prevention." The interventions may be designed to shorten the duration of the disorder by reducing the time between onset and presentation for treatment. This is termed "secondary prevention." Or the goal may be the reduction of impairments that result from the disorder. This is termed "tertiary prevention." Clearly secondary prevention is necessary only if primary prevention fails to eradicate the disorder. Similarly, tertiary prevention has a place only if treatment is not fully effective. In practice, all three forms of preventive intervention are relevant to most disorders, and this is certainly the case with respect to eating disorders.

PRIMARY PREVENTION

Primary prevention is the ideal. It requires the application of an intervention capable of preventing the onset of disorder. Generally, but not necessarily, such an intervention requires a knowledge of the processes involved in the development of the disorder. As explained in Chapter 35, this knowledge is lacking or, at best, incomplete with respect to eating disorders. From the findings of retrospective studies, we have some knowledge of proximal events in the development of eating disorders, with dieting being the most common behavioral precursor, but exactly how and at what stage in the development of these disorders other risk factors operate is not known.

Given current knowledge, the only option is to employ preventive interventions that seem likely to have a beneficial effect and test whether the effects are as predicted. To date researchers have focused on attempting to modify common behavioral precursors of eating disorders among the most vulnerable age group, namely schoolchildren. The goal has been to reduce the prevalence of dieting and related weight-control behavior such as self-induced vomiting and the misuse of laxatives. Various educational programs have been devised for this purpose, several of which include complex combinations of procedures such as inoculation against the influence of the media and peer-resistance training. There have been five studies of the effectiveness of these programs, the most notable by Killen and coworkers. Without exception, the results have been disappointing. An increase in knowledge about eating disorders, dieting, and related behavior and concerns has been achieved but this has not been accompanied by any change in the target behaviors.

Since eating disorders commonly start during school-age years, a priority must be to develop effective school-based interventions. However, it is important not to lose sight of the fact that interventions that reduce the prevalence of dieting and related behavior will not necessarily result in a reduced incidence of eating disorders. Only a small minority of those who diet go on to develop an eating disorder, and it may be that this minority will prove resistant to prevention programs of this type. Until it has been established that reducing the prevalence of dieting and related behavior results in a decrease in the incidence of eating disorders, the premise on which these school-based interventions are founded remains open to doubt.

It can be argued that a different preventive strategy is needed. Rather than developing interventions for use with schoolchildren in general, it might be more productive to focus on subjects known to be at especially high risk for developiing eating disorders. Assuming that such subjects could be made aware of their high-risk status, they might be more likely to see the relevance of interventions designed to reduce their risk and might therefore be more likely to change. Unfortunately, there are two related problems with this approach. First, since few risk factors for eating disorders are known with any confidence, it is not yet possible to define such a high-risk group; and second, even if it were possible to reduce the incidence of eating disorders among high-risk individuals, this strategy would be likely to have little impact on their overall incidence, since high-risk groups generally contribute only a small proportion of the cases in the entire population.

Some writers have advocated a political approach to primary prevention, namely, focusing on social factors of presumed etiological importance. These authors point out that sociocultural factors are strongly implicated in the etiology of eating disorders (see Chapter 15) and on this basis argue that the fashion and diet industries should be the target of preventive interventions. Although there has been some progress in this regard in that the claims of the weight loss industry are now being more carefully scrutinized than before, it is doubtful whether the idealization of thinness can be so easily modified, given the vested interests that support it.

SECONDARY PREVENTION

Despite its potential, remarkably little attention has been paid to the secondary prevention of eating disorders. It is well established that in most cases a considerable period elapses between the onset of the disorder and the seeking of help, if indeed help is sought at all. The goal of secondary prevention is to shorten the interval between onset and obtaining effective help. To achieve this goal, a knowledge of the factors that promote and retard seeking help is needed, a topic which has been largely ignored.

Obstacles to seeking help are likely to include the following:

1. The person suffering from the disorder does not view it as a problem. This attitude appears to be especially common among individuals with anorexia nervosa. As a result it is often concerned others who persuade the sufferer to seek help.
2. The hope that the problem will go away of its own accord. In some cases this will indeed happen. Little is known about the natural history of anorexia nervosa and bulimia nervosa, so it is not possible to identify in advance those cases with a benign course ahead of them.
3. Some people think that their eating problem is not sufficiently severe to merit treatment or that they do not deserve help.
4. Shame, guilt, and secrecy are common among people with bulimia nervosa. By seeking treatment, sufferers run the risk of others finding out about the problem and the years of deceit and subterfuge that may have been required to keep it hidden.
5. Difficulty telling doctors. Previous problems (e.g., menstrual or gastrointestinal problems, depression, or low self-esteem) for which a doctor was consulted may actually have been a result of the eating problem, yet the doctor was not informed of their true cause. Some people go to their doctor planning to divulge the problem but lose their nerve at the last moment.
6. Fear of treatment. It is common for people with anorexia nervosa or bulimia nervosa to be concerned that treatment will involve weight gain.
7. Financial barriers to seeking help.

The relative importance of these and other obstacles to seeking help need to be known so that a rational approach to secondary prevention can be planned. A clear priority must be to increase general awareness of the nature and early features of eating disorders so that sufferers and others can recognize when there is a problem. Those who are most likely to come in contact with individuals who have eating disorders should be particularly well informed; such contacts include teachers, sports coaches, and doctors. These professionals should be taught ways of broaching the subject and helping sufferers admit to their eating problem.

Improving access to effective help is also important. Research on the applicability and effectiveness of self-help is especially relevant, since it has the potential of being readily accessible and since it circumvents some of the obstacles to seeking help. It is likely that individuals suffering from eating disorders would respond to sound education and advice that was provided in a self-help format.

TERTIARY PREVENTION

The notion of tertiary prevention has rarely been considered with respect to eating disorders. Doubtless the reason for this neglect is the negative connotation of a focus on reducing the impairments associated with established disorder. Yet it is a reality that some patients with anorexia nervosa gain little benefit from treatment, and relapse is also common. The situation with regard to bulimia nervosa seems more positive, although some cases prove refractory and run a chronic course. Reducing the morbidity and mortality associated with chronic eating disorders is an important objective (see Chapter 65).

CONCLUSION

It has been said that programs for the prevention of eating disorders are based on faith. The present lack of knowledge of the risk factors for the development of eating disorders, together with the absence of any evidence that preventive interventions work, mean that this is certainly the case. Such faith has nevertheless led certain countries (e.g., Norway) to implement sophisticated, multifaceted prevention programs designed to reduce both the incidence and prevalence of eating disorders. While programs of this type are to be welcomed, it is to be hoped that they will eventually be underpinned by research findings that support their use.

ACKNOWLEDGMENTS

I am grateful to the Wellcome Trust for their support (Senior Lectureship award 13123). I also wish to acknowledge the helpful comments of Jacqueline Carter and Zafra Cooper.

FURTHER READING

Fairburn, C. G. (1995). *Overcoming binge eating*. New York: Guilford Press. A self-help book designed to contribute to the secondary prevention of binge eating problems.

Fairburn, C. G., & Cooper, P. J. (1982). Self-induced vomiting and bulimia nervosa: An undetected problem. *British Medical Journal, 284,* 1153–1155. The first study to show that the great majority of those with bulimia nervosa are not in treatment.

Killen, J. D., Barr Taylor, C., Hammer, L. D., Litt, I., Wilson, D. M., Rich, T., Hayward, C., Simmonds, B., Kraemer, H., & Varady, A. (1993). An attempt to modify unhealthful eating attitudes and weight regulation practices of young adolescent girls. *International Journal of Eating Disorders, 13,* 369–384. The most sophisticated of the studies evaluating school-based prevention programs.

Levine, M. P., & Hill, L. (1991). *A 5-day lesson plan on eating disorders: Grades 7–12*. Columbus, OH: National Eating Disorders Organization (formerly National Anorexic Aid Society). A leading school-based prevention program.

Moreno, A. B., & Thelen, M. H. (1993). A preliminary prevention program for eating disorders in a junior high school population. *Journal of Youth and Adolescence, 22,* 109–124. An evaluation of a school-based prevention program.

Moriarty, D., Shore, R., & Maxim, N. (1990). Evaluation of an eating disorder curriculum. *Evaluation and Program Planning, 13,* 407–413. An evaluation of a school-based prevention program.

Paxton, S. J.(1993). A prevention program for disturbed eating and body dissatisfaction in adolescent girls: A 1-year follow-up. *Health Education Research, 8,* 43–51. An evaluation of a school-based prevention program.

Rose, G. (1992). *The strategy of preventive medicine*. Oxford: Oxford University Press. An extended essay in which the limitations of the "high-risk" approach to prevention are discussed; instead, an argument is made for a population-based strategy.

Shisslak, C. M., Crago, M., & Neal, M. E. (1990). Prevention of eating disorders among adolescents. *American Journal of Health Promotion, 5,* 100–106. An evaluation of a school-based prevention program.

Striegel-Moore, R. H. (1992). Prevention of bulimia nervosa: Questions and challenges. In J. H. Crowther, D. L. Tennenbaum, S. E. Hobfoll, & M. A. P. Stephens (Eds.), *The etiology of bulimia nervosa: The individual and familial context* (pp. 203–223). Washington, DC: Hemisphere. An upbeat account of various approaches to the primary prevention of eating disorders.

Striegel-Moore, R. H., & Silberstein, L. R. (1989). Early identification of bulimia nervosa. In W. G. Johnson (Ed.), *Advances in eating disorders* (2nd ed., Vol. 2, pp. 267–281). Greenwich, CT: JAI Press. A discussion of the value of early intervention in bulimia nervosa and methods for achieving it.

• 52 •

FEMINIST INFLUENCES ON THE TREATMENT OF EATING DISORDERS

Susan C. Wooley

Feminism is first and foremost a political movement that seeks to expand women's rights and opportunities, making them commensurate with those of men. But feminism is also an intellectual movement whose adherents have redefined the content, premises, and methods of inquiry in a number of fields. Feminist literary criticism, for example, has influenced what is considered literature, the interpretation of literary texts, and the methods of criticism. Similar influences have been felt in such fields as history, anthropology, sociology, and linguistics, where feminism as a sensibility has stimulated discovery and challenged longstanding habits of thought, a shift given momentum by postmodernist epistemologies emphasizing the socially constructed nature of historical and scientific "truth."

In psychology, as in other fields, the feminist influence is pervasive and profound. It includes an attempt to rescue women from the generic "man" of traditional research and theory and to study the impact of gender on social, intellectual, and physical development; on values; and on cultural and familial roles. In addition, feminists have sought to remove barriers to women's entry to, and full participation in, the field; to eradicate sexist language in our literature; and to name, investigate, and influence sexist practices that produce psychological distress in women. The following sections describe some of the main influences of the feminist sensibility on the understanding and treatment of eating disorders. It should be recognized, however, that we are in a period of rapid change; there is no clear consensus among feminists about the goals and methods of psychotherapy, nor can the feminist influence on psychotherapy be reduced to a few concrete prescriptions.

CULTURAL EMBEDDEDNESS OF EATING DISORDERS

Most traditional theories of eating disorders recognize dieting as a risk factor (see Chapter 35) and attribute widespread dieting to the cultural idealization of thinness (see Chapters 15 and 39). Few have asked why thinness is so overvalued, what other features of such illnesses besides striving for thinness are culturally induced, or how therapy might assist women in resisting a pathogenic culture. In contrast, feminist theorists have held that cultural constructions of gender are central to the understanding and treatment of eating disorders.

Noting the historical role of hunger in the oppression of peoples, writers of the 1970s "fat underground" were the first to question the social implications of cultural overvaluation of thinness in women. This theme has permeated much subsequent analysis that relates increasing cultural pressure for thinness to women's increasing social power, noting that the former tends to eradicate the latter. By this view, weight loss simultaneously reflects women's efforts to escape the role constraints traditionally associated with the ample female body and their capitulation to a covert demand for self-diminishment.

Other suggested metaphorical meanings of self-starvation include a "hunger strike" against an oppressive culture, a wordless cry for help in the face of abuse or neglect, an attempted demonstration of personal power, an avoidance of sexuality and/or sexual exploitation, and a symbolic protest against the materialism of consumer-oriented society. These formulations raise serious questions about the culture: whether there is a backlash against women's progress; whether sexual exploitation has pushed women into a mass retreat from maturity; whether the culture supports values that can give meaning to women's lives; and whether women yet have a voice strong enough to obviate the need to speak through their bodies.

FEMALE DEVELOPMENT: BEYOND FOOTNOTES

Traditionally most developmental theories have included women as an afterthought, if at all. Few have gotten far past Freud's dismissive treatment, expressed in the witless query, "What do women want?" In recent years theorists such as Nancy Chodorow, Carol Gilligan, and Jean Baker Miller have begun to define differing lines of male and female development, arguing that primary nurturance by a same-sex parent causes girls to identify with the nurturing role, often learning to put others' needs above personal success; that moral development of girls differs from that of boys, being informed primarily by an "ethic of care" rather than an "ethic of justice"; that sense of self for girls is more defined by relationships than it is for boys; that girls, but not boys, undergo a crisis in adolescence during which they become less assertive and self-confident; and that achievement by girls is limited by social stereotyping, prejudicial treatment, and fear that the price of success may be abandonment and emotional isolation. As many have noted, female development has long been dominated by a degree of appearance anxiety almost unknown to males.

These observations have influenced the treatment of eating disorders in many ways. Family therapists have begun to question theoretical models that pathologize attachment; that undervalue women's contributions to the emotional welfare of their families; and that deny power imbalances, holding all family members accountable for such unwanted outcomes as parental alcoholism or battering. A particular effort is made by therapists to avoid blaming mothers for failures inherent in their role: the impossibility of modeling attributes that have only recently begun to be demanded of women; the pressure women experience to teach daughters to conform to pathogenic appearance and behavior norms; and the psychological burden of their own unfulfilled dreams.

There has been increased attention to relationships, reflected in more frequent involvement of the families of origin of adult patients (see Chapter 56), greater use of therapeutic groups, and renewed interest in the therapeutic relationship in individual therapy. Personal empowerment and resistance against pathogenic cultural norms have emerged as common goals across modalities, and psychoeducational components of therapy have increasingly included exposure to feminist analyses of relevant issues (see Chapter 53). Feminist therapy, like the feminist movement from which it springs, is informed by the maxim that the personal is political.

TREATMENT: DIFFERENT GOALS

Feminist theorists have tended to construct different accounts of their female patients' lives and, as a result, have emphasized different issues in therapy. A striking example is the importance attached by feminists to sexual abuse (see also Chapter 40). Before 1980, sexual abuse had received little if any attention in theories of eating disorders and was, in fact, all but unknown. The discovery—or rediscovery after Freud—of widespread abuse was largely an accomplishment of feminist therapists and their patients. Feminist treatment of sexual abuse has diverged from the traditional agenda of private working through in individual therapy to include family therapy, victim support services, confronting perpetrators, and the exploration of social and legal remedies. Other issues that received little attention in the past but have figured prominently in work by feminist therapists include physical abuse, inadequate fathering, conflicting messages regarding sexuality, differential treatment within families of sons and daughters, the gender-role implications of puberty, and the implicit expectation that daughters serve as emotional care givers in their families.

Feminist therapies typically place less emphasis on insight and more on empowerment; the goal of "adjustment" is supplanted by self-differentiation, self-determination, and informed refusal. The effectiveness of these approaches often depends on the accurate anticipation of, and preparation for, others' resistance to the patient's change, for the woman who emerges from feminist therapy is rarely still "the best little girl in the world."

THE MEDIUM IS THE MESSAGE

The methods by which therapeutic goals are pursued carry important metamessages about gender. Feminist therapists typically stress the replacement of the hierarchical doctor–patient relationship—which reinforces female patients' sense of dependency and helplessness—with a more egalitarian one. But even therapists who find it misleading to deny the inevitable power differential between patient and therapist nonetheless often dispense with some of the trappings. The distant, unexpressive stance historically deemed necessary for the development of transference is largely avoided by feminist therapists, who are usually more self-disclosing, more informal, more overtly nurturing, and more willing to advocate on behalf of patients who have been or are currently being victimized. Inherent in these shifts is a belief that the decreased risk of sexualization and the inevitable identification between same-sex persons permits, and calls for, more flexible and permeable boundaries.

Aware that in Western culture, emotion has been devalued—defined as weak and womanly—and contrasted with such "male virtues" as strength and independence, many feminist therapists explicitly strive to revalue affect, giving permission and direction to patients' expressions of grief, longing, shame, and rage. The preference for affective expression over intellectual interpretation has led to a revived interest in experiential therapies such as guided imagery, art therapy, music therapy, writing therapy, Gestalt techniques, and psychodrama. Body image therapies, a collection of altogether new approaches, illustrate the shift away from exclusively cognitive interventions to body-centered and affectively evocative ones.

Feminists have paid particular attention to the ways in which therapy can unwittingly reinforce gender-role stereotypes. Adjunctive pharmacotherapy and hospitalization, for example, often become destructive reenactments of family patterns in which male physicians, cast in the role of consulting experts to female therapists, recreate the daughter's experiences with a distant father whose opinions were valued over those of her more available but less respected mother. Therapy teams whose hierarchy replicates the common social pattern of male dominance can subtly undermine the goal of empowering female patients.

Many writers have examined issues related to therapist gender, noting influences on both the content and the process of therapy. One commonly noted problem is the reluctance of some sexually abused patients to disclose their experiences to male therapists, suggesting the necessity of involving female therapists in order to improve detection and facilitate the working through of abuse. Therapist gender may also exert more subtle influences on therapeutic content, such as the concealment from male therapists of feelings that patients believe will brand them as weak. Although patients suffering from gender ambivalence or shame may find a male therapist a more comfortable object for identification, such a choice can be destructive if relationships with women have been too long avoided or if the male therapist subtly joins with the patient in devaluing women and/or "female behaviors."

Understandably male and female therapists tend to experience different counter-transference reactions to the anorexic patient who staunchly resists the female developmental line, the bulimic patient who appears to be hopelessly enmired in its demands, or the victim of male abuse who calls forth distinctly gendered emotional responses. Such gender effects can be put to good use if attended to, but they become problems if ignored.

CONCLUSION

Only in hindsight will it be possible to trace the lasting influence of feminist thought on the theory and treatment of eating disorders, and it is doubtful that this influence will ever be entirely separable from the natural evolution of the field or the broader influence of feminism on psychology and on the larger culture. The persistent posing of the question, "What does this have to do with gender?" might be as good a marker as any for a sensibility that seeks not so much to impose a set of rigid rules and expectations but rather to enlarge the way we think about issues, recognizing that gender remains the single most powerful organizing influence on behavior. Concern with gender requires that we direct our attention back in time to the historically massive force of gender-role prescriptions that blindly propel us even today; to the present moment with its power either to rigidify or to mindfully challenge gender constraints; and to a future that is almost impossible for us to imagine, so profoundly imprinted are the images of gender willed to us from the past. But imagine we must; the reimagining of gender is arguably the most important intellectual and emotional challenge of our age.

FURTHER READING

Brown, L., & Rothblum, E. (1989). Fat oppression and psychotherapy: A feminist perspective. *Women and Therapy, 8*(3). A special issue devoted to the stigmatization of fatness in women and to feminist therapies addressing these issues.

Fallon, P., Katzman, M. A., & Wooley, S. C. (Eds.). (1994). *Feminist perspectives on eating disorders.* New York: Guilford Press. An anthology representing most American feminists in the field that includes historical analyses of relevant topics, discussions of body image, feminist reexaminations of treatment issues, firsthand accounts of female experience, and prevention and research agendas.

Hornyak, L. M., & Baker, E. K. (Eds.). (1989). *Experiential therapies for eating disorders.* New York: Guilford Press. A comprehensive description of the varieties of experiential therapies for eating disorders that have been adopted by many feminist therapists.

Johnson, C. (Ed.). (1991). *Psychodynamic treatment of anorexia nervosa and bulimia.* New York: Guilford Press. The section on feminist psychodynamic perspectives contains discussions of female development, countertransference and gender, and the role of the therapist in feminist psychodynamic therapy.

Kearney-Cooke, A. (1978). Group treatment of sexual abuse among women with eating disorders. *Women and Therapy, 7,* 5–21. One of the first reports of high rates of sexual abuse in eating-disorder patients and still one of the best discussions of experiential treatment techniques useful with abuse victims in this population.

Laurence, M. (1987). (Ed.). *Fed up and hungry: Women, oppression and food.* New York: Peter Bedricks. A collection of feminist essays representing British feminists and the Women's Therapy Centre in London.

Orbach, S. (1984). Accepting the symptom: A feminist psychoanalytic treatment of anorexia nervosa. In D. M. Garner & P. E. Garfinkel (Eds.), *Handbook of psychotherapy for anorexia nervosa and bulimia* (pp. 83–104). New York: Guilford Press. A succinct summary of the developmental theories and treatment recommendations of this well-known and influential author.

Root, M. P. P., Fallon, P., & Friedrich, W. N. (1986). *Bulimia: A systems approach to treatment.* New York: W. W. Norton. A feminist examination of family dynamics and family therapy.

Schoenfielder, L., & Weiser, B. (Eds.). (1983). *Shadow on a tightrope: Writings by women on fat oppression.* Iowa City: Ann Lute. One of the few accessible sources of articles by members of the original "fat underground."

Steiner-Adair, C. (1986). The body politic: Normal female adolescent development and development of eating disorders. *Journal of the American Academy of Psychoanalysis, 14,* 95–114. The first and fullest attempt to relate Gilligan's theories on female development to the conflicts experienced by women with eating disorders.

Wooley S. C., & Kearney-Cooke, A. (1986). Intensive treatment of bulimia and body image disturbance. In K. Brownell & J. Foreyt (Eds.), *Handbook of eating disorders: Physiology, psychology and treatment of obesity, anorexia and bulimia.* New York: Basic Books. A brief description of a comprehensive treatment program informed by a feminist perspective.

• 53 •

PSYCHOEDUCATION IN THE TREATMENT OF EATING DISORDERS

MARION P. OLMSTED
ALLAN S. KAPLAN

DEFINITION AND RATIONALE

Psychoeducation was originally conceptualized as an integral component of cognitive-behavioral therapy based on the premise that some maladaptive beliefs grow out of incorrect or absent information. Over the years, however, the educational approach has filtered into other treatment modalities and currently represents an important aspect of most interventions for eating disorders.

Pure psychoeducation is defined as the provision of information to the patient about the patient's disorder and methods of overcoming it for the purpose of promoting attitudinal and behavioral change. An important corollary is the clinician's attitude that the patient is entitled to the information and will be able to make use of it to make informed decisions about her own care. This attitude is directly antithetical to the outdated paternalistic notion that the clinician should make the decisions about the patient's care: It is an acknowledgment that the locus of control resides with the patient.

Training for psychoeducation requires significant preparation by clinicians, since they must be completely familiar with the scientific literature they intend to present. They must also be prepared to answer questions honestly, and to admit the limitations of their own knowledge. The stance the clinician aims for is a firm, empathic, noncritical attitude that avoids confrontation yet does not collude with the patient's disturbed thinking about weight and shape. An initial "agreement to disagree" about issues such as caloric intake and weight expectations is often a useful approach that allows the patient to hear what the clinician has to say without being provoked into opposition by a more dogmatic, authoritarian style. A psychoeducational approach imparts the feeling to the patient that she is a respected and valued part of the collaborative effort aimed at helping her recover. The clinician offers expertise and the sincere belief that change is possible, while the patient proceeds at her own pace and is encouraged to take credit for any changes she makes.

CONTENT

A wide range of information has the potential for great value to eating-disorder patients, and a full dose of psychoeducation should include at least the following topics:

1. *The multidetermined nature of eating disorders.* Eating disorders are multidetermined and self-perpetuating disorders that develop and persist as the result of a complex interplay among biological, psychological, familial and sociocultural factors (also see Chapter 35). The specific combination and relative emphasis of the different factors varies among individuals. In individual therapy, the therapist may work with the patient to identify the predisposing and maintaining factors that are relevant to her, while in group psychoeducation the model is presented didactically, and patients are encouraged to apply it to their own situation. It is important for patients to understand that what was responsible for their initial vulnerability to develop an eating disorder may be quite different from what is maintaining the problem.

2. *Medical complications and the effects of vomiting, laxative, and diuretic abuse* (see also Chapters 47 and 48). Many of the physical symptoms patients experience are a direct result of the body's attempt to conserve energy in the face of starvation. Decreased heart rate and blood pressure account for dizziness and fainting; decreased body temperature accounts for cold intolerance. Peristalsis decreases, and constipation results. Many of the more unpleasant gastrointestinal symptoms patients experience are directly attributable to vomiting or laxative use. Vomiting causes a disruption of the integrity of the lower esophageal sphincter, leading to reflux and esophagitis, which the patient experiences as extreme heartburn and regurgitation of food. Regurgitation of hydrochloric acid along with the vomitus leads to an erosion of dental enamel and poor oral hygiene. Swollen parotid glands are probably also the result of purging behaviors and may be mislabeled by the patient as a "fat" face.

Laxative use disrupts the normal functioning of the large bowel and in the terminal stages can lead to a totally flaccid, nonresponsive bowel requiring surgical resection. Vomiting and laxative use may lead to bleeding and anemia or even esophageal or bowel perforation and death. Vomiting as well as laxative and diuretic abuse deplete the body of electrolytes such as potassium, which can lead to symptoms such as muscular cramps and weakness, heart arrhythmias, and sudden cardiac arrest. It is important for patients to understand that laxative abuse is an ineffective means of weight control, since laxatives exert their action on the large bowel, well after calories have been absorbed in the small bowel. Whatever weight loss occurs with laxatives or diuretics is associated with the shift of fluid out of the body. This use of laxatives thus may set up a vicious cycle in which the body reabsorbs fluid over a period of 24 to 48 hours following the acute dehydration, translating into a regain of weight because of fluid retention. This weight gain may, in turn, stimulate further laxative or diuretic use.

3. *Set-point theory and the consequences of dieting.* Set-point theory (see Chapter 9) is diametrically opposed to the culturally pervasive belief that an individual is personally responsible for what she weighs. It is therefore important to provide patients with rigorous evidence for its validity. A comprehensive review of the Keys' study, in which healthy volunteers were starved, provides a strong foundation, since it illustrates the physical, psychological, and social consequences of starvation. In the study, a description of the associated changes in eating behavior, both during the starvation phase and during the refeeding phase when some of the male subjects experienced binge eating and increased hunger after eating, provides critically important information for women with eating disorders. The Sims study demonstrates the homeostatic regulation of weight following intentional weight gain and provides compelling reassurance that set point includes bidirectional weight regulation and not, as most patients fear, universal weight gain. Evidence that obesity is largely genetically determined and not simply explained by overeating (see Chapters 1 to 8) supports set-point theory and challenges

the notion that weight is a moral issue. The metabolic adaptation to dieting should be described (see Chapter 11), and the connection between dieting and bingeing should be emphasized (see Chapter 16). One of the goals is to provide a scientific framework to help the patient organize what she is experiencing in terms of cause and effect. In this regard, extreme weight preoccupation and stringent dieting and overexercising need to be explicitly defined as eating disorder symptoms similar to the more ego-dystonic symptoms such as bingeing and purging.

4. *Nondieting and basic nutritional information.* Myths abound in this area, and many patients' fears are addressed by the provision of basic information regarding the way various food components are processed by the body. Patients should be encouraged to eat a normal amount of food—1,900 to 2,200 calories daily for women of average height—to schedule and plan meals thoughtfully and then follow through with "mechanical" eating, regardless of how they feel at the time. Eventually the meal plan should include all foods in moderation, but in the short-term avoided foods may need to be introduced gradually and at planned times. It may be useful to show pictures depicting both appropriate and inappropriate amounts and kinds of food so that patients have a clear mental image of nondieting meals and snacks.

5. *Sociocultural factors and body image issues.* A slide show that illustrates the pressures on women to be thin and the changing nature of the ideal female body over the years can help link patients' drive for thinness with its sociocultural context (see Chapter 15). A discussion of the way the female body is used in advertising and in the media can serve to arouse righteous indignation about the objectification of women's bodies, which can serve as a balance for patients' feelings of powerlessness to resist the current cultural ideal. Many women with eating disorders acknowledge feeling both body image disparagement (see Chapter 64) and low self-worth, but they tend to see these feelings as relatively separate problems. It is important to describe how body image disparagement can be amplified by displaced feelings of unhappiness in other domains. A desire to be happy and feel better about oneself is normal, but efforts to achieve this end through weight control are either unsuccessful or demand too high a price. Since patients have already tried the "weight control method of improving self-esteem," they should be encouraged to try a different approach for a period of time. This effort involves focusing on themselves as agents or "doers" rather than as passive objects valued mainly for their appearance.

6. *Cognitive and behavioral strategies.* Behavioral self-control strategies and cognitive coping strategies can often be applied by patients who receive instructional information. In many cases patients have already used similar strategies to promote dieting and other symptomatic behavior; retaining these methods while shifting the goal allows some patients to transfer a whole set of usable skills. These strategies are described in Chapters 54, 57, and 60. It may also be useful to present information about thinking errors, belief systems, and cognitive restructuring, although the changes patients are able to make without associated therapy may be quite limited. Nevertheless, even purely didactic exposure to these topics may stimulate thought and prime the patient for cognitive-behavioral therapy.

7. *Relapse prevention.* It is important for patients to have realistic expectations about the course of recovery; they need to know that symptoms may fluctuate and that the whole process takes time. Care should be taken to differentiate "slips" from relapse. If the patient slips, she should be prepared to label her behavior appropriately; return to normalized eating at the next mealtime; and, if necessary, apply strategies she found

helpful in the early stages of recovery. A discussion of circumstances that might increase the probability of relapse is also helpful; these circumstances include physical illness, stress, being overextended, and any other situation that might influence the patient not to have regular meals.

EFFICACY OF PSYCHOEDUCATION

The provision of some kind of educational information is mentioned explicitly as a component of treatment in about 75% of the published treatment studies for bulimia nervosa, suggesting there is some consensus about its importance. However, since the vast majority of these studies are multimodal treatment packages, they provide little information about the specific efficacy of psychoeducation. The effectiveness of a relatively pure psychoeducational group treatment for bulimia nervosa has been studied in only one investigation. The psychoeducational intervention consisted of five lectures accompanied by slides, and patients were asked not to introduce themselves or reveal personal information in the group. Twenty-one percent of the patients had no symptoms during the month after the intervention; this figure did not differ significantly from the 36% abstinence rate observed for a comparison treatment consisting of 18 weeks of individual cognitive-behavioral therapy. However, the two treatments were differentially effective for more severely ill patients; patients who were vomiting more than once a day tended to improve more with individual cognitive-behavioral therapy, while the two treatments were equally effective for patients who were vomiting less often. After a 3-month uncontrolled follow-up, the patients who had received psychoeducation were doing about as well as the patients who had received individual cognitive-behavioral therapy; there was some shifting across outcome categories in each condition, but the proportion of patients with a good outcome was similar in both groups, immediately after treatment and at 3-month follow-up. No information about the long-term effects of a purely psychoeducational intervention is currently available.

THE ROLE OF PSYCHOEDUCATION

The collaborative attitude promoted by a psychoeducational approach may form the basis for a solid therapeutic alliance and may therefore be beneficial across a variety of interventions. This attitude is especially important in the initial assessment of patients with eating disorders. Patients with anorexia nervosa may be coerced into seeking help, whereas patients with bulimia nervosa may want to restrict attention to their ego-dystonic symptoms such as bingeing. In either case insistence on nutritional rehabilitation is not likely to be well received and may discourage the patient from returning for a second visit. Adopting a collaborative educational approach during the initial encounter encourages the patient to feel that she is an active participant in the therapeutic process. It is useful to present some information related to the multidetermined nature of eating disorders; the effects of starvation; the connection between dieting and bingeing; medical complications; and the ineffectiveness of vomiting, laxatives, and diuretics for weight control, although the time available to discuss these topics is necessarily limited. It is our clinical impression that a few patients do make significant behavioral changes following an initial consultation and assessment that might span two or three sessions. However, at this stage the primary goal is not symptom control but rather to have the patient leave with the feeling that a helpful therapeutic process is available to her.

Psychoeducation is also a useful component of treatment directed toward symptom interruption. As described above, there is limited evidence that a brief period of group-psychoeducational therapy is sufficient for a small subgroup of less symptomatic bulimia nervosa patients, but the primary role of psychoeducation is to act as a foundation or structure for other interventions. Although access to the relevant information is critical, patients may also require personalized assistance in applying it, the opportunity to express their fears and ventilate their emotions, and the support of a trusting therapeutic relationship.

METHODS OF DELIVERY

Pure psychoeducation is ideally delivered in a group format; in fact, for the psychoeducation to remain "pure," the group must be large enough to avoid intimacy. Even when purity is not important, it is easier for the clinician to ensure comprehensive coverage of the material if she or he follows a structured presentation accompanied by visual aids and has a group of patients expecting to receive the information at a specified time. Another advantage of group psychoeducation is that it is highly cost-effective, since groups can be much larger than is typical for therapy groups.

As a component of treatment, psychoeducation may be combined with either individual or group therapy offered either simultaneously or sequentially. Integrated treatment programs have been the norm to date, but a sequencing approach might be advantageous. As a first stage of treatment, a brief psychoeducational group session might prime patients to use subsequent therapy more efficiently. Also, a progression of interventions allows the patient to opt out when she has met her treatment goals.

TARGET GROUPS

As part of a stepped-care model, a psychoeducational group may be a cost-effective first stage of treatment for all eating-disorder patients. Our untested intuition is that it would be less effective as a sole treatment for anorexia nervosa, in which the symptoms are more ego syntonic, than for bulimia nervosa. Psychoeducational groups for parents and spouses of eating-disorder patients have also been conducted at our center and are highly valued by participants. In addition to offering educational material about eating disorders, psychoeducation provides family members with information about setting appropriate limits and boundaries and separating symptoms from family interactions. Another function of psychoeducation is to serve as a prevention strategy for high-risk groups of women and female children in general. The aim here is to deglamorize eating disorders and stress the negative consequences of unhealthy weight control practices. Controlled studies of the effects of psychoeducation for various target groups are just beginning, and although the approach appears to be promising, it requires empirical validation.

MECHANISMS OF CHANGE

Theoretically, when educational information has an effect, it should be through the alteration of beliefs that are based on incorrect or absent information. There are many reasons why the beliefs or the ensuing behavior of anorexia nervosa or bulimia nervosa patients might not change: Patients may minimize or discount the information given, show a psychological resistance to change, or have insufficient psychological and emotional resources to challenge their ingrained thinking and behavioral patterns. Some of these barriers are undoubtedly circumvented by other therapeutic interventions in multimodal treatment approaches. However, it is equally plausible that pure psychoeducation might facilitate change in patients who find a therapeutic relationship difficult or threatening.

Patients who are able to follow the recommendations offered in psycoeducation and make some initial changes in their eating behavior may experience a sense of increased self-efficacy, since their improvement is the product of their own efforts. Similarly, the knowledge that some of their previous self-expectations were unrealistic may bolster their feelings of personal competence. When improvement occurs early in treatment, it may serve as a catalyst for an upward spiral in which progress facilitates further progress.

SUMMARY

Psychoeducation is frequently included as one component in multimodal treatment packages and may also have limited use as an independent intervention. The efficacy of a purely psychoeducational intervention has been examined in only one study, and there is no information about its long-term effects. Although it is highly valued by clinicians, it is not known whether psychoeducation is a "necessary" component of treatment when used in conjunction with other modalities. Its mechanisms of action are, at present, uncertain. The approach holds great promise but requires substantial empirical validation.

FURTHER READING

Bennett, W., & Gurin J. (1982). *The dieter's dilemma: Eating less and weighing more.* New York: Basic Books. This is a very easily read introduction to weight regulation issues.

Davis, R., Dearing, S., Faulkner, J., Jasper, K., Olmsted, M. P., Rice, C., & Rockert, W. (1992). The road to recovery: A manual for participants in the psychoeducation group for bulimia nervosa. In H. Harper-Guiffre & K. R. MacKenzie (Eds.), *Group psychotherapy for eating disorders* (pp. 281–284). Washington, DC: American Psychiatric Press. This is a manual for patients and is intended to supplement material presented in treatment.

Davis, R., & Olmsted, M. P. (1992). Cognitive-behavioral group treatment for bulimia nervosa: Integrating psychoeducation and psychotherapy. In H. Harper-Guiffre & K. R. MacKenzie (Eds.), *Group psychotherapy for eating disorders* (pp. 71–103). Washington, DC: American Psychiatric Press. This chapter is intended for use as a therapist's manual.

Garner, D. M., Fairburn, C. G., & Davis, R. (1987). Cognitive-behavioral treatment of bulimia nervosa: A critical appraisal. *Behavior Modification, 4,* 398–431. This review includes a component analysis of the treatments that have been studied and shows the wide use of psychoeducation.

Garner, D. M., Rockert, W., Olmsted, M. P., Johnson, C., & Coscina, D. V. (1984). Psychoeducational principles in the treatment of bulimia and anorexia nervosa. In D. M. Garner & P.E. Garfinkel (Eds.), *Handbook of psychotherapy for anorexia nervosa and bulimia* (pp. 513–572). New York: Guilford Press. This is an early review of some of the scientific literature that forms the basis for psychoeducation. It includes references to many of the primary sources.

Kaplan, A. S. (1993). Medical and nutritional assessment of eating disorders. In A. S. Kaplan & P. E. Garfinkel (Eds.), *Medical issues and the eating disorders*. New York: Brunner/Mazel. This chapter includes detailed information about nutritional and medical issues that are important in the initial assessment of eating-disorder patients.

Olmsted, M. P., Davis, R., Rockert, W., Irvine, M. J., Eagle, M., & Garner, D. M. (1991). Efficacy of a brief group psychoeducational intervention for bulimia nervosa. *Behaviour Research and Therapy, 29,* 71–83. This is the only published study of the efficacy of pure psychoeducation as a treatment for bulimia nervosa.

THE NUTRITIONAL MANAGEMENT OF ANOREXIA AND BULIMIA NERVOSA

PIERRE J. V. BEUMONT
STEPHEN W. TOUYZ

THE NEED FOR NUTRITIONAL COUNSELING

Little has been written about the nutritional management of anorexia nervosa and bulimia nervosa. This is surprising, since it is the perversion of eating or, more accurately, of dieting behavior and the resulting undernutrition that leads to serious complications that distinguish these illnesses from other disorders. It has been assumed that the abnormal eating pattern will correct itself once the psychological problems are addressed, and it has even been suggested that attention to dietary issues is deleterious because it focuses the patient on the "symptom" rather than the "pathology." Such advice is as ridiculous as prohibiting the discussion of drinking behavior with patients with alcohol related disease!

The metabolic effects of dieting disorders have been described in Chapters 44 and 46. Although the nutritional disturbance may be serious and complicated, with varying degrees of protein depletion, deficiencies in essential foodstuffs and electrolyte imbalance, it is essentially a state of undernutrition resulting from a diet that is inadequate to meet energy demands. Energy insufficiency may lead to emaciation (in anorexia nervosa patients) or may trigger a chaotic pattern of eating, with alternating episodes of restriction and compensatory hyperphagia (in bulimia nervosa patients). In either instance, the patient is likely also to use purging behaviors. Except in the most severe cases, however, the digestive system is intact, and the main obstacles to nutritional restoration are behavioral and psychological. The prescription of a modified diet is likely to be counterproductive, since it reinforces the patient's belief that she should not eat normally. It is not so much the management of the patient's diet that is complex as the treatment of the patient embarking on that diet.

The appropriate person to direct nutritional rehabilitation and to provide dietary counseling is a dietician, who should be an integral member of the treatment team. Unlike psychiatrists, psychologists, nurses, other doctors, or lay counselors, dieticians have a truly expert knowledge of dietary matters, and their nonthreatening status helps make their advice readily acceptable to patients. On the other hand, dieticians may be handicapped by their prior experiences. They are accustomed to dealing with the ill effects of overeating and of diets too high in energy and relatively low in essential nutrients. For dieticians, the dieting-disordered individual poses a paradox by practicing the very behaviors dieticians espouse for their obese patients. To be effective, the dietician must be able to go beyond the prescription of idealistic diets and promote instead a return to normal, sensible "good enough" eating.

Patients' trust must be won if they are to reveal the extent of their fears about eating and follow the advice they are given. Such trust is engendered not only by providing strictly accurate nutritional information but also by being a sympathetic listener. However, there is no place for compromise about the patient's unhealthy beliefs and attitudes about food or any point in trying to bargain over the goals of treatment. These goals should be clearly stated from the outset. They are:

1. To attain and maintain normal nutritional status in adults and normal growth in adolescents
2. To establish normal eating behavior
3. To promote a normal attitude toward food
4. To promote normal responses to hunger and satiety cues

THE DIETARY HISTORY

The first step in the nutritional management of eating disorders is to take the patient's dietary history. This history entails a detailed analysis of the patient's eating patterns and weight fluctuations from childhood to the present, the methods of weight control that have been used, the foods avoided (usually red meat, dairy products, and sweet and fatty foods) and the reasons for so doing, and the occurrence of purging and binge eating. The various behavioral abnormalities found in anorexia and bulimia patients are described in Chapter 27. It is important to elicit these details in the history so they can be addressed in future counseling sessions. A semistructured interview such as the Eating Disorder Examination may be useful in obtaining some of this information (see Chapter 22).

Patients' beliefs about nutrition and attitudes toward eating should also be explored, as well as the beliefs and eating behaviors of other members of the family. Faddish beliefs are often strongly held, particularly that foods are either "good, healthy, and nonfattening" or "bad, unhealthy, and fattening." Patients manifest extreme fussiness by their numerous food dislikes and aversions or even in their recital of alleged allergic responses to certain foodstuffs.

Of course dietary histories are not always accurate, since patients may be untruthful about their behavior, but there is no reason to believe that these histories are any less reliable than other forms of clinical data, such as psychiatric and medical histories. Nevertheless, it is appropriate to meet with important family members (usually the patient's mother or spouse) to confirm the patient's story, ascertain whether family members too have problems with eating, and ensure that they are not condoning the patient's abnormal practices.

NUTRITIONAL REHABILITATION OF PATIENTS WITH ANOREXIA NERVOSA

Many anorexic patients are admitted to the hospital (see Chapter 59), and for reasons of convenience this section has been written from that perspective. However, increasingly patients are being treated in outpatient or day-patient centers. The principles of nutritional management are similar, irrespective of the setting.

Nutritional rehabilitation entails the restoration of a normal body weight. For adults this may be defined as the weight at which one is physically healthy and which one can maintain by eating a normal, healthy diet without restrictions. This weight should be within the range of a body mass index (BMI = weight in kilograms per height in meters^2) between 20 and 25. For children or younger adolescents, the target weight is one at which the patient will continue to grow at a normal rate. A set BMI value is not appropriate for children; instead pediatric growth tables should be consulted. However, it is important to bear in mind that the patient's growth may already have been stunted by the illness, so the clinician should not accept a target weight that merely reflects such stunting.

An eating program to bring about the necessary weight gain is drawn up by the dietitian, but the responsibility for its implementation is shared by all the members of the management team. Special foods are not required; rather, regular normal meals should be planned. The aim is to effect a gain of 1 to 1.5 kilograms a week. Initially, a daily intake of as little as 1,500 kilocalories (6,000 kilojoules) is prescribed because larger amounts may cause discomfort after the prolonged restriction these patients have experienced. Food quantities are increased only when the patient manages to complete each meal. The energy intake needed to bring about full weight restoration eventually may go as high as 3,500 kilocalories per day, depending on how active the patient is. At these high levels, some energy may be provided in the form of concentrated, high-calorie products, but the emphasis is always on resuming normal eating. Dietary supplements are seldom needed, and tube feeding or parenteral nutrition should be avoided unless absolutely necessary. Such procedures are invasive, are not without physical danger, and do not help patients resume responsibility for their own health. Similar criticisms may be made of high-energy liquid diets.

Eating behavior must be the focus of explicit attention. The earlier practice of isolating anorexia nervosa patients at mealtimes was ill advised, since it merely reinforced the abnormalities of their eating behavior. It is far better that patients eat in a communal setting so that other patients and staff may provide them with appropriate role models. Their actual eating behavior should be carefully monitored, and our Eating Behavior Rating Scale provides a fairly objective means of doing so. It is important to provide encouragement and counseling to correct a patient's abnormal eating practices, but rather than repeat the conflicts that may have taken place between the patient and her family before admission, confrontation should be avoided during mealtimes themselves, and patients should be encouraged to interact socially in an appropriate way. Specific eating difficulties are addressed later in individual counseling sessions with a nurse or dietitian. In some instances, it is helpful to videotape a patient during meals and then use the tapes in feedback sessions. If the reasons for making such tapes are carefully explained to the patient, the procedure is usually quite acceptable.

The management of anorexia nervosa is not complete just by the attainment of a healthy weight. Both inpatients and outpatients need continuing dietary guidance to assist them in adjusting to an appropriate energy intake for weight stabilization while maintaining normal eating behavior. The maintenance period is often an unsettling time, since the security of a structured weight gain program is no longer in place, and a resurgence of anorexic eating behaviors at this time is not uncommon. It is important that patients be helped to develop a spontaneous, relaxed eating pattern so that their weight maintenance does not depend on adherence to a strict "therapeutic" diet. Any return to restrictive practices must be avoided, since it will inevitably lead to relapse. All diet foods, such as artificially sweetened drinks or fat-reduced foodstuffs, should be avoided. They are unnecessary if the patient is eating normally, and they encourage the return of an anorexic attitude toward food.

It is often beneficial for inpatients to stay in the hospital for a specified 2- to 3-week maintenance phase, during which they are given short periods of home leave. This provides them with the opportunity to practice eating at home prior to discharge. Occasional meals in restaurants are also useful in allowing patients to adjust to eating outside the protective hospital environment.

Educational Sessions

The assumption that dieting disordered patients are well informed about nutritional matters is a dangerous myth. They may have a superficial knowledge of diets and of the various means of losing weight, but this knowledge is highly selective, derived from dubious sources (such as popular magazines), usually extreme, and often incorrect. Dieting-disordered patients are frequently highly opinionated in their views, but few have even a basic understanding of nutritional matters. It is important that their misinformation is corrected and that they learn the truth about their energy and nutrient requirements.

These issues should be discussed, either individually or in a group setting, throughout the treatment period (also see Chapters 53 and 54). Topics that need to be explored are the dynamics of energy input, activity, and weight control; the nutrient content of foods; the dangers of dieting and of purging behaviors; the changing dietary requirements as weight is regained; and the nutritional requirements for good health and weight maintenance. Many of our patients have been astonished to learn that a daily intake of 1,000 kilocalories is insufficient for a healthy young woman!

The beliefs and attitudes of patients with anorexia nervosa do not change automatically with weight gain. Understanding that is based on correct information, the personal experience of the benefits of well-being resulting from improvement in diet and the restoration of nutrition, and continual support and reassurance are all needed to effect change. It is here that the counseling and educational skills of the dietician are tested.

Key members of the patient's family should be involved in at least some of these educational sessions. Their own knowledge of nutritional matters may also be defective, with the result that they have contributed to the patient's misinformation and unhealthy attitudes. Or, on the other hand, these family members may have been deceived by the patient concerning the advice she has been given. It is important that these key family members, too, have a clear idea of what the dietitian actually recommends.

Family members should be advised on how to help the patient readjust to a normal life-style after discharge. They should let the patient take responsibility for her own eating, since "stand-over" tactics at home are likely to be counterproductive. However, they must not condone anorexic practices or ignore evidence that the patient is relapsing. If any of these problems occur, family members must encourage the patient to return for further counseling sessions.

Anorexia nervosa is an illness that usually persists for some years. Just as continued psychotherapy is required, so is persistent nutritional counseling. A skilled and experienced dietician, working on an outpatient basis, is as important in the long-term care of these patients as in their acute rehabilitation period.

NUTRITIONAL REHABILITATION OF PATIENTS WITH BULIMIA NERVOSA

There are far more similarities than there are differences between the nutritional management of bulimia and anorexia nervosa. Although bulimia nervosa patients are at an apparently normal weight and do not need to go on a weight gain program, they do need to resume normal and relaxed eating, avoid restrictive practices, and tolerate being at a weight that may be considerably higher than they would like.

There are several reasons why nutritional counseling should be undertaken early in the course of treatment of bulimia nervosa. The chaotic eating pattern that characterizes bulimia nervosa can be so distressing that patients must regain control over it before they can be involved in meaningful psychotherapy. Patients often view their problem as primarily one of overeating, and they do not understand that the episodic gorging is largely a response to their restrictive eating practices. These patients have many fears and misconceptions about food and weight control that must be identified and corrected. Bulimics firmly believe they will get fat if they take regular meals or any high-energy foods. And often their eating has been disordered for so long that they have lost the ability to eat normally. They must relearn the answers to such basic questions as, What is hunger? When should I eat? How much food is enough? and, What is normal eating?

As is done with the anorexic patient, the dietician first takes a detailed dietary history of the bulimic patient and fully explores the patient's eating behavior, dietary knowledge, and attitudes toward food. Rather than accept the patient's protestation that the problem is solely one of overeating, the dietician should emphasize that the overeating is but one aspect of a complex pattern of disordered behavior. In fact, it is persistent and excessive dietary restraint that is the primary trigger to the disorder. Binge eating is a response to unrealistic restraint, and the binge eater is really a "disinhibited dieter." If she can be persuaded to relinquish her restrictive eating practices and resume normal eating, the urge to binge eat will gradually dissipate.

The line between bulimia and anorexia nervosa is very fine, and many of the patients who seek help for bulimic symptoms are slightly underweight, albeit not so thin as to warrant a diagnosis of anorexia nervosa. In order to maintain their low weights, they would need to continue to restrict their food intake, and this dieting would preclude the return to normal eating practices. For that reason, the dietitian should encourage the patient not to focus on maintaining a particular weight but rather to accept that her healthy weight is the weight she will maintain when eating a healthy diet and being reasonably active. Of course, this message is difficult for weight-preoccupied patients to accept. Part of the skill of nutritional counseling is to be able to present it persistently and persuasively.

Between binge eating episodes, bulimia patients not only curtail the absolute amounts of food they eat, but they also limit their food choices, avoiding what they consider to be unhealthy or frightening foods—invariably, foods that have a high energy content. (These become the foods on which they binge.) The therapist's aim is to alter this misconceived perfectionism about food. Normal eating does not mean eating only "health" foods; it means taking in a mixed and balanced diet containing the essential nutrients and sufficient calories for the body's needs. It is accepting a "good enough" diet, rather than repeatedly failing to maintain an unrealistic, perfectionist, "optimal" diet. Perhaps the most important message to convey is that the amount of food needed to meet daily energy demands is greater than that necessary for essential nutrient requirements, so that good health is achieved by supplementing a diet of healthy, "nutritionally" sound foods with a selection of some high-energy, less "nutritious" foods. If patients can be persuaded to take small amounts of high-energy foods every now and then, they are less likely to binge on them later.

A meal plan is drawn up, and the patient is persuaded to adhere to it and not to try to compensate for episodes of binge eating by further restriction or purgation. Time is set aside for regular educational sessions, during which the patient is given accurate information about nutritional matters. Where appropriate, responsible family members are involved in these meetings.

Laxatives, both chemical and "natural," are frequently abused by bulimics. The futility of this behavior in regard to effecting enduring weight loss, and its manifest dangers to physical health, need special emphasis.

If the patient follows this dietary advice, she will begin to feel better. The therapist capitalizes on this improvement, pointing out that many of the patient's symptoms have been the direct result of poor eating. In most instances, the resumption of normal meals and the cessation of purgation lead to only a slight gain of weight (usually between 1 and 3 kilograms), and that gain is due largely to a degree of rehydration. Patients are often amazed and delighted to realize that they can eat normally without becoming obese.

Most bulimic patients are treated as outpatients. They should be seen on a weekly basis to start, then less frequently as they gradually resume control over their eating. A regular review of patients' food diaries offers a convenient means of providing continued support and reassurance and further educational material. Patients are advised of strategies to help regulate their eating, such as avoiding missing meals or snacks, using appropriate utensils, and not picking at food. They are encouraged to introduce feared binge foods into their diet and to not feel guilty about occasional, planned indulgences. They are told that minor relapses into bulimic behavior are not to be interpreted as total failure but rather as stages in the process of recovery. Advice is given on meal planning, preparation, and eating in various situations so patients will be able to conform with social expectations. The use of alcohol or drugs such as marijuana is discouraged, since these substances are likely to induce a resumption of disrupted eating.

When therapy is terminated, the potential for relapse needs to be recognized; relapse may occur at times of stress or if the patient again embarks on a pursuit of thinness. If and when relapse does occur, the patient should immediately return to a structured meal plan. Ready access to the dietician should be assured.

While most anorexia patients are treated by a multidisciplinary team, of which a dietician should be a valued member, the treatment of bulimia patients may sometimes be undertaken by a dietician working alone. Of course, underlying psychological problems must not be overlooked, but in many instances these problems are not major, and the provision of sound nutritional advice and continued support constitute sufficient treatment.

ACKNOWLEDGMENTS

We wish to thank our dietician colleagues for all they have taught us about the nutritional management of dieting disorders, in particular Mrs. Hazel Williams, Ms. Maureen O'Connor, Mr. Peter Talbot, and Ms. Janet Conti.

FURTHER READING

Beumont, P. J. V., Chambers, T., Rouse, L., & Abraham, S. F. (1981). The diet composition and nutritional knowledge of patients with anorexia nervosa. *Journal of Human Nutrition, 35,* 265–273. An objective analysis of the food choices and nutritional knowledge of anorexia nervosa patients.

Beumont, P. J. V., O'Connor, M., Touyz, S., & Williams, H. (1987). Nutritional counselling in the treatment of anorexia and bulimia nervosa. In P. J. V. Beumont, G. D. Burrows, & R. Casper (Eds.), *The handbook of eating disorders: Part 1. Anorexia and bulimia nervosa* (pp. 349–359). Amsterdam: Elsevier/North-Holland.

Fairburn, C. G., & Cooper, Z. (1987). The Eating Disorder Examination (12th Edition). In C. G. Fairburn & G. T. Wilson (Eds.), *Binge eating: Nature, assessment, and treatment* (pp. 317–360). New York: Guilford Press. An excellent instrument that provides a wealth of useful information about patients' particular difficulties with eating.

Laessle, R. G., Beumont, P. J. V., Butow, P., Lennerts, W., O'Connor, M., Pirke, K. M., Touyz, S. W., & Waadt, S. (1991). A comparison of nutritional management with stress management in the treatment of bulimia nervosa. *British Journal of Psychiatry, 159,* 250–261. An account of an outpatient treatment trial in which a psychological approach to the treatment of bulimia was compared with focused nutritional counseling, both delivered in a group setting.

O'Connor, M. A., Touyz, S. W., & Beumont, P. J. V. (1989). Nutritional management and dietary counselling in bulimia nervosa. *International Journal of Eating Disorders, 7,* 657–662. A practical guide to nutritional counseling for bulimia nervosa patients.

O'Connor, M. A., Touyz, S. W., Dunn, S., & Beumont, P. J. V. (1987). Vegetarianism in anorexia nervosa: A review of 116 consecutive cases. *Medical Journal of Australia, 147,* 540–542. A study of vegetarianism in anorexia nervosa patients.

Williams, H., & Beumont, P. J. V. (1990). Eating disorders. In *Principles of nutritional management of clinical disorder,* Handbook No. 6 of the Dietitians Association of Australia, Canberra, ACT (pp. 63–75). Detailed guidelines for the treatment of anorexia and bulimia nervosa patients, aimed primarily at dietitians.

Wilson, A. J., Touyz, S. W., Dunn, S. M. & Beumont, P. J. V. (1989). The eating behavior rating scale (EBRS): A measure of eating pathology in anorexia nervosa. *International Journal of Eating Disorders, 8,* 583–592. An objective measure of the abnormal eating behaviors seen in anorexia nervosa patients.

Wilson, A. J., Touyz, S. W., O'Connor, M., & Beumont, P. J. V. (1985). Correcting the eating disorder in anorexia nervosa. *Journal of Psychiatric Research, 19,* 449–451. A description of nutritional counseling for patients with anorexia nervosa.

• 55 •

PHARMACOTHERAPY
OF EATING DISORDERS

B. Timothy Walsh

In this chapter I will review our current knowledge of the utility of medication in the treatment of the eating disorders anorexia nervosa and bulimia nervosa. Although there has been substantial research on the pharmacotherapy of these eating disorders, and although medication has been demonstrated to be beneficial, particularly for patients with bulimia nervosa, significant questions remain about when and for which patients pharmacotherapy should be employed.

ANOREXIA NERVOSA

As described in Chapters 27 and 28, individuals with anorexia nervosa exhibit a variety of psychological disturbances, some of which bear a strong resemblance to symptoms or conditions known to respond to pharmacotherapy. The occurrence of such disturbances, coupled with the often refractory nature of anorexia nervosa, has led to clinical trials of a variety of pharmacological agents for this eating disorder. For example, the disturbed thinking about shape and weight of those with anorexia nervosa at times becomes so severe as to suggest the presence of a delusion. It is not unreasonable to wonder whether antipsychotic medication might be of help in reducing these patients' preoccupation with such thoughts. Similarly, depressed mood is commonly observed in patients with anorexia nervosa. Since many forms of depression respond well to treatment with medication, antidepressant medication would, on theoretical grounds, seem likely to be valuable. Unfortunately there have been only a few controlled trials of medication in anorexia nervosa, and none of the trials has demonstrated a dramatic efficacy of any agent.

In the decade after the introduction of the first antipsychotic medication chlorpromazine, the potential utility of this class of medication for a number of psychiatric disorders, including anorexia nervosa, was enthusiastically touted. However, the initial optimism about the benefits of chlorpromazine, which was sometimes combined with insulin, in anorexia nervosa was short-lived. In the only two double-blind, placebo-controlled trials of antipsychotic medications, one of pimozide and the other of sulpiride, neither showed a statistically significant effect favoring weight gain or any clear improvement in the core psychopathological features of anorexia nervosa, including the distorted thinking about shape and weight. The lack of scientific evidence for benefit, coupled with the growing appreciation of the side effects of the currently available antipsychotic agents, has led to a loss of interest in the use of this class of medication for the treatment of anorexia nervosa.

In the 1970s, increased attention focused on the presence of mood disturbance in individuals with anorexia nervosa. In part this attention was prompted by the growing recognition of the utility of antidepressant medications for the treatment of mood disturbance. In addition, it was noted that some individuals who received tricyclic antidepressants for the treatment of depression described a marked increase in appetite and gained significant amounts of weight. Since patients with anorexia nervosa frequently exhibited depressed mood and would obviously benefit from gaining weight, the use of tricyclic antidepressants, particularly amitriptyline, was appealing. Results of open clinical trials of this medication were promising, but two double-blind, placebo-controlled trials produced minimal evidence of substantial clinical utility for most patients with anorexia nervosa. In light of the common occurrence of mood disturbance in patients with anorexia nervosa, of the increased frequency of mood disorders in their relatives, and of the known efficacy of antidepressants in the treatment of depression, it is surprising that the double-blind trials conducted to date have shown so little evidence for the utility of this class of medication in the treatment of this disorder.

The presence of mood disturbance in anorexia nervosa patients and the propensity of lithium to cause weight gain also prompted a controlled trial of this agent. While there was a hint of faster weight gain for patients taking lithium compared with those taking placebo, this effect was not statistically significant, and clinically the overall response to lithium was not impressive.

The only other agent whose utility in cases of anorexia nervosa has been examined using controlled trials is cyproheptadine, an agent that has no established role in the treatment of other psychiatric disorders. Cyproheptadine is an antihistamine and anti-serotonergic agent that is employed in the treatment of a variety of allergic conditions. It was noted that individuals treated with cyproheptadine for allergic conditions sometimes gained weight, and the utility of cyproheptadine for the treatment of anorexia nervosa was therefore explored. A series of three controlled trials conducted in the 1970s and 1980s suggested that cyproheptadine, particularly in relatively high doses such as 32 milligrams per day, was of some small but statistically detectable benefit to hospitalized patients in promoting weight gain and relieving depression. In addition, unlike the other agents examined in controlled trials, cyproheptadine was relatively free of side effects in this medically ill population.

Recently investigators have turned their attention away from the acute "weight gain" phase of treatment of anorexia nervosa to the maintenance of recovery. Many patients who regain weight in a structured setting, such as an inpatient unit, relapse soon after the end of this phase of treatment. Based in part on the similarities between anorexia nervosa and obsessive–compulsive disorder (see Chapter 28) and on the utility of serotonergic agents in the treatment of obsessive–compulsive disorder, it has been suggested that the specific serotonin reuptake inhibitor fluoxetine may be useful in preventing relapse in patients who have gained weight. A controlled trial to examine this intervention is currently under way.

In summary, despite the manifold biological and psychological disturbances of patients with anorexia nervosa, controlled medication trials have been few, and no pharmacological agent has yet been demonstrated to have clinically significant use in this disorder. For that reason, the use of medication in anorexia nervosa at present is dictated not by the diagnosis of anorexia nervosa, but by other clinical features and by the judgment of the responsible physician. One reasonable approach is not to initiate medication until any acute medical problems, such as disturbances of electrolytes or of liver function, have been addressed and hopefully resolved and the patient has gained a significant amount of weight. The presence of moderate or more severe depression at that point might prompt consideration of treatment with an antidepressant. Because their side effects are relatively few, and because of the suggestions of their utility in preventing relapse, the specific serotonin reuptake inhibitors such as fluoxetine may be preferable to other classes of antidepressant medication. The use of antianxiety agents to relieve these individuals' distress around mealtimes has been suggested and may occasionally be useful, but it is usually not of great value. Cyproheptadine appears benign, but its utility is unclear. Antipsychotic agents should be used only in the most difficult and refractory patients. It should be emphasized that our knowledge of pharmacotherapy for anorexia nervosa is based on fewer than 10 double-blind, placebo-controlled trials. Additional research is needed to identify other interventions that may be of use in treating anorexia nervosa.

BULIMIA NERVOSA

In contrast to the rather disappointing state of pharmacotherapy for anorexia nervosa, there have been more fruitful investigations of the utility of medication in the management of bulimia nervosa. The most convincing evidence supports the use of antidepressant medications. The results of controlled trials of other agents, including anticonvulsants, lithium, and the serotonin agonist fenfluramine, have been either negative or equivocal, and these agents are only rarely used in the treatment of the disorder.

Investigations of antidepressant medication in the treatment of bulimia nervosa were prompted by the now widely accepted observation that there is an increased frequency of mood disturbance associated with this eating disorder. These observations eventually led to a series of double-blind, placebo-controlled trials of antidepressant medication. Most classes of antidepressant medication have been examined, including the tricyclic antidepressants, MAO inhibitors, specific serotonin reuptake inhibitors, and atypical antidepressants such as bupropion and trazodone. In almost all the controlled trials, antidepressant medication has proven superior to placebo in terms of reduction of binge frequency. Generally, mood disturbance and preoccupation with shape and weight also show greater improvement with medication than with placebo.

While the data from these studies represent a significant contribution to our knowledge of treatment strategies for bulimia nervosa, they have also raised a number of provocative and important questions. One major question that remains unresolved is why antidepressant medications are effective in the treatment of bulimia nervosa. Although the use of antidepressant medication was initially prompted by the observation of depressed mood in many patients, it does not appear that the "antibulimic" efficacy of antidepressants is related to their effects on mood. In none of the controlled studies has the presence or the degree of mood disturbance been found to be a significant predictor of response to antidepressant medication. In several studies, the response of patients with bulimia nervosa who were not depressed was compared with the response of similar patients who were depressed at the time of randomization. In general the nondepressed patients obtained benefit equivalent to that obtained by the depressed patients. Thus it does not appear the pretreatment presence of depression is of any use in identifying those patients whose eating behavior is most likely to benefit from antidepressant medication.

Studies of the specific serotonin reuptake inhibitor fluoxetine have provided another indication that the mechanism by which antidepressants lead to improvement in bulimia nervosa patients may differ from the mechanism responsible for relief of depression. In a clinical trial involving almost 400 patients, it was found that 60 milligrams of fluoxetine per day, but not 20 milligrams of fluoxetine per day, was clearly superior to placebo. Since fluoxetine at a dose of 20 milligrams per day is known to be effective in the treatment of depression, the observation that a higher dose was needed to treat bulimia nervosa suggests that the mechanism by which fluoxetine produces improvement in bulimia nervosa may be different from that by which it relieves depression.

The controlled trials of antidepressants for bulimia nervosa have also revealed two significant clinical problems with the use of this class of medication as the sole intervention. First, in most studies, only a minority of patients achieve remission from binge eating and purging. Second, it is not clear that the improvement attained during medication treatment is sustained with continued medication, and it is even less clear that a time-limited course of medication will produce lasting improvement.

In addition, as is described elsewhere (see Chapter 60), structured forms of psychotherapy, particularly those using cognitive-behavioral techniques, are clearly effective in the treatment of bulimia nervosa. The work conducted to date suggests that a course of psychotherapy focused on the treatment of bulimia nervosa yields superior results than a single course of a single antidepressant agent. There are hints that when such forms of psychotherapy are combined with antidepressant medication, small additional gains are accrued, for example, in relief of depression. However, for most patients, the gains are small and must be balanced against the risk of side effects.

In presenting treatment options for a patient with bulimia nervosa, it may be helpful to summarize the current knowledge of the efficacy of both psychotherapy and pharmacotherapy. For patients who have not been treated previously and who are not seriously depressed, it is generally appropriate to recommend a trial of psychotherapy before initiating treatment with medication. Antidepressant medication should be considered particularly when the patient has failed or is failing to respond adequately to a course of good psychotherapy or when the patient has a depressive syndrome sufficiently severe to merit treatment independently of its association with bulimia nervosa. While there is no evidence that one antidepressant is superior in the treatment of bulimia nervosa than any other, fluoxetine has two advantages. It is of established efficacy when used at a dose of 60 milligrams per day and is relatively free of side effects. Additional studies are required to identify patient characteristics that will help in selecting those most likely to benefit from treatment with antidepressant medication.

FURTHER READING

Agras, W. S., Rossiter, E. M., Arnow, B., Schneider, J. A., Telch, C. F., Raeburn, S. D., Bruce, B., Perl, M., & Koran, L. M. (1992). Pharmacologic and cognitive-behavioral treatment for bulimia nervosa: A controlled comparison. *American Journal of Psychiatry, 49*, 82–87. Report of a study in which cognitive-behavioral treatment was found to be superior to a course of desipramine, suggesting the combination of medication and psychotherapy may be advantageous.

American Psychiatric Association. (1993). Practice guideline for eating disorders. *American Journal of Psychiatry, 150,* 208–228. An authoritative review of the treatment of eating disorders, with suggestions regarding medication.

Mitchell, J. E., Pyle, R. L., Eckert, E. D., Hatsukami, D., Pomeroy, C., & Zimmerman, R. (1990). A comparison study of antidepressants and structured group psychotherapy in the treatment of bulimia nervosa. *Archives of General Psychiatry, 47,* 149–157. The first controlled comparison of medication, psychotherapy, and their combination in the treatment of bulimia nervosa. The intensive group psychotherapy program was superior to a course of imipramine in producing changes in eating behavior, but the active medication produced detectable improvement in mood and anxiety.

Walsh, B. T. (1992). Pharmacological treatment of eating disorders. In K. Halmi (Ed.), *The psychobiology and treatment of anorexia nervosa and bulimia nervosa* (pp. 329–340). Washington, DC: American Psychiatric Press. A detailed review of the place of medication in the treatment of eating disorders.

Walsh, B. T., & Devlin, M. J. (1992). The pharmacologic treatment of eating disorders. In D. Shaffer (Ed.), *Psychiatric clinics of North America* (pp. 149–160). Philadelphia: W. B. Saunders. Another detailed review, with comments regarding the use of medications in younger patients.

• 56 •

FAMILY THERAPY AND EATING DISORDERS

Christopher Dare
Ivan Eisler

For many years clinicians have believed that in a complete management plan for anorexia nervosa, the family of the patient had an important role to play. The first modern accounts of the syndrome in the late 19th century (see Chapter 25) referred to the need to "deal" with the family, which was generally seen to have a negative role. This view is exemplified by the comments made by the famous neurologist Charcot on the need to limit the contact between the patient and her family if the physician was to be able to effect a successful treatment. During the early part of this century psychological models of eating disorder were temporarily replaced by physical etiological models, but by the middle of the 20th century, the tide had again changed and the patient's family experiences were seen as having a pivotal role in the development of the disorder. A major influence in this period was the work of Hilde Bruch, in particular her notion of the formative experiences of early mother–infant interaction, in which, according to her, the child's needs received insufficient and inaccurate feedback from the mother, leading to poor development of the child's interoceptive awareness, a distorted perception of self, and a pervasive sense of ineffectiveness.

Although these very specific, clinically derived theoretical conceptualizations have not been backed up by systematic research, results of a growing number of studies in the past 30 years seem to support the general notion that family factors contribute to the development or maintenance of eating disorders. For example, it has been demonstrated in a study at the Maudsley Hospital in London that the presence of overt psychiatric illness in a parent, or of marked family disharmony, influences the long-term outcome of patients admitted to the hospital with a severe eating disorder.

The accumulating clinical observations have been supplemented, in a significant way, by the ideas and practice of family therapy. A number of influential figures in the family therapy field (most notably Mara Selvini-Palazzoli and Salvador Minuchin) have given their attention to the treatment of eating disorders. Selvini-Palazzoli has advocated a move away from an individual therapy approach to whole family intervention, and Salvador Minuchin has produced systematic clinical data to show the effectiveness of family therapy. The clinical practice of both Minuchin and Selvini-Palazzoli has been instrumental in the development of family therapy as a widespread treatment modality for mental health and psychological problems in children, adolescents, and young adults. The high level of prestige the observations of these two great innovators have earned has given great impetus to the application of family therapy to the treatment of anorexia nervosa. These developments have given strong support to a specific belief about the etiology of anorexia in particular and of eating disorders in general, a belief not confined to the adherents of the "family therapy movement": that the disorders originate in specific, pathogenic family processes, despite the fact that Minuchin himself drew attention to the role of a variety of factors other than family processes in the etiology of anorexia nervosa. Selvini-Palazzoli also viewed the wider processes of social change as influencing the upsurge of anorexia nervosa cases in northern Italy.

The theory of a single cause leading to a single treatment can have strong appeal. The different clinical evocations of Minuchin and Selvini-Palazzoli have been augmented by comments from other influential family therapists. Carl Whitaker has identified the role of family uncertainty about the balance of individuality and separateness in characterizing the context in which anorexia nervosa develops. Michael White has added important concepts about the three-generational family process in which the eating disorder develops. He has also incorporated views of the familially transmitted pressures of social process concerning food and the distinctive differences in socially derived role expectations that adolescent males and females experience. Cumulatively, family therapists and clinicians who are convinced by these arguments have come to believe that anorexia nervosa is the exemplar of a disorder originating in known family disturbance that can be treated by forms of therapy targeting these apparently well-established causative factors. In fact, a careful examination of the research literature does not reveal data to support the notion that there is a distinctive and consistent pattern of family structure and family functioning in eating-disorder patients (see Chapter 38). The differences that have been reported between eating-disorder families and control groups are probably best understood as being associated with more severe or more chronic illness than as consistent etiological factors. Somewhat paradoxically, while the accumulating empirical evidence is against a family etiological model, the evidence for the importance of involving the family in the treatment is increasingly strong.

CLINICAL STUDIES OF FAMILY THERAPY FOR EATING DISORDERS

Over the years, in clinical practice in departments of child and adolescent psychiatry, family therapy techniques have been used in working with both anorexic and bulimic nonadult patients, which is much less true of departments of adult mental health or internal medicine. Results of several follow-up studies support the efficacy of family therapy, particularly in adolescent anorexic patients. The strongest evidence has come from a series of randomized controlled trials of family therapy conducted at the Maudsley Hospital. In the first study, a series of 80 patients consecutively admitted to an inpatient refeeding program were randomly assigned, on discharge from the hospital, to a 1-year course of family therapy or supportive, individual treatment. Patients with an early onset (before the age of 19 years) and a short history (less than 3 years at the time of admission presentation) of illness had a significantly better outcome when treated with family therapy than did patients who received the control treatment, both at the end of the treatment program and at a 5-year follow-up. Figure 56.1 shows the patients' progress in terms of weight change over the course of treatment and at a 5-year follow-up. The good progress in terms of weight in this younger group of patients is paralleled in other areas, so that 9 out of 10 in this group were categorized as having

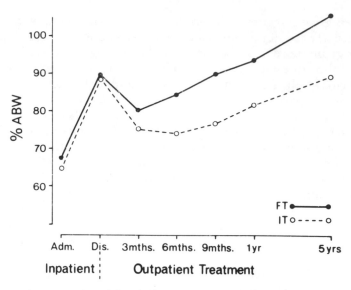

FIGURE 56.1. Changes in average weight during treatment and follow-up of early-onset, short-history patients with anorexia nervosa. (ABW, average body weight; FT, family therapy; IT, individual therapy.)

recovered from the illness at the time of the long-term follow-up. In comparison, nearly half the patients who received the control treatment had a level of symptoms (low weight or the development of bulimic symptoms) that warranted the designation of a poor outcome. Family therapy in this study was not, however, universally beneficial. The patients with more chronic illness, patients with a late onset of illness, and those with severe bulimia nervosa, did not gain specific benefit from family therapy in comparison with the control treatment.

The results of the study have some important practical and theoretical implications. From a practical, clinical standpoint, it appears that family therapy might be used for the initial treatment of adolescent anorexia nervosa, leaving hospital admission and other interventions for those individuals with life-threatening physical symptoms and those who failed to respond to the outpatient program.

The implications of the efficacy of family therapy in adolescence led to a further controlled study comparing two forms of family therapy: the conjoint family therapy so far found to be effective and a comparison form termed "family counseling," in which the parents are seen as a couple but separately from their daughter. The aim of this study was to elucidate the mechanisms underlying an effective family intervention. Both the conjoint form of family therapy and the family counseling had similar aims and generally followed a similar course. From the start there was a strong focus on helping the parents manage the symptomatic behavior of their daughter or son. The therapist had to help the parents overcome their sense of helplessness and find a way of mobilizing the family's resources to help themselves. The therapist at the same time made it very clear that the family was not considered by the therapist as the source of the problem but rather as the best resource for effective treatment. Later in the treatment, as the patient regained weight, wider adolescent and family issues were discussed. Similar topics came up for discussion in both the conjoint family therapy and the family counseling sessions, although in the latter the therapist did not meet with the patient and the parents together; rather, the therapist would see the patient alone for half the treatment session and the parents for the other half. The counseling that took place involved the exploration of the patient's feelings and beliefs about her/his problems with food, body image, self-esteem, relationships (especially those with the parents as they change their attitudes toward her dieting, bulimic, or other eating behaviors). A pilot study of this comparison, involving 18 patients, and a definitive study of 40 patients showed that overall both treatments were equally effective in bringing about a return to normal weight without recourse to inpatient treatment.

This work also produced some evidence that challenges the present traditional view of the family as a pathogenic agent as described above. The measure taken to evaluate family affective communication, expressed emotion (EE), turned out to be a strong predictor of outcome of family intervention. As has been found in previous studies, families in which one or the other parent displays an above-average level of "critical comments" that does not lessen during the course of the treatment tend to have a poorer response to treatment. However, when the results were examined separately for "high EE" and "low EE" families, the surprising finding was that family counseling was associated with greater improvement than was conjoint family therapy.

Two other findings from the earlier pilot study suggest a possible explanation. A 2-year follow-up of the families revealed important differences in how the families experienced the therapy of the two treatment modalities. While parents as well as patients in both treatments had found the major thrust of the therapy (which highlighted the serious, life-threatening nature of the illness and helped the parents take charge) helpful, those in the conjoint family therapy group were much more likely to report having open conflicts or struggles with the daughter and were also more likely to feel blamed. This finding was particularly true in families whose initial levels of criticism as measured by the EE scales were relatively high. Moreover, a measure of family satisfaction (derived from the Family Adaptation and Cohesion Evaluation Scales [FACES III]) suggested that the families who were most satisfied with family life at the beginning of therapy had the best outcome in terms of their child's eating disorder.

The very low levels of affective communication, as measured by EE, in these families can be seen, possibly, as an aspect of what Minuchin describes as showing conflict avoidance. The findings of the Maudsley study suggest that a form of family therapy that does *not* challenge the family's characteristic patterns is associated with as good an outcome for anorexic patients as is the family therapy that has access to and challenges those family qualities. Furthermore, in some families, family counseling may in fact be more effective. This finding challenges the notion that the efficacy of family therapy stems from its ability to alter the characteristic patterns of family interaction and family organization.

Family Therapy and Adult Anorexia Nervosa

Further treatment studies at the Maudsley Hospital are continuing to refine our knowledge of the potential benefits of family therapy and its mode of action in groups other than the adolescent anorexic. Two studies (one completed and one still in progress) have as their focus the question of the role of family therapy in adult and mostly chronic anorexia nervosa sufferers. Contrary to the findings of the earlier study, family therapy appears to lead to a better outcome than does individual psychodynamic therapy and individual supportive treatment in the whole age range of patients. This finding seems to be most clearly so for those in whom the illness starts before adulthood. While these findings are of interest, they should be viewed as tentative, since they are based only on results recorded at the end of treatment; these results need to be confirmed in longer-term follow-up.

Family Therapy and Bulimia Nervosa

While the role of family therapy in the treatment of anorexia nervosa is now well established, its place in the treatment of bulimia nervosa is less clear. Two of the Maudsley studies discussed above included subgroups of low-weight patients with severe cases of bulimia nervosa. In the first study, their outcome both in family therapy and in the control individual supportive therapy was generally quite poor, while in the second study a comparable patient group responded better to family therapy than to either individual psychodynamic psychotherapy or individual supportive therapy. A small pilot study of family therapy for adolescent bulimia nervosa patients showed a response to treatment similar to that found in adolescent anorexia nervosa patients. Fairburn has recently shown that an individual therapy that focuses primarily on the patient's personal relationships (interpersonal therapy) is highly effective in treating bulimia nervosa. This finding indicates that family therapy ought to be explored more systematically as a possible treatment for bulimia nervosa.

CONCLUSIONS

Family therapy is now well established as an effective treatment for anorexia nervosa in adolescence, and there is growing evidence that it may have an important role in the treatment of adult anorexia nervosa as well as bulimia nervosa. The model of family therapy that has been shown to be effective in adolescent anorexia nervosa may also be effective in the treatment of young bulimics, but systematic research in this area has not yet been conducted. The family therapy approaches that have been used with adults (for both bulimia nervosa and anorexia nervosa) tend to be less symptom oriented than those used with adolescents, and the evidence for the effectiveness of any particular approach is at present weak. In clinical practice the use of family therapy is widespread, and a variety of theoretical approaches are employed. The systematic evaluation of the efficacy of family therapy in treating eating disorders, however, has been limited to one treatment/research center in which, inevitably, the focus has been on a particular style of family therapy. Replications and/or modifications of the research described in this chapter would greatly enhance our knowledge in this area.

ACKNOWLEDGMENTS

The authors wish to acknowledge the very generous support given to the work reported here by the trustees of the Bethlem Royal and Maudsley Hospital, the Medical Research Council of Great Britain, the Mental Health Foundation, and the Leverhulme Trust.

FURTHER READING

Bruch, H. (1974). *Eating disorders: Obesity, anorexia nervosa and the person within.* London: Routledge and Kegan Paul. An important book that influenced much of the later thinking about families and eating disorders.

Crisp, A. H., Norton, K., Gowers, S., Halek, C., Bowyer, C., Yeldham, D., Levett, G., & Bhat, A. (1991). A controlled study of the effect of therapies aimed at adolescent and family psychopathology in anorexia nervosa. *British Journal of Psychiatry, 159,* 325–333. A controlled clinical trial of combined therapies that included family interventions.

Dare, C., Eisler, I., Russell, G. F. M., & Szmukler, G. I. (1990).The clinical and theoretical impact of a controlled trial of family therapy in anorexia nervosa. *Journal of Marital and Family Therapy, 16,* 39–57. In this paper the approach to family therapy developed at the Maudsley Hospital is described in some detail.

Eisler, I. (1995). Family models of eating disorder. In G. I. Szmukler, C. Dare, & J.Treasure (Eds.), *The eating disorders: Handbook of theory, treatment and research* (pp. 155–176). Chichester: John Wiley & Sons. A detailed review of the research into family factors in the etiology of eating disorders.

Le Grange, D., Eisler, I., Dare, C., & Hodes, M. (1992). Family criticism and self-starvation: A study of expressed emotion. *Journal of Family Therapy, 14,* 177–192. The crucial and deleterious effect that family criticism of the patient has on the outcome of family therapy challenges the clinical descriptions of the "psychosomatic family."

Minuchin, S., Rosman, S. L., & Baker, L. (1978). *Psychosomatic families.* Cambridge, MA: Harvard University Press. This classic work presents both a clinical picture of families of anorexic patients and suggestions for a treatment model for changing the family pattern.

Russell, G. F. M., Dare, C., Eisler, I., & Le Grange, D. (1992). Controlled trials of family treatments in anorexia nervosa. In K. A. Halmi (Ed.), *Psychobiology and treatment of anorexia nervosa and bulimia nervosa* (pp. 237–261). Washington, DC: American Psychiatric Press. This chapter contains a description of a series of controlled trials of family therapy conducted in the Maudsley Hospital in London and includes preliminary data from the two more recent studies.

Russell, G. F. M., Szmukler, G., Dare, C., & Eisler, I. (1987). An evaluation of family therapy in anorexia nervosa and bulimia nervosa. *Archives of General Psychiatry, 44,* 1047–1056. This is the first published account of a controlled trial of family therapy for patients with an eating disorder.

Selvini-Palazzoli, M. (1974). *Self-starvation: From the intrapsychic to the transpersonal approach.* London: Chaucer. This book influenced the development of family therapy, showing its evolution from psychoanalytic psychotherapy. The work propounded a view of the family etiology of anorexia nervosa.

Schwartz, R. C., Barrett, M. J., & Saba, G. (1985). Family therapy for bulimia. In D. M. Garner & P. E. Garfinkel (Eds.), *Handbook of psychotherapy for anorexia nervosa and bulimia* (pp. 280–310). New York: Guilford Press. This chapter from an important handbook contains a useful review of clinical practice in the treatment of bulimia nervosa.

• 57 •

COGNITIVE-BEHAVIORAL THERAPY FOR ANOREXIA NERVOSA

Kelly Bemis Vitousek

The cognitive-behavioral approach to understanding and treating anorexia nervosa was first described in detail in 1982. Over the ensuing 12 years, some elements of the theoretical model have been tested empirically and generally supported; the recommended treatment strategy has been further elaborated and widely adopted in clinical practice. A majority of eating disorder specialists endorse the cognitive-behavioral approach for anorexic clients, either as the primary psychotherapeutic modality or in combination with psychodynamic techniques. The influence of this model on the treatment of anorexia nervosa appears equivalent to that of a related approach proposed independently and almost simultaneously for bulimia nervosa (see Chapter 60). Yet while the latter application of cognitive-behavioral principles has garnered extensive support through controlled trials, the efficacy of similar strategies for anorexia nervosa has not been established. At present cognitive-behavioral intervention in cases of anorexia nervosa can be advocated only with reference to the appeal of its comprehensive theoretical and therapeutic model; to clinical impressions of its applicability; or, by extrapolation, to data on the effectiveness of a related approach to a kindred disorder. Clearly none of these grounds is compelling; however, in the absence of strong empirical support for any alternative form of psychotherapy, they are sufficient to justify the inclusion of this modality in comparative trials currently underway.

COGNITIVE-BEHAVIORAL THEORY

Reduced to its essence, the cognitive model holds that anorexic symptoms are maintained by a characteristic set of beliefs about weight and eating. The central premise of anorexia nervosa is that the worth of the self is represented in the weight and shape of the body. This belief arises from a complex interaction among more basic views of the self and a sociocultural context that supports the linkage between weight and personal values (see Chapter 15). Once formed, the dominant anorexic idea influences individuals to engage in stereotypic eating disordered behaviors, to endorse subsidiary irrational beliefs, to be responsive to eccentric reinforcement contingencies, to process information in accordance with predictable cognitive biases, and to manifest starvation-induced physiological changes—all of which serve to strengthen the underlying premise. The cognitive model suggests that the core features of anorexia nervosa acquire their positively and negatively reinforcing properties because they fulfill aspects of the more general belief systems of vulnerable individuals, accounting for the fiercely "egosyntonic" quality of anorexic symptoms.

Self-statement inventories, semistructured interview schedules, and think-aloud procedures have established that eating disordered subjects differ from normal control subjects in the frequency, intensity, and nature of their concerns about weight, shape, and food. Scores on cognitive measures have been shown to decrease during the course of treatment, to predict response to treatment, and to correlate with other indices of eating disorder symptomatology. Much of the cognitive assessment research reported to date is marred by serious methodological and conceptual flaws, including the use of subclinical or mixed diagnosis samples and the omission of psychiatric or dieting control groups. Self-statement measures are typically heterogeneous compilations of the kinds of peculiar ideas clients verbalize in psychotherapy; few of these measures have been designed or administered in ways that make it possible to determine whether beliefs represent symptoms or mediating variables.

More recently, researchers have begun to apply the methods of cognitive science to the study of the eating disorders, moving beyond cognitive content to explore the processes through which eating disorder beliefs may develop, proliferate, and become autonomous. The cognitive model postulates that anorexics develop weight-related self-schemas that act to prolong symptoms in a relatively automatic way, by directing the manner in which affected individuals perceive, interpret, and remember their experience.

Results of recent studies are consistent with hypothesized differences in information processing. Anorexics (and bulimics) have been found to remember food- and weight-related information preferentially after reading descriptive passages, to attend selectively to the food- and weight-related meanings of ambiguous words, and to manifest delayed response times to food- and/or weight-related stimulus sets on the Stroop task. It remains unclear whether these paradigms are assessing statelike salient concerns instead of or in addition to the more stable attentional biases predicted by cognitive theory.

COGNITIVE-BEHAVIORAL INTERVENTION

The principles of cognitive-behavioral therapy for anorexia nervosa are derived from the approach delineated by Beck and his coworkers; however, conventional cognitive strategies have been adapted to address the specific features of the anorexic patient. These features include: (1) the egosyntonic nature of symptoms; (2) the interaction between physical and psychological elements; (3) the idiosyncratic beliefs related to food and weight; and (4) the prominence of deficits in self-concept.

Engaging the Anorexic Client in Treatment

A prerequisite to work on any of the causal variables specified by the cognitive model is the engagement of the anorexic client as an active participant in the therapeutic enterprise. In descriptions of cognitive-behavioral therapy, considerable space is devoted to outlining recommended strategies for the crucial initial phase. It is suggested that the guiding principle of "collaborative empiricism" may make the cognitive approach particularly suitable for this wary and resistant population. Clients are not required to surrender their tenuous sense of control to the authoritative judgments of an expert; rather, they are encouraged to join in an experimental process of discovering how their own beliefs and behaviors actually affect their experience. They are not asked to concede the irrationality of cherished values but simply to take a closer look at the *means* they have chosen to secure them and the full range of *consequences* that result. The establishment of a sound, supportive therapeutic relationship is viewed as essential for success in this endeavor, since its quality profoundly influences the client's willingness to confront the terrifying prospect of weight gain.

A substantial portion of the first few sessions of therapy may be devoted to helping the client develop an exhaustive list of both the "pros" and the "cons" of her eating disorder, phrased in her own terms. The construction of this list is intended to serve a number of purposes. First, the inclusion of the perceived advantages of symptomatology is often disarming to clients who are accustomed to being warned about the dangers of their behavior by family members and physicians. The cognitive therapist explicitly acknowledges that weight loss must confer some significant benefits that will be missed and emphasizes that therapy will be unsuccessful if the patient is not fully compensated for these losses. Second, the exercise provides an opportunity to insert psychoeducational material about the symptoms the patient does find distressing (see Chapter 53). Experiences such as depression, irritability, impaired concentration, and food preoccupation are linked to the common cause of starvation pathology. The therapist begins to articulate a theme that will recur throughout treatment; that is, that such symptoms are inextricably connected to restrictive dieting and suboptimal weight, and it is not within the client's power to eliminate them selectively while retaining the benefits she associates with the attainment of her thin ideal. Third, the identification of pros and cons can serve an important assessment function, providing information about an individual client's motivational system and experience of her disorder. Finally, the technique allows the therapist to start introducing the change strategies of cognitive-behavioral therapy. Each claimed advantage and disadvantage is cast as a hypothesis that can be examined for its validity and adaptiveness or used as the basis for prospective data collection. The functional emphasis inherent in this exercise reflects one of the most distinctive features of cognitive therapy for anorexia nervosa, which remains evident during the entire course of treatment.

Managing Eating and Weight

Clients who are starving or engaging in chaotic eating behavior are unable to participate actively in the therapeutic process; therefore, efforts to improve nutritional and weight status are an integral part of the clinical agenda from the inception of treatment. The processes of dietary rehabilitation and weight restoration are not carried out in isolation from the "real work" of cognitive-behavioral therapy; rather, they are closely integrated with the ongoing examination of the client's core beliefs.

A goal weight range clearly above the menstrual threshold and a target rate of weight gain are established for each client early in treatment. Although these goals may be modified on the basis of emerging evidence about the client's individual metabolism and natural weight, they are not negotiated in concession to the client's pathological fears about normal weight status. Progress toward these objectives is monitored regularly by the therapist and may be supported by operant contingencies, particularly with hospitalized patients.

In the beginning stages of recovery, clients are encouraged to eat in a "mechanical" fashion according to prescribed guidelines for the composition, quantity, and spacing of meals, rather than to attempt to interpret the signals of hunger and satiety that have become confused by their belief systems and starved state. "Forbidden foods" that have been avoided because of fears that they will cause weight gain or precipitate binge eating episodes are gradually reintroduced.

Modifying Beliefs about Weight and Food

The essence of cognitive-behavioral therapy involves teaching clients to test the validity of the thoughts, perceived reinforcement contingencies, and information-processing styles that influence them. A formal strategy for evaluating beliefs is imparted in therapy sessions and is practiced through the completion of homework exercises.

The first step involves operationalizing specific beliefs. Clients are enlisted in mapping out the network of associations attached to their concerns about weight and food and in articulating their expectations about what will occur if they violate or conform to their assumptions. The material clients provide in therapy and through self-monitoring records is then explored through both deductive and inductive techniques.

Logical errors in information processing, such as selective attention, dichotomous reasoning, and confirmatory bias, are identified and discussed, and clients are taught to be more alert to occasions when schema-driven processing impairs their ability to interpret data accurately. Decentering techniques are used to help clients recognize discrepancies between the standards they set for themselves and others and to establish concrete criteria for determining when their own behavior or appearance has particular effects on the environment.

Clients are trained to apply four questions to the distressing cognitions they experience: (1) What is the evidence for my belief? (2) Are there any alternative explanations? (3) What are the implications if my belief is accurate? and (4) Is it adaptive for me to act in accordance with my belief? The first three questions follow a conventional format for analyzing automatic thoughts in cognitive therapy; the fourth has been added to address the special problems posed by clients who are unable or unwilling to subject overvalued ideas to tests of rationality or accuracy.

Many of the predictions expressed by clients can be translated into formal hypotheses and evaluated by collecting data in a prospective fashion. The therapist and client work together to devise informative experiments that bear on specific beliefs. For example, an anorexic who maintains that people respond more favorably to her when she loses 2 pounds might decide to gather information about whether others are capable of detecting such minute fluctuations, or she might vary her own behavior to assess whether the social environment reacts more to her weight or to other aspects of her appearance, behavior, or affect.

Modifying Views of the Self

During the course of therapy, attention gradually shifts away from the focal symptomatology of anorexia nervosa to the more general aspects of the self that may have predisposed the individual to the development of her disorder. While none of these underlying disturbances is unique to anorexia nervosa, characteristic themes can be discerned, prominently featuring deficits in self-concept and self-awareness and concerns about achievement, maturity, and morality. It is not necessary to shift from a cognitive to a dynamic paradigm to remediate these deficits—all can be addressed through techniques consistent with cognitive-behavioral principles, such as the exploration of logical inconsistencies between values, the examination of the functional consequences of setting unattainable goals, the design of prospective tests. In the later stages of therapy, clients are encouraged to experiment with new strategies for achieving their goals, new sources of positive reinforcement for experiencing pleasure and pride, and new standards for gauging personal worth.

The recommended duration of cognitive-behavioral therapy for anorexic clients is considerably longer than that recommended for bulimic clients—often 1 to 2 years of weekly sessions, with more intensive treatment in the first several months. This extended course is necessary to accommodate the greater resistance of anorexic clients to the change process, as well as to accomplish weight restoration. In addition, cognitive-behavioral therapy for bulimia nervosa is typically restricted to disorder-specific behaviors and self-statements; treatment for anorexia nervosa makes more extensive use of cognitive restructuring techniques for the modification of higher order beliefs. It is not clear whether these disparities in the recommended depth and breadth of cognitive-behavioral therapy address fundamental distinctions between the two disorders or whether they simply reflect the orientations of the specialists who developed the respective approaches.

Effectiveness

A few systematic case studies of cognitive-behavioral therapy for anorexia nervosa have been reported. The only controlled study published to date yielded equivocal evidence for its relative efficacy. Few differences were found between cognitive-behavioral, behavioral, and "treatment-as-usual" conditions, although cognitive therapy was associated with higher rates of compliance; no group could be considered clinically recovered at 1-year follow-up. Unfortunately a number of methodological problems make it difficult to draw clear conclusions from this single comparative trial. The sample size was small, the cell composition unequal, the treatment duration limited, and the principal therapist served as the sole evaluator of clinical status. Moreover it appears that the primary focus in the cognitive-behavioral condition was the disputation of specific beliefs about weight and shape, which represents only a portion of the complex treatment package proposed for anorexia nervosa.

The persistent lack of data on the effectiveness of cognitive-behavioral therapy is embarrassing for an approach with a commitment to empiricism—but it is, at least, nothing singular for the field. Astonishingly, there have been only four controlled studies of psychotherapy of any kind for anorexia nervosa—perhaps reflecting clinical pessimism about the prospects of obtaining satisfactory results as well as the daunting problems involved in assessing the long-term effects of a long-term treatment for a relatively rare disorder. While these considerations make the absence of data more understandable, formal trials of the utility of cognitive therapy for anorexia nervosa are clearly long overdue.

FURTHER READING

Beck, A. T., Rush, A. J., Shaw, B. F., & Emery, G. (1979). *Cognitive therapy of depression.* New York: Guilford Press. Basic principles of cognitive-behavioral treatment.

Channon, S., deSilva, P., Hemsley, D., & Perkins, R. (1989). A controlled trial of cognitive-behavioral and behavioral treatment of anorexia nervosa. *Behaviour Research and Therapy, 27,* 529–535. The sole comparative outcome study of cognitive-behavioral treatment for anorexia nervosa.

Cooper, P. J., & Fairburn, C. G. (1984). Cognitive behaviour therapy for anorexia nervosa: Some preliminary findings. *Journal of Psychosomatic Research, 28,* 493–499. A series of case studies using cognitive-behavioral techniques.

Garner, D. M. (1986). Cognitive therapy for anorexia nervosa. In K. D. Brownell & J. P. Foreyt (Eds.), *Handbook of eating disorders: Physiology, psychology, and treatment of obesity, anorexia, and bulimia.* New York: Basic Books (pp. 301–327). Further description of cognitive therapy techniques.

Garner, D. M., & Bemis, K. M. (1982). A cognitive-behavioral approach to the treatment of anorexia nervosa. *Cognitive Therapy and Research, 6,* 123–150. The initial proposal of a cognitive-behavioral model for understanding and treating anorexia nervosa.

Garner, D. M., & Bemis, K. M. (1984). Cognitive therapy for anorexia nervosa. In D. M. Garner & P. E. Garfinkel (Eds.), *Handbook of psychotherapy for anorexia nervosa and bulimia.* (pp. 107–146). New York: Guilford Press. A more detailed presentation of the therapeutic strategies outlined in Garner and Bemis (1982), including excerpts of therapy sessions.

Garner, D. M., Rockert, W., Olmstead, M. P., Johnson, C., & Coscina, D. V. (1984). Psycho-educational principles in the treatment of bulimia and anorexia nervosa. In D. M. Garner & P. E. Garfinkel (Eds.), *Handbook of psychotherapy for anorexia nervosa and bulimia* (pp. 513–572). New York: Guilford Press. A compendium of the psychoeducational material employed in cognitive therapy for the eating disorders.

Vitousek, K. B., & Ewald, L. S. (1993). Self-representation in eating disorders: A cognitive perspective. In Z. Segal & S. Blatt (Eds.), *The self in emotional disorders: Cognitive and psychodynamic perspectives.* New York: Guilford Press (pp. 221–257). An extended presentation of the cognitive theoretical model of restricting anorexia nervosa.

Vitousek, K. B., & Hollon, S. D. (1990). The investigation of schematic content and processing in the eating disorders. *Cognitive Therapy and Research, 14,* 191–214. A theoretical discussion of the role of information processing in the onset and maintenance of the eating disorders; presents an agenda for research on the properties of weight-related schemas.

Vitousek, K. B., & Orimoto, L. (1993). Cognitive-behavioral models of anorexia nervosa, bulimia nervosa, and obesity. In P. C. Kendall & K. Dobson (Eds.), *Psychopathology and cognition.* New York: Academic Press. (pp. 191–243). A review of the status of cognitive theory and therapy for the eating disorders.

• 58 •

PSYCHODYNAMIC PSYCHOTHERAPY FOR ANOREXIA NERVOSA

David B. Herzog

Long-term psychotherapy is probably the most commonly prescribed outpatient treatment for anorexia nervosa in the United States. Short-term trials with cognitive-behavioral therapy, family therapy, and adjunctive psychotropic medication may be recommended first, but since these interventions often produce only modest improvement, the anorexic is frequently referred for long-term psychotherapy.

DEFINITION AND GOALS

Psychodynamic psychotherapy has a lengthy history in the treatment of anorexia nervosa. Although various well-studied therapies use psychodynamic principles, psychodynamic psychotherapy for anorexia nervosa has not been the subject of scientific investigation because it is an expensive and time-consuming form of treatment, and its effectiveness is difficult to demonstrate. In this chapter, the term "psychodynamic psychotherapy" will refer to all long-term therapies that explicitly use the relationship between the patient and therapist as the primary treatment tool and that attend to transference and countertransference reactions. The goals of psychodynamic psychotherapy are to restore the capacity to feel and care; develop modes of feeling and expressing power and dependency; attenuate the severe superego along with primitive guilt; develop strategies for coping that are more adaptive than the current eating behaviors; and return the patient to a healthy nutritional, physiologic, cognitive state. In more difficult cases, the goal may be to keep the patient alive and relatively free of medical harm until the patient is more able to use psychotherapy.

MODELS OF THERAPY

The psychodynamic model may be classically analytic, self-psychological, interpersonal, or objects-relations oriented. The traditional psychodynamic psychotherapist employs a neutral stance with the patient and interprets and clarifies patient-generated transference material. Yet these psychodynamic modes permit considerable flexibility in the therapist role as long as the therapist attends to the patient/therapist relationship. The therapist's level of activity may depend on the theoretical orientation and the developmental phase of the patient. The therapist may be active; support or prescribe medication; give homework; take vital signs or weigh the patient; set expectations; develop contracts regarding the minimal state of health for outpatient care to continue; support the patient's defenses; and help coordinate care through the team of clinicians, including the internist, nutritionist, and family therapist. No developmental phase has been consistently implicated in the etiology of anorexia nervosa, yet the scientific literature contains numerous case reports associating anorexia nervosa with specific developmental failures and describes corresponding treatment approaches. Moreover, each school of psychodynamic therapy has its own language. The classical psychoanalytic psychotherapist may focus on impasses in the patient's earliest developmental phase, the symbiotic phase, and confirm the patient's perceptions or correct her/his distortions. The self psychology psychotherapist may focus on the patient's failures in mirroring or empathy. The object-relations psychotherapist may address splitting as a developmental failure.

ROLES

Psychodynamic psychotherapy has several roles in the treatment of anorexia nervosa. It can provide a matrix of relationships within which other therapies can be administered. It can provide a unified stance that precludes splitting among the various treaters. In the context of alliance and a reassurance that the therapy will be there even when the symptoms have subsided, the anorexic can begin to take risks toward health. In the context of supportive psychotherapy, the anorexic patient who refuses medication because it is "unnatural" or "it will make me fat" may later accept it in a reservoir of trust. The psychodynamic psychotherapy perspective is also critical in helping to manage the intense countertransference reactions that these patients frequently evoke through their hostility, help rejection, neediness, relapsing symptoms, medical complications, and suicidality. Attention to countertransference may prevent potentially untherapeutic responses, including boundary violations, coercion, or rejection of the patient.

QUALITIES OF THE THERAPIST

What qualities should the psychodynamic psychotherapist possess? The therapist above all should be empathic and should accurately mirror the perceived wants, needs, and feelings of the patient. The therapist should be patient, undemanding, reliable, consistent, and flexible. The therapist should be able to bear the patient's affect and demonstrate that relationships can sustain anger, conflict, and misunderstanding. The therapist should be aware that empathic failures are inevitable and should be mended promptly. The therapist should provide explanations about the eating disorder, coaching, and encouragement. Anorexics uniformly react negatively to inexplicit goals, inactivity, and formality. The anorexic patient may require a mixture of general support, vigilant beneficial care, and firm behavioral limits to sustain psychotherapy.

INITIATING THERAPY

Psychodynamic psychotherapy should be offered as the primary treatment for anorexic patients who demonstrate significant character pathology and as an adjunct to other treatments for those patients who experience chronic symptoms or experience residual problems following successful response to other treatments. The patient who has been prescribed psychodynamic psychotherapy needs to be educated about therapy so she can make a rational choice about participating. A 10-session trial of psychodynamic psychotherapy can be extremely helpful in establishing a psychodynamic formulation and in defining treatment goals and options. In psychodynamic psychotherapy, normalizing the eating behavior is not the single defined goal. In contrast to cognitive-behavioral and psychopharmacological approaches, the psychodynamic psychotherapist must balance the requirements of medical safety with the goal of creating an alliance with a suspicious, reluctant patient. This difficult balancing act is made somewhat easier if the clinician can create a safety envelope that can contain the medical and nutritional damage while the therapeutic effort proceeds. The safety envelope clearly delineates the minimal medical requirements, such as weight and vital signs, to continue in outpatient treatment.

The approach in psychotherapy depends on a thorough assessment of what the symptoms and their function mean to the patient. It takes a number of sessions to gather a sufficiently detailed history from the anorexic patient to formulate this complex dynamic. The anorexic is generally private, guarded, and fearful of being controlled. She will need time to develop an alliance with the psychotherapist before revealing her understanding of the symptoms, what kind of therapy she wants, how willing she is to participate, and how ready she is to change. The patient's reservoir of coping skills may be limited, leaving her quite dependent on her anorexic symptoms. For her to feel safe in the therapy, the patient may need to know that her anorexic behaviors will not disappear before she begins to develop other compensatory processes. Severely anorexic patients who have been in and left treatment more than once as part of a lifelong pattern of unsustained relationships may require their therapy to proceed very slowly. The mistrustful patient who cannot comply with others' requests that she gain weight may benefit from her therapist adopting the position of an interested but neutral party with regard to weight gain. The therapist might request that the patient provide the time to talk by not losing any additional weight: "I would like to get to know you. All I ask is that you don't lose any additional weight so that we can continue to talk."

What are the conflicts anorexia nervosa attempts to solve? Anorexic symptomatology can simultaneously represent loyalty to the family and be a manifestation of passive–aggressive rebellion toward the family. It can stabilize the family system. It can be a way of seeking help for the parents. It can convey power. It can hold back suicidal impulses. It can reverse the pressures of sexuality, remove one from relationships, delay growing up, and undo separation. It can make one feel special. It can elevate self-esteem by abstinence, exercise, control, and perfectionism. It can be a way of somatizing anxiety, anger, or the need for help.

What are some of the key features of psychodynamic psychotherapy in anorexia nervosa? Developing an alliance with the anorexic patient is often slow and difficult. The parents of an anorexic child or adolescent may coerce their child into therapy at first, although it becomes the therapist's role to help the patient become curious about her symptoms and to establish a therapeutic alliance. Treatment of adult anorexia nervosa must be voluntary, and involuntary aspects such as mandatory hospitalization must be clearly detailed and spelled out. The therapist must make it abundantly clear that the success of psychotherapy depends on at least minimal nutritional and physical requirements. Patients are often reassured by the therapist's knowledge about anorexia nervosa and are relieved that the therapist is neither minimizing nor repulsed by her symptoms. The therapist should emphasize feelings in the context of a friendly, open, non-judgmental atmosphere. The therapist should clarify that psychotherapy can proceed only with the patient's cooperation and collaboration. It is helpful to describe anorexia nervosa as a puzzling phenomenon and that the therapist will need the patient to take an active role in trying to determine how these symptoms developed and what would facilitate change.

Some features of psychoanalytic therapy may be harmful to the anorexic patient. The silence and neutral stance of traditional psychoanalytic therapy are often understood by the anorexic patient as rejection. Moreover, the anorexic often has a deep mistrust of others and their motives; this distrust is thought to be due to a fundamental problem in the earliest dyadic relationship. Thus the therapist's interpretations may generate considerable discomfort in the patient because of concern regarding how the therapist reached that conclusion, what judgments the therapist is making, and what are the therapist's expectations.

Controversy exists about whether psychodynamic psychotherapy should be initiated with the acutely ill anorexic, because the starved state is associated with poor judgment and the inability to use abstract thought. However, since the development of a therapeutic relationship with the anorexic patient is a slow process, the sooner the building of an alliance is initiated, the better. Moreover, the relationship with the therapist may help the patient tolerate some of the eating, weight, and body shape changes that will be expected of her by the general physicians and dietitians.

TRANSFERENCE

Are there common transferential themes in the psychotherapy with anorexic patients—that is, does the patient have common feelings resulting from early childhood experiences that are projected onto the therapist? As a result of the patient's inability to tolerate any flaws in herself, she may idealize the therapist as she has idealized her parent(s). Such idealization may contribute to the anorexic feeling of being more flawed unless she can be the perfect anorexic. The transference has its benefits and dangers. The therapist may use the idealization to support the patient's acceptance of other potentially useful interventions, such as nutritional counseling or pharmacotherapy. The idealized transference may increase the patient's need to please and might make her feel more subject to being judged and at risk for disappointing others and herself. The therapist has the opportunity to clarify the idealization by being open about his/her "errors," which may allow the patient to become less self-critical. The patient may also experience the therapist as the parent who did all the right things but never really understood her. Such feelings toward the therapist may interfere with the patient's regular attendance at therapy sessions or with her acceptance of the therapist's recommendations. The therapist may respond by being too permissive or by being overcontrolling. Clarification of these feelings frees the patient to accept the therapist's intentions and fosters the growth of interpersonal relationships.

COURSE OF THERAPY

Effective psychodynamic psychotherapy permits risk-taking both in the session and in outside relationships. It is useful to coach the patient on how to interact with others. The therapist can convey such instructions based on an empathic understanding of the patient and not on stock formulas. As the therapy becomes an important proving ground for the patient to test new ways of relating, the therapist should be aware of the real patient–therapist relationship in addition to the transference and refrain from excessively controlling the patient. During the course of therapy, the anorexic will experience the empathic, nonjudgmental understanding of another person; will separate from a pathological family system, if that exists; will resolve her hostile dependent attachment to her parents, should that be present; and will engage in the trials of adolescent psychosexual development in order to enter adulthood with the beginnings of a firm, cohesive sense of self.

What makes psychodynamic psychotherapy for anorexia nervosa distinct from long-term psychotherapy for any other disorder? The disorder is commonly ego syntonic, and the tenacity with which some patients hold onto the symptoms is unique. The potential medical complications and life-threatening nature of the symptoms (see Chapter 47) are unusual for most psychiatric disorders. The enigmatic nature of the syndrome makes therapy challenging. Such intense countertransference responses are uncommon in most psychiatric disorders. Thus it is essential for the therapist to proceed cautiously (and often slowly), to be friendly, to be as open as possible to acknowledging errors, and to be modest about expectations.

Psychodynamic psychotherapy for anorexia nervosa is usually conducted at a frequency of one to two times per week but may vary from once a month to three to four times per week. Some patients will be functioning well after 1 to 2 years of psychotherapy, while others may require up to 8 to 10 years of treatment. Some patients will improve their anorexic symptomatology early in the course of psychodynamic psychotherapy but may warrant additional treatment for a depressive core, for excessive rigidity in noneating spheres of life, for an inability to play, for difficulty in forming intimate relationships, or for family problems. The great majority of patients will substantially improve. Some will be persistently symptomatic, particularly those with greater ego deficits, more comorbidity, and purging behaviors. The psychotherapist should regularly review the status of treatment with the patient and, in the case of a teenager, with the family. Sometimes the use of self-report questionnaires can be helpful in demonstrating change (see Chapter 22). When there are impasses in therapy (and they are likely to occur), the therapist should review the treatment with a trusted colleague and, if the impasse persists, seek a formal consultation. Psychodynamic psychotherapy can be exhausting, but the long-term results are often rewarding for both the patient and the therapist.

FURTHER READING

Bemporad, J. R., & Herzog, D. B. (Eds.). (1989). *Psychoanalysis and eating disorders*. New York: Guilford Press. A collection of chapters covering the etiology of anorexia nervosa from a self psychological perspective, the role of the parents' relationship in the development of anorexia nervosa, and the process of recovery from anorexia nervosa as described in the retrospective accounts of 13 recovered women.

Boris, H. (1984). On the treatment of anorexia nervosa. *International Journal of Psycho-Analysis, 65,* 435–442. The author elucidates the difficulties of analytic work with the anorexic patient, who strives to be free of personal wants and projects her own desires onto others. Helpful approaches for the therapist to use in interpretating these projections are presented.

Bruch, H. (1982). Anorexia nervosa: Therapy and theory. *American Journal of Psychiatry, 139,* 1531–1538. In this article, active patient participation is encouraged, in contrast to a traditional psychoanalytic approach that emphasizes interpretation of unconscious processes. The absence of confirming responses in early mother–child interactions may be related to the effectiveness of initiative, autonomy, and being listened to in the therapy of anorexic patients.

Goodsitt, A. (1984). Self psychology in the treatment of anorexia nervosa. In D. M. Garner & P. E. Garfinkel (Eds.), *Handbook of psychotherapy for anorexia nervosa and bulimia* (pp. 55–82). New York: Guilford Press. Presents anorexia nervosa as a disruption of the self and a disorder of separation–individuation. The therapist's function as a self-object for the patient and the various stages of dynamic individual psychotherapy are discussed, as are associated psychodynamic issues and symptom management.

Herzog, D. B., Brotman, A., & Hamburg, P. (1987). Psychotherapy: An affirmative view. *International Journal of Eating Disorders, 6,* 545–550. Discusses the value of long-term psychodynamic psychotherapy for anorexia nervosa patients, both as a primary form of treatment and as an adjunct to other treatments. The anorexic patient's need for an ongoing therapeutic relationship is suggested by the chronicity, variability, and functional complexity of the disorder.

Johnson, C., (Ed.). (1991). *Psychodynamic treatment of anorexia nervosa and bulimia.* New York: Guilford Press. A collection of writings that include comments on traditional psychoanalytic treatments of eating disorders, interpersonal psychoanalytic techniques, feminist psychodynamic perspectives, and integrative approaches that combine psychodynamic and behavior therapies.

Palazzoli, M.S. (1978). *Self-starvation: From individual to family therapy in the treatment of anorexia nervosa.* New York: Jason Aronson. A review of the historical, diagnostic, sociological, and developmental aspects of the disorder. The author discusses in detail the individual therapy of anorexic patients with attention to such related topics as the anorexic's experience of space and time and the existentialist contribution to the treatment of anorexia nervosa.

Rizzuto, A. M., Peterson, R. K., & Reed, M. (1981). The pathological sense of self in anorexia nervosa. *Psychiatric Clinics of North America, 4,* 471–487. A characterization of anorexia as a particular form of schizoid personality, originating in a disturbance in the "mirroring phase" in which the mother is unable to see the child as a psychic being. Case material and an approach to treatment are presented.

Sours, J. (1980). *Starving to death in a sea of objects: The anorexia nervosa syndrome.* New York: Jason Aronson. A fictional case study of an anorexic adolescent girl, followed by a historical review of the anorexic syndrome and its phenomenological aspects. Four distinct developmental patterns of anorexia are presented, as well as a psychoanalytic treatment approach designed to explore and resolve disturbed ego defenses.

Swift, W., & Stern, S. (1982). Psychodynamic diversity in anorexia nervosa. *International Journal of Eating Disorders, 2,* 17–35. A proposal for a conceptual model for understanding the heterogeneity of anorexic patients consisting of three psychodynamic subtypes of the more severely disturbed patients: those with a concomitant borderline personality organization, those who appear empty and understructured, and those who are emotionally conflicted and identity confused.

• 59 •

INPATIENT TREATMENT
OF ANOREXIA NERVOSA

Manfred M. Fichter

Hospitalization has long been one aspect of the management of anorexia nervosa. William Gull, one of the first physicians to describe the syndrome of anorexia nervosa, recommended hospital admission so that the physician in charge could gain control of the situation. Other early writers like Janet advocated inpatient treatment in order to separate the patient from her home environment (i.e., the parents).

GENERAL ISSUES AND AREAS OF CONSENSUS

Although in former decades many quite different forms of treatment have been described and advocated for anorexia nervosa (ranging from electroconvulsive therapy to treatment with high-dose neuroleptics and from hypophysectomy to psychotherapy), there is today consensus concerning the overall management of the disorder. It is generally agreed that:

1. Psychological treatment/psychotherapy is the treatment of choice (whether on an inpatient or an outpatient basis). However, the philosophical background and treatment school of the therapist appear to be less important than his or her competence and experience in treating eating disordered patients.
2. The patient will gain little benefit from psychotherapy when body weight is very low. Therefore weight gain should be an early goal.
3. It is usually helpful to involve significant others (parents, partner) in the treatment process.
4. Treatment must be adapted to suit the patient's needs.
5. There should be as much continuity of care as possible.

Intensity of Care

Inpatient treatment is the most intensive form of intervention that can be offered to a patient. There has been little research on the relative indications for inpatient and outpatient treatment. Most clinicians agree that in many cases of anorexia nervosa treatment should be conducted at least partially on an inpatient basis. However, when outpatient or day hospital facilities are available, both the necessity for inpatient treatment and the length of stay can be reduced.

INDICATIONS FOR INPATIENT TREATMENT

Serious Physical Complications or Suicide Risk

Some patients come to medical attention because of the consequences of the eating disorder, such as anemia, edema, cachexia, or acute dilation of the stomach with danger of rupture (see Chapter 47), or because of suicidal risk or acts. Such patients should be referred to a specialist knowledgeable about eating disorders so that treatment can be started as early as possible.

Very Low Body Weight and Other Medical Complications[1]

Physicians, therapists, family members, and friends should make it clear to the patient that a very low body weight is unacceptable. Clinicians who are not experienced in the management of eating disorders will want to know at what weight admission for in-patient treatment should be arranged. To decide, several variables should be taken into account. Substantial weight loss will practically always be accompanied by signs of starvation (bradycardia, hypotension, cold extremities when outside temperatures are low, and difficulties in concentration). The selective diet of anorexic patients makes it unlikely that protein malnutrition or neuropathies exists, but over half vomit or abuse laxatives, so that electrolyte disturbance may be encountered. The electrolyte disturbance has usually developed gradually and should not lead to overreaction on the part of the physician, although hospital admission for stabilization may be indicated. Situational variables are also relevant to the decision of whether or not to admit the patient. When weight loss is extreme (body mass index [BMI] below 13) or has been rapid; when other medical complications are present; and when the patient, parents, and others feel unable to control the situation, the patient should be admitted.

Lack of Response to Outpatient Treatment

While some patients respond well to outpatient treatment, others deteriorate or have temporary crises; both these situations may make inpatient treatment necessary.

Outpatient Treatment Is Not Available

When no satisfactory outpatient facility is available, the patient may have to be admitted to the hospital.

Severe Behavioral Disturbance

Hospital admission may help to disrupt persistent behavioral problems such as fasting and frequent bingeing and vomiting. Being in a new environment, and one in which change is reinforced, can help patients make changes that cannot be made on an outpatient basis.

The Need for Separation from the Family or Partner

One reason for hospitalization of an anorexic may be to relieve the burden on helpless relatives. In other cases, such as in families whose members are very involved with each

[1]See also Chapter 47.

other or where relatives express a high degree of negative emotion toward the patient, admission serves to distance the patient from relatives. The patient's problems can then be worked on step by step in a protected atmosphere.

Other Reasons

Hospital admission may be indicated for diagnostic observation, for the treatment of comorbid disorders, to confront the patient with his/her denial, and as preparation for subsequent outpatient treatment. The issue of inpatient versus outpatient treatment is often debated in a dichotomous "either/or" form. However, inpatient and outpatient treatment actually complement each other, and health services should be organized so that the transition from one to the other can be made without major disruption. Many eating disordered patients have relapsed or even died because no appropriate outpatient treatment was available following the end of an inpatient admission.

TREATMENT SETTING

Inpatient treatment should be performed by a trained team of nurses, psychologists, doctors, and other specialists who have experience in treating such patients. It appears that the type of hospital discipline (e.g., psychiatric or general medical) is of less importance than the degree of experience and level of training of the staff. However, since the emphasis of treatment is on psychological approaches, sufficient training of the staff in psychological treatment methods is essential.

DURATION OF TREATMENT

There has been very little research on the appropriate duration of inpatient treatment. Patients who complete inpatient therapy and are discharged at a normal weight appear to have a better prognosis than those who discontinue treatment early. However, inpatients who gain weight as rapidly as possible just to get out of hospital (i.e., by eating their way out of the hospital) tend to relapse and resist rehospitalization.

NATURE OF THE ILLNESS AND PHASES OF INPATIENT TREATMENT

Nature of the Illness

Hilde Bruch, in her important book *Eating Disorders: Anorexia Nervosa, Obesity and the Person Within,* described three main features of anorexic patients:

1. *Body-image disturbance:* The overestimation of body dimensions associated with an intense fear of becoming fat in spite of being cachectic.
2. *Other perceptional disturbances:* Proprioceptive and interoceptive perception and insufficient perception of emotions associated with a dissociation between patients' thoughts and their bodily sensations and feelings. To a large extent these patients are

out of touch with their bodies and emotions and are therefore unable to act appropriately in situations of conflict or stress and when emotions such as anger or loneliness are stimulated.

   3. *An all-pervasive feeling of ineffectiveness:* This feeling may be denied in early phases of the illness. The illness has been described as an (inappropriate) attempt to cope with feelings of inadequacy. By maintaining strict control over their weight, patients feel they can demonstrate control in at least one area of their lives. Fasting or bingeing and purging become the primary response to *all* threatening events; the patient no longer needs to respond differentially. If therapy is to be effective, patients must learn and accept that the illness is not a true solution but a false one; they must get in touch with their bodily sensations and emotions and must learn what their needs are and how these needs can be achieved in a socially acceptable way. The phases of treatment are based on this general background.

Phases of Treatment

Preparation Phase

Anorexics who are being hospitalized for the first time are usually frightened about the new setting and about being under the control of others. Patients who have been hospitalized in the past may have had negative experiences. Since some time often elapses between the initial contact with a physician and the decision to be admitted, this time should be used to inform patients about the treatment so they will have the chance to talk with other patients who have been admitted and to become acquainted with the (inpatient) therapist. A preadmission session and tour through the unit helps dispel patients' irrational fears and thereby encourages them to have realistic expectations.

   Therapists should be flexible in designing individual patients' treatment programs and should pay attention to their fears and preferences. For patients with very low weight, the message must be clear: "We will give you help and support, but we will not let you starve yourself to death." In this early phase, parents, partner, and significant others should also be involved and should (generally) be informed about the strengths and limitations of inpatient treatment. Frequently parents or partners feel guilty, believing they may have done something wrong that caused the patient's problem. They should receive the message that they have done the best they could, that nobody can be blamed for having caused this multifactorial disorder, but that it is important that from this time on the treatment team, the patient, and the relatives must work jointly together. The more transparent the treatment is for patients and relatives, the better they will understand the basis for the treatment approach and the better will be their compliance.

Admission and Start of Inpatient Treatment

Forming a trusting therapeutic relationship is of major importance for the success of treatment. In the early phase of treatment, the therapist must be considerate and sensitive to the patient's needs and anxieties. Once a positive trusting relationship has been established, it can be used to encourage the patient to move in the right direction with determination (achieving weight gain or tackling situations that will arise once the patient has achieved a normal weight, such as being approached by people of the opposite sex).

Main Inpatient Treatment Phase

Anorexic patients have many things to learn. Treatment would not be successful if it merely undermined the patients' defenses. During the main inpatient treatment phase, patients need to accomplish the following:

1. Enhance their bodily perceptions (i.e., get in touch with their bodily sensations and feelings).
2. Learn appropriate ways of expressing emotions.
3. Acquire important social skills (e.g., saying no; drawing clear boundaries; and conveying their own needs, wishes, and decisions to others).
4. Tackle situations that enhance their psychosexual development.

It is not possible to recommend a specific duration of inpatient treatment. It can be relatively brief when the patient is highly motivated to change, when there is no additional psychopathology or family problems, and when good follow-up outpatient facilities are available. Economic factors are also relevant.

To induce weight gain, several different approaches have been used. Dally and Sargant decades ago advocated a triad of neuroleptic medications in high dosage combined with bed rest and feeding through a nasogastric tube. This approach is experienced as threatening and highly aversive by many patients and is clearly outdated. When used by an experienced, well-trained team, behavior therapy with operant reinforcement for weight gain (e.g., access to certain privileges desired by the patient) are effective in practically all patients (Halmi). When they are not effective, it is usually because mistakes have been made by the therapist and the team (e.g., insufficient reinforcement, inconsistency, rifts between team members). Other therapy possibilities include the use of nasogastric feeding (some patients even prefer this method to having to eat more) or total parenteral hyperalimentation. Generally the chronic starvation syndrome and the consequences of purging should not be treated too forcefully: There is increasing recognition of the dangers of too-rapid refeeding, especially when parenteral methods are used. In spite of their severe emaciation, patients with anorexia nervosa are rarely willing to stay in bed when bed rest is prescribed. Whether or not bed rest beneficial has not been assessed.

The patient should be informed in advance about the possible transient side effects of weight gain (e.g., dependant edema and nonspecific gastrointestinal discomfort). Laxative-dependent patients should be withdrawn from laxatives gradually; they should receive a diet with a high fiber content and possibly should be instructed in the technique of stomach massage ("colonic massage").

Crises in treatment occur even in the most experienced units. For example, patients may pretend to gain weight by drinking water or using hidden weights, or they may secretly misuse laxatives. These crises require action, but not overreaction, from the therapeutic team. It should be kept in mind that each crisis is an opportunity for the patient to learn more about his/her illness and to learn to trust others. In such situations, the team should be consistent and clear, but also supportive and not punishing.

At the beginning of treatment the patient may not want to gain weight but may rather want to work on improving of self-esteem and social skills. While the issue of weight gain cannot be put aside for very long, there is—with the exception of life-threatening cachexia—no need to put pressure on the patient right at the start. As time proceeds the patient will understand better why weight gain is important. Also, the fear of gaining weight may diminish with the acquisition of new social skills, so that the patient can more easily be persuaded to normalize eating and gain weight. If the patient fails to eat enough and gain weight, a behavioral weight gain program or medical hyperalimentation (tube feeding) may need to be implemented. In principle, behavioral weight gain programs are very similar to each other. Nevertheless, each program should be designed to suit the individual, incorporating the preferences of the patient as much as possible. Virtually all programs for weight gain in anorexics contain behavior therapy principles at least implicitly. In behavior therapy, these principles are applied systematically. Behavior therapy for anorexia nervosa is often cited in the context of weight programs only. However, present-day behavioral inpatient or outpatient treatment in eating disorders usually employs a wider, broad-spectrum approach that addresses disturbances in perception and expression of emotion, and depressive symptoms and thoughts, in addition to low weight.

Practically all the studies in which the efficiency of different kinds of psychotropic medication for anorexia nervosa have been assessed have shown disappointing results (see Chapter 55). Neuroleptics, antidepressants, lithium, and tranquilizers are all of little value.

While anorexics are experts in counting calories, they usually know little about healthy nutrition. In former decades, talking with the patient about food and eating during therapy sessions was considered taboo in many treatment centers. Today it is recommended that the anorexic patient be informed and educated concerning nutrition (see Chapters 53 and 54). The patient is taught to consume a wide variety of foods containing sufficient nutrients and other essential ingredients and to eat adequate amounts of carbohydrates. Previously avoided foods must be incorporated into their diet. Some treatment programs offer courses in which shopping and cooking truly healthy food are practiced.

Stabilization Phase

In most inpatient programs, patients are encouraged to increase their body weight to at least near their normal weight and to stabilize at this weight. During the weight-stabilization phase (when the BMI is between 19 and 24) patients should be fully educated about eating disorders (see Chapter 53). Treatment centers that specialize in eating disorders have an advantage in that they can usually offer other relevant group therapies, such as an antidieting group, and groups focusing on social skills training; on enhancing interoceptive, proprioceptive, and emotional awareness; and on assertiveness training. Generally families should be involved in the treatment of young anorexic patients and of selected older anorexics who appear extremely involved with their families or partners (see Chapters 38 and 56).

Transition from Inpatient to Outpatient Treatment

As the end of inpatient treatment approaches, many patients become anxious and need support in taking the step from the hospital to everyday life. The transition is easier if there is continuity of care, with the same therapist involved with both the inpatient and the outpatient care. For organizational reasons, discharge from inpatient treatment is frequently associated with separation experiences (separation from other patients, from the therapy team, and from the main therapists). The patient's reactions to these separations should be addressed, especially with patients who are especially sensitive to this issue. Patients must not be allowed to fall into a therapeutic vacuum after discharge: Where necessary, they should receive help in finding an outpatient therapist. Given these patients' "all-pervasive feelings of personal ineffectiveness" (Bruch), problems should be anticipated and possible solutions explored. Once conflicts with parents or partner have been solved, and when better and healthier ways of interaction have been established, the patient will be less vulnerable to relapse.

GENERAL ISSUES AND OBSTACLES

Involuntary Treatment

What should be done when an anorexia nervosa patient refuses treatment? When treatment goes well in a good, trusting patient–therapist relationship, this issue rarely arises. However, it does occur at times. The legal system in most countries makes it possible to commit a severely emaciated anorexic patient to a hospital against his/her will because of the risk of death. However, when an anorexic patient who refuses treatment is forced to gain weight, she may "eat herself out of the hospital" or oppose all constructive therapeutic measures, so that there is little long-term progress. Therefore, compulsory hospitalization should be avoided if at all possible. It takes time and effort to build up motivation in therapy-resistant patients, but it is usually possible to arrive at a point at which they will make their own choice and gradually find a constructive way to deal with their illness (also see Chapter 57). Therapists should do their best to avoid becoming involved in power struggles with their patients.

Staff-Related Problems

Staff who are not experienced in the treatment of eating disorders may be provoked by an anorexic patient's behavior and react in a way similar to that of the patient's family members. When anorexics are deceitful (e.g., hiding laxatives or food, drinking water before being weighed, and vomiting in secret) staff may be tempted to punish the patient. Sometimes such behavior results in divisiveness amongst therapeutic team members. This situation must be avoided. Neither a punitive response nor one of pity will induce maturation and therapeutic progress in the anorexia nervosa patient. Non-judgmental confrontation, in the context of understanding the patient's extreme fears of weight gain and other relevant dynamics, is the approach needed. Anorexic patients usually exhibit pronounced dichotomous thinking (see Chapter 57). Things and people are either totally good or totally bad. Staff must be made aware of this tendency so they can understand and counteract it sensibly.

   Another issue calling for staff sensitivity is that of the feelings of guilt in anorexic families. The parents may have been accused by professionals, neighbors, or friends of being responsible for their daughter's illness. Many parents are highly sensitive to the suggestion that family conflicts may in some way be associated with the illness. The therapist and the rest of the team should maintain an understanding, nonjudgmental attitude toward the patient and her family. It is difficult to enlist the parents' true cooperation and support if they fear they will be blamed.

Another problem may arise in units where there are several anorexic patients. Competition may arise among the anorexics concerning issues such as who eats the least, who loses the most weight, who is the most seriously ill, who needs the most staff attention, who is the most special case, and who is the thinnest. If this situation arises, it should be addressed openly. Well-trained, experienced staff will be able to build up and create a positive climate and structure for change, giving positive reinforcement to those patients who are working constructively in therapy. Positive reinforcement for positive change is much more productive than focusing on acting-out behaviors such as drinking alcohol or acts of self-mutilation. There are many major advantages to treating anorexic patients in specialized eating disorder units that have well-trained staff, whereas in units with few such patients, resentment among the other patients may build up because of the special attention the eating-disorder patients demand. Nevertheless, it must be acknowledged that anorexics with multi-impulsive behaviors (concomitant alcoholism, stealing, deliberate self-harm) can be a real challenge even to well-trained, experienced staff.

FURTHER READING

Andersen, A. E. (1985). Inpatient treatment of anorexia nervosa. In A. E. Andersen (Ed.), *Practical comprehensive treatment of anorexia nervosa and bulimia* (pp. 54–90). Baltimore: The Johns Hopkins University Press. A good account on inpatient treatment of eating disorders.

Bruch, H. (1973). *Eating disorders.* New York: Basic Books. A classic book on eating disorders. Essential reading.

Fichter, M.M. (1990). *Bulimia nervosa: Basic research, diagnosis and therapy.* New York: John Wiley & Sons. Provides an up-to-date account of bulimic syndromes.

Garner, D. M., & Garfinkel, P. E. (Eds.). (1984). *Handbook of psychotherapy for anorexia nervosa and bulimia.* New York: Guilford Press. A valuable book on the various forms of treatment for anorexia nervosa and related eating disorders.

Halmi, K. A. (1984). Behavioral management for anorexia. In D.M. Garner & P.E. Garfinkel (Eds.), *Handbook of psychotherapy for anorexia nervosa and bulimia* (pp. 147–159). New York: Guilford Press. This chapter describes the behavioral approach to the treatment of anorexia nervosa.

Russell, G. F. M., Szmukler, G. E., Dare, C., & Eisler, I. (1987). An evaluation of family therapy in anorexia nervosa and bulimia nervosa. *Archives of General Psychiatry, 44,* 1047–1057. One of the first studies of family therapy as a treatment for anorexia nervosa.

• 60 •

SHORT-TERM PSYCHOLOGICAL TREATMENTS FOR BULIMIA NERVOSA

CHRISTOPHER G. FAIRBURN

There has been considerable interest in the treatment of bulimia nervosa since its emergence in the second half of the 1970s. Indeed, its treatment has been the subject of more than 30 controlled trials. From the outset it has been clear that the great majority of patients can be managed on an outpatient basis. The emphasis of research has therefore been on identifying the optimal form of outpatient treatment, with two approaches attracting the most interest: antidepressant drugs and a specific form of cognitive-behavioral therapy. The current standing of antidepressant drug treatment is discussed in Chapter 55. In brief, these drugs have a beneficial effect in the short-term, but the degree of improvement is not as great as that obtained with cognitive-behavioral therapy and, more important, improvement appears to be poorly maintained. In contrast, the gains made with cognitive-behavioral therapy seem to be well maintained, at least in the short-to-medium term. For this reason, cognitive-behavioral therapy must be regarded as the leading treatment for the disorder.

COGNITIVE-BEHAVIORAL THERAPY

The cognitive-behavioral approach to the treatment of bulimia nervosa was first described in 1981. A detailed treatment manual was published in 1985 and has been periodically revised on the basis of further experience (see "Further Reading").

The treatment is based on a cognitive view of the processes involved in the maintenance of the disorder. According to this view, the disorder persists largely because of the influence of certain cognitive characteristics, specifically a tendency to judge self-worth almost exclusively in terms of shape and weight, the presence of low self-esteem and perfectionism, and a dichotomous ("black-and-white") way of thinking. These features result in patients living in fear of fatness and weight gain, being acutely sensitive to changes in their shape and weight, and continually attempting to maintain strict control over their eating. This dieting creates a vulnerability to binge eating through several interacting physiological and psychological mechanisms (see Chapter 16). For example, these patients react adversely to even minor deviations from their self-imposed dietary goals and typically respond by temporarily abandoning control over their eating and then renewing their determination to diet.

The cognitive view of the maintenance of bulimia nervosa is supported by evidence that among those who have recovered, in behavioral terms, the chances of relapse are directly related to the presence of continuing concerns about shape and weight. Indirect support of this view comes from the finding that purely behavioral versions of the treatment are less effective than the full treatment.

In the cognitive-behavioral treatment of bulimia nervosa a sequence of cognitive and behavioral procedures is used to erode the cognitive and behavioral aspects of the disorder. The treatment has three stages. In the first the emphasis is on helping patients regain control of their eating and on establishing a pattern of regular eating. The main elements are behavioral and educational. The second stage is broader in scope and includes procedures for tackling dieting and the main precipitants of binge eating. In addition, problematic ways of thinking are addressed using standard cognitive restructuring procedures. The third stage is concerned with consolidating progress and ensuring that changes are maintained in the future. In this stage, relapse prevention procedures are used.

Treatment is generally conducted on a one-to-one basis and involves about 20 50-minute sessions over a period of 4 to 5 months. There are advantages to having two sessions a week for the first few weeks; they help to interrupt the habitual binge eating of the more severe cases. Generally the final sessions are held biweekly as treatment is phased out.

The effectiveness of the treatment has been demonstrated in numerous studies. It has been found to be more effective than a variety of other treatments, including behavioral versions of the treatment, exposure with response prevention, supportive psychotherapy, supportive expressive psychotherapy, and treatment with antidepressant drugs. Comparing results across studies is difficult, but it seems that cognitive-behavioral therapy results on average in at least a 70% reduction in the frequency of binge eating and purging, and between one-third and one half of patients cease to binge altogether. Accompanying the behavioral changes are a lessening of the concerns about shape and weight and a marked improvement in psychosocial functioning. Some data are available on the maintenance of change. Several studies have had 6-month to 1-year follow-up periods, and in one study patients were followed up for an average of 6 years. The findings suggest that the changes are well maintained and that relapse is uncommon. Few predictors of outcome have emerged, although patients with severe personality disturbance appear to do less well and are more likely to drop out. Low self-esteem is another poor prognostic feature.

OTHER SHORT-TERM PSYCHOLOGICAL TREATMENTS

Behavior Therapy

Two forms of behavior therapy have been studied. One is a type of exposure with response prevention designed for patients who vomit after binge eating. The therapy involves having such patients eat until the point at which they would ordinarily vomit and then helping them develop skills to resist doing so. Sessions of this type can take several hours and must be practiced repeatedly; they also usually include other behavioral and cognitive procedures.

Not surprisingly, exposure with response prevention is not popular with patients. While it does result in substantial change, there is no evidence that it adds anything to the standard cognitive-behavioral treatment. Exposure with response prevention is therefore not widely used.

The other behavioral treatment is an exclusively behavioral form of the cognitive-behavioral approach. Several versions have been devised, including one designed specifically for dietitians (called "nutritional counseling"; see Chapter 54). On balance, these simplified treatments do not seem to be as effective as cognitive-behavioral therapy. For example, in two studies it was found that while cognitive-behavioral therapy and behavior therapy were comparable in their effects at the end of treatment, there was a tendency to relapse among those patients who received behavior therapy. However, it is important to point out that a proportion of patients do respond to these simplified behavioral treatments. In other words, not everyone needs the full cognitive behavioral treatment.

Psychoeducational Treatments

Psychoeducational therapy is usually conducted in a group setting and involves educating patients about bulimia nervosa and ways of overcoming it (see Chapter 53). The advice generally follows that used in cognitive-behavioral therapy.

Again, for some people education alone is sufficient. Olmsted and colleagues evaluated a particularly unusual form of this treatment, in that it was presented in a lecture format. They found that for the less disturbed patients the results were comparable to those obtained with cognitive-behavioral therapy. However, little is known about the maintenance of change following purely educational treatments.

Focal Psychotherapy

Several forms of focal psychotherapy have been evaluated as treatments for bulimia nervosa including interpersonal psychotherapy (IPT) and supportive–expressive psychotherapy. Interpersonal psychotherapy is a short-term psychotherapy devised originally for the treatment of depression. It focuses on identifying and modifying those interpersonal problems thought to be responsible for episodes of depression. These problems include unresolved grief, disputes with friends or relatives, difficulties forming or maintaining relationships, and problems in coping with life transitions (e.g., leaving home, getting married, or becoming a parent). Interpersonal difficulties of this type are common among patients with bulimia nervosa and may contribute to its maintenance.

To date there has been just one study of the use of IPT in the treatment of bulimia nervosa. It was found that while IPT was not as effective as cognitive-behavioral therapy at the end of treatment, it "caught up" to such an extent that it was as effective 1 and 6 years later. These findings suggest that IPT has a delayed but powerful effect.

Supportive–expressive psychotherapy is another brief psychotherapy. It, too, is designed to address interpersonal issues, but it is not as focused as IPT. Like IPT, it has been the focus of one study. It was found to produce significant change, but the results were not as good as those produced by cognitive-behavioral therapy. No data have been published on the maintenance of change following supportive–expressive psychotherapy.

Family Therapy

Family therapy is not widely used in the treatment of bulimia nervosa. The findings of the one controlled study were not promising, but the patient group was atypical. There are practical obstacles to this form of treatment, since most patients with bulimia nervosa are in their 20s and are living away from their family of origin. On the other hand, there is consensus that the families of young patients should be involved with their treatment.

Group Therapy

For several reasons group therapy seems an attractive way of treating patients with bulimia nervosa. Many patients are demoralized by the thought that she/he is the only person with this type of problem; and because these patients have never before discussed the problem with anyone, it can be difficult to dispel this view. Sharing the problem with others can be helpful by reducing the stigma, shame, and sense of isolation these patients feel. Another advantage of group therapy is that in properly run groups, members can learn vicariously from each other. Treating people in groups also makes practical sense, since much of the education and advice used in the cognitive-behavioral approach is suitable for presentation in a standard form. There are also financial considerations that favor group therapy, since it may be a cost-effective alternative to individual treatment

At present, however, the relative effectiveness of group and individual therapy is uncertain. What is needed are direct comparisons of group and individual versions of the same form of treatment. No such comparisons have been made.

Guided Self-Help

Guided self-help is a new approach to the treatment of bulimia nervosa. It is designed to be an initial intervention in a "stepped-care" program (see below) in which the patient follows a self-help program with the support and guidance of a therapist. The treatment sessions need not be long (no longer than 30 minutes), and there can generally be fewer of them than in more conventional short-term treatments (5 to 10 sessions). Guided self-help has several potential strengths. First, it empowers patients, since they feel they are in control of their treatment. Second, since a specialist therapist is not required, it is suitable for use in primary care. And third, it involves relatively little therapist and patient time.

Two self-help programs based on the cognitive-behavioral approach have been published and may be used in this way. Guided self-help has yet to be satisfactorily evaluated.

STEPPED CARE

What are the implications of the research findings for the overall management of bulimia nervosa? For people who seek professional help, the implications are clear. The treatment of choice is cognitive-behavioral therapy on a one-to-one basis. Most people benefit substantially and, in the majority of cases, the changes appear to last. It is important to add, however, that cognitive-behavioral therapy is not a panacea: Some people do not improve or make only limited gains. For these people, additional or alternative treatments are needed. On the other hand, it seems that others respond to simpler forms of treatment usually involving education and advice.

Some years ago I proposed that a stepped-care strategy be adopted. This strategy involves offering patients a simple treatment first, since there are grounds for thinking that a significant number will respond. Only those who do not benefit move on to the next "step," which involves a more intensive treatment. Again, a significant number are likely to respond. Those who do not move on to the next step, and so on.

This strategy makes obvious sense, but what should the steps be? Guided self-help would seem a good first step. An alternative might be a psychoeducational group, although such groups are difficult to set up in the absence of substantial numbers of referrals. Logically the second step would be the full cognitive-behavioral approach conducted on a one-to-one basis. However, it is less clear what should follow. Possibilities include IPT, drug treatment, and partial or full hospitalization. In the absence of any research on the treatment of those who fail to respond to cognitive-behavioral therapy, the decision must depend on the preferences of the therapist and patient and on what resources are available.

ACKNOWLEDGMENT

C. G. F. is supported by Wellcome Trust Senior Lectureship (13123).

FURTHER READING

Cooper, P. J. (1993). *Bulimia nervosa: A guide to recovery.* London: Robinson. The first self-help version of the standard cognitive-behavioral treatment for bulimia nervosa.

Fairburn, C. G. (1981). A cognitive behavioral approach to the management of bulimia. *Psychological Medicine, 11,* 707–711. The original report on cognitive-behavioral therapy for bulimia nervosa.

Fairburn, C. G. (1993). Interpersonal psychotherapy for bulimia nervosa. In G. L. Klerman & M. M. Weissman (Eds.), *New applications of interpersonal psychotherapy* (pp. 353–378). Washington, DC: American Psychiatric Press. A description of the use of interpersonal psychotherapy to treat bulimia nervosa.

Fairburn, C. G. (1995). *Overcoming binge eating.* New York: Guilford Press. A self-help version of the standard cognitive-behavioral treatment for bulimia nervosa. It is designed for all types of binge eating problem.

Fairburn, C. G., Agras, W. S., & Wilson, G. T. (1992). The research on the treatment of bulimia nervosa: Practical and theoretical implications. In G. H. Anderson & S. H. Kennedy (Eds.), *The biology of feast and famine: Relevance to eating disorders* (pp. 317–340). San Diego: Academic Press. A review of the research on the treatment of bulimia nervosa.

Fairburn, C. G., Jones, R., Peveler, R. C., Hope, R. A., & O'Connor, M. (1993). Psychotherapy and bulimia nervosa: The longer-term effects of interpersonal psychotherapy, behavior therapy and cognitive behavior therapy. *Archives of General Psychiatry, 50,* 419–428. A comparison of three leading psychological treatments for bulimia nervosa.

Fairburn, C. G., Marcus, M. D., & Wilson, G. T. (1993). Cognitive behavior therapy for binge eating and bulimia nervosa: A comprehensive treatment manual. In C. G. Fairburn & G. T. Wilson (Eds.), *Binge eating: Nature, assessment, and treatment* (pp. 361–404). New York: Guilford Press. A detailed description of the cognitive behavioral approach to the treatment of binge eating problems.

Garner, D. M., Rockert, W., Davis, R., Garner, M. V., Olmsted, M. P., & Eagle, M. (1993). Comparison of cognitive-behavioral and supportive–expressive therapy for bulimia nervosa. *American Journal of Psychiatry, 150,* 37–46. The comparison of cognitive-behavioral therapy and supportive expressive psychotherapy.

Olmsted, M. P., Davis, R., Rockert, W., Irvine, M., Eagle, M., & Garner, D. M. (1991). Efficacy of a brief group psychoeducational intervention for bulimia nervosa. *Behaviour Research and Therapy, 29,* 71–83. A study of the effectiveness of a purely educational treatment for bulimia nervosa.

Wilson, G. T., & Fairburn, C. G. (1993). Cognitive treatments for eating disorders. *Journal of Consulting and Clinical Psychology, 61,* 261–269. An account of the nature, effectiveness, and mechanism of action of cognitive-behavioral treatments for bulimia nervosa.

• 61 •

PSYCHODYNAMIC TREATMENT OF BULIMIA NERVOSA

CRAIG JOHNSON

When the editors of this book invited me to write about psychodynamic treatment of bulimia nervosa, I enthusiastically accepted the task. The editors then mentioned they were seeking a rather brief account. I immediately panicked. Parsimony is not one of the cardinal features of therapists who are psychodynamically oriented. Psychodynamic explanations of psychopathology are indeed complex. In essence, psychodynamic theory is an attempt to clarify the unique, multilayered, conscious, and unconscious adaptations individuals make to their environment from birth to death. This attempt to capture the complexity of human development through the life span, however, is both the theory's greatest strength and its greatest weakness. In the theorists' efforts to avoid being too reductionistic, psychodynamic theory may become too complicated and even esoteric, with the result that many clinicians find the conceptualizations unwieldy and not clinically useful. The willingness of psychodynamic theorists to grapple with complexity, however, is one of the reasons I have become progressively interested in the model. Therefore, I have some fear that my effort to be succinct will do a disservice to the richness, complexity, and diversity of thinking represented among psychodynamically oriented clinicians.

This chapter has several sections. I have attempted to highlight aspects of psychodynamic therapy that are unique. In the first section I review how psychodynamic therapists view the development and meaning of symptoms. In the next two sections I discuss the importance of transference and countertransference analysis in resolving these symptoms. In the final section I offer suggestions to aid in the selection of those for whom psychodynamic treatment is most appropriate.

THE MEANING OF SYMPTOMS

Psychodynamic theorists offer a variety of explanations of how normal development and psychopathology occur. Popular contemporary formulations include self psychology, object relations theory, ego psychology, and Jungian theory. In my mind, the thread that binds most of these theories together is the focus on how individuals' interactions with their environment shape the way they think and act, and how over time individuals progressively consolidate a sense of self or identity that regulates these interactions with the environment. This sense of self and other then faces repeated tests of its adaptiveness throughout the various stages of lifetime development. If these patterns are adaptive enough, given the cultural context, and the individuals are content enough with these adaptations, they will neither seek help nor be brought for help. If, however, these patterns are sufficiently maladaptive, symptoms will develop that demand attention. The way in which these symptoms are viewed and treated does set psychodynamic theory somewhat apart from other theories of psychopathology.

Among psychodynamic theorists, symptoms are often viewed as "windows to the mind" of the individual. Symptoms may be conscious or unconscious, perhaps symbolic efforts to communicate the nature and extent of the individual's struggle. Psychodynamically oriented therapists' interest in understanding the symbolic/adaptive meaning of patients' symptoms often results in therapists shying away from directly intervening out of fear that if the underlying deficit or conflict is not resolved the patient will quickly return to the symptoms or substitute other symptoms. For example, the drive for thinness or fear of fat that is characteristic of patients with eating disorders may have a variety of meanings. For some patients the pursuit of a prepubertal look is an active attempt to control a maternal introject that is experienced as intrusive and controlling. Such patients achieve this goal both symbolically and concretely by not allowing their bodies to attain an adult female form similar to that of their mothers. In essence, these eating disordered individuals attempt to control their fear of being controlled by their mothers by refusing to look like the mothers.

If these patients' drives for thinness are an attempt to defend themselves against overcontrol by a powerful outside figure, then the intrusive and aggressive treatment of the symptoms (i.e., rapid weight restoration), without regard for their meaning to the patients, will probably result in their increasing opposition or temporary compliance. Patients who simply comply are likely to return to their previous low weight once they have escaped the treatment setting, or they might engage in purging behavior to undo the experience of intrusive control (i.e., forced calorie intake). In this example, if a well-intentioned therapist makes suggestions or interventions to change these symptoms he/she will most likely experience a range of reactions from the patient that seem inappropriate to the current circumstances. From a psychodynamic perspective, the therapist would be experiencing a transference reaction from the patient that would require analysis. Working through the transference with their therapists would then allow patients to understand these symptoms as their efforts to adapt. This insight, along with the positive relational experience with the therapists, would then free these patients to pursue other, more adaptive, coping strategies. The use of analysis of transference is, once again, a technique that sets psychodynamic treatment apart from other treatments.

INTEGRATING SYMPTOM MANAGEMENT
AND ANALYSIS OF TRANSFERENCE

The term "analysis of transference" may evoke an image of a passive, silent therapist who speaks to the patient only to offer genetic interpretations regarding the patient's unconscious, impulse-laden motives. Although this characterization of psychoanalysis has certainly persisted over the years, I do not consider it a good technique for exploring transference with eating-disorder patients. For me, the term "analysis of transference" is used to describe the process whereby therapists are committed to attempting to understand on an ongoing basis how the patient is experiencing the immediate actions or nonactions of the therapist. This process operates on the assumption that whenever a therapist engages in a therapeutic relationship, patients will respond in ways that reflect their characteristic perceptions of self and others. These perceptions are amalgams of years of interactions with others, some of which may have been quite destructive. Unquestionably these previous experiences with others will bias the patient's experience of the therapist, perhaps in a negative way. Thus, when a therapist offers a symptom management suggestion, the patient may experience that offer in a multitude of ways, some of which might deviate from what the therapist intended. Unless the therapist is alert to this possibility and is willing to process it with the patient, the transference issues arising out of the interpersonal interaction may prevent patients from using the suggestion. I cannot overemphasize the importance of this process in facilitating change for eating-disorder patients. I believe it is this attentiveness to understanding the patient's experience of the therapist that consolidates the therapeutic alliance and allows patients to relinquish their resistance to change.

How transference is allowed to develop and is managed usually differentiates psychoanalysis from psychodynamic psychotherapy. In psychoanalysis the therapist strives to achieve as neutral a "frame," or "therapeutic environment," as possible. The hope is that patients will project upon this "blank screen" their characteristic thoughts and behaviors (transference). The therapist is then able to interpret or make conscious the conflicts or deficits that are troubling the patient. As these conflicts or deficits are resolved, symptoms remit. In this model, the therapist is reluctant to become too active out of fear of biasing the patient's projections. This pure form of psychanalysis has been appropriately criticized for erring too much in the direction of nonactivity regarding symptom management. Many eating disordered patients have been allowed to languish for long periods of time at extremely low weights or to persist in frequent bingeing and vomiting.

I, as well as others, have sought to modify psychoanalytic technique not only to avoid having patients languish symptomatically but also to preserve the very useful concepts of transference and countertransference analysis. I have previously argued that for optimal treatment, the therapist must simultaneously offer patients specific symptom management strategies—cognitive-behavioral (see Chapter 60), psychoeducational (see Chapter 53), psychopharmacological (see Chapter 55), 12-Step—and be prepared to analyze any resistance by patients that may occur, using a psychodynamic perspective. Applying this integrated perspective to the earlier example, the therapist would necessarily try to prevent the patient from continuing to lose weight. This attempt may require progressively restrictive, invasive interventions on the therapist's part. As these interventions unfold, however, the therapist should be prepared to try, thoughtfully and patiently, to understand how the patient experienced and understood the therapist's actions. The very fact that the therapist considers the patient's feelings important is often quite healing.

Psychoanalysts whose practice reflects a purer perspective have argued that activity by the therapist disturbs the therapeutic frame, thus precluding the possibility of analyzing transference. It has been my experience that the introduction of symptom management techniques actually facilitates rather than interferes with the therapist's ability to analyze transference. By using specific cognitive and behavioral skills, the therapist can often help frame a patient's pattern of interpersonal difficulty or illustrate the functional nature of a symptom. For example, giving up binge and purge behavior may allow the patient's feelings to surface or may increase the patient's awareness of expectations about receiving help from others. If therapists are committed to simultaneously offering behavioral symptom management suggestions and understanding the patients' experience of being offered these suggestions, they are in what I consider to be the most favorable position to facilitate change and to analyze patients' resistance to change.

THE IMPORTANCE OF COUNTERTRANSFERENCE THEORY

Countertransference theory has many dimensions to it. Three that I feel are particularly important are discussed below. First, therapists as well as patients have self/other schemas. These schemas affect therapists' relationships with their patients, and it is incumbent upon therapists to monitor how their own psychology might interfere with their patients' growth. Second, a therapist's reactions to a patient are important sources of information regarding the nature and extent of the patient's struggle. Finally, implicit in the concept of countertransference is the acknowledgment that there are two people in the consulting room and that each brings his/her own intrapsychic and interpersonal baggage to the dialogue. The emphasis on a two-person process helps humanize the psychotherapy, which in turn generally strengthens the collaboration between patient and therapist. I am not aware of any other treatment technique that places this level of emphasis on using and monitoring the therapist's reactions to the patient to help understand the patient.

TREATMENT EFFECTIVENESS

The effectiveness of psychodynamic techniques in the treatment of bulimia nervosa has been somewhat hard to assess. The nuances of the technique are difficult to control experimentally, and there are many variations of it. Results of the few studies designed to compare psychodynamically oriented treatment with cognitive-behavioral therapy have shown a slight advantage in favor of cognitive-behavioral techniques. I am not aware of any studies in which the blending of techniques was attempted along the line suggested in this paper.

Overall, the outcome literature reveals that approximately one-half to two-thirds of patients who are offered an informed cognitive-behavioral and/or psychopharmacological intervention respond favorably (see Chapters 55 and 60). I feel that the use of psychodynamic techniques is most relevant to the remaining one-third to one-half of patients who do not fully respond to these briefer approaches. Most of these "difficult-to-treat" patients have significant Axis II personality disorders that need to be managed concomitantly with their eating-related symptoms. The physical and/or psychological traumas they have experienced result in a conflicted or impoverished ability to regulate themselves adaptively and to engage in mature, interdependent relationships. In my experience, psychodynamic theory and techniques have proved to be the most useful model for working with this group of patients.

ACKNOWLEDGMENT

Dr. Johnson's contribution to this book is supported by the William K. Warren Research Foundation, Tulsa, Oklahoma.

FURTHER READING

Bemporad, J. R., & Herzog, D. B. (Eds.). (1989). *Psychoanalysis and eating disorders*. New York: Guilford Press. Traditional psychoanalytic perspectives on the etiology of eating disorders, including obesity.

Bruch, H. (1973). *Eating disorders: Obesity, anorexia nervosa and the person within*. New York: Basic Books. Seminal psychoanalytic work on the etiology and treatment of anorexia nervosa from an ego psychology perspective. The work is a precursor to contemporary objective relations and self psychological theories of eating disorders.

Fairburn, C. G. (1984). Cognitive-behavioral treatment of bulimia. In D. M. Garner & P. E. Garfinkel (Eds.), *Handbook of psychotherapy for anorexia nervosa and bulimia* (pp. 160–192). New York: Guilford Press. Classic formulation of bulimia nervosa using the principles of cognitive-behavioral therapy.

Garner, D. M., & Bemis, K. M. (1984). Cognitive therapy for anorexia nervosa. In D. M. Garner & P. E. Garfinkel (Eds.), *Handbook of psychotherapy for anorexia nervosa and bulimia* (pp. 107–146). New York: Guilford Press. Classic formulation of the treatment of anorexia nervosa using the principles of cognitive-behavioral therapy.

Garner, D. M., Rockert, W., Olmsted, M. P., Johnson, C., & Coscina, D. V. (1985). Psychoeducational principles in the treatment of bulimia and anorexia nervosa. In D. M. Garner & P. E. Garfinkel (Eds.), *Handbook of psychotherapy for anorexia nervosa and bulimia* (pp. 513–572). New York: Guilford Press. A review chapter with information about factors that lead to and perpetuate eating disorders that was meant to be used in manual form to teach patients about anorexia nervosa and bulimia nervosa.

Johnson, C. (Ed.). (1991). *Psychodynamic treatment of anorexia nervosa and bulimia*. New York: Guilford Press. An edited volume that addresses a variety of issues regarding eating-disorder patients from a psychodynamic perspective.

Johnson, C., & Connors, M. (1987). *The etiology and treatment of bulimia nervosa: A biopsychosocial perspective*. New York: Basic Books. This volume is a comprehensive biopsychosocial approach to understanding and treating bulimia nervosa.

Johnson, C. L., & Sansone, R. A. (1993). Integrating the 12-step approach with traditional psychotherapy for the treatment of eating disorders. *International Journal of Eating Disorders, 14* (2), 121–134. Clinical discussion of the advantages and disadvantages of integrating the 12-Step approach into traditional treatment settings.

Schwartz, H. J. (1988). *Bulimia: Psychoanalytic treatment and theory*. New Haven, CT: International Universities Press. This volume represents an ultratraditional psychoanalytic perspective on the etiology and treatment of anorexia nervosa and bulimia.

Selvini-Palazzoli, M. (1974). *Self-starvation: From the intrapsychic to the transpersonal approach to anorexia nervosa*. London: Chaucer-Human Context Books (American ed.: Jason Aronson, New York, 1978; German translation: Klett-Cotta, Stuttgart, 1982). This work is an interesting blend of systemic and objective relations theory regarding anorexia nervosa.

Wachtel, P. L. (Ed.). (1982). *Resistance: Psychodynamic and behavioral approaches*. New York: Plenum Press. A comprehensive theoretical discussion of the interface between behavioral and psychodynamic approaches.

· 62 ·

INTENSIVE BRIEF INPATIENT TREATMENT OF BULIMIA NERVOSA

BRUNNA TUSCHEN
HINRICH BENTS

The intensive brief inpatient treatment[1] of bulimia nervosa is based on the assumption that bulimic symptoms are maintained by a vicious cycle of extreme anxiety regarding body weight and shape, unhealthy strategies to reduce weight (e. g., periods of extreme restrained eating, vomiting, and excessive exercise), and binge eating.

Bulimic patients often start this cycle with restrained eating, which often has its origin in a strong desire to be slim. The idealized body image, for instance, may be a response to low self-esteem, social conflicts, emotional disturbance, or peer-group standards. Restrained eating also produces physiological changes, which in turn may increase the probability of binge eating. It is assumed that dysregulations in the perception of hunger and satiation may also encourage binge eating (see Chapter 43).

Binge eating is often followed by paniclike fears of gaining weight. As a consequence, bulimics try to reduce these fears by vomiting, dieting, abusing laxatives, or exercising excessively. The vicious cycle is thus completed. The binge–diet cycle is also maintained by psychological processes, such as distraction from negative mood states, stress relief, and avoidance of social conflicts. In addition, the social isolation that often accompanies bulimia nervosa may prevent alternative coping strategies and thus maintain the vicious cycle.

Based on an anxiety-reduction model of bulimia nervosa, the intensive brief inpatient treatment focuses on lowering body-weight and shape-related anxieties in order to establish normal eating behavior. Additionally, simultaneously exposing the patient to stressful situations and to binge food that the patient is not to eat effectively reduces the association between stress and binge eating.

THE INTENSIVE BRIEF INPATIENT TREATMENT

With exposure as a main therapeutic strategy, the program is characterized by a short duration of treatment, a focus on target symptoms, and highly individualized interventions. The treatment program has the following phases: assessment, cognitive preparation, exposure and cognitive interventions, and relapse prevention and self-management.

[1]The concept was developed by Brunna Tuschen and Irmela Florin at the University of Marburg.

Assessment

The treatment program starts with a comprehensive psychological and medical assessment that lasts about 2 days. After a psychological screening interview, a medical examination is carried out to identify medical conditions that may require further treatment or—in unfavorable cases—may even preclude the use of exposure therapy.

In the second stage of the assessment process, a semistructured interview is conducted to make the diagnosis of bulimia nervosa and/or other psychiatric disorders on the basis of DSM-IV criteria. In addition, a variety of diagnostic tools, including psychophysiological assessments, measurements of body image disparagement, and a battery of psychometric tests, is used to assess bulimic symptoms and their associated psychopathology.

Based on the results of the assessment, a decision is made for or against exposure therapy. Patients with serious medical diseases, such as coronary heart disease, are excluded; to date, none have been excluded.

Cognitive Preparation

To enhance the credibility of the treatment and facilitate a goal-oriented motivation for therapy, considerable attention is given to the cognitive preparation of the patients. In this therapeutic session (duration: 2 to 3 hours) the therapist and the patient develop a plausible model to explain the etiology and maintenance of his/her bulimic symptoms. The structure of this model is based on the vicious cycle already mentioned, plus some individualized hypotheses concerning the etiology. The specific components of the vicious cycle (e. g., the kind of stressors associated with binge episodes) are personalized.

The aim during the cognitive preparation, as well as during the entire treatment, is to integrate the patient's core assumptions about the etiology of her/his bulimic symptoms into the scientific model. The therapist must avoid disputing the patient's ideas. Rather, the therapist's aim should be to develop the model in collaboration with the patient. A cooperative working atmosphere is, for instance, facilitated by using a flip chart to keep in mind the therapist's as well as the patient's ideas about the factors that maintain the eating disorder. To enhance the credibility of the developed model and facilitate the patient's compliance, the therapist uses specific psychological strategies, including anticipating the patient's doubts, evaluating bulimic symptoms as plausible and understandable, reinforcing the patient's ideas concerning the vicious cycle, and using explanations that may reduce the patient's feelings of shame and guilt.

Based on the resulting model of bulimia nervosa, implications for possible behavior change are cooperatively worked out. Moreover—using, for instance, a so-called mental experiment—possible positive or negative outcomes of treatment are discussed.

The patient is given detailed information concerning the possible effects of exposure therapy. No pressure is exerted on the patient to participate in treatment. The patient is allowed a few days to think about the pros and cons of the proposed treatment program and to decide whether or not he/she will take part. If the patient decides to participate, the intensive phase of treatment starts immediately.

EXPOSURE THERAPY AND COGNITIVE INTERVENTIONS

The inpatient treatment takes 10 to 14 days. It is not unusual for the patient to have direct contact with the therapist for up to 10 to 12 hours per day during the early stages of treatment. The following daily timetable is typical of the beginning of treatment:

8:00 A.M.	Planning the patient's eating schedule and calorie intake (2,000 calories)
9:00	Exposure: Breakfast (500 calories)
10:30	Evaluation and cognitive interventions
11:00	Exposure: Snack (200 calories)
12:00 P.M.	Exposure: Weighing patient, with simultaneous or subsequent cognitive interventions
12:30	Exposure: Lunch (600 calories)
2:00	Exposure: Body image with simultaneous or subsequent cognitive interventions
4:00	Exposure: Snack (200 calories)
4:30	Evaluation and cognitive interventions
5:00	Exposure: Binge food
6:30	Exposure: Dinner (500 calories)
7:30	Evaluation, preparation of evening and next day's schedules

From the very beginning, patients may perform certain parts of the treatment alone. However, close therapeutic supervision is necessary to achieve habituation of anxiety during exposure. A similar program is carried out in the following days but with increased self-control during exposure sessions. The patient is encouraged to experiment with normal eating behavior. The conditions are made as similar as possible to the natural environment. For instance, the patient is confronted with social or mental stressors that typically trigger his or her binges. Throughout treatment the patients keep diaries of their eating behavior as well as their emotional and cognitive reactions.

To achieve habituation effects, the exposure therapy focuses on situations and behaviors that induce the anxieties associated with gaining weight and that increase the patient's craving for binge food: exposure to subjectively "forbidden" food, exposure to binge food, and exposure to specific triggers of binges as well as to body shape and weight.

Exposure to "Forbidden" Food

Patients are confronted throughout the day with "forbidden" food such as high-calorie snacks and normal meals. They are asked to eat this forbidden food and to verbalize its taste, smell, appearance, and consistency. To obtain habituation, any avoidance behavior is prevented. The primary goals of these exposure sessions are to reduce anxiety and enhance self-control over regular eating as well as to encourage the consumption of moderate portions of high-calorie food.

The exposure sessions are repeated several times a day and are performed under various conditions: The patients eat their meals together with their therapist as well as alone or in the company of other patients. Eating takes place in the clinic's cafeteria; in the training kitchen; in various restaurants, even fast-food restaurants; at the patient's home; and, of course, with a broad variety of food.

Exposure to Binge Food and to Specific Triggers of Binge Eating

These therapeutic sessions are designed to achieve habituation of craving evoked by food consumed during binge episodes. The exposure to binge food also takes place at different times of the day and under various conditions. As already mentioned, patients are confronted with a variety of binge foods and must taste, smell, and describe the consistency and appearance of the food. During the sessions, patients repeatedly rate their desire to binge. A session is finished as soon as a steep decrease in the desire to binge occurs.

Considerable attention is paid to the simulation of natural conditions as triggers of craving and binge eating. For example, a patient's binges may be triggered by negative thoughts concerning her inability to become a musician or by accusing herself of being unable to establish stable relationships. In this case, the patient is required to listen to audiotapes in which these negative thoughts are repeated over and over. Simultaneously, prolonged exposure to a variety of binge foods takes place. By repeating these exposure sessions several times a day, the relationship between specific triggers of craving (e.g., negative thoughts) and sensations related to food intake is broken down.

The focus concerning situational triggers of binge eating lies in exposure therapy. If the behavioral analysis reveals distinct skill deficits (e.g., assertiveness problems), components of traditional behavioral programs (e.g., problem solving or assertiveness training) are added.

Exposure to Body Shape

Exposure to body shape is done using a special mirror that provides a full view of the body. A videocamera is also used. At the beginning of the exposure therapy session, patients wear their normal clothes. While standing in front of the mirror or watching the videotape they describe their physical appearance in detail; for example, the size and form of the nose, mouth, hips, breasts, arms, legs, and the color of skin and hair. The therapeutic interventions, such as asking specific questions, modeling, or preventing avoidance behavior, help the patients extend their criteria of self-evaluation regarding body shape and physical attractiveness. Additionally, during the prolonged sessions, anxieties concerning body shape are habituated.

The conditions are varied from session to session. For example, in later sessions, patients wear tight fitting clothes that emphasize their figures. The body confrontation using the mirror is also designed to help the patients recognize and accept the attractive as well as the less attractive parts of their bodies. Patients are therefore encouraged to experiment with their outfits, their hair, and their makeup. To enrich the patients' ideas of their attractiveness, they are also asked to experiment with self-expression (e.g., expressing a positive mood or experimenting with their gestures and facial expressions in interpersonal situations). These sessions, which take place in various situations (e.g., walking through the town, speaking with a waiter) are videotaped. Afterward the videotapes are discussed.

These exposure sessions are always performed by a female therapist or at least are assisted by a female therapist.

Exposure to Body Weight

Weighing is also performed under varying conditions (e.g., weighing in the morning or in the evening or weighing before or after a rich meal). Patients learn that fluctuations in body weight are quite normal, and as the sessions progress, their anxieties decrease. Through this process, the anxiety-provoking cognitions become apparent to the patient and therapist. The therapist focuses on these cognitions during the cognitive interventions.

Cognitive Interventions

The cognitive interventions are guided by a set of specific principles. For example, the therapist never argues against the patient's thoughts or goals, nor does he/she directly suggest alternative cognitions. Instead, one therapeutic principle is to show the patient that his/her assumptions or goals are plausible and not unusual. In light of the patient's cognitive system—for example, the patient's idealization of a slim body shape—behaviors such as dieting and vomiting become understandable.

As a second therapeutic principle, the therapist seemingly incidentally verbalizes possible negative outcomes of certain behaviors or questions whether certain goals may be compatible (e.g., to go on with extreme dieting while reducing craving and thoughts about eating). Through this strategy the patient's internal conflicts become salient. Thus the patient feels a kind of cognitive conflict or cognitive dissonance (e.g., the wish to continue dieting coexisting with the desire to stop binge eating). The therapist then confirms that it is difficult to change one's goals and that it would be understandable if the patient decided not to change his or her goals. As a consequence, changing goals becomes a challenge to the patient, and resistance breaks down.

RELAPSE PREVENTION

During the entire treatment, typical cues in the patient's usual environment that may provoke relapse are anticipated and simulated (see above). To provide the patients with strategies that may help them to cope with relapse, typical dysfunctional feelings and cognitions regarding relapse are anticipated. Using specific cognitive strategies (see above), the patients are helped to interpret relapses as opportunities to practice the newly learned strategies.

SELF-MANAGEMENT

The inpatient treatment phase is followed by a period of 6 to 8 weeks of structured self-management therapy. During this phase, patients live at home and have contact with their therapist by telephone. If necessary, a personal consultation or even a repeated short inpatient stay is possible at any time.

EVALUATION

To evaluate the effectiveness of this form of treatment, follow-ups are carried out 6 weeks, 1 year, and 5 years after therapy. Measures include relevant psychometric assessments of eating behavior, psychiatric disorder, and mood as well as information about the patient's social adjustment. Preliminary results suggest that this intensive brief inpatient treatment, which involves approximately 35 therapist–patient hours, is efficient in facilitating habituation and extinction processes and in preventing avoidance behavior. Thus a high percentage of patients maintain their normalized eating pattern and show a significant decline in their frequency of binge eating. However, based on case reports, patients with severe abuse of alcohol and psychoactive substances, symptoms of anorexia nervosa (e.g., low body weight), and severe psychiatric disorders (e.g., posttraumatic stress disorder) need more therapy sessions and seem to have a higher probability of relapse.

The long-term effects of this treatment have yet to be evaluated. The promising early results will hopefully be maintained in follow-up studies.

DISCUSSION

It can be assumed that the mechanisms described below facilitate change. The exposure therapy is extremely intensive and has almost no time limit. These qualities may help facilitate the habituation and extinction processes. Because avoidance behavior is prevented, patients change their eating behavior quickly, which increases their positive self-evaluation and self-efficacy and elevates their mood.

The repeated and varied introduction of new ways of eating may help the patient review and restructure such cognitive components as expectations about gaining weight, attitudes, and evaluations. This process is supported by specific cognitive interventions that enhance alternative perceptions of, and attitudes toward, body image and interpersonal attractiveness.

The construct of self-efficacy is generally considered to be of fundamental importance for the long-term stability of behavioral change. The process of cognitive preparation and the specific cognitive interventions during therapy continuously focus on the patient's self-efficacy. No external pressure is exerted on the patients to change their goals or thoughts about body shape and weight. Last but not least, the short duration of the inpatient treatment should contribute to the experience of self-efficacy.

In the future it will, of course, be necessary to clarify the relative contributions of each of these and other specific components to the overall treatment outcome. Future research should also focus on the differential effects of exposure therapy in patients with specific comorbidity such as severe personality disorder, dissociative disorder, or self-destructive behaviors. (An alternative approach to the inpatient management of such patients is described in Chapter 63.)

FURTHER READING

Carter, F. A., & Bulik, C. M. (1994). Exposure treatments for bulimia nervosa: Procedure, efficacy and mechanisms. *Advances in Behavior Research and Therapy, 16,* 77–129. A comprehensive review of exposure-based treatments.

Fairburn, C. G., Marcus, M. D., & Wilson, G. T. (1993). Cognitive-behavioral therapy for binge eating and bulimia nervosa. In C. G. Fairburn & G. T. Wilson (Eds.), *Binge eating: Nature, assessment, and treatment.* New York: Guilford Press. A detailed description of the cognitive-behavioral treatment of bulimia nervosa and binge eating disorder.

Fiegenbaum, W. (1988). Long term efficacy of ungraded versus graded massed exposure in agoraphobics. In I. Hand & H.-U. Wittchen (Eds.), *Panic and phobias. Treatment and variables affecting course and outcome* (Vol. 2, pp. 83–88). New York: Springer. Ungraded massed exposure treatment was shown to be more effective in reducing anxiety symptoms than a graded version of the treatment. The exposure treatment program consists of a diagnostic phase, a cognitive preparation phase, an intensive training phase, and a self-control phase. The structure of the intensive brief inpatient treatment of bulimia nervosa was adapted from this exposure treatment program.

Jansen, A., Broekmate, J., & Heymans, M. (1992). Cue-exposure vs self-control in the treatment of binge eating: A pilot study. *Behaviour Research and Therapy, 30,* 235–241. Six obese bulimic patients were treated with cue exposure and response prevention. Another group of six patients was guided to escape the binge-related cues by using self-control strategies. The group treated with cue-exposure showed a higher rate of abstinence regarding binge eating.

Pirke, K. M., Vandereycken, W., & Ploog, D. (Eds.). (1988). *The psychobiology of bulimia nervosa.* Berlin, Heidelberg, New York: Springer. A collection of studies on the metabolic, endocrine, and behavioral aspects of eating disorders and the treatment of bulimia nervosa (including exposure-based treatment).

Polivy, J., & Herman, C. P. (1993). Etiology of binge eating: Psychological mechanisms. In C. G. Fairburn & G. T. Wilson (Eds.), *Binge eating: Nature, assessment, and treatment* (pp. 173–274). New York: Guilford Press. A comprehensive account of the mechanisms underlying binge eating.

• 63 •

INPATIENT TREATMENT OF MULTI-IMPULSIVE BULIMIA NERVOSA

J. Hubert Lacey

Normal-weight bulimia nervosa patients respond well to short, time-limited outpatient treatment programs (see Chapter 60). It is rarely necessary to consider inpatient or day-care programs for these patients. Such programs do have a role, however, when a patient who is otherwise motivated is unable to benefit from outpatient treatment or needs physical care. Such admissions are brief. Longer admissions must be considered, however, when the patient demonstrates significant comorbidity. It is about this latter group that this chapter is concerned.

PREVALENCE OF COMORBID SYMPTOMATOLOGY

The St. George's bulimia clinic is situated in a section of London where the population is demographically representative of a British urban area. The prevalence of self-damaging and addictive behavior in the clinic population, all of whom are from the local area, is extensive—although few need admission. In a recent study, one-quarter of these clinic patients reported consuming over 36 units of alcohol a week, and 8% drank more than 50 units. Just fewer than 30% abused drugs, over one-fifth repeatedly stole, and a similar number had overdosed more than twice. Just fewer than 1 in 10 regularly cut themselves. These behaviors were not random in the patients, and most were statistically associated. Thus alcohol abuse was significantly associated with drug abuse and repeated overdosing; and repeatedly, cutting was significantly associated with drug abuse. Repeated stealing and overdosing did not occur in isolation and are markers of the severity of the illness. When an account of such behavior is elicited from a patient, the clinician must inquire carefully about the full range of the patient's comorbid behavior. In all, 40% of this unselected and representative sample reported comorbid behavioral symptoms. Most of these patients benefit from outpatient treatment, and few need admission. However, for the 8% to 10% of the clinic population who have a severe core disorder, admission is self-evident or becomes so after a trial of outpatient help. These patients I have termed "multi-impulsive bulimics."

Multi-Impulsive Bulimia

Diagnosis

I define these patients as exhibiting at least three of the following behaviors: drinking at least 36 units of alcohol a week; taking heroin, LSD, or amphetamines or purchasing "street" tranquilizers on at least four occasions in the previous year; stealing at least 10 times in the previous year; at least one overdose in the previous year; and severe regular self-cutting or self-burning. These behaviors are associated with a sense of being out of control. The frequency of each may fluctuate, each behavior is interchangeable with another, and each is perceived by the patient as impulsive. The patient's affects are depression and intense anger, which are particularly declared when the behaviors are controlled.

Clinical Features

Multi-impulsive bulimics are older when they first seek help than the majority of bulimia nervosa patients. These women report drifting down the social scale and are less likely than other bulimics to be in employment. They are also less likely to be married or have a stable union. Relationships, when present, tend to be abusive or to be with a "safe" man, that is, with a man to whom they have little commitment. Multi-impulsive bulimics are more likely than other bulimics to have an alcohol-abusing partner or come from a family with a history of alcohol abuse, particularly by fathers. It is this group of bulimics that commonly reports having been sexually abused (see Chapter 40).

Personality

The multi-impulsive bulimic is different from the majority of bulimia nervosa patients who appear to have little personality disturbance (see Chapter 30). Indeed, in articles I wrote in the early 1980s, I described multi-impulsives as "personality disordered," and most warrant such a diagnosis. Lack of control and impulsivity are frequently cited as fundamental elements of the psychopathic or sociopathic personality disorders in the psychiatric literature. Impulsivity forms the first factor in the factor analysis of Hare's checklist for psychopathy. Multi-impulsive bulimics show symptoms that have obvious similarities to the explosive personality disorder described in ICD-9 and DSM-IV. Many might be described as having the hysterical personality disorder described in ICD-10.

It needs to be established whether the multi-impulsive bulimic is merely a variant of the borderline personality disorder (BPD). The DSM-III-R diagnostic criteria for BPD include multiple impulsive behaviors, affective instability, and self-harm. Hostility and impulsive anger are important aspects of BPD, and they are associated with high rates of impulsive self-harm, substance abuse, and eating disorders. It appears that BPD is quite prevalent among alcoholics, and simultaneous diagnoses of eating disorders, mood disorders, and substance abuse are common.

Multi-Impulsive Personality Disorder

Some years ago, I suggested that multiple substance abuse or the combination of dependence, self-damaging behavior, bulimia, and apparent sociopathy might be related to a common mechanism of failure to control impulse behavior (when that behavior is defined as a failure to consider risks and consequences coupled with a lack of deliberation). I argued that within each "uni-impulsive" disorder, (bulimia, alcoholism, drug addiction, and others), there is a distinct subgroup of patients with multiple disorders of impulse control. Such individuals suffer from a "multi-impulsive personality disorder." The term is essentially shorthand, but the distinction between it and the uni-impulsive disorders is based on the previous or current evidence of other areas of impaired control, such as repeated self-harm, overdoses, or alcohol or other substance abuse. This theory has received support in a variety of studies, and, indeed, in eating-disordered patients impulsivity has been shown to be a predictor of long-term outcome.

THE TREATMENT PROGRAM

Although multi-impulsive bulimics constitute only a minority of the bulimic patients attending the eating disorders clinic, they present a major treatment problem. The recognition of the diagnosis of multi-impulsive bulimia has facilitated the development of treatment methods that give more importance to the management of delayed gratification and control of impulsivity than is possible in the outpatient clinic. This recognition has allowed the development of treatments to deal with the interchangeable nature of the symptoms. If the binge eating of the multi-impulsive bulimic is addressed in treatment, the patient moves to self-harm or drug abuse. Such symptom substitution tends to thwart therapies, and, in my view, only by focusing on all symptoms simultaneously can the underlying psychopathology be tackled.

The treatment program described below is one attempt to deal with this problem. It is suitable not only for multi-impulsive bulimics but also for patients with multi-impulsive personality disorder who are attending alcohol- or drug-dependence clinics.

Initial Assessment

All patients are assessed by questionnaire and interview. In the questionnaire the severity and duration of all symptoms are explored and linked to life events and emotions. The questionnaire provides a full personal, family, menstrual, and sexual history. During the subsequent interview, the diagnosis is confirmed, a psychodynamic formulation is made, and motivation is engendered. A preadmission visit provides the prospective patient the opportunity to meet other patients with whom she can discuss the program. As a result of the visit, the patient makes her own decision about entering the program. Many spend considerable time on the waiting list, and during this time they are seen regularly, but infrequently, in the outpatient clinic. These visits are not part of "treatment," rather, they engender motivation and are educative.

The patient joins 10 other multi-impulsives among a total of 23 eating-disordered inpatients and day patients at the Atkinson Morley Hospital (St. George's Hospital Medical School).

The program consists of four stages: a 2-week assessment period, a 16-week inpatient treatment program, a day-patient program over a 15-week period, and a follow-up program.

Inpatient Assessment Period

Each permanent member of the clinical team meets and assesses the new patient to assist in determining her suitability for the full program. Of note are the patient's motivation and insight, as well as her ability to engage on a deeper psychological level. Her reactions to the restraints placed on her are assessed, as is her behavior in groups. The patient in turn assesses the program and her own suitability. To this end, she is helped by her key nurse. Together they determine and write down the psychological and social aims of the patient's admission.

At the end of the assessment period, the patient is discharged if continued admission is unwanted or thought inappropriate; either situation is rare. However, occasionally a patient returns to attending the outpatient clinic and awaits readmission when her motivation is more manifest. Should the joint decision (i.e., the patient and staff together) be for continued admission, the patient agrees to the verbal contract to take part in the full nursing and dietary program, the ward psychotherapy program, and the occupational therapy program.

Inpatient Treatment Program

The Contract

The contract is verbal and rests between the patient and all members of the team. The patient agrees not to binge eat, vomit, or attempt to lose weight; not to be violent to herself, others, or hospital property; not to use unprescribed drugs; not to drink alcohol on the unit (and, if alcohol abuse is an issue, off the unit as well); not to form any sexual relationships on the unit; and to become actively involved in the treatment program. The patient knows that if she does not adhere to this agreement, her admission is jeopardized.

The Nursing and Dietary Program

With the key nurse, the patient examines her diet and food diaries and discusses the feelings they engender. Initially menus are controlled by the staff, but gradually, according to a set schedule, choice is returned to the patient. The patient contracts to eat a prescribed diet, the aim of which is to establish a normal eating pattern: three balanced meals, each containing adequate amounts of carbohydrates. The patient uses a food diary to record all food eaten and any binge eating, vomiting, or associated thoughts and feelings. She is expected to take the diary with her everywhere and to record events as they occur, rather than at the end of the day. She works through this diary with her key nurse, who is the primary staff member helping the patient with the dietary program.

The patient is weighed twice a week. She is expected to maintain her weight within a weight band that is set at 1 kilogram above and below that of the fourth weighing after admission. This weight band allows for rehydration following normal eating, as well as the giving up of vomiting and laxative abuse.

The key worker gives day-to-day support and encouragement and counseling on present-day issues and also acts as the patient's advocate. He/she guides the patient, directing emotions to the appropriate therapies, and plays an important role in educating the patient about her illness. Since the key worker and the patient have a close relationship, the former is in a good position to confront the patient if she returns to her old ways. It is explained to the patient that she is putting her emotions into behavior rather than into the psychotherapies being offered. If this problem persists, the patient leaves the unit temporarily for a week of "time out."

Time Out

Time out is not ordered lightly. The decision is made during the ward round, with the patient and staff present. It is not punitive but gives the patient the option of determining whether she is ready to pursue the treatment. It is emphasized that it is in no sense a failure if she decides she cannot return to the unit, and she is told that outpatient support will be provided. The patient is given questionnaires designed to help her identify other options she might have chosen instead of the addictive or self-damaging behavior. The questionnaires are designed to examine feelings, attitudes, and options. This period of rustication is insisted upon even if the patient has suicidal ideation. The patient knows that any self-damaging behavior while she is at home will lead to immediate discharge. Usually, after a week away from the unit, the patient returns determined to regain control.

Occupational Therapy Program

The occupational therapy program is designed to help patients overcome the fear of eating and the fear of eating with others. It addresses low self-esteem and encourages pride in self and body.

Shop/Cook Group and Shop/Clothes Group

The patient shops for food that may include previously (self-) forbidden or binge foods. She learns to prepare and feed herself appropriate amounts without anxiety. The shop/cook group and its associated shop/clothes group are under the overall control of the occupational therapist, with the support of the nursing staff and dietician.

Communication and Assertion Group

This group uses interaction exercises, role play, social-skills training, and anger management. The group facilitates communication and addresses low self-esteem. Patients are asked to set personal goals and are encouraged to give regular feedback to each other.

Leisure Group

A wide range of creative therapies such as enameling, pottery, and batik are used. The aims include helping the patient socialize and interact, working on problems of impulsivity and frustration when faced with a practical task, increasing concentration and attention, learning new skills, working at problems of perfectionism and failure, and learning realistic goals.

Movement Therapy

Among the issues commonly examined are the patient's personal feelings about her body, sexuality, and taking initiative and her fears of physical contact and self-expression. Self-massage or paired massage is used.

Exercise Group

This therapy is introduced cautiously. The aim is to have the patient experience exercise as a means of relaxation and enjoyment rather than as a form of weight control. Swimming and team sports are encouraged.

Ward Psychotherapy Program

The unit is run on milieu therapy lines. The patient is encouraged to analyze her behavior on the unit. Staff endeavor to explore the underlying psychological processes that determine the patient's interaction with peers and staff and feed this information back to her. There are numerous ward meetings, some practical, some interpretive. Emergency meetings are called for crisis management.

The patient's treatment aims are repeatedly reassessed, and she is assisted in developing alternative coping mechanisms to deal with distress.

Psychodynamic Groups

There are twice-weekly groups facilitated by the nurse and the ward doctor. In these sessions, group-analytic principles are used and are under the supervision, via a one-way screen, of a psychodynamic psychotherapist. There are separate groups for day patients.

Topic Groups

These groups are cognitive-behavioral in orientation, and there are separate groups for inpatients and day patients. The groups are run by a psychologist with a variable coleader, and each topic runs for 4 to 6 weeks. The topics include fathers, mothers, families, sexuality, separation and loss, and food.

Individual Psychotherapy

As the eating disorder and other impulsive behaviors are becoming controlled by the ward regime, underlying emotional issues emerge. Each patient has weekly psychodynamic psychotherapy beginning at the third week of the program (entrance into the inpatient program) and ending at the end of the day-patient program, making an average of 30 sessions. With the development of a therapeutic relationship, use is made of the transference, and emotional factors associated with the development and maintenance of the disorder are revealed.

Art Therapy

The techniques of art therapy and psychodrama have been developed to a particular level of sophistication on the unit. They are designed specifically for multi-impulsive patients. In art therapy, patients are helped to find ways of expressing conflicts externally through an art medium such as paint, crayon, or clay. Art therapy allows for alternative means of communication and self-expression and is particularly useful for those patients who find verbal work intimidating. The patients work together to help each one explore her own work in depth.

Psychodrama

One patient in each session explores a personal issue, such as a family relationship, anger, feelings about her body, or sexual abuse. The enactment of various scenes helps all patients trace the roots of a particular issue within themselves as well as explore habitual maladaptive patterns in order to effect changes.

Outside Groups

Patients with alcohol or drug problems are encouraged to attend Alcoholics Anonymous (AA) or similar groups.

Didactic Lectures

Patients attend didactic lectures given by speakers (who may or may not be associated with the hospital) on bulimia, alcohol abuse, the physical complications of eating disorders, media exploitation of women, and other pertinent subjects.

Day-Patient Program

Patients attend at least 60 sessions of day-patient treatment over the course of 15 weeks, each session lasting half a day. These sessions follow discharge from the inpatient program. A minimum of four sessions must be attended each week, one of which must be the day-patient psychodynamic group and one the day-patient topic cognitive group. The program is tailored for individual needs. Patients usually continue with psychodrama and art therapy, and their individual therapy is maintained. The day-patient psychotherapy group concentrates on the difficult transition to day-patient and, subsequently, outpatient status.

Follow-Up Outpatient Support

Patients are seen regularly but infrequently (monthly to every 3 months) by a joint medical and nursing team. Some patients continue with their individual therapy, but this rarely extends beyond 15 weeks. The patient may attend an outpatient support group specifically geared for multi-impulsive patients. This group operates as a drop-in center. The organizers of the group may refer a patient for relapse-prevention courses during difficult periods. Some patients are encouraged to attend AA. A small percentage of patients, who are likely to benefit from ongoing psychotherapy, are referred to the psychotherapy department.

Efficacy of Treatment

Two follow-up studies have been conducted on this treatment program. Details of the article describing the first study are given in the "Further Reading" section. The second, and major, study involved reinterviewing patients 3 and 9 years after admission. Their symptoms and life-styles had changed profoundly, with statistically significant reductions in the severity and frequency of measured behavior. All patients claimed to have benefited from treatment, with few engaging in self-harm during the follow-up period, whether cutting, burning, or overdosing. Only a minority continued with alcohol or street-drug abuse, and the episodes were more circumscribed. All were in employment or caring for children. Most were capable of sustaining a relationship. All had women friends, and most were, or felt capable of, sustaining a relationship with a man. No relationship was abusive. Details are to be published shortly.

CONCLUSION

Inpatient and day-care programs are necessary only for bulimic patients who show substantial comorbid behavioral dysfunction. Multi-impulsive patients can give up their self-damaging, addictive, and eating-disordered behavior during the treatment program described in this chapter, and these benefits are maintained over many years. The treatment is lengthy and expensive, but insurers and national health purchasers will accept claims for this treatment if the overwhelming majority of normal-weight bulimic patients are treated briefly, effectively, and cheaply in the outpatient department (see Chapter 60).

FURTHER READING

Evans, C. D. H., & Lacey, J. H. (1992). Multiple self-damaging behavior among alcoholic women: A prevalence study. *British Journal of Psychiatry, 161,* 643–647. A prevalence and clinical study in which the similarities between alcoholic and eating-disordered populations are demonstrated.

Johnson, C., Tobin, D., & Dennis, A. (1990). Differences in treatment outcome between borderline and non-borderline bulimics at one-year follow-up. *International Journal of Eating Disorders, 9,* 617–627. Good on management issues.

Lacey, J. H. (1992). Homogamy: The relationships and sexual partners of normal-weight bulimic women. *British Journal of Psychiatry, 161,* 638–642. A necessary introduction to one of the major problems faced in therapy.

Lacey, J. H. (1993). Self-damaging and addictive behavior in bulimia nervosa: A catchment area study. *British Journal of Psychiatry, 163,* 190–194. A detailed clinical description of patients of the type admitted to this inpatient program.

Lacey, J. H., & Evans, C. D. H. (1986). The impulsivist: A multi-impulsive personality disorder. *British Journal of Addiction, 81,* 641–649. The first published paper referring to the multi-impulsive bulimic and setting the clinical problem in the context of other self-damaging behavior.

Lacey, J. H., & Read, T. R. C. (1993). Multi-impulsive bulimia: Description of an inpatient eclectic treatment program and a pilot follow-up study of its efficacy. *Eating Disorders Review, 1,* 22–31. The only published report on the efficacy of the treatment described in this chapter.

Waller, G. (1994). Childhood sexual abuse and borderline personality disorder in the eating disorders. *Child Abuse and Neglect, 18,* 97–101. An excellent research paper that introduces the reader to the association between childhood sexual abuse and borderline personality disorder.

Westen, D. (1991). Cognitive-behavioral interventions in the psychoanalytic psychotherapy of borderline personality disorders. *Clinical Psychology Review, 11,* 211–230. A valuable multimodel approach to therapy with patients with borderline personality problems.

Wonderlich, S. A., & Swift, W. J. (1990). Borderline versus otherpersonality disorders in the eating disorders: Clinical description. *International Journal of Eating Disorders, 9,* 629–638. A good, broad description of personality disorders in patients with eating disorders.

• 64 •

ASSESSMENT AND TREATMENT OF BODY IMAGE DISTURBANCE

James C. Rosen

"Body image" refers to a person's mental image and evaluation of his or her physical appearance and the influence of these perceptions and attitudes on behavior. A disturbance in body image is one of the essential features of anorexia nervosa and bulimia nervosa (see Chapter 23). Although abnormalities of eating behavior can occur in other mental disorders as well, the unique aspect of anorexia and bulimia nervosa is the meaning that eating has for the patient in relation to her concerns about body weight and physical appearance.

BODY IMAGE IN THE DEVELOPMENT OF AND RECOVERY FROM EATING DISORDERS

Of all psychological factors that are believed to cause eating disorders, body image dissatisfaction is the most relevant and immediate antecedent. Weight control is the patient's remedy for the defect she perceives in her appearance and is secondary to the body image problem. The importance of body image has been confirmed in longitudinal studies of at-risk populations. Fluctuations in eating disorder symptoms over time in adolescent girls are best predicted by body image. Other psychological variables believed to be important in the etiology of eating disorders, such as psychopathology, stress, and family dysfunction, are associated with concurrent symptoms but add little to the prediction of eating disorders over time after controlling for body image.

Starvation, binge eating, vomiting, and other eating behaviors are typically the most obvious and frightening problems for eating-disordered patients and their loved ones. Consequently, these behaviors are generally the immediate targets for intervention, especially in cases of life-threatening weight loss. However, patients may gain weight in the hospital or stop vomiting for many reasons other than having come to terms with their underlying body image disorder. Without significant body image change, maintenance of recovery will be a struggle. The importance of body image in recovery from eating disorders has been confirmed in studies of treatment outcome: Body image is the most consistent predictor of improvement and relapse after treatment for anorexia and bulimia nervosa. Also, a program that targeted only eating and vomiting behavior in bulimia nervosa was dramatically inferior to one that also targeted body image attitudes (see Chapter 60).

DEVELOPMENT OF BODY IMAGE DISORDER

The following cognitive behavioral model of body image disorder is based on case studies of anorexia and bulimia nervosa and body dysmorphic disorder (BDD). No prospective, longitudinal studies of body image disorder are available at present. The literature on BDD is relevant because it, too, is a body image disorder, and the clinical features overlap considerably with those of anorexia and bulimia nervosa.

All individuals are exposed to cultural messages about physical appearance, but only a small number develop serious body image disorders (see Chapters 15 to 17). Therefore it is important to examine individual risk factors. Adolescents who have distinctive physical features (e.g., obesity, early maturity) often receive much attention because of their physical development, triggering self-consciousness. The risk of developing a body image problem is even greater if this attention is coupled with especially negative feedback or more traumatic incidents such as being teased or humiliated for one's looks or being sexually assaulted (see Chapter 40). These experiences can trigger dysfunctional assumptions about the normality of one's physical appearance and its importance to personality, self-worth, and acceptance.

Several mechanisms maintain the preoccupation with appearance. The patient rehearses negative and distorted self-statements about physical appearance to such an extent that they become automatic and believable. Avoidance behavior prevents the patient from habituating to the sight of her appearance, especially in social situations where there is the possibility of attention from other people. Finally, checking behavior may provide immediate relief but, in the long run, keeps the person's attention focused on aspects of appearance that elicit anxiety.

ASSESSMENT AND TREATMENT OF BODY IMAGE IN EATING-DISORDER PATIENTS

Most popular body image questionnaires have acceptable reliability and validity, but their usefulness in assessing eating-disorder patients is limited. The attitudes assessed are superficial complaints of body dissatisfaction (e.g., "I feel dissatisfied with the shape of my body"). Body image behavior is not assessed, especially repetitive checking behavior and avoidance of situations that provoke self-consciousness about appearance. Preoccupation with physical features other than weight or body shape is not assessed. No objective criterion is provided for a pathological degree of body image symptoms, and the questionnaires are not directly comparable to the DSM-IV diagnostic criteria pertaining to body image symptoms in anorexia and bulimia nervosa. Recently my colleagues and I developed a more clinically oriented measure, the Body Dysmorphic Disorder Examination, that taps into the full range of body image disorder symptoms and addresses these limitations.

Types of Appearance Complaints

Initially it may seem that the patient is simply concerned about her overall weight or body shape. However, with further questioning, body dissatisfaction usually can be localized to specific areas. Thighs, abdomen, and buttocks are the most common areas of complaint. Breast size or shape, facial features, and skin blemishes are common as well. Other complaints that occur with some frequency concern head or body hair, aging, scars, teeth, height, hips, arms, and hands. Reducing body dissatisfaction to specific perceived defects makes the problem more concrete and available for cognitive intervention. Awareness of other types of appearance concerns will help the patient understand that losing weight will not eliminate all her negative body image feelings and that the problem is preoccupation with appearance in general.

Body Image Distortion

To measure the sensory–perceptual disturbance of body image, the subject estimates her body size with some type of adjustable marker. Relative to an objective measurement of body dimensions, the eating-disorder patient typically overestimates her size, indicating that she sees herself as out of proportion and bigger than is realistic. These and other sensory distortions are even more pronounced when body image is challenged by eating, physical activity, or wearing certain clothes. Showing the discrepancy between her real and imagined size can help persuade the patient that body image is a subjective experience and that feelings of being huge or misshapen do not necessarily correspond with actual appearance.

Size-distortion techniques have acceptable reliability, correlate significantly with other body image measures, and show change in conjunction with treatment. However, they do not always discriminate eating disordered women from other weight-preoccupied women. There are other limitations: (1) size distortion is measured during resting conditions as if it were a trait rather than a state variable that fluctuates with exposure to body image challenges; (2) size distortion is not the only type of sensory–perceptual abnormality in eating disorders, but experiences such as exaggerated visceral sensations would be difficult to measure; and (3) the cognitive processes that control body image distortion are uncertain.

Body Image Attitudes

Eating-disorder patients are either dissatisfied with their appearance or fear they might easily become unattractive, repulsive, deviant looking, and so on, if they were to gain weight. What follows is a typical cognitive scenario: Intrusive thought of body dissatisfaction; other people will notice the defect and be critical; the relationship will be damaged; and the physical defect is visible proof of a defect in character. To facilitate cognitive therapy, the patient should keep a body image diary and record situations that provoke concerns about appearance, body image beliefs, and the effect of both on mood and behavior. Eventually the patient should be taught to recognize maladaptive thoughts and to record adaptive thoughts in the diary.

The patient can make "body talk"—such as, "I don't like my disgusting jelly belly"—less negative by switching to more self-accepting, objective, yet believable self-statements. For example, "My stomach is round and soft." Distraction by focusing on more pleasing aspects of appearance is also useful. Ultimately intrusive body thoughts are difficult to suppress completely, and some degree of this type of thinking is normal. Therefore therapy should help the patient correct the more damaging beliefs concerning self-worth that trigger feelings of shame and embarrassment. In particular, attention might be focused on beliefs that physical appearance proves the patient is unlovable, foolish, stupid, lazy, incompetent, lacking in self-respect, promiscuous, immoral, disgusting, and so on. For obese bulimics, do not discount the fact that their thoughts of discrimination because of their obesity are based on reality (see Chapter 73). However, help them to develop more self-enhancing attitudes in response to these negative experiences and to learn not to exaggerate or accept negative stereotypes about obesity.

Body Image Behavior

Despite being preoccupied with weight, most eating-disorder patients avoid looking at their own bodies or do so only with great distress. Before she is asked to confront even more frightening situations, the patient needs to feel comfortable with the sight of her appearance in privacy. The patient should gradually expose herself to a hierarchy of distressing aspects of appearance, first in her imagination and then in reality, with a full-length mirror, clothed and unclothed. Negative body talk should be replaced with nonjudgmental self-descriptions.

Examples of other exposure assignments are wearing a form-fitting outfit, being nude in front of others, not hiding the stomach with folded arms, exercising in public while wearing workout clothes, eating in public, accentuating a distressing feature (e.g., wearing a colorful necklace around a fat neck), and not only trying on clothes in stores but also asking sales clerks for feedback. Such assignments should gradually be made more difficult, for example, by varying circumstances such as the familiarity of the people involved, physical proximity to others, and the type of social interaction (e.g., wearing a bathing suit in the backyard as opposed to a public swimming pool).

Self-defeating body-checking behaviors should be reduced. Some ways of doing so are to set a fixed time for dressing; to refrain from multiple changes of clothes; to stop asking people for reassurance; to stop comparing one's appearance with that of other people; and to eliminate excessive measuring with weight scales, tapes, or special clothes. An exposure-plus-response prevention format is needed when the anxiety and urge to check are strong. For example, a patient might first accentuate her desire to check by tucking in her blouse or eating and then refraining from self-inspection in the mirror.

CONCLUSION

Surprisingly, body image has been neglected in treatment studies of eating disorders, and there is much more to learn about this important component of anorexia and bulimia nervosa. The cognitive-behavioral treatment model described here has been evaluated with several different populations and has proved to be more effective than nondirective educational or supportive therapy approaches. A thorough assessment and treatment of body image will greatly facilitate recovery from eating disorders.

FURTHER READING

Cash, T. F. (1991). *Body image therapy: A program for self-directed change* (Audiocassette series including client workbook). New York: Guilford Press. A cognitive-behavioral program for the patient to use in conjunction with therapy.

Cash, T. F., & Pruzinsky, T. (Eds.). (1990). *Body images: Development, deviance, and change.* New York: Guilford Press. Covers the entire field of body image and its manifestation in different clinical populations.

Rosen, J. C. (1992). Body image disorder: Definition, development, and contribution to eating disorders. In J. H. Crowther, D. L. Tennenbaum, S. E. Hobfoll, & M. A. P. Stephens (Eds.), *The etiology of bulimia: The individual and familial context* (pp. 157–177). Washington, DC: Hemisphere Publishing. Detailed presentation of the concept of body image disorder in eating disorders.

Rosen, J. C. (1995). The nature of body dysmorphic disorder and treatment with cognitive behavior therapy. *Cognitive and Behavioral Practice, 2,* 145–168. A review of body dysmorphic disorder, a condition similar to body image problems in eating disorders, and details on treating body image disturbance.

• 65 •

THE MANAGEMENT OF PATIENTS WITH INTRACTABLE EATING DISORDERS

Joel Yager

Despite advances in treatment, many patients with eating disorders have intractable problems. Such cases may or may not have seemingly volitional components: Some patients are unable to recover in spite of their best efforts, good motivation, and excellent treatment. Others avoid treatment for reasons that may be capricious. Some may try to maintain a sense of self-efficacy by convincing themselves that they *want* their symptoms. Discussions of factors that augur poor prognoses appear in Chapters 41 and 42.

Intractability may take several forms: unremitting core symptoms with persistent psychological, behavioral, physiological and/or social impairments; repeated relapses and clinical instability; and complicating comorbid conditions. Some patients maintain high social functioning despite severe, ongoing eating disorder symptoms; whereas others, with fewer eating disorder symptoms *per se,* remain impaired. Intractability may be related to such factors as the nature and intensity of eating disorder symptoms, temperament and personality, coping styles, enduring attitudes, comorbidity, and the quality of social supports. Clinical improvement occasionally occurs even in patients who have suffered for many years. Exactly what accounts for unexpected turnarounds in such patients is uncertain: Hopelessness can never be predicted with complete certainty.

THERAPEUTIC GOALS

Treatment goals are relatively easy to establish for patients exhibiting acute deterioration such as life-threatening medical problems in habitually marginal patients. These goals may be achieved through short-term, life-saving interventions, with or without the patient's cooperation, via hospitalization and nutritional support. Therapeutic goal setting may be more difficult for long-term, intractable problems. Clinicians must avoid both grossly overestimating what achievements are possible and underestimating the patient's potential. Clear goals are needed for weight gain or maintenance; for reducing specific psychopathological features such as obsessional thinking, rituals, depression, anxiety and panic attacks; for reducing specific physical symptoms; for improving social

374

functioning; and so forth. Although improvement in one area may bring improvement in others, no assurances exist that general recovery will occur even when seemingly central problems abate, such as malnutrition and anorexic attitudes.

When facing intractable problems, clinicians must take special care to monitor any propensity they may have for undue therapeutic zeal. Clinicians should avoid naively attributing intractability to inept treatment at the hands of former caregivers, immodestly assuming that they can do better, and overreaching in therapeutic goals. Unrealistically high expectations may generate terrible performance pressures in patients, resulting in even greater shame, guilt, resentment, hopelessness, sense of failure and, occasionally, suicide. Similarly, when patients fail to improve, clinicians may feel defeated, self-critical, and resentful toward the patients; these emotions may result in the clinician blaming the patient and in therapeutic neglect.

On the other hand, setting therapeutic expectations too low may lead to inadequate attention to patients and sometimes to unintentional attempts to undermine patient behaviors that might actually represent positive changes. Steering between these two poles requires constant assessment; setting and resetting explicit, modest, stepwise goals; and consolidating gains along the way. Previously untried treatments may be offered if clinician and patient (and often family) agree that the potential advantages clearly outweigh the foreseeable risks. The clinician must be particularly thoughtful when the patient's goals differ from those of the clinician and/or family, as when the patient desires to be left alone but the family wants aggressive intervention. If the patient is not in acute danger and accepts herself as unlikely to change, the clinician should still describe the remaining treatment options. Should the patient reject them all, the most humane course may be to accede to her wishes without punishing her and help the family accept the situation. The following specific strategies may be helpful:

- Efforts should be made to establish the heartfelt rapport necessary for durable, effective working alliances. Lacking this rapport, attempts to help may be experienced as coercive fights for control and be therapeutically futile.
- Fully review previous treatments, and seek the patient's, clinicians,' and family's explanations for the successes and failures of each past approach.
- Assess the patient's current goals, expectations and explanations regarding the likelihood of the success or failure of future treatments, as well as the patient's concerns about treatment. Assess the extent to which the patient's desire to be left alone may reflect her depressive distortions of realistic prognostic appraisals. Where possible and appropriate, treatment should mirror the patient's requests.
- Clinicians should never impose any treatment that may put patients at undue risk. Patients and families should give full informed consent regarding all interventions and should not be coerced into accepting any expensive or time-consuming treatment that is unlikely to effect much sustained improvement. When an unorthodox treatment is contemplated, extensive consultation and review, as well as the signed consent of patients—and of families, when necessary—should be obtained and documented.
- Establish treatment teams that include primary care physicians and dieticians in addition to mental health clinicians. Team members should communicate frequently to share information and strategies and to avoid splitting.
- Develop clear expectations of patient and caregiver roles and limitations, using behavioral contracts where appropriate. Regarding weight and medical severity,

basic limits should be established with the patient beyond which the treatment team will insist that the patient be hospitalized for medical stabilization.

• Interventions that patients might experience as dehumanizing control battles should be avoided, except if they are necessary in life-threatening situations. Even in such cases, programs should never be inherently punitive.

• Reconsider the patient's past psychotherapies and their nature, timing, acceptance, and value. Many interpersonal, cognitive, family, behavioral, and psychodynamic psychotherapies are available, and, as with medications, additional trials may offer benefits. However, clinicians and patients should be honest about the likelihood that the benefits from such therapies will be supportive or palliative, rather than "curative." Each clinician must decide how much time to spend listening compassionately to and supporting emotionally and socially isolated patients with intractable disorders. Certainly the history of medicine provides many precedents for such work.

• Family assessment should be undertaken when possible, education and counseling offered, therapy considered, and encouragement given to the patient to join support groups.

• Rethink past medication trials and consider medications not used before. Patients with intractable eating disorders are often more likely to accept medications than are recent-onset patients. The potential value of medications should not be oversold. Patients should be given reading material about suggested medications. Medications worth judicious consideration include specific serotonin reuptake inhibitors, tricyclic antidepressants, monoamine oxidase inhibitors, cyproheptadine, low-dose neuroleptics, lithium, naltrexone, antianxiety agents, and anticonvulsants. Clearly, the use of medications requires judgment of medical safety; precedent and justification in the literature; full informed consent; and ongoing, close supervision.

• Legal interventions should be used only to save the patient's life and to demonstrate the clinician's devotion to the patient.

• Consultations for patients and for clinicians should be sought liberally. Clinicians may especially need help managing negative countertransference reactions.

• If all has failed, continue to treat the patient with compassion, minimizing her suffering and unrealistic expectations while maintaining some measure of realistic positivity. Patients may burn out on treatment and may wish simply to be left alone. Without justifiable alternatives, clinicians should offer these patients an open door and ask permission to keep in touch. These patients should be kept comfortable, with no undue restrictions or impositions (except as necessary to sustain life). Food, clothing, and shelter should always be made available.

• If a food-refusing patient's medical situation is urgently life threatening, the patient should be offered alternatives such as complete liquid diets; nasogastric tube feedings; or, very rarely, total parenteral nutrition. In the face of imminent death because of food refusal, the staff may institute nasogastric feedings on a "good Samaritan" basis while seeking legal conservatorship. Such interventions may avert imminent death and are therefore warranted and justified. However, without patients' willing cooperation, treatment plans using nasogastric tubes or parenteral nutrition are usually short-lived and likely to fail. Some patients pull out tubes placed against their will. However, after one or two nasogastric tube feedings, some patients do agree to take food by mouth.

- The murky legal situation of food-refusing and/or purging patients who constantly flirt with death parallel those of other chronically suicidal patients. Few facilities are able to keep such patients hospitalized indefinitely, and few patients or families can pay for prolonged confinement. Furthermore, the only effect of sustained coercive confinement may be to prolong life but not necessarily to improve its quality. In cases where patients act out anger-generating "sub-intentional suicide" games, their dynamics and corresponding clinical strategies should be fully discussed among staff to prevent destructive countertransference and splitting.
- Although clinicians should not actively assist suicide, compassionate clinicians understand that for some patients the pain of struggling against an unrelentingly miserable existence is more than they can bear. In these rare situations, as with patients suffering from other pain-laden terminal conditions, clinicians should alleviate pain and discomfort. Clinicians and families, often unable to accept the "rational" nature of the patient's desire to die, should be helped to accept the possibility of a fatal outcome compassionately, and after death occurs, staff and family should deal with these same issues.
- Keep a long view. For as yet inexplicable reasons, symptoms and resistance in even very chronic patients may change or evolve over time, so that such patients begin to show greater interest and participate in specific new treatments, or treatment in general, and also begin to improve.

TALKING WITH PATIENTS AND THEIR FAMILIES

When talking with patients and their families about prognosis and treatment in the face of an intractable disorder, the clinician should integrate a realistic assessment of the likely outcome while providing some degree of hope and comfort, all based on a great deal of uncertainty. It is clinically unsound and humanistically untenable to offer either undue optimism or harsh, unfiltered pessimism. Some clinicians justify giving patients and their families blunt descriptions of worst-case scenarios as likely outcomes by suggesting that this kind of presentation occasionally provokes a paradoxically opposite reaction. In these cases, patients are supposed to refuse to do badly just to spite their clinicians. However, proof that paradoxical approaches have ever been successful with chronic patients is entirely lacking. At the same time, the danger of presenting unrelentingly bleak prognoses lies in potentially depriving patients and their families of any shred of hope that might facilitate improvement. One may compassionately provide patients and their families with available knowledge filtered through a prism of reality-bound optimism, cloaked in the fact that our prognostic abilities are severely limited by considerable ignorance. Such prognostications should always contain broad statements that include the possibility of change.

FURTHER READING

Dresser, R. (1984). Legal and policy considerations in treatment of anorexia nervosa patients. *International Journal of Eating Disorders, 3,* 43–51. A good review of the legal interventions to be considered when treating resistant, intractable patients in life-threatening situations.

Garfinkel, P. E., & Garner, D. M. (Eds.). (1987). *The role of drug treatment for eating disorders*. New York: Brunner/Mazel. An excellent clinical discussion of research studies and clinical practices regarding virtually all classes of psychiatric medications for eating disorders.

Garner, D. M., & Garfinkel, P. E. (Eds.). (1984). *Handbook of psychotherapy for anorexia nervosa and bulimia*. New York: Guilford Press. A gold mine of effective psychosocial interventions, described in considerable detail.

Goldner, E. (1989). Treatment refusal in anorexia nervosa. *International Journal of Eating Disorders, 8,* 297–306. A thoughtful review of why patients with anorexia nervosa refuse treatment.

Hamburg, P., Herzog, D. B., Brotman, A. W., & Stasior, J. K. (1989). The treatment resistant eating disordered patient. *Psychiatric Annals, 19,* 494–499. Another good review that also synthesizes the combined experiences of several experienced clinicians.

Hornyak, L. M., & Baker, E. K. (Eds.). (1989). *Experiential therapies for eating disorders*. New York: Guilford Press. A collection of articles on potentially useful adjuncts for the treatment of eating disordered patients. Patients with intractable conditions may respond to some of the less traditional psychological interventions that depend less on introspection and verbalization than do traditional psychotherapies.

Luby, E. D., Marrazzi, M. A., & Kinsie, J. (1987). Case reports—Treatment of chronic anorexia nervosa with opiate blockade. *Journal of Clinical Psychopharmacology, 7,* 52–53. An interesting account of seven patients with intractable disorders who were treated with naltrexone—with a few successes.

Ludwig, A. M. (1971). *Treating the treatment failures: The challenge of chronic schizophrenia*. New York: Grune & Stratton. A humbling account of how the best efforts of competent, hard-working, and well-intentioned clinicians dealing with intractable patients, in this case patients with chronic schizophrenia, may often lead to frustrating failures and sometimes to a few modest gains. For these cases at least, careful behavioral strategies occasionally effected at least some modest improvement in some patients.

Pope, H. G. Jr., McElroy, S. L., Keck, P. E., & Hudson, J. I. (1989). Long term pharmacotherapy of bulimia nervosa. *Journal of Clinical Psychopharmacology, 9,* 385–386. On the basis of their experience, these authors suggest that if at first you don't succeed, try, try again.

Ratnasuriya, R. H., Eisler, I., Szmukler, G. L., & Russell, G. F. M. (1991). Anorexia nervosa: Outcome and prognostic factors after 20 years. *British Journal of Psychiatry, 158,* 495–502. A classic long-term follow-up study.

· VIII ·
SCOPE, CONSEQUENCES, AND PHYSIOLOGY OF OBESITY

• 66 •

HISTORY OF OBESITY

Kelly D. Brownell

Only in the past several years have attempts been made to chronicle historical developments in the obesity field. While this omission is surprising in some ways, one might claim that only a recent history exists because obesity is a product of modern-day affluence, lack of physical activity (through energy-saving devices), and access to highly processed, widely advertised, energy-dense, and readily available foods.

In fact there is a rich history dating back thousands of years indicating striking changes in the way excess weight has been viewed. From the famous Venus of Willendorf, a small 25,000-year-old statue of a very heavy female figure, to the exceedingly lean ideal of today, numerous shifts have occurred, even within this century, in conceptualizations of obesity.

Understanding this history is important from a number of perspectives. Modern-day concepts have been shaped by history and exist within a prevailing cultural context. Understanding the roots of current thinking can suggest new directions for the future. In addition, the key issue of societal values and how these values affect both science and practice becomes more comprehensible when one understands the past.

This chapter provides a brief overview of the history of obesity and then incorporates a discussion of the influence of this history on modern thinking. The discussion of early history is drawn mainly from a 1992 chapter by Bray on the topic—the most extensive history available.

EARLY HISTORY

Prehistoric Times through the 17th Century

Some of the earliest historical references to obesity draw a connection between weight and fertility. The Venus of Willendorf, for example, was thought to be a fertility symbol or a characterization of a revered mother. This opinion may reflect an early observation, supported by modern evidence, that low body weight is associated with cessation of menses and hence with infertility.

This view later changed, as illustrated by the suggestion of Hippocrates that obesity was associated with menstrual irregularities and infertility. At that time, obesity was considered a medical peril; Hippocrates' text states that "sudden death is more common in those who are naturally fat than in the lean." Among Hippocrates' suggestions for the remedy of obesity were to perform hard labor, sleep on a hard bed, eat only once each day, eat fatty food for greater satiation, and walk naked as long as possible.

In Bray's history of obesity, similarities were seen between Greco-Roman views of obesity and the later Arabic views prevalent from the 12th to the 15th centuries. Personal shortcomings (the moralistic approach) began to be cited as a cause of obesity, and hard work, eating bulky foods with few calories, and taking frequent baths were recommended for weight loss.

In the 16th and 17th centuries, the first writings specifically on obesity appeared. The moral approach waned as obesity began to be considered an internal problem, with the imbalance of bodily chemicals or a mechanical malfunction as its cause.

18th and 19th Centuries

Prominent physicians of this period agreed with their predecessors that altered diet and increased activity were the key features of treating obesity. The moralistic view re-emerged, however, with the concept that it was *problems* with eating and exercise that caused obesity. Advice such as limiting the selection of foods and leaving the dining area while still hungry were given.

Theories of etiology at this time also emphasized fat tissue, including inadequate oxidation of fat, along with specific aspects of nutrient intake. In 1785, Rigby noted the importance of energy balance, stating that if more nutrients were taken into the body than were necessary for "animal support," weight gain would occur as organs became distended. Gluttony ("intemperance") was considered the cause of excess ingestion of nutrients.

It was also at this time that the concept of types of obesity was introduced, resembling modern-day attempts to classify obesity. Although not yet named, clusters of symptoms similar to Prader–Willi syndrome and Pickwickian syndrome were described. At least two causes of obesity were then considered possible—physical malfunction and overeating because of personality and temperamental shortcomings. Work during this era was carried out in Edinburgh; Paris; and, somewhat later, Germany.

The interest in obesity in Germany during the 19th century led to a number of physiological theories of obesity, some still discussed today. Body composition was a popular topic as anthropometric measurements were made, energy conservation was discussed, and the attribution of obesity to an excessive number of fat cells was suggested. Physical anthropology and measurements of populations were applied to obesity, most notably by Quetelet in Belgium, who developed an index of weight corrected for height. Known originally as the Quetelet Index it is now referred to as the body mass index.

English physicians in the 19th century had a great deal of interest in obesity. The specific role of body fat was discussed, the theory of thermodynamics became influential, and Chambers wrote a monograph on obesity in which four types based on age of onset were discussed. This work had an important influence on American medicine in the next century.

20TH-CENTURY HISTORY

An explosion of research on obesity has occurred in the 20th century. The research has touched nearly every aspect of the disorder and in recent years has delved more deeply into the issue of etiology, with studies on genetics and molecular biology. In his history of the field, Bray cites two major areas in which the major advances have occurred during this century: the study of food intake and its control, and the use of behavioral methods for weight loss.

Changes in Treatments for Obesity

While previously the treatment for obesity consisted of little more than urging lowered intake and increased exercise, dramatic changes have occurred in the 1900s. While the ultimate goal is still to alter energy balance, the means for accomplishing this goal have varied widely. Beginning in the 1950s, psychiatry joined medicine in the treatment of obesity. Psychiatry was dominated by psychoanalytic theory, so obesity was considered an acting out of unconscious impulses, which themselves reflected disturbed personality development. Then, and still today, the theory has not been tested, and with almost no empirical support for treating obesity with psychoanalysis, it is surprising indeed that this practice still exists.

Psychologists entered the picture in the 1960s and 1970s with the application of learning theory. Obesity became an appealing target for behavioral interventions because the outcome (weight loss) was so easily measured. Many studies were undertaken showing that behavioral approaches aimed at life-style modification were more effective than other approaches to which they were compared.

One positive outcome of the behavior therapy movement was the demand for controlled trials, random assignment to groups, use of meaningful controls, and assessment of maintenance of weight loss (see Chapter 85). This commitment to empirical research and evaluation was a major conceptual advance, as earlier treatments simply had not been tested. On the negative side, early studies focused on statistical as opposed to clinical significance, so small weight losses with no follow-up were the basis for proclaiming behavior therapy as the treatment of choice for mild to moderate obesity. In the intervening years, behavioral approaches have been integrated into nearly every treatment program for obesity, but as Wilson notes in Chapter 85, they alone have not fulfilled the promise suggested by the optimism of the 1970s.

Advances in physiology in the 1970s and 1980s had a strong impact on thinking about treatment. The discovery that body weight is governed by a complex network of neural, hormonal, and metabolic factors, and that genetics are influential in determining body weight and shape, led to pessimism about whether personal efforts at weight control could be effective. Simultaneously, medicine reemerged as a leading force in treating obesity. Very-low-calorie diets and surgery were widely used and tested during this era.

The 1990s have seen even more pessimism about the ability of obese persons to lose weight and keep it off, yet there is more optimism about the promise of combining and integrating treatments. The pessimism is expressed as a strong antidieting movement in which some individuals claim that dieting is never effective and creates many more problems than it solves (see Chapter 17). The optimism is seen in new hope for pharmacotherapy (see Chapter 89), the possibility that treatments derived from basic research will be effective, the recognition that different treatments may work for different individuals (see Chapter 98), and the application of psychotherapeutic methods such as interpersonal psychotherapy.

CONSEQUENCES OF THE MEDICAL PERSPECTIVE ON OBESITY

It is clear from this history that various specialties within medicine have dominated the obesity field. The roots of the field lie in medicine because physicians have been called upon over the centuries to explain and "cure" this problem. The eating disorders field, in contrast, has much stronger roots in the behavioral and social sciences, and even within medicine, psychiatry has greater involvement than other specialties.

An example of how this history affects prevailing practices is the way research funding is dispensed in the United States by the National Institutes of Health. Nearly all obesity research is funded by institutes oriented toward physical diseases, such as the National Institute of Diabetes and Digestive and Kidney Diseases. Nearly all research on eating disorders is funded by the National Institute of Mental Health.

Among the virtues of a medical conceptualization of obesity are that the effects of obesity on health have been documented in great detail and that considerable thought has been given to the medical management of the obese individual. Considering the strong effect of excess weight on risk factors such as hypertension and diabetes, and on diseases such as coronary heart disease and cancer, the attention to medical issues is necessary. Yet the medical perspective is confining in some ways.

Limitations

The strong role of the medical and biological sciences in shaping obesity research has strengthened the field in many ways and has limited the field in others. One limitation has been in the conceptualization of risk. The negative consequences of obesity (risk factors and disease endpoints) are generally defined in medical terms only. The psychological and social consequences may be at least as debilitating for some individuals and may have a strong impact on disease (e.g., depression), factors related to disease (e.g., social support, income), and quality of life.

There are several consequences of this focus on medical risk. First, individuals are thought to require intervention based on medical risk, while other important aspects of their lives are ignored. Hence nearly all treatment programs for obesity do not attempt to assess or intervene with psychological and social issues. In fact, very little is known about how these issues should be approached. Nearly all funding for treatment research has been oriented toward reducing medical risk, while the literature contains almost no information on reducing psychosocial risk.

A second limitation has occurred in work on how to match individuals to treatments (see Chapter 98). Current thought in this area has focused on weight as the sole criterion for matching. Because increasing weight is associated with increasing risk, two concepts have prevailed. The first is that the priority for treatment should be given to people with the highest weights, thus yielding the largest potential for risk reduction.

The second concept is that aggressive treatments such as very low calorie diets and surgery, because they carry some medical risk, are thought to be appropriate only for people with high weights, hence producing a positive benefit–risk ratio. What may be a more important matter—whether such a scheme actually produces the best results (which will depend to a great extent on psychosocial factors)—has not been addressed.

The Need for Integrating Disciplines

There is a compelling need for better integration of the medical, behavioral, and social sciences in the treatment of obesity. At a superficial level, such integration would appear to be occurring at present. Rosters at professional meetings and in journals represent different disciplines. However, presentations at international obesity meetings and publications in journals such as the *International Journal of Obesity* and *Research* involve little in the way of psychosocial work and, to some extent, of treatment itself. One could reasonably argue that this situation simply reflects current interests in the field, which poses an even stronger argument for having funding agencies sponsor more research and training opportunities related to psychological and social issues.

SUMMARY

Unlike the eating disorders field, in which psychology and psychiatry have been the driving forces, medicine has been the dominant influence in the obesity field. This focus advanced the field in some ways and limited it in others. Modern conceptualizations of obesity as a disorder with multiple etiologies, consequences, and treatments make it clear that multidisciplinary work will be necessary for understanding the etiology and for developing methods for prevention and treatment of obesity.

FURTHER READING

Bray, G. A. (1990). Obesity: Historical development of scientific and cultural ideas. *International Journal of Obesity, 14,* 909–926. A remarkable history of the obesity field, with extensive historical referencing, a strong focus on periods prior to the 20th century, and discussions of the moral stigma of obesity and obesity as a pathological medical condition.

Brownell, K. D., & Rodin, J. (1994). The dieting maelstrom: Is it possible or advisable to lose weight? *American Psychologist, 49,* 781–791. Article in which the dieting controversy is discussed and specific recommendations are offered for the role of dieting in different segments of the population.

Brownell, K. D., & Wadden, T. A. (1992). Etiology and treatment of obesity: Understanding a serious, prevalent, and refractory disorder. *Journal of Consulting and Clinical Psychology, 60,* 505–517. Coverage of current conceptualizations of obesity, with a discussion of changes in treatments for obesity from 1950 to the present.

French, S. A., & Jeffery, R. W. (1994). Consequences of dieting to lose weight: Effects on physical and mental health. *Health Psychology, 13,* 195–212. Review and conceptual article on the effects of dieting on medical and psychosocial outcomes, along with both clinical and public health recommendations regarding the role of dieting in the management of weight and eating problems.

Schwartz, H. (1986). *Never satisfied: A cultural history of diets, fantasies, and fat.* New York: Free Press. A view from a historian of the development over the past 150 years of cultural ideals of beauty and their impact on body image, dieting practices, and societal norms.

DEFINITION AND CLASSIFICATION OF OBESITY

Kelly D. Brownell

DEFINITION

Defining obesity is straightforward: It is an excess of body fat. Obesity is to be distinguished from overweight, which refers to weight in excess of some standard, generally life insurance company actuarial tables. Measuring weight is easy and inexpensive, while measuring body fat is not. Consequently overweight is often used as a proxy for obesity. Because body weight and body fat are highly correlated, in most cases an individual classified as overweight would also meet the criterion for obesity. There are exceptions, however, so the choice of measuring weight or body fat must be made in the context of specific research or clinical questions (see Chapters 8 and 18).

Defining the levels at which body fat and body weight cross thresholds and become obesity and overweight is not straightforward and has generated considerable debate in the field. The precise point at which scientists and health officials believe increasing weight threatens health ranges from 5% to 30% above ideal weight, a considerable spread. Furthermore, different tables of "ideal" weights have been embraced by different figures in the field (see Chapters 13 and 69).

The use of the body mass index (BMI) has become more common in recent years. The BMI is expressed as weight in kilograms per height in meters^2, and is more strongly associated with percent body fat and health complications than is weight. A means for calculating BMI from height and weight, and of estimating risk, is shown in Figure 67.1.

Presently there appears to be most support for the BMI figures adopted by the National Center for Health Statistics. These figures define overweight as a BMI of 27.3 in women and of 27.8 in men, and severe overweight as 32.3 or more in women and 31.1 or more in men. These cutoffs for overweight and severe overweight represent, respectively, roughly 20% and 40% above ideal weight using the 1983 Metropolitan Life tables.

A RATIONALE FOR CLASSIFICATION

Attempts at classification date back at least to the early 1900s, when a distinction was made between endogenous and exogenous obesity. Over the years, numerous systems of typing obesity have been proposed, including those based on cellularity (hyperplastic vs.

NOMOGRAM FOR BODY MASS INDEX

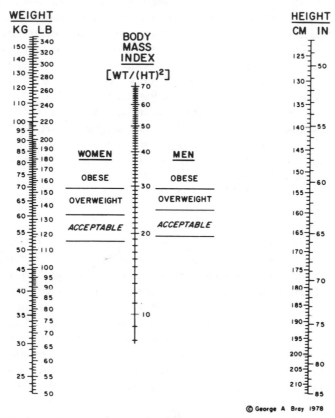

FIGURE 67.1. Nomogram for determining body mass index. Place a straightedge between the column for weight and the column for height. The BMI value is indicated at the point the straightedge crosses the Body Mass Index line. Copyright 1978 by George A. Bray. Reprinted by permission.

hypertrophic obesity), body fat distribution (upper vs. lower body obesity), age at onset, and degree of obesity (using weight, BMI, and body composition).

Underlying these systems is the recognition that obesity is a heterogeneous disorder with multiple etiologies, physical consequences, and possibilities for treatment. It has often been proposed often in the past 10 years that the word "obesity" be abandoned in favor of "obesities."

The benefits of a valid classification system would be impressive. The etiology of obesity may become more clear, groups requiring special medical management would be more readily recognized, and treatments might be targeted in a more effective manner. It is an area where much more research is needed.

SYSTEMS FOR CLASSIFICATION

Systems Based on Weight

Most proposed classification schemes are based on some index of body weight, the assumption being that increasing weight is related to medical risk and/or the need for more aggressive treatment. One such scheme was proposed in the mid-1980s by Stunkard, who argued that three categories were justified: mild, moderate, and severe obesity. As shown in Table 67.1, Stunkard suggested that the categorization should be based on percentage above ideal weight, that adipose-tissue cellularity and medical complications would differ across groups, and that treatment would range from behavior therapy provided by lay leaders in the case of mild obesity to surgery for severe obesity.

Several investigators have proposed systems based on the BMI. Blackburn and colleagues have proposed a classification scheme based on BMI that would have more categories than the Stunkard system, arguing that increasing medical risk with increasing levels of BMI argue for more immediate and aggressive treatments.

Bray proposed a system similar to the one by Blackburn and colleagues, with levels of BMI segmented by increasing levels of risk (Figure 67.1). These categories are then used by Bray to suggest the caloric intake to be prescribed in treatment and whether drugs, exercise, or surgery would be indicated (Table 67.2).

Strengths and Limitations of Systems Based on Weight

Both the greatest strength and the major limitation of these systems is that obesity is conceived entirely in medical terms and that the driving force of treatment is medical risk. It is true that risk increases with increasing levels of weight, so these weight-based systems are helpful in defining which individuals should be top priorities for treatment.

The corollary of this view is that increasing medical risk justifies increasingly aggressive treatment (which itself carries some risk). While in principle more serious disease requires more serious treatment, this concept has not transferred well to the clinical management of obesity. Even the most aggressive treatments can now be undertaken with relative safety (see Chapter 86 on very-low-calorie diets and Chapter 90 on surgery), and it is not clear that less demanding treatments are risk free (if not of medical then of psychosocial risk).

A related notion is that more aggressive treatments will be more effective. With the exception of surgery, which clearly produces large weight losses, treatments cannot be distinguished from one another in the ultimate magnitude of weight loss, except that behavioral approaches seem to offer the most hope for maintenance. As discussed in

TABLE 67.1 A Classification Scheme Based on Percentage Overweight, Showing Prevalence, Pathology, Complications, and Recommended Treatments

	Classification of obesity		
Type	Mild	Moderate	Severe
Percentage overweight	20%–40%	41%–100%	>100%
Prevalence (among obese women)	90.5%	9.0%	0.5%
Pathology	Hypertrophic	Hypertrophic, hyperplastic	Hypertrophic, hyperplastic
Complications	Uncertain	Conditional	Severe
Treatment	Behavior therapy (lay)	Diet and behavior therapy (medical)	Surgical

Note. From Stunkard (1984). Copyright 1984 by Raven Press. Reprinted by permission.

TABLE 67.2. Recommendations for the Treatment of Obesity Based on Classification by Levels of Risk

Risk	Caloric intake (kcal/d)			Choice of treatments		
	<200	200–800	>800	Exercise	Drugs	Surgery
Low	NA	3	2	1	NA	NA
Moderate	NA	2	1, 2	1	3	NA
High	NA	1	2	3	2	NA
Very high	2	1	1	3	2	1, 2

Note. NA, not appropriate; 1, first choice; 2, second choice; 3, third choice. From Bray (1992). Copyright 1992 by Lippincott. Reprinted by permission.

Chapter 98, different treatments are likely to be effective for different people, and the degree of obesity is only one possible matching criterion. Considering this to be the only criterion is likely to lead to inadequate classification schemes.

Systems Based on Psychological/Behavioral Factors

Nearly 15 years ago, Garrow discussed a classification scheme based on the degree of control an individual has over eating. Garrow conceived of a dimension of control ranging from extreme control, where no weight problem exists, to no control, where chaotic, compulsive eating occurs. He proposed that treatments emphasizing self-control skills (e.g., behavior modification) would be effective for people who already exhibit moderate control. Individuals with less control might require programs with more structure and fewer choices (e.g., very low calorie diets, jaw wiring [which was in use at the time] and surgery). This system has not been tested.

More recently, binge eating has become a prominent issue, and some investigators have proposed that obese individuals with and without binge eating form distinct groups (see Chapter 78). Because binge eating disorder is considered an eating disorder, it is possible that obese binge eaters must be treated for their eating disorder prior to treatment for their obesity. Research is now under way to test this concept.

What is noteworthy about these approaches is that they are grounded in behavioral and psychological issues. It is possible that these latter issues are more important criteria than weight *per se* in determining which treatments should be recommended.

CONCLUSIONS ABOUT CLASSIFICATION

Many classification systems have been proposed, but none has prevailed; perhaps in part because of a lack of research that would justify the selection of one approach. There is a real deficit in knowledge that must be remedied, but in addition I believe this effort has faltered for conceptual reasons. One of these reasons is that most systems rely on weight as the single criterion for classification. There are countless other possibilities that should be explored. These possibilities include a broad array of medical issues (e.g., genetics, metabolic rate), psychological variables (e.g., self-esteem, body image), and behaviors (e.g., diet composition, binge eating, history of physical activity).

Another reason is that the systems are wedded to defining risk and treatment recommendations simultaneously. However, a system may be effective in defining risk but not in defining effective treatments. There may be points where the BMI crosses thresholds at which risk increases, but these same points may not be relevant to treatment decisions. It will be important in the future to disengage these goals of classification.

The third reason relates to the medical perspective on obesity (see Chapter 66). The obese person confronts more than medical risk and is made up of more than blood pressure, lipids, and visceral fat. Two obese people may have the same medical risk but have entirely different psychosocial risk for factors such as depression, poor self-esteem, and deficits in social skills. It is important, therefore, that classification systems encompass more than medical risk and that medical risk is acknowledged as only one of many variables that may be important to understanding the etiology of obesity and its risk, treatment, and prevention.

FURTHER READING

Blackburn, G. L., & Kanders, B. S. (1987). Medical evaluation and treatment of the obese patient with cardiovascular disease. *American Journal of Cardiology, 60,* 55g–58g. Discussion of a classification scheme based on the association of rising levels of BMI with health risk.

Bray, G. A. (1992). An approach to the classification and evaluation of obesity. In P. Bjorntorp & B.N. Brodoff (Eds.), *Obesity* (pp. 294–308). Philadelphia: Lippincott. Discussion of various factors to be considered in developing a classification system, with a focus on systems based on medical risk.

Brownell, K. D., & Wadden, T. A. (1992). Etiology and treatment of obesity: Understanding a serious, prevalent, and refractory disorder. *Journal of Consulting and Clinical Psychology, 60,* 505–517. Review of the obesity field in which the importance of classification for matching individuals to treatments is emphasized.

Callaway, C. W., & Greenwood, M. R. C. (1984). Introduction to the Workshop on Methods for Characterizing Human Obesity. *International Journal of Obesity, 8,* 477–480. Overview of the proceedings of a conference sponsored by the National Institutes of Health and aimed at identifying different types of obesity and proposing treatment based on these characterizations.

Garrow, J. S. (1981). *Treat obesity seriously: A clinical manual.* London: Churchill-Livingstone. Detailed discussion of classification schemes, with one of the first proposals of a scheme based on a behavioral factor (control over eating).

Stunkard, A. J. (1984). The current status of treatment for obesity in adults. In A. J. Stunkard & E. Stellar (Eds.), *Eating and its disorders* (pp. 157–173). New York: Raven Press. Proposal of a classification scheme for defining risk and targeting treatment involving three categories relating to the degree of obesity (mild, moderate, and severe).

• 68 •

PREVALENCE AND DEMOGRAPHICS OF OBESITY

David F. Williamson

Prevalence is the proportion of a population that has a health condition at a given point in time. It is a function of three factors: the case definition, the incidence rate of the condition (the rate at which new cases occur in the population), and the mean duration of the condition (the average time that an individual in the population has the health condition). Differences in the prevalence of a condition will occur between populations or within a population over time if any of these three factors changes.

The prevalence of obesity might change spuriously because different case definitions are applied at different times or in different populations. Currently a number of different definitions of obesity are used (see Chapter 67); hence it is important to state the definition used explicitly when reporting the prevalence of obesity. A true change in the prevalence of obesity might occur because the incidence rate has changed; that is, because people are becoming obese at a faster or slower rate than before. The prevalence of obesity might also change because obese people are remaining obese for a longer or shorter period of time, because it has become more or less difficult to treat obesity, or because the case fatality of obese persons has changed as a result of either poorer or better medical management of obesity.

Although the prevalence of obesity is well documented in the United States, very little is known about the incidence or mean duration of obesity in any population. Thus it is difficult to determine why the prevalence of obesity changes over time or why it is different between populations. With these limitations in mind, in this chapter I will review current knowledge of the prevalence and demographic correlates of obesity from population-based surveys carried out in the United States.

CASE DEFINITIONS OF OBESITY USED IN U.S. POPULATION SURVEYS

In contrast to clinical studies in which obesity is often defined on the basis of direct measures of adiposity (e.g., using underwater weighing, computed tomography), in large-scale, population-based surveys obesity is most often defined on the basis of weight and height, because these measures are less expensive to collect under field conditions. The most recently available national data on the height and weight of U.S. adults 18 to 74 years old comes from the Second National Health and Nutrition Examination Survey (NHANES II), which was conducted between 1976 and 1980 by the National Center for

Health Statistics (NCHS). These data indicate that the average man was 1.75 meters (5′9″) tall and weighed 77 kilograms (170 pounds) and the average nonpregnant woman was 1.63 meters (5′4″) tall and weighed 63 kilograms (138 pounds). These height and weight data can be expressed in terms of the body mass index (BMI = weight in kilograms per height in meters^2). This index has a very low correlation with height and a very strong correlation with weight, thus allowing the comparison of body weight among persons of differing heights. The average American man has a BMI of 25.1, and the average American woman has a BMI of 23.7.

Because women generally have smaller bones and less muscle tissue than men, women's BMIs would be expected to be less than those of men for any given percentile of the BMI distribution. However, this generalization only holds true below the 75th percentile of the BMI distribution. In the upper quarter of the BMI distribution, women's BMIs are higher than men's. For example, at the 95th percentile of the two distributions, the BMI of women (36.0) is nearly 3.5 units higher than that of men (32.6), which is approximately equal to a 9-kilogram (20-pound) weight difference.

It is possible for an individual to have a high weight-for-height ratio but not be obese because he/she is very muscular (see Chapters 8 and 18), so the term "overweight" rather than "obesity" is often used when the BMI is employed to estimate the prevalence of obesity. The misclassification of obesity may have real implications in clinical practice, but it is unlikely that many highly muscular individuals will be misclassified as obese when the prevalence of obesity at the population level is estimated.

The NCHS has defined overweight as a BMI of 27.8 or more in men and of 27.3 or higher in women. "Severe overweight" was defined as a BMI of 31.1 or higher in men and a BMI of 32.3 or higher in women. The lower cutoffs correspond to approximately 20% above desirable body weight in the 1983 Metropolitan Life Insurance Company tables, whereas the upper cutoffs correspond to 40% above desirable body weight. For persons of average height (men, 5′9″; women, 5′4″), overweight is equivalent to a body weight greater than 85 kilograms (187 pounds) in men and greater than 72 kilograms (158 pounds) in women, whereas severe overweight is equivalent to a body weight greater than 95 kilograms (210 pounds) in men and greater than 85 kilograms (188 pounds) in women. "Morbid obesity" has also been defined as a BMI of 39.0 or more for both sexes. For persons of average height this BMI would correspond to a weight of 120 kilograms (265 pounds) or more in men, and a weight of 103 kilograms (226 pounds) or more in women.

PREVALENCE OF OVERWEIGHT, SEVERE OVERWEIGHT, AND MORBID OBESITY

In the United States it is currently estimated that the prevalence of overweight is 24.2% in men (15.4 million) and 27.1% in nonpregnant women (18.6 million), yielding 34 million overweight U.S. adults. Severe overweight affects 8.0% (5.1 million) of men and 10.6% (7.4 million) of women, while morbid obesity affects 0.6% (327,000) of men and 2.5% (1.7 million) of women. For morbid obesity, the prevalences may be substantially underestimated, since it is likely that morbidly obese persons have lower participation rates in health surveys than is the case with the general population.

For both men and women, the greatest increase in the prevalence of overweight occurs between the ages of the early twenties and the early thirties. In men, the peak prevalence of overweight reaches 31.0% between 45 and 54 years of age; subsequently, the prevalence of overweight decreases with increasing age (see Chapter 13). In contrast, women experience a monotonic increase in the prevalence of overweight throughout the entire age range, which reaches a peak of 38.5% between 65 and 74 years of age. Similar age- and sex-related trends are observed in the prevalence of severe overweight; there are no published data on the age- and sex-related trends in the prevalence of morbid obesity in the United States population.

There is only modest ethnic variation in the prevalence of overweight among men, with the highest prevalence found in Mexican Americans (31.2%), followed by African Americans (26.3%) and European Americans (24.4%). Similar ethnic differences are found in the prevalence of severe overweight in men: 10.8% in Mexican Americans, 10.4% in African Americans, and 7.8% in European Americans. In contrast, there is strong ethnic variation in the prevalence of overweight in U.S. women. The highest prevalence of overweight is found in African Americans (45.1%), followed by Mexican Americans (41.5%), and European Americans (24.6%). For severe overweight, the ethnic-specific prevalences are, respectively, 19.7%, 16.7%, and 9.6%. There are no published data on the ethnic-specific prevalence of morbid obesity in the U.S. population.

SECULAR TRENDS IN OVERWEIGHT

Secular trends in the prevalence of overweight have been estimated from three U.S. national health surveys carried out from 1960 to 1962, 1971 to 1974, and 1976 to 1980. In European Americans the prevalence has increased by only about 1 percentage point during this 20-year period, but it has increased by 5.1 percentage points among African Americans. The most striking increase has occurred in African American men, who experienced a 6.0 percentage-point increase (a relative increase of 28%) during this period. Among African American women, the increase was 3.2 percentage points (a relative increase of 7%). There are no published data on secular trends in the prevalence of severe overweight or morbid obesity in the U.S. population.

Results of more recent studies suggest that there may have been a marked increase in the prevalence of obesity in the United States during the 1980s. Based on data collected in three communities in the upper midwestern United States from 1980 to 1987, strong evidence was found for a secular trend in both mean BMI and in the prevalence of overweight in both sexes. Preliminary analysis of data collected from 1990 to 1991 by the Third National Health and Nutrition Examination Survey (NHANES III) estimates that the current prevalence of overweight in U.S. adults is approximately 34%. If this preliminary estimate holds, the prevalence of overweight in the U.S. has increased by approximately 33% during the decade of the 1980s.

ESTIMATES OF THE INCIDENCE OF OBESITY

To estimate the incidence rate of obesity directly, it is necessary that body weight be measured longitudinally in a cohort of nonobese individuals. If the body weights of the individuals in the cohort are measured frequently (e.g., weekly or monthly), a true incidence "rate" can be estimated, because the actual time at which a person *first* "becomes obese" (i.e., the time at which the individual's body weight rises above the case definition cutoff) will be known accurately. However, continuous monitoring of body weights is very expensive, especially for large, nationally representative surveys, and is thus unlikely ever to be carried out. An alternative is to measure body weights of individuals in an initially nonobese cohort at two points in time and then compute the proportion of the cohort who are obese at the second measurement. This method will not provide an estimate of the incidence rate; rather, it gives an approximate estimate of the "risk" of developing obesity. This measurement is likely to be an underestimate of the true risk of obesity because it will not include persons who became obese during the study but who then lost weight and became nonobese before their weights were remeasured.

Data are available from a nationally representative sample of U.S. adults who were 25 to 74 years old during the period from 1971 to 1975 when their body weights were first measured and whose weights were remeasured an average of 10 years later, in the period from 1982 to 1984. In both sexes, the net change in mean weight during the 10-year period was a modest gain of 0.9 kilograms (2 pounds). There were substantial differences, however, in mean weight change with age: persons aged 25 to 34 years had the largest mean weight gain, while persons aged 65 to 74 years had the largest mean weight loss. There were also marked differences in weight change between men and women, with women experiencing larger weight gains or losses than men, regardless of age. Among persons aged 25 to 34 years, women gained 3.4 kilograms (7.4 pounds) and men gained 2.8 kilograms (6.1 pounds), whereas among persons aged 65 to 74 years, women lost 4.4 kilograms (9.7 pounds) and men lost 3.4 kilograms (7.5 pounds) during the 10-year period. African American women had substantially greater variation in their 10-year weight change than did European American women. At the 5th (loss) and 95th (gain) percentiles of the 10-year weight-change distribution, African American women lost or gained about twice as much weight as their European American counterparts.

These same data were used to estimate the 10-year risk of becoming overweight. Among men and women who were not overweight during the period 1971 to 1975, those who were 35 to 44 years old had the highest risk of becoming overweight (men: 16.3%, women: 13.5%), while those who were 65 to 74 years old had the lowest risk of becoming overweight (men: 4.7%, women: 4.0%) during the next 10 years. There are no published data on the risks of becoming severely overweight or morbidly obese in U.S. adults.

SUMMARY

Based on U.S. nationally representative data collected in the late 1970s, the prevalence of overweight in U.S. adults is currently estimated to be about 24% of men and 27% of women. In men and women the prevalence of severe overweight is estimated to be about 8% and 11%, respectively, and the prevalence of morbid obesity is estimated to be 0.6% and 2.5%. Preliminary analysis of nationally representative data collected in the early 1990s suggests that the prevalence of overweight in the United States may have increased to about 34% of men and women. After being adjusted for differences in height, the figures show that women tend to have a more variable distribution of body weight than men (see Chapter 11), and African American women tend to have more variable distribution of body weight and higher levels of obesity than European American women. This same pattern holds for distributions of weight change; women have a more variable distribution than men, and African American women have a more variable distribution than European American women. Based on nationally representative data collected between the early 1970s and the early 1980s, the 10-year risk of becoming overweight was found to be highest in persons aged 35 to 44 years, among whom 16.3% of men and 13.5% of women became overweight.

FURTHER READING

Kuczmarski, R. J. (1992). Prevalence of overweight and weight gain in the United States. *American Journal of Clinical Nutrition, 55,* 495s–502s. Includes age- and race-specific prevalence estimates.

Najjar, M. F., & Rowland, M. (1987). *Anthropometric reference data and prevalence of overweight, United States, 1976–1980. Vital and health statistics* (Series 11, No. 238. Public Health Service Publication No. 87-1688). Washington, DC: U.S. Government Printing Office. Provides detailed estimates of height, weight, and other anthropometric measures for the U.S. population.

Williamson, D. F. (1993). Descriptive epidemiology of body weight and weight change in U.S. adults. *Annals of Internal Medicine, 119,* 646–649. A concise but fairly detailed summary of body weight statistics for the U.S. population.

Williamson, D. F., Kahn, H. S., Remington, P. L., & Anda, R. F. (1990). The 10-year incidence of overweight and major weight gain in U.S. adults. *Archives of Internal Medicine, 150,* 665–672. The first article to contain estimates of the age-, sex-, and race-specific "incidence" of obesity in the U.S. population.

• 69 •

EPIDEMIOLOGICAL STUDIES OF HEALTH RISKS DUE TO EXCESS WEIGHT

Walter C. Willett
JoAnn E. Manson

HEALTH RISKS AND EXCESS WEIGHT

The relationships between body weight and the risk of the development of significant disease as well as total mortality have been examined in many epidemiological studies. Such studies provide insight into biological relationships and are also used to develop ranges of desirable weights. The definition of desirable weights and the application of such guidelines to individuals have become a controversial topic during the last several years (see Chapters 13 and 67). The debate was precipitated by a substantial increase in the upper limit of the recommended weight range for persons over age 35 in the 1990 U.S. guidelines. In this chapter we examine methodological issues related to the study of associations between adult body weight and health outcomes, briefly review known associations, and attempt to synthesize available data relating to desirable weights.

Measures of Body Weight in Epidemiological Studies

As many thousands of subjects are needed for epidemiological studies relating fatness to health outcomes, measurements must be simple and widely available. Thus the vast majority of available data are based on weight and height. Such measures are usually combined to provide relative weights, which are standardized for height and sometimes for sex, or body mass index (BMI = weight in kilograms per height in meters^2), which is then converted to weight-for-height tables to be generally understandable. While often criticized, such simple measures do correlate highly with fat mass in young and middle-aged adults and are strongly predictive of important health outcomes (see Chapters 18 and 70). In elderly groups, however, changes in weight often also reflect important decreases in lean body mass as a result of inactivity or chronic disease, thus complicating the interpretation of data based on weight and height (see Chapter 13).

Recently measurements of body fat distribution, particularly waist and hip circumferences, have received much attention as possible independent predictors of serious disease (see Chapters 70 and 79). The rationale for such measurements is largely based on evidence that intra-abdominal fat may have distinct metabolic features; however, it is also possible that in an aging population, abdominal circumferences may be a better indicator of overall adiposity than indices based only on weight and height. BMI is not only strongly correlated with abdominal adiposity and waist-to-hip circumference ratio, it is also the most modifiable of these parameters. *Changes* in weight are also a potentially useful predictor of disease risk (see Chapter 72); because differences in weight are observed within the same person, they will tend to be uncorrelated with frame size, which is difficult to characterize.

Methodological Issues

Studies of body weight in relation to the risk of death and disease are conceptually simple: A large population is weighed and measured and then followed to determine who dies or develops specific diseases. Rates of death or disease can then be calculated for various levels of body weight (appropriately adjusted for height, age, and gender) to determine a quantitative dose–response relationship; the nadir defines the range of optimal weights. In practice, however, several problems can potentially distort true causal relationships between weight and health outcomes.

Although total mortality is attractive as the primary outcome, or "bottom line," in determining optimal weights, studies of this endpoint are particularly prone to distortion and misleading conclusions. The first problem is that many persons lose weight before death, so that low weight may be the result rather than the cause of the underlying disease. Investigators have attempted to deal with this problem by eliminating from the study subjects who have known conditions, such as cancer, that might cause both weight loss and premature death and also by eliminating from the analysis the first years of follow-up. However, such steps will be incomplete because some unrecognized conditions that increase the chances of dying, such as preclinical cancers, depression, or early pulmonary or cardiac failure, may cause reductions in weight for many years before death.

A second problem is that other variables, or confounders, may be related to both weight and health outcomes and may thus distort the causal relationship. Smoking is a prime example; smokers tend to be lean but also are at greatly increased risk of death, thus making the group of lean individuals appear to have an elevated mortality rate. Alcoholism and depression are likely to have the same effect but are harder to characterize in an epidemiological study. These effects can be controlled partially by statistical methods, but the best solution is to study "never smokers" and nonalcoholics.

A third problem affecting a number of epidemiological studies is that statistical methods have sometimes been used to control for metabolic consequences of obesity such as hypertension, hyperglycemia or diabetes, and hyperlipidemia. This approach results in "overcontrol," which statistically removes the biological consequences of obesity that mediate its effects on disease incidence (see Chapter 70).

In addition to the methodological problems noted above, studies of total mortality are also inherently insensitive because obesity, and almost any other factor, is not likely to influence all specific causes of death. Thus even important health effects will be diluted by unrelated causes of death, making them more difficult to detect or study in detail except in extremely large investigations. For example, we would probably be interested in avoiding a factor that caused all leukemias, but we would not be able to detect the elimination of that factor by studying total mortality. Further, many conditions such as angina pectoris, degenerative arthritis, and nonfatal strokes cause major disability and suffering even though they do not count as deaths. Finally, the use of total mortality alone as an endpoint does not contribute to biological understanding; ultimately we want to relate what we observe epidemiologically to knowledge in pathophysiology and basic biology. This goal requires information about the types of disease and metabolic perturbations caused by excess weight.

Studies of Mortality

Whether the relation between body weight and total mortality is linear, J-shaped, or U-shaped has been a focus of controversy. Fundamentally this argument is not fruitful because overwhelming evidence exists that substantial degrees of obesity increase morbidity and mortality and that at some levels, extremely low body weight is deleterious. Thus the question is better focused on defining the range of weights associated with optimal health.

Although the relation between weight and mortality has been examined in many studies, until recently in none have the methodological problems described above been fully addressed. For example, data used to compile the Metropolitan Life tables of desirable weights did not include information on cigarette smoking, thus biasing these tables toward higher recommended weight levels. Notably this bias is more serious in more recent data, since the full effect on health is not experienced until after many decades of smoking. Such an effect might account for the revision to recommended weight levels in the 1983 tables that were higher than those of the 1959 tables. Until recently the best available data were from the large American Cancer Society cohort of nearly 1 million persons. Although the analysis did not account for early deaths due to preclinical disease, it did provide information separately for smokers and nonsmokers; among nonsmokers mortality was minimal at or somewhat below average relative weight. Notably the overall excess mortality among the leanest persons was mainly due to cancers of the lung, bladder, and pancreas, strongly suggesting that this was artifact due to smoking.

Superimposed, the earlier (1959) Metropolitan Life data and the American Cancer Society data both suggest optimal mortality at a level corresponding to a BMI of approximately 20 to 23, although both are probably biased toward a higher nadir. This "optimal weight" range is also supported by a 27-year follow-up of middle-aged men in the Harvard Alumni Study. Although some have argued that the optimal weight increases with age (see Chapter 13), this observation is probably an artifact of the increasing prevalence of weight loss secondary to chronic disease among older persons and the cumulative effects of cigarette smoking. Studies from Framingham and a population of Seventh-Day Adventists indicate that, although the strength of the association between body weight and mortality decreases with age, being leaner than average is still advantageous.

Excess Body Weight and Morbidity

The incidence of myocardial infarction, still the most important disease in the United States, is strongly related to excess weight in both men and women. The relationship appears to be linear, and even persons of average weight (i.e., a BMI of 24 to 26) at midlife have excessive risks. Not surprisingly, excess weight is strongly associated with the major metabolic risk factors for coronary disease. Adult-onset diabetes is most sensitive to excess weight; a gradient in risk of more than 50-fold is seen from the leanest to the heaviest men and women, and even modest gains in weight from age 18 to midlife (e.g., 5 kilograms) are associated with an increase in risk several times greater than that of a person who maintained a stable weight. Excess body weight accounts for a high proportion of cases of hypertension, lowers HDL-cholesterol levels, and increases triglyceride and LDL-cholesterol levels. Excess body weight is also associated with the risk of stroke, although not as strongly as for coronary heart disease. Consistent with the excess risk of coronary heart disease at even average U.S. levels of BMI, it was found in the Framingham Heart Study that, in contrast to those with a BMI of less than 23, many individuals with a BMI of 23 to 25 had abnormalities in serum lipids, glucose tolerance, and blood pressure. Almost all persons with a BMI higher than 25 had such abnormalities. In support of a causal association between obesity and these metabolic abnormalities, even modest degrees of weight loss are associated with favorable alterations in insulin sensitivity, glucose tolerance, blood pressure, and lipids.

Incidence rates of endometrial and gall bladder cancer are several times higher among obese than among lean persons; however, these are relatively uncommon causes of cancer death. The incidence of the more common cancers, including those of the lung, breast, colon, and prostate, are at most weakly associated with body weight. Weight is somewhat more strongly related to mortality from breast cancer, in part because of the later detection of tumors in more obese women as well as a worsened prognosis independent of stage. Breast cancer during the premenopausal years is one of the few diseases that is inversely associated with body weight, perhaps because of the increased occurrence of anovulatory menstrual cycles at higher weights. However, even among premenopausal women there is no reduction in breast cancer mortality with higher weight.

Incidence rates of gallstones and osteoarthritis of the knees and hips are strongly associated with body weight. Fractures of the hip, in contrast, are only about one-fourth as common in obese women as in lean women, presumably because of a combination of the formers' padding during falls, higher bone mass related to increased weight bearing, and higher endogenous estrogen levels. This apparent benefit from obesity, which is experienced primarily at the end of life, does not, however, outweigh the deleterious effects of overweight, because cardiovascular disease and diabetes are far more important causes of death, and even the orthopedic complications of overweight counterbalance the mortality due to hip fractures.

CONCLUSIONS

For most adults, optimal health will be experienced if a lean body weight is maintained throughout life by means of regular physical activity and, if needed, modest dietary restraint. The optimal range of weights appears to correspond to a BMI from about 18 to 23, which is similar to the 1959 Metropolitan Life desirable weights for medium-frame persons. This range is considerably lower than those in the 1990 U.S. guidelines, which increase the BMI to 27 at age 35. This rather narrow range is most appropriately used as a guide for persons who wish to prevent obesity-related morbidity and mortality as they pass through adult life. Individuals and care providers should regard even modest weight gain after age 21, for example 5 kilograms, as an important signal indicating the need for adjustments in activity and eating patterns to prevent further gains in weight.

The range of weights associated with optimal health may represent an unrealistic goal for persons who are already substantially outside this range (see Chapter 98); treatment of overweight and the benefits of even modest reductions in weight are discussed elsewhere in this book (see Chapters 70 and 71).

FURTHER READING

Garrison, R. J., Feinleib, M., Castelli, W. P., & McNamara, P. M. (1983). Cigarette smoking as a confounder of the relationship between relative weight and long-term mortality. The Framingham Heart Study. *Journal of the American Medical Association, 249,* 2199–2203. An analysis of body weight and mortality in the Framingham Heart Study population that includes age-specific analyses.

Garrison, R. J., & Kannel, W. B. (1993). A new approach for estimating healthy body weights. *International Journal of Obesity, 17,* 417–423. A detailed study of the metabolic effects of overweight in the Framingham population.

Lee, I-M., Manson, J. E., Hennekens, C. H., & Paffenbarger, R. S. (1993). Body weight and mortality: A 27-year follow-up of middle-aged men. *Journal of the American Medical Association, 270,* 2823–2828. A large-scale study of body weight and all-cause mortality in men that includes a separate analysis of never smokers, excludes the first several years of follow-up, and provides a long duration of follow-up.

Lew, E. A., & Garfinkel, L. (1979). Variations in mortality by weight among 750,000 men and women. *Journal of Chronic Diseases, 32,* 563–576. The largest study of body weight and mortality, it also includes analyses relating to nonsmokers.

Linsted, K., Tonstad, S., & Kuzma, J. W. (1991). Body mass index and patterns of mortality among Seventh-Day Adventist men. *International Journal of Obesity, 15,* 397–406. A study of body weight and mortality that largely accounts for methodological biases because the population contains few smokers and follow-up is carried out for more than two decades.

Manson, J. E., Stampfer, M. J., Hennekens, C. H., & Willett, W. C. (1987). Body weight and longevity: A reassessment. *Journal of the American Medical Association, 257,* 353–358. A critical review of studies of weight and total mortality.

Willett, W. C. (1990). *Nutritional epidemiology.* New York: Oxford University Press. An overview of issues in nutritional epidemiology.

• 70 •

MEDICAL COMPLICATIONS OF OBESITY

F. Xavier Pi-Sunyer

Obesity is a public health concern because of its association with a number of medical complications that lead to both increased morbidity and increased mortality. The most common complications are diabetes mellitus, hypertension, dyslipidemia, cardiovascular disease, gallstones and cholecystitis, respiratory dysfunction, and increased incidence of certain cancers.

DIABETES MELLITUS

There is a strong positive correlation between the average weight in a population and the presence of type 2 (non-insulin-dependent) diabetes mellitus. In a population divided into mild, moderately, and severely obese, the risk for diabetes increases 2 , 5 , and 10-fold, respectively. The severity of the obesity is a determinant, as is the length of time obesity has been present.

The pathogenesis of the diabetes is related to the insulin resistance caused by the obesity, which increases in severity as the body mass index rises. The organs primarily sensitive to the action of insulin are muscle, adipose, and liver. As excess fat accumulates in the body, the ability of insulin to act at the cellular level is impaired. The cellular effect is manifested both at the insulin receptor and at the postreceptor level. At the insulin receptor, there is a down regulation of the receptors, so that the total number of receptors at the membrane surface are decreased, as is the affinity of the insulin for the receptors. These changes lower the ability of circulating insulin to bind to the receptors and to initiate the signals that lead to the many intracellular actions of insulin.

There are also postreceptor abnormalities in obese individuals, so that the signals for initiating glucose transport, glucose oxidation, and, particularly, glucose storage as glycogen are impaired. The net effect is to decrease glucose entrance and use by insulin-sensitive cells. This effect is particularly true in muscle. The islet cells respond to the resultant increased blood glucose levels by making and secreting more insulin. This process continues day in and day out as long as an individual is overweight. Finally, in those individuals who have the appropriate genetic predisposition to the disease, frank diabetes supervenes.

HYPERTENSION

Epidemiological studies have demonstrated that for every 10-kilogram rise in body weight over normal there is an increase of 3 mm Hg in systolic and 2 mm Hg in diastolic pressure. In the Framingham Heart Study, for every 10% increase in relative weight, systolic blood pressure increased by 6.5 mm Hg. Some studies have shown even greater effects. The longer the duration of obesity, the greater the risk of developing hypertension. Using data from the U.S. National Health Examination II survey (in which obesity was defined as a weight for height above the 85th percentile of that of men and women in the third decade of life), the prevalence of hypertension in those who were 20% or more overweight was twice that of those who were normal weight. The distribution of body fat is an important determinant of blood pressure risk, with central or intra-abdominal body fat being a greater risk than peripheral fat (see Chapter 79).

The causes for the relationship between obesity and hypertension are not clear, although various mechanisms have been invoked. First, sodium retention may occur because of decreased renal filtration surface. Second, insulin enhances the tubular reabsorption of sodium, and insulin levels are high in obese persons because of the prevailing insulin resistance. Third, a number of studies have suggested an increased catecholamine tone in obesity, leading to hypertension. (These data, however, are controversial.) Fourth, in some reports it has been suggested that plasma renin levels may be inappropriately elevated in obese persons. More information is needed on the pathogenesis of hypertension related to excess fat accumulation.

STROKE

Directly linked to the increased prevalence of hypertension in obese persons is an increased risk of stroke. In the Framingham study, for instance, there was a steeply rising curve of stroke with increasing weight. For example, in the male group under 50 years, the risk of stroke rose from 22 to 30 to 49 per thousand as relative weights rose from 110 to 129 to higher than 130, respectively.

DYSLIPIDEMIA

Obesity is associated with two particular abnormalities of circulating lipids: the elevation of triglyceride levels and the depression of high-density lipoprotein cholesterol (HDL-C) levels. Hypertriglyceridemia seems to be abetted by both increased production at the liver and decreased clearance of triglycerides at the periphery. Triglycerides are transported predominantly as very-low-density lipoproteins (VLDLs). These VLDLs are produced in the liver by hyperinsulinemia, the high levels of free fatty acids (FFA) arriving at the liver from the abdominal fat depot, and the glucose precursors available to the liver as glycerol. In addition, with obesity there is often a decreased activity of lipoprotein lipase at the muscle level. This enzyme hydrolyzes triglyceride and allows it to be cleared from the plasma either into muscle for use as fuel or into adipose for storage. As clearance of triglycerides is decreased, higher circulating levels result.

Since HDL-C levels are low in obese persons, while low-density lipoprotein cholesterol (LDL-C) levels are usually only mildly elevated or within normal range, the ratio of LDL-C to HDL-C is always elevated. This combination raises the risk of coronary heart disease.

CARDIOVASCULAR DISEASE

Coronary heart disease is usually described epidemiologically as cardiovascular disease (CVD). Included in CVD is angina pectoris, nonfatal myocardial infarction, and sudden death. These conditions occur more frequently in obese persons. There has been much controversy as to how important obesity is in CVD morbidity and mortality. It is well known, as mentioned above, that obesity enhances the risk of hypertension, dyslipidemia, and diabetes, all of which are strong independent risk factors for CVD. When these factors are controlled for in statistical multivariate analysis, obesity often does not emerge an independent risk factor. This finding is more common in the shorter prospective studies, while in studies carried out for longer than 15 years, obesity consistently shows itself as an independent risk factor. In addition, many epidemiologists believe that it is a mistake, when assessing obesity risk, to control for just those conditions that are made worse by obesity (see Chapter 69).

GALLBLADDER DISEASE

A number of changes occur with obesity that predispose an individual to gallstone formation. The bile becomes supersaturated with cholesterol as cholesterol excretion from the liver increases. Also, the motility of the gallbladder decreases, so that the sac is emptied much less efficiently. Whether this condition is due to a decreased sensitivity to the cholecystokinin released with each meal is unclear. The net effect is to increase the formation of predominantly cholesterol-containing stones. These stones enhance the propensity to gallbladder inflammation, so that acute and chronic cholecystitis is much more common in obese persons. The incidence of this condition is higher in women than in men, partly because the prevalence of obesity is higher in women, but there may be other reasons as yet undiscovered. The need for surgery to remove diseased gallbladders is much more common in obese persons and more so in women than in men.

RESPIRATORY DISEASE

The increased weight of the chest in obesity leads to poor respiratory motion and also decreased compliance of the respiratory system, so that both vital capacity and total lung capacity are often low. As the overweight becomes more severe, ventilation–perfusion abnormalities occur that impair adequate oxygenation of the blood, even though carbon dioxide escape is adequate. With continued and persistent obesity, sleep apnea, either peripheral or central, may occur. Peripheral apnea is manifested by obstruction of the airway caused by excess fatty tissue and the relaxation of the pharyngeal and glossus muscles. Central apnea is the result of a cessation of the signals that initiate inspiration. The mechanism for this cessation of signals is unclear, but apneic episodes may occur many times during the night, causing significant hypoventilation. The severity of all the above abnormalities may lead to progressively more severe hypoxemia and hypercapnia, which in turn may lead to pulmonary hypertension, right heart failure, and cor pulmonale.

CANCER

The relationship of obesity to cancer is somewhat unclear, and more data are required. However, there is an association between some cancers and overweight. It is not known whether the association may be due to other relationships, such as high fat in the diet, elevated total calories, or other specific components of the diet. However, the associations, leaving causality unclear, have been well described.

In women, higher rates have been described for endometrial, gallbladder, cervical, and ovarian cancers. Premenopausal women who are obese are less at risk, and postmenopausal women are at greater risk, for breast cancer. It is possible that some of this postmenopausal effect is related to the increasing estrogenicity that occurs with increasing obesity as women age. This increased estrogenicity is the result of estrogen production in adipose tissue from sex-hormone precursors that are soluble in fat, are deposited in fat, and are converted there to active estrogen. This combined estrogenicity might affect breast cancer incidence. An increased incidence of colorectal and prostate cancers has been found in obese men. The mechanisms of this effect are unknown.

ARTHRITIS AND GOUT

Because of the increased stress on the weight-bearing joints caused by increased weight, degenerative disease of these joints is quite common in obese persons, particularly as the duration and severity of the obesity increases.

While the reason for the increased incidence of gout in persons who are overweight is not clear, such an association has been found repeatedly in cross-sectional studies. This association of gout and overweight is manifested to a much greater degree in men than in women, in whom higher levels of excess fat are needed for the disease to develop.

EFFECTS OF FAT DISTRIBUTION

Recent epidemiologic data from many countries has established fat distribution as an important determinant of disease risk (see Chapter 79). As a result, it is not only the degree of obesity but also where the fat is deposited that is important. Results of available studies suggest it is the intra-abdominal, or visceral, fat that is crucial in this regard. The pathophysiology may be related to the increased lipolytic activity of fat cells in this region, which release large amounts of FFA to the liver and the periphery. The combination of the hyperlipacidemia and hyperinsulinemia leads to increased VLDL production with resultant hypertriglyceridemia. The lipacidemia also inhibits glucose transport and oxidation in muscle, increasing the insulin resistance and the propensity for diabetes. The hyperinsulinemia leads to increased sodium absorption and increases the risk of hypertension.

CONCLUSION

The medical complications of obesity are considerable. It must be realized that diabetes mellitus, hypertension, dyslipidemia, cardiovascular disease, and stroke are, aside from cancer, AIDS, and violence, the leading causes of morbidity and mortality in the developed world. If cancer, a condition in which obesity often plays a part, is added, obesity is a large contributor to the burden of disease affecting industrialized countries. Whether the effect of these diseases is direct and independent or indirect through enhancing other risk factors is essentially irrelevant from a public health perspective. If obesity could be prevented, a very significant and positive impact on chronic disease and mortality would occur.

FURTHER READING

Bjorntorp, P. (1990). "Portal" adipose tissue as a generator of risk factors for cardiovascular disease and diabetes. *Arteriosclerosis, 10,* 493–496. A review of the pathophysiology of central visceral adipose tissue in enhancing health risks.

Burton, B. T., Foster, W. H., Hirsch, J., & VanItallie, T. B. (1985). Health implications of obesity: An NIH Consensus Development Conference. *International Journal of Obesity, 9,* 155–170. A summary report of an important NIH conference on obesity and its medical risks.

Higgins, M., Kannel, W., Garrison, R., Pinsky, J., & Stokes, J. III. (1988). Hazards of obesity—The Framingham experience. *Acta Medica Scandinavica 723* (Suppl.), 23–36. A review of the effects of obesity as seen in one of the largest and most carefully done longitudinal studies of a population group.

Manson, J. E., Colditz, G. A., Stampfer, M. J., Willett, W. C., Rosner, B., Monson, R. R., et al. (1990). A prospective study of obesity and risk of coronary heart disease in women. *New England Journal of Medicine, 322,* 882–889. An interim report of one of the best ongoing longitudinal studies of heart disease in women.

Manson, J. E., Stampfer, M. J., Hennekens, C. H., & Willett, W. C. (1987). Body weight and longevity: A reassessment. *Journal of the American Medical Association, 257,* 353–358. A discussion of epidemiological methodological pitfalls in evaluating the impact of obesity on health.

Pi-Sunyer, F. X. (1991). Health implications of obesity. *American Journal of Clinical Nutrition, 53,* 1595s–1603s. A somewhat more extensive review of the hazards of obesity.

Pi-Sunyer, F. X. (1993). Medical hazards of obesity. *Annals of Internal Medicine, 119,* 655–660. A review of the medical hazards of obesity.

VanItallie, T. B. (1985). Health implications of overweight and obesity in the United States. *Annals of Internal Medicine, 103,* 983–988. An earlier, well-balanced review of the health implications of obesity.

• 71 •

EFFECTS OF WEIGHT LOSS ON WEIGHT-RELATED RISK FACTORS

George L. Blackburn

WEIGHT LOSS AND RISK FACTORS

Obesity is an independent risk factor for cardiovascular disease, hypertension, and diabetes and is associated with several other medical and psychological disorders (see Chapter 70). Weight loss is known to reduce these risks and to improve or resolve comorbid disorders. Although most dieters strive to achieve "ideal" body weight—whether defined by life insurance height-for-weight mortality tables or by a more stringent social ideal—clinical and laboratory evidence clearly supports the value of modest weight loss to attain health and emotional benefit.

Weight loss as low as 5% of body weight has been shown to reduce or eliminate disorders associated with obesity, and a 10% to 20% reduction in body weight with maintenance of this weight loss over 2 to 5 years can reduce health risks and maintain health benefits. Most obese patients can achieve this weight loss in 12 to 16 weeks on a balanced, hypocaloric diet or on a very-low-calorie diet combined with regular physical activity and behavior modification, and this degree of weight loss can be maintained for at least 18 months. Successful treatment of obesity should therefore not be defined as "reduction to desired weight and maintenance of this weight for 5 years," as has been suggested (*Weighing the Options,* 1995) but should instead focus on that amount of weight loss necessary to promote health and prevent disease—a reasonable yet targeted weight loss goal.

Diabetes

The association between obesity and non-insulin-dependent diabetes mellitus (NIDDM) is well known (see Chapters 70 and 92). Both obesity and NIDDM result in insulin resistance and subsequent hyperinsulinemia. In the obese patient, the principal target tissues for insulin (liver, skeletal muscle, and adipose tissue) do not respond appropriately to the hormone, and the body compensates for this impairment of hormone action by secreting increased amounts of insulin, resulting in hyperinsulinemia. When the obese person becomes unable to compensate for the insulin resistance, hyperglycemia and NIDDM ensue.

While the interactions between obesity and NIDDM remain unclear, weight loss has been shown to ameliorate insulin resistance, improve carbohydrate tolerance, and reduce hyperglycemia and hyperinsulinemia. Frequently, hyperglycemia lessens as soon as a hypocaloric diet is initiated, suggesting that caloric restriction has a beneficial effect independent of weight loss. Furthermore, several studies have shown that a weight loss of 10% to 20% greatly improves glycemic control in obese NIDDM subjects and that such improvements can last from 1 to 3 years, even if some weight is subsequently regained. Weight maintenance has been shown to improve insulin sensitivity as well. Outcome can best be monitored by the use of radioimmunoassay and fasting serum insulin tests, with the goal being to achieve normalization of insulin levels and glycosylated hemoglobin.

Hypertension

Results of many studies have revealed that weight reduction in both normotensive and hypertensive obese individuals is associated with decreases in blood pressure, although the exact mechanisms by which obesity elevates blood pressure and weight loss reduces blood pressure remain unknown. Some investigators studying obese hypertensive populations have described alterations in the fluid volume distribution, hemodynamic changes, and cardiac morphological alterations; others have shown variations in adrenergic, metabolic, and endocrine factors. Another theory suggests that obesity leads to worsening of insulin resistance, development of hyperinsulinemia (which increases adrenergic activity), and the reabsorption of sodium at the renal tubular levels. Clearly more research is needed to better understand the complex role of obesity in the pathogenesis of hypertension and its association with hyperinsulinemia.

Whatever the mechanism, it is well known that weight loss in overweight hypertensive individuals leads to a fall in arterial pressure. While some investigators have attributed the change in blood pressure to a concomitant reduction in sodium levels, which typically occurs on a hypocaloric diet, the results of more recent studies show that weight loss has an independent, antihypertensive effect in the absence of sodium restriction and that significant reduction in blood pressure among obese subjects does not require the attainment of ideal body weight.

A loss of only 10% of initial body weight has been shown to reduce blood pressure significantly in overweight adults, and weight loss can prevent blood pressure elevation in individuals at risk for developing hypertension. In long-term studies, weight loss has been effective in slowing or preventing the return of hypertension. Nonpharmacological treatment of hypertension involving weight loss tends to ameliorate other risk factors as well (e.g., the lipid profile improves, insulin resistance improves, or the patient may quit smoking or start an exercise program). Weight loss can also reduce left ventricular hypertrophy.

Cardiovascular Disease

The relationship between body weight and morbidity and mortality from heart disease was first noted in data collected from the insurance companies, with the death rate attributed to cardiovascular disease noted to be higher among overweight men than among normal-weight men. In more recent studies obesity has been identified as an independent determinant of coronary heart disease, even among mildly to moderately overweight middle-aged women (see Chapter 70). Obesity is associated with elevated serum triglyceride levels, lowered high-density (HDL) cholesterol levels, and an increased ratio of low-density cholesterol (LDL) to HDL cholesterol, which entails the greatest atherosclerotic risk.

Modest weight loss is associated with an increase in HDL cholesterol levels and an improvement in the ratio of total cholesterol to HDL cholesterol. Even a 5% to 10% weight loss can improve both the total cholesterol level and the more important LDL:HDL ratio; hypertriglyceridemia is also reversible with weight loss. As with other risk factors for cardiovascular disease, weight loss is known to reduce plasma estrogen levels. In obesity, momentary coagulation status and antitrypsin III level may be more sensitive risk factors for myocardial infarction than serum lipid levels in patients who do not display hyperlipidemia.

Gallstone Formation

Media reports linking dieting and symptomatic gallstones led to a widespread belief that weight loss causes gallbladder disease. Indeed, dieting and rapid weight loss particularly have been reported to increase the risk of gallstones in the obese population, which is already at increased risk for symptomatic and asymptomatic gallstones. The proposed mechanisms for this increased risk include supersaturation of biliary cholesterol and gallbladder stasis, both of which can occur during severe caloric restriction. However, weight loss need not lead to gallstone formation in the obese: Diets that provide 14 grams of protein and 10 grams of fat in at least one meal daily (to ensure adequate gallbladder contraction), that limit weight loss to 2% or less per week, and that last 12 or fewer weeks reduce or eliminate the risk of gallstone formation. Reduced-obese patients have a risk of gallstone formation that is comparable to that in the nonobese population.

Sleep Apnea

Obstructive sleep apnea is a syndrome in which the pharyngeal airway collapses during sleep. While the airway is collapsed, patients cannot breath and eventually have a brief arousal, gasp for breath, and fall back asleep until the cycle repeats itself. This cycle leads to fragmented sleep with little or no slow-wave sleep. Modest weight loss (9%) has been shown to reduce the frequency of apnea, to improve sleep quality, and to reduce daytime somnolence, although the degree of improvement often depends on the length of time the condition has been present. Although the exact mechanism remains unknown, such improvement might result either from changes in the anatomy of the airway (increased airway size) or from changes in the ventilatory drive (increased activation of the upper airway muscles).

Other Benefits

Excess weight places obese patients at increased risk for complications during and following surgery. A 5% to 10% reduction in weight and concomitant diuresis can shorten length of hospital stay and reduce the incidence of postsurgical complications. Modest weight loss will also, depending on the existing structural damage, alleviate low back pain and osteoarthritis, particularly of the knees. Finally, weight loss has been shown to improve mood, body image, self-esteem, and interpersonal functioning. A major targeted goal for sequential weight loss should result in the loss of one-third to one-half of excess body fat.

Body Fat Distribution

Available data strongly suggest that obese patients whose fat is predominantly in the upper body or abdomen (android) are at greater risk of morbidity and mortality than are those whose fat is predominantly in the lower body or femoral-gluteal regions (gynoid) (see Chapter 79). Prospective studies of regional patterns of obesity have shown that the waist:hip ratio is a risk factor for ischemic heart disease, stroke, hyperlipidemia, insulin resistance, diabetes, and death independently of total body fat mass in randomly selected men and women. Additional research has associated this increased risk with visceral rather than subcutaneous fat deposition. Results of recent studies also indicate that body fat is preferentially lost from the abdominal area, particularly in patients with an android distribution, which significantly reduces the associated risk factors. Metabolic studies have shown that insulin resistance that results in hyperinsulinemia represents an important biomarker for the health risks of obesity, including those related to body fat distribution.

Population Differences

The influence of ethnic differences on the effect of degree of weight loss on health benefits remains poorly understood. Moderate weight loss (as low as 3%) achieved with dietary change, physical activity, behavior modification, and group support has been shown to reduce blood pressure and serum cholesterol, fasting glucose, and insulin levels in obese African American women.

Age differences, as they affect health outcomes following weight loss, must also receive more attention, particularly in older adults for whom prospective data are lacking. Studies in children have shown significant health benefits following 3% to 16% weight loss.

TREATMENT EFFECTS

In very few studies has it been possible to separate the effects of caloric restriction, increased exercise, and weight reduction on health outcomes. Caloric restriction alone can improve glycemic control independently of weight loss. Diet composition (particularly the fatty-acid profile) has been shown to influence insulin concentration and insulin resistance independently of weight loss. Data on the health effects of dietary fat are extensive, and because most obesity treatment programs emphasize reduction in fat intake, the differential effects are again hard to identify. Similar difficulties are encountered in considering the role of exercise, which has independent favorable effects on cardiovascular disease, cancer, diabetes, and risk factors for other chronic disease. Other issues that must be studied for their impact on health following modest weight loss include rapidity of weight loss, frequency of feeding, and the effect of prior weight cycling (see Chapter 11).

CURRENT KNOWLEDGE, FUTURE DIRECTIONS

In summary, the available evidence strongly supports the use of modest weight-loss goals (i.e., 10% of initial body weight) in the treatment of obese patients. Preliminary evidence even suggests that weight loss resulting in the depletion of adipocytes below their normal size may cause these cells to overcompensate when restoring lipid levels, leading to weight gain. However, several questions remain partially or completely unanswered regarding the impact of the method for achieving this loss and population differences in outcome.

Primary indicators of successful treatment include lower fasting and postprandial serum insulin levels, diastolic and systolic blood pressure, serum triglycerides levels, and LDL:HDL cholesterol ratios. Treatment must include a reduction in fat intake, an increase in physical activity, and an emphasis on making permanent behavioral changes that support a healthier life-style. Treatment must also be appropriate to the patient's age, ethnic background, and education level.

FURTHER READING

Blackburn, G. L. (1993). Comparison of medically supervised and unsupervised approaches to weight loss and control. *Annals of Internal Medicine, 119,* 714–718. Reviews the role of the physician in effecting a 10% reduction in body weight to improve health and reduce weight-related disease risk factors.

Blackburn, G. L., & Kanders, B. S. (Eds.). (1994). *Obesity: Pathophysiology, psychology, and treatment.* New York: Chapman Hall. Examines the treatment of obesity, with an emphasis on underlying pathophysiology and etiology.

Goldstein, D. J. (1992). Beneficial health effects of modest weight loss. *International Journal of Obesity, 16,* 397–415. Literature review summarizing the effects of a 10% weight loss on NIDDM, hypertension, hyperlipidemia, hypercholesterolemia, and cardiovascular disease.

Kanders, B. S., & Blackburn, G. L. (1992). Reducing primary risk factors by therapeutic weight loss. In T. A. Wadden & T. B. VanItallie (Eds.), *Treatment of the seriously obese patient* (pp. 213–230). New York: Guilford Press. Reviews the short- and long-term medical outcomes associated with a 10% to 20% reduction in initial body weight.

Wadden, T. A., & Stunkard, A. J. (Eds.). (1993). *Obesity: Theory and therapy* (2nd ed.). New York: Raven Press. An important review of the roles of diet, exercise, behavior modification, and adjunct use of drugs and surgery in the treatment of obesity.

Weighing the Options: Criteria for evaluating weight-management programs. (1995). Washington, DC: National Academy Press. An important review of the criteria used to evaluate the effectiveness of various approaches to preventing and treating the problems of overweight and obesity.

• 72 •

THE ASSOCIATION OF WEIGHT LOSS WITH MORBIDITY AND MORTALITY

David F. Williamson

Approximately 25% of men and 40% of women in the United States report that they are trying to lose weight, making intentional weight loss one of the most common health-related practices. It is likely that two factors account for the high prevalence of intentional weight loss: a culturally determined esthetic ideal (see Chapter 15) and the well-documented salutary effects of intentional weight loss on physiological risk factors such as blood pressure, serum lipids, insulin, and glucose (see Chapter 71). The beneficial physiological effects of intentional weight loss are consistent and have been established on the basis of a number of well-designed randomized, controlled trials. Hence it has been reasonable to assume that intentional weight loss in obese persons will result in concomitant reductions in morbidity and mortality. No randomized controlled trials have been published, however, to demonstrate that intentional weight loss in the obese actually reduces morbidity or increases longevity. In fact, the large majority of published epidemiological studies show that persons who experience a "net loss" of weight over time have shorter life spans than those whose body weights remain relatively stable.

Many persons who have intentionally lost weight report that they ultimately gain back some or all of the weight they originally lost. For some persons this pattern of weight loss followed by regain will be repeated over many years of dieting. Thus an additional source of concern is what we have learned from epidemiological studies in which morbidity and mortality rates of persons with stable body weights were compared with those of persons whose weights have fluctuated over time (see Chapter 11). The finding in most of these "weight cycling" studies is that morbidity and mortality rates are higher in those with fluctuating body weights.

Before summarizing the major results of the epidemiological studies of weight loss, weight fluctuation, and morbidity/mortality I will review the methodological issues that are important for a proper interpretation of the studies.

METHODOLOGICAL ISSUES

Assessment of Intentionality

In no published epidemiological study have the separate effects of intentional versus unintentional weight loss been reported. In virtually all the published epidemiological studies, intentionality of weight loss is not assessed. Because unintentional weight loss can result from preexisting illness, those who experience weight loss or weight fluctuation may be in poorer health than their weight-stable counterparts. This methodological shortcoming may seriously bias epidemiologic studies toward a finding of a spuriously increased risk of morbidity and mortality associated with general weight loss.

Effect Modification by Level of Obesity

In most studies the problem of whether the effects of weight change are different for obese persons compared with leaner persons has not been examined. If the adverse effects of weight loss on morbidity and mortality are found only in leaner persons, weight loss is more likely to be a consequence than a cause of disease. In the absence of direct information on intentionality, however, such a finding could not rule out the possibility that intentional weight loss in leaner persons is harmful.

Control for Preexisting Illness and Related Factors

Even if in an epidemiological study intentional weight loss were separated from unintentional weight loss, it is still important to control for differences in underlying illness between intentional weight losers and people with stable weights. It is probable that many persons who intentionally lose weight have been told to do so by a physician who has discovered either preexisting illness or elevated risk factors for illness. Thus "successful" intentional weight loss might also result from an underlying disease proccess that is coincident with the dieter's weight loss attempt.

The ability of the investigator(s) conducting an epidemiological study to control adequately for preexisting illness depends on the quality of data available from each individual's health history and current signs or symptoms of disease. In lieu of such information, many investigators have attempted to control for preexisiting illness in their studies by exluding deaths that occurred "early" in the follow-up period of the study, under the assumption that persons with preexisting illness would be more likely to die sooner than healthier persons. Unfortunately there is no generally accepted definition of early mortality, and it is not clear that such exclusions control for differences in health status between individuals who lose weight and those who remain stable.

It is also critical to control for smoking in studies of weight loss and morbidity/mortality (see Chapter 69). Smokers are more likely to lose weight over time than nonsmokers because of the metabolic effects of nicotine and because smokers are more likely to develop serious illness. Heavy alcohol consumption may also be related to both weight loss and increased morbidity and mortality, and any epidemiological study should also contain measures to control for these factors.

HEALTH OUTCOMES

Intentional weight loss in obese persons may not extend their life-spans but might improve other intermediate measures of their health status and overall quality of life. In the vast majority of weight loss studies, however, only associations with mortality have been examined. A few studies have included measures of disease incidence or morbidity, and in only one study has the contribution of weight loss to mobility disability in older women been examined. Information on morbidity and other measures of health status are more difficult to ascertain and quantify than mortality. It is critical, however, that such information be assessed in future studies, especially in those in which intentionality of weight loss is known.

In epidemiological studies of weight loss and weight fluctuation, relatively weak or nonexistent associations with cancer mortality have been found, while associations with cardiovascular mortality have consistently been strong. This is a puzzling finding, because if preexisting illness is responsible for the deleterious effects of weight loss, then preexisting cancer should play a major role. It is also ironic that cardiovascular mortality is increased in association with weight loss, when intentional weight loss is most often recommended to obese persons to prevent cardiovascular disease. It is possible, however, that preexisting cardiovascular disease is a stronger cause of unintentional weight loss than is generally appreciated.

Assessment of Weight Fluctuation

Epidemiological studies have included measures of exposure to weight fluctuation in two ways. In some studies statistical summaries have been used, such as the intraindividual coefficient of variation, standard deviation, or root mean square error from the regression of each person's body weight on the time of each weight measurement. These statistical summaries give little insight into the patterns of weight fluctuation that may be related to morbidity or mortality, and each summary measure has somewhat different statistical properties. In other studies a priori categories of weight change have been developed based on the percentage change in body weight observed from measurement to measurement. Such categorizations make it possible to distinguish among persons with "stable" body weight, those whose weight fluctuates, and those whose weight shows monotonic increases or decreases over time. Each investigator, however, tends to classify patterns of weight change in different ways, and often there are a substantial number of persons whose patterns of weight change do not fit neatly into a predefined category. Thus it is difficult to compare results from study to study.

MAJOR RESULTS OF STUDIES OF NET WEIGHT LOSS

In two recently published reviews, data from 19 epidemiological studies of the association between weight loss and longevity were examined. Six of these studies were purported to demonstrate a positive benefit of weight loss on mortality, but after close examination only one study, the 1950 Metropolitan Life Insurance Study, was found to have consistent results. Results of this study showed that formerly obese persons who had been "re-rated" for life insurance at a lower premium because they had lost weight (intentionality of weight loss was only assumed) experienced substantially lower mortality rates over a 16- to 25-year period than did their counterparts who had remained obese. Former moderately overweight men and women had 20% and 37% lower mortality rates, respectively, and former severely overweight men and women had 39% and 16% lower mortality rates, respectively. In contrast, the results of the remaining 18 studies showed either inconsistent associations between weight loss and longevity (i.e., in some subgroups weight loss was weakly protective while in others it was deleterious) or consistently deleterious associations.

In two recently published studies that were not included in these reviews it was also found that weight loss is associated with increased mortality. In a nationally representative cohort of U.S. adults followed up between 1971 and 1975 and 1982 and 1984 it was found that men and women who reported having lost 15% or more of their maximum lifetime body weight experienced an approximate twofold increase in mortality rates compared with indiviuals who had lost less than 5% of their lifetime maximum weight. This result was modified, however, by the level of lifetime maximum body weight, with little increase in weight-loss-associated mortality found in those with the highest lifetime maximum body mass index ($\geq$29 kilograms/meters^2). In a prospective analysis of the Framingham cohort of men and women aged 35 to 54 years at baseline, weight change over a 10-year period was related to subsequent 20-year survival. It was found that cardiovascular and coronary heart disease and all-cause mortality rates were 33% to 61% higher for men who had lost weight than for their counterparts whose weight had changed least. In women, all-cause mortality rates were 38% higher in those who had lost weight.

MAJOR RESULTS OF STUDIES OF WEIGHT FLUCTUATION

Since 1989 there have been six published prospective epidemiologic studies of the association between weight fluctuation and morbidity/mortality (see Chapter 11). In four of these studies substantial increases in mortality associated with weight fluctuation were found, while in the remaining two studies, which had very small sample sizes, no association with mortality was found. Of those in which an association was found, two had especially strong research designs and are described below (see also Chapter 11).

In the Framingham cohort eight biennial measures of weight and recalled weight at age 25 were used to compute the intraperson coefficient of variation of body weight as a measure of weight fluctuation. All deaths that occurred in the first 4 years after the last measured weight were excluded in order to control for preexisting disease, and mortality rates were compared between those in the lowest tercile of variation in body weight and those in the highest tercile of body weight variation. Among men, weight variability was associated with the following increases in mortality and morbidity rates: +65% in all-cause mortality, +78% in coronary heart disease morbidity, +93% in coronary heart disease mortality, and +33% in cancer morbidity. Among women, the following increases were found: +27% in all cause mortality, +38% in coronary heart disease morbidity, and +55% in coronary heart disease mortality; but no effect was found for cancer morbidity.

In the Multiple Risk Factor Intervention Trial in middle-aged men, the intrapersonal standard deviation of body weight was computed from measured weights taken annually for 6 to 7 years, and in a subgroup of men the intrapersonal standard deviation was based on measured weights taken every 4 months for 6 to 7 years. In this study five categories of weight "cycling" were defined *a priori*, based on percent changes in weight between weighings. The major finding of this study was that all-cause mortality was increased by 64% in men who were in the highest quartile of the intrapersonal standard deviation of weight compared with those in the lowest quartile. In addition, compared with those whose weight changed by less than 5% from the baseline weight at any weighing, those who exhibited weight "cycling" (had losses followed by gains that were both 5% or more than baseline weight) had 16% to 150% increases in all-cause mortality. The authors did note, however, that the deleterious effects of weight fluctuation were much weaker in men whose body mass index was in the upper tercile (>28.8 kilograms/ meters^2).

SUMMARY

In the large majority of prospective epidemiologic studies it was found that weight loss and weight fluctuation are associated with substantial increases in morbidity and mortality rates. In no studies, however, have the effects of intentional weight loss been separated from unintentional weight loss. Thus current knowledge based on the published epidemiological literature is not adequate to conclude that intentional weight loss is harmful to obese persons; neither, however is current knowledge adequate to conclude that intentional weight loss in the obese decreases their morbidity or mortality.

FURTHER READING

Andres, R., Muller, D. C., & Sorkin, J. D. (1993). Long-term effects of change in body weight on all-cause mortality: A review. *Annals of Internal Medicine, 119,* 737–743. A thorough methodological review of the published studies on net weight change and mortality.

Blair, S. N., Shaten, J., Brownell, K., Collins, G., & Lissner L. (1993). Body weight change, all-cause mortality, and cause-specific mortality in the multiple risk factor intervention trial. *Annals of Internal Medicine, 119,* 749–757. This study has the strongest analytic design of any study of weight fluctuation and morbidity/mortality.

Hamm, P. B., Shekelle, R. B., & Stamler J. (1989). Large fluctuations in body weight during young adulthood and 25-year risk of coronary death in men. *American Journal of Epidemiology, 129,* 312–318. One of the original articles on "weight cycling" and longevity in which categories of weight fluctuation were defined *a priori.*

Higgins, M., D'Agostino, R., Kannel W., & Cobb J. (1993). Benefits and adverse effects of weight loss: Observations from the Framingham Study. *Annals of Internal Medicine, 119,* 758–763. The only study in which the association of weight loss with changes in physiological risk factors and with subsequent morbidity and mortality were examined in the same individuals.

Launer, L. J., Harris, T., Rumpel, C., & Madans, J. (1994). Body mass index, weight change, and risk of mobility disability in midddle-aged and older women: The epidemiologic follow-up study of NHANES I. *Journal of the American Medical Association, 271,* 1093–1098. The only nationally representative cohort study in which the relationship between weight loss and mobility disability was examined.

Lee, I. M., & Paffenbarger, R. S. (1992). Change in body weight and longevity. *Journal of the American Medical Association, 268,* 2045–2049. A clearly presented study of the association between net weight change (both gain and loss) and longevity in male Harvard alumni.

Lissner, L., Odell, P. M., D'Agostino, R. B., Stokes, J. III, Kreger, B. E., Belanger, J. A., & Brownell, K.D. (1991). Variability of body weight and health outcomes in the Framingham population. *New England Journal of Medicine, 324,* 1839–1844. The best analyzed study of weight fluctuation and morbidity/mortality to report results for women.

Pamuk, E. R., Williamson, D. F., Madans, J., Serdula, M. K., & Byers, T. E. (1992). Weight loss and mortality in a national cohort of adults, 1971–87. *American Journal of Epidemiology, 136,* 686–697. The first nationally representative study of net weight loss and mortality in the United States.

Williamson, D. F., & Pamuk, E. R. (1993). The association between weight loss and increased longevity: A review of the evidence. *Annals of Internal Medicine, 119,* 731–736. A methodological review of the six published studies that purport to show a positive benefit of weight loss on mortality.

Wing, R. R. (1992). Weight cycling in humans: A review of the literature. *Annals of Behavioral Medicine, 14,* 113–119. A thorough review of studies on the effects of "weight cycling" in humans, including metabolism, body fat distribution, physiologic risk factors, and morbidity/ mortality.

• 73 •

PSYCHOSOCIAL CONSEQUENCES OF OBESITY

ALBERT J. STUNKARD
JEFFERY SOBAL

"Obesity creates an enormous psychological burden . . . in terms of suffering, the burden may be the greatest adverse effect of obesity."

This conclusion of the 1985 National Institutes of Health Consensus Conference on Obesity put the establishment on record as recognizing the devastating psychosocial consequences of obesity in our society. While it was an important step, it was only a first step, painfully short of what is necessary to cope with the problem. For *obesity* does not create a psychological burden. Obesity is a physical state. *People* create the psychological burden.

THE ORIGIN OF THE PSYCHOSOCIAL EFFECTS

Social Bias

The untoward psychosocial consequences of obesity, unlike its physical ill effects, are not the inevitable consequence of obesity but derive from culture-bound values by which people view body fat as ugly and unhealthy (see Chapter 15). One need look no further than the many societies in developing countries in which fatness is highly valued to see that the derogation of obesity in Western society is a function of social attitudes specific to particular times and places.

The psychological burden of obese persons is created in an age-old way, by the action of stigma, a mark of infamy or disgrace. In recent years, in most countries, social controls have greatly reduced the stigma formerly directed toward many minority groups. Both custom and legal measures have made it unfashionable to stigmatize persons on the basis of race, ethnic origin, or sexual orientation. Obesity remains the last socially acceptable form of prejudice, and obese persons remain perhaps the only group toward whom social derogation can be directed with impunity.

This derogation is widespread and intense. Thus children as young as 6 years of age describe silhouettes of an obese child as "lazy, dirty, stupid, ugly, cheats, and lies." When shown black-and-white drawings of a normal-weight child, an obese child, and children with various handicaps, such as missing hands and facial disfigurement, children and adults both rated the obese child as the least likable. Not only does this prejudice extend across the population spectrum, but it also, sadly, afflicts obese persons themselves.

Obesity is a significant impediment to marriage: Over a 7-year period, Gortmaker, Must, Perrin, Sobol, and Dietz found that young obese women were far less likely to marry than were nonobese women who differed from them in no way except for their body weight. When obese women do marry, they are far more likely to fall in social class than are nonobese women.

Prejudice and Discrimination

Obese persons must also contend with discrimination, the behavioral enactment of prejudice. Thus obese high school students are accepted less frequently into prestigious colleges than are nonobese students from whom they do not differ in school performance. When obese persons enter the job market, the discrimination is as severe. In one study, 16% of employers surveyed said that they would not hire obese women under any circumstances, and an additional 44% would not hire them under certain circumstances.

One aspect of the stigma afflicting obese persons is particularly painful. It is the prejudice and discrimination directed by health care personnel toward the obese persons for whom they care. Rand and MacGregor found that 78% of their patients reported that they had "always, or usually, been treated disrespectfully by the medical profession because of (their) weight." Formal and informal assessments of the attitudes of physicians toward obese persons suggest that these perceptions are fully justified. One survey of physicians found that they viewed their obese patients as "weak-willed, ugly, and awkward."

The negative attitudes of physicians have been ascribed to their unsuccessful efforts at the treatment of obesity. This explanation may possibly apply to the small number of physicians who actually treat obesity. It does not, however, apply to the far larger number of physicians whose contacts with obese persons have not included efforts at weight reduction. This number includes practicing physicians, physicians in training, and even, remarkably, medical students before they have treated a single obese patient. It appears that the antipathy of physicians toward their obese patients derives from their assimilation of the prevailing negative social attitudes towards obesity rather than from their experiences in the treatment of obesity.

PSYCHOLOGICAL EFFECTS

Results of several studies have shown that obese persons' scores on standard psychological tests differ little if at all from those of nonobese persons. In the face of the intense psychological assault to which they are subjected, this is a truly surprising finding, a tribute to the resilience of the human spirit. The stigma attached to being overweight does, however, take its toll on the emotional health of some obese persons. Although they show no greater disturbance on conventional measures of psychopathology, many obese persons suffer from psychological problems specific to their obesity, including disparagement of the body image and binge eating.

Body Image

Persons with disparagement of the body image view their bodies as grotesque and loathsome and believe that others can view them only with hostility and contempt. Such persons may be completely preoccupied with their obesity and feelings of self-loathing. Given the widespread prevalence of weight-related prejudice, one might expect all obese persons to despise their physical appearance, but such is not the case. The disturbance occurs most often in young women of middle and upper middle socioeconomic status, groups in which obesity is less prevalent and for which the sanctions against it are far stronger. The disturbance is generally confined to persons who have been obese since childhood, who have other neurotic disturbances, and whose parents and friends have derogated them for their overweight. Adolescence appears to be the period of greatest risk for the development of these problems, which afflict a majority of severely obese persons.

Binge Eating

A second psychological disorder that occurs with increased frequency among obese persons is binge eating (see Chapter 78). The disorder, although relatively uncommon in the general obese population, afflicts as many as 30% of persons entering weight reduction programs, and its prevalence increases with increasing degrees of overweight. Obese binge eaters report significantly greater psychological distress than do obese nonbingers, including depression, anxiety, and obsessivelike behaviors. Finally, obese binge eaters are more likely to terminate weight reduction programs prematurely and to regain the weight they had lost in treatment than are obese non-binge-eaters.

General Self-Perceptions

A dramatic example of how severely obese persons perceive their disorder has been provided by Rand and MacGregor's quantification of these perceptions by an imaginative method, "owning one's disability." In this method, patients are asked a series of forced-choice questions as to whether they would prefer their current disability to a number of other handicaps. In previous tests of this method, 62% to 95% of respondents selected their own disability when it was randomly paired with other severe disabilities; evidently most people prefer the devil they know to one they do not.

Obesity is a striking exception, as revealed by a study of severely obese persons who lost 45 kilograms by surgery and who had maintained their weight loss for at least 3 years. Not a single patient preferred being obese to being deaf, dyslexic, diabetic, or having heart disease. In only two conditions did any formerly obese persons prefer their obesity to other disorders, and then it was only a small number. Thus only 10% preferred to be legally blind to being obese, and no more than 8% preferred having a limb amputated to being obese.

WHAT TO DO ABOUT THE PROBLEM

It is clear that our obese patients are suffering from a grievous social ill. The time is past when we can ignore this suffering or place our hopes on some new treatment that will make our patients thin and deliver them from stigma. We must attack the stigma itself.

For many years the primary focus of those health professionals and social scientists interested in stigma has been to document it. In the course of these efforts valuable information has been acquired. Now these persons are enlarging their focus and using the knowledge they have obtained to explore measures designed to combat stigma. An example of these new developments is Sobal's four-component model for coping with the stigmatization of obesity: (1) helping persons recognize the presence of stigma, (2) preparing them to respond to stigmatizing acts, (3) reacting to these acts, and (4) repairing the damage done by stigmatization.

A scientific approach to combating stigma may be most useful in informing the actions of lay advocacy groups. The leading advocacy group, the National Association to Advance Fat Acceptance (NAAFA), has performed invaluable service in its attacks on the sources of stigma. These attacks include the application of legal sanctions against discrimination where such sanctions exist and the advocacy of such laws where they do not. They involve public education and action such as boycotts of the products of insensitive manufacturers.

A promising compact for the future may include scientists learning how to minimize the stigma of obesity and lay organizations putting into practice what we know. If such a compact succeeds, future generations may not have to suffer as grievously from the psychosocial consequences of their obesity.

FURTHER READING

Blumberg, P., & Mellis, L. P. (1985). Medical students' attitudes towards the obese and morbidly obese. *International Journal of Eating Disorders, 4*, 169–175. This important article describes how negative attitudes toward obese persons are firmly ingrained in future physicians as early as medical school.

Canning, H., & Mayer, J. (1966). Obesity: Its possible effect on college admissions. *New England Journal of Medicine, 275*, 1172–1174. This paper was ahead of its time in using an objective measure—college admissions—to demonstrate discrimination towards obese adolescents.

Gortmaker, S. I., Must, A., Perrin, J. M., Sobol, A. M., & Dietz, W. H. (1993). Social and economic consequences of overweight in adolescence and young adulthood. *New England Journal of Medicine, 329*, 1008–1012. This widely cited article has brought the psychosocial burdens of obese people to the recognition of the medical profession.

Price, J. H., Desmond, S. M., Krol, R. A., Snyder, F. F., & O'Connell, J. K. (1987). Family practice physicians' beliefs, attitudes and practices regarding obesity. *American Journal of Preventive Medicine, 3*, 339–345. It is not just specialists who treat their obese patients badly: Price and his colleagues show that the family practitioner is equally at fault.

Rand, C. S. W., & MacGregor, A. M. C. (1990). Morbidly obese patients' perceptions of social discrimination before and after surgery for obesity. *Southern Medical Journal, 83*, 1390–1395. This paper provides what we believe to be the most devastating evidence of the untoward psychosocial consequences of obesity.

Richardson, S. A., Goodman, N., Hastorf, A. H., & Dornbusch, S. M. (1961). Cultural uniformity in reaction to physical disabilities. *American Sociological Review, 26*, 241–247. This report, which is still widely cited, was the first to document the terrible psychological price paid by obese children.

Sobal, J. (1991). Obesity and nutritional sociology: A model for coping with the stigma of obesity. *Clinical Sociological Review, 9*, 125–141. This review, which presents approaches to coping with the stigma of obesity, is one of the few signs of hope on the horizon for obese people.

Spitzer, R. L., Devlin, M. J., Walsh, B. T., Hasin, D., Wing, R. R., Marcus, M. D., Stunkard, A. J., Wadden, T. A., Yanovski, S., Agras, W. S., Mitchell, J., & Nonas, C. (1992). Binge-eating disorder: A multisite field trial of the diagnostic criteria. *International Journal of Eating*

Disorders, 11, 191–203. This article is important in that it was the report that established binge eating as a serious problem for obese people.

Wadden, T. A., & Stunkard, A. J. Psychosocial consequences of obesity and dieting. In A. J. Stunkard & T. A. Wadden (Eds.), *Obesity: Theory and therapy* (pp. 163–167). New York: Raven Press. This chapter is the latest and perhaps the most thorough description of the unfortunate psychosocial consequences of obesity and dieting.

• 74 •

METABOLIC EFFECTS OF EXERCISE IN OVERWEIGHT INDIVIDUALS

Wim H. M. Saris

EXERCISE, BODY WEIGHT CONTROL, AND ENERGY BALANCE

It is appealing to postulate that exercise may be a key factor in weight control (see Chapter 84). Athletes in most sports are lean, and increased body fatness is frequently seen in those who leave sports. Obese individuals are normally not physically active, and if they start an exercise program, they lose weight.

Exercise is linked to power output and heat production and thus with energy expenditure. According to the laws of thermodynamics, obesity is a result of a positive energy balance in which energy intake has exceeded expenditure over a prolonged period. Although this equation of energy balance is simple, it is not clear which part of the equation is mostly affected in obesity. There are many factors associated with energy intake, expenditure, and their interaction.

The difference in physical activity between normal and overweight individuals has been examined in a plethora of studies, but the available data are by no means conclusive. It appears that in the majority of studies no relation was found between inactivity and obesity. The studies are severely hampered by methodological problems and a lack of clarity about the definition of physical activity. Reduced activity may be balanced partly by the increased energy cost of weight-bearing activities. In fact, moving around with a higher body mass implies a higher energy cost. This fact was demonstrated in a weight loss study in which, during the weight reducing regime, each experimental subject wore a vest with weights compensating for his/her weight loss. The decrease in energy expenditure during weight loss was only half that of the control subjects who did not compensate for their identical weight loss.

Until recently the methods available to quantify physical activity (see Chapter 21), such as questionnaires, movement counters, or heart rate recorders, were invalid for measuring the relatively small differences in activity that may lead to a positive energy balance and ultimately to weight gain. Recently data have been published on the doubly labeled water technique, now considered the gold standard method for quantifying energy expenditure under free-living conditions. Almost no differences in physical activity, expressed as a multiple of the resting metabolic rate (RMR), have been found between obese and nonobese subjects, indicating that inactivity is not the prime factor that causes the positive energy balance. However, most studies are cross-sectional and thus use subjects with different genetic and environmental backgrounds. Prospective studies are needed to quantify the role of inactivity in the imbalance between energy input and output.

An alternative conclusion can be drawn from the many epidemiological studies showing a consistent negative relationship between level of activity and body mass index or skinfold thickness. In addition, the results of animal studies provide overwhelming evidence of the importance of activity in the regulation of body weight. Finally, the long-term outcome for the treatment of obesity supports the importance of exercise in controlling body weight (see Chapter 84). Although the long-term results of weight loss programs are generally disappointing, individuals who become regular exercisers (a minimum of three sessions a week), have a fairly good chance of controlling their weight. Those who cease exercising regain weight.

The main question, then, seems to be settled: Exercise is a key factor in weight control. But questions of considerable importance remain. What is the mechanism by which exercise enhances weight control? Is it just a question of counting the extra calories in the energy balance or does it affect other aspects of metabolism leading to a better regulation of body weight and body fatness?

FACTORS LINKING EXERCISE TO WEIGHT CONTROL

Exercise Expends Energy

In most textbooks on exercise physiology one can find tables or figures showing the energy costs of recreational activities such as swimming, walking, cycling and running at different speeds. Since the RMR for the average adult is fairly close to 35 milliliters of oxygen per kilogram per minute, or 1 kilocalorie per kilogram per hour, the energy costs of activities are frequently expressed as multiples of RMR. MET is defined as the ratio of the metabolic rate for a specific activity divided by the RMR.

The highest energy expenditure during walking is 9.6 kilocalories per kilogram per hour, during running it is 16.2 kilocalories per kilogram per hour, and during breast-stroke swimming it is 19.2 kilocalories per kilogram per hour, indicating that in 1 hour of exercise, more energy is expended during running, cycling, and swimming than during walking. However, to expend about 18 kilocalories per kilogram per hour for a longer period of time, the maximal oxygen consumption of an individual must be more than 60 milliliters per kilogram per minute, which indicates that in general only well-trained young subjects will be able to expend this amount of energy per minute. An individual with a maximum oxygen consumption per unit time (VO_{2max}) of 35 milliliters per kilogram per minute (the average for a 40-year old female) is not able to expend more than about 7.2 kilocalories per kilogram per hour (corresponding to 70% VO_{2max}). For this individual, fast walking may be as effective as running or cycling.

To exercise while covering a certain distance (for instance from home to office), cycling is the most efficient way. Walking or running the same distance will cost considerably more energy. If the net energy expenditure during exercise is calculated by subtracting RMR, the energy cost of exercise varies between 2 and 17 kilocalories per kilogram per hour, which means that a 70-kilogram person can spend somewhere between 130 and 1,200 kilocalories extra during 1 hour of exercise depending on the activity and the person's work capacity.

Exercise Affects Food Intake

Many studies have shown that energy intake remains relatively constant during an exercise training program for obese individuals, indicating that the effects of exercise are not offset by a corresponding increase in appetite. However, the physiological response appears to be different between lean and obese individuals. Lean individuals maintain weight by an accurate adjustment of energy intake to increasing expenditure levels, while in the obese, intake remains fixed, suggesting an uncoupling of energy intake from expenditure.

A possible physiological explanation can be found in the postexercise effect of exercise on hunger and satiety. Hunger is typically depressed after intense exercise. Postexercise satiety signals, mainly from the gastrointestinal tract, seem to be potent enough to prevent an increase in food intake as long as the energy stores in the body are sufficient. In athletes this phenomenon may become the pathological "exercise-induced anorexia."

Another interesting phenomenon observed in individuals who begin regular exercise is a change toward a relatively carbohydrate-rich diet at the expense of fat. This change in food habits may also affect hunger and satiety. It is now well established that equicaloric amounts of carbohydrate have a stronger satiety effect than fat. This finding also implies that exercise does not automatically lead to a postexercise energy deficit if the fat content of the diet is excessive.

Exercise Affects Macronutrient Balance

Recent experimental evidence suggests that the postexercise regulation of body weight can be better understood by taking into account the effects of exercise on the carbohydrate and lipid balance as well as on the energy balance. As a result of physical training, several metabolic adaptations occur that may facilitate weight control. In a number of studies, the relationship between muscle fiber type, carbohydrate/fat oxidation rate, and weight control has made the muscle compartment the focus of attention. About half the energy is expended through skeletal muscle. Sympathetic–adrenergic response and fiber type are influenced by exercise training. Longitudinal and cross-sectional studies have demonstrated that dramatic changes can occur in skeletal muscle in response to training, which increases the capacity of several metabolic pathways to meet higher performance demands. During exercise there is a shift to a greater use of fat as fuel to spare glycogen, which may be considered the fuel of preference for exercising muscle. Another important adaptation is increased insulin sensitivity. Insulin resistance related to obesity results both in diminished glucose oxidation and decreased glucose storage in muscle. These phenomena lead to a blunting of the facultative thermogenic response to feeding. The postexercise resynthesis of glycogen leads to a decrease in carbohydrate oxidation and a compensatory increase in lipid oxidation.

These physiological adaptations are focused on one point: The body does not appear to tolerate prolonged carbohydrate imbalance. This difference in sensitivity in maintaining macronutrient balance between carbohydrate and fat suggests that exercise can induce a substantial increase in lipid oxidation both during and after exercise at the expense of fat stores. As a consequence, weight maintenance programs using exercise may emphasize diet composition. The beneficial effects will be rather small if the fat:carbohydrate ratio (food quotient) is too high.

This new concept of macronutrient balance is also relevant to exercise prescription.

Prolonged regular exercise at a moderate level of intensity (3 to 6 MET) will maximize the relative lipid content of the fuel mix oxidized, inducing a lipid and energy deficit. Regular low-to-moderate-intensity prolonged-endurance exercise does not invalidate other effects by which exercise has been shown to confer health benefits on obese individuals. These benefits include an improvement of the plasma lipid profile and insulin sensitivity, as well as blood pressure control.

CONCLUSIONS

Although many factors are involved in the delicate balance between energy intake and expenditure, exercise is a key part of weight control. Activity facilitates weight reduction through direct energy expenditure. Besides this action, regular exercise alters metabolism so that the release or storage of energy in both muscle and adipose tissue is facilitated. Exercise also increases the capacity to oxidize carbohydrate and especially fat in muscle by improving free fatty acid metabolism and enhancing tissue insulin sensitivity. In addition, regular exercise induces appetite suppression with a concomitant preferential intake of carbohydrate, since carbohydrate balance is more tightly regulated than fat balance.

In the context of a weight-reducing exercise program, a body fat deficit should be reached by regular low- to moderate-intensity prolonged exercise and by reducing the fat content of the diet. In this way exercise seems to be one of the most powerful factors in the complex and delicate balance between energy input and energy output.

FURTHER READING

Bouchard, C., Despres, J. P., & Tremblay, A. (1993). Exercise and obesity. *Obesity Research, 1,* 133–147. A critical review of the evidence for a role of regular exercise in the prevention and treatment of obesity and its metabolic complications.

Flatt, J. P. (1987). Dietary fat, carbohydrate balance and weight maintenance: Effect of exercise. *American Journal of Clinical Nutrition, 45,* 296–306. The first study in which the concept of macronutrient balance in relation to exercise is discussed.

Montoye, H. J., Kemper, H. C. G., Saris, W. H. M., & Washburn, R. A. (1995). *Measuring physical activity and energy expenditure.* Champaign, IL: Human Kinetics. A handbook of the state of the art and science of estimating energy expenditure and physical activity, including all methods, devices, questionnaires, and MET tables.

Saltin, B., & Gollnick, P. D. (1983). Skeletal muscle adaptability: Significance for metabolism and performance. In L. D. Peach, R. H. Adrian, & S. R. Geiger (Eds.), *Handbook of physiology: Skeletal muscle* (pp. 555–631). Baltimore: William & Wilkins.

Saris, W. H. M. (1993). The role of exercise in the dietary treatment of obesity. *International Journal of Obesity, 17,* 17–21. An overview of the role of exercise during the dietary treatment of overweight.

Schutz, Y., Flatt, J. P., & Jequier, E. (1989). Failure of dietary fat intake to promote fat oxidation: A factor favoring the development of obesity. *American Journal of Clinical Nutrition, 50,* 307–314. A detailed study of the metabolic effects of a high fat intake on substrate utilization.

• 75 •

SOCIAL AND PSYCHOLOGICAL EFFECTS OF WEIGHT LOSS

GARY D. FOSTER
THOMAS A. WADDEN

Understanding the psychosocial effects of weight loss is central to evaluating the benefits and risks of treatment. Many patients enter weight reduction programs seeking improvements in mood, self-concept, or social relationships. The expectations of both patients and practitioners must be realistic and must take into account both the positive and the negative effects of weight loss. In this chapter we summarize research findings regarding the psychosocial effects of weight loss and weight regain, discuss our clinical impressions of the relationship between weight loss and psychosocial functioning, and identify areas for further research.

EFFECTS OF WEIGHT LOSS AND WEIGHT REGAIN

Research Findings

Studies conducted between 1950 and 1970 found that weight loss was associated with adverse emotional reactions, including "dieting depression," anxiety, irritability, and nervousness. Most of these articles were written by psychiatrists who reported the experiences of their obese psychotherapy patients, a sample unlikely to represent the obese population in general.

Later studies presented a much different clinical picture. Weight loss was associated with improvements in mood or, at a minimum, with no worsening. Results reported by Brownell and Stunkard are typical. Mean scores of 9.3 on the Beck Depression Inventory (BDI) declined to 3.4 after an 8.5-kilogram weight loss—a change from mild dysphoria to normal mood. The most salient difference between early and later studies was the use of behavior therapy in the latter investigations, suggesting some protective or even mood-enhancing effect of behavior therapy (see Chapter 85). The positive effect of behavioral treatment has been confirmed in controlled trials in which subjects treated with diet combined with behavior therapy showed significantly greater improvement in mood than did those treated by diet alone.

Other factors such as the method and frequency of assessment, may also contribute to the divergent findings between earlier and later studies. Studies that assessed mood by standardized psychometric instruments, such as the BDI and the State–Trait Anxiety Inventory, found improvements or no change in mood, while open-ended assessments, usually by psychiatric interview, revealed adverse mood changes. The frequency of assessment also affected outcome. Pretreatment to posttreatment assessment of mood revealed positive or benign changes, whereas more frequent, concurrent assessment found both positive and untoward changes. End-of-treatment assessment may capture the positive effect of weight loss on mood, while more frequent assessment may measure the transient stresses associated with decreasing energy intake (i.e., dieting) and increasing exercise. The effects of the method and frequency of assessment were clearly demonstrated in a study using multiple and varied assessments of mood in the same sample of patients. Across methods, positive changes were reported after weight loss in the group as a whole, although some individuals reported difficulties while dieting.

Weight Regain

Despite the high prevalence of weight regain, there are few studies of its psychological effects. Patients in one study reported that weight regain adversely affected their mood, self-esteem, and satisfaction with appearance, although a second study found no significant difference in psychological status between persons with or without a marked history of weight cycling. There is a pressing need for research on this topic.

CLINICAL IMPRESSIONS

Weight Loss

Research on the psychosocial effects of weight loss and weight regain lags behind our clinical knowledge. In this section, we briefly summarize our clinical impressions, which are consistent with research findings of both positive and untoward responses to weight loss. In terms of benefits, obese women who lose weight report almost universally that they are pleased by their improved appearance, their opportunity to buy more fashionable clothes, and their positive feelings about themselves. They are justifiably proud of their weight loss and the hard work required to achieve it, and they enjoy praise from family and friends. Weight loss also brings a sense of well-being for many as their medical conditions improve.

Concomitant with these very positive changes, some patients experience untoward responses ranging from annoyance to serious distress. One common problem is the increased attention they receive. Such attention and praise are especially difficult for shy patients who are not accustomed to receiving compliments. Some resent being treated so differently based solely on a change in weight.

Attention from the opposite sex, while sought by some, is occasionally disconcerting, particularly to those who have a history of sexual or physical abuse. Weight loss may bring a sense of increased vulnerability, especially when excess weight has served a protective function. It may also change a person's marital, social, and occupational roles. These changes are often positive, although they may not appear to be. For example, the finding that the divorce rate increased for women who had undergone surgery for obesity was viewed more favorably when studies revealed that these divorces were limited to marriages that were rated as unsatisfactory before weight loss.

The adverse consequences described above occur in only a minority of patients. They occur frequently enough, however, to require that clinicians be alert and intervene promptly.

Weight Regain

It is difficult to imagine that weight regain is not associated with adverse psychosocial consequences, given its public nature and society's negative attributions about the causes of obesity (e.g., lack of willpower, weakness; see Chapter 73). Our clinical impressions are that as patients regain weight, they experience a variety of emotions, including anger, frustration, shame, and hopelessness. Unfortunately these emotions prevent patients from seeking help to stop or reverse their weight gain. Thus it is important to help patients identify these potential emotional barriers to seeking additional treatment.

FUTURE RESEARCH

The limits of our current knowledge about the psychosocial effects of weight loss are both surprising and disturbing. Current data leave several important questions unanswered: (1) Do most obese patients experience significant psychosocial changes as a result of weight loss? (2) What is the specific nature of these changes? and (3) What are the subject or treatment characteristics that may modulate specific changes?

We believe these questions may be addressed in several ways. The first is to consider the remarkable heterogeneity of obese persons. Although a variety of factors differentiate the obese, several are especially relevant for the investigation of the psychosocial effects of weight loss. The first is the patient's initial level of psychopathology. It is possible that the greatest harm or benefit may occur in patients with the highest levels of psychopathology. This may be especially true in patients with weight-related psychopathology such as body image disparagement or binge-eating disorder (see Chapter 73). Independent of psychopathology, those who experience the most distress because of their weight may experience the most dramatic benefits of weight loss, as suggested by the extremely positive changes in persons who are distressed enough to seek surgical treatment for their obesity.

Differences in the psychosocial effects of weight loss may also be related to differences in the patient's age of onset and/or the duration of the obesity. The effects of reversing a recent weight gain are likely to differ from those associated with reversing a lifetime history of significant obesity. The circumstances surrounding the onset of obesity may also play a role. Someone who has gained weight during successive pregnancies may feel differently about weight loss than would a person who gained weight after an emotional or physical trauma.

Cognitive factors are another source of significant heterogeneity. Patients vary greatly in their expectations about changes following weight loss. These expectations (e.g., specific goal weight, medical changes, improved social functioning) are likely to affect how weight loss is viewed. Thus identical changes in weight may be viewed by patients as a "success" or a "failure" depending on their specific cognitive styles. Such characterizations will probably modulate changes in self-efficacy and psychological status.

A second general strategy to improve research in this area is to assess the psychosocial effects of different treatment regimens. Such a strategy should include assessing the effects of different degrees of caloric restriction, type and intensity of exercise programs, and psychotherapeutic modalities, such as group versus individual care or cognitive-behavioral versus interpersonal therapy. It will be important in conducting these studies to isolate the psychosocial effects of weight loss from those associated with the therapeutic intervention. It is possible, for example, that large weight losses affect mood negatively when they occur in individual dieters in traditional outpatient practice settings but that these ill effects are prevented by group cognitive-behavioral therapy. Weight loss may not be the mechanism for psychosocial change, as suggested by reports of positive changes in patients' psychosocial status despite no weight loss. For example, interpersonal and cognitive-behavioral treatments of obese binge eaters result in significant psychosocial improvements without any change in weight.

A third general strategy to improve research in this area concerns the use of specific, rather than global, outcome measures. In most research, global measures of self-concept or mood are used. Such measures are less likely to be sensitive to weight loss than those that address psychological or social constructs more closely related to weight, such as body image, perceived health, or size discrimination. For example, studies of adolescent females demonstrate that obese girls experience more weight and body dissatisfaction than average-weight girls but show no differences in global measures of self-esteem or mood. Both global and specific measures can be used to assess whether changes in weight- or diet-related constructs (e.g., dieting self-efficacy) influence more global constructs (general self-efficacy).

In summary, increased satisfaction with one's appearance and improved self-esteem are probably two of the most significant factors motivating people to lose weight. Despite the fact that millions of people diet yearly, we know little about whether they achieve these psychological goals. Moreover, we know even less about whether the failure to lose weight or maintain weight loss may harm, rather than improve, psychological functioning. These questions are central to the responsible and ethical treatment of obese persons and await the concerted efforts of researchers and practitioners.

FURTHER READING

Brownell, K. D., & Stunkard, A. J. (1981). Couples training, pharmacotherapy, and behavior therapy in the treatment of obesity. *Archives of General Psychiatry, 38,* 1224–1229. A study that demonstrated the positive changes in mood that accompanied weight loss when these changes were assessed by global, standardized methods.

Foster, G. D., & Wadden, T. A. (1994). The psychology of obesity, weight loss, and weight regain: Research and clinical findings. In: G. L. Blackburn & B. S. Kanders (Eds.), *Obesity: Pathophysiology, psychology and treatment* (pp. 140–166). New York: Chapman and Hall. A review of the psychosocial consequences of weight loss and weight regain. It includes clinical descriptions of positive and untoward responses to weight loss, as well as suggestions for their clinical management.

French, S. A., & Jeffery, R. W. (1994). The consequences of dieting to lose weight: Effects on physical and mental health. *Health Psychology, 13,* 195–212. A review of the physical and psychological consequences of dieting, with particular attention to the methodological issues of defining a "diet."

Jasper, J. (1992.) The challenge of weight control: A personal view. In T.A. Wadden & T.B.

VanItallie (Eds.), *Treatment of the seriously obese patient* (pp. 411–436). New York: Guilford Press. An eloquent description of the psychosocial effects of weight loss by a patient who experienced them.

O'Neil, P. M., & Jarrell, M. P. (1992). Psychological aspects of obesity and dieting. In T. A. Wadden & T. B. VanItallie (Eds.), *Treatment of the seriously obese patient* (pp. 252–271). New York: Guilford Press. A review of the psychological effects of dieting, with particular attention to the effects of very-low-calorie diets on mood, body image, and hunger.

Smoller, J. W., Wadden, T. A., & Stunkard, A. J. (1987). Dieting and depression: A critical review. *Journal of Psychosomatic Research, 31,* 429–440. Contains the proposal that factors in addition to behavior therapy, such as the method and frequency of assessment, might have accounted for the differences in results between early and more recent studies.

Stunkard, A. J., & Rush, A. J. (1974). Dieting and depression reexamined: A critical review of untoward responses during weight reduction for obesity. *Annals of Internal Medicine, 81,* 526–533. A review of studies up to the early 1970s that suggested that dieting was frequently associated with a variety of untoward emotional responses, particularly depression.

Stunkard, A. J., Stinnett, J. L., & Smoller, J. W. (1986). Psychological and social aspects of the surgical treatment of obesity. *American Journal of Psychiatry, 143,* 417–429. A comprehensive review of psychosocial changes following the surgical treatment of obesity.

Wadden, T. A., Stunkard, A. J., & Smoller, J. W. (1986). Dieting and depression: A methodological study. *Journal of Consulting and Clinical Psychology, 54,* 869–871. A study clearly demonstrated the confounding effects of the method and frequency of assessment techniques.

Wilson, G. T. (1993). Relation of dieting and voluntary weight loss to psychological functioning and binge eating. *Annals of Internal Medicine, 119,* 727–730. A review of the psychological effects of dieting in both obese and nonobese populations, including a thoughtful analysis of the potential role of dieting in the development of eating disorders.

Wing, R. R., Epstein, L. H., Marcus, M. D., & Kupfer, D. J. (1984). Mood change in behavioral weight loss programs. *Journal of Psychosomatic Research, 28,* 189–196. A review of 10 studies that suggested that objective measures of mood revealed positive changes following weight loss. The authors suggested that the difference between their findings and those of Stunkard and Rush (1974) was the use of behavior therapy in the more recent studies.

• 76 •

OBESITY IN MINORITY POPULATIONS

SHIRIKI K. KUMANYIKA

This chapter on "minority populations" refers to a set of diverse subpopulations of non-Caucasian or Hispanic ancestry living in the United States (Table 76.1). In 1990 the U.S. population included approximately 12% black Americans, 9% Hispanic Americans, 3% Asian and Pacific Islander Americans, and 1% American Indians and Alaskan Natives. The consideration of obesity in these diverse populations adds an additional layer of complexity to many questions that remain unresolved in the overall obesity literature. There is substantial demographic variation in obesity among non-Hispanic whites, but studies of obesity in minority populations are helping to underscore the full range of relevant biological and psychosocial variation in obesity that may apply both within the United States and globally.

PREVALENCE OF OBESITY IN MINORITY POPULATIONS

There is generally a high burden of obesity among adults in minority populations (Tables 76.2 and 76.3), regardless of the definition used. The prevalence of obesity among children in minority populations varies with both age and race/ethnicity. For both adult and childhood obesity, the possibility that racial/ethnic differences in obesity are entirely or partly driven by measurement artifacts is a continuing issue. Large differences in obesity prevalence cannot be explained away by ethnic differences in stature, conformation, or other skeletal characteristics. Measurements of children are particularly sensitive to error and to the reference standard chosen, but again, not to the point of explaining differences among groups.

HEALTH IMPLICATIONS OF OBESITY IN MINORITY POPULATIONS

Possible racial/ethnic differences in the significance of obesity to morbidity and mortality are an active area of inquiry. Not all the health consequences of obesity that have been observed in non-Hispanic white populations are associated with obesity in minority populations. The resulting implication of a lesser need to treat a given level of obesity in some minority populations must be evaluated with extreme caution, however. Obesity can contribute to many health problems, all of which may be relevant to the overall

TABLE 76.1. Origins or Ethnic Classification of Persons in U.S. Racial/Ethnic Minority Categories

Black Americans	Hispanic Americans	Asian and Pacific Islander Americans	American Indians and Alaska Natives
Black Americans	Mexico	China, Japan, Korea	American Indians (>500 tribes)
Caribbean islands	Puerto Rico	Philippines, Vietnam, Cambodia	Eskimos
African countries	Cuba	Laos, Thailand, Malaysia, Singapore	Alaskan Indians
	Central America	Indonesia, India, Pakistan	Aleuts
	Latin America	Bangladesh, Sri Lanka, Burma	
	Spain	Hawaii, Guam, Samoa, Tonga, Fiji, other Micronesian islands	

Note. Native Hawaiians are an additional ethnic group not appropriately included in any of the above four categories.

benefit : risk ratio of treatment. Moreover, the apparent benefit : risk ratios of obesity treatment in minority populations may change with the increasing acquisition of risk factors in these populations and with improvements in the efficacy of obesity treatment.

Diabetes mellitus occurs with substantially greater frequency among minority populations than among non-Hispanic white populations (this greater frequency of diabetes applies to Asian Americans as well, even though excess obesity is not usually observed in these populations). Other obesity-related conditions such as heart disease, hypertension, and hypercholesterolemia occur more frequently among blacks than among whites, but this excess risk is not observed consistently in the other minority groups. The incidence of endometrial cancer among black women does not fit the expected picture with respect to obesity. Obesity is associated with a substantially increased risk of endometrial cancer, based on data for white populations. However, black women, who are twice as prone to obesity as white women, have only half the incidence of endometrial cancer.

The ability to tie rates of obesity in minority populations to excess all-cause mortality, the "gold standard" on which the traditional actuarial definitions of obesity have been based, has also been limited. This limitation may be partly due to the conspicuous paucity of obesity-mortality studies in minority populations. Currently available evidence has been interpreted by some as suggesting that the optimum body mass index for survival is higher for minority than for white populations and should be estimated separately within each racial or ethnic group. One possible explanation for the discrepancies in the association of obesity and health outcomes between minority and white populations is that one or more critical corisk factors necessary for the harmful effects of obesity to be expressed are absent or less prevalent in some minority populations. These corisk factors include cigarette smoking, high-fat diets, low-fiber diets, or very low levels of physical activity.

This line of reasoning implies that the health significance of obesity in minority populations may increase over time and emphasizes the importance of attending to secular trends. In a contrasting view, ethnic differences in the health consequences of

TABLE 76.2. Prevalence of Overweight (Body Mass Index $\geq$ 27.3) in Females by Age and Race/Ethnicity

	18–24 yr	25–34 yr	35–44 yr	45–54 yr	55–64 yr	65–74 yr
Non-Hispanic white	10	18	25	30	35	37
Non-Hispanic black	24	34	41	61	59	61
Mexican American	22	32	44	52	57	50
Puerto Rican	24	27	43	50	49	61
Cuban American	14	24	33	37	51	40
Native Hawaiian	50	61	62	84	33	—
Pima Indian	81	84	87	81	74	60
American Samoan	—	82	91	91	96	73

	20–29 yr	30–39 yr	40–49 yr	50–59 yr	60–69 yr
Mexican American, <poverty	26	45	58	62	59
Non-Hispanic, <poverty	16	41	53	54	43
Mexican American, >poverty	24	37	45	49	57
Non-Hispanic, >poverty	14	20	28	34	37

Note. Data are from Ernst and Harlan (1991) and U.S. Department of Health and Human Services and U.S. Department of Agriculture. *Nutrition Monitoring in the United States* (DHHS Publication No. [PHS] 89-1255).

TABLE 76.3. Prevalence of Overweight (Body Mass Index ≥ 27.8) in Males by Age and Race/Ethnicity

	18–24 yr	25–34 yr	35–44 yr	45–54 yr	55–64 yr	65–74 yr
Non-Hispanic white	13	21	28	31	29	26
Non-Hispanic black	6	18	41	41	26	26
Mexican American	16	29	37	37	38	30
Puerto Rican	16	19	33	33	26	32
Cuban American	21	28	26	35	32	31
Native Hawaiian	50	79	61	65	69	—
Pima Indian	61	76	78	61	53	31
American Samoan	—	80	85	87	91	60

	20–29 yr	30–39 yr	40–49 yr	50–59 yr	60–69 yr	
Mexican American, <poverty	20	38	46	35	32	
Non-Hispanic, <poverty	10	22	36	24	27	
Mexican American, >poverty	21	33	37	37	36	
Non-Hispanic, >poverty	15	25	34	29	28	

Note. Data are from Ernst and Harlan (1991) and U.S. Department of Health and Human Services and U.S. Department of Agriculture. *Nutrition Monitoring in the United States* (DHHS Publication No. [PHS] 89-1255).

obesity are interpreted as the result of underlying genetic differences in susceptibility or protection. Neither of these explanations can be fully supported or refuted at present; it is possible that both may be applicable in some cases. Genetic explanations cannot, however, be pursued using the census bureau classifications of race/ethnicity listed in Table 76.1. These classifications are often not appropriate for drawing inferences about heredity.

ETIOLOGICAL AND TREATMENT PERSPECTIVES

The common susceptibility to obesity is surprising in view of the extensive demographic, cultural, and genetic diversity among and within minority populations. This shared susceptibility may reflect exposure to certain determinants of obesity that are common to these populations. These determinants may be innate (genetic or congenital), developmental, macroenvironmental (available food supply and the demands of occupational physical activity), or microenvironmental (reproductive history, customary eating and activity practices, cigarette and alcohol use, and attitudes or behaviors that affect voluntary weight control). All three types of determinants may predispose U.S. minority populations to excess obesity.

GENETIC OR DEVELOPMENTAL FACTORS

The "thrifty genotype" theory attributes high rates of obesity and diabetes in certain ethnic groups to superefficient mechanisms for fat storage resulting from evolutionary adaptations to cycles of feast and famine. The validity of this theory remains open to question, because a genetic basis for such metabolic adaptation has not been identified and other viable explanations not dependent on a thrifty gene can also be advanced. Marked increases in the prevalence of obesity have occurred in many minority groups within a relatively short time frame, suggesting that whatever genetic predisposition is operating must leave room for considerable influence by the environment. Patterns of obesity among children in some racial/ethnic groups are consistent with exposure to obesity-promoting variables in utero or during early childhood. As examples, exposure to high circulating insulin levels in utero may affect some children because of the high prevalence of obesity and hyperinsulinemia among women in some minority populations in their childbearing years; artificial feeding and early introduction of solid food appear to be more prevalent in some minority populations.

MACROENVIRONMENTAL FACTORS

In comparison to U.S. non-Hispanic white populations, minority populations may also have in common a relatively recent and less complete transition from conditions in which food availability was limited or cyclic to a situation of a relative abundance of food. These transitions are also characterized by decreased energy expenditure because of lesser demands for occupational physical activity. The net result is an increased potential for higher intake and lower output of calories, shifting the energy balance and requiring voluntary weight control efforts to counteract this effect. Presumably these factors establish a context in which those who are behaviorally and biologically susceptible become obese in proportion to their degree of susceptibility.

MICROENVIRONMENTAL FACTORS

The third and innermost circle of obesity-promoting factors operates at the individual level. The reproductive histories of minority-group women are often different from those of non-Hispanic white women (see Chapter 10). However, explorations of reproductive variables such as timing of menarche, childbearing, menopause, and lactation have not provided clear answers. The role of eating behaviors in the genesis of obesity is another area that remains difficult to resolve, and there are no good data on this point related to obesity in minorities. There is evidence in some minority populations that physical activity is lower than average, perhaps explaining at least part of the picture. Patterns of alcohol consumption and cigarette smoking in minority populations may also be important. For example, black women are more likely to abstain from alcohol use and to be lighter smokers than white women, consistent with an obesity-inhibiting effect attributed to both these practices.

The literature on voluntary weight control practices is currently expanding to cover the population at large (rather than primarily persons who seek obesity treatment) and to consider more variables relating to dieting practices and body image. Findings from studies of minority populations are making a unique contribution to this literature, because persons in racial/ethnic minority populations appear to be more likely to place some positive or neutral values on obesity compared to persons in white populations whose attitudes toward obesity may be more uniformly negative (see Chapter 15). The effect of these more mixed cultural values relating to obesity in minority populations may be to offer some protection from the extreme fear or stigmatization of obesity that may contribute to the development of eating disorders in the larger culture. Cultural values in minority populations concerning obesity may also present a qualitatively different context for weight control or weight reduction attempts, resulting in a lesser ability to counteract the tendency to gain weight with aging in these populations.

FURTHER READING

Brown, P. J., & Konner, M. (1987). An anthropological perspective on obesity. *Annals of the New York Academy of Sciences, 499,* 29–46. Reviews anthropological findings related to cultural views of obesity and gender differences in obesity in both industrialized and nonindustrialized societies.

Dowse, G., Zimmet, P., Collins, V., & Finch, C. (1992). Obesity in Pacific populations. In P. Bjorntorp & B. N. Brodoff (Eds.), *Obesity* (pp. 619–639). Philadelphia: J. B. Lippincott. A review of the epidemiology of obesity in Pacific Islander populations.

Ernst, N. D., & Harlan, W. R. (Eds.). (1991). Obesity and cardiovascular disease in minority populations. Proceedings of a conference held in Bethesda, MD, August 26–28, 1990. *American Journal of Clinical Nutrition, 53,* 1507S–1561S. This supplement is entirely devoted to articles about various aspects of obesity in specific minority populations.

Harrison, G., & Ritenbaugh, C. K. (1992). Obesity among North American Indians. In P. Bjorntorp & B. N. Brodoff (Eds.), *Obesity* (pp. 610–618). Philadelphia: J. B. Lippincott. A discussion of possible reasons for the widespread prevalence of obesity among American Indians from a nutritional epidemiological perspective.

Kumanyika, S. (1993). Ethnicity and obesity development in children. *Annals of the New York Academy of Sciences, 699*, 81–92. A consideration of the possible determinants of the observed differences in patterns of childhood obesity in U.S. minority populations.

Kumanyika, S. K. (1994). Obesity in minority populations: An epidemiologic assessment. *Obesity Research, 2*, 166–182. An evaluation of obesity in minority populations as an epidemiological rather than a clinical problem.

Kumanyika, S. K., & Golden, P. M. (1991, Winter). Cross-sectional differences in health status in U.S. racial/ethnic minority groups: Potential influence of temporal changes, disease, and life-style transitions. *Ethnicity and Disease, 1*, 50–59. A discussion of methodological and conceptual issues relevant to comparisons of minority and white populations, with a particular emphasis on the importance of attending to secular trends in the acquisition of risk factors.

Kumanyika, S. K., Morssink, C., & Agurs, T. (1992). Models for dietary and weight change in African-American women: Identifying cultural components. *Ethnicity and Disease, 2*, 166–175. A discussion of the potential influence of underlying cultural assumptions on the efficacy of weight reduction program models in minority populations.

Savage, P. J., & Harlan, W. R. (1991). Racial and ethnic diversity in obesity and other risk factors for cardiovascular disease: Implications for studies and treatment. *Ethnicity and Disease, 1*, 200–211. A comprehensive review article including a discussion of possible mechanisms.

Sobal, J., & Stunkard, A. J. (1989). Socioeconomic status and obesity: A review of the literature. *Psychological Bulletin, 105*, 260–75. A detailed review of patterns of obesity in relation to socioeconomic status among adults and children in many populations.

• 77 •

CHILDHOOD OBESITY: PREVALENCE AND EFFECTS

William H. Dietz

PREVALENCE

Childhood obesity is now among the most prevalent nutritional diseases of children and adolescents in the United States. Estimates based on triceps skinfold data collected from representative samples of the U.S. population between 1962 and 1980 indicated that the prevalence among U.S. children had increased by over 50% and the prevalence in adolescents had increased by over 40%. Based on these data, it appears that one in five children in the United States is now obese. These data were subsequently challenged because they were based on measurements of the triceps skinfold, which may be less reliable than a measure such as the body mass index, which is based on weight and height. However, several surveys of less representative populations over the same time period have also documented increases in the prevalence of obesity in children, consistent with the marked increases that have occurred in adults over the same time period.

The same national data have been used to examine specific subsets of the population that may be at risk. For example, despite consistent data from several surveys that obesity is more prevalent among white than among African American children, the recent increases in prevalence have been greater among African American children.

EFFECTS

Persistence

The consequence of greatest concern in association with childhood obesity is the likelihood of its persistence. The two factors that predict the persistence of obesity are age of onset and severity. Severe obesity at any age is likely to persist. Early age of onset also appears to increase the risk of persistence, particularly among females. Approximately one-third of all adult obesity in women began in adolescence. Furthermore, the likelihood of spontaneous remission of obesity in women is approximately 30%, whereas 70% of obesity in men remits spontaneously. Adult obesity that had its onset in adolescence is associated with more severe adult obesity than is adult-onset obesity. If the severity of adult obesity predicts morbidity, these observations would suggest that adolescent-onset obesity may be associated with increased adult morbidity. Obesity that develops at other times in childhood, such as the obesity seen in infants of diabetic mothers, may also be associated with an increased risk of adult disease. Whether morbidity is affected by age of onset remains to be determined.

Psychological Consequences

The psychosocial consequences of obesity are among the most widespread adverse effects of the disease (see Chapter 73). Children in kindergarten have already learned to associate obesity with a variety of less desirable traits, and they rank obese children as those they would least like to have as friends. College acceptance rates for obese adolescent girls are lower than those for nonoverweight girls of comparable academic backgrounds. Adult women who are obese as adolescents or young adults earn less, marry less frequently, complete fewer years of school, and have higher rates of poverty than their nonobese peers. Few of these effects occur among obese men. These results persist when controlling for obese children's IQ, self-esteem at baseline, or income and educational level of their parents. The effects on IQ and self-esteem therefore appear related to an extension of the discrimination that begins in early childhood.

Medical Consequences

Obesity has multiple effects on growth and function in children and adolescents. For example, obese children tend to be taller, their bone ages are advanced, their fat-free mass is greater, and menarche in girls occurs earlier than in their nonobese counterparts. The origin of these effects is unclear. Increased height, advanced bone age, and earlier menarche may reflect the auxotrophic effects of increased food intake, whereas the increase in fat-free mass may result from both the increased muscle mass needed to support the increased weight and the increased nuclear mass of the adipocytes. No adverse effects have yet been attributed to these consequences of increased body fat. However, the increased stress of weight bearing may cause bowing of the tibia (Blount disease) or femur in young children and may predispose to slipped capital femoral epiphysis.

Obesity also affects a variety of cardiovascular risk factors. As in adults, obesity affects blood pressure, lipid levels, and glucose tolerance. Obesity appears to be the leading cause of hypertension in children. As in adults, obesity is associated with hypercholesterolemia. Low-density lipoprotein levels are increased, and high-density lipoprotein levels are low. In contrast to adults, in whom fat distribution affects the risk of many of these abnormalities, fat distribution in children does not become centralized until adolescence. As a result, clear evidence that links fat distribution in childhood to morbidity is lacking. For example, although hyperinsulinemia and glucose intolerance characterize childhood obesity, no clear relationship exists between fat distribution and insulin levels, or the area under either the glucose or the insulin curves following glucose tolerance tests in adolescents. Likewise, non–insulin-dependent diabetes rarely occurs in obese children. When present it is usually accompanied by a strong family history.

Two of the most malignant consequences of childhood-onset obesity are pseudotumor cerebri and sleep apnea. Obesity accounts for a significant proportion of pseudotumor cerebri cases, although the mechanism remains unclear. The diagnosis is established by a history of headaches and the presence of papilledema. The most important sign of sleep apnea is daytime somnolence. Apnea is rarely mentioned spontaneously by parents, despite their apprehension and clear recognition of the difficulty their child has breathing at night. If the tonsils are enlarged, a tonsillectomy may cure sleep apnea. However, both unremitting sleep apnea and pseudotumor cerebri warrant the aggressive use of a restrictive hypocaloric diet in conjunction with vigorous family therapy.

Obesity present in adolescence also appears to entrain a variety of morbid consequences. For example, in a cohort of adults originally studied from the time of their enrollment in elementary school through high school, all-cause and cardiovascular mortality were increased among men who were obese when they were in high school but not among women who were obese during high school. The risk of diabetes and subsequent atherosclerosis was increased among both men and women who were obese during high school. Except for diabetes, the risk of death or subsequent morbidity was only modestly attenuated when the effect of adolescent obesity on adult weight was controlled. These results suggest that the effect of adolescent obesity on adult morbidity and mortality is not mediated by the effect of adolescent obesity on adult obesity. Either adolescent obesity had a direct impact on adult morbidity and mortality, or a third factor predisposed to both adolescent obesity and adult disease. Body fat distribution may represent the mechanism whereby obesity present in adolescence affects morbidity and mortality. Body fat distribution in adolescent males is more strongly centralized than it is in adolescent females. Therefore one possibility is that the regionalization of fatness that occurs in obese adolescent males may increase the risk of later complications of obesity.

SUMMARY

Obesity in children and adolescents is growing in prevalence. Childhood obesity itself is associated with serious medical and psychosocial consequences, but may exert its most negative impact by increasing the likelihood that an individual will be obese later in life. It is an issue of major public health significance.

FURTHER READING

Gortmaker, S. L., Dietz, W. H., Sobol, A. M., & Wehler, C. A. (1987). Increasing pediatric obesity in the United States. *American Journal of Diseases of Childhood, 141,* 535–540. Results of this study demonstrate substantial changes in the prevalence of childhood obesity over a 20-year period.

Gortmaker, S. L., Must, A., Perrin, J. M., Sobol, A. M., & Dietz, W. H. (1993). Social and economic consequences of overweight in adolescence and young adulthood. *New England Journal of Medicine, 329,* 1008–1012. A comprehensive demonstration of the adverse effects of obesity on income and marital status.

Must, A., Jacques, P. F., Dallal, G. E., Bajema, C. J., & Dietz, W. H. (1992). Long-term morbidity and mortality of overweight adolescents: A follow-up of the Harvard Growth Study of 1922 to 1935. *New England Journal of Medicine, 327,* 1350–1355. This article represents the most convincing study of the effects of adolescent obesity on morbidity and mortality in adults.

Pettit, D. J., Baird, H. R., Aleck, K. A., Bennett, P. A., & Knowler, W. C. (1983). Excessive obesity in offspring of Pima Indian women with diabetes during pregnancy. *New England Journal of Medicine, 308,* 242–245. One of several studies whose results demonstrate that factors operating prior to birth may have a long-term impact on body fat.

• 78 •

BINGE EATING AND OBESITY

Marsha D. Marcus

Clinically significant binge eating problems—the frequent and regular intake of an objectively large amount of food with an associated sense of loss of control over eating—affects between 20% and 30% of individuals seeking treatment for obesity in university centers. Some meet DSM-IV criteria for bulimia nervosa, but most do not report the regular inappropriate compensatory behaviors (i.e., fasting, purging, or excessive exercising) required for that diagnosis. Obese binge eaters frequently do meet criteria for a new diagnosis, binge eating disorder, which appears in an appendix of DSM-IV as a proposed diagnostic category requiring further study (see Chapter 24). Binge eating disorder is characterized by a pattern of regular (an average of two or more episodes per week) and sustained (episodes for at least 6 months) binge eating without regular inappropriate compensatory behaviors. Although there has been considerable controversy about the specifics and utility of the proposed diagnosis, considerable data indicate that the pattern of binge eating among obese individuals described by the binge eating disorder criteria is a prevalent problem that is associated with significant morbidity.

EPIDEMIOLOGY

Although the exact prevalence of binge eating among obese individuals is not known, data from multisite field studies of binge eating disorder and several obesity clinical research centers provide reasonably concordant estimates that 20% to 30% of obese individuals who seek treatment report serious problems with binge eating. The prevalence of binge eating disorder among obese individuals in the general community is much lower, with estimates ranging from 5% to 8%. Nevertheless, given that obesity affects 34 million American adults, the prevalence of this problem is substantial.

Available evidence suggests that binge eating affects more women than men (the ratio identified in the binge eating disorder field trials was three women to two men) and that prevalence rates are equivalent for white and African American subjects. Binge eating is associated with more severe adiposity. In one study, 10% of subjects with a body mass index (BMI) of 25 to 28, but 40% of those with a BMI of 31 to 42, reported serious binge eating problems. Moreover, when binge eaters are compared with equally obese non-binge-eaters, the binge eaters report an earlier onset of obesity and dieting and more frequent episodes of significant weight loss and regain. Future epidemiological research is needed to establish the prevalence and clinical correlates of the problem as well as to clarify the demographic characteristics of patients.

EATING DISORDER PSYCHOPATHOLOGY

Results of a growing number of studies have revealed significant differences between obese binge eaters and equally obese non-binge-eaters in the ability to control eating behavior and other aspects of eating disorder psychopathology such as the concern with eating, shape, and weight. Thus the eating disordered behavior of obese binge eaters is not an artifact of obesity.

There are both similarities and differences in the eating disorder psychopathology of obese binge eaters and normal-weight bulimia nervosa patients. In structured clinical interviews for eating disorders, the two groups report comparable severity of binge eating behavior (although obese binge eaters report fewer binge episodes) and a similar level of their concern with shape, weight, and eating, concerns that are pathognomonic of eating disorders. Obese binge eaters do not report the high levels of dietary restraint that characterized bulimia nervosa patients.

Obese binge eaters do not, on the average, compensate for binge episodes by restricting food intake between episodes. In fact, when compared with equally obese non-binge-eaters, binge eaters eat more during regular meals as well as during episodes of overeating. These findings must be reconciled with other data indicating that obese binge eaters diet more frequently and have more weight fluctuations than obese non-binge-eaters. Clinical evidence suggests that periods of dietary restriction among obese binge eaters may alternate with sustained periods of binge eating and lack of dietary restraint. In fact, dieting may represent an effort to regain control over eating behavior. Several studies have shown that participation in structured weight loss programs is associated with a reduction of binge eating among obese individuals with clinically significant binge eating problems.

The relationship between dieting behavior and binge eating has conceptual and theoretical relevance. Dieting has been implicated in the etiology of both binge eating and bulimia nervosa, in the latter, dieting behavior almost always precedes the onset of binge eating (see Chapters 16 and 35). In contrast, results of several studies indicated that up to one-half of obese binge eaters retrospectively report that the onset of binge eating occured before any effort to restrict intake. These data, when taken together with findings of the absence of regular dietary restriction among obese binge eaters, suggest that the etiology and course of binge eating in a substantial number of obese individuals may differ from those of bulimia nervosa patients. Prospective studies of obese and normal-weight binge eaters are needed to clarify the onset and course of binge eating problems as well as the relationship among binge eating, obesity, and dieting behavior.

Psychiatric Comorbidity

Numerous questionnaire studies, and now studies using structured interviews, confirm that obese binge eaters report more psychosocial dysfunction and psychiatric symptomatology, particularly depression, than do obese non-binge-eaters. Binge eaters report higher lifetime rates of psychiatric disorders, including anxiety, mood, and personality disorders. In contrast to studies in which bulimia nervosa patients and normal-weight controls were compared, results of other studies to date have not confirmed differences between binge eaters and non-binge-eaters in alcohol or other substance abuse disorders, obsessive–compulsive disorder, or history of sexual victimization.

The differences between obese binge eaters and obese non-binge-eaters in lifetime history of major depression are particularly striking. In one recent study, binge eaters were 12.9 times as likely to report a history of major depression. Moreover, mood and eating problems may be related. Clinical experience is that obese binge eaters have problems with mood modulation as well as with the regulation of food intake. Patients frequently report that binge eating occurs in the context of negative mood states and serves a self-soothing or mood-regulating function.

Although there have been no studies of the eating behavior of obese binge eaters during depressive episodes, there is a consistent pattern of significant weight gains during lifetime episodes of major depression among obese patients in weight control programs. Finally, in a recent study in our laboratory, 23% of a group of obese binge eaters met the criteria for atypical depression, a syndrome characterized by the maintenance of mood reactivity, overeating, oversleeping, severe fatigue, and sensitivity to rejection. These individuals demonstrated significantly more severe binge eating behavior than did binge eaters who did not meet the criteria for atypical depression. Thus future research is needed to elucidate the relationship among depression, binge eating, and weight gain in obese individuals.

Although it is clear that obese binge eaters suffer substantial morbidity from both eating disorders and other psychiatric symptomatology, other work has shown that normal-weight bulimia nervosa patients report higher rates of psychiatric comorbidity than do obese binge eaters (see Chapter 28). It has therefore been suggested that there is a continuum of severity among binge eaters, with purging bulimia nervosa patients showing the greatest degree of disturbance and obese binge eaters the least disturbance. This may be the case, but it is difficult to draw firm conclusions from available studies, in which divergent definitions of comparison groups and widely differing methodologies have been used. Moreover, the obese binge eaters studied to date have been significantly older than bulimia nervosa patients; this age difference has further complicated between-group comparisons. Additional work that focuses on the description of a broad spectrum of disordered eating is necessary to elucidate similarities and differences among variants of disordered eating.

CONCLUSIONS

In summary, although additional epidemiological studies are needed, it appears that serious binge eating is a common problem among obese individuals. The etiology of binge eating among obese binge eaters is unknown, although a biological predisposition for obesity and/or mood problems may be risk factors for the development of the problem. The relationships among obesity, binge eating, mood disorder, and dieting behavior are also unknown but may be clarified by prospective studies of the onset and course of the disorder. Finally, since both obesity and disordered eating are associated with significant morbidity, effective treatments for these patients are urgently needed. It appears that an effective program for obese binge eaters must include amelioration of the eating disorder and depressive symptomatology, and it must produce moderate weight loss for most patients as well.

FURTHER READING

Bruce, B., & Agras, W. S. (1992). Binge eating in females: A population-based investigation. *International Journal of Eating Disorders, 12*, 365–373. A study using the Eating Disorder Examination, a state-of-the-art assessment of disordered eating used to describe obese binge eaters.

Marcus, M. D. (1993). Binge eating in obesity. In C. G. Fairburn & G. T. Wilson (Eds.), *Binge eating: Nature, assessment, and treatment* (pp. 77–96). New York: Guilford Press. A comprehensive review of clinical and research issues relating to binge eating in obese individuals.

Marcus, M. D., Smith, D., Santelli, R., & Kaye, W. (1992). Characterization of eating disordered behavior in obese binge eaters. *International Journal of Eating Disorders, 12*, 249–255. A community-based study of binge eating behavior in a random sample of 455 women.

Marcus, M. D., Wing, R. R., & Hopkins, J. (1988). Obese binge eaters: Affect, cognitions and response to behavioral weight control. *Journal of Consulting and Clinical Psychology, 56*, 433–439. A description and prospective outcome study of obese binge eaters and non-binge-eaters in a behavioral weight loss program.

Yanovski, S. Z. (1993). Binge eating disorder: Current knowledge and future directions. *Obesity Research, 1*, 306–324. An excellent review of studies pertaining to binge eating disorder.

Yanovski, S. Z., Leet, M., Yanovski, J. A., Flood, M., Gold, P. W., Kissileff, H., & Walsh, B. T. (1992). Food selection and intake of obese women with binge eating disorder. *American Journal of Clinical Nutrition, 36*, 975–980. One of the first laboratory studies of the eating behavior of obese binge eaters.

Yanovski, S. Z., Nelson, J. E., Dubbert, B. K., & Spitzer, R. L. (1993). Binge eating disorder is associated with psychiatric comorbidity in the obese. *American Journal of Psychiatry, 150*, 1472–1479. A controlled study of the psychiatric comorbidity of binge eating disorder.

· 79 ·

THE IMPORTANCE OF BODY FAT DISTRIBUTION

PER BJÖRNTORP

BODY FAT DISTRIBUTION AND HEALTH

Several prospective population studies show that abdominal fat distribution, usually measured as the waist:hip circumference ratio (WHR), is an independent risk factor for cardiovascular disease (CVD), non-insulin-dependent diabetes mellitus (NIDDM), stroke, and premature death. In addition, the WHR is closely associated statistically with other risk factors for these diseases, including elevated very-low-density lipoprotein levels, low high-density lipoprotein levels, insulin resistance, and hypertension.

The WHR is a convenient way to measure visceral fat accumulation in epidemiological studies, although it is not a precise measurement of intra-abdominal fat mass. Visceral fat accumulation is more strongly associated with risk but has not been possible to analyze in most prospective studies because it must be determined using computerized tomography. The mentioned risk factors and diseases constitute what is now usually called syndrome X or, more clearly, the metabolic syndrome. In the absence of measurements of visceral fat, body fat distribution can serve as an indicator of one or several factors of the metabolic syndrome. It is thus an easily measurable, or even directly visible, indicator of a high probability of ill health.

It is possible that visceral fat accumulation may cause or amplify the metabolic risk factors via effects on the liver. Hepatic metabolism of insulin, glucose, and lipoproteins is probably influenced by portal free fatty acids (FFA), mobilized in abundance from visceral adipose tissue depots. Adipocytes in these tissues are particularly sensitive to lipolytic stimuli and are relatively insensitive to insulin inhibition of lipolysis. The mobilization of FFA from these depots is therefore pronounced, particularly when the visceral fat stores are enlarged. In this way visceral adipose tissue may, via portal FFA, generate hyperinsulinemia, hyperglycemia, and hyperlipidemia as well as hypertension via hyperinsulinemia, all metabolic risk factors for CVD, NIDDM, and stroke. Visceral-depot fat may in this way actually generate the metabolic syndrome.

An elevated WHR is also associated statistically with nonmetabolic risk factors for disease, such as smoking, excess alcohol consumption, coagulation factors, and psychosocial factors. In these cases, factors other than portal FFA must be involved. It is likely that some of these factors are indicators of processes involved in the mechanisms for the accumulation of visceral fat. There is now considerable evidence that a multiple endocrine abnormality, related to a neuroendocrine disturbance, might be primarily

445

involved in this cluster of risk factors and diseases. The nonmetabolic statistical associates of an elevated WHR, mentioned above, may contribute to the endocrine abnormalities, as discussed below.

Visceral obesity associated with the metabolic syndrome is also associated with disturbances along the axes from the hypothalamus to the adrenals and gonads, as well as with growth hormone secretion and sympathetic nervous system activity. The hypothalamic–adrenal axis seems to be particularly sensitive to stimulation, at different levels, by the adrenals, ACTH, corticotropin-releasing factor (CRF) secretion, and physical as well as psychological stressors.

Steady-state cortisol levels may not be elevated in patients with visceral obesity and metabolic syndrome; in fact, these levels have been reported to be low. Under the influence of life stressors, daily cortisol secretion should be elevated. Subjects with visceral accumulation of body fat and associated metabolic syndrome have a number of symptoms, personality characteristics, and psychosomatic diseases in common, suggesting that they are often subjected to stressful situations. These situations may be related to poor socioeconomic conditions and/or to psychosocial problems. Such subjects also drink more alcohol and often smoke; these behaviors are also accompanied by an increased secretion of cortisol.

The hypothalamic–gonadal axis is also involved, and here an inhibition is seen, resulting in irregular menses in women and relative hypogonadism in men. In addition, relative hyperandrogenism is frequently seen in women. This condition is caused by an increased production of androgens in these women, the origin of which is not known. It is suspected, however, that these increased androgen levels may be associated with the other neuroendocrine abnormalities, either at the level of the central nervous system or by interactions between the CRF and the gonadotropin releasing factor. This important area clearly needs more exploration.

Growth hormone (GH) secretion is particularly blunted in persons with visceral obesity and the metabolic syndrome. This blunting effect influences the number, area, and amplitude of GH secretion peaks but seems to be partly reversible by the amelioration of the hypogonadism in men by testosterone substitution.

Finally, the central regulation of hemodynamic variables after stress is changed in persons with visceral obesity. Instead of the classic fight–flight reaction, with increased heart rate and blood pressure combined with a compensatory decrease of peripheral resistance, these individuals experience an abnormal reaction: an increase in peripheral resistance along with a more depressed reaction of central hemodynamics. This reaction of hemodynamics has been observed in experimental animals subjected to uncontrollable, cortisol-producing stress.

Effects of Abnormalities

There are several consequences of these multiple abnormalities. First, insulin resistance is well known as a consequence of increased cortisol secretion. Furthermore, recent evidence strongly suggests that both hyperandrogenicity in women and a relative hypogonadism in men are followed by insulin resistance. The evidence supporting this statement comes from intervention studies in humans and rats, in which the respective abnormalities were produced or ameliorated. The mechanisms for these effects are found at the level of muscle insulin sensitivity. These observations suggest a "window" of normal, sex-specific concentrations of testosterone within which muscular insulin sensitivity is optimal. Being outside (above or below) this window seems to be followed by insulin resistance in men and women, suggesting a U-shaped dose–response curve of testosterone in relation to insulin sensitivity. The explanation for this reaction is not known and is another important area for further research.

These endocrine abnormalities probably cause a direction or redistribution of body fat stores to visceral depots. Cortisol in the presence of insulin, the level of which is found to be elevated in persons with visceral obesity, increases the potential of adipocytes to accumulate triglycerides, while testosterone and growth hormone (both at low levels in men with visceral obesity) prevents this triglyceride accumulation and instead amplifies lipid mobilization. These steroid hormone effects appear to be mediated by the stimulation of the transcription of several appropriate genes. For example, the lipolysis stimulation of testosterone and growth hormone is expressed at levels of beta-adrenergic receptors, adenylate cyclase, and protein kinase A (or hormone-sensitive lipase). These hormonal effects are probably more pronounced in visceral fat because of its combination of high cellular density, innervation, and blood flow, as well as the characteristics of the adipocytes, which seem to have a high density of receptors for cortisol and androgens.

The influence of female sex steroids on human adipose tissue is enigmatic. Receptors for estrogens and progesterone are probably absent. Nevertheless, exposure of the hormones in question changes the fat distribution in women. It seems that female sex steroid hormones may interact with the metabolism and distribution of human adipose tissue by indirect mechanisms of unknown nature.

In summary, there is now considerable evidence that in cases of visceral obesity, the secretion of cortisol is periodically elevated because of a sensitive hypothalamic–adrenal axis and that there is also low testosterone secretion in men and hyperandrogenicity in women. These abnormalities, combined with elevated FFA concentrations from enlarged, lipolytically sensitive fat depots, provide powerful mechanisms for the creation of insulin resistance and its associated metabolic aberrations. In conjunction with a low secretion of growth hormone and hyperinsulinemia, the abnormal regulation of sex steroid hormone levels also seems to have the capability of directing storage lipids to visceral fat. This action, then, seems to provide the basis for visceral fat accumulation and the metabolic syndrome, by which visceral fat itself may then amplify the metabolic abnormalities.

Possible Reasons for Hormonal Abnormalities

A major problem then emerges: Why do the hormonal abnormalities occur? The pattern of endocrine disturbances in these individuals, as well as the hemodynamic abnormalities, are reminiscent of those seen in persons after they experience submissive reactions to stress. Persons with visceral obesity and metabolic syndrome also show other signs of the effects of stress, such as frequent absenteeism and psychosomatic and psychiatric diseases. There is now evidence that socioeconomic background factors are also operative in these individuals, which may provide a basis for the type of stress reactions discussed. Many of our findings on this topic have recently been confirmed.

It is difficult to proceed in this area with human research; the evidence will have to be descriptive. Intervention studies to induce or ameliorate a chronically stressful environment are not ethically or practically feasible. Such studies are possible in primates, and recent studies have shown that chronic stress, leading to submissive reactions, is followed essentially by the same neuroendocrine abnormalities as are seen in humans, although the regulation of testosterone levels, growth hormone levels, and circulation in primates has not yet been measured. This is then associated with insulin resistance, elevated blood pressure as well as plasma lipid levels, and visceral fat accumulation. Also associated with these findings in primates are early signs of coronary atherosclerosis and decreased glucose tolerance. It thus seems as if the entire syndrome may in fact be reproducible in these primate studies. This evidence lends strong support to the contention that a stress reaction in humans may promote a dangerous metabolic syndrome.

We have recently labeled this condition a "civilization syndrome," because the underlying, primary pathogenetic factors appear to be overeating, low physical activity, stress, smoking, and alcohol. These are signs of an unhealthy life-style and are often seen in urbanized society today.

IMPLICATIONS

There are several scientific and practical implications of the elucidation of this visceral obesity syndrome, its metabolic complications, and its effects on serious morbidity and mortality. First, human obesity is clearly not a homogenous entity. As a consequence, the medical profession should be selective in the work-up and treatment of obesity patients (see Chapters 82 and 98). Second, endocrine and neuroendocrine abnormalities may be of pathogenetic importance for the development of NIDDM as well as a major factor in the development of CVD. The recognition of these relationships might lead to new avenues for understanding these prevalent and serious diseases. Finally, better knowledge of the pathogenetic mechanism may lead to new developments in prevention and therapy.

FURTHER READING

Björntorp, P. (1988). The associations between obesity, adipose tissue distribution and disease. *Acta Medica Scandinavica* (Suppl. 723), 121–134. Provides an overview of the field with a full list of references.

Björntorp, P. (1990). "Portal" adipose tissue as a generator of risk factors for cardiovascular disease and diabetes. *Arteriosclerosis, 10,* 493–496. Provides an overview of the field with a full list of references.

Björntorp, P. (1991). Metabolic implications of body fat distribution. *Diabetes Care, 14,* 1132–1143. A review of body fat distribution data emphasizing specific associations with metabolic variables.

Björntorp, P. (1991). Adipose tissue distribution and function. *International Journal of Eating Disorders, 15,* 67–81. Provides an overview of the field with a full list of references.

Björntorp, P. (1992). Psychosocial factors and fat distribution. In G. Ailhaud et al. (Eds.), *Obesity in Europe, 91* (pp. 377–387). London: John Libbey. Provides an overview of the field with a full list of references.

Björntorp, P. (1992). Biochemistry of obesity in relation to diabetes. In K. G. M. M. Alberti, R. A. DeFronzo, H. Keen, & P. Zimmet (Eds.), *Textbook of diabetes mellitus* (pp. 551–568). London: John Wiley. Provides an overview of the field with a full list of references.

Björntorp, P. (1993). Androgens, the metabolic syndrome and non-insulin dependent diabetes mellitus. *Annals of the New York Academy of Sciences, 676,* 242–252. Discussion of the cluster of variables known as metabolic syndrome.

Björntorp, P. (1993). Visceral obesity: A "civilization syndrome." *Obesity Research, 1,* 206–222. A detailed review of the body fat distribution literature, with a focus on how physiological factors interact with health habits associated with modern life.

Jayo, J., Shively, C., Kaplan, J., & Manuck, S. (1993). Effects of exercise and stress on body fat distribution in male cynomolgus monkeys. *International Journal of Obesity, 17,* 597–604. In these monkeys, stress was followed by visceral fat accumulation and endocrine and metabolic perturbations similar to those found in abdominal obesity in humans, strongly supporting the concept of a similar pathogenesis in the human condition.

Mårin, P., Darin, N., Amemiya, T., Andersson, B., Jern, S., & Björntorp, P. (1992). Cortisol secretion in relation to body fat distribution in obese premenopausal women. *Metabolism, 41,* 882–886. This report provides evidence for a hypersensitive hypothalamic–pituitary–adrenal axis in abdominal obesity.

· 80 ·

THE MOLECULAR BIOLOGY OF OBESITY

RUDOLPH L. LEIBEL
JULES HIRSCH

GENES AS MEDIATORS OF ENVIRONMENTAL INFLUENCES ON BODY COMPOSITION

The human haploid genome comprises approximately three billion nucleotide base pairs encoding an estimated 100,000 genes. Until the recent advent of molecular genetic techniques capable of following the segregation of multiple relatively small regions of the genome, the extent of the contributions of nature and nurture to obesity could not be examined in a reductionist fashion. Studies of the concordance of somatic phenotype among monozygous and dizygous twins, adopted children, and their respective parents, as well as segregation analysis of body mass index in families, indicate a substantial genetic contribution to the degree of body fatness (see Chapter 4). Although single-gene/ locus mutations that produce obesity are well known (e.g., in Prader–Willi, Alstrom– Hallberg, and Bardet–Biedl syndromes) most human obesity appears to reflect the results of complex interactions between *multiple* genes and the environment.

The relevant question, then, is not whether genes play a role in the determination of body composition, but rather which genes are involved and how they function. For genetic disorders such as cystic fibrosis or sickle cell anemia, the disease phenotype, while partly dependent on developmental or environmental factors, will nonetheless be apparent in virtually all individuals who are homozygous for mutant alleles. This virtual concordance of genotype and phenotype is not true in the case of phenylketonuria, for example, in which the phenotype can be prevented or markedly ameliorated by altering the environment (preventing exposure to excessive phenylalanine).

Obesity resembles phenylketonuria in that the phenotype is absolutely dependent on the environment. Obesity cannot develop unless the environment permits energy intake to exceed output over a sufficient period of time. This fact greatly complicates the task of identifying the genes that are responsible for susceptibility to obesity. The genes that must be identified are those that convey susceptibility in particular environmental circumstances. Such critical interactions of genes and environment to produce phenotype are elegantly described by the so-called norm of reaction, which treats genotype as a mirror that reflects environmental circumstances to generate the phenotype of an individual organism. Rather than being the sole or even the most important determinant of phenotype, genotype mediates, environmental influences on development and on other phenotypes of the individual.

The amount of fat stored in the body at any time is the result of many processes impinging on the net energy balance (see below). Different genes (or groups of genes) may play a role in this balance at different points in development and in different environmental/metabolic contexts. The shape of the norm of reaction "surface" of a gene (or of a group of genes that determines a metabolic process) will dictate the magnitude of the genotypic impact in any environmental circumstance. Thus the same aspect of a phenotype may be influenced by different genes under different environmental circumstances.

THE INFLUENCE OF GENES ON ENERGY STORAGE

By considering obesity from the perspective of the first law of thermodynamics we can identify the physiological processes that must be under the control of obesity-related genes in whatever environmental context they are acting, as in the equation

$$\Delta U = E - W$$

where U is stored energy, E is energy input, and W is metabolic and physical work performed. Most of the body's potential chemical energy (U) is stored as fat, which has the advantages of high caloric density and hydrophobicity. Energy input (E) occurs by food intake; energy output (W) results from resting metabolic processes (e.g., maintenance of transmembrane ion gradients), thermic effects of feeding, and physical activity (see Chapter 6). Changes in stored energy (ΔU) are due to imbalances between E and W.

Physiological studies in animals and humans suggest that energy intake and expenditure are interrelated, so that changes in one lead to compensatory changes in the other, which tends to hold body energy stores relatively constant over time. Because of the existence of these compensatory processes, it seems unlikely that genes that determine long-term energy storage would *primarily* influence the afferent or effector limbs of this apparent control loop. Rather, the major relevant genes more likely influence a central comparator, or "set point," which integrates afferent signals and coordinates efferent traffic that affects food intake and energy expenditure. However, cogent arguments can be made for a model of weight regulation that does not rely on a set point but is based on the detection of the level of energy storage. If, for example, meal initiation is affected by the status of hepatic glycogen stores, then equilibrium points for hepatic glycogen, which may be genetically/developmentally determined, may be the basis for body weight regulation. Of course, biochemical biasing of glycogen storage might be achieved by alterations of body fat, thus allowing for metabolic "cross talk" between hepatic biochemistry and adipose tissue energy stores. In any event, the physiological areas involved in the control of fat storage or of processes leading to fat storage are the likely sites for genetic alteration in human obesity.

IDENTIFICATION OF GENES RELEVANT TO HUMAN OBESITY SYNDROMES

A few types of human obesity are clearly related to defects in single genes or small regions of the genome. Prader–Willi syndrome, for example, is due to the absence (or lack of expression) of one or more paternal alleles of genes on the short arm of chromosome 15. Bardet–Biedl syndrome is transmitted as an autosomal recessive. The obesity in Bardet–Biedl and Prader–Willi patients is highly penetrant—that is, if the genotype is present, obesity is very likely to occur. In a large Bedouin family, recently reported, the Bardet–Biedl locus was mapped to chromosome 16. However, the Bardet–Biedl phenotype was not linked to this locus in an affected subkindred of this family. Similar pleiotropism has been detected in some of the families in which either the glucokinase gene (chromosome 7p) or a locus on chromosome 20q has been linked to the maturity-onset diabetes of the young (MODY) phenotype. This degree of genetic pleiotropism in disorders with distinct phenotypes suggests that there will be considerable heterogeneity of genotypes contributing to common phenotypes such as obesity and non–insulin-dependent diabetes mellitus. The recent demonstration that four distinct phenotypes (including multiple endocrine neoplasia and Hirschprung disease) result from different mutations in one gene, the receptor tyrosine kinase gene, indicates yet another layer of complexity with which efforts to identify obesity-related genes may have to contend.

Genetic Analysis of Complex Phenotypes

A major problem now confronting geneticists is the molecular dissection of the genetic bases for complex phenotypes such as obesity. Molecular tools and analytic techniques are needed for identifying the genes that, in the aggregate, lead to quantitative traits whose medical consequence is related to degree of affectation rather than the presence or absence of a discrete phenotype. The substantial phenotypic complexity of single-gene/locus mutations is still far less than that which arises when phenotypes determined by multiple genes are analyzed. Here one contends not only with multiple alleles per locus but also with the interactions among loci. The existence of highly polymorphic molecular marker sets that span the genome at increasingly smaller intervals has enabled the mapping of the quantitative trait loci (QTLs) that determine aspects of fruit (tomato) phenotype, hypertension in rats, insulin-dependent diabetes milletus in rats and mice, seizure susceptibility in mice, and fat content in pigs.

The genes that are primarily responsible for the regulation of body weight in mammals are not known (see Chapter 4). Given the importance of this system to survival and reproduction, the relevant physiological systems are likely to be redundant and overlapping. Because obesity itself results in profound and protean metabolic changes, the primary components of this system have proven difficult to isolate by conventional biochemical and physiologic approaches.

Identification of such genes can be approached in two general ways: (1) "candidate genes" for the phenotype can be identified by biochemical analyses of relevant metabolic processes in animals and humans and/or by looking for human homologues of genes that cause obesity in animals; and (2) the relevant genomic regions can be "mapped" in human families by segregating for phenotypes of interest (e.g., obesity), which can be done by tracking the cosegregation of polymorphic markers with the phenotype(s).

The first approach relies on the prior identification of genes or genomic regions that may play a role in energy balance. Processes believed to be relevant to the phenotype in affected and unaffected individuals (humans or animals) are examined for differences that might reflect the primary metabolic or structural basis for the phenotype. The genes for these proteins can be examined either directly (by looking for biologically significant differences in gene sequence or expression between affecteds and unaffecteds) or indirectly (by looking for genetic linkage between these genes and relevant aspects of phenotype). Such efforts are complicated by the fact that the phenotype that is used to identify the presence of the gene(s) frequently perturbs the function of many other organs. Obesity is a clear example of this phenomenon. The presence of excessive body fat, from whatever cause, results in secondary increases in the concentration of circulating insulin and a variety of other metabolic changes. Any effort to identify the primary etiology of the obesity is confounded by the biochemical changes the obesity itself induces in the organism.

The second approach requires no *a priori* assumptions about the physiological functions of the relevant gene(s). The gene is identified by its location in the genome rather than by its structure or function. If a sufficiently fine genetic map and then a physical map of a region linked to a specific aspect of phenotype can be made, the responsible gene can be cloned. Such a "positional" strategy was used to clone the genes responsible for cystic fibrosis, Huntington's disease, and muscular dystrophy. The isolation of a gene in circumstances where the current understanding of the relevant biochemistry/cell physiology does not point to a specific molecular mechanism may result in a situation where the gene is in hand, but the molecular pathogenesis of the disease remains a mystery (e.g., Huntington's disease, muscular dystrophy). Alternatively, if in physiological studies a specific mechanism (e.g., chloride transport in cystic fibrosis) has been implicated, then isolation of the gene can at once confirm the validity of such postulates and provide the basis for the creation of rational therapeutics (e.g., adenovirus-mediated chloride transporter gene transfection of respiratory epithelium).

Positional strategies are currently being used to clone the genes for several rodent mutations that cause obesity (see below). Once cloned, these genes can be examined as candidate genes for specific instances of human obesity.

RODENT MODELS OF OBESITY

Genetic models of deranged energy balance may provide insights into various elements of the control processes. A considerable number of apparent single-gene mutations resulting in obesity have been described in rodents. The phenotypes of these animals include early-onset hyperphagia, reduced energy expenditure, insulin resistance, and diabetes of variable severity (depending on the strain of the rodents in which the obesity mutation is carried). Normal alleles of the genes involved appear to produce tonic suppression of body weight/fat, since their recessive, loss-of-function mutations result in the maintenance of a greater amount of body fat. An understanding of the molecular bases for one or more of these mutations would identify the molecules that are central in the integrated control of energy balance. The dominant yellow mutation (A^y), which is associated with obesity and an increased frequency of various cancers, has recently been shown to result in the expression of the normal agouti gene product in tissues where it is not normally expressed (e.g., the brain). This finding suggests that a normal brain contains receptors for a molecular homologue of the agouti protein and that this receptor/ligand system may play a role in the regulation of energy balance.

The rodent mutations may be used in several ways. A study of the molecular physiology of organs (e.g., brain, pancreas, muscle, fat) from preobese, homozygous affected animals may reveal genes that play a seminal role in the development of the obese phenotype. By examining organ-specific early differences in gene expression between affected and wild-type animals one might even identify the mutant gene. Positional cloning strategies may also be used to isolate the responsible genes without the need for prior knowledge of the gene product. And finally, precise genetic mapping of these mutations by interstrain genetic crosses can be used to identify regions of synteny-homology between rodent and human. This information can be used to select polymorphic molecular markers, which in turn can be used to determine (by linkage analysis) the possible roles of such genes in human obesity.

RELATIONSHIPS OF MOLECULAR MAPS TO PHENOTYPE

In essence, the identification of genes that play a role in obesity (or any other phenotype) requires the location of those areas of the genome that are common among affecteds or that are different between affecteds and unaffecteds. These differences/similarities can be tracked using DNA sequence variation to mark specific regions of chromosomes. The availability of sets of polymorphic markers that span the genome now permits such tracking across the entire genome of an individual. Maps with 15-centiMorgan (cM) resolution permit the localization of a highly penetrant simple, single-gene Mendelian trait. With a 1-centiMorgan map one can find regions of homozygosity by descent (regions of shared identical DNA sequence) in inbred children affected with a recessive disease. Denser maps will permit linkage disequilibrium (association) studies to identify regions of identity by descent in affected subjects. This is the degree of resolution (e.g., 0.1 centiMorgan) needed for efficient study of polygenic traits. This use of high-density maps has been described by Lander as "enlightened brute force." Newer approaches such as representational difference analysis (RDA) and genome mismatch scanning (GMS) will, in theory, permit direct cloning of regions of similarity or difference between two genomes without the need for prior detailed genetic or physical maps.

THE CRITICAL ROLE OF QUANTITATIVE PHENOTYPING

Molecular genetics provides the tools and techniques for the ultimate in reductionist biology—determining the relationship of any phenotype to specific sequences of nucleotides. The monogenic diseases are currently being described in this way at an accelerating rate. The polygene phenotypes will be much more difficult to solve, but they are more important from the point of view of quantitative burden of illness. In the genetic assault on these complex phenotypes, clinical characterization will be of critical importance. We will be looking at quantitative traits (continuous variables) that are determined by a number of genes, each with a relatively small effect. For single-gene diseases, the investigator need only make a decision (admittedly often difficult) regarding the presence or absence of the disease. For continuous traits such as obesity, the situation is far more complex. The powerful effects of development, environment, and other genes on the degree of obesity (and its medical consequences) will make it necessary to select clinical subgroups for analysis based on detailed historical, anthropometric and metabolic data.

Far from marking the end of the need for clinical investigation, the advent of tools for monitoring the segregation of very small regions of the genome places enormous and unprecedented emphasis on the ability to accurately quantify the components of complex phenotypes for the purpose of identifying individuals most likely to have the same genetic basis for the phenotype of interest. The use of isolated (from an interbreeding point of view), genetically homogeneous populations may be of significant help in reducing phenotypic "noise" in such studies. Failure to give sufficient emphasis to these aspects of the analysis of polygene effects on continuous phenotypic traits will result in experimentally fatal mismatches between the resolution of genotypic (nucleotide level) and phenotypic measures. It is also likely that, as these studies proceed, genotypic analysis will provide a powerful tool for the selection of individuals on whom to perform such detailed phenotypic characterization. In this way, a reciprocal interaction between clinical analysis and molecular genetics will build an understanding of the fundamental pathophysiology of obesity.

FURTHER READING

Andersson, L., Haley, C. S., Ellegren, H., Knott, S. A., Johansson, M., Andersson, K., Andersson-Eklund, L., Edfors-Lilija, I., Fredholm, M., Hansson, I., Hakansson, J., & Lundstrom, K. (1994). Genetic mapping of quantitative trait loci for growth and fatness in pigs. *Science, 263,* 1771–1774. The application of QTL analysis to the identification of the region of the pig genome that affects body fat.

Bultman, S. J., Michaud, E. J., & Woychik, R. P. (1992). Molecular characterization of the mouse agouti locus. *Cell, 77,* 1195–1204. The agouti gene is promiscuously expressed in the obese yellow (A^y) mouse—the first demonstration of a molecular basis for obesity.

Collins, F. (1992). Positional cloning: Let's not call it reverse anymore. *Nature Genetics, 1,* 3–6. The basic strategy for identifying genes based solely on their location in the genome.

Friedman, J., & Leibel, R. (1992). Tackling a weighty problem. *Cell, 69,* 217–220. Strategies for the cloning of rodent obesity genes and relating them to human obesity.

Griffiths, A. J. F., Miller, J. H., Suzuki, D. T., Lewontin, R. C., & Gelbart, W. M. (1993). *An introduction to genetic analysis*. New York: W. H. Freeman. Chapter 23 describes the "norm of reaction" as a model for environment-by-genome interaction.

Jacob, H., Lindpainter, K., Lincoln, S., Kusumi, K., Bunker, R., Mao, Y., Ganten, D., Dzau, V., & Lander, E. (1991). Genetic mapping of a gene causing hypertension in the stroke-prone spontaneously hypertensive rat. *Cell, 67,* 213–224. Identification of a rodent hypertension-related gene by positional strategy.

Lander, E. (1993). Finding similarities and differences among genomes. *Nature Genetics, 4,* 5–6. The basic principles of RDA and GMS.

Silver, L. M. (1992). Bouncing off microsatellites. *Nature Genetics, 2,* 8–9. The identification and use of microsatellite (SSR, or simple sequence repeat motifs) markers for genetic mapping in various species.

Weissenbach, J., Gyapay, G., Dib, C., Vignal, A., Morissette, J., Millasseau, P., Vaysseix, G., & Lathrop, M. (1992). A second-generation linkage map of the human genome. *Nature, 359,* 794–801. Molecular genetic linkage maps of the human genome that employ highly polymorphic molecular markers based on recurring simple sequence repeat motifs (SSRs, microsatellites).

GLOSSARY

Autosomal Recessive: A mutation, located on a nonsex chromosome, whose phenotype is apparent only when both copies (alleles from both parents) of the gene are mutated.

CENTIMORGAN (cM): The distance between two genetic loci measured by the frequency of meiotic recombination between the loci. 1 centiMorgan = 1% recombination ("crossing over") frequency. In humans, 1 centiMorgan is equivalent to approximately 1×10^6 nucleotide base pairs.

DIFFERENTIAL DISPLAY: A technique for identifying messenger RNAs (mRNAs) that are differentially expressed as a result of mutation, cell specificity, or treatment difference.

GENOME MISMATCH SCANNING: A method of linkage analysis that does not require conventional polymorphic molecular markers. The technique entails looking for regions of similarity in DNA from different individuals who share a phenotype.

LINKAGE ANALYSIS: The effort to demonstrate the cosegregation of genes, molecular polymorphisms, or phenotypic characteristics on a region of the same chromosome.

MAPS:

1. GENETIC: Shows the location and order of genes on specific chromosomes. Distances are determined by the frequency of meiotic recombination between loci.

2. PHYSICAL: Shows the ordering of genes based on their relationships in cloned, contiguous fragments of DNA.

NORM OF REACTION: The pattern of phenotypes produced by a specific genotype under different environmental conditions.

PLEIOTROPISM: Several aspects of phenotype affected by a single mutation, or similar phenotypes produced by different mutations.

POLYMORPHIC MARKER: A variation in the DNA sequence or protein phenotype (e.g., amino acid sequence, charge, mass, gross physical structure) that occurs in a genomic region or gene near a genetic locus of interest. Such variation can be used to identify the precise region of a chromosome on which a gene is located.

REPRESENTATIONAL DIFFERENCE ANALYSIS (RDA): A technique for isolating DNA fragments that are unique to one population of DNA fragments but not to another. Can be used to short-cut more tedious genetic techniques for isolating DNA from specific regions of the genome.

SEGREGATION ANALYSIS: The delineation of the mode of inheritance of a trait by the application of genetic models of inheritance to patterns of familial aggregation of phenotypes.

• 81 •

IMPACT OF SUGAR AND FAT SUBSTITUTES ON FOOD INTAKE

Barbara J. Rolls

Supermarket shelves are replete with foods and drinks that are sugar-free or fat-free. According to a recent survey conducted by the Calorie Control Council, four out of five Americans are consuming these products. Most consumers expect such reduced-calorie foods to help them lower their intake of sugar, fat, and total energy and to help with weight control.

SUGAR SUBSTITUTES

Many people believe that sugar contributes to overeating and obesity. However, there is little evidence that sugar is involved in the etiology of obesity or that obese individuals eat excessive quantities of sweet foods. Nevertheless, the wide availability of sugar substitutes has meant that a reduction in sugar intake is a relatively easy strategy to employ when dieting to lose weight.

Sugar substitutes (also referred to as "nonnutritive," "artificial," or "intense" sweeteners) have been available for decades. Saccharin was the first widely available sweetener. It has largely been replaced by aspartame, which is used to reduce sugar in a wide range of foods and drinks. Acesulfame K has also been approved for use. Other sweeteners, ranging from 400 to 10,000 times sweeter than sucrose, are awaiting approval. Recently there has been considerable debate about the effectiveness of intense sweeteners as an adjunct to weight control. This debate began with reports that sweet taste can increase appetite and food intake.

Although there have been reports of increased hunger ratings associated with intense sweeteners, a number of investigators have found that the most widely used sweetener, aspartame, is generally associated with decreased or unchanged ratings of hunger. Even when aspartame increased ratings of hunger, there was no evidence of an impact on the regulation of food intake and body weight. Aspartame has not been found to increase food intake; indeed, several studies have shown that consumption of aspartame-sweetened foods or drinks was associated with either no change or a reduction in energy intake.

Data from long-term studies of the use of sugar substitutes are limited. Laboratory studies in which aspartame replaced sugar indicate that if the calorie reduction is substantial—that is, if a number of sugar-free foods are consumed during the day, compensation for this reduction will be incomplete and daily energy intake will be reduced. The studies suggest that the substitution of only a few sugar-reduced foods may not reduce daily energy intake. Thus the casual use of foods with sugar substitutes is unlikely to be of benefit in weight control.

Also at issue is whether intense sweeteners affect diet composition. Although results of several laboratory studies show that the consumption of intense sweeteners is associated with reduced daily sugar intake, data from population-based diet surveys do not show that sugar consumption has decreased as sweetener use has increased. More controlled long-term studies of the effects of sweeteners on diet composition and on daily energy intake are required.

In one study, foods that incorporated sugar substitutes formed a valuable part of a balanced weight control program that included behavioral interventions and exercise in addition to dietary modification. The use of aspartame-sweetened products increased satisfaction with the diet by providing a range of palatable foods with reduced energy, and aspartame use was associated with better long-term control of body weight.

FAT SUBSTITUTES

While there is little evidence that sugar consumption is associated with obesity, sugar increases the palatability of many high-fat foods, and the consumption of fat is associated with obesity. Results of several studies have shown that the development of obesity is more strongly related to fat intake than to total energy intake. Obese individuals have an enhanced preference for dietary fat, and they appear to be relatively insensitive to the satiety value of fat. Furthermore, any excess fat consumed is more likely to be deposited as body fat in obese persons than in lean individuals.

Despite concerted efforts to encourage a reduction in fat in the daily diet, fat comprises approximately 37% of the average diet in the United States. Because taste is the primary determinant of food choices, and since eating habits are difficult to change, a key to fat reduction may be to provide reduced-fat foods that mimic the full-fat versions. In one assessment of dietary changes associated with several years of successful compliance with a low-fat diet it was found that trimming fat from foods and substituting low-fat foods for the higher-fat versions were the best strategies for long-term fat reduction.

A wide range of fat substitutes, including gums, emulsifiers, starches, and proteins, are used to produce palatable low-fat or fat-free products. On the horizon, but not yet approved for consumption, are zero-calorie fat substitutes having the same physical and sensory properties as traditional fats. These fat substitutes are suitable for a wide range of applications, including frying. Thus the potential for a change in the nutrient composition of the food supply is enormous.

Since fat substitutes represent a new technology, there is little information on their effects on food intake and food selection. Several recent studies in which olestra (a zero-calorie fat substitute) was covertly incorporated into a meal or several meals showed that both lean young men and children compensated for the calorie reduction later in the test day so that there was no reduction in daily energy intake. Olestra consumption was associated with a dose-dependent reduction in fat intake and a reciprocal increase in carbohydrate intake; subjects did not eat more fat to make up for the fat reduction associated with olestra. It seems likely that the most important health benefit associated with the use of fat substitutes will be a reduction in the percentage of calories from fat in the diet.

The role of fat substitutes in weight reduction has not yet been examined. In one study, the results led to the suggestion that the incorporation of olestra into foods reduces the feelings of "deprivation" associated with low-fat diets and also reduces the number of foods that are considered "tempting." Studies are needed to determine whether fat substitutes have long-term value for dietary modification or weight loss.

CONCLUSIONS

The key to whether sugar and fat substitutes will improve diet composition or reduce energy intake is the way the consumer uses them. These products can help with compliance to, and satisfaction with, low-energy diets by increasing the range of palatable foods available for consumption. If reduced-sugar foods are substituted for foods with a high sugar content, there should be a reduction in the sugar content of the diet. Likewise, if reduced-fat foods are substituted for foods with a high fat content, there should be a reduction in the fat content of the diet. However, there may be no beneficial changes in either diet composition or energy intake if a consumer uses the consumption of such reduced-energy foods as an excuse to eat other high-fat foods or to overeat high-calorie, low-fat foods. Further studies of the psychological and physiological effects of sugar and fat substitutes are critical for developing appropriate nutritional counseling strategies to promote acceptance of, and adherence to, dietary modifications.

FURTHER READING

Birch, L. L., Johnson, S. L., Jones, M. B., & Peters, J. C. (1993). Effects of a nonenergy fat substitute on children's energy and macronutrient intake. *American Journal of Clinical Nutrition, 58*, 326–333. A description of the effects on food intake of a zero-calorie fat substitute in children.

Drewnowski, A., Brunzell, J. D., Sande, K., Iverius, P. H., & Greenwood, M. R. C. (1985). Sweet tooth reconsidered: Taste responsiveness in human obesity. *Physiology and Behavior, 35*, 617–622. A study showing that obese individuals have a preference for high-fat foods, not sweet foods.

Foreyt, J. P., & Goodrick, G. K. (1992). Potential impact of sugar and fat substitutes in American diet. *Journal of the National Cancer Institutes Monographs, 12*, 99–103. A review of the potential impact of sugar and fat substitutes.

Kanders, B. S., Lavin, P. T., Kowalchuk, M. B., Greenberg, I., & Blackburn, G. L. (1988). An evaluation of the effect of aspartame on weight loss. *Appetite, 11* (Suppl.), 73–84. The first clinical trial to assess the effects of the incorporation of aspartame into a weight loss program.

Mela, D. J. (1992). Nutritional implications of fat substitutes. *Journal of the American Dietetic Association, 92*, 472–476. A review of the potential impact of fat substitutes on nutrition.

Porikos, K. P., Booth, G., & VanItallie, T. B. (1977). Effect of covert nutritive dilution on the spontaneous intake of obese individuals: A pilot study. *American Journal of Clinical Nutrition, 30*, 1638–1644. The first study of the long-term effects of a sugar substitute on food intake.

Rolls, B. J. (1991). Effects of intense sweeteners on hunger, food intake and body weight: A review. *American Journal of Clinical Nutrition, 53*, 872–878. A comprehensive review of the effects of sugar substitutes on food intake and body weight.

Rolls, B. J., Pirraglia, P. A., Jones, M. B., & Peters, J. C. (1992). Effects of olestra, a non-caloric fat substitute, on daily energy and fat intake in lean men. *American Journal of Clinical Nutrition, 56,* 84–92. The first controlled study of the effects of olestra on food intake in lean men.

Rolls, B. J., & Shide, D. J. (1992). The influence of dietary fat on food intake and body weight. *Nutrition Reviews, 50,* 283–290. A review of the effects of dietary fat on food intake and body weight.

· IX ·
ASSESSMENT AND TREATMENT OF OBESITY

· 82 ·

CLINICAL ASSESSMENT OF OBESE PATIENTS

Roland L. Weinsier

The clinical assessment of patients who are seen for treatment of obesity is critical for understanding the etiology of the disorder in each case and for establishing a reference point for response to therapy. Not all clinical assessments must be conducted by a physician, although the person who does the assessment must be qualified to rule out neuroendocrine causes of obesity, determine the presence and extent of comorbidities, if any, recommend further medical and laboratory evaluation as needed, and recognize which individuals are at high risk for complications of obesity and/or its treatment. The clinical assessment consists of a focused medical history, a careful physical examination, and appropriate laboratory studies.

MEDICAL HISTORY

The focused medical history should identify: (1) potential factors contributing to the individual's obesity (e.g., familial, behavioral, or endocrinological); (2) current medical complications; (3) past treatment responses; and (4) factors that should preclude weight reduction intervention. Table 82.1 is an outline of the factors generally to be considered under each of these categories. Although endocrine abnormalities associated with obesity are listed, identifiable endocrinological disorders that cause obesity are quite uncommon, occurring in fewer than 1% of cases. Second, when present, the endocrine disorders that are most likely to cause weight gain (i.e., Cushing syndrome, hypothyroidism, polycystic ovary syndrome) rarely cause severe degrees of obesity.

When searching for medical complications of the patient's obesity, the clinician should remember the following: (1) not all obese persons have medical complications or are unhealthy; (2) there is still controversy over the extent of the contribution of obesity per se to some medical problems, such as hypertension and hypercholesterolemia; and (3) the known comorbidities of obesity are not evenly distributed among all obese persons. Consequently, it cannot be assumed that all obese persons are ill or that their overweight condition is the primary cause of any comorbid states that may exist.

TABLE 82.1. Factors to Be Considered in the Medical History of an Obese Patient

Factors predisposing to/associated with obesity
Family history of obesity (number of first-degree relatives who are obese)
Age of onset
In children: growth pattern, mental and physical maturation
Potential endocrine abnormalities
   Hypothyroidism: symptoms include cold intolerance, menstrual abnormalities, constipation, weakness
   Cushing's syndrome: symptoms include hypertension, glucose intolerance, menstrual dysfunction, weakness, back pain, compression fractures, bruising
   Polycystic ovarian syndrome: symptoms include reduced/absent menses shortly after menarche, hirsutism
Life-style changes concurrent with onset of weight gain (e.g., job change, marriage/divorce, childbirth, relocation)
Dietary pattern (best reviewed with diet records)
Pattern of physical activity (best reviewed with exercise records)

History of medical complications of obesity
Cancer (especially of endometrium and breast)
Glucose intolerance and diabetes mellitus
Hepatobiliary disease (especially gallstones, hepatic steatosis and enlargement)
Hypertension, hyperlipidemia, coronary artery disease
Osteoarthritis (especially, but not exclusively, of weight-bearing joints)
Respiratory disease (especially periodic apnea due to obstruction, or alveolar hypoventilation)

Previous treatment responses
Past successes, failures; weight-cycling pattern
Past medical and surgical therapies for obesity

Factors warranting precaution/precluding weight reduction
< 20 or > 65 years of age
History of anorexia nervosa
Pregnancy or lactation

PHYSICAL EXAMINATION

Assessment of Degree of Obesity

Normative reference values for defining obesity do not necessarily indicate optimum health (see Chapters 13 and 67). Nevertheless it is important to attempt to classify individuals according to their "desirable" weight. A variety of data sets have been developed for reference weights, although none is considered ideal. Table 82.2 provides weight–height reference values for men and women derived from Metropolitan Life Insurance Company actuarial data. The degree of obesity can be expressed as percentage overweight, with desirable body weight usually set between 90% and 120% of "ideal" weight. Another method for assessing the degree of obesity is the body mass index (BMI), taken as weight in kilograms per height in meters^2. Although individuals with unusually large muscle mass or short legs for their height may be misclassified as obese (see Chapters 8 and 18), the guidelines listed below are useful. Grades II and III are clearly associated with increased health risk.

Degree of obesity	Body mass index
Grade 0	<25
Grade I	25–29.9
Grade II	30–40
Grade III	>40

TABLE 82.2. Weight–Height Reference Chart (Adults)

Height (no shoes)		Reference weight			
		Women		Men	
Feet/inches	Centimeters	lb	kg	lb	kg
4'10"	147	101	46	—	—
4'11"	150	104	47	—	—
5'0"	152	107	49	—	—
5'1"	155	110	50	—	—
5'2"	157	113	51	124	56
5'3"	160	116	53	127	58
5'4"	162	120	54	130	59
5'5"	165	123	56	133	60
5'6"	167	128	58	137	62
5'7"	170	132	60	141	64
5'8"	172	136	62	145	66
5'9"	175	140	63	149	68
5'10"	178	144	65	153	69
5'11"	180	148	67	158	71
6'0"	183	152	69	162	74
6'1"	185	—	—	167	76
6'2"	188	—	—	171	78
6'3"	190	—	—	176	80
6'4"	193	—	—	181	82

Note. Data adapted from Metropolitan Life Company: Build and Blood Pressure Study, 1959. In Weinsier, Heimburger, and Butterworth (1989, p. 147). Copyright 1989 by C. V. Mosby Co. Reprinted by permission.

Skinfold measurements afford more specificity in classifying the degree of obesity and tracking change in body fat (see Chapter 18). One approach is that of Durnin and Womersley, which is based on the sum of four skinfold measurements: biceps, triceps, subscapular, and suprailiac. The percentage of body fat of men and women is then estimated by making reference to Table 82.3. Below are the recommended criteria for normal percent of body fat for men and women:

	Percent body fat	
Category	Men	Women
Normal	12%–20%	20%–30%
Borderline	21%–25%	31%–33%
Obese	>25%	>33%

Body fat distribution, independent of the amount of fat, is an important predictor of medical problems (see Chapter 79). The easiest measurement is the waist:hip ratio, taken as their circumferences. A ratio of >0.85 for women and >1.00 for men reflects anb abdominal, or android, pattern, which is associated with increased visceral fat and risk for hypertension, hyperinsulinemia, diabetes, anh cardiovascular disease.

Medical Examination of the Obese Patient

The following aspects are particularly important in identifying coexistent medical disorders and helping rule out endocrinologic abnormalities and should be part of the more comprehensive physical examination.

TABLE 82.3. Equivalent Fat Content, as Percentage of Body Weight, for a Range of Values for the Sum of Four Skinfolds

Skin-folds (mm)	Men (age in years)				Women (age in years)			
	17–29	30–39	40–49	50+	16–29	30–39	40–49	50+
15	4.8				10.5			
20	8.1	12.2	12.2	12.6	14.1	17.0	19.8	21.4
25	10.5	14.2	15.0	15.6	16.8	19.4	22.2	24.0
30	12.9	16.2	17.7	18.6	19.5	21.8	24.5	26.6
35	14.7	17.7	19.6	20.8	21.5	23.7	26.4	28.5
40	16.4	19.2	21.4	22.9	23.4	25.5	28.2	30.3
45	17.7	20.4	23.0	24.7	25.0	26.9	29.6	31.9
50	19.0	21.5	24.6	26.5	26.5	28.2	31.0	33.4
55	20.1	22.5	25.9	27.9	27.8	29.4	32.1	34.6
60	21.2	23.5	27.1	29.2	29.1	30.6	33.2	35.7
65	22.2	24.3	28.2	30.4	30.2	31.6	34.1	36.7
70	23.1	25.1	29.3	31.6	31.2	32.5	35.0	37.7
75	24.0	25.9	30.3	32.7	32.2	33.4	35.9	38.7
80	24.8	26.6	31.2	33.8	33.1	34.3	36.7	39.6
85	25.5	27.2	32.1	34.8	34.0	35.1	37.5	40.4
90	26.2	27.8	33.0	35.8	34.8	35.8	38.3	41.2
95	26.9	28.4	33.7	36.6	35.6	36.5	39.0	41.9
100	27.6	29.0	34.4	37.4	36.4	37.2	39.7	42.6
105	28.2	29.6	35.1	38.2	37.1	37.9	40.4	43.3
110	28.8	30.1	35.8	39.0	37.8	38.6	41.0	43.9
115	29.4	30.6	36.4	39.7	38.4	39.1	41.5	44.5
120	30.0	31.1	37.0	40.4	39.0	39.6	42.0	45.1
125	31.0	31.5	37.6	41.1	39.6	40.1	42.5	45.7
130	31.5	31.9	38.2	41.8	40.2	40.6	43.0	46.2
135	32.0	32.3	38.7	42.4	40.8	41.1	43.5	46.7
140	32.5	32.7	39.2	43.0	41.3	41.6	44.0	47.2
145	32.9	33.1	39.7	43.6	41.8	42.1	44.5	47.7
150	33.3	33.5	40.2	44.1	42.3	42.6	45.0	48.2
155	33.7	33.9	40.7	44.6	42.8	43.1	45.4	48.7
160	34.1	34.3	41.2	45.1	43.3	43.6	45.8	49.2
165	34.5	34.6	41.6	45.6	43.7	44.0	46.2	49.6
170	34.9	34.8	42.0	46.1	44.1	44.4	46.6	50.0
175	35.3					44.8	47.0	50.4
180	35.6					45.2	47.4	50.8
185	35.9					45.6	47.8	51.2
190						45.9	48.2	51.6
195						46.2	48.5	52.0
200						46.5	48.8	52.4
205							49.1	52.7
210							49.4	53.0

Note. Biceps, triceps, subscapular, and suprailiac of men and women of different ages. From Durnin and Womersley (1974), *British Journal of Nutrition, 32,* 77–97. Copyright 1974 by The Nutrition Society. Published by Cambridge University Press. Reprinted by permission.

Blood pressure: Should be taken using cuff size appropriate for the patient's arm circumference (this information is shown on the cuff itself; if in doubt, use a larger cuff to avoid a spuriously high reading).

Skin: Red to purple depressed striae, hirsutism, acne, and moon facies with plethora suggest Cushing syndrome; mild hirsutism is seen in cases of polycystic ovarian syndrome; dry, coarse, cool, and pale skin suggests hypothyroidism.

Fat distribution: Truncal distribution with fat accumulation around the supraclavicular areas and dorsocervical spine ("buffalo hump") suggests Cushing syndrome.

Thyroid gland: Enlargement is suggestive of hypothyroidism.

Edema: Boggy, nonpitting edema of the eyes, tongue, hands, and feet suggests the myxedema of hypothyroidism.

Neurologic examination: Slow ankle reflex with delayed relaxation phase suggests hypothyroidism; muscle weakness suggests Cushing syndrome and hypothyroidism.

LABORATORY ASSESSMENT

No laboratory test done on the obese patient should be considered routine and certainly does not replace a good medical history or physical examination. Tests should be dictated by individual findings, as indicated in Table 82.4.

CLINICAL CLASSIFICATION OF OBESITY

The appropriate clinical classification of the obese patient is, unfortunately, still based on ill-defined criteria. Nevertheless the following categories are frequently used and provide information about predisposition, duration, severity, and risk of medical complications associated with the obese state.

- Age of onset: juvenile versus adult-onset
- Familial predisposition: considered positive if at least one first-degree relative has a history of obesity
- Neuroendocrine disorder: presence/absence of underlying disease state
- Severity of obesity: as percent of desirable weight, grade of obesity by BMI, and/or percent of body fat

TABLE 82.4. Laboratory Assessment of Medical Conditions Associated with Obesity

If suspicion of . . .	Consider . . .
Cushing's syndrome	24-hour urine collection to be tested for free cortisol (>150 micrograms/24 hours; abnormal), plus low-dose dexamethasone suppression test of 0.5 milligrams every 6 hours for 2 days, with collection of 24-hour urine to test for 17-hydroxycorticosteroid levels on second day (>3.5 milligrams/24 hours; abnormal)
Hypothyroidism	Serum TSH level (normal, generally < 5 microunits/milliliter)
Diabetes	Fasting serum glucose level
Hyperlipidemia	Fasting total levels of cholesterol, triglycerides, HDL cholesterol
Gallstones	Ultrasonography
Periodic/sleep apnea	Sleep studies for oxygen desaturation; ENT exam for upper airway obstruction

Note. TSH, thyroid-stimulating hormone; HDL, high-density lipoprotein; ENT, ear, nose, and throat.

- Fat pattern: gynoid versus android (or upper body vs. lower body) according to waist:hip ratio (or other method of assessment)

As an example, a patient might be classified as having adult-onset, positive familial predisposition, no evidence of endocrine abnormality, Grade II severity, gynoid pattern of obesity.

SUMMARY

A thorough clinical assessment is central to understanding the complex etiological factors involved in an individual's obesity, to identify medical consequences requiring special attention, and to develop a comprehensive treatment plan. The heterogeneous nature of this disorder requires that assessment be undertaken at the level of the individual.

FURTHER READING

Björntorp, P. (1993). Visceral obesity: A "civilization syndrome." *Obesity Research, 1*, 206–222. A review of the relationship between body fat distribution and disease.

Bray, G. A. (1993). Fat distribution and body weight. *Obesity Research, 1*, 203–205. A discussion of guidelines for healthy body weights and body fat patterns.

Pi-Sunyer, F. X. (1994). Obesity. In M. Shils, J. Olson, & M. Shike (Eds.), *Modern nutrition in health and disease* (8th ed., pp. 984–1006). Philadelphia: Lea & Febiger. A review of obesity encompassing classification, assessment of severity, pathogenesis, and therapy.

Weinsier, R. L. (1989). Obesity. In R. Weinsier, D. Heimburger, & C. Butterworth (Eds.), *Handbook of clinical nutrition* (pp. 244–263). St. Louis: C. V. Mosby. An overview of obesity including guidelines for estimating desirable body weight, etiological factors, disease associates, prevention, and treatment.

• 83 •

STANDARDS FOR THE TREATMENT OF OBESITY

ADAM DREWNOWSKI

The provision of products and services to aid in weight loss represents a multibillion-dollar industry. Market analysts estimate that over $4.5 billion was spent in 1988 on hospital-sponsored clinics and programs for weight reduction. Nonclinical weight loss programs, both commercial and nonprofit, claimed a further $1.5 billion market, with over 13,000 such programs in operation.

The issue of consumer protection in the largely unregulated weight loss industry was the topic of congressional hearings in 1990. Subsequent investigations of products and services by the Food and Drug Administration and the Federal Trade Commission (FTC) have resulted in a number of cease-and-desist orders, aimed at protecting both the health and the finances of the consumer. To protect the consumer from false advertising claims, the FTC required the substantiation of claims regarding the efficacy of the weight loss program, the likelihood of permanent weight loss, and disclosure of the potential health risks of weight reduction.

The Michigan Task Force to Establish Weight Loss Guidelines grew out of failed attempts in that state to pass legislation protecting consumers from unsafe weight loss practices. Its primary goal was to establish a consensus within the health care community regarding acceptable standards of health care in weight loss programs. Task force members represented professional groups of physicians, dietitians, nurses, psychologists, research scientists, sports medicine specialists, and eating disorder experts. Additional input was sought from representatives of the weight loss industry. The final version of the Michigan guidelines was endorsed by 44 health organizations in Michigan and published in December 1990. A summary of the recommendations is provided in Table 83.1.

THE MICHIGAN GUIDELINES

The chief aim of the Michigan guidelines was to protect the consumer. Whether their managers acknowledge it or not, weight loss programs and services are effectively in the business of health care. In the view of the task force, such care should meet certain standards. Potential clients should be screened for health risks prior to weight loss, and programs should be staffed by competent professionals prepared to deliver the appropriate level of care.

TABLE 83.1. Final Recommendations for Adult Weight Loss Programs

Screening: The client should be screened, and the level of health risk should be identified: low, moderate, or high.

Individualized treatment plan: Factors contributing to the client's weight status should be identified. These factors should determine the relative importance of diet, exercise, behavioral change, medical monitoring or supervision, and health supervision in each individualized treatment plan.

Staffing: Weight loss service providers should be trained and appropriately supervised for each level of health risk of clients receiving care.

Full disclosure: The client should give informed consent, having been informed of any potential physical and psychological risks of weight loss, the probable long-term success of the program, the full cost of the program, and the professional credentials of the service providers.

Reasonable weight goal: The weight goal for the client should be based on personal and family history and not exclusively on height and weight charts.

Rate of weight loss: The advertised and actual rate of weight loss, after the first 2 weeks, should not exceed an average of 2 pounds per week.

Calories per day: The daily caloric intake should not be lower than 1,000 kilocalories without medical supervision. If the daily caloric intake is below 800 kilocalories, additional safeguards should be in place. Even with medical supervision, 600 kilocalories per day is the lowest recommended intake.

Diet composition
• Protein: between 0.8 and 1.5 grams protein per kilogram of goal body weight, but no more than 100 grams protein per day.
• Fat: 10% to 30% of energy as fat.
• Carbohydrate: at least 100 grams per day without medical supervision; at least 50 grams per day even with medical supervision.
• Fluid: at least 1 quart water daily.

Nutritional adequacy: The food plan should allow the client to obtain 100% of the Recommended Dietary Allowances (RDAs). If nutritional supplements are used, nutrient levels should not greatly exceed 100% of the RDA.

Nutrition education: Nutrition education encouraging permanent healthful eating patterns should be incorporated into the weight loss program.

Formula products: The food plan should consist of foods available from the conventional food supply. Formula products are not recommended for the treatment of moderate obesity and should not be used at low-calorie formulations without specialized medical supervision.

Exercise component: The weight loss program should include an exercise component that is safe and appropriate for the individual client:
• The client should be screened for conditions that would require medical clearance before starting an exercise program.
• The client should be instructed on how to recognize and deal with potentially dangerous physical responses to exercise.
• The client should work toward 30 to 60 minutes of continuous exercise five to seven times per week, with gradual increases in intensity and duration.

Psychological Component: Appropriate behavior modification techniques should be incorporated into the individualized weight loss program.

Appetite suppressants: Appetite suppressant drugs are not recommended and should not take the place of changes in diet, exercise, and behavior.

Weight maintenance: A maintenance phase should be included. Programs should place as high a priority on helping clients maintain weight loss as on achieving initial weight loss.

Note. Data from Task Force to Establish Weight Loss Guidelines for Michigan (1990).

Current research reflects the recognition that human obesity is a medical disorder of complex origin with multiple antecedents and predisposing factors (see Chapters 4 and 70). Accordingly the task force favored an individualized and multimodal approach to the treatment of obesity, based on diet, exercise, and behavioral change. Weight history and familial factors were also taken into account. The task force recommended that the target weight should be based on personal and family weight history and not simply height- and weight-chart data (see Chapter 98). Indeed, the target weight should be determined by the health benefits likely to be achieved through weight loss.

Among task force recommendations regarding treatment standards were items dealing with client screening, professional staffing of weight loss programs, and full disclosure. The task force recommended that weight loss centers screen potential clients. Depending on the client, such screening might range from a simple symptom checklist to a full physical examination (see Chapter 82). Obese clients should be classified not only by excess body weight but also by associated medical conditions and overall health risk.

While some obese patients may be healthy, others have a variety of medical symptoms or suffer from chronic disease. Health problems may arise when an at-risk client is admitted to a weight loss program that does not offer adequate health supervision or provide medical care. The task force distinguished among three levels of health care, intended for clients at progressively higher risk, and specified the minimum professional qualifications for the health service personnel.

In the interest of consumer protection, the task force recommended that managers of weight loss programs disclose all components of treatment to clients, including the outline of the treatment plan, its duration, and its cost. Cost estimates should include any products, services, supplements, laboratory tests, and other costs that are a part of the weight loss program. The professional credentials of the service providers should be listed in the disclosure statement. The potential risks and benefits associated with weight reduction should be explained, and the long-term success of the program should be substantiated by clinical studies.

The dietary guidelines endorsed by the task force were conservative. The recommended diet was a balanced, restricted-calorie (800–1,000 kilocalories per day) diet containing 10% to 30% of energy from fat and no less than 100 grams of carbohydrate per day. Restricted-calorie diets of less than 600 kilocalories per day were not recommended, even under medical supervision. Formula products were not recommended for the treatment of moderate obesity, and appetite-suppressant drugs were not recommended at all (see Chapter 89).

APPLICATIONS

The Michigan guidelines, released in 1990, were aimed at establishing a voluntary consensus among health professionals regarding the standards of health care in weight loss. Since their release, other legislative attempts to regulate the weight loss industry have addressed the same concerns and have at times employed similar language. A consumer protection bill aimed at the weight loss industry, currently before the Michigan legislature, addresses the issues of professional credentials of health care providers, the need for full disclosure of the benefits and risks of weight loss, and the nature of the contract between the consumer and the health care provider. The FTC has focused its complaints on misleading advertising, notably the advertised rapid rate and the purported permanence of weight loss. As a result, "lose weight forever" is no longer the major advertising theme, and it is to be hoped that the standards of care will improve as well.

FURTHER READING

Petersmarck, K. A. (1992). Building consensus for safe weight loss. *Journal of the American Dietetic Association, 92,* 679–680. Useful background information about the origin of the Michigan guidelines, plus a summary table of the main recommendations.

Rock, C. L., & Coulston, A. M. (1988). Weight-control approaches: A review by the California Dietetic Association. *Journal of the American Dietetic Association, 88,* 44–48. An early position paper by the California Dietetic Association regarding the safety and efficacy of weight loss.

Subcommittee on Regulation, Business Opportunities and Energy of the Committee on Small Business. (1990). *Juvenile dieting, unsafe over-the-counter diet products, and recent enforcement efforts by the Federal Trade Commission* (House of Representatives, Serial No. 101-80, pp. 240–246). Washington, DC: U.S. Government Printing Office. Congressional testimony regarding unhealthy dieting practices and risk to health.

Task Force to Establish Weight Loss Guidelines. (1990). *Toward safe weight loss: Recommendations for adult weight loss programs in Michigan.* Lansing, MI: Michigan Department of Public Health. Full text of the Michigan guidelines, published by the Michigan Department of Public Health, Center for Health Promotion.

• 84 •

EXERCISE IN THE TREATMENT OF OBESITY

Kelly D. Brownell

If there is one universal truth in current conceptualizations of the treatment of obesity, it is that exercise is a key component of any treatment program. Whether this should be the case and why, whether inactivity is causally related to obesity, and how the thorny problem of exercise adherence is best addressed are the main topics of this chapter.

ASSOCIATION OF PHYSICAL ACTIVITY WITH OBESITY

Epidemiological and survey studies have shown consistently that the level of physical activity is inversely related to weight. The correlation does not prove causation, however, so an important issue in the field has been whether low activity causes obesity or whether the excess weight causes a person to be less active. While the issue has not been resolved, it appears that both relationships occur. Therefore it is safe to say that individuals who are inactive are at increased risk for becoming obese. The causation hypothesis is further supported by a doubling in the prevalence of obesity in the United States since 1900, despite a 10% decline in food intake.

IS EXERCISE LINKED TO SUCCESS IN WEIGHT CONTROL?

Whether participants in weight control programs are exercising is the single strongest correlate of the long-term maintenance of weight loss. This connection has been documented in correlational studies and in randomized trials in which individuals are assigned to exercise and no-exercise conditions. The effect of exercise is more often evident in long-term weight loss than in the initial stages of programs. There is no longer doubt that the likelihood of long-term weight loss is enhanced in individuals who exercise.

Mechanisms

A number of mechanisms have been proposed to explain the association between exercise and weight control. The most frequently advanced are (1) increased lean body mass resulting in a higher metabolic rate; (2) increased metabolic rate that is produced by the exercise and endures beyond specific bouts of exercise; and (3) the energy expenditure of the activity itself. Data can be marshalled to supported each position, but one does not rise above the others as the definitive mechanism.

A Possible Psychological Mechanism

My hypothesis, admittedly speculative, is that the psychological impact of exercise is a key mechanism that links physical activity to weight control. This hypothesis is based on (1) my belief that the metabolic effects of exercise, while beneficial, will explain much less variance in weight control than does energy intake, thus pointing to a nonmetabolic factor as the key mechanism; and (2) clinical observations that many people who exercise and maintain weight loss are doing regular but low-level activities that are unlikely to have significant metabolic effects.

Should this psychological hypothesis be correct, it will be essential to identify the specific psychological factors that link exercise to weight control. Again, only speculation is possible, but likely candidates are self-esteem, modulation of mood, and improved body image. As discussed below, recommending the optimal types and amounts of exercise will depend on identifying mechanisms.

A NEW EXERCISE PRESCRIPTION FOR OBESITY

Traditional Prescriptions

The traditional prescription for exercise, including that for obese persons in treatment, is a regimen of aerobic activities. From this tradition, the widely known formula for improving fitness has infiltrated the thinking of overweight individuals and the people who design programs for them. The formula indicates that exercise must be done with sufficient frequency (typically three times per week), intensity (bringing the heart rate to at least 70% of maximum), and duration (20 minutes for each bout).

This prescription was born of studies in exercise physiology designed to identify a threshold of activity needed to improve cardiovascular fitness. What has been lost in its translation to the obesity field is that most individuals exercise to lose weight and to look better; improving cardiovascular fitness is a lower priority. The belief that exceeding the threshold is necessary for exercise to have any value is so ingrained, and attaining this level is so difficult for many people, that exercise is either not attempted or is quickly abandoned.

Regular, Low-Level Activity with Adherence as the Focus

If psychological factors are what connect exercise to weight control, questions about which types of activity produce the most sustained elevation in heart rate or are most effective at building lean body mass should give way to a different question: What exercise will produce the desired psychological effects? Duration and intensity may not be the vital considerations.

Each time a person is active, as long as the person defines the effort as "exercise," an opportunity for reinforcement and affirmation of life-style change is present. The mandate, therefore, is to maximize the number of such opportunities and to encourage cognitive changes such that the individual has a broad definition of exercise and sees any attempt to increase activity as a positive development. Activities like golf, bowling, and leisurely walking may in fact "count" as exercise if they register with the individual as bouts of activity.

In addition to the psychological benefits of selecting activities a person enjoys and can maintain, epidemiological data suggest that modest activity may have impressive health benefits. Blair and colleagues calculated mortality ratios for more than 13,000 individuals who were assessed for physical fitness based on a maximal stress test and were then followed up for an average of 8 years. Mortality ratios were compared across individuals at five levels of fitness, from the least fit to the most fit. While increasing levels of fitness were associated with declining mortality, the largest drop in mortality occurred between the least fit group and the group with only moderate fitness.

These data and others have led the Centers for Disease Control and Prevention (CDCP) and the American College of Sports Medicine (ACSM) to lower the amount of exercise said to be necessary for health and fitness. In 1993, the ACSM and the CDCP released new exercise guidelines for Americans. The new guidelines recommend 30 minutes or more of incremental, moderate-intensity exercise for most days of the week (at least 5 days). Six 5-minute bouts would add up to 30 minutes, and activities that "count" include walking, gardening, cleaning house, playing golf, and raking leaves, as well as the usual sports activities such as swimming, cycling, and running.

THE ADHERENCE CHALLENGE

Obstacles to Exercise

Overweight individuals face a combination of physical and psychosocial burdens when they begin to exercise. Beyond the fact that excess weight makes exercise more difficult, many people have negative feelings about exercise because of past experiences. They may have been teased as children or selected last for teams, and they may be embarrassed by their lack of coordination, inexperience with athletics, or appearance when dressed for exercise.

Professionals must be sensitive to these obstacles and should anticipate hesitation when exercise prescriptions are given. Changing the typical prescription can be helpful (as discussed above), but it may also be necessary to work with the person to overcome these barriers.

Methods for Improving Adherence

Considerable research has been done on exercise adherence. Interventions have targeted cognitive issues (e.g., goal setting and relapse prevention), behavior changes (e.g., stimulus control and reinforcement), and the social environment (e.g., spouse involvement). Table 84.1 presents recommendations for enhancing exercise adherence in overweight individuals.

It is also likely that developmental factors are involved in adherence and that a life-span perspective will suggest different exercise prescriptions depending on the age and accompanying physical and psychological status of the individual. Table 84.2 presents features of various developmental stages and the resulting suggestions for exercise.

TABLE 84.1. Recommendations for Maximizing Exercise Adherence by Obese Persons

General principles
    Be sensitive to psychological barriers
    Be sensitive to physical barriers
    Decrease focus on exercise threshold
    Increase focus on enhanced self-efficacy
    Emphasize consistency and enjoyment, not amount and type
    Begin at person's level of fitness
    Encourage person to define routine activities as "exercise"
    Focus on compliance and avoid emphasis of minor metabolic issues (e.g., whether to
        exercise before or after a meal)
    Consider life-span developmental context
    Consider sociocultural issues
    Evaluate social support network

Specific interventions
    Prescription
        Provide clear information about importance of activity, including the psychological
            benefits
        Maximize routine activity; daily activities are exercise
        Maximize walking (e.g., park a greater distance from work)
        Increase use of stairs in lieu of escalators
        Incorporate a programmed activity that is enjoyable, fits with lifestyle, and is feasible
            as client's fitness improves
    Behavioral
        Introduce self-monitoring, feedback, and goal-setting techniques
        Identify important targets other than weight loss, including physical changes,
            increased endurance, lowered resting heart rate
        Use physical activity when tempted to overeat or when distressed
        Stimulus control: Increase exercise cues (e.g., reminders for increasing activity) and
            decrease competing cues (e.g., do not schedule exercise when it might conflict with
            work or social obligations)
    Maintenance and relapse prevention
        Use flexible guidelines and goal-setting, but avoid rigid rules
        Identify potential high-risk situations for skipping exercise (e.g., stressful times, busy
            schedule)
        Develop plans to cope with high-risk situations
        Use exercise following dietary lapses to counteract caloric effects physically and, more
            importantly, to regain psychologically a sense of control, mastery, and commitment
        Convey philosophy that one day lapsed does not a failure make
        Use of minimal intervention strategies including phone contacts may foster exercise
            maintenance

Note. From Grilo, Brownell, and Stunkard (1993, p. 366). Copyright 1993 by Raven Press. Reprinted by permission.

SUMMARY

Exercise is touted as a necessary and central feature in weight control programs, a notion supported by abundant evidence. This finding underscores the need for research to identify the mechanisms linking physical activity to weight control, so that types and amounts of exercise can be prescribed in an informed manner. Very different approaches might be adopted if the effect is found to be psychological rather than metabolic. Low-level activity, if done regularly, is likely to have beneficial effects and may produce better adherence than would typical exercise prescriptions.

TABLE 84.2. Features and Examples of Physical Activity Programs for Several Major Developmental Milestones

Milestone (critical period)	Specific features	Goals/strategies
Adolescence	Rapid physical and emotional changes	Exercise as part of a program of healthy weight regulation (both sexes)
	Increased concern with appearance and weight	Noncompetitive activities that are fun, varied
	Need for independence	Emphasis on independence, choice
	Short-term perspective	Focus on proximal outcomes (e.g., body image, stress management)
	Increased peer influence	Peer involvement, support
Initial work entry	Increased time and scheduling constraints	Choice of activities that are convenient, enjoyable
	Short-term perspective	Focus on proximal outcomes
	Employer demands	Involvement of work site (environmental prompts, incentives)
		Realistic goal setting/injury prevention
		Coeducational noncompetitive activities
Parenting	Increased family demands and time constraints	Emphasis on benefits to self and family (e.g., stress management, weight control, well-being)
	Family-directed focus	
	Postpartum effects on weight, mood	Activities appropriate with children (e.g., walking)
		Flexible, convenient, personalized regimen
		Inclusion of activities of daily living
		Neighborhood involvement, focus
		Family-based public monitoring, goal setting
		Availability of child-related services (child care)
Retirement age	Increased time availability and flexibility	Identification of current and previous enjoyable activities
	Longer-term perspective on health; increased health concerns, "readiness"	Matching of activities to current health status
		Emphasis on mild- and moderate-intensity activities, including activities of daily living
	Caregiving duties, responsibilities (parents, spouse, children, or grandchildren)	Use of "life path point" information and prompts
		Emphasis on activities engendering independence
		Garnering support of family members, peers
		Availability of necessary services (e.g., caretaking services for significant other)

Note. From King (1991, p. 364). Copyright 1991 by Williams & Wilkins. Reprinted by permission.

FURTHER READING

Blair, S. N., Kohl, H. W., Paffenbarger, R. S., Clark, D. G., Cooper, K. H., & Gibbons, L. W. (1989). Physical fitness and all-cause mortality: A prospective study of healthy men and women. *Journal of the American Medical Association, 262,* 2395–2401. Landmark study showing that even moderate levels of fitness confer significant advantages for long-term mortality.

Brownell, K. D., & Wadden, T. A. (1992). Etiology and treatment of obesity: Understanding a serious, prevalent, and refractory disorder. *Journal of Consulting and Clinical Psychology, 60,* 505–517. A review of the obesity field that includes information on the importance of exercise in treatment.

Dishman, R. K. (Ed.). (1994). *Advances in exercise adherence.* Champaign, IL: Human Kinetics Press. An excellent edited book with chapters on basic and applied issues in exercise adherence.

Grilo, C. M., Brownell, K. D., & Stunkard, A. J. (1993). The metabolic and psychological importance of exercise in weight control. In A. J. Stunkard & T. A. Wadden (Eds.), *Obesity: Theory and therapy* (2nd ed., pp. 253–273). New York: Raven Press. A thorough review of the literature on exercise and obesity, with attention to both metabolic and psychosocial issues and to the key issue of adherence.

Kayman, S., Bruvold, W., & Stern, J. S. (1990). Maintenance and relapse after weight loss in women: Behavioral aspects. *American Journal of Clinical Nutrition, 52,* 800–807. Study showing the association of exercise and other behavioral factors with the long-term maintenance of weight loss.

King, A. (1991). Community intervention for promotion of physical activity and fitness. In K. B. Pandolf & J. O. Holloszy (Eds.), *Exercise and sports sciences reviews* (pp. 211–259). Baltimore: Williams & Wilkins. A public health perspective on exercise and exercise adherence, with a developmental perspective on designing exercise programs.

McArdle, W. D., Katch, F. I., & Katch, V. L. (1991). *Exercise physiology: Energy, nutrition and human performance.* Philadelphia: Lea & Febiger. Text with excellent coverage of energy intake, energy expenditure, and metabolic issues influencing body weight and general health.

Pavlou, K. N., Krey, S., & Steffee, W. P. (1989). Exercise as an adjunct to weight loss and maintenance in moderately overweight subjects. *American Journal of Clinical Nutrition, 49,* 1115–1123. A controlled study showing the benefits of exercise for the maintenance of weight loss.

Shah, M., & Jeffery, R. W. (1991). Is obesity due to overeating, inactivity, or to a defective metabolic rate? *Annals of Behavioral Medicine, 13,* 73–81. A scholarly review of the role energy intake and expenditure play in obesity.

Wood, P. D., Stefanick, M. L, Williams, P. T., & Haskell, W. L. (1991). The effects on plasma lipoproteins of a prudent weight-reducing diet with or without exercise in overweight men and women. *New England Journal of Medicine, 325,* 461–466. A well-designed randomized study showing the effects of diet with and without exercise on weight loss and metabolic variables.

• 85 •

BEHAVIORAL APPROACHES
TO THE TREATMENT OF OBESITY

G. Terence Wilson

Behavioral treatment has as its primary goal the modification of eating habits and level of physical activity. The emphasis is on changing behavior to restrict caloric consumption and increase energy expenditure through physical exercise, thereby producing a negative energy balance and consequent weight loss. In this pragmatic rationale it was recognized that genetic predisposition and biological mechanisms might make behavioral therapy unusually difficult for many obese individuals (see Chapter 4).

Since their introduction in the late 1960s, behavioral treatment programs have become increasingly intensive, multifaceted, and sophisticated. Behavioral change methods aimed at altering eating habits and restricting caloric intake were increasingly complemented by a focus on better nutrition and on strategies designed to increase physical exercise, improve interpersonal relationships, and develop less dysfunctional attitudes about eating and weight control. Most recently, specific strategies for maintaining treatment-induced weight loss have been incorporated into such programs. Beginning in the 1980s, behavioral treatment has also been combined with pharmacotherapy (see Chapter 89) and very-low-calorie diets (VLCDs) of 800 calories or less to produce substantially greater amounts of weight loss (see Chapter 86). This development signaled a more aggressive approach to weight loss than the principle of gradualism that had characterized earlier treatment.

Behavioral treatment has been more intensively researched, and its effects more thoroughly documented, than any other intervention for obesity. Treatment principles and procedures have been clearly specified in "user friendly" treatment manuals for professionals and the public alike. As a result the treatment has been widely disseminated and accepted. Behavioral treatment has, for some time now, been regarded as a necessary component of any adequate obesity treatment program.

DESCRIPTION OF TREATMENT

A core feature of behavioral treatment is self-monitoring: the detailed, daily recording of food intake and the circumstances under which it occurs.

Self-monitoring is the mainstay of the behavioral assessment of obesity. It provides the information that allows the therapist to determine when and where the episode took place; what the patient was thinking, feeling, and doing at the time; and the nature of the interpersonal context. This information is essential for selecting and implementing intervention strategies. Self-monitoring is also part of the behavior change process. Patients use this self-monitoring of performance to evaluate their progress against realistic weight loss goals. Attaining these goals motivates continued adherence to treatment procedures. By learning to identify the personal and environmental influences that regulate their eating, patients can take specific actions to break unhealthy habits. The same behavioral principles are used to encourage increased physical activity. Other self-regulatory strategies include stimulus control, which is designed to limit exposure to cues that prompt overeating. For example, patients are instructed to do nothing else while eating (e.g., they are not to watch television) so that they remain fully aware of their actions and are not distracted from their consumption goals.

Comprehensive behavioral treatments include several therapeutic components in addition to self-control strategies for altering eating habits and increasing exercise. There is a focus on improved nutrition. Rigid dieting is discouraged in favor of balanced and flexible food choices designed to reduce the consumption of saturated fat and increase the intake of complex carbohydrates. Cognitive restructuring is used to identify and modify dysfunctional thoughts and attitudes about weight regulation. Interpersonal relationships are addressed in order to cope with specific triggers for overeating and to increase social support for weight control. Finally, relapse prevention strategies are used to promote the maintenance of treatment-induced weight loss (see Chapter 96).

EVALUATION OF TREATMENT OUTCOME

Short-Term Effects

Of all approaches to the treatment of obesity, behavioral interventions have been the most intensively evaluated. This commitment to the systematic and objective assessment of the short-term, and even more important, the long-term effects of treatment is one of the major contributions of the behavioral approach to the study and treatment of obesity. Behavioral treatment consistently produces significant weight loss in patients with mild (20% to 40% overweight) to moderate (40% to 100% overweight) obesity. The longer treatment programs have become (to accommodate more intensive and comprehensive interventions), the greater has been the amount of weight loss. Furthermore, treatment results in generalized improvement in psychological well-being (e.g., reductions in depression, improvement in body image, and enhanced interpersonal functioning; see Chapter 75) and in biological variables such as blood pressure and serum lipid levels (see Chapter 71).

Weight loss at posttreatment is maintained well at 1 year follow-up (and up to 3 years in a controlled study in Japan), with roughly two-thirds of weight loss sustained. Combining behavioral treatment with a VLCD produces significantly better maintenance at 1 year than the diet alone.

Predictors of weight loss have proven elusive. Personality traits, measures of psychopathology, presence of binge eating, dietary restraint, and history of weight cycling have all proven unreliable in this respect. The process variables of early weight loss and compliance with self-monitoring are the most useful predictors. Patients who do neither are very poor risks for treatment. Although not strictly a predictor variable, adherence to an exercise regimen is a reliable correlate of the maintenance of weight loss (see Chapter 84).

Long-Term Effects

Relatively few studies have included evaluations of the long-term effects of the treatment of obesity. Of the different forms of treatment, behavioral methods have been scrutinized more thoroughly than any others. The results indicate that some programs have produced good maintenance of weight loss for as long as 2 years following treatment. Yet 5-year follow-up data have shown that virtually all patients return to their pretreatment baseline, even though many have participated in alternative treatments during this period. Proponents of behavioral treatment correctly point out that the disappointing 5-year findings come from a single major study and that additional studies are needed before it can be concluded that behavioral treatment is ineffective in the long haul. Nevertheless, all follow-up studies showed the same pattern, namely, gradual regain of weight over time. The pace at which this weight regain occurs may vary across studies, but the trend toward a return to baseline values is clear. This trend is even seen in studies in which specific maintenance strategies have been implemented during the follow-up period (see Chapter 97).

It has been argued that negative long-term outcomes may underestimate the effectiveness of behavioral treatment. First, it has been noted that in measuring the long-term success of treatment by the extent to which patients are below the pretreatment baseline there is an implicit assumption that the maintenance of a stable weight in the absence of treatment. Yet there is evidence that people gain weight over time and that this tendency is greater in the obese. Second, it may be that the patients in predominantly university-based treatment programs that have yielded disappointing long-term results are not representative of the full spectrum of obese people trying to control their weight. Third, it has been claimed that superior weight maintenance will result from matching specific treatments to particular subgroups of more homogeneous patients (see Chapter 98).

In contrast to the negative outcomes with adults, the behavioral treatment of childhood obesity has yielded very promising results (see Chapter 91). A series of related studies was used to evaluate a family-based program for children (ages 6 to 12 years) that emphasized life-style change and weight control in both the children and their parents. Ten years after treatment, fully 34% of the obese children showed a decrease in percent overweight; 30% were no longer obese. Treatment that was focused solely on changes in the children's behavior resulted in relapse by the 5-year follow-up. Consistent with other research, the obese parents who were treated in the same program showed the all-too-familiar pattern of initial weight loss followed by relapse. By 5 years virtually all had returned to baseline, and at 10 years, the parents in all groups showed increases in percent overweight.

One explanation of why children but not adults show lasting treatment effects is that it is simply easier to teach healthy eating and activity habits to young children than to adults. A second possibility is that parents find they can exert external control—including social support and food management—on children and even adolescents living at home. However, obese adults who lose weight regain it because the *self*-control on which they have to rely gradually erodes. The children in these studies did not have to rely as much on self-control because they then grew up in an environment that was restructured to support changes in eating and exercise habits. The treatment that focused on weight and life-style change in both children and parents produced long-term results superior to that which focused only on the children.

THE LIMITS OF BEHAVIORAL TREATMENT

The critical question is: Why does behavioral treatment succeed in the short-term but prove ineffective in the long-term? It appears that relapse is attributable to patients' failure to adhere to the self-regulatory strategies they learn in treatment. By definition, for most patients, weight loss is insufficiently reinforcing to sustain compliance with a pattern of food intake and exercise that produces a negative energy balance. Continual external structure and support is required (see Chapter 97). Therefore, investigators have called for what amounts to lifelong "treatment." Continued contact of one form or another with a treatment program is the best means of maintaining weight loss. Nonetheless, clinical experience suggests that attendance and adherence to continual treatment would taper off.

Obesity is influenced strongly by genetic factors and, once established, is maintained by several potent and probably irreversible biological mechanisms. Genetic influence is only predisposition, not predetermination (see Chapter 4), but it is expressed in an environment that exacerbates the risk to the vulnerable person. Obese people have to impose endless control (be it cognitive, behavioral, or more broadly environmental) on energy intake and expenditure. Behavioral interventions provide training and support in shoring up this control. In principle it could be maintained for a lifetime, and a small number of patients seem to be able to do just that, especially with the help of social support and physical exercise. But these efforts are up against an environment that increasingly favors weight gain because of the ready availability of highly palatable, high-fat foods and of a sedentary life-style.

Despite its limitations in producing long-term weight loss, behavioral treatment is of value in modifying behaviors that are linked to adverse health effects and psychological distress without necessarily causing weight loss in obese individuals. It reduces, if it does not eliminate, binge eating, a behavioral abnormality that occurs in roughly 30% of patients who seek therapy (see Chapter 78). This effect on binge eating has several favorable consequences independent of weight loss. It may make it easier for individuals to participate and remain in more conventional weight control treatments, the putative benefits of which are discussed below. It might also prevent future weight gain. If binge eating is a risk factor for obesity in some individuals, then the successful treatment of binge eating before the person becomes overweight might prevent obesity. Such treatment of binge eating should increase patients' sense of personal control, which has a variety of positive psychological sequelae, including improved adherence to behavior change strategies. Finally, it should improve mood and reduce associated psychopathology, important goals in their own right (see Chapter 75).

A second benefit is that behavioral treatment can modify behaviors that bear directly on health, such as reducing fat intake and increasing exercise, although there are also problems in sustaining these changes on a long-term basis. Even if behavioral treatment does not contribute to weight loss during pharmacotherapy for obesity, it has been shown to have incremental value in lowering cholesterol and triglyceride levels.

Finally, behavioral treatment can be used to help obese patients become more assertive in coping with the adverse social sequelae of being overweight, in enhancing their self-esteem, and in reducing their dissatisfaction with body image regardless of their weight loss.

FURTHER READING

Brownell, K. D. (1994). *The LEARN program for weight control* (6th ed.). Edmonds, WA: American Health Press. A comprehensive, state-of-the-art treatment manual for obesity.

Brownell, K. D., & Wadden, T. A. (1992). Etiology and treatment of obesity: Understanding a serious, prevalent, and refractory disorder. *Journal of Consulting and Clinical Psychology, 60,* 505–517. An evaluation of the current status of behavioral treatment.

Epstein, L. H., Valoski, A., Wing, R. R., & McCurley, J. (1994). Ten-year outcomes of behavioral family-based treatment of childhood obesity. *Health Psychology, 13,* 573–583. A summary of successful treatment studies of childhood obesity.

Garner, D. M., & Wooley, S. C. (1991). Confronting the failure of behavioral and dietary treatments for obesity. *Clinical Psychology Review, 11,* 729–780. A critique of the effectiveness and suitability of dietary and behavioral treatment of obesity.

Lichtman, S. W., Pisarska, K., Berman, E. R., Pestone, M., Dowling, H., Offenbacher, E., Weisel, H., Heshka, S., Matthews, D. W., & Heymsfield, S. B. (1992). Discrepancy between self-reported and actual caloric intake and exercise in obese subjects. *New England Journal of Medicine, 327,* 1893–1898. A description of sophisticated experimental research showing that some obese patients substantially underestimate their food intake.

National Institutes of Health Technology Assessment Conference Panel. (1993). Methods for voluntary weight loss and control. *Annals of Internal Medicine, 119,* 764–770. Summary recommendations from the National Institutes of Health conference on the treatment of obesity.

Wadden, T. A., & Bartlett, S. J. (1992). Very low calorie diets: An overview and appraisal. In T. A. Wadden & T. B. VanItallie (Eds.), *Treatment of the seriously obese patient* (pp. 44–79). New York: Guilford Press. A comprehensive review of behavioral treatment combined with VLCDs.

Weintraub, M. (1992). Long-term weight control: The national Heart, Lung, and Blood Institute funded multimodal intervention study. *Clinical Pharmacological Therapy, 51,* 581–646. A large, 4-year study in which the effects of pharmacological therapy combined with behavioral treatment were evaluated.

Wilson, G. T. (1993a). Behavioral treatment of obesity: Thirty years and counting. *Advances in Behaviour Research and Therapy, 16,* 31–75. A critical analysis of the history and limitations of behavioral treatment.

Wilson, G. T. (1993b, June). *Behavioral and psychological predictors of treatment outcome in obesity.* Paper presented at NATO/NIH Conference on Treatment of Obesity, New York. An up-to-date review of the evidence on predictors of treatment.

• 86 •

VERY-LOW-CALORIE DIETS: APPRAISAL AND RECOMMENDATIONS

Thomas A. Wadden

For dieters, the 1980s were a time of high expectations and large weight losses, perhaps best reflected by the popularity of very-low-calorie diets (VLCDs). The use of VLCDs has declined sharply in the 1990s with the rise of antidieting sentiments (see Chapter 17). Nevertheless these diets remain an important treatment option for significantly obese individuals, as described in this chapter.

VERY-LOW-CALORIE DIETS: AN OVERVIEW

A scientific panel recommended in 1979 that the term "very-low-calorie diet" be reserved for diets providing fewer than 800 kilocalories daily. This definition is widely accepted, and most commercially produced diets provide approximately 400–800 kilocalories per day. The definition, however, does not take into account the fact that obese individuals differ markedly in their daily energy requirements and that the use of the same diet in different individuals can create vastly different caloric deficits. Thus a 700-kilocalories-per-day VLCD induces a deficit of only 500 kilocalories per day in a short but obese woman with a daily energy requirement of 1,200 kilocalories. The same diet, however, induces a deficit of 2,500 kilocalories per day in a tall, obese man with a daily energy expenditure of 3,200 kilocalories. Thus Atkinson has suggested that a VLCD be defined in terms of the energy requirements of the individual receiving it and that it provide 10 kilocalories per kilogram of ideal body weight (see Chapter 93). Thus taller individuals and those with larger frames should receive more calories.

Composition of the Diet

Larger individuals should also receive more protein to preserve lean body mass. Most commercially prepared VLCDs provide 70–90 grams of protein daily, but a more appropriate practice is to prescribe 1.2–1.5 grams of protein per kilogram of ideal body weight. Protein is usually obtained from egg or dairy sources and is provided as a powdered-protein formula that is mixed with water. These "liquid diets" usually also provide 30–45 grams of carbohydrate per day, 2–5 grams of fat, and 100% of the daily recommended allowance for essential vitamins and minerals. Liquid VLCDs are consumed three to five times daily, along with 2 liters of noncaloric fluid, and are the dieter's sole source of nutrition; no other foods are usually allowed. Alternatively, protein may be obtained from a diet of lean meat, fish, or fowl, served in food form, that is known as a "protein-sparing modified fast." This diet must be supplemented with 2–3 grams of potassium daily and a multivitamin supplement. Both dietary approaches produce excellent short-term weight losses, which makes the choice of diets a matter of personal choice.

Patient Selection

VLCDs are usually limited to persons who are a minimum of 30% overweight, because mildly obese patients do not retain bodily protein as satisfactorily as do heavier individuals during severe caloric restriction. Excessive losses of bodily protein may be associated with serious complications, including death. Moreover, mildly obese individuals can reduce using less aggressive approaches (see Chapter 98). In addition to meeting the weight requirement, patients must undergo a thorough medical examination to ensure they do not suffer from contraindications that include a recent myocardial infarction; a cardiac conduction disorder; a history of cerebrovascular, renal, or hepatic disease; cancer; Type I diabetes; or pregnancy. Behavioral/psychiatric contraindications include bulimia nervosa (i.e., binge eating followed by purging), significant depression (including bipolar disorder), acute psychiatric illness, and substance abuse disorders (excluding cigarette smoking).

Safety

Current VLCDs are generally safe when administered under appropriate medical supervision that includes a physician visit and blood test every 2 weeks during the period of severe caloric restriction. No increase in cardiac complications has been observed in patients treated for up to 16 weeks, a record of safety that contrasts sharply with the fatal cardiac arrhythmias associated with the use of liquid protein diets in the 1970s. Patients treated by current VLCDs frequently report fatigue, dizziness, muscle cramping, gastrointestinal upset, or cold intolerance during the first few weeks, but these symptoms cause only minor discomfort and are readily managed. Of greater concern is the increased risk of gallstones, the incidence of which has been as high as 26% in some studies. Only a minority of patients, however, develop symptomatic gallstones that require treatment (see Chapter 70). The risk of this complication can be reduced by using a diet that ensures gallbladder contraction by providing a minimum of 14 grams of protein and 10 grams of fat at one meal.

Multidisciplinary Approach

Typically VLCDs are delivered by a multidisciplinary team that includes a physician, dietitian, and behavioral psychologist. The physician is responsible for monitoring patients' health, whereas the dietitian provides instruction in consuming the VLCD and the "reseeding" diet that follows, in which conventional foods are gradually reintroduced. Patients are usually treated weekly in groups of 8 to 15 persons that are led by a behavioral psychologist who instructs participants in the modification of eating and exercise habits. A typical course of treatment lasts 20 to 30 weeks and includes three principal phases: (1) the VLCD (12–16 weeks), (2) the refeeding period (4–6 weeks), and (3) weight maintenance (4–8 weeks).

RESULTS OF TREATMENT

VLCDs produce mean weight losses in women of approximately 20 kilograms in 12 to 16 weeks and losses in men of 30 kilograms. These reductions are two to three times greater than those produced by a conventional 1,000–1,500 kilocalorie-per-day diet during the same period of time and are associated with marked improvements in blood pressure, cholesterol and blood glucose levels, and other indices of health, including psychological status.

Long-Term Results

These favorable short-term results differ markedly from long-term findings. On the average, patients treated by VLCDs regain 35% to 50% of their lost weight in the year following treatment, even when they receive the program of life-style modification described above. Approximately 10% to 20% of participants maintain all of their weight loss during this time, but an equal number regain it all. Unfortunately investigators are currently unable to predict who will be successful. Long-term studies show that patients gain increasing amounts of weight over time.

Our research team recently assessed the effectiveness of maintenance therapy following a VLCD program. Obese women were randomly assigned to either a 1,200-kilocalorie-per-day balanced deficit diet (BDD) or a VLCD for the first 4 months, followed by a 1,200-kilocalorie-per-day diet. All patients attended treatment weekly for the first 12 months and then biweekly for an additional 6 months. Figure 86.1 shows that patients who received the VLCD lost approximately twice as much weight during the first 6 months as those on the BDD. In the year that followed, however, they regained more than 50% of their lost weight, even while attending weekly or biweekly weight maintenance sessions. Thus at 18 months their mean weight loss was less than that of the BDD patients.

In a second study, we randomly assigned patients who had lost approximately 20 kilograms on a VLCD to either 1 year of biweekly maintenance sessions or the same therapy combined with 200 milligrams daily of sertraline, a selective serotonin reuptake inhibitor currently approved (as Zoloft) for the treatment of depression. Regrettably patients in both conditions regained 50% or more of their lost weight while receiving maintenance therapy.

VERY-LOW-CALORIE DIETS: A REAPPRAISAL

These and other findings raise questions about the benefits of VLCDs as compared with traditional reducing diets. A 26-week VLCD program costs a minimum of $2,500 and yet provides results 1 year later that are no better than those produced by less expensive approaches.

Results of a recent double-blind study indicate that it is not necessary to use severely

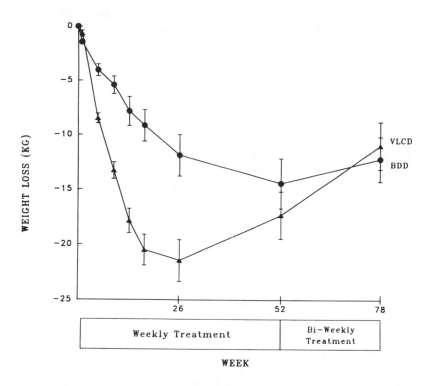

FIGURE 86.1. Mean weight losses of subjects treated by a VLCD or a BDD during 1 year of weekly treatment and 6 months of biweekly maintenance therapy.

restrictive VLCDs. Obese women who were randomly assigned to consume liquid diets providing 420, 660, or 800 kilocalories per day lost an average of 18.2, 18.5, and 16.6 kilograms, respectively, after 12 weeks—differences that were not statistically or clinically significant. We cannot explain why women on the 420-kilocalorie-per-day diet failed to lose 4.1 kilograms more than those on the 800-kilocalorie-per-day diet, as would have been predicted from differences in the caloric content of the two diets. Perhaps patients on the 420-kilocalorie-per-day regimen had larger reductions in resting metabolic rate that slowed their rate of weight loss, or they may not have been as adherent or as physically active as participants on the 800-kilocalorie-per-day diet. Regardless of the reason(s), these findings are consistent with those of other investigators and suggest that there is little benefit in outpatient practice to restricting VLCDs to fewer than 800 kilocalories per day.

Portion-Controlled Servings

These findings further suggest that the effectiveness of VLCDs, compared with conventional 1,000–1,200-kilocalories-per-day reducing diets, may be more attributable to the form and manner in which VLCDs are consumed than to their severe caloric restriction. Liquid diets in particular provide overweight individuals a choice-free menu of portion-controlled meals that allows them to avoid contact with conventional foods. This approach is likely to facilitate excellent dietary adherence. Moreover, portion-controlled diets provide patients a precise estimate of their calorie intake. By contrast, research using doubly labeled water has shown that when obese individuals are asked to keep a food diary, they typically underestimate their calorie intake by 30% to 40%. Thus, when instructed to consume a 1,000-kilocalorie-per-day diet, they may actually eat closer to 1,400 kilocalories per day. Differences in adherence may well explain why obese women who consume a traditional 1,200-kilocalorie-per-day reducing diet for 12 weeks lose an average of only 7 kilograms, whereas our patients who received an 800-kilocalorie-per-day liquid diet for the same period lost almost 17 kilograms.

Frozen-food dinners and other portion-controlled foods may well facilitate dietary adherence in a manner similar to VLCDs. In our most recent study, we obtained excellent weight losses in women who consumed a liquid diet combined with an evening meal of conventional food (i.e., a preportioned dinner entree). This 925-kilocalorie-per-day mixed diet was associated with minimal health complications, which allowed us to reduce the frequency and cost of medical monitoring. Moreover, the mixed diet was not associated during the refeeding period with any increase in binge eating, a problem that has been described by Telch and Agras (see Chapter 94).

RECOMMENDATIONS

Our research teams' current recommendations concerning the use of VLCDs are summarized in the four points that follow:

1. The use of VLCDs, as commonly defined, should be discontinued with most patients in favor of low-calorie diets that provide at least 800 kilocalories per day (and ample protein) but retain the form of traditional VLCDs (i.e., portion- and calorie-controlled servings).

2. All significantly obese individuals seeking treatment using a low-calorie diet should have a thorough medical examination. If found to be in good health, the individual's schedule of medical monitoring can be reduced, in contrast to that of persons treated by a traditional VLCD.

3. Preliminary findings indicate that it may be beneficial to add a daily meal of conventional food to liquid-diet regimens. The inclusion of this meal is likely to reduce patients' anxiety and problem eating during the refeeding period.

4. Low-calorie formula diets should be used only in a program of life-style modification designed to increase physical activity, reduce the consumption of dietary fat, and improve coping skills. Moreover, these diets should be used only after patients have failed to reduce using more conservative interventions. With either approach, patient and practitioner must be prepared to devote as much effort to the maintenance of weight loss as to its induction.

These recommendations are based on the belief that less severe caloric restriction and the inclusion of a daily meal of conventional foods will produce robust weight losses while avoiding the dietary deprivation and other factors that are associated with the rapid regaining of weight following VLCDs. Controlled clinical trials, however, are needed to test these hypotheses and to provide data that will inform the treatment of seriously obese patients.

ACKNOWLEDGMENT

Preparation of this chapter was supported by Grant No. MH49451-02 from the National Institute of Mental Health and by a Research Scientist Development Award (K02 MH00702-06).

FURTHER READING

Atkinson, R. L. (1992). Medical evaluation and monitoring of patients treated by severe caloric restriction. In T. A. Wadden & T. B. VanItallie (Eds.), *Treatment of the seriously obese patient* (pp. 273–289). New York: Guilford Press. This chapter provides an excellent description of the medical evaluation and monitoring required for persons treated by a VLCD.

Foster, G. D., Wadden, T. A., Peterson F. J., Letizia, K. A., Bartlett, S. J., & Conill, A. M. (1992). A controlled comparison of three very-low-calorie diets: Effects on weight, body composition, and symptoms. *American Journal of Clinical Nutrition, 55,* 811–817. Patients randomly assigned to consume liquid diets providing 420, 660, or 800 kilocalories per day lost comparable amounts of weight, a finding that raises the question of whether severe caloric restriction is needed.

Miura, J., Arai, K., Tsukahara, S., Ohno, M., & Kideda, Y. (1989). The long-term effectiveness of combined therapy by behavior modification and very low calorie diet: 2-year follow-up. *International Journal of Obesity, 13,* 73–77. A Japanese team of investigators reports the most successful long-term findings to date for the use of VLCDs combined with behavior modification.

National Task Force on the Prevention and Treatment of Obesity. (1993). Very-low-calorie diets. *Journal of the American Medical Association, 270,* 967–974. This article provides a thorough review of the historical development and safety and efficacy of VLCDs. The authors conclude that these diets are neither more nor less effective than other dietary interventions for the treatment of significantly obese individuals.

Perri, M. G., McAllister, D. A., Gange, J. J., Jordan, R. C., McAdoo, W. G., & Nezu, A. M. (1988). Effects of four maintenance programs on the long-term management of obesity. *Journal of Consulting and Clinical Psychology, 56,* 529–534. This is the best study in a series designed to improve the maintenance of weight loss by having participants attend biweekly group meetings in the year following their weight loss. The use of this approach with VLCDs has not been encouraging.

Telch, C. F., & Agras, W. S. (1993). The effects of a very-low-calorie diet on binge eating. *Behavior Therapy, 24,* 177–193. Binge eating is reported by clinicians to be a frequent outcome of treatment using VLCDs. This study confirms that a small minority of persons may develop the problem.

Wadden, T. A., Foster, G. D., & Letizia, K. A. (1994). One-year behavioral treatment of obesity: Comparison of moderate and severe caloric restriction and the effects of maintenance therapy. *Journal of Consulting and Clinical Psychology, 62,* 165–171. Biweekly maintenance therapy was effective in maintaining a 12-kilogram weight loss achieved with a conventional reducing diet but not in maintaining a 21-kilogram loss induced by a VLCD. Eighteen months after treatment began, subjects treated by the former method had a larger weight loss than those treated by the VLCD.

Wadden, T. A., & VanItallie, T. B. (Eds.). (1992). *Treatment of the seriously obese patient.* New York: Guilford Press. This comprehensive volume contains a review of the development of VLCDs, descriptions of the biological and psychological responses to severe caloric restriction, a detailed guide to treatment using this approach, and an examination of methods to improve the maintenance of weight loss.

Wing, R. R., Marcus, M. D., Salata, R., Epstein, L. H., Miaskiewicz, S., & Blair, E. H. (1991). Effects of a very-low-calorie diet on long-term glycemic control in obese Type II diabetics. *Archives of Internal Medicine, 151,* 1334–1340. Long-term glycemic control was significantly better 1 year after treatment in persons who received a VLCD than in those who received a conventional reducing diet, despite the fact that subjects in the both conditions regained substantial amounts of weight.

• 87 •

POPULAR DIETS

Johanna Dwyer

WHAT WE KNOW

The best way to judge the effectiveness of popular diets is to have well-controlled clinical trials of their outcomes in reducing fatness at 1 and 5 years. Unfortunately such data are rarely available. We know enough to describe general principles by which diets work and the criteria for selecting popular diets, however.

General Principles by Which Popular Diets Work

Diets work by decreasing energy intake, increasing energy output, or altering both simultaneously to create an energy deficit.

Weight control, not weight reduction, is essential. Reducing diets alone are not enough. For health, long-term weight control and management systems are needed, since not only is weight loss important, but so is maintenance of the lowered weight.

Popular diets are not for everyone. Some people are able to control their weight on their own, but others need additional help. Popular diets that people embark on by themselves may not provide sufficient assistance. Success or failure depends on many factors, chief among them the degree of overweight, the duration of the overweight, and coexisting illnesses.

Some processes and strategies needed for weight loss differ from those required for maintenance once healthier weights have been reached. Many different diets, varying in energy levels and nutrient composition, can be used for initial weight loss. Diets for maintaining lowered weights once fatness is lost must be lower in energy than that of diets followed prior to weight reduction, since both resting metabolism and the energy cost of moving the lighter body are less. In general, low-fat, high-fiber, high-carbohydrate, nutritionally adequate diets, a physically active life that includes exercise, and behavior modification are best for maintenance (see Chapter 97). Both weight loss and maintenance diets should be adequate in other nutrients and should include behavior modification and physical activity.

Safe and effective weight loss begins by considering individual needs and risks (see Chapters 82 and 98). The level of care and staff support provided to dieters must be based on each client's health and emotional needs and risks. Safe and effective weight loss begins by screening out those for whom weight loss is contraindicated. Those who have medical problems that may require additional help, or who express the need for extensive help and support, are also poor candidates for embarking on popular diets on their own.

The lowest weight goal is not necessarily the best. Weight goals should be reasonable (see Chapter 98). Even modest weight loss goals, if sustained, may be sufficient to achieve a realistic and important health benefit. Often the level of such weight losses are above the so-called ideal or desirable weights of the population.

The fastest weight loss is not the best for health. Weight loss should be no more than 0.5–1 pound per week, or 1% of body weight, for efforts that people embark upon by themselves. More rapid rates of loss are difficult to sustain, and nutrient intakes may be inadequate unless supplements are used.

MANAGEMENT PLAN: SELECTION CRITERIA FOR POPULAR DIETS

Consider the 10 essential criteria discussed below in evaluating whether popular diets are likely to contribute to safe and effective weight control.

Calories

Calculate a rough estimate of energy needs, using the following rule of thumb:

1. Calculate the resting metabolic rate (RMR):
   Male RMR = 900 + 10 (weight in kilograms)
   Female RMR = 700 + 7 (weight in kilograms)

2. Multiply the resulting RMR by the appropriate estimate for physical activity level:
   1.2: very sedentary
   1.4: moderately active
   1.8: very active

The total of the RMR times the estimate for physical activity gives a rough approximation of the individual's total energy needs in energy balance.

Energy Deficit Approach

Energy deficits of 500 kilocalories from energy balance levels (intakes at which the individual is neither gaining nor losing weight) will cause a loss of about 1 pound of fat tissue per week; usually deficits greater than this are not suggested for self-initiated efforts of the type that are involved with most popular diets. A deficit of 1,000 kilocalories per day will cause a 2-pound loss per week. But such a rapid loss, since it may give rise to profound psychological and physiological sequellae, is not advisable without medical supervision.

Fixed-Energy-Level Diets

Another approach to weight reduction is to use diets with fixed caloric levels. Prescribed fixed low-calorie eating plans limit intake by controlling portion sizes, menu choice, and composition. This option involves less active involvement on the part of the dieter in the self-monitoring of the intake of individual food constituents than does the energy-deficit approach. But it also limits choices and spontaneity in dietary selection. Popular diets of this type include prepackaged and portion-controlled foods such as low-calorie canned or frozen entrees and other products available in supermarkets. Fixed low-calorie diet programs are also operated by commercial and nonprofit weight loss management systems.

Fat Gram Counting and Other Strategies

Another way to control intake is to self-monitor by counting and limiting calories or some other constituent, with the end result that energy intakes are decreased. The person limits daily intake of kilocalories or grams of fat or sugar to a predetermined number. Dietary fat, which provides 9 kilocalories per gram, twice that of protein and carbohydrate, is often targeted for reduction. Fat gram counting proved effective in studies such as the Women's Health Trial and the Multiple Risk Factor Intervention Trial, reducing energy intakes by 150 to 400 kilocalories per day.

Another technique is to permit only certain foods. Particularly effective techniques for limiting fat include using leaner cuts of meat (especially among men), increased intake of fat-modified foods, low-fat food preparation methods, and combinations of substitution, reduction, and modification of fat-containing foods (popular among women).

For individuals used to high-fat omnivorous diets, the adoption of a vegetarian, and especially a vegan, eating plan also usually causes weight loss (since the substitution of lower-fat items takes longer than the reduction of high-fat items), at least over the short term. For those who eat large amounts of sweet foods, either limitating simple sugar intake or sugar-gram counting often produces the desired calorie deficits. Abstinence from alcohol is recommended on reducing diets because alcohol is very high in calories (approximately 7 kilocalories per gram of absolute alcohol). To determine the caloric contribution of alcohol to intake, multiply the number of ounces of alcohol consumed by 0.8 and by the proof (the latter is defined as twice the percent alcohol in the product).

Predicting Weight Loss

The amount of weight lost on reducing regimens depends on energy intake and output levels as well as on the usual energy needs of the individual. Therefore, on equivalent energy intakes, weight losses may differ substantially, since energy needs do also.

Moderate Hypocaloric Plans

Moderate hypocaloric reducing plans, often 1,800 kilocalories for men and 1,200 kilocalories for women, offer the calorie levels used in many of the more responsible commercial weight reduction programs and the sounder weight control books.

One moderately low-calorie regimen is based on balanced deficits in protein, fat, and carbohydrate. Foods may be chosen from among recipes, frozen entrees, or items sold through a commercial weight loss program. Formal moderately low-calorie diet programs are operated in a variety of locations, including health care facilities and business settings. Those in health care facilities have the advantage of providing liaison with and referral to health professionals. In both settings group support, nutritional advice, and physical activity can and should be incorporated. In addition to commercial and health-care-center based services, self-help programs are available at low or no cost, such as Take Off Pounds Sensibly (TOPS) and Overeaters Anonymous (OA). Reasonable moderately low-calorie diets are also available in some books.

Low-Calorie Diets

Low-calorie diets (LCDs) provide from 800 to 1,200 kilocalories per day. They require some medical supervision, since the lower the energy level, the greater are the physiological and psychological effects. Using a diet containing less than 1,200 kilocalories it is almost impossible to meet vitamin and mineral needs from food sources alone. Diets that are this hypocaloric should also not be embarked upon on one's own, since they have noticeable effects on metabolism as well as on loss of fat. These diets are most suitable for individuals who have significant medical reasons for losing weight rapidly, such as non-insulin-dependent diabetes mellitus, hyperlipidemias, high blood pressure, and orthopedic problems, all conditions that may also require physician guidance.

There are two major types of LCDs. First are those based on regular foods, which require vitamin and mineral supplementation (with iron, calcium, vitamin B-6, riboflavin, and others) to be adequate. These LCDs include those offered in commercial weight loss programs. There are also some good books that advocate LCDs.

Specially formulated or fortified food products that require vitamin and mineral supplementation make up the second type of LCD. One variety of this type is the diet meal replacement, often a milk-based formula product that is either liquid or solid. This variety now includes liquid formulas and dried, canned, and frozen microwavable meals. These products are also available in drugstores. If used according to directions and consumed at levels of 1,100–1,200 kilocalories they provide a complete diet. However, many dieters do not use them as the directions on the package specify and thus may run the risk of deficiencies. Many people now use LCD meal replacements. If they are used appropriately they may provide a helpful and safe low-calorie interlude for those who are able to sustain the regimen. If used inappropriately, as for only one or two meals a day and without the recommended supplemental foods, they may be inadequate and fail to meet the recommended dietary allowances (RDAs).

Very-Low-Calorie Diets

Very-low-calorie diets (VLCDs) are those that provide 600–800 kilocalories per day or less. Total fasting or starvation are discussed elsewhere (see chapter 86). Any diet that of less than 800 kilocalories is below that required for resting metabolism. Such diets lead to dramatic shifts in fluid and electrolyte balances, resting metabolism, and exercise tolerance. They require supplementation to be nutritionally adequate. If VLCDs are not correctly formulated, the loss of lean body mass can be great. Since the risk of side effects, compromised metabolism, or other problems is great for some individuals, it is vital that VLCDs be used carefully and be medically supervised, with frequent monitoring.

For those who use VLCDs, frequent health supervision is needed because such patients may become dehydrated, especially if the diet is very low in carbohydrate and is ketogenic. If the dieting is unsupervised, lean body mass and linear growth may decrease, and cardiac changes may occur. In addition, if their VLCDs are not supplemented, patients may experience disorders in water balance, which may cause diuresis, dehydration, ketosis, electrolyte imbalances, and nutrient deficiencies. The lowering of resting metabolism causes lethargy, which results in decreased voluntary physical activity and exercise tolerance, light-headedness, dizziness, weakness, and feeling faint on standing. In addition anemia, constipation, menstrual irregularity, and hair loss may result.

VLCDs are not appropriate for self-initiated dieting efforts. They are also inappropriate for most obese children and adolescents under 18 years of age (especially those who are pubertal), pregnant and lactating women, the elderly, those who are ill, and those with emotional problems. As energy deficits increase, so too do the homeostatic mechanisms that regulate food intake. Resting metabolic rates fall—by as much as 15% in total starvation—and the voluntary energy output during physical activity also falls. The end result is that on VLCDs the energy deficit is somewhat less than anticipated.

Total Fasting

Total fasting starvation (no food intake) starvation (no food intake) is contraindicated for all patients, especially for those who are embarking on regimens of their own, because such fasting causes excessive loss of lean body mass. This drastic weight reduction method has profound metabolic effects, including diuresis, kaliuresis, saliuresis, and nutrient deficiency, unless the total fasting is supplemented. The large loss of lean body mass and the extreme energy deficit lead to a greater decline in the RMR, voluntary physical activity (so that lethargy is common), and exercise tolerance.

Composition of the Diet

Dietary composition can affect weight loss, nutrition, and hydration status, especially when energy intake is very low (e.g., less than 800 kilocalories). Protein intake is necessary to spare nitrogen, and the lower the energy intake the greater the need for protein.

Carbohydrate levels are important in low-calorie diets, since adequate carbohydrate is needed to maintain the blood sugar level and the fluid balance. At least 50 grams of carbohydrate per day (the amount provided by 4 tablespoons of sugar) is required to spare protein and to avoid large shifts in weight due to changes in water balance. When carbohydrate intake is less than 100 grams per day, insulin levels fall and protein is catabolized to provide the glucogenic amino acids, which can be converted to glucose, the fuel for cells that require glucose. When protein must be catabolized to maintain blood glucose levels, additional water is liberated as the protein is degraded. For each gram of protein or glycogen that is broken down, 3 grams of water is released.

Adequate dietary fiber levels are also important to avoid constipation and to add bulk to the diet. Electrolytes, including potassium and sodium, must be included, particularly for persons on VLCDs. Diets must incorporate sufficient fluids, and vitamins and minerals must meet RDA levels.

Consumer Issues

The costs of popular diets vary. It is important that consumers be aware of the costs and that they match consumers' needs. Cost and effectiveness are not necessarily related. The most expensive weight management systems are not necessarily the most effective or the safest from the standpoint of health.

Consumer friendliness involves ethical business practices in marketing and advertising the diet. Programs should explicitly and fully disclose the physiological and psychological risks associated with weight loss and regain and a realistic estimate of the long-term success of the program after 1 and 5 years.

Incorporation of Components of Sound Weight Management

The components of sound weight management include healthful hypocaloric and maintenance diets, physical activity and exercise, and behavior modification. Physical activity and exercise are increasingly recognized as important in both the loss and the maintenance phases (see Chapter 84).

Many persons with weight problems have comorbidities that require simultaneous dietary or pharmacological treatment and must be considered in planning the therapeutic diet. Drug dosages may need to be adjusted during the hypocaloric phase of the weight program.

MAINTENANCE OF HEALTHY WEIGHTS

The factors that seem to be associated with long-term success in keeping weight off are physical activity and exercise, gradual changes in diet, therapy that deals with obesity as a disorder that will respond to an altered social milieu, and individualization of treatment to fit patients' life-style realities. Weight loss should be maintained for at least 1 year before renewed efforts to lose even more weight are attempted.

Many other measures must also be acted on to reduce the risk of chronic degenerative diseases; these measures include nonsmoking and physical activity. Popular diets that stress broad-based health promotion and disease prevention programs are desirable.

AREAS NEEDING RESEARCH

We know enough to assist people in distinguishing between sound and unsound popular diets. However, much remains to be discovered. We need to determine the processes by which people interpret weight-related recommendations and select diets to attain healthy and desirable/ideal weights.

Weight goals for the prevention of obesity differ from those that are optimal for cure once overweight is present. We need to understand how people classify themselves and select their weight goals, as well as the factors that influence their choice of diets to attain healthier weights.

It is important to evaluate how best to help people choose and implement weight control programs that are best for them. We need to improve our ability to predict who is likely to have the best outcomes from different types of self-help efforts. It is also essential to develop better reporting and monitoring systems. Most people who lose weight do not maintain these losses. Presently the national nutrition monitoring system does not include systematic monitoring and reporting mechanisms for gathering information on either the beneficial or the adverse effects of popular self-help dieting programs or on the long-term effects of weight loss efforts on health. There is a need for research to determine the best ways of developing such data collection mechanisms and of using them both to enhance good outcomes and to avert problems.

The final suggestion is for better regulation of the promotion and advertising of popular diets. Both practice and ethical standards for the treatment of the different types of obesity, especially those that are complicated by various risk factors, should be established and validated.

FURTHER READING

Brownell, K. D. (1991). Dieting and the search for the perfect body: Where physiology and culture collide. *Behavior Therapy, 22,* 1–12. Provides insights into the motivations behind the use of popular diets.

Brownell, K. D., & Wadden, T. A. (1992). Etiology and treatment of obesity: Understanding a serious, prevalent and refractory disorder. *Journal of Consulting and Clinical Psychology, 60,* 505–517. Describes the motivations for dieting and suggests some criteria for treatment selection, including the use of low-calorie popular diets.

Dwyer, J. T. (1992). Treatment of obesity: Conventional programs and fad diets. In P. Björntorp & B. N. Brodoff (Eds.), *Obesity* (pp. 662–676). Philadelphia: J. B. Lippincott. Provides examples of reasonable, questionable, and unreasonable popular diets.

Dwyer, J. T., & Lu, D. (1993). Popular diets for weight loss: From nutritionally hazardous to healthful. In A. J. Stunkard & T. A. Wadden (Eds.), *Obesity: Theory and therapy* (2nd ed., pp. 231–232). New York: Raven Press. Provides a detailed description of schemes for analyzing popular diets.

Kayman, S., Bruvold, W., & Stern, J. S. (1990). Maintenance and relapse after weight loss in women: Behavioral aspects. *American Journal of Clinical Nutrition, 52,* 800–807. A discussion of our lack of knowledge of the individual differences in successful treatment modalities, the relapse problem, and the importance of behavioral factors in avoiding it.

King, A. C., Frey-Hewitt, B., Dreon, D. M., & Wood, P. D. (1989). Diet vs. exercise in weight maintenance: The effects of minimal intervention strategies on long-term outcomes in men. *Archives of Internal Medicine, 149,* 2741–2746. Shows the beneficial effects of off-the-job physical activity and exercise in weight control.

Report of the Task Force on the Treatment of Obesity. Canadian Department of Health and Welfare. (1991). Ottawa, Ontario: Author. Provides guidelines for safe and effective weight loss.

Schacter, S. (1982). Recidivism and self-cure of smoking and obesity. *American Psychologist, 84,* 436. An early study that calls attention to the importance of self-help efforts.

Smith-Schneider, L. M., Sigman-Grant, M. J., & Kris-Etherton, P. M. (1992). Dietary fat reduction strategies. *Journal of the American Dietetic Association, 92,* 34–38. Shows the caloric effects of dietary fat reduction strategies.

St. Jeor, S. T., Brownell, K. D., Atkinson, R. L., Bouchard, C., Dwyer, J. T., Foreyt, J. P., Heber, D., Kris-Etherton, P., Stern, J. S., Willett, W., Wilson, G. T., & Wood, P. D. (1993). Obesity: Workshop III. *Circulation, 88,* 1391–1396. Describes special considerations in choosing popular diets when lipid disorders are present.

Thomas, P. R. (Ed.). (1991). *Improving America's diet and health: From recommendations to action: A report of the Committee on Dietary Guidelines Implementation.* Washington, DC: National Academy Press. Provides the background for constructive community and self-help efforts in weight management.

• 88 •

COMMERCIAL AND SELF-HELP APPROACHES TO WEIGHT MANAGEMENT

Alberto Cormillot

In recent years there has been a significant increase in the use of commercial and self-help approaches to weight loss. The origin of this movement can be traced back to two developments, namely, the visibility of lay-led self-help groups for addictive disorders and the introduction of behavioral technologies for the treatment of these disorders.

In the United States alone, a prominent self-help group, Take Off Pounds Sensibly (TOPS), enrolled over 300,000 members at the height of its influence, and Weight Watchers enrolled 1,000,000 people each week in 16,000 separate meetings. There was an explosive growth in the income of commercial programs in the 1980s, with total revenues of $3 billion per year for just four of these organizations in the United States (Diet Center, Jenny Craig, Nutri/System, and OptiFast).

Spurred in part by the growth of an antidieting mentality (see Chapter 17), congressional hearings on advertising practices in the industry, and general skepticism of commercial programs, revenues for many programs plunged in the 1990s. Nutri/System closed many centers, and business for Jenny Craig was reported to be down by 50%.

COMMERCIAL AND SELF-HELP GROUPS: AN OVERVIEW

The self-help movement is an outgrowth of attempts to cope with physical and mental health problems using peer and personal resources with little or no professional help. This movement, in its varied expressions, has become paramount in the delivery of health care services because of its low cost and accessibility and also because it offers an efficient complement or alternative to more conventional service delivery programs.

Self-help and commercial groups have the potential to offer the personal involvement and comprehensive approach needed to promote behavior changes in complex problems such as obesity. This potential, combined with the vast numbers of people who can be reached, make the programs of these groups the most influential approaches to weight management currently available.

On the negative side, these groups often generate expectations greater than can be reasonably achieved, sometimes through misleading advertising. Moreover, evaluations of the programs have not been made public. Recent moves in the United States to regulate the commercial weight loss industry might, in the future, enable patients and/or professionals to make informed choices about treatment. Unfortunately, such action has not taken place in other countries.

Groups: A Brief Description

Self-Help Groups

These groups gather people with weight or eating problems and operate at little or no cost, generally without professional intervention. Examples are Overeaters Anonymous (OA) and TOPS in the United States; GRACO in Italy; and Anonymous Fighters Against Obesity (ALCO), which operates in Argentina, Uruguay, Chile, Paraguay, Spain, and Israel. The groups all offer considerable social support but vary in their philosophy. A group such as TOPS includes more behavioral principles, while OA is based on the 12-Step model used in addiction programs and focuses on "compulsive overeating" as the core problem.

Commercial Programs.

These programs provide information on dieting and nutrition and may include physical activity, behavioral techniques to change eating patterns, psychotherapy, the provision of food, and group support. The programs vary widely in cost, from those requiring a small program fee for each meeting to those charging for dietary supplements or prepackaged food (where the total costs can be several thousand dollars). The most prominent programs are Weight Watchers, Jenny Craig, OptiFast, Diet Center, Nutri/System, all in the United States; Libra in Norway; Slimming Magazine in Great Britain; and Dieta Club in Argentina.

The Striking Absence of Evaluation

Considering that many millions of individuals have enrolled in commercial and self-help programs for weight loss, that the problem they seek to remedy has important effects on their health and psychological functioning, and that billions of dollars are spent annually, it is striking indeed how little is known about the effectiveness of such approaches. A few scattered papers have been published on such groups, but the focus has been on the attrition (the dropout rate) experienced by these groups rather than on the weight loss and maintenance of their clients. The results suggest that attrition in some programs is high (50% or more clients drop out in the first few weeks), but even here, our knowledge is incomplete.

One can only speculate about why there has not been more evaluation of these programs. It has not because of a lack of interest among investigators, since many have expressed interest in undertaking such work. More likely it is due to problems with confidentiality in the self-help groups and with protecting the financial interests of the commercial programs. In self-help groups such as OA, clients cannot be identified and therefore their progress (or lack of it) would be difficult to follow. As for the commercial programs, which saw remarkable growth in the 1980s, reporting lackluster or even poor results would only stand to reduce their profits. The closed atmosphere that now surrounds these programs will probably remain so until regulatory action forces a scrutiny of their results.

It is clear that the evaluation of commercial and self-help programs is a major research priority. This research should have as its objective the examination not only of the obvious factors such as attrition and short- and long-term weight loss but also of the effects of these programs on clients' health and psychosocial factors.

AN INTEGRATED APPROACH

Competition rather than cooperation between commercial and self-help programs has been the rule. This is a discouraging situation and has led to a failure to exploit the full range of opportunities that might be available to people with serious eating and weight problems. In Argentina, by adopting a more cooperative philosophy, we have developed a network that includes self-help and commercial groups, both with some degree of professional involvement. Among the array of services are outpatient individual or group treatments, inpatient treatment, food provision, and information dissemination through courses and the mass media, always placing the consumer at the center of the network.

The network consists of a variety of programs involving assistance, prevention, research, and teaching. The network is displayed in Figure 88.1. Commercial and self-help treatments are important parts of the total system. Over 1,000,000 persons have made direct use of the system.

Three Programs within the Network

To illustrate the range of services available through the integrated network, three of its key programs will be discussed here.

ALCO

Founded in Argentina in 1967, ALCO is a nonprofit self-help organization based on a philosophy similar to that of Alcoholics Anonymous (AA). The 12 steps of AA have been

Intervention channel	Program
Clinical services	Inpatient or outpatient program
Self-help group	ALCO
Family support	FAMALCO
Commercial/self-help program	Dieta Club
Program for eating disorders	ABAN
Provision of healthy food	Dieta Service
Mass media	Radio, television, newspapers
Restaurant menus	Alternative menus for restaurants
Research	CINAS (research support, library)
National nutrition policy	National policy, advice to food industry

FIGURE 88.1. A list (developed and/or coordinated by me) of comprehensive services available in Argentina. The self-help (ALCO, FAMALCO) and commercial (Dieta Club) programs are among the potential resources and may be the most appropriate choices for some individuals, thus underscoring the need for criteria for matching individuals to treatments.

modified in ALCO; less emphasis is placed on the concept of a "higher power" so as to reinforce personal involvement and responsibility. Essentially nonprofessional, ALCO is a variation of typical self-help groups, its unique feature being that leaders use guidelines developed by experts and receive training from experts. Supported mainly by donations from members, ALCO also derives some profit from the sale of low-priced written materials.

Dieta Club

Established in 1981, Dieta Club in both a professional and a nonprofessional institution, a cross between self-help and commercial programs. Many of the leaders were formerly overweight. Professional participation includes experts other than physicians (psychologists, nutritionists, etc.). Special obesity programs are offered for children, adolescents, pregnant and postpartum women, and the handicapped. Dieta Club also offers treatment for other addictive and eating disorders (gambling, smoking, alcoholism, bulimia, and anorexia nervosa). The program primarily involves group meetings, which the average client attends weekly.

FAMALCO

Loosely translated, FAMALCO stands for "Families of Anonymous Fighters Against Obesity." As Al-Anon is an organization for family members of alcoholics involved in AA, FAMALCO is a group for family members of obese persons involved with ALCO. It is a self-help group that provides support for family members and friends in a group context. Its main aim is to offer ideas and resources for coping, which are developed with input from professionals.

Key Aspects of the Integrated Approach

Several conceptual issues are important across the network of programs. These issues, outlined below, guide the development of program content and structure.

1. *Linguistic implications.* The terms "recovery" and "cure" must be used carefully. It is our position that the condition of being obese remains the same even after weight loss. In addition,4obesity is considered a disease, not a vice (morality model), a sin (religious model), or a fashion (exclusively esthetic model).

2. *Possible weight.* Because in practice many patients cannot reach the expected conventional values represented by ideal, desirable, or healthy weights, we have developed the concept of "possible weight" (PW) (see also Chapter 98). The PW enables both patient and physician to define treatment goals that come much closer to the patient's actual possibilities, thus minimizing frustration and dropout caused by unattainable goals. Maximum weight (MW), ideal weight (IW), length of obesity (LO), and age beyond 20 years are used to calculate the PW, using the following formula:

$$PW = IW + 0.1 (MW - IW) + 0.1 (LO \text{ in years}) + 0.1 (\text{age in years} - 20)$$

3. *Training.* Within our network, we consider the training of both professionals and lay leaders to be of utmost importance. Effective management of obesity does not

primarily rest on a knowledge of its pathophysiology. Controversy still exists on this issue, but currently there are no proven therapies that can modify the putative etiological mechanisms of obesity.

Our training emphasizes ethical and humanistic approaches based on principles discussed by Carl Rogers and Abraham Maslow and on a need for a change in the physician's attitude. It is important for professionals to realize that while obesity may be biosocial in origin, its treatment lies in psychosocial issues.

4. *Matching the treatment to the individual.* Several issues are considered in selecting the most suitable program for an individual (see also Chapter 98). The first concerns the aspects of weight itself, such as the degree of overweight; comorbidity; years of obesity; and the possible influence of heredity on the patient's condition. The greater these aspects are, the greater the need for professional intervention, at least during the initial stages of treatment.

Other factors include the degree of the patient's involvement with treatment (professional intervention may be necessary to strengthen the initial "liaisons"), the number of previous treatments (the more often a patient has been in treatment, the higher the risk of dropout), spontaneous demand, and geographical and financial issues (these last two factors sometimes leave lay groups as the only alternative).

CONCLUSIONS

To provide comprehensive services for overweight individuals, professionals should consider commercial and self-help groups as viable options at any stage of treatment. The utility of these groups is often overestimated by commercial advertisements but is also often underestimated by professionals. Among the virtues of commercial and self-help programs is low cost, the availability of long-term support, flexibility that allows a person to move from one program to another, and collaboration with professionals. Finally, it is important for researchers to break the barrier of doubt in order to provide the systematic research needed to identify the individuals most likely to benefit from such assistance.

ACKNOWLEDGMENTS

My thanks to Dr. Kelly Brownell for his helpful suggestions and to Drs. Claudia Chaufan and Ruben Zuckerfeld for our discussion of ideas and the organization of the contents of this chapter.

FURTHER READING

American Cancer Society. (1984). *Guidelines on self-help and mutual support groups.* New York: American Cancer Society. An update on self-help and mutual support groups, focusing on the reparative nature of such groups.

Cormillot, A. (1983). *Obesity: Follow-up of three systems in the medium-term.* Paper presented at the Fourth International Congress on Obesity, New York. A comparison of the changes in obese patients treated by means of three systems during 1 year.

Cormillot, A., Fuchs, A., & Zuckerfeld, R. (1986). *A network for multifaceted treatment of obesity based on the addictive behavioral model.* Paper presented at the Fifth International Congress on

Obesity, New York. A description of a network for treating obesity, based mainly on an addiction model, with contributions from other fields, including biology, behavior therapy, addictive disorders, eating disorders, and physical activity.

Feuerstein, M., Dobkin, P. L., Shapiro, S., & Tannenbaum, S. (1989). A strategy to predict outcomes in a comprehensive weight loss program. *International Journal of Obesity, 13* (Suppl. 1), 101. An article on predictors of attrition and weight loss of 224 women enrolled in a commercial program (Nutri/System).

Garb, J. R., & Stunkard, A. J. (1972). Effectiveness of a self-help group in obesity control: A further assessment. *Archives of Internal Medicine, 134,* 716–720. One of the earliest articles in which a nonclinical program was evaluated, in this case the TOPS self-help group.

Mallory, L. (1984). *Leading self-help groups: A guide for training facilitators.* New York: Family Service America. A helpful guide for training facilitators within self-help groups, covering all the topics essential to the experiences that are sought in such groups.

Stunkard, A. J., & Wadden, T. A. (1992). Psychological aspects of human obesity. In P. Björntorp & B. N. Brodoff (Eds.), *Obesity* (pp. 352–360). Philadelphia: Lippincott. A review of the psychological aspects of obesity that are important to consider in developing weight control programs.

Taylor, C. B., & Stunkard, A. J. (1993). Public health approaches to weight control. In A. J. Stunkard & T. A. Wadden (Eds.), *Obesity: Theory and therapy* (pp. 335–353). New York: Raven Press. A discussion of approaches to weight control from a public health perspective, including a detailed review of commercial and self-help programs.

Vandereycken, W. (1990). The addiction model in eating disorders: More critical remarks and a selected bibliography. *International Journal of Eating Disorders, 9,* 91–101. A discussion of the addiction model as applied to eating disturbances.

Volkmar, F. R., Stunkard, A. J., Woolston, J., & Bailey, B. A. (1981). High attrition rates in a commercial weight loss program. *Archives of Internal Medicine, 141,* 426–428. The documentation of an attrition rate of approximately 50% within the first 6 weeks of enrollment in a major commercial weight loss program.

Wolfe, B. L. (1992). Long-term maintenance following attainment of goal weight: A preliminary investigation. *Addictive Behaviors, 17,* 469–478. A study of 517 individuals who had lost weight in a commercial program (Jenny Craig).

• 89 •

PHARMACOLOGICAL TREATMENT OF OBESITY

STANLEY HESHKA
STEVEN B. HEYMSFIELD

OVERVIEW OF PHARMACOLOGICAL TREATMENT

Pharmacological agents have long been available for the short-term treatment of obesity. The rationale is that such agents may be necessary to assist in the treatment of patients with resistant/recalcitrant cases of obesity, but once a reduced weight is achieved the patient can then be assigned the task of maintaining the lower weight. Overweight is viewed as the result of a temporary behavioral excess or abnormal physiological condition, and once the proper weight has been attained the patient is then in approximately the same position as a person who had always been of normal weight. The task is then simply to avoid the problems that would again produce obesity.

This view of obesity is challenged by an alternative view—that obesity is a enduring disorder requiring continued intervention, in a manner similar to hypertension and non-insulin-dependent diabetes mellitus (NIDDM). This is the model physicians have followed in treating obesity resulting from certain types of hypothyroidism. Exogenous thyroid hormone and thyroid supplementation is continued indefinitely. Termination of the intervention would result in the return of the imbalance that caused the obesity. This alternative view has stimulated the search for obesity treatments that can be applied for longer periods of time without necessarily addressing the original physiological basis of the imbalance.

Off in the future lies the hope that a better understanding of obesity through molecular biology will allow us to address the causes of the disorder rather than just the symptoms (see Chapter 80). For the moment this understanding remains a hope rather than a certainty, and the increasing prevalence of the disorder in the developed nations makes it imperative to apply and perfect existing interventions that can be shown to be safe and effective.

CLASSES OF PHARMACOLOGICAL ANTIOBESITY AGENTS

Since obesity is a disorder of energy balance, pharmacological agents can be initially classified as those that reduce net energy intake and those that increase energy expenditure. A third category usually not considered might be agents that alter fuel storage and the mixture of fuels that is used. While it might seem appropriate to identify the nature of the disorder in an individual, that is, whether the cause of excess energy stores is an abnormally high intake and/or abnormally low expenditure, this capability is usually not possible given the current state of the art. Small errors in energy balance that are within the range of measurement error may have large cumulative effects on actual fuel storage in the body. Furthermore, it does not follow that such identification would then make treatment more effective: One of the two components may be more easily altered than the other (e.g., intake may be more easily modified than expenditure). Thus, aside from attending to the usual contraindications for a particular medication, little distinction is currently made among types of obesity in designing a pharmacological treatment.

Medications that alter net energy intake may be classified as appetite suppressants (anorexiants), satiety enhancers, or agents that alter the absorption of ingested nutrients. Medications that affect energy expenditure are thermogenic agents or agents that increase the rate of futile cycles, thereby decreasing metabolic efficiency. A third category consists of medications that affect fat storage and oxidation.

Agents That Reduce Net Energy Intake

Anorexiants

One major category of anorexiants is the amphetamines (e.g., dextroamphetamine sulfate). Amphetamines are now rarely used for weight reduction because of their high potential for abuse and the possibility of drug dependence. They are noncatecholamine sympathomimetic amines that slow central nervous system (CNS) stimulant activity. Their effects include blood pressure elevations, so they are contraindicated for persons with cardiovascular disease and hypertension. Their most evident antiobesity action is that of appetite suppression; however, other concomitant effects on metabolism and the nervous system have not been definitively ruled out.

A second major grouping consists of pharmacological agents closely related to amphetamines but whose CNS stimulatory action and abuse potential are greatly reduced. In this grouping are:

Phentermine (hydrochloride and resin): A sympathomimetic amine with pharmacological activity similar to that of an amphetamine. Its actions include CNS stimulation and blood pressure elevation, as well as occasional tachyphylaxis. Its contraindications are similar to those for amphetamines. This medication should not be used within 14 days of discontinuing the use of a monoamine oxidase inhibitor.

Phenmetrazine (hydrochloride): A compound from the oxazine group whose actions include CNS stimulation and blood pressure elevation. As with other sympathomimetic amines, tachyphylaxis has been observed to occur.

Phendimetrazine (tartrate): A phenylalkylamine sympathomimetic with actions similar to those of the amphetamines.

Diethylpropion (hydrochloride): A sympathomimetic amine that stimulates the CNS and produces anorexia. As with other agents in this class, some tolerance to the medication's appetite-suppressing effects develops over time.

Mazindol: An imidazoisoindole sympathomimetic anorectic agent with CNS stimulant activity that appears to exert its primary effects on the limbic portion of the CNS.

Phenylpropanolamine: A nonprescription beta-phenylethylamine derivative in the sympathomimetic category that has few significant CNS stimulant effects and does not produce dependence. When used as part of a comprehensive management program that includes diet, exercise, and behavior modification, phenylpropanolamine significantly increased the rate of weight loss for up to 16 weeks in a controlled clinical trial.

Another category of anorexiants acts mainly through serotonergic pathways:

Fenfluramine (hydrochloride): A serotonin reuptake inhibitor that tends to have slightly depressant CNS effects. Its main antiobesity effect is appetite suppression; however, other mechanisms and modes of action may be involved.

All the agents listed above are approved by the Food and Drug Administration for use in short-term treatment. Other anorexiant drugs awaiting approval, or in advanced stages of development in the United States, include:

Dexfenfluramine: The dextroisomer of *dl*-fenfluramine. Dexfenfluramine stimulates the release of serotonin and inhibits its reuptake, thereby increasing serotonin concentrations in the synaptic cleft. Although the molecule resembles an amphetamine, no CNS stimulation is observed and a slight drowsiness may be induced. There are many different classes and subgroups of serotonin receptors, and the serotonergic system is involved in a wide variety of functions such as depression, anxiety, pain, and sleep. The precise causal chain leading from increased CNS serotonin levels to appetite suppression is not known. Immediate effects of improved glycemic control and lowered of blood pressure, independent of weight loss, have been observed.

Fluoxetine: A serotonergic agent, currently available as an antidepressant drug. At higher doses it has an effect on body weight.

Sibutramine (hydrochloride): Originally investigated as an antidepressant agent, sibutramine acts on monoamine reuptake systems in the brain and down regulates both beta-adrenoceptors and the associated noradrenaline-linked adenylate cyclase. Sibutramine does not have a sedative effect. A small but statistically significant rise in blood pressure and heart rate may occur.

Satiety Enhancers

Some research has been conducted on agents that are meant to enhance satiety rather than suppressing appetite. For example, agents that delay gastric emptying (e.g., chlorocitrate and cholecystokinin) may thereby prolong feelings of satiety and fullness and may delay the onset of hunger and eating. No products with delayed gastric emptying as the principal mechanism of action are presently available, although some of the existing medications may have this mechanism as one of their modes of action.

Altered Nutrient Absorption

Several medications inhibit nutrient absorption and thereby increase fecal energy losses. Among the medications of this kind that are under investigation is the following:

Tetrahydrolipstatin: This agent binds with pancreatic and other gastrointestinal lipases, thereby preventing them from playing their usual roles in the absorption of fat.

Consequently the net absorption of dietary fat is reduced. To prevent the appearance of side effects related to excessive malabsorption, the intake of dietary fat should be limited to no more than about 30% of total calories.

Other presently experimental compounds (e.g., acarbose and AO-128) block carbohydrate digestion.

Agents That Increase Energy Expenditure

Thermogenic Agents

The use of thermogenic agents has long seemed a promising avenue for altering energy balance, but the difficulty has been to find an agent that increases thermogenesis without affecting cardiac function. At present ephedrine is the only available drug in this category. Ephedrine combined with caffeine produces greater weight loss than placebo. Newer synthetic agents such as the beta-agonist BRL 26380A are more promising but as yet have not been comprehensively studied. Thyroid hormone administration during dieting may cause excessive protein loss and cardiac hypertrophy and should not be prescribed.

Altered Storage/Fuel Utilization

Body composition can be manipulated in growing animals by the selective use of hormones. Similarly fat can be reduced and muscle increased in athletes who inappropriately use anabolic steroid medications. At present there are no approved medications that selectively reduce the storage or increase the oxidation of fat stores.

TREATMENT WITH COMBINATIONS OF MEDICATIONS

There has been one well-publicized, long-term clinical trial in which a combination of two medications (phentermine and fenfluramine) was used. The results suggest that a combination of medications that have relatively different modes of action may be effective in reducing and maintaining a lower weight for a long duration with an acceptable level of side effects. At present such treatment should be undertaken only in the context of a research protocol and should provide close patient monitoring for unanticipated adverse events.

The protocol for combination long-term (>4 months) treatment with phentermine resin and fenfluramine that is used at our center is shown in Table 89.1. The starting drug and maintenance dosages can be varied according to the patient's baseline characteristics and treatment response.

GENERAL GUIDELINES

Medication treatment is usually reserved for patients who fail to lose weight or maintain their weight loss following conventional therapy. A thorough physical examination and history should reveal whether any particular agent is contraindicated on the basis of its

TABLE 89.1. Combination Treatment Used at the Obesity Research Center

Level	Fenfluramine (Pondimin)		Phentermine (Ionamin)	
	Dose (mg)	Schedule	Dose (mg)	Schedule
I	20	1 hr before dinner	15	Take before breakfast
II	20	1 hr before dinner	30	Take before breakfast
III	20	1 hr before dinner	30 8	Take before breakfast 1 in the midafternoon
IV	20 20	Take before breakfast 1 hr before dinner	30 8	Take before breakfast 1 in the midafternoon
V	20 20 20	Take before breakfast 1 hr before lunch 1 hr before dinner	30 8	Take before breakfast 1 in the midafternoon
VI	20 20 20(2)	Take before breakfast 1 hr before lunch 1 hr before dinner	30 8	Take before breakfast 1 in the midafternoon

Note. Adapted with permission from Dr. Morton Maxwell.

mode of action (e.g., sympathomimetic agents would not be appropriate for patients with hypertension).

After a medication regimen has been initiated, the patient should make regular visits for monitoring body weight, vital signs, blood chemistry, and other factors appropriate for the specific medication. Frequent monitoring visits are recommended immediately after the medication is started. Rapid rates of weight loss should be avoided (i.e., >1 kilogram per week after the first few weeks) because they may be an indication of inadequate levels of nutrition and/or loss of body components other than fat. Prolongation of the electrocardiographic QT_c interval in particular has been associated with fatalities in cases of rapid weight loss.

There is some suggestion in the data from long-term drug trials that tolerance may develop after long periods on a medication. Thus it would be most useful for long-term treatment to have drugs with different modes of action available so that medications may be alternated if one loses its efficacy.

The usual practice is to prescribe drugs as an adjunct to a program of caloric restriction and exercise. It is not clear how much these latter elements enhance weight loss over and above the simple effect of medication. Exercise, however, clearly confers benefits to the patient apart from any contribution to weight reduction.

FURTHER READING

American medical association drug evaluations. (1992). Chicago, IL: American Medical Association. An excellent, annually updated resource for obesity medications with an emphasis on clinical work.

Blundell, J. E. (1992). Serotonin and the biology of feeding. American Journal of Clinical Nutrition, 55, 155S–159S. A review of the neurotransmitter serotonin's role in appetite behavior.

Bray, G. (1993). Use and abuse of appetite-suppressant drugs in the treatment of obesity. Annals of Internal Medicine, 119, 707–713. A current overview of how diet medications work and their role in obesity treatment.

Drug information for the health care practitioner: USPDI 1993 (13th ed., pp. 438–445). (1993). Rockville, MD: United States Pharmacopeial Convention. Medication characteristics, including composition, are summarized in this periodical.

Guy-Grand, B. (1992). Clinical studies with *d*-fenfluramine. *American Journal of Clinical Nutrition, 55*, 173S–176S. An overview of the serotonergic agent *d*-fenfluramine.

Hauptmann, J. B., Jeunet, F. S., & Hartmann, D. (1992). Initial studies in humans with the novel gastrointestinal inhibitor Ro 18-0647 (tetrahydorlipostatin). *American Journal of Clinical Nutrition, 55*, 309S–313S. An analysis of this important new medication that partially inhibits fat absorption.

Levitsky, D. A., & Troiano, R. (1992). Metabolic consequences of fenfluramine for the control of body weight. *American Journal of Clinical Nutrition, 55*, 167S–172S. A good review of the widely used medication fenfluramine with an emphasis on its metabolic effects.

Sullivan, A. C., & Comai, K. (1978). Pharmacological treatment of obesity. *Internal Journal of Obesity, 2*, 167–189. A classic in-depth review of medications for obesity treatment and their mechanisms of action.

Weintraub, M., Sundaresan, P. R., Schuster, B., Moscucci, M., & Stein, E. C. (1992). Long-term weight control study: III. An open label study of dose adjustment of fenfluramine and phentermine. *Clinical Pharmacological Therapeutics, 51*, 602–607. An impressive study in which the long-term use of combined pharmacological treatment is examined.

Wellman, P. (1992). Overview of adrenergic anorectic agents. *American Journal of Clinical Nutrition, 55*, 193S–198S. A review of andrenergically active obesity treatment medications.

• 90 •

SURGICAL INTERVENTIONS FOR OBESITY

John G. Kral

Most texts on surgical treatment of obesity start with an apologia that points out the severity of the disease and the inability of nonsurgical treatments to maintain significant weight loss over a meaningful period of time. These points have been made in other chapters, more or less explicitly, in this book.

Currently patient mortality associated with the surgical treatment of obesity in competent hands is less than 0.5%, and the morbidity associated with widely accepted operations is trivial compared with the morbidity of obesity itself. Epidemiological data are becoming available that demonstrate that the mortality (3 to 12 times normal) of severe obesity not treated or treated nonsurgically exceeds operative mortality. Thus it would seem that the surgical treatment of obesity passes the "acid test" required for the acceptance of any therapy. A different test this surgery also passes is that of providing improved quality of life to the majority of patients who undergo the procedure and who with few exceptions, would elect to have it done again if necessary, regardless of physicians' assessments of outcome. These observations attest to both the severe psychological burden of obesity (see Chapter 73) and the efficacy of the surgery.

GASTRIC RESTRICTION

There are two forms of purely restrictive gastric procedures currently in use: vertical stapled gastroplasty with banded outlet, and circumgastric banding. Both function by limiting the capacity of the stomach to 15 milliliters of solids and by delaying the emptying of these solids through the banded opening that has a diameter of 9–10 millimeters (Figure 90.1). These operations do *not* effectively restrict the intake of caloric liquids or semisolids unless solid food is already filling or obstructing the upper stomach, or "pouch." With time the pouch stretches, allowing ingestion of larger quantities of solids.

A modification of circumgastric banding uses an inflatable band connected to a subcutaneous reservoir or port, easily accessible to the surgeon for the injection or removal of fluid to adjust the diameter of the opening in the stomach. The inventor, Dr. Kuzmak, has just developed a technique for placing these bands laparoscopically, paving the way for increasingly less invasive (and thus safer) antiobesity surgery. Remarkably,

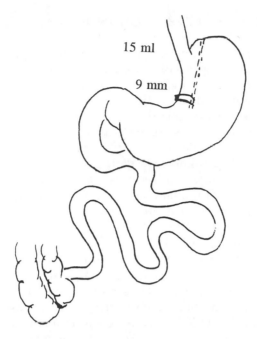

15 ml

9 mm

FIGURE 90.1. Vertical stapled gastroplasty with a banded outlet from the 15-milliliter pouch.

with proper instruments, laparoscopic procedures are particularly suited to obese patients because there is better exposure than is the case with open surgery.

There are limitations to purely restrictive operations: (1) They can be defeated by the "soft-calorie syndrome," (2) the pouch expands, and (3) many patients are unwilling or unable to accept the constraints on their eating behavior.

There is great variation in the outcome of these operations based on the characteristics of the population being studied. Superobese patients (those who are ≥ 225% of desirable weight), individuals who are "addicted to sweets," and black Americans have less successful weight loss experiences than others.

MALABSORPTION

The rationale behind intestinal bypass operations was that excess consumed energy would pass unabsorbed into the stools, in essence enabling patients to maintain their eating habits. Subsequently it was demonstrated that intestinal bypass actually influences ingestive behavior through mechanisms involving the release of gastrointestinal "satiety" peptides from the small intestines (see Chapter 2), toxins from bacterial overgrowth, and undetermined factors. Weight stabilization or regain occurs because of the morphological adaptation of the intestinal mucosa in the form of lengthening and thickening of the villi and/or deepening of the crypts to compensate for the excluded jejunum and ileum. Numerous complications of intestinal bypass, most of them preventable, and the development of gastric operations as alternative procedures, led to the virtual discontinuation of the jejuno-ileal bypass after 1980.

COMBINED GASTRIC RESTRICTION AND MALABSORPTION

Gastric bypass operations combine the gastric restriction of a small proximal gastric pouch (15 milliliters) with the bypass of more than 90% of the stomach, the duodenum, and a limb of jejunum of varying length (Figure 90.2). The rapid rush of liquid and soft, high-caloric food "dumping" into the limb of small intestine causes the release of polypeptides, which evokes discomfort (nimiety) and/or satiety. For this reason gastric bypass operations consistently cause greater weight loss than pure gastric restriction.

The limitations of conventional gastric bypass are: (1) a widening of the (unbanded) gastrojejunostomy, (2) the expansion of the gastric pouch (as in gastroplasty), (3) and the adaptation of the limb of intestine that receives the food. This adaptation is morphological and/or hormonal through the blunted release of peptides or the development of resistance to hormone action. By excluding the food from digestion by gastric acid, gastric bypass operations cause malabsorption of calcium, iron, and vitamin B_{12} and thus have the potential to cause deficiencies.

Because of dissatisfaction with maintenance of weight loss beyond 5 years postoperatively, surgeons have performed increasingly aggressive gastric bypass operations, either by banding the outlet of the small gastric bypass, thus combining the gastric restriction of a gastroplasty with the malabsorptive gastric bypass, or by lengthening the bypassed limb of the small bowel, thus causing substantially more malabsorption.

These modifications are modeled on the biliopancreatic diversion operation of Scopinaro. This procedure consists of a resection of approximately two-thirds of the stomach and the bypass of all of the duodenum and jejunum, which are drained into the

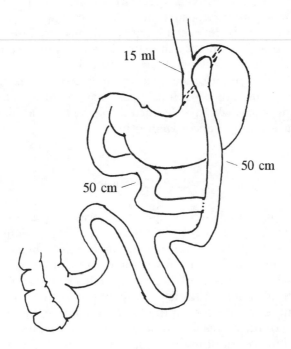

FIGURE 90.2. Gastric bypass excluding most of the stomach, the duodenum, and a 40–50-centimeter segment of proximal jejunum.

last 50 centimeters of the ileum. The proximal ileum is attached to the gastric remnant as a conduit for the (undigested) food. The resection makes this operation anatomically irreversible, although reanastomosis leads to functional restitution. The maldigestion and malabsorption associated with this type of operation requires diligent monitoring for life and often entails multiple hospitalizations during the first 2 postoperative years.

OUTCOME

Surgeons require higher standards for the evaluation of outcome than do other physicians or health professionals who treat obesity. In articles on diet, behavioral modification, drugs, and exercise, the expression "long-term" is frequently used to refer to periods of 6 months to 1 year, and rarely is data provided for as long as 2 years. Furthermore, dropout rates are seldom presented; when they are, they reach levels of 25% to 50% after the completion of the weight loss and maintenance phases of the study (see Chapters 85 and 86). "Success" of nonsurgical treatment is most often referred to in terms of weight loss expressed in percentage of original weight (commonly < 10%) or in pounds or kilograms lost.

The simplest outcome measure to quantitate is mortality. However, a mortality statistic does not necessarily measure "success." Some severely obese patients without the diagnostic criteria of depression clearly express a preference for guaranteed weight loss with the possible risk of early death to living as obese for the rest of their lives. It is true that a follow-up evaluation cannot be performed to validate such a choice, but it demonstrates some of the complexity in defining success. Similarly, a qualitative comparison between the side-effects and complications of antiobesity surgery on the one hand and the side-effects and complications of remaining obese on the other can really only be done by the patient. There is substantial evidence that it is exceedingly rare for patients who have had antiobesity surgery to regret having had an operation even in the face of medically significant complications.

It is true that absolute weight loss is relatively easy to measure and is perceived by obese patients as the primary goal of treatment. However, medical goals should be related to the reduction of comorbidity rather than to weight loss, and success will be defined differently by patients, internists, psychiatrists, surgeons, insurance companies, and government agencies.

Table 90.1 outlines the effects of surgical treatment on prevalent and serious morbidity in severely obese patients. Beneficial effects are being documented on other,

TABLE 90.1. Effects of Antiobesity Surgery on Comorbidity

	% Cured[a]	% Improved[b]
Hypertension	60–65	90
Diabetes	90–95	100
Dyslipidemia	70	85
Asthma	>95	100
Heart failure	60	90
Sleep apnea	100	100

Note. Pooled data from reports on >1,000 patients in published series.
[a]No further need for treatment.
[b]Reduced dosage of medication.

less well-known conditions such as urinary stress incontinence, osteoarthritis of the knees, reflux esophagitis, and venostasis ulcers. Relapse rates remain to be determined, although weight loss achieved by surgical treatment appears to bring patients well below the threshold levels for the appearance of most comorbidities. Weight loss at 5 years after gastric restrictive operations amounts to 40% to 50% of excess weight. After gastric bypass, the loss of excess weight is between 50% to 60%.

Problems

If agreement could be reached on four outcome measures—longevity; comparative morbidity; quality of life, expressed as quality-adjusted life years (QALY); and economy—it would still be necessary to determine relative values to allow a comparison of different groups of patients and different types of operations.

Patient selection still leaves much to be desired. Improved methods for characterizing eating behavior might provide a basis for the selective assignment of patients to a particular type of procedure. At this point, it seems as if the prevalence of binge eating disorder varies among populations of severely obese patients. This variance might explain discrepancies among published studies and might lead to fewer disagreements over the "method of choice" or the "gold standard."

Standards for performing antiobesity surgery with respect to patient assessment and pre- and postoperative education should be set. Improved techniques for obtaining follow-up with a view to monitoring safety as well as providing information on outcome are germane to all forms of treatment of obesity. Although in most surgical series, 75% follow-up rates are attained for 5 or more years, and in some more than 90% follow-up is achieved, there is always room for improvement. The characterization of dropouts has not yet been performed in any large series.

OUTLOOK

The perfection of laparoscopic circumgastric banding will provide an even greater margin of safety, thus allowing the inclusion of patients presently considered poor operative risks. A wider acceptance of these less invasive procedures should lead to earlier intervention, before serious comorbidity has occurred.

A staged approach, or step-care strategy, might start with laparoscopic banding after the failure of nonoperative treatment. If laparoscopic banding fails, patients might be offered a combined gastric-malabsorptive procedure, with the degree of malabsorption tailored to the severity of the obesity. Such a staged approach should reduce the number of patients who have a very aggressive operation as their primary procedure, thus reducing the number of patients exposed to the risk of significant iatrogenic malnutrition.

Attempts at combined modality treatment that includes surgery might well have considerable benefits. The addition of pharmacological treatment to gastric restrictive procedures after patients have reached a weight loss nadir might potentiate the effects of the surgery and provide prolonged maintenance of the weight loss.

Among surgical techniques, a small operative series has demonstrated the potentiation of weight loss by combining truncal vagotomy with gastroplasty in patients who were followed up for 5 to 10 years. Other surgical techniques may be developed that will have effects on the satiety cascade, although the strongest effects would be expected from procedures that cause nimiety or aversion.

FURTHER READING

Brolin, R. E., Kenler H. A., Gorman, J. H., & Cody, R. P. (1992). Long-limb gastric bypass in the superobese. *Annals of Surgery, 215,* 387–395. A controlled study of increasing malabsorption in gastric bypass.

Kuzmak, L. I. (1992). Stoma adjustable silicone gastric banding. *Problems in General Surgery, 9,* 298–317. A gastric restrictive procedure recently adapted for laparoscopic surgery.

National Institutes of Health Consensus Development Conference. (1992). Gastrointestinal surgery for severe obesity. *American Journal of Clinical Nutrition,* 55(Suppl.), 487S–619S. A collection of definitive reviews of this topic, including one article on quality of life (pp. 611–614).

Sjostrom, L., Larsson, B., Backman, L., et al. (1992). Swedish obese subjects (SOS): Recruitment for an intervention study and a selected description of the obese state. *International Journal of Obesity, 16,* 465–479. The first prospective epidemiological study of severe obesity.

• 91 •

MANAGEMENT OF OBESITY IN CHILDREN

Leonard H. Epstein

Obesity is a major pediatric health problem (see Chapter 77), and the prevalence of obesity in children is rising. Currently 27.1% of children 6–11 years old and 21.9% of adolescents 12–18 years old are obese. Childhood obesity affects health, resulting in lowered fitness, increased blood pressure, increased total cholesterol levels, and decreased high-density lipoprotein concentrations.

In addition to the immediate health effects of being an obese child, prospective epidemiological research has shown that being obese in adolescence increases the risk of adult morbidity and mortality more than 50 years later independently of adult obesity status. Finally, obesity in childhood predicts adult obesity. Thus, even if obesity was not associated with immediate and long-term health changes, the increased risk of becoming an obese adult, along with the limited availability of effective treatments, should be incentives for developing powerful treatments for obese children.

The goal in this chapter is to provide an overview of the comprehensive treatment of obesity in children, covering information on diet, exercise, and behavior management. The focus will be on children, but areas for adaptation to adolescents will be noted.

CONCEPTUALIZING AND DESIGNING TREATMENT

The Role of Child Development in Treatment Plans

Treatment for obesity in children must be adapted to the specific developmental stages and capabilities of the child, as well as the role of parents and peers as social influences on eating and exercise regulation. A program for an obese 4-year-old must be considerably different from a program for a 15-year-old in what can be expected from the child and the degree of parental support that is needed.

Treatments designed to modify eating and exercise habits in children should focus on changing both caloric intake and energy expenditure. Interventions should promote the development of improved eating and exercise habits that will track into adulthood. Thus energy balance will shift, but there must be a strong focus on the long-term maintenance of eating and exercise behaviors.

Consider the goal of having a child lose weight with a nutritionally balanced diet of

1,200 calories per day, derived from the new food pyramid. The focus might be on the caloric and macronutrient content of the diet, with discretionary use of diet foods as long as they fit within the calorie goal. If the goal is to modify taste preferences along with caloric intake, it might be advisable to control access to these foods and teach the children to make better food choices. Similar questions pertain to exercise. Is it sufficient to encourage children to exercise regularly even if they do not like the exercise?

Dietary Goals

The general goal of diets should be to lower the typical caloric intake to promote weight loss while providing adequate calories for growth. There has been little research on the use of very-low-calorie diets in children, and they are probably not advisable until research has documented their safety (see Chapter 77). We use different diets and degrees of caloric restriction based on age and developmental status. Younger children have a minimal caloric restriction of 100–200 kilocalories per day, while older children have caloric restrictions that may reduce intake by 500–1,000 kilocalories per day. It is important to monitor growth, keeping in mind that obese children are often taller than their peers; also, height percentile charts that take into account the parents' height should be used.

Little is known about whether access to foods of lower nutritional quality should be limited during development in the effort to encourage choice of foods that promote weight regulation. We use the stoplight (or traffic-light) diet program. In the program foods from the standard food exchange programs are divided into color-coded food groups that correspond the stoplights: red, yellow, and green. High-calorie red foods should be eaten in limited quantities, and the number of servings of red foods per week and the setting in which those foods are eaten (outside of the home) are to be controlled. The clinician should also consider how food is used by the child and limit the use of food as a reinforcer, either by the parent or by the child himself/herself.

Activity Goals

Children should be as active as possible; the type of activities should promote an active life-style. We emphasize a life-style activity program rather than more structured aerobic exercise, since the goal is to increase daily expenditure rather than to engage in structured exercise at intensities that promote fitness. The life-style approach uses the choice of normal daily activities to develop new exercise habits.

A corollary of being active is being less sedentary. Sedentary behaviors such as watching television are incompatible with being active and are associated with increased caloric intake. Thus limiting access to sedentary behaviors would have the dual function of making more opportunities to be active and fewer opportunities for excess eating. We have found that limiting access to sedentary behaviors improves weight loss beyond attempts to increase activity.

Behavior Management Goals

The methods used to change eating and exercise behavior may have a more profound effect than the specifics of caloric reduction or the amount of exercise prescribed. The long-term effectiveness of treatment depends on changing behavior, not simply on modifying energy balance.

Among the many complex issues to be considered in the treatment of childhood obesity is who in the family should be treated. Our research suggests it is critical to include at least one parent in the treatment. This parent should be provided a full diet and exercise program and be expected to make the same changes required of the obese child. In many families one or both parents are often obese and could also benefit from weight loss and habit change. For all but the youngest children, parents and children should be seen separately so as to maximize the degree of responsibility the child will take for behavior change. Even if the parents are not obese, having them model appropriate behaviors and restructure the family environment offer significant benefits.

There are numerous components to most family-based treatments, but there has been little controlled research to indicate which should be emphasized. Several factors that involve the individual child or adult should be included, such as self-monitoring and goal setting. Self-monitoring is the variable most often related to long-term outcome, and even after 10 years, people who report continued self-monitoring have better long-term weight regulation than individuals who do not.

It is important to consider the behavioral factors that can be used to best advantage in family-based treatments and can best promote joint parent–child change. There are three sets of such factors to consider. First, modeling allows parents to make changes that set the stage for changes by the child. The "do as I say, not as I do" strategy will not be effective, and children will not follow a program if they observe their parents engaging in problem behaviors. Second, stimulus control, in which environmental stimuli are changed, can have effects across generations. For example, if high-calorie foods are not stored in the house, or if access to television viewing is limited, both parents and children must choose new behaviors. Third, and perhaps most important, the inclusion of both parents and children in the treatment provides the opportunity for the joint reinforcement of a change in habits. Parents can be trained to reinforce new behaviors in their children while children can do the same for their parents. In fact, conjoint reinforcement should be considered as a way of maintaining correct parental behavior. In a typical family-based intervention, the parents must make many behavior changes, and these behaviors must be reinforced if they are to be maintained. Some support can come from the therapist and spouse, but it may be particularly effective coming from the child.

CONCLUSIONS

The treatment of obese children can have an important impact on current and future health and can reduce the risk of obese children becoming obese adults. In developing treatments, therapists should consider the specific developmental characteristics of the children, use treatments that maximize the possibility for long-term behavior change, and meet the energy balance requirements for weight loss.

ACKNOWLEDGMENTS

Preparation of this chapter was supported in part by Grant Nos. HD20829, HD23713, and HD25997. I extend my appreciation to Debbie Muoio for her comments on an earlier version of this chapter.

FURTHER READING

Brownell, K. D., Kelman, S. H., & Stunkard, A. J. (1983). Treatment of obese children with and without their mothers: Changes in weight and blood pressure. *Pediatrics, 71,* 515–523. A well-controlled study in which the importance of treating both parents and children is documented; mothers and children were separated during treatment.

Dietz, W. H., & Gortmaker, S. L. (1985). Do we fatten our children at the television set? Obesity and television viewing in children and adolescents. *Pediatrics, 75,* 807–812. The best documentation of the cross-sectional and prospective influences of sedentary behaviors on obesity.

Epstein, L. H., Valoski, A., Wing, R. R., & McCurley, J. (1990). Ten-year follow-up of behavioral, family-based treatment for obese children. *Journal of the American Medical Association, 264,* 2519–2523. The first controlled study in which it was shown that the effects of using family-based treatments persist through extended follow-up intervals.

Epstein, L. H., & Wing, R. R. (1987). Behavioral treatment of childhood obesity. *Psychological Bulletin, 101,* 91–95. A comprehensive review of the treatment of obese children.

Epstein, L. H., Wing, R. R., Koeske, R., & Valoski, A. (1985). A comparison of lifestyle exercise, aerobic exercise and calisthenics on weight loss in obese children. *Behavior Therapy, 16,* 345–356. A controlled demonstration of the importance of increasing activity levels in the treatment of childhood obesity.

Garn, S. M., & Clark, D. C. (1976). Trends in fatness and the origins of obesity. *Pediatrics, 57,* 433–456. The best general review of developmental and familial contributions to obesity.

Israel, A. C., Stolmaker, L., & Andrian, C.A.G. (1985). The effects of training parents in general child management skills on a behavioral weight loss program for children. *Behavior Therapy, 16,* 169–180. A controlled study of the importance of teaching parents behavior management skills as part of treating childhood obesity.

Rolland-Cachera, M-F., Deheeger, M., & Guilloud-Bataille, M. (1987). Tracking the development of obesity from one month of age to adulthood. *Annals of Human Biology, 14,* 219–229. A detailed examination of the pattern of development of obesity from childhood to adulthood.

Sasaki, J., Shindo, M., Tanaka, H., Ando, M., & Arakawa, K. (1987). A long-term aerobic exercise program decreases the obesity index and increases the high density lipoprotein cholesterol concentration in obese children. *International Journal of Obesity, 11,* 339–345. A controlled study of the important role of regulated exercise in childhood obesity.

Stark, O., Atkins, E., Wolff, O. H., & Douglas, J. W. B. (1981). Longitudinal study of obesity in the National Survey of Health and Development. *British Medical Journal, 283,* 13–17. The best demonstration that obese children are at risk for becoming obese adults.

• 92 •

TREATMENT OF OBESITY IN THE DIABETIC PATIENT

Rena R. Wing

Diabetes is a major health problem in the United States, affecting approximately 12 million Americans and costing $20 billion per year. Most individuals with diabetes have Type II, or non-insulin-dependent diabetes mellitus (NIDDM); 60% to 90% of these individuals are overweight (see Chapter 70).

Weight loss is the treatment of choice for obese patients with NIDDM. Weight loss reduces hyperglycemia as well as abnormalities in hepatic glucose production, insulin sensitivity, and insulin secretion. Even modest weight losses of 15–30 pounds are sufficient to produce long-term improvements in glycemic control (see Chapter 71).

Weight loss and maintenance are difficult to achieve with overweight NIDDM patients; recent data from our research group suggest that weight maintenance may be a greater problem for diabetic than for nondiabetic individuals. Efforts are therefore needed to develop more effective interventions for these patients.

BEHAVIORAL WEIGHT CONTROL FOR NIDDM PATIENTS

For the most part, weight loss strategies for obese NIDDM patients parallel those used with nondiabetics and involve a combination of diet, exercise, and behavior modification. Some of the differences in the treatment of diabetic and nondiabetic individuals are highlighted in this chapter.

The Need for Medical Monitoring

Caloric restriction produces dramatic, immediate improvements in glycemic control; 3 to 7 days of dieting can decrease fasting glucose levels from 220 to 170 milligrams per deciliter. Since most NIDDM patients are treated with oral medication or insulin, these sudden changes in glycemic control require careful adjustments in diabetes medication to prevent hypoglycemic reactions. Before starting NIDDM patients on low-calorie diets, we decrease insulin doses by up to 50% and stop oral diabetes medication entirely. Blood sugar levels are monitored frequently to permit further adjustments in diabetes medications. Likewise, medications for hypertension and/or hyperlipidemia must be adjusted as the patient loses weight.

Some investigators have observed poorer weight losses in patients who use insulin;

our data do not support this finding. We have found no differences in weight loss between subjects treated with diet only and those who are taking oral medication or using insulin, perhaps because of the frequent adjustments we make in the medication regimen.

Dietary Regimen

The major dietary goal for obese patients with NIDDM is to decrease their caloric intake. The magnitude of the caloric deficit appears to be related to the degree of improvement in glycemic control and is independent of weight loss. In our treatment programs, we have used both balanced diets of 1,000–1,500 kilocalories per day and very-low-calorie diets (VLCDs; 400 kilocalories of lean meat, fish, or fowl or liquid formula diets) combined with behavior modification. We found that the use of VLCDs increased the magnitude of initial weight loss, the percent of patients who achieved significant weight loss, and the initial improvements in glycemic control. Like other investigators who have studied VLCDs with nondiabetic subjects, we unfortunately found no significant differences in weight loss at 1-year follow-up between subjects treated with VLCDs and those who received balanced low-calorie diets (see Chapter 86). However, despite their comparable long-term weight losses, we found that subjects treated with VLCDs had better long-term improvement in glycemic control than did subjects treated with a balanced low-calorie diet. Since this finding was not replicated in a second study, further research is needed to determine whether VLCDs have a long-term impact on glycemic control.

There are also questions regarding the macronutrient composition of the diet for NIDDM patients. Given that diabetics are at increased risk for cardiovascular disease, a low-fat diet is advised; however, some studies have shown that low-fat, high-carbohydrate diets actually worsen triglyceride levels and glycemic control in NIDDM patients. In these studies, weight maintenance regimens were used. In a study we conducted with a calorie-restricted weight loss diet, we found that by emphasizing a low dietary fat intake (<20% of calories from fat) weight loss was increased in NIDDM patients, with no adverse effects on their glycemic control or lipid levels.

Exercise

The other key component of a weight loss regimen for NIDDM patients is exercise. As with nondiabetic subjects, diabetics have better long-term weight losses when treated with the combination of diet plus exercise than with diet alone (see Chapter 84). Exercise, independent of weight loss, also reduces insulin resistance and, in some studies, improves glycemic control in diabetic subjects. We found that obese NIDDM subjects who were randomly assigned to diet plus exercise lost significantly more weight than those on a diet-only regimen at 10-week, 20-week, and 1-year follow-up. Moreover, self-reported level of activity at 1-year follow-up was related to improvements in HbA_1 levels, independent of weight loss.

Since many overweight diabetics are older and suffer from other health problems, increasing their exercise levels may be difficult. Gradual changes in activity level and low-intensity exercises such as walking clearly make the most sense for these older, sicker individuals (see Chapter 84 for a discussion of exercise adherence).

Home Blood-Sugar Monitoring and Behavioral Self-Regulation

Self-blood-sugar monitoring (SBGM) devices are now available that allow diabetic patients to monitor their blood-sugar levels accurately. It has been suggested that the feedback from SBGM regarding the effect of diet and exercise on blood-sugar control will produce greater success in self-regulation. Unfortunately, results of controlled trials of SBGM have not supported this hypothesis. There is no evidence that NIDDM patients who are taught to monitor their blood-sugar levels adhere more closely to their diet and exercise regimens, lose more weight, or achieve better glycemic control than do subjects who are given comparable attention and education but are not taught SBGM. Clearly the information obtained from SBGM is useful to the physician in adjusting a patient's diabetes medication, but this technique does not appear to lead automatically to increased self-regulatory behavior on the part of the diabetic patient.

Frequent Contact

Recently obesity researchers have begun to stress that obesity is a chronic disease that may require lifelong treatment (see Chapters 89, 93, and 97). This chronic disease model is particularly appropriate for obese individuals with NIDDM. Our most recent weight loss programs for NIDDM patients involved weekly contact for a full year. The program produced our most successful outcomes to date. However, when treatment was stopped at the end of the year, subjects regained weight. Thus some type of ongoing intervention model must be developed (see Chapter 97).

WEIGHT CONTROL IN THE PREVENTION OF NIDDM

In the preceding section the emphasis was on the importance of weight loss in the *treatment* of NIDDM. However, it should be noted that weight loss and exercise may also be important in *preventing* this disease. Results of numerous prospective studies have indicated that obesity is related to the risk of the development of NIDDM (see Chapter 70). Moreover, obesity interacts with a family history of diabetes, so that the greatest risk occurs in those individuals who are obese and have a parental history of diabetes. Upper body fat distribution and low activity levels are also important independent risk factors for NIDDM.

Given these findings, it is reasonable to hypothesize that weight loss might prevent or delay the occurrence of NIDDM in individuals at risk for this disease. In a recent study, individuals with impaired glucose tolerance were treated in a weight loss and exercise program. Only 11% of individuals in the intervention program developed diabetes during 6 years of follow-up, compared with 22% of those in a nonrandomized control group. Moreover, improvement in glucose tolerance was significantly correlated with weight loss and with increased physical fitness in patients in the intervention group. The benefit of weight loss was obtained despite a mean weight loss in intervention subjects of only 2.3% to 3.7% of initial body weight, whereas weight increased by 0.5% to 1.7% in nontreated subjects. Results of this study strongly support the possibility that weight loss may reduce the risk of developing NIDDM. A controlled clinical trial to test whether weight loss and/or exercise can prevent or delay diabetes in high-risk individuals is clearly warranted.

FURTHER READING

Bonadonna, R. C., & Defronzo, R. A. (1992). Glucose metabolism in obesity and Type II diabetes. In P. Björntorp & B. N. Brodoff (Eds.), *Obesity* (pp. 474–501). Philadelphia: Lippincott. A review of the literature on glucose metabolism in obesity and NIDDM.

Hamman, R. F. (1992). Genetic and environmental determinants of non-insulin-dependent diabetes mellitus (NIDDM). *Diabetes/Metabolism Reviews, 8,* 287–338. A review of the research on the genetic and environmental determinants of NIDDM.

Henry, R. R., Scheaffer, L., & Olefsky, J. M. (1985). Glycemic effects of intensive caloric restriction and isocaloric refeeding in non-insulin-dependent diabetes mellitus. *Journal of Clinical Endocrinology and Metabolism, 61,* 917–925. Demonstrates the benefits of caloric restriction or glycemic control.

Kriska, A. M., & Bennett, P. H. (1992). An epidemiological perspective of the relationship between physical activity and NIDDM: From activity assessment to intervention. *Diabetes/Metabolism Reviews, 8,* 355–372. A review of the literature on exercise and NIDDM.

Tuomilehto, J., Knowler, W. C., & Zimmet, P. (1992). Primary prevention of non-insulin-dependent diabetes mellitus. *Diabetes/Metabolism Reviews, 8,* 339–353. A discussion of the determinants of diabetes and the results of intervention studies to reduce the risk of diabetes.

Vinik, A., & Wing, R. R. (1992). The good, the bad, and the ugly in diabetic diets. In J. H. Karam (Ed.), *Endocrinology and metabolism clinics of North America* (pp. 237–279). Philadelphia: Saunders. A discussion of the issues related to the dietary component of treatment intervention for patients with diabetes.

Wing, R. R. (1989). Behavioral strategies for weight reduction in obese Type II diabetic patients. *Diabetes Care, 12,* 139–144. A discussion of behavioral strategies for the treatment of obese patients with NIDDM.

Wing, R. R. (1993). Behavioral treatment of obesity: Its application to Type II diabetes. *Diabetes Care, 16,* 193–199. A review of the progress made in the behavioral treatment of NIDDM.

Wing, R. R., Koeske, R., Epstein, L. H., Nowalk, M. P., Gooding, W., & Becker, D. (1987). Long-term effects of modest weight loss in Type II diabetic patients. *Archives of Internal Medicine, 147,* 1749–1753. Shows that even modest weight losses can have long-term benefits for obese NIDDM individuals.

· 93 ·

MANAGING CHRONIC REFRACTORY OBESITY

Richard L. Atkinson

We may define "refractory obesity" as a return to and maintenance of an obese body weight despite multiple attempts to lose weight. In this chapter the reasons for the refractory nature of obesity are evaluated, the limitations of current treatments are discussed; and methods of determining which patients need aggressive treatments are explored, as well as the options for the clinician who is faced with an individual who has not responded to the usual treatment methods.

CURRENT MEDICAL APPROACHES TO OBESITY TREATMENT AND THEIR LIMITATIONS

The current standard treatment for obesity is a combination of diet, exercise, and behavior modification. Because dietary fat is thought to enhance the deposition of fat, and dietary fiber is thought to increase satiety and help reduce insulin resistance, the recommended diet contains 20% to 35% of calories as fat and about 20–40 grams of dietary fiber. The exercise prescription given to most obese people trying to lose weight is to walk or perform similar-intensity activities for about 30 minutes per day, at least 5 days per week. Finally, patients are told to alter their life-styles to follow the diet and exercise regimen, to increase their activity during daily life (see Chapter 84), and to maintain emotional stability during the stress of constant deprivation. This treatment is successful for most patients in producing short-term weight loss but is based on the hypothesis that obesity is a behavioral problem. The high percentage of long-term failure of behavioral treatments suggests that this hypothesis is not correct (see Chapter 85).

Genetic factors clearly play a major role in the etiology of obesity, and many investigators now believe that most cases of obesity are due to a genetic predisposition to obesity that is expressed when a susceptible individual is exposed to the environment of Western civilization (see Chapter 4). If so, biochemical pathways in obese people should be different than those in normal-weight individuals, and behavioral treatments would not be expected to alter these pathways. For patients who chronically fail with such approaches, it is unlikely that their obesity is primarily a behavioral problem; and aggressive treatment of obesity, such as very-low-calorie diets (VLCDs), obesity drugs, or obesity surgery must be considered.

DETERMINING WHICH PEOPLE NEED
AGGRESSIVE TREATMENT OF OBESITY

It is necessary to determine the population for whom aggressive treatment is indicated. Although there is great debate about optimal body weight and whether body weight should increase with age (see Chapter 13), there is agreement that a body mass index (BMI) above 27 is associated with an increased incidence of the complications of obesity and with increased mortality (see Chapters 67 and 72). Individuals who have medically significant obesity are candidates for more aggressive treatments, and the greater the obesity, the more aggressive the clinician may become. A National Institutes of Health Consensus Development Conference panel concluded that obesity surgery is justified in individuals with a BMI greater than 40, or a BMI greater than 35 if major complications of obesity are present (see Chapter 90). Conversely, clinicians must think very carefully about treatment with a VLCD or with obesity drugs for patients with a BMI of less than 27.

There is general agreement that the complications of obesity that justify aggressive treatment of obesity include hypertension, diabetes mellitus, hyperlipoproteinemia, and sleep apnea (see Chapter 70). Other complications, such as arthritis, gout, a family history of vascular disease or cancer, or significant emotional problems due to obesity (see Chapter 73) may enter into the decision to use aggressive treatments. Purely cosmetic reasons for weight loss must be very carefully considered because all these aggressive treatments of obesity are associated with side effects, some very serious, and the benefits may not justify the risks.

AGGRESSIVE APPROACHES TO OBESITY TREATMENT

Very-Low-Calorie Diets

Many clinicians define a VLCD as a diet containing less than 800 kilocalories per day. In this definition, first advanced in 1979 by the Expert Panel of the Life Sciences Research Office of the Federation of American Societies for Experimental Biology, differences in body size are ignored, making the definition difficult to defend (see Chapter 86). A large man and a small woman each eating 800 kilocalories per day will be under different restrictions. It would be more rational to define a VLCD based on the number of calories per kilogram of metabolically active lean body mass. However, because it is not practical to measure the lean body mass of individual patients, calorie prescriptions may arbitrarily may be based on the medium-frame "desirable" weight as defined by the 1959 Metropolitan Life Insurance tables. Using this arbitrary definition, a VLCD is defined as a diet that provides 10 kilocalories or less per kilogram of "desirable" body weight.

The VLCDs are described in detail in Chapter 86, so only a brief summary will be presented here. A VLCD may consist of either regular foods or a formula preparation, and each approach has its proponents. Most clinicians agree that protein intake should be higher than the recommended dietary allowance, in the range of 1.0–2.0 grams of protein per kilogram of desirable weight. Proponents of protein-sparing modified fasting diets, which consist mainly of meats with a very low carbohydrate intake insist that higher levels of protein (1.5–2.0 grams per kilogram) are needed to preserve nitrogen balance and to provide the natural micronutrients that presumably are not present in defined formula diets. Proponents of formula diets note that a patient is guaranteed an adequate intake of essential nutrients if he/she takes the prescribed number of meals of formula. Formula diets that do not have adequate protein or other nutrients are not designed for use as VLCDs and should not be used for this purpose. Supplements are needed for many VLCDs, especially food-based diets, to meet the requirements for an adequate intake of vitamins and minerals.

Medical histories should be obtained for all patients, and all should undergo a physical examination by a physician before starting a VLCD. Physician follow-up is mandatory (see Chapter 86), although much of the care can be given by nurses and dietitians. The details of exclusion criteria and the scheduling of follow-up visits and tests are given in Chapter 86.

VLCDs produce rapid weight loss, and there is a modest amount of evidence that this rapid loss may confer greater advantages than less rapid weight loss. In one study, diabetic control 1 year later was better in patients who were treated with a VLCD than in those who received a low-calorie diet (see Chapter 92). In other studies, long-term improvements of blood pressure are reported for patients who were previously on VLCD; but such improvements were not seen with low-calorie diets. The mechanisms for these phenomena are not yet known, and additional research is needed to confirm them.

The advantages of VLCDs are rapid weight loss and the fact that a VLCD requires behavior so different from normal that it is easier for patients to adhere to the regimen. The disadvantage is that patients may consider a VLCD an end unto itself, not simply a temporary measure to achieve weight loss. The use of VLCDs does not teach patients to modify their life-styles, and there is a great temptation to return to pretreatment eating habits when they cease the VLCD. Because most obese patients cannot eat as "normal" people do and remain lean, they rapidly regain weight.

Numerous complications of VLCDs have been reviewed elsewhere. In the past there has been the fear that the use of VLCDs presents unacceptable risks for morbidity and mortality. Modern VLCDs, used under a physician's care, generally are safe, and there does not appear to be an increased mortality associated with their use (see Chapter 86).

Drug Treatment

Because of current laws in most states in the United States, drugs for obesity have no role in the treatment of obesity. Most states prohibit the use of obesity drugs for longer than 12 weeks, regardless of whether or not they are effective. Bray has editorialized about the irrationality of such laws, but until these laws are repealed, the disadvantages of intermittent use of obesity drugs outweigh the advantages. There is new evidence that drugs may be effective for obesity, and additional research needs to be done (see Chapter 89). Single-drug therapy for obesity produces average weight losses that are about 0.5 pounds greater than that achieved with placebo. Weight losses of this magnitude are a poor justification for the use of drugs, considering their potential side effects. However, careful evaluation of the data from drug trials suggests there are subgroups of patients who respond with greater weight losses than the placebo group. These data suggest that specific drugs may correct the biochemical differences of specific subtypes of obesity.

The drugs currently approved by the U.S. Food and Drug Administration (FDA) for the treatment of obesity in the United States, along with drugs approved by the FDA for other problems but known to cause weight loss, are discussed in detail in Chapter 89.

All available drugs, used alone, produce approximately similar weight loss, and there is little rationale for the use of one over another. There also is little difference in the risks associated with these drugs, and the rationale for assigning these drugs to particular Drug Enforcement Agency categories is poorly justified. Studies in animals suggest that the addictive potential of all these drugs is limited, although there are individual differences. Phenylpropanolamine and fenfluramine are said to have no reinforcement potential when given to monkeys. There is definite abuse potential for dextroamphetamine and methamphetamine, and these drugs, although approved by the FDA, should never be used for the treatment of obesity.

Since no drug has been approved by the FDA for the treatment of obesity since 1972, all approved obesity drugs are available as generic preparations. Other drugs are in various phases of research and development (see Chapter 89). The three closest to being clinically useful are dexfenfluramine, orlistat, and sibutramine. Dexfenfluramine is the dextroisomer of *dl*-fenfluramine and has fewer side effects. Orlistat blocks lipase action in the small intestine, thus reducing fat absorption and presumably reducing calorie absorption. Sibutramine appears to enhance energy expenditure and reduce food intake. If clinical trials do not reveal any major adverse reactions, these drugs are likely to be submitted for approval to the FDA and may come available for clinical use within the next 5 to 10 years.

Drug therapy is the most common treatment for almost all chronic diseases. For most such diseases, if one drug is not effective or only marginally effective, one or more additional drugs are added. Numerous trials of obesity drugs have been conducted, but in only a handful of these studies has more than one drug been used simultaneously. Reports of only two combinations of obesity drugs have been published in the medical literature: those of ephedrine–methylxanthines–aspirin combinations and fenfluramine–phentermine combinations (see Chapter 89).

Combinations of ephedrine with methylxanthines and/or aspirin have been shown to produce modest, long-term weight losses. The most commonly used methylxanthine studied is caffeine, but theophylline and other agents have also been evaluated. Ephedrine appears to stimulate beta-2 and beta-3 adrenergic receptors, resulting in the loss of fat mass with only modest losses of lean mass. These drugs have not been used in large numbers of patients for an extended time, and there is concern that the stimulative effects of ephedrine may produce cardiac arrhythmias in a small number of susceptible individuals. Ephedrine has been approved by the FDA as an over-the-counter drug for cold symptoms. Despite its widespread use, not many fatal arrhythmias have been recorded, so the risk of adverse reactions appears to be quite low. Because caffeine enhances the effects of ephedrine, the total amount of caffeine and other methylxanthines ingested in coffee, soft drinks, tea, chocolate, and the like should be limited by patients, and clinicians should warn patients to avoid extra intake of these substances.

Weintraub and colleagues have published reports of seminal studies in which a combination of fenfluramine and phentermine resin was used (see Chapter 89). Fenfluramine and phentermine have different mechanisms of action: Fenfluramine is a serotonin agonist, and phentermine is a centrally active catecholaminergic agent. The rationale for the study was that this combination would have additive or synergistic effects. Results of their preliminary studies showed that half-strength doses of each drug (fenfluramine: 20 milligams three times daily; phentermine resin: 15 milligrams once daily) were as effective as full-strength doses of either drug alone, and all groups had greater weight losses than the placebo group. Despite comparable weight losses, the subjects taking the combination of two drugs had significantly fewer side effects than did subjects taking either of the drugs in full doses. The side effects of the combination were not different from those seen in the placebo group.

In a complex, long-term study, subjects on a standard program of diet, exercise, and behavior modification were randomized to placebo or to the combination of fenfluramine and phentermine. Weight loss was greater in the group taking the drug combination than in the group taking placebo during the first 34 weeks of the trial. After 34 weeks, all subjects went on the drug treatment. Subjects formerly on placebo promptly began losing weight, and weight losses persisted for as long as 3.5 years. Upon cessation of treatment, the subjects regained the lost weight. Preliminary data by the author and colleagues on over 1,000 patients treated with the combination of these two drugs for up to 18 months confirm Weintraub's results in producing weight loss and reducing the complications of obesity.

The usefulness of drugs as a primary treatment of obesity is unclear. There have been few long-term studies of any obesity drug, and most such drug trials had simultaneous programs of diet, exercise, and behavior modification. Additional research is needed to determine if combinations of drugs are safe and effective for the long term. Additional combinations of drugs need to be tested, and it seems likely that regimens of different combinations will be needed for people with different etiologies for their obesity. However, it is premature to conclude that obesity drugs will play a major role in the treatment of obesity, and the general feeling among scientists is that any long-term use of these agents should be performed as part of a research protocol.

Surgery

Surgery may be justified for massively obese individuals whose obesity is refractory to other treatments (see Chapter 90). The two most commonly used types of surgery for obesity in the United States are vertical banded gastroplasty (VBG) and gastric bypass surgery. Both involve partitioning the stomach into a small upper pouch and a large lower pouch. With VBG, a vertical row of surgical staples is placed along the lesser curvature of the stomach, and a mechanical obstruction is produced between the upper and lower pouches by inserting a band around the stomach that limits the diameter of the opening to approximately 1 centimeter. The small size of the upper pouch (volumes constructed to about 15–30 milliliters) limits the size of a meal, but once food passes through the obstruction, motility and digestion proceed normally. In contrast, in gastric bypass the stomach is completely divided by two rows of staples. The upper jejunum is transected and the distal end is pulled up to the small upper gastric pouch and anastomosed with a 1-centimeter opening. The lower stomach and duodenum do not receive food, and their secretions enter the nutrient stream via an end-to-side anastomosis to the distal jejunum.

The mechanisms of action of the two types of surgery are quite different. In VBG, a mechanical obstruction to food passage is produced, and there may be some limitation of food intake by neural or humoral signals from the upper pouch, which quickly becomes distended when the patient begins eating. Gastric bypass produces obstruction and distension of the upper pouch, but it also results in the rapid passage of nutrients into the jejunum. A majority of patients experience symptoms of the "dumping syndrome" in which these nutrients pass down the small intestine rapidly and may be associated with nausea, diarrhea, and abdominal cramping. These symptoms tend to improve with time, but weight loss correlates with the severity of the dumping syndrome. Weight loss is superior with gastric bypass, as is long-term weight maintenance.

FUTURE HORIZONS FOR OBESITY TREATMENT

The current treatment of obesity is hindered by inadequate knowledge of the etiology of obesity. The mechanisms that promote fat accumulation and the defense of body weight at an elevated level are mediated by biochemical differences in the obese, and an understanding of these mechanisms may allow the development of more effective drugs than currently are available. Also we have only begun to explore the effects of combinations of existing drugs. As with drug therapy in most other chronic diseases, for obesity combinations of drugs are likely to be more effective than single drugs, and genetic or biochemical markers may be identified for the different subtypes of obesity that will allow more specific drug treatment. The identification of the genes that regulate body weight, body fatness, and food intake for the different subtypes of obesity may allow high-technology solutions for obesity. Finally, more effective surgical procedures may be developed for the very obese who cannot be treated by any other method. With the identification of the humoral and neural alterations produced by intestinal bypass surgery, it may be possible to develop surgical techniques that will not have the side effects of intestinal bypass.

FURTHER READING

Atkinson, R. L. (1989). Low and very-low-calorie diets. *Medical Clinics of North America, 73*, 203–215. A comprehensive review of low and very-low-calorie diets, with suggestions for the clinical use of these regimens.

Bray, G. A. (1991). Barriers to the treatment of obesity. *Annals of Internal Medicine, 115*, 152–153. An interesting editorial with a discussion of the reasons obesity drugs have not received more support and more widespread use.

Guy-Grand, B., Apfelbaum, M., Crepaldi, G., Gries, A., Lefebvre, P., & Turner, P. (1989). International trial of long-term dexfenfluramine in obesity. *Lancet, ii*, 1142–1145. One of the largest long-term trials of a drug for obesity in the medical literature.

Silverstone, T. (1992). Appetite suppressants: A review. *Drugs, 43*, 820–836. A comprehensive review of the use of drugs for treating obesity.

Sugerman, H. J., Londrey, G. L., Kellum, J. M., Wolf, L., Liszka, T., Engle, K. M., Birkenhauer, R., & Starkey, J. V. (1989). Weight loss with vertical banded gastroplasty and roux-y gastric bypass for morbid obesity with selective versus random assignment. *American Journal of Surgery, 157*, 93–102. Probably the best study in the literature in which gastric bypass and vertical banded gastroplasty are compared in a scientific manner.

Toubro, S., Astrup, A. V., Breum, L., & Quaade, F. (1993). Safety and efficacy of long-term treatment with ephedrine, caffeine, and an ephedrine/caffeine mixture. *International Journal of Obesity, 17*(Suppl. 1), S69–S72. A long-term study of one of two combinations of drugs that have been used for treating obesity.

Wadden, T. A., Sternberg, J. A., Letizia, K. A., Stunkard, A. J., & Foster, G. D. (1989). Treatment of obesity by very-low-calorie diet, behavior therapy, and their combination: A five-year perspective. *International Journal of Obesity, 13*(Suppl. 2), 39–46. The most definitive study in the literature done to evaluate the long-term success of standard medical treatment of obesity and demonstrating that the success rate is very low.

Weintraub, M. (1992). Long-term weight control: The National Heart, Lung, and Blood Institute funded multimodal intervention study. *Clinical Pharmacological Therapy, 51,* 581–646. A seminal study of obesity drugs showing that the continuous use of phentermine and fenlfluramine is effective for up to 3.5 years.

Wing, R. R., Marcus, M. D., Salata, R., Epstein, L. H., Miaskiewicz, & Blair, E. H. (1991). Effects of a very-low-calorie diet on long-term glycemic control in obese Type 2 diabetic subjects. *Archives of Internal Medicine, 151,* 1334–1340. Although treatment with VLCDs is rarely indicated, this study provides some justification for the use of VLCDs in selected patients.

• 94 •

TREATMENT OF THE OBESE BINGE EATER

W. Stewart Agras

These are early days in our attempts to characterize the best treatment for overweight individuals with binge eating disorder (see Chapter 78). Less than a handful of controlled treatment studies have been done, and in all only short-term results are reported for what is evidently a chronic disorder. Hence we have only an initial understanding of which treatments work. The principal research question at present is whether treating the eating disorder and overweight is better than treating overweight alone. As we shall see, the answer to this question is unclear. Research into the treatment of binge eating disorder leans heavily on the findings of the past decade concerning the treatment of bulimia nervosa (see Chapters 55 and 60), findings suggesting that cognitive-behavioral therapy, interpersonal therapy, and antidepressant medication are likely candidates for the treatment of binge eating disorder.

EXISTING TREATMENTS

Cognitive-Behavioral Therapy

In two published studies, together with several studies in progress, cognitive behavioral therapy was confirmed as an effective treatment for reducing binge eating in binge eating disorder. In contrast to trials conducted on the treatment of bulimia nervosa, in the published studies of cognitive-behavioral therapy, which show the influence of the obesity treatment literature (see Chapter 85), group rather than individual treatment has been used. Moreover, treatment of binge eating disorder in the obese has been of shorter duration than is the case in those with bulimia nervosa, and shorter periods of time have been used to assess abstinence from binge eating.

These points are illustrated in the first controlled study in which the effectiveness of cognitive-behavioral therapy was measured by comparing patients who had undergone cognitive-behavioral therapy with a waiting-list control group. For those receiving cognitive-behavioral therapy, therapy was provided in a group format and lasted 10 weeks, and abstinence was assessed for a 1-week period. At the end of treatment, nearly 80% of the participants met the criteria for abstinence in the treatment group, compared with 9% in the control group. The number of binge eating episodes declined by 94% in the treatment group. These results were replicated when the waiting-list control group was treated. There was some evidence of relapse by the time of the 10-week follow-up, not particularly surprising given the brevity of treatment. Nonetheless, the results of this study suggest that cognitive-behavioral therapy may well be an effective treatment for binge eating disorder. The effectiveness of cognitive-behavioral therapy was confirmed in a small-scale uncontrolled study using a 16-week group program. Abstinence was assessed over a 4-week period. Binge eating was reduced by 81%, and 50% of the patients became abstinent from binge eating. It was also noted that if a 1-week assessment had been used, 75% of the participants in this latter study would have been considered abstinent. Results of these studies suggest that cognitive-behavioral therapy will promote abstinence in about the same proportion of individuals who have binge eating disorder as those who have bulimia nervosa.

Interpersonal Therapy

The surprising finding that interpersonal therapy, when adapted to an eating disordered population, is as effective as cognitive-behavioral therapy in the treatment of bulimia nervosa (see Chapter 60), has been replicated in binge eating disorder. There are several reasons why such a therapy may work in bulimia nervosa and binge eating disorder. The eating disorders emerge during adolescence, often in a context of interpersonal disturbance, particularly role transitions such as becoming independent. Additionally, negative affects such as depression, anger, or anxiety, have been found to provoke binge eating. Such feelings may well arise from interpersonal conflict. Hence it is reasonable to suppose that interpersonal therapy would be effective in both bulimia nervosa and binge eating disorder. In the one controlled study designed to examine this question in binge eating disorder, a group adaptation of interpersonal therapy, meeting for 16 weekly sessions, was used. Participants were allocated at random to cognitive-behavioral therapy, interpersonal therapy, or a waiting-list control condition. Both cognitive-behavioral therapy (28% abstinent) and interpersonal therapy (44% abstinent) were superior to the waiting-list control condition (0% abstinent) but were not significantly different from one another. Some relapse occurred in both groups during the 1-year follow-up.

It is tempting to speculate that cognitive-behavioral therapy and interpersonal therapy exert their therapeutic effects through different mechanisms. It would seem likely, therefore, that patients with binge eating disorder who fail cognitive-behavioral therapy might respond to interpersonal therapy. This hypothesis is being tested in an ongoing study, and initial findings suggest it is not true.

Pharmacological Treatment

Desipramine was found to be effective in a double-blind, placebo-controlled study of patients with binge eating disorder. Treatment lasted for 12 weeks, with a mean dose of desipramine of 188 milligrams per day. Binge eating was reduced by 63%, and 60% of the group receiving active medication became abstinent from binge eating, compared with 15% of those receiving placebo. Both hunger and disinhibition were also reduced significantly for those in the active medication group. The reduction in hunger is interesting, since it confirms results of other work that suggests that antidepressants may have a weak appetite suppressant effect in the treatment of eating disorders.

In another controlled study, imipramine and naltrexone (an opiate antagonist) were used in a double-blind, placebo-controlled study, with both bulimia nervosa patients and binge eaters. Neither medication was found to reduce the frequency of binge eating more effectively than placebo, but both significantly shortened the duration of binges. The lack of efficacy of the antidepressant in bulimia nervosa patients is surprising, given the large amount of literature demonstrating the effectiveness of the tricyclic anti-depressants in treating that condition. Dosage and attained blood levels both appeared adequate.

In an ongoing study, in which desipramine was added to cognitive-behavioral therapy in the treatment of binge eating disorder, no additive effects on binge eating were found, a finding similar to those in studies of bulimia nervosa. Two studies, albeit with rather small sample sizes, have been reported in which the effectiveness of seroto-nin reuptake inhibitors (fluoxetine in one study and fluvoxamine in the other) in reducing weight was examined. In both studies weight losses of obese binge eaters and obese non–binge-eaters were compared. In neither study was an advantage found for the obese binge eater, although the frequency of binge eating was not reported in either study.

Effects on Weight

Does treatment of the eating disorder lead to weight loss? An examination of the treatment studies aimed at reducing binge eating in binge eating disorder, reveals that patients in the treatment group do not lose weight, and in some instances gain weight, although not to a greater extent than do those in the control group. This finding has led to the addition of simple elements of weight control to cognitive-behavioral therapy for BED, such as weekly weighing, an exercise program, and the substitution of low-fat foods for high-fat food.

On the other hand, in several studies it has been noted that patients with binge eating disorder who stop, or nearly stop, binge eating tend to lose significantly more weight than those who do not stop binge eating. This finding suggests that the eating disorder should be treated first, followed by weight loss therapy. Against this suggestion is the finding from two ongoing studies that cognitive-behavioral therapy combined with weight loss therapy is no more effective in reducing either binge eating or weight. One interesting finding is that weight loss therapy, perhaps because it leads to more orderly eating, is associated with reductions in binge eating.

THE CLINICAL MANAGEMENT OF BINGE EATING DISORDER

Given the relatively small amount of research on the treatment of binge eating disorder and the conflicting results concerning the advantage of treating the eating disorder, the following guidelines must be regarded as tentative. It continues to appear logical first to treat the eating disorder and then to treat overweight, remembering that the goal in treating the eating disorder should be the attainment of abstinence from binge eating, which has been shown to facilitate weight loss.

Suitably adapted for this group of patients, cognitive-behavioral therapy should be regarded as the first-line therapy. This choice is based on the findings of research on bulimia nervosa and the replication of the effectiveness of cognitive-behavioral therapy in binge eating disorder. The most effective mode of treatment (individual vs. group) is unknown at this time. Because most weight control programs are offered in a group format, such a format will probably remain the most used, since it has been demonstrated to be effective and is a less costly form of therapy. The optimal length of treatment has not been delineated, but it seems likely that most of the published studies were conducted for too short a time period; hence a duration of 16–24 weeks of cognitive-behavioral therapy is suggested here.

The Content of Cognitive-Behavioral Therapy

The content of cognitive-behavioral therapy for binge eating disorder is similar to that for bulimia nervosa—both are divided into three phases: (1) altering chaotic eating habits, (2) identifying and changing attitudes toward weight and shape, and (3) relapse prevention. Since a number of manuals describing cognitive-behavioral therapy for bulimia nervosa are available, only the necessary adaptations for its application to binge eating disorder will be outlined here.

In the first phase of treatment, since a number of individuals with binge eating disorder tend to gain weight during cognitive-behavioral therapy, it seems reasonable to add a weekly weighing and recording of that weight, as well as an exercise program consisting of a minimum of four daily 20-minute walks each week (see Chapter 84). It may be advantageous to point out that attaining abstinence from binge eating is important and to set the goals of therapy as attaining abstinence, keeping weight stable or declining, and having at least a minimal exercise program in place. These criteria should be achieved before the move is made to the weight loss phase of treatment. In dealing with the self-monitoring records of these patients, the therapist should concentrate on patients reducing the length of time between meals and broadening their food choices, but some effort should also be made to help the patient select foods of lower fat content. It should be noted here that the need for dietary restraint is less severe for patients with binge eating disorder than for bulimia nervosa patients, and that restraint appears to increase during treatment, a finding opposite to that for bulimia nervosa. The increase in restraint is probably due to the lessening of the chaotic eating style observed in many patients with binge eating disorder.

The second phase of treatment needs less modification. Patients with binge eating disorder have rigid food rules similar to those of patients with bulimia nervosa, although binge eating disorder patients' attitudes toward weight and shape may differ markedly because of the presence of obesity. Some patients may deny they have negative attitudes toward weight and shape. However, most patients with binge eating disorder are clearly overly concerned with their weight and appearance, have suffered considerable rejection because of their overweight, and they exhibit a high degree of negative affect associated with these attributes (see Chapter 73). An exploration of these attitudes and affects is important, with the goal of reducing the degree to which binge eating disorder patients' self-esteem is based on weight and shape. The final phase of treatment, relapse prevention, is similar to that outlined for bulimia nervosa.

FURTHER READING

Alger, A., Schwalberg, D., Bigaouette, J. M., Michalek, A. V., & Howard, L. J. (1991). Effect of a tricyclic antidepressant and opiate antagonist on binge eating behavior in normoweight bulimic and obese, binge eating subjects. *American Journal of Clinical Nutrition, 53,* 865–871. A controlled pharmacological study of binge eaters.

McCann, U. D., & Agras, W. S. (1990). Successful treatment of nonpurging bulimia nervosa with desipramine: A double-blind, placebo-controlled study. *American Journal of Psychiatry, 147,* 1509–1513. The first controlled study in which the effectiveness of an antidepressant in treating binge eating disorder is described.

Smith, D. E., Marcus, M. D., & Kaye, W. (1992). Cognitive-behavioral treatment of obese binge eaters. *International Journal of Eating Disorders, 12,* 257–262. A detailed description of the use of cognitive-behavioral therapy for binge eating disorder.

Telch, C. F., Agras, W. S., Rossiter, E. M., Wilfley, D., & Kenardy, J. (1990). Group cognitive-behavioral therapy for the nonpurging bulimic: An initial evaluation. *Journal of Consulting and Clinical Psychology, 58,* 629–635. A controlled study of the use of cognitive-behavioral therapy in binge eating disorder.

Wilfley, D. E., Agras, W. S., Telch, C. F., Rossiter, E. M., Schneider, J. A., Cole, A. G., Sifford, L., & Raeburn, S. D. (1993). Group cognitive-behavioral therapy and group interpersonal therapy for the nonpurging bulimic: A controlled comparison. *Journal of Consulting and Clinical Psychology, 61,* 296–305. An interesting comparison of the effectiveness of cognitive-behavioral therapy and interpersonal therapy in binge eating disorder with a 1-year follow-up, replicating the findings in studies of bulimia nervosa.

Yanovski, S. Z. (1993). Binge eating disorder: Current knowledge and future directions. *Obesity Research, 1,* 306–324. A thoughtful review of the current knowledge concerning the psychopathology and treatment of binge eating disorder.

• 95 •

WEIGHT LOSS PROGRAMS FOR MINORITY POPULATIONS

John P. Foreyt

The prevalence of obesity in minority populations in the United States generally exceeds that of the majority white population (see Chapter 76). Among females, for example, approximately 35% of whites, 44% of African Americans, 42% of Mexican Americans, 40% of Puerto Ricans, and 40% of Native Americans are obese. Among males, these figures are 31% of whites, 26% of African Americans, 31% of Mexican Americans, 26% of Puerto Ricans, and 34% of Native Americans. All these figures appear to be increasing as new data become available. We are losing, not winning, the obesity war.

Obesity is a serious health concern. It is a major risk factor affecting mortality and morbidity, especially from cardiovascular disease (CVD) (see Chapters 69 and 70). Hypertension, diabetes, and high blood cholesterol levels, all risk factors for CVD, are more commonly found among the obese than the nonobese. Other health problems associated with obesity include gallbladder disease, osteoarthritis, gout, and abnormal pulmonary function. Obesity is linked to colorectal and prostate cancers in men and to endometrial, gallbladder, cervical, ovarian, and breast cancers in women. Although some data suggest that these relationships are less strong in minority populations than in the white population at this time, these differences may be only temporary while these populations are undergoing current epidemiologic transitions (see Chapter 76). Other methodological issues, such as selective nonresponsiveness to surveys or cohort effects, also may be responsible for the observed differences.

DETERMINANTS OF OBESITY

Poverty and lower levels of education are associated with higher levels of obesity, and these factors affect proportionately more individuals in minority populations than individuals in the white population (see Chapter 14). Different minority populations appear to share the same high-fat diet and low-exercise pattern and, in general, seem to be less concerned about weight than the white population. Minorities have less access to health care, including counseling about potentially effective weight management principles. Proportionately, fewer members of minorities perceive themselves to be obese than do whites. The primary factor associated with higher levels of obesity in minorities appears to be lower socioeconomic status.

BEHAVIORAL TREATMENT OF OBESITY

Behavioral intervention programs for the treatment of obesity have been the state of the art for over 20 years (see Chapter 85). Behavioral treatment focuses on changing dietary and exercise habits to achieve realistic weight losses and maintenance of those losses. The primary components of current interventions include (1) self-monitoring of eating and exercise patterns and of the cognitive patterns associated with those behaviors, (2) modifying the antecedent factors associated with inappropriate eating and exercise patterns, and (3) restructuring the reinforcing or punishing consequences of the appropriate or inappropriate behaviors. Building social support is also an important component of the program.

Intervention is usually conducted in groups of about 10 individuals, and the weekly meetings last about an hour. The groups are typically led by a health care professional, such as a registered dietitian. The entire treatment lasts about 4 to 6 months. The average overweight individual loses about 22 pounds and maintains two-thirds of the loss at a measurement 1 year later (see Chapter 85). Without continued treatment, the average individual gains back most of the initial weight lost over the following year or two. Newer trends in the behavioral treatment of obesity include better screening of individuals who would be likely to benefit from the programs being offered, matching of individuals to specific treatments (see Chapter 98), increasing the length of intervention (see Chapter 97), building stronger social support systems, and combining behavioral interventions with other approaches such as very-low-calorie diets (VLCDs), pharmacotherapy, and surgery.

TREATMENT OF OBESITY IN MINORITY POPULATIONS

Few data have been reported on the use of behavioral treatments for weight reduction among minority populations. Minorities participate far less in formal behavioral treatment programs than do whites. Of the few results published to date, those of two large clinical trials indicated that African American women lost less weight than did white women when enrolled in the same obesity treatment program, and that in the control group, African American women gained more weight than did their white counterparts. A weight loss intervention with Mexican American women resulted in losses about half of what are seen with white women over an equal time period. No long-term, controlled, prospective data have been published on screening or matching minority individuals to specific programs, or on long-term, controlled studies using VLCDs, pharmacotherapy, or surgery with minority populations.

Current behavioral approaches, either by themselves or combined with VLCDs, pharmacotherapy, or surgery, may not be applicable to minority populations. What data exist suggest that simply applying the commonly used behavioral principles to minority individuals does not work very well, as evidenced by less weight loss and more attrition. Attempts to make interventions culturally specific to minorities have been sparse. There is clearly a need to develop a behavioral analysis of weight management for minority populations within their own cultures. A major unanswered question in this field is how to design programs to help minorities change their eating and exercise habits using what is already known and translating this knowledge into culturally relevant interventions.

CONVENTIONAL VERSUS CULTURALLY RELEVANT INTERVENTIONS

Most behavioral interventions for the treatment of obesity are conducted in groups of unrelated individuals. Such an approach may be less relevant with many minority populations, which place high value on extended families, such as grandmother/mother/daughter/granddaughter. Interventions that exploit intergenerational ties may be more effective than more conventional approaches.

The primary dietary intervention in conventional programs includes an emphasis on the basic food groups. In approaches used with minority populations more attention should be focused on the special dietary problems of these individuals, including concerns related to their lactose intolerance; low intake of fresh fruits, vegetables, and fiber; the use of "soul" food; and frequent snacking. Some minority groups have their own folk systems of food classification that can be incorporated into, rather than excluded from, dietary programs. Some individuals will have poor nutritional status, including insufficient calcium and iron, which will require special intervention. The church, in relation to food habits, the extended family, and other social factors, may play a more prominent role with many minorities than is currently emphasized in conventional programs.

Barriers to change will need to be recognized and addressed. Poverty, current higher acceptable weight standards associated with health risks, and the lack of knowledge of the relationship between obesity and some cancers may play a more prominent role in treatment.

Current counseling methods that typically use a didactic approach may be less effective with members of minority groups than more indirect strategies, such as emphasizing story telling, more role playing, linking of folk beliefs to current scientific facts, sharing experiences, and more active learner participation.

A PUBLIC HEALTH APPROACH

Differences between the prevalence of obesity in minorities and the white population would be minimized by reducing the socioeconomic differences. However, the prevalence of obesity in whites is also high and getting higher (see Chapter 68). A population approach to treating obesity appears the only practical strategy for achieving a significant reduction in this serious risk to health (see Chapters 99 and 101). Several public health approaches might be helpful in reducing obesity in the population in general (and minority populations specifically). Education is one key to weight management. Required health education in the schools that includes information about the management of obesity, equal access to treatment, increased availability of healthy foods (especially fruits and vegetables), and opportunities for physical activity would further reduce socioeconomic differences.

Limiting access to unhealthy foods may also be required for controlling obesity at the societal level. Excise taxes on foods high in fat may not be such a far-fetched idea. Limiting or forbidding advertisements on television for such foods or placing warning labels on them, similar to strategies used in this country for the sale of cigarettes, may be effective.

It will be important to evaluate the impact of new food labeling requirements on the buying habits in different populations. How much impact will food labeling have on minorities who tend to be loyal to certain brand names? School breakfast and lunch programs and other food subsidy programs disproportionally affect minorities; the modification of these programs has the potential to affect the development of lifelong dietary habits.

Finally, direct modification of the food supply significantly affects what we eat. It is essential to assess the effects of the large-scale availability to minority populations of low-fat and no-fat foods containing artificial fats and nonnutritive sweeteners.

SUMMARY AND CONCLUSIONS

The prevalence of obesity in minority populations is generally higher than in the white population. The lack of strong social pressure to lose weight, despite an awareness of the health risks of obesity, and little exercise contribute to the problem. Published data suggest that relatively few minorities participate in formal intervention programs. Among those individuals who do join obesity treatment programs, attrition is higher and weight losses are lower than among white participants given the same interventions. Few intervention programs have been designed specifically to treat obese minorities. The design of such programs requires a behavioral analysis of the factors and barriers that affect weight within a culturally relevant context. Both clinical and public health approaches are urgently needed to combat this growing threat to the health of minority populations in this country.

FURTHER READING

Brown, P. J. (1993). Cultural perspectives on the etiology and treatment of obesity. In A. J. Stunkard & T. A. Wadden (Eds.), *Obesity: Theory and therapy* (2nd ed., pp. 179–193). New York: Raven Press. A thoughtful discussion of the cultural factors to be considered in the treatment of obesity.

Cousins, J. H., Rubovits, D. S., Dunn, J. K., Reeves, R. S., Ramirez, A. G., & Foreyt, J. P. (1992). Family versus individually oriented intervention for weight loss in Mexican American women. *Public Health Reports, 107*, 549–555. An example of a culturally relevant intervention program for obese Mexican American women.

Ernst, N. D., & Harlan, W. R. (1991). Executive summary. Conference highlights, conclusions, and recommendations. *American Journal of Clinical Nutrition, 53*, 1507S–1511S. The executive summary of the National Heart, Lung, and Blood Institute's Conference on Obesity and Cardiovascular Diseases in Minority Populations, held in Bethesda, Maryland, August 28–29, 1990.

Foreyt, J. P., & Cousins, J. H. (1993). Primary prevention of obesity in Mexican-American children. *Annals of the New York Academy of Sciences, 699*, 137–146. Part of the conference Prevention and Treatment of Childhood Obesity, held in Bethesda, Maryland, March 9–11, 1993, by the New York Academy of Sciences and published by the academy in a book with the conference's title, edited by C. L. Williams and S. Y. S. Kimm.

Jeffery, R. W. (1991). Population perspectives on the prevention and treatment of obesity in minority populations. *American Journal of Clinical Nutrition, 53*, 1621S–1624S. A discussion of the problems of inequities in access to health education, treatment services, and environmental opportunities in the prevention and treatment of obesity in minority populations.

Kanders, B. S., Ullmann-Joy, P., Foreyt, J. P., Heymsfield, S. B., Heber, D., Elashoff, R. M., Ashley, J. M., Reeves, R. S., & Blackburn, G. L. (1994). The Black American Lifestyle Intervention (BALI): The design of a weight loss program for working-class African-American women. *Journal of the American Dietetic Association, 94,* 310–311. An example of a culturally relevant intervention program for obese African American women.

Kumanyika, S. K. (1994). Obesity in minority populations: An epidemiologic assessment. *Obesity Research, 2,* 166–182. An excellent review of the issues relating to the prevalence, health implications, and prevention and treatment of obesity in minority populations.

Kumanyika, S. K., Morssink, C., & Agurs, T. (1992). Models for dietary and weight change in African-American women: Identifying cultural components. *Ethnicity and Disease, 2,* 166–175. An exploration of the cultural factors that potentially influence the effectiveness of weight control programs for African American women.

Kumanyika, S. K., Obarzanek, E., Stevens, V. J., Hebert, P. R., & Whelton, P. K. (1991). Weight-loss experience of black and white participants in NHLBI-sponsored clinical trials. *American Journal of Clinical Nutrition, 53,* 1631S–1638S. An examination of the race-specific weight loss differences from two randomized, multicenter trials: the Hypertension Prevention Trial and the Trials of Hypertension Prevention.

McGinnis, J. M., & Ballard-Barbash, R. M. (1991). Obesity in minority populations: Policy implications of research. *American Journal of Clinical Nutrition, 53,* 1512S–1514S. A study of the broad, relevant social and research issues regarding obesity in minority populations.

• 96 •

RELAPSE:
A COGNITIVE-BEHAVIORAL MODEL

G. Alan Marlatt

RELAPSE: DEFINITIONS AND MODELS

"Relapse" is a term with many negative connotations. The derivation of the word is Latin, *relabi,* which means "to slip" or "to fall back." Its antonym is "prolapse" ("fall forward"), used primarily in a medical context (e.g., prolapse of the uterus). In medical parlance, "relapse" usually refers to a recurrence of a disease after a period of improvement (e.g., a relapse of cancer or malaria). But the term also carries moral overtones, perhaps because in early theological usage, "relapse" was defined as "to fall back into paganism, evil, error, heresy, or unbelief; to backslide."

"Relapse" is also a central concept in the addictions field, where it has traditionally been used to describe a recurrence of "bad habits" after a period of abstinence. Research on the treatment outcome of people treated for alcoholism, smoking, or heroin addiction clearly demonstrates that relapse rates are not only high (over two-thirds return to drug use within 1 year after treatment) but that they are remarkably similar across different addictive behaviors. In the field of addiction treatment, relapse has often been equated with failure, a terminal state, a "dead end."

In a penetrating analysis of different approaches to behavior change and therapy, Brickman and his colleagues described four basic models, each of which provides a different contextual definition of "relapse." According to Brickman, the four models can be placed in a 2×2 matrix based on the response to two basic questions: (1) Does this model assume that an individual is personally responsible (yes or no) for the development of his/her problem (e.g., alcoholism, obesity)? (2) Does this model assume that the person is responsible for changing the problem once it has developed (yes or no)?

In the moral model, the person is judged responsible both for the development of the problem and for doing something to change it. Viewed from this perspective, an alcoholic is both responsible for how the problem developed ("You drink because you lack the moral willpower to resist temptation") and for changing his/her behavior ("It's completely up to you to stop"). Failure to change or relapse is also blamed on the person, who typically responds by feeling guilty about his/her inability to control this morally unacceptable, or "sinful," behavior.

The disease model avoids the "blaming the victim" approach inherent in the moral model. Because the disease (e.g., obesity) is considered to be rooted in genetic/biological factors beyond the control of the individual, an obese person is alleviated of blame for the development of the problem. To change, the patient needs treatment (e.g., therapy, medication, surgery), usually administered in a medical setting; patients are discouraged from trying to "cure themselves." Relapse is viewed as a return of the underlying disease, again due largely to circumstances beyond the patient's personal control (biological causation).

Brickman defines the "enlightenment," or spiritual model (as expressed in 12-Step programs such as Alcoholics Anonymous or Overeaters Anonymous), as follows: Although one may be held responsible for letting the problem develop in the first place, change is facilitated by turning one's personal responsibility over to a Higher Power represented by God and/or the spiritual fellowship of a group. In order to change, one must replace personal willpower with a spiritual Higher Power to be enlightened on the path to salvation. Often the 12-Step programs endorse a disease model that renders the victim powerless (acceptance of personal powerlessness over the disease is the first step). Since the underlying disease cannot be cured, one must come to rely on lifelong attendance at self-help groups in order to arrest future development of the disease. Relapse is thus defined as an inevitable consequence of missing meetings or getting "out of touch" with one's Higher Power.

In the "compensatory" model, Brickman's fourth category, it is assumed that although a person is not to held fully responsible for the initial development of the problem, that person can assume major responsibility for change. Most problems have multiple determinants, including the interactive roles of heredity, environment, and psychosocial factors. Once a problem has developed, however, an individual can assume responsibility and learn to compensate for the problem by acquiring more adaptive coping behaviors. Change can occur both through one's own efforts (e.g., quitting smoking on one's own) and/or by seeking assistance or guidance in learning better self-management strategies. Since learning plays a critical role in change, relapse is defined within this context as a mistake or error in acquiring or maintaining new behavior patterns. Mistakes can play a corrective role in the learning process (e.g., learning to ride a bicycle often involves several painful slips or mistakes that facilitate compensatory responses).

THE RELAPSE PROCESS: A COGNITIVE-BEHAVIORAL MODEL

Rather than supporting the view of relapse as an end-point or terminal outcome, recent research has highlighted the advantages of approaching relapse as a process of events that unfold in a temporal dimension. The process of relapse has multiple determinants, consistent with a biopsychosocial model of addictive behavior. A study of both the antecedents and the consequences of relapse points to the critical interaction of psychological factors (e.g., cognition, affect, motivation, and coping), environment (e.g., sociocultural milieu, availability of substances), and biological factors (e.g., genetic predisposition, somatic effects of drug or food consumption). The biopsychosocial model provides a good fit with Brickman's compensatory model described above.

The process of relapse can be considered as a chain of events over time, often referred to as the "relapse chain." The relapse chain consists of a series of distal and proximal determinants. Proximal factors include the precipitating or "trigger" event preceding a lapse. Proximal triggers, or high-risk situations for relapse, impact the individual's motivation and coping capacity. In some cases, relapse is precipitated by sudden, unexpected exposure to a high-risk situation (e.g., a person trying to quit smoking runs across an old friend who offers a cigarette). In other cases, events leading to an eventual relapse build up over time, often involving a series of rationalized decisions ("seemingly irrelevant decisions") that lead the individual closer to the brink (e.g., a newly abstinent alcoholic who buys a bottle of sherry to keep in the house "just in case guests drop by for a drink").

Interviews conducted with individuals who experienced relapse after a period of successful progress in abstaining from either alcohol, tobacco, or opiates have revealed a number of common high-risk situations. A high-risk situation is defined broadly as any situation that poses a threat to the individual's sense of control or ability to maintain abstinence. Here it is not merely the objective situation itself but the person's subjective appraisal of and reactions to the event that are critical to the outcome. Some of the more common high-risk situations for substance abuse relapse include:

1. *Negative emotional states.* Here individuals report that their initial lapse occurred in reaction to a negative or unpleasant mood state such as anger, anxiety, depression, boredom, or frustration. Negative emotional reactions to interpersonal conflict (arguments, criticism, separation) are included in this category. More than half of interviewees report lapses that are triggered by negative emotional states.

2. *Social influence situations.* Situations in which the individual's lapse is a response to the influence of another person or group so that the individual engages in the otherwise prohibited behavior (e.g., direct social pressure or exposure to models engaged in the target behavior). About 20% of interviewees report giving in to social influence at the time of their initial lapse.

3. *Positive emotional states.* Some relapses occur when the person is feeling good instead of bad. The use of a substance to enhance positive emotional states accounted for 12% of initial lapses reported in an interview study conducted by my group. People involved in weight loss programs appear to be particularly susceptible to interpersonal positive emotional states. In a sample of dieters in Overeaters Anonymous who were interviewed concerning the circumstances of their dietary relapse, almost one-third identified positive emotional states as the primary trigger (e.g., birthday celebrations, holiday family gatherings). This trigger category was second only to negative emotional states (47% of lapses).

Although other high-risk triggers have been identified (e.g., testing personal control, or "willpower tests"; exposure to substance or food cues), the majority of high-risk situations fall into the three categories described above. In this regard, relapse may be considered a maladaptive coping response, particularly if the individual has a history of substance use or food consumption as a "self-medication" strategy in response to stress. If the individual is able to execute an effective coping response in the high-risk situation (e.g., cognitive or behavioral coping), the probability of relapse decreases. "Self-efficacy" refers to the individual's expectancy of being able to cope with different high-risk situations as they develop. Self-efficacy ratings for coping with prospective high-risk situations have been found to be a strong predictor of relapse across a variety of addictive behaviors.

If a person is unable to cope with a high-risk trigger situation, because of either motivational conflict or skill deficit, he/she may experience a corresponding decrease in self-efficacy (often experienced as a sense of helplessness or a tendency to "give in" to temptation). The probability of relapse is further increased to the extent that the individual holds positive outcome expectancies about the initial effects of the activity or substance. Often such a person will anticipate the immediate positive effects of indulging, based on "euphoric recall" of past experiences, while at the same time ignoring or neglecting to attend to the delayed negative consequences. A failure to cope effectively with a high-risk situation, coupled with positive outcome expectancies for indulgence, sets the stage for an initial lapse in the presence of substance or food cues.

In traditional disease models of addiction, relapse is defined in absolute terms: Either one is totally abstinent or one has relapsed; even one drink or one cigarette is enough to throw the person "off the wagon" into relapse. In this dichotomous model of relapse there is a failure to take into account a critical distinction between lapse and relapse. In the cognitive-behavioral model of the relapse process, a "lapse" is defined as a single, discrete episode in which abstinence is violated or a rule governing consumption is broken (e.g., violation of dietary restrictions). "Relapse," on the other hand, is associated with a full return of the target behavior to baseline levels (e.g., pretreatment drinking rates or prediet weight levels). Between a single lapse and a total relapse, a wide range of "in-between" responses, or patterns, have been identified. Not all lapses lead to total relapse. Some people respond to a lapse as a warning signal or discriminative cue for renewed coping efforts. A lapse can be viewed as an error or mistake that calls for learning new coping strategies.

For others, particularly those who believe in a dichotomous, "all-or-none" view of abstinence, a lapse is tantamount to a total relapse. The requirement of abstinence is viewed as an absolute dictum; once one has crossed over the line, there is no going back. Efforts to regain control are often abandoned and the person is at greater risk for giving up or dropping out of treatment. Often a sense of guilt and self-blame is associated with the lapse. To account for this reaction to a personal transgression of an absolute rule, we have described an attributional dimension called the "abstinence violation effect" (AVE). There are two components of the AVE: a cognitive attribution as to the perceived cause of the lapse combined with an affective reaction to this attribution. As I have described elsewhere:

> An increased AVE is postulated to occur when the individual attributes the cause of the lapse to internal, stable, and global factors that are perceived to be uncontrollable (e.g., lack of willpower and/or the emergence of the symptoms of an underlying addictive disease). The intensity of the AVE is decreased, however, when the individual attributes the cause of the lapse to external, unstable (changeable), and specific factors that are perceived to be controllable (e.g., a transitory deficit in coping with a specific high-risk situation).

Research has documented the influence of the AVE as a mediating factor in the relapse process.

RELAPSE PREVENTION

Viewing relapse as an ongoing process rather than a terminal event has a number of advantages. Habit change can be likened to a journey, with many choice points, or "forks in the road," where the individual can make renewed commitments or decisions that lead to a "fresh start." Vulnerability or resistance to relapse can be assessed at various stages along the relapse chain, from distal factors associated with the individual's general life-style and personal relationships to proximal factors associated with high-risk trigger situations. Even if lapses occur, the motivation for renewed coping efforts may attenuate the relapse process and prevent treatment attrition.

Relapse prevention methods have been developed for a variety of treatment programs to enhance the maintenance of behavior change. Basically two goals are involved: (1) to help people maintain their initial goals and prevent the occurrence of lapses, and (2) to assist individuals who are experiencing lapses and setbacks to get "back on track" and prevent either further relapse or treatment dropouts. A variety of cognitive-behavioral interventions have been described in the relapse prevention literature. Examples include:

1. Providing clients with an understanding of the relapse process and their own relapse chains.
2. Assessing and enhancing motivation with particular emphasis on self-efficacy and outcome expectancies.
3. Assessing high-risk situations and training clients in more effective planning and coping skills.
4. Helping clients to identify and modify their own cognitive rationalizations and distortions that may sabotage their efforts to maintain behavior change.
5. Cognitive reframing of lapses as mistakes that prompt restorative coping (and avoiding the motivational debilitation associated with the AVE).
6. Developing functional alternatives to the addictive behavior (e.g., relaxation, exercise) to facilitate a balanced life-style.
7. Using metaphor and imagery to enhance awareness and coping (e.g., using "relapse road maps" to illustrate relapse chains).
8. Enlisting social support and significant others to provide assistance in coping with relapse crises.
9. Modifying unrealistic distal goals for change and establishing manageable proximal subgoals.
10. Enhancing awareness or mindfulness of the interaction of one's life-style habits and their consequences.

In summary, relapse prevention is a cognitive-behavioral approach to preventive self-management designed to enhance the maintenance of behavior change. Many current treatment programs for habit change use relapse prevention in individual or group therapy as a means of enhancing successful treatment outcome or to help clients cope with setbacks and to get "back on track" after a lapse. Although much research is needed to evaluate the efficacy and effectiveness of relapse prevention, recent reviews show promising results in the treatment of addictive behaviors.

FURTHER READING

Bandura, A. (1977). Self-efficacy: Toward a unifying theory of behavior change. *Psychological Review, 48,* 191–215. This theoretical article provides an overview of the social–cognitive theory of self-efficacy and behavior change.

Bandura, A. (in press). *Self-efficacy.* New York: W. H. Freeman. This new book provides a detailed presentation of self-efficacy theory and related research.

Brickman, P., Rabinowitz, V. C., Karuza, J. Jr., Coates, D., Cohn, E., & Kidder, L. (1982). Models of helping and coping. *American Psychologist, 37,* 368–384. This article provides a description of different models of addictive behaviors: disease, moral, compensatory, and spiritual.

Brownell, K. D., Marlatt, G. A., Lichtenstein, E., & Wilson, G. (1986). Understanding and preventing relapse. *American Psychologist, 41,* 765–782. In this article the theoretical framework for understanding the relapse process across a variety of behaviors is set forth.

Chiauzzi, E. J. (1991). *Preventing relapse in the addictions: A biopsychosocial approach.* New York: Pergamon Press. Presents practical and helpful information about relapse prevention using a biopsychosocial approach.

Cummings, C., Gordon, J. R., & Marlatt, G. A. (1980). Relapse: Strategies of prevention and prediction. In W. R. Miller (Ed.), *The addictive behaviors: Treatment of alcoholism, drug abuse, smoking, and obesity* (pp. 291–321). Oxford: Pergamon Press. This material presents a description of high-risk situations for relapse.

Marlatt, G. A., & Gordon, J. R. (1980). Determinants of relapse: Implications for the maintenance of behavior change. In P. O. Davidson & S. M. Davidson (Eds.), *Behavioral medicine: Changing health lifestyles* (pp. 410–452). New York: Brunner/Mazel. This was the first article to present the cognitive-behavioral model of relapse that serves as the foundation for relapse prevention.

Marlatt, G. A., & Gordon, J. R. (Eds.). (1985). *Relapse prevention: Maintenance strategies in the treatment of addictive behaviors.* New York: Guilford Press. This is the main text on relapse prevention; it provides a review of the literature and describes numerous relapse intervention strategies.

Wanigaratne, S., Wallace, W., Pullin, J., Keaney, F., & Farmer, R. (1990). *Relapse prevention for addictive behaviors.* Oxford: Basil Blackwell. A useful, practical "how to do it" description of the relapse prevention methods that would be applied in the clinic.

Wilson, P. H. (Ed.). (1992). *Principles and practice of relapse prevention.* New York: Guilford Press. Describes how relapse prevention can be used in the treatment of relapse problems across a variety of target behaviors (including nonaddictive behaviors).

• 97 •

METHODS FOR MAINTAINING WEIGHT LOSS

Michael G. Perri

Poor maintenance of weight loss represents the most pressing challenge in the management of obesity. Following the conclusion of weight loss treatments, most participants gradually abandon their dieting and exercise routines and eventually regain weight. Indeed, the regaining of weight that almost inevitably follows weight loss treatment has frustrated both obese people and the professionals who treat them. However, some individuals do succeed in maintaining significant weight loss, and an increasing number of studies show that maintenance is most likely to occur when clients receive interventions designed specifically to enhance long-term progress.

The problem of poor maintenance appears to stem from a complex interaction of physiological, environmental, and psychological variables. Physiological factors, such as adaptive thermogenesis, an excessive number of fat cells, and increased adipose tissue lipoprotein lipase activity, prime the obese person to regain lost weight. Continuous exposure to an environment rich in fattening foods, combined with a dieting-induced heightened sensitivity to palatable foods, further disposes the individual to setbacks in dietary control (see Chapter 16). Most obese persons cannot, *on their own,* sustain the substantial degree of psychological control necessary to cope effectively with this unfriendly combination of environment and biology. Moreover, during the period following treatment, there are fewer reinforcers to maintain adherence to dietary goals. Consequently, many individuals become discouraged by the difficulties they encounter in sustaining their lower weights, and their negative psychological reactions to initial weight gains contribute further to the maintenance problem. Individuals often ascribe their lack of success to personal failings. Such attributions can trigger feelings of depression and guilt and precipitate a sense of hopelessness that leads to an abandonment of the weight loss effort and ultimately to a total relapse (see Chapter 96).

What then can be done to improve the long-term management of obesity? Table 97.1 presents the major behavioral procedures that have been tested as maintenance

---

[1]Most of the research in this area has been conducted in university settings using group treatment approaches with help-seeking obese volunteers. Consequently it may not be possible to generalize the findings to other clinical settings, to individual therapy approaches, or to obese individuals who are not seeking professional treatment.

TABLE 97.1. Maintenance Strategies for Long-Term Weight Management

Ongoing professional contact

Purposes:	Continued focus on key behaviors
	Support for adherence to program
	Help with problem solving of obstacles to maintenance
Methods:	Personal meetings between client and professional
	Telephone conferences
	Communication by mail
	Combinations of the above

Skills training

Purposes:	Identification of high-risk situations
	Training to avoid lapses
	Positive coping with slips and relapses
Methods:	Review of past patterns of relapse
	Formal training in problem solving
	Practice in coping with high-risk situations
	Cognitive restructuring of a lapse

Social support

Purposes:	Additional guidance
	Emotional support
	Social reinforcement
Methods:	Couples training
	Buddy systems
	Self-help groups
	Telephone networks

Physical activity

Purposes:	Additional caloric expenditure
	Prevention of a decrease in metabolic rate
	Improvement in mood and self-concept
Methods:	Life-style changes
	Aerobic training
	Resistance training

Multicomponent programs

Purposes:	Effectiveness of multiple methods
	Lack of data for "matching" strategies to clients
	"Interest" value of multiple strategies
Method:	Combinations of strategies listed above

Note. From Perri, Sears, and Clark (1993). Copyright 1993 by the American Diabetes Association. Adapted by permission.

strategies. A knowledge of the existing research on maintenance strategies can provide the clinician with important information for long-term treatment planning in the care of the obese individual.[1]

MAINTANENCE STRATEGIES

Professional Contact

A consistent finding in the obesity literature is a strong association between the duration of professional contact and the maintenance of weight loss. The longer obese clients are in contact with treatment providers, the longer they adhere to the behaviors necessary for weight control. Indeed, most individuals who seek professional treatment will require some form of long-term clinical contact to manage their weight effectively. At the present time, in "state-of-the-art" maintenance programs, clients meet with their therapists every other week during the year following the initial course of weight loss treatment. Programs of this intensity and frequency typically enable the obese individual to maintain 80% to 100% of the weight lost during the initial treatment. Without continuing professional contact, clients maintain only 50% to 60% of their initial losses within 1 year.

Several factors may contribute to the beneficial impact of continued professional contact. First, ongoing contact fosters continued vigilance and active awareness of the eating and exercise behaviors that are crucial to weight maintenance. Second, such contact entails a social demand for clients to meet the positive expectations and specific goals they have set with their therapists. Third, posttreatment contact allows clients an opportunity to receive strategic advice in dealing with obstacles to progress. Finally, such contact serves as a positive motivational influence to reinforce continued adherence and to help clients avoid "burnout" in their long-term battle with obesity.

Skills Training

The obese individual must acquire the skills to anticipate and cope with circumstances that increase the risk of relapse. After treatment concludes, clients inevitably face situations that tempt them to eat more, exercise less, and forgo the self-control techniques taught in treatment. If an individual lacks the skills to negotiate these "high-risk" situations, a slip or lapse in self-control is likely. Moreover, a sense of hopelessness and a decrease in self-efficacy will result if the person interprets the lapse as evidence that he/she is a "failure" at self-control, and an initial setback can become the start of a full-blown relapse (see Chapter 96).

Training in specific cognitive-behavioral strategies has been suggested as a way of preventing or minimizing relapse following treatment. Clients can be taught to recognize situations that pose a "high risk" for a lapse in self-control; problem-solving techniques can be employed to generate ways of coping with high-risk situations, and practice in dealing with actual high-risk situations can be used to improve the client's ability to avoid initial lapses. In addition, clients can be taught cognitive restructuring techniques to overcome the negative affect and sense of failure that often accompany lapses in self-control.

Available research results indicate that teaching clients relapse-prevention techniques during an initial course of therapy does *not* have a beneficial effect on long-term progress. However, combining relapse prevention training with a systematic program of professional contacts during the follow-up period seems to improve the long-term maintenance of weight loss. To implement relapse prevention skills effectively, many clients may need the assistance of a health-care professional at the time they are coping with a lapse or relapse. Thus training in relapse prevention skills is most effective when combined with posttreatment professional contact.

Social Support

As an alternative to professional care, other persons in clients' social environment may assist them in the maintenance of weight loss. Self-help groups such as Take Off Pounds Sensibly (TOPS) and Overeaters Anonymous (OA) are widely available to assist overweight people with ongoing social support, but little research has been done on the effectiveness of these groups as aids in maintenance (see Chapter 88). Several studies are available regarding the use of partners and peers in the management of obesity. Results of some research have indicated that *cooperative* partners can have a beneficial impact on outcome, and in other studies results suggest that groups of obese individuals may be taught how to run their own peer support groups and that such groups can have a positive impact on maintenance.

Exercise

Increased physical activity is often associated with long-term success in weight management (see Chapter 84). In addition to increasing energy expenditure, exercise may also facilitate weight loss by minimizing the decline in metabolic rate that usually accompanies weight loss (see Chapter 74). Regular exercise also produces psychological benefits, including an increased sense of well-being and improvement in mood and self-concept. Recommendations for exercise, most often regimens of brisk walking or stationary cycling, are regularly incorporated into obesity treatment programs. Several studies have demonstrated the beneficial short- and long-term impact of increased exercise on weight management. However, such changes in exercise patterns are themselves subject to poor long-term maintenance. The problem of maintaining an increase in physical activity can be managed in part by including adherence to exercise goals as a key component of a multifaceted approach (see Chapter 84).

Multicomponent Programs

The ideal maintenance program would involve matching treatment methods to the specific needs of particular clients (see Chapter 98). Unfortunately an empirical database that would describe those procedures best suited to particular clients is not yet available. Consequently multicomponent maintenance programs have been developed in the hope that at least some aspects of a multifaceted approach will benefit a particular individual. Empirically tested multicomponent programs have typically included ongoing professional contact, training in problem-solving or relapse-prevention skills, social support through peer-group networks, and a high frequency of moderate-intensity aerobic exercise. From the results of several studies it appears that weight loss treatments supplemented with multicomponent maintenance programs produce superior long-term results than do treatments without maintenance programs. Although multicomponent programs hold "interest" appeal for clients and therapists alike, the addition of facets such as social support, skills training, or greater opportunity for exercise may not produce incremental benefits beyond the positive effects provided by a systematic program of ongoing professional contacts.

CONCLUSION

The long-term management of obesity presents a daunting challenge to health care professionals. When initial weight loss therapy is supplemented with posttreatment strategies, clients exhibit greater adherence to weight control techniques and better maintenance of weight loss. Indeed, the most consistent finding in the maintenance literature is that structured programs of posttreatment therapist contacts help clients sustain weight loss. For most obese individuals, the successful management of obesity requires the implementation of maintenance strategies over long periods of time. Thus the health care professional must be prepared to systematically and compassionately aid the obese client in identifying effective methods to sustain the behavioral changes needed for long-term success. Equipped with a variety of strategies to enhance the persistence of changes in diet and exercise, clinicians will be better able to assist their clients in the long-term management of obesity.

FURTHER READING

Bjorvell, H., & Rossner, S. (1985). Long-term treatment of severe obesity: Four-year follow-up of results of a combined behavioural modification programme. *British Medical Journal, 291,* 379–382. Outcome study describing a comprehensive, multicomponent intervention for the long-term management of obesity.

Brownell, K. D., Marlatt G. A., Lichtenstein, E., & Wilson, G. T. (1986). Understanding and preventing relapse. *American Psychologist, 41,* 765–782. Review article describing the benefits of relapse prevention training across a variety of addictive behaviors.

Fremouw, W., & Damer, D. (1992). Obesity. In P. H. Wilson (Ed.), *Principles and practice of relapse prevention* (pp. 69–84). New York: Guilford Press. A review of the effects of maintenance strategies on the management of obesity.

Marlatt, G. A., & Gordon, J. R. (Eds.). (1985). *Relapse prevention: Maintenance strategies in the treatment of addictive behaviors.* New York: Guilford Press. The landmark text outlining the principles and procedures of a social learning perspective on the problem of relapse.

Perri, M. G., McAllister, D. A., Gange, J. J., Jordan, R. C., McAdoo, W. G., & Nezu, A. M. (1988). Effects of four maintenance programs on the long-term management of obesity. *Journal of Consulting and Clinical Psychology, 56,* 529–534. Outcome study documenting the beneficial long-term effects of posttreatment maintenance programs.

Perri, M. G., Nezu, A. M., & Viegener, B. J. (1992). *Improving the long-term management of obesity: Theory, research, and clinical guidelines.* New York: John Wiley. A comprehensive overview of the theory, research, and clinical strategies for improving the long-term treatment of obesity.

Perri, M. G., Sears, S. F., & Clark J. E. (1993). Strategies for improving maintenance of weight loss: Toward a continuous care model of obesity management. *Diabetes Care, 16,* 200–209. Summary of research suggesting the need for a "continuous care" approach to obesity treatment.

Wadden, T. A., Sternberg, J. A., Letizia, K. A., Stunkard, A. J., & Foster, G. A. (1989). Treatment of obesity by very low calorie diet, behavior therapy, and their combination: A five-year perspective. *International Journal of Obesity, 13,* 39-46. Outcome study documenting the poor long-term maintenance of weight loss.

· 98 ·

MATCHING INDIVIDUALS
TO TREATMENTS

Kelly D. Brownell

A RATIONALE FOR MATCHING

Ranging from hypnosis to surgery, many programs are available for weight loss. In professional settings alone there are many choices, and if books, commercial and self-help programs, health clubs, and programs and devices advertised in the popular media are factored in, the list of approaches is long indeed.

Health professionals have traditionally adopted two stances regarding this array of approaches. First, there has been skepticism and criticism of approaches offered outside the medical setting, particularly money-making enterprises. The assumption is that a profit motive generates inappropriate, fraudulent, or even dangerous practices.

The second position has been that research will identify one treatment that rises above others, yielding a "treatment of choice" for all individuals. An example of the product of this mind-set is a survey of obesity experts by Bray and colleagues in which those surveyed were asked to rate the effectiveness of seven treatments for obesity, not whether certain treatments would be most effective for certain individuals. What emerged was predictable—different experts expressed different choices for treatments, and no one treatment received consistently superior ratings.

Studies using random assignment of subjects to programs and then parametric statistics to compare one program with another will produce, by definition, treatments that on average are better than others. Many such studies were done in the 1970s and 1980s to compare behavior therapy with other approaches. When behavior therapy won the majority of these statistical horse races, many experts proclaimed it the treatment of choice for mild to moderate obesity.

What has been lost in this pursuit is that while one program may be statistically superior to another, the difference may not be clinically meaningful, and that even a statistically inferior program may be most effective for some individuals. The search for a best fit between individuals and treatments, as opposed to the search for a best treatment, argues for different designs, hypotheses, and statistical analyses than have been used traditionally. Such work is only beginning in obesity research, so it is instructive to turn first to work done in other fields.

MATCHING WORK IN OTHER FIELDS

The importance of matching treatments to individuals has been recognized in several other fields, where both conceptual and empirical work are advanced beyond what is known in the obesity field.

Prochaska and colleagues have developed a model in which stages of change are defined for individuals who are in the process of modifying their behavior. Individuals are said to be at one of five stages of readiness and change: (1) "precontemplation," where no action is being considered; (2) "contemplation," where serious thought is given to change, but no specific action has yet been taken; (3) "preparation," where there is intent to change and early signs of behavior change; (4) "action," where behavior change is occurring; and (5) "maintenance," where changes have been consolidated and are permanent. This model has been applied extensively in fields other than weight control, but only preliminary work exists in the weight control field.

A logical extension of this "stages-of-change" model is that intervention should be targeted at an individual's stage, and that a program will fail if it has been designed for individuals at different stages. Nearly all approaches to weight control have been designed according to the assumption that individuals are in the action stage. Thus programs are "mismatched" to individuals who are in earlier stages.

The alcoholism area is where the most advanced matching work has occurred. In several early studies psychological variables were identified that suggested different treatments, a concept being tested presently in a multicenter study called Project MATCH. Obesity researchers may be well advised to follow this example, because so little is known about selecting a treatment for an individual.

EXISTING KNOWLEDGE IN THE OBESITY FIELD

Classification Schemes

In the obesity field, little attention has been paid to the issue of matching in the context of classification (see Chapter 67). The philosophy has been that types of obesity can be identified and that treatments will be prescribed accordingly. The prevailing approach has been to classify individuals according to their degree of obesity and then to recommend that the most aggressive treatments be used for people with the most severe obesity.

While this approach has promoted the idea of different treatments for different individuals, it has serious limitations. Only a small minority of obese persons are sufficiently overweight to warrant the most aggressive approaches, such as surgery, leaving little guidance for the management of nearly all people who seek help. In addition, systems based on weight are not derived from data on how individuals respond to treatment; rather, they are based on the supposition that the medical risks of a person's excess weight must exceed the risks associated with a given treatment. Only a few treatments increase risk in a meaningful way, so this concept of comparing the risks of obesity with those of treatment is helpful only occasionally.

A Comprehensive Scheme

A scheme that takes into account more factors than body weight was proposed by Brownell and Wadden and is displayed in Figure 98.1. This scheme begins with a

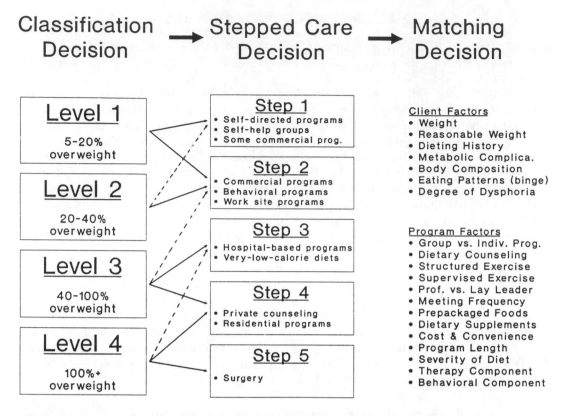

Classification Decision → **Stepped Care Decision** → **Matching Decision**

Level 1
5-20% overweight

Level 2
20-40% overweight

Level 3
40-100% overweight

Level 4
100%+ overweight

Step 1
• Self-directed programs
• Self-help groups
• Some commercial prog.

Step 2
• Commercial programs
• Behavioral programs
• Work site programs

Step 3
• Hospital-based programs
• Very-low-calorie diets

Step 4
• Private counseling
• Residential programs

Step 5
• Surgery

Client Factors
• Weight
• Reasonable Weight
• Dieting History
• Metabolic Complica.
• Body Composition
• Eating Patterns (binge)
• Degree of Dysphoria

Program Factors
• Group vs. Indiv. Prog.
• Dietary Counseling
• Structured Exercise
• Supervised Exercise
• Prof. vs. Lay Leader
• Meeting Frequency
• Prepackaged Foods
• Dietary Supplements
• Cost & Convenience
• Program Length
• Severity of Diet
• Therapy Component
• Behavioral Component

FIGURE 98.1. A conceptual scheme showing the three-stage process in selecting a treatment for an individual. The first step, the Classification Decision, groups individuals into four levels according to percent overweight. Each level dictates which of the five steps would be reasonable in the second stage, the Stepped Care Decision. This process indicates that the least intensive, costly, and risky approach will be used from among alternative treatments. The third stage, the Matching Decision, is used to make the final selection of a program and is based on a combination of client and program variables. The dashed lines with arrows between the Classification and Stepped Care stages show the lowest level of treatment that may be beneficial, but more intensive treatment is usually necessary for people at the specified weight level. From Brownell and Wadden (1991, p.162). Copyright 1991 by Association for Advancement of Behavior Therapy. Reprinted by permission.

classification decision based on percentage overweight. This classification defines a range of treatments that are potentially effective for individuals in a given range of weights. As with traditional classification schemes, aggressive treatments with some risk are considered suitable only for persons who are significantly overweight, since for such persons treatments known to result in small weight losses would be considered inadequate.

The second stage of decision making involves a stepped-care philosophy in which the least expensive, costly, difficult, and dangerous approaches would be undertaken as the first line of intervention, reserving approaches that rate higher on these dimensions for treatment failures. A stepped-care approach is designed to maximize cost-effectiveness, but cost and effectiveness are not necessarily related; hence the need for a third decision stage.

The third stage is a final matching decision, in which individual matching factors are used to select from among eligible treatments defined by the first two stages. A list of possible factors is shown to the far right of Figure 98.1 and include program factors (e.g., convenience) and client factors (e.g., binge eating).

Brownell and Wadden have provided an example of the means by which the entire process would be used. An individual who is 50% overweight would be considered to be at level 3 for the classification decision, which would effectively rule out the treatments listed in levels 1, 2, and 5 in making the stepped-care decision. The eligible treatments from stepped-care levels 3 and 4 would be considered in the third step, which involves the individual matching factors. For instance, a person may need professional nutrition instruction and medical monitoring, suggesting the suitability of a hospital-based program.

The authors of this matching scheme acknowledge that it has not been tested. The same is true of other matching schemes that, as noted above, rely on weight as the only matching criterion. Given limitations in the effectiveness of current treatments for obesity, a study of the utility of matching schemes is a top priority.

A Survey of Obesity Experts

The matching schemes discussed above have been proposed but not tested, so it is unknown whether the criteria chosen for matching are optimal. Schwartz and Brownell conducted a survey of 25 leading experts in the obesity field to determine whether there was a consensus on matching factors. The experts were asked about 11 approaches: dieting on one's own, 12-Step programs (e.g., Overeaters Anonymous), exercise programs, commercial programs with group support (e.g., Weight Watchers), commercial programs with food (e.g., Jenny Craig), university-based behavioral programs, very-low-calorie diets (VLCDs), residential programs, medication, and surgery.

Summed across the responses of the 25 experts, 170 matching criteria were suggested. Of these, only five factors were listed by more than 50% of the experts: (1) mild to moderate obesity is an indication for dieting on one's own; (2) except when medical complications exist, everyone should exercise; (3) VLCDs are appropriate only when moderate to morbid obesity exists; (4) private counseling is indicated when a psychiatric disturbance exists; and (5) massive/morbid obesity is necessary to justify surgery.

These results are striking in the lack of guidance they provide for matching. Exercise is recommended in all cases; hence it provides no means for distinguishing among different approaches. Three of the five criteria are based on weight and follow the general and untested classification sentiment that dominates the field. The need for individual counseling is somewhat more helpful, although this criterion applies to a minority of the individuals who seek treatment.

Even with their collective clinical and research experience, which is vast, these experts did not generate consistent matching criteria. This observation emphasizes both the absence of and the need for data from which to make matching judgements.

MATCHING INDIVIDUALS TO WEIGHT LOSS GOALS

The aim of nearly all weight loss programs is to reduce weight to the ideal level. In spite of the lofty, if not impossible, nature of this ambition, the practice of assigning goal weights using height–weight tables is very common. Even when such tables are not used, programs generally do little to explore and modify the unrealistic goal weights many individuals set for themselves.

Several investigators have proposed a focus on "reasonable weights." These are weights based on a realistic assessment of the likelihood that a person will lose enough to reach a specific weight, the degree of effort and restraint necessary to remain at that weight, a family history of obesity, and other factors (see Chapter 88). The guiding principle is that some individuals will not or cannot attain ideal weights and will suffer from repeatedly losing and regaining weight or become resigned to the excess weight. Establishing reasonable goals may lead to smaller losses initially but to better maintenance eventually. Given the medical benefits of modest weight losses (see Chapter 71), the need for research on the effectiveness of setting reasonable goals is clear.

Criteria for establishing reasonable weights have been proposed but have not been tested extensively (see Chapter 88). One approach is represented by the questions listed in Table 98.1. These questions are the kind a clinician might pose to a client to open a discussion about establishing a reasonable weight goal.

CONCLUSIONS AND RECOMMENDATIONS FOR FUTURE WORK

The traditional approach to treating obesity, which involves a search for one best program that can applied en masse, has been disappointing. Obesity is a heterogenous disorder with many causes and consequences; hence the likelihood that different individuals will respond to different treatments.

The study of matching individuals to treatments is at a very early stage, so even the most descriptive work is necessary. Possible matching criteria must be generated and then tested. Ultimately, controlled studies are needed in which subjects who are characterized according to matching variables are randomly assigned to different treatments or are matched and mismatched to different treatments in some systematic way.

The public health burden of obesity is so high that bold steps must be taken to explore not only new methods for prevention and treatment but new conceptual approaches to how these methods will be targeted toward individuals. Because work on this topic is so challenging, only a concerted effort to organize and support such research by governmental agencies will advance the field in a significant way.

TABLE 98.1. Questions Used to Develop a Reasonable Weight Goal for an Individual

1. Is there a history of excess weight in your parents or grandparents?
2. What is the lowest weight you have been able to maintain as an adult for at least 1 year?
3. What is the largest clothing size in which you feel comfortable and can say, "I look pretty good considering where I have been?"
4. Think of a time when you were at a lower weight. What degree of food restriction and/or exercise did it require to stay at that weight? Could you maintain the same degree of effort for the long term? If not, what level of effort do you feel would be reasonable?
5. Think of a friend or family member with your frame and age who you feel looks normal. What does this person weigh?

Note. These questions are based on data from Brownell and Rodin (1990) and are based on clinical impressions. Research on the topic has not been done.

FURTHER READING

Bray, G. A., York, B., & DeLany, J. (1992). A survey of the opinions of obesity experts on the causes and treatment of obesity. *American Journal of Clinical Nutrition, 55,* 151S–154S. A survey of obesity experts who attended a scientific meeting, in which respondents were asked which treatments they believed were most effective.

Brownell, K. D., & Rodin, J. (1990). *Weight maintenance survival guide.* Dallas: American Health Publishing. A practical guide to the maintenance of weight loss, with a focus on how to determine a reasonable weight.

Brownell, K. D., & Wadden, T. A. (1991). *Behavior Therapy, 22,* 153–177. An early discussion of a matching scheme in which other factors besides weight were used as matching criteria. The proposed scheme involved an integrated, three-stage approach involving classification, stepped care, and matching stages.

Brownell, K. D., & Wadden, T. A. (1992). Etiology and treatment of obesity: Understanding a serious, prevalent, and refractory disorder. *Journal of Consulting and Clinical Psychology, 60,* 505–517. An overview of the etiology and treatment of obesity, with special attention to the issues of "reasonable weight" and of matching individuals to treatments.

Prochaska, J. O., DiClemente, C. C., & Norcross, J. C. (1992). In search of how people change: Applications to addictive disorders. *American Psychologist, 47,* 1102–1114. A major review and theoretical article on the stages and processes of change across different addictive disorders.

Project MATCH Research Group. (1993). Project MATCH: Rationale and methods for a multisite clinical trial matching patients to alcoholism treatment. *Alcoholism: Clinical and Experimental Research, 17,* 1130–1145. A description of the most ambitious research project yet undertaken on matching individuals to treatments (in this case, for alcoholism).

Schwartz, M. B., & Brownell, K. D. (in press). Matching individuals to treatments: A survey of obesity experts. *Journal of Consulting and Clinical Psychology.* A survey of experts in the obesity field that showed surprisingly little agreement on criteria for matching individuals to treatments.

· 99 ·

PUBLIC HEALTH APPROACHES TO THE MANAGEMENT OF OBESITY

Robert W. Jeffery

The prevalence of obesity in the United States is high and has increased steadily in recent years. This situation, in combination with evidence linking obesity to a variety of negative health and social consequences, makes it an important public health problem. The purpose in this chapter is to discuss the treatment of obesity from a public health perspective. Its primary thesis is that there are important differences between the medical and the public health views on the problem and that these differences have implications for treatment.

Public health interventions for obesity should not simply be thought of as medical interventions disseminated on a larger scale. A public health perspective leads to a consideration of environmental strategies that are quite different from those used in the clinical management of obesity. Here the success of the current generation of community programs for obesity control is described and alternative public health approaches are proposed.

PUBLIC HEALTH VERSUS MEDICAL MODELS

Differences between medical and public health models of obesity begin with the definition of obesity itself. From a medical perspective, obesity is an individual-level variable. Patients are obese because their body fatness is high compared with population norms or biological ideals. From a public health perspective, however, obesity is defined in terms of average fatness in the population as a whole or the percent of the population who exceed a certain fatness level (prevalence). Obesity is a public health problem when its prevalence in a population is higher than that of other groups.

Following from the differences between public health and medical models in defining obesity are differences in the emphasis given to causal variables. Because the medical model is conceptually predicated on the individual, in it the search for the causes in variables that differ between individuals is emphasized. These causes include individual differences in genetic endowment and in acquired characteristics (biological, psychological, and behavioral) that make some individuals more susceptible to obesity than others.

In the public health model of obesity individual differences are also recognized as a source of variability. To determine why some populations are more obese than others, however, focus of the model has been also on factors outside the individual, in particular on the environmental conditions that lead to differences in the exposure of populations as a whole to factors that promote obesity.

It is not totally clear at this juncture what specific types of exposure contribute to population obesity. However, plausible suspects are certainly a food supply that is high in energy density, high in palatability, and low in cost, and the widespread availability of labor-saving technologies that have eliminated the need for physical activity as part of everyday life. In the public health model of obesity individual- and population-level causes are seen as intertwined. The main driving force behind the prevalence of obesity in the general population is its exposure to environmental conditions that promote high energy intake and a sedentary life-style. The extent to which specific individuals are affected by exposure to these conditions, however, is dictated to a large degree by individual differences in susceptibility.

MODELS FOR INTERVENTION

Intervention strategies for obesity are derived from causal models. Interventions derived from the medical model are based on the attempt to alter individual susceptibilities, treating the environment as a constant. In some interventions in this domain, the aim is to modify biological susceptibility through pharmacological or surgical methods. In others, still within the same framework, the focus is to strengthen people's ability to cope with an adverse environment by providing education and skills training to develop psychological and behavioral adaptations.

Public health interventions for obesity can also be approached from an individual perspective. Indeed, virtually all public health efforts to date have been in this domain. These efforts have focused on strategies for disseminating education and behavioral-skills training programs to wide audiences at a low unit cost. Among these strategies are school-based education programs for youth, mass media education, work-site interventions, home correspondence approaches, and community programs involving multiple component programs.

Unfortunately the results of these programs have not yet been impressive in addressing the public health problem of obesity. The general population is acutely aware of the problem of obesity, and a high proportion report taking direct action to control their weight. Individual programs have also been successful in inducing large numbers of people to participate, and those who do usually achieve some weight loss. Nevertheless, at the population level these programs have so far had only a negligible effect on the prevalence of obesity.

TREATING THE ENVIRONMENT

An as yet unexplored aspect of the public health model of obesity intervention is one in which the environment rather than the individual is treated as the focus of change. In intervention strategies in this domain the focus is to reduce the exposure of the entire population to factors that promote obesity.

A wide range of strategies have been employed in public health to address population exposure to disease-promoting agents. By way of illustration and to stimulate further inquiry, six that may have applicability to population obesity are briefly discussed below. For purposes of illustration, dietary fat is singled out as an obesity-causing agent, although similar arguments would be applicable to other environmental causes as well.

Modifying Environmental Abuse Potential

The first of these public health strategies is to reduce the abuse potential of the environment. In this strategy it is recognized that people are exposed to many potentially harmful substances in the environment and efforts are made to reduce the potential for harm by imposing environmental safety standards. Successful examples of this strategy include mandating safety glass in automobiles to reduce crash injuries and regulating the lead content of paint. For obesity, two possible strategies in this domain are suggested. One would be to regulate the calorie or fat density of food products so that their consumption in normal quantities would be less likely to contribute to obesity. A second would be to regulate the size of the packages in which high-fat products are sold, in an effort to reduce the likelihood that purchasers will consume too much of such a product.

Controlling Advertising

A second public health strategy is to control commercial advertising practices. The principle behind the regulation of advertising practices is to limit the ability of special interest groups to encourage the use of products by population groups for whom they would constitute a significant hazard, or to require that factual information be provided to consumers to help them make wiser decisions about the use of these products. The limitation of cigarette advertising is a current example of such a strategy, as is the recent addition of health warning labels on alcoholic beverages. For obesity, two possible uses of this strategy are again suggested. One is to improve nutrition labeling or product packaging so that people are better able to assess whether food products have abuse potential, and some progress is being made in this area. A second is to directly restrict the promotion of high-fat food items (e.g., the advertising of high-fat foods on children's television programs).

Controlling Sales Conditions

A third public health strategy is to control the conditions under which products are sold. The purpose of this measure is to limit exposure to hazardous substances, either in vulnerable subgroups or in the population as a whole. Children are a particularly vulnerable group for a variety of products. Thus we have minimum age laws for the use of tobacco, alcohol, and automobiles. More broadly, we also recognize that unlimited access to alcohol poses a threat to the general population, and in most jurisdictions there are restrictions on the number of outlets and the hours of sale. Similar restrictions might be directed at products that contribute to obesity. For example, high-fat, low-nutrient foods might be removed from school vending machines and publicly supported school lunch programs, and the number of outlets for the distribution of foods with high abuse potential might be reduced through licensing policies.

Controlling Prices

The fourth public health strategy is to control exposure by controlling prices. Excise taxes on alcohol and tobacco, for example, are in place partly because they reduce consumption. An analogous strategy might be adopted with respect to dietary fat. Excess dietary fat contributes to obesity as well as to other negative health outcomes. An excise tax on fat would increase the cost of high-fat foods and act as a disincentive to fat consumption. For producers, it would encourage the development of a wider array of low-fat products.

Improving Environmental Controls

A fifth public health strategy is to impose environmental controls to minimize adverse consequences. Environmental control strategies are those in which both the risks inherent in the use of certain products and the likelihood of their use are recognized. These measures would be an attempt to modify the environment so as to reduce the degree of harm. Successful examples of environmental control strategies are roadway and home engineering standards, which reduce the likelihood that individual carelessness will result in dire consequences. For obesity, environmental control strategies might focus on exercise. Exercise appears to protect against obesity. Thus policies that increase the availability and affordability of exercise participation might have a positive influence on population obesity.

Improving Public Health Education

The final strategy is public health education. It seems likely, based on current data, that educational strategies in which individuals are simply exhorted to change their behavior will have limited utility as either a clinical or a public health approach. However, education can have other functions; it can help destigmatize the problem of obesity and accurately portray the costs and probability of success of alternative treatment options. In addition, education can help develop a greater awareness in the general population of the extent to which broader environmental conditions contribute to the problem and the potential that exists for changing the environment.

One problem in discussing public health interventions for obesity in the environmental domain is that hard data to support these ideas is scarce. However, the results of a recent small-scale study that bears on one of these issues will be described. The study took place in a public cafeteria over a 9-week period. In the first 3 weeks, daily purchases of fruit and salad were observed. In the next 3-week period, the variety of salad and fruit selections was increased and their price was reduced by 50%. In the final 3 weeks, baseline conditions were reinstated. This environmental manipulation had a dramatic impact on the purchasing behavior of cafeteria patrons. There were no changes in the number of cafeteria patrons throughout the study. However, the amount of both fruit and salad purchases tripled during the period of environmental change. Although this study was clearly limited in scope, it highlights the important point that substantial changes in eating behavior can be achieved in a defined population without any educational efforts at all concerning the healthiness of fruit or of salad, simply by changing the choices available and their relative cost.

CONCLUSIONS

I have argued here that medical and public health models of obesity differ in important ways. They differ in the way they define the problem of obesity, in the variables that are emphasized in their etiological models, and also in treatment approach. The medical model focuses on individual difference variables, whereas the public health model also incorporates the manipulation of a broad range of environmental influences. To date, public health interventions have been focused largely on mass dissemination of individual-oriented change strategies. These strategies have not been markedly effective. An area that deserves further study is whether environmental strategies, some of which have been quite successful in other health domains, might not also be successfully applied to the management of obesity as a population problem.

FURTHER READING

Bush, P. J., Zuckerman, A. E., Theiss, P. K., Taggart, V. S., Horowitz, C., Sheridan, M. J., & Walter, H. J. (1989). Cardiovascular risk factor prevention in black schoolchildren: Two-year results of the "Know Your Body" program. *American Journal of Epidemiology, 129,* 466–482. Describes the results of a large study in which the effectiveness of a multicomponent, school-based intervention in reducing cardiovascular risk factors, including obesity, were evaluated.

Flegal, K. M., Harlan, W. R., & Landis, J. R. (1988). Secular trends in body mass index and skinfold thickness with socioeconomic factors in young adult women. *American Journal of Clinical Nutrition, 48,* 535–543. Describes the recent trend in the population prevalence of obesity in young women, using a nationally representative cohort sample.

Jeffery, R. W., & Forster, J. L. (1987). Obesity as a public health problem. In W. G. Johnson (Ed.), *Advances in eating disorders* (pp. 253–271). Greenwich, CT: JAI Press. A theoretical/conceptual article in which the public health perspective on obesity and implications for intervention are outlined.

Jeffery, R. W., Forster, J. L., French, S. A., Kelder, S. H., Lando, H. A., McGovern, P. G., Jacobs, D. R., & Baxter, J. E. (1993). The Healthy Worker Project: A work-site intervention for weight control and smoking cessation. *American Journal of Public Health, 83,* 395–401. Results of a 2-year work-site intervention program for obesity and smoking in which a combination of education and payroll-based incentives were used. It is unique among work-site studies in that a randomized design was used and results were assessed based on the entire work force rather than on program participants.

Jeffery, R. W., Gray, C. W., French, S. A., Hellerstedt, W. L., Murray, D., Luepker, R. V., & Blackburn, H. (in press). Evaluation of weight reduction in a community intervention for cardiovascular disease risk: Changes in body mass index in the Minnesota Heart Health Program. *International Journal of Obesity, 18.* An evaluation of the results of the Minnesota Heart Health Program, as well as those of the Stanford Five-Cities Project (see Taylor et al., below). These two studies represent the state of the art in community trials conducted during the 1980s.

Price, R. A. (1987). Genetics of human obesity. *Annals of Behavioral Medicine, 9,* 9–14. A brief review of genetic studies on obesity.

Stunkard, A. J., Cohen, R. Y., & Felix, M. R. J. (1989). Weight loss competitions at the worksite: How they work and how well. *Preventive Medicine, 18,* 460–474. A compilation of several research projects undertaken to examine weight control programs in work sites that use team competition as a motivational procedure.

Taylor, C. B., Fortmann, S. P., Flora, J., Kayman, S., Barrett, D. C., Jatulis, D., & Farquhar, J. W. (1991). Effect of long-term community health education on body mass index. *American Journal of Epidemiology, 134,* 235–249. Findings on obesity from the Stanford Five-Cities Project, a 10-year research project designed to reduce cardiovascular risk factors in entire communities.

VanItallie, T. B. (1985). Health implications of overweight and obesity in the United States. *Annals of Internal Medicine, 103,* 983–988. A review of health risks associated with obesity. The review was prepared for a National Institutes of Health (NIH)-sponsored consensus conference on the topic.

Wadden, T. A., & Stunkard, A. J. (1985). Social and psychological consequences of obesity. *Annals of Internal Medicine, 103,* 1062–1067. A review of the social–psychological correlates of obesity, prepared for an NIH-sponsored consensus conference on the topic.

· 100 ·

COMPASSIONATE TREATMENT OF THE OBESE INDIVIDUAL

Thomas A. Wadden
Barbara J. Wingate

It is hard to imagine the prejudice and discrimination that overweight individuals endure (see Chapter 73). Having read the literature on this topic, a skeptical reporter donned a new hairstyle and a special body suit that appeared to more than double her petite figure and then set off for an afternoon of shopping. She was shocked by what she encountered. "Here I was, a 250-pound *invisible* woman. People in stores and elevators, even my own colleagues at work, refused to make eye contact with me; they treated me as if I didn't exist. The only time I was acknowledged was with dirty looks, snickers, and nasty remarks."

Nasty remarks can be found even in our nation's respected news weeklies. Thus the author of a recent "My Turn" column in *Newsweek* wrote, "This information (about genetic determinants of obesity) should be withheld from the fat multitudes because the obese will latch onto any excuse for failing to lose weight. . . . Face it Chubbo, when was the last time you were force-fed." These sentiments illustrate all too clearly that obesity is still regarded by lay persons, and many practitioners, as a moral rather than a medical problem. It is attributed to indulgence, lack of willpower, and similar failings, accusations that allow lean individuals to feel morally superior. Regrettably, many overweight individuals have internalized this view at the expense of their self-esteem and self-respect.

For most overweight individuals, efforts to lose weight often exacerbate rather than heal their psychological injuries (see Chapters 16 and 17). A small percentage enjoy lasting weight control, but the great majority experience shame, frustration, and humiliation as they lose and regain weight in full view of family, friends, coworkers, and heath care providers. Rather than criticizing treatment programs for their inadequacies, most dieters blame themselves, an attribution frequently echoed by professionals in comments such as, "I guess you weren't ready to be thin," or, "You must not have worked hard enough on your eating and exercise habits." Such remarks only add insult to injury, particularly since neither patient nor practitioner fully understands the complex interaction of behavioral and biological factors responsible for weight regain.

COMPASSIONATE TREATMENT: RESPECT AND CONCERN

Traditionally the principal goal of obesity treatment has been to reduce excess weight to control health complications such as diabetes and hypertension. This goal should be

564

complemented, however, by efforts to reduce weight-related distress. This latter goal can be accomplished in two general ways. First, the practitioner must understand patients' frustration and disappointment with their weight and communicate this understanding to the patients. Second, the practitioner should not add further injury to patients' self-esteem by criticizing, directly or indirectly, their weight control efforts when success eludes them. Adherence to the principles described below should help establish a favorable patient–practitioner relationship and convince overweight individuals that they have been treated with respect and concern. Thus practitioners should strive to:

1. Understand that overweight individuals are not all the same. They differ in the factors that have contributed to their weight problem and in the effect their obesity has on their lives. This realization is as important for patients as it is for practitioners.

2. Foster autonomy by actively involving patients in the decisions about the goals and methods of treatment. Patients who embrace weight control are usually more successful than those who feel it is imposed upon them. Moreover, inviting patients to participate in treatment decisions acknowledges their competence and value.

3. Treat with respect patients' reports of their eating and exercise habits, particularly when such reports are inconsistent with changes in their weight or health status.

4. Encourage patients to discuss their feelings about their weight and listen nondefensively when they report disappointment or frustration with their treatment and weight loss.

5. Provide a consistent and supportive relationship throughout all phases of treatment, particularly during periods of relapse.

6. Help patients realize their self-worth and that it is independent of their weight.

7. Examine their own feelings about obesity, as well as their successes and failures in working with this problem, all of which will affect their interactions with overweight individuals.

In the remainder of this chapter, we highlight the application of these principles during the initial assessment, weight reduction, and long-term care. The chapter is written primarily with women in mind, who generally suffer more than men from the pain of obesity (see Chapters 15 and 73). Regardless of the nearly equal prevalence of obesity between the sexes, women outnumber men four to one in commercial weight loss programs, despite the fact that they usually have fewer health complications (because of their lower-body fat patterning). Whatever the cultural or biological influences, our society still encourages women to believe they cannot be attractive or desirable unless they are thin (see Chapter 15).

INITIAL ASSESSMENT

Weinsier has described in Chapter 82 the initial medical evaluation of the overweight individual, while Stunkard, as well as Wadden and Foster, have outlined a behaviorally-oriented interview designed to assess the patient's weight and dieting histories, eating and exercise habits, psychosocial status, and goals and expectations of treatment. Both types of assessment are required to make informed decisions about patients' treatment needs and options. Practitioners in both settings should remember that at an initial visit patients are often anxious about the practitioner's reaction to their obesity, whether the provider can help them, and whether they deserve help, given their history of perceived failure. Patients appreciate the practitioner's acknowledgement of these worries.

Psychosocial History

The initial part of a behavioral interview should be devoted to getting to know the individual. Thus the practitioner may inquire about the patient's: (1) satisfaction with work; (2) intimate relationships (i.e., partner, children, and friends) and social functioning; (3) hobbies and interests; and (4) current life goals and challenges. The patient should be encouraged to discuss how weight affects and is affected by these factors and what changes are anticipated with weight reduction.

In addition, the practitioner should determine what has led the patient to seek weight reduction at this particular time. Most obese individuals have been overweight for months, if not years, before seeking treatment. Usually something has happened that now makes their obesity intolerable. Such precipitants may include poor physical health or depression, prodding by a spouse or employer, or the hope that their job opportunities and social lives will improve with weight loss. Each individual has a personal story to tell. Frequently patients have experienced disappointment, sadness, or other emotions that should be addressed before weight loss is considered. Brief paper-and-pencil tests, such as the Beck Depression Inventory, provide a useful assessment of mood that can be followed by specific inquiries, including those about the history and duration of the problem.

Eating Disorders

The assessment of the patient's weight and dieting history, as well as eating and exercise habits, provides important information concerning the etiology and type of the patient's obesity (as described by Wadden and Foster). In obtaining such information, the practitioner should assess whether the patient has an eating disorder. Binge eating disorder occurs in approximately 20% to 30% of overweight persons who seek professional help for weight control and is frequently accompanied by depression, body image disparagement, and other difficulties (see Chapter 78). This disorder represents a clear case in which "overweight individuals are not all the same." A history of bulimia or anorexia similarly presents a more complicated clinical picture that requires careful treatment planning.

Summary and Treatment Decisions

Patients benefit greatly from receiving, near the end of the interview, a verbal summary of the practitioner's findings. The summary illustrates that the practitioner has listened carefully and also provides an opportunity to educate patients about the specific causes and consequences of their obesity. The summary might include information about the genetics of obesity, which frequently reduces feelings of guilt and failure in severely obese persons by suggesting that "it's not all my fault." Not all the news will perhaps be as welcome—for example, that food intake is greatly underestimated by both obese and lean individuals—but it will be useful. At the conclusion, the practitioner should invite the patient's feedback concerning the summary.

The patient should also be invited at this time to discuss goals concerning weight and health. Janet, a patient treated with a very-low-calorie diet pondered the following questions before treatment:

"How thin do I want to be? How thin can I become? What weight can I maintain? How much exercise will I have to do? How much food will I have to forego? In short, what am I willing to sacrifice for thinness? All these questions assume that I have answered the most fundamental question for anyone who has been grossly overweight and who losses weight: What is thinness?"

The practitioner's task is to help patients clarify their goals and assess whether these goals are reasonable (see Chapters 88 and 98). Thus the practitioner might suggest that a goal weight of 80 kilograms seems more reasonable than one of 60 kilograms for a woman who currently weighs 100 kilograms and has not weighed 60 kilograms since age 12. On the other hand, the need for weight reduction might be emphasized to an overweight, unmotivated 30-year-old man, given the clear hazards of his upper body fat patterning. In both cases, the clinician should provide information that allows the patient to make an informed decision, rather than making the decision for the individual. Treatment options should be reviewed and selected in a similar manner.

WEIGHT REDUCTION

In the next two sections it is assumed that patient and practitioner have decided that weight loss is desirable (although other decisions are possible) and have selected a treatment approach. The practitioner should discuss the general course and duration of therapy to enable the patient to establish realistic expectations and understand the goals for behavior change. It is critical that patients participate in treatment planning from the outset because it is they, not the practitioner, who implement therapy. It is also important to address several related issues. How frequent will office visits be? Will patients weigh in at each visit, and, if so, will they measure themselves or be weighed by the practitioner? What happens when the patient cannot keep an appointment? Will treatment visits generally follow a set agenda or a more open-ended course? These are relatively minor issues, but they can present problems later on if not addressed at the outset.

Difficulties during Weight Loss

Treatment is usually gratifying for both patient and practitioner as long as the patient loses weight consistently. Both, however, may become frustrated and discouraged when the patient fails to lose weight satisfactorily for 2 or more weeks. Two situations are common; they are addressed below.

Excellent Adherence

The patient may report excellent adherence and expect the practitioner to explain (and correct) the lack of weight loss. All too often, clinicians react by impugning the accuracy of the patient's self-reports, saying something to the effect of, "It's impossible not to lose weight if you're really sticking to the diet." Thus a frustrated practitioner criticizes an already frustrated and demoralized patient with a statement that can only undermine their alliance.

A more appropriate response, if the practitioner suspects nonadherence, might be: "I can understand why you're frustrated. You're not losing weight and you don't have a good answer for it. It is frustrating. Let's concentrate on the things that you can control here, your eating and exercise habits. Let's examine your portion sizes and calories to make sure that we're not missing anything. Would that be okay?"

Alternatively, if the practitioner is confident about the patient's adherence, he or she might encourage the patient to evaluate success on the basis of behavior change, not weight, with the expectation that the two will eventually fall in line. This approach should only be taken, however, after the practitioner first acknowledges the patient's frustration and disappointment. It is difficult to seek new solutions until such feelings have been expressed and heard.

Poor Adherence

In a second common situation, a patient who has not lost weight for several weeks reports that she has been eating "junk" and has not been exercising. "I don't know what's going on. I just haven't been able to get into it lately."

Practitioners frequently find such patients difficult because they appear unmotivated and do not make good use of their treatment. Thus a provider might be tempted to state, "You don't really seem to be trying. You're the only one who can help yourself." Such statements do little to help the individual understand the difficulties she is having. Such help might be provided by exploring the circumstances of her overeating, mood and social interactions, or feelings about treatment.

Pride and Prejudice

A patient's failure to lose weight or, more often, to maintain a weight loss, implicitly challenges the practitioner's professional competence and self-esteem. Practitioners present themselves as experts who deserve patients' confidence, trust, and substantial remuneration. They may strongly believe that their training and skills are far superior to those of "counselors" who staff commercial weight loss programs. A patient's failure to lose weight threatens the practitioner's self-esteem. This threat is heightened, sometimes to the point of being intolerable, by a patient's statement that the practitioner does not "seem to have any new answers" or is otherwise unhelpful.

Practitioners often fail to realize that the emotions they experience at such times (e.g., frustration, annoyance, incompetence) are the very same feelings experienced by patients. Practitioners may attempt to preserve their professional esteem at the expense of the patient. Rather than acknowledging the patient's feelings of frustration and inadequacy, practitioners may accentuate these feelings with dismissive pronouncements such as, "This program has worked for dozens of other people. I don't know why it's not for you." Too often, professionals' own prejudices toward overweight individuals are brought to bear in defense of their treatment.

What is required is an honest, constant, and supportive relationship in which patients can discuss their troubled feelings and be secure that the practitioner will not be defensive. Such a relationship permits the practitioner to challenge a patient's motivation without injuring self-esteem. For example, after hearing that a patient has not exercised or maintained a food diary for the past month and has gained 3 pounds, the practitioner might state, "Tell me what happened with your exercise this month. You said at our last meeting that you thought exercise was the most important activity for your success."

What should practitioners do when they experience frustration, annoyance, or related feelings in working with overweight patients? Talk with their colleagues. Speaking with a colleague can be of invaluable assistance, not only in "letting off steam" but in identifying the specific patient–practitioner interactions that are causing difficulty. Starting a weekly case supervision group, attending conferences, and reading the weight-control literature can all support practitioners in their efforts to support their patients.

LONG-TERM CARE

Most significantly overweight individuals require long-term treatment, similar to the treatment of hypertension and diabetes. Research to explore the optimal structure and components of long-term care has only just begun.

It is essential to maintain a supportive, accepting relationship that encourages patients to return for help when they need it. The relationship must be able to overcome the feelings of shame, guilt, and isolation that accompany relapse (see Chapters 96 and 97). During weight loss, the practitioner and patient should discuss the possible occurrence of overeating and weight regain and the resulting thoughts and emotions the patient is likely to experience at such times. They should identify the specific factors that might inhibit the patient from contacting the practitioner and then rehearse methods to facilitate such contact. Regularly scheduled meetings—on a monthly, bimonthly, or quarterly basis—are also likely to increase patients' feelings that they have support and can ask for help whenever they need it.

Support Groups

Patients should also be encouraged to explore whether a support group might be helpful (see Chapters 88 and 97). Such groups differ markedly in their treatment philosophies and in the experiences they offer. An understanding of the patient's specific needs will help determine the most appropriate group, whether it is Weight Watchers (which takes an educational approach to weight loss), Overeaters Anonymous (which addresses compulsive eating using group support), or the National Association to Aid Fat Acceptance (NAAFA; which seeks to foster self-acceptance).

WEIGHT AND SELF-ACCEPTANCE

Some might argue that compassionate treatment and weight reduction are at odds with each other. If most diets end in failure, then truly compassionate treatment should encourage obese individuals to accept their size and themselves (see Chapters 16 and 17). The emotional energy saved in relinquishing this battle could then be used to enjoy other activities (and perhaps to fight the weight-related prejudice and discrimination that afflict our society).

This view deserves consideration. It is embraced by the members of NAAFA, whose diligent efforts have helped reduce prejudice and discrimination against overweight Americans and have prompted practitioners to examine their usual bias that "thinner is better." Thus practitioner and patient together must weigh the costs and benefits of weight control. For persons with clear and significant medical complications, efforts to control weight may seem imperative, whereas for those without such complications, the battle may not be worth the costs. Different patients often make different choices, reflecting that overweight individuals are not all the same.

ACKNOWLEDGMENTS

Preparation of this chapter was supported by National Institute of Mental Health Research Scientist Development Award No. KO2 MH00702-06 and by Grant No. RO1 MH49451-02, both to Dr. Wadden.

FURTHER READING

Brownell, K. D. (1991). Dieting and the search for the perfect body: Where physiology and culture collide. *Behavior Therapy, 22*, 1–12. The author describes our nation's preoccupation with weight and dieting, the assumptions that underlie it, and the compromises that many must reach with their bodies.

French, S. A., & Jeffery, R. W. (1994). Consequences of dieting to lose weight: Effects on physical and mental health. *Health Psychology, 13*, 195–212. In this review the authors conclude that the adverse effects of dieting have been overstated in many cases.

Garner, D. M., & Wooley, S. C. (1991). Confronting the failure of behavioral and dietary treatments for obesity. *Clinical Psychology Review, 11*, 729–780. The authors argue that "all diets fail" and that most weight control efforts rob overweight individuals of their self-esteem and well-being.

Jasper, J. (1992). The challenge of weight control: A personal view. In T. A. Wadden & T. B. VanItallie (Eds.), *Treatment of the seriously obese patient* (pp. 411–434). New York: Guilford Press. The author describes her efforts to achieve an acceptable weight and the methods she uses to maintain it.

Rand, C. S. W., & Macgregor A. M. C. (1990). Morbidly obese patients' perceptions of social discrimination before and after surgery for obesity. *Southern Medical Journal, 83*, 1390–1395. Approximately 80% of subjects surveyed reported that, because of their obesity, they had been treated disrespectfully by health care providers.

Stunkard, A. J. (1993). Talking with patients. In A. J. Stunkard & T. A. Wadden (Eds.), *Obesity: Theory and therapy* (pp. 355–363). New York: Raven Press. In this chapter the author alerts practitioners to the importance of listening to their overweight patients and provides a model for obtaining weight, dieting, and psychosocial histories.

Wadden, T. A., & Foster, G. D. (1992). Behavioral assessment and treatment of markedly obese patients. In T. A. Wadden & T. B. VanItallie (Eds.), *Treatment of the seriously obese patient* (pp. 290–330). New York: Guilford Press. The authors provide an overview of an initial behavioral assessment and a method for summarizing key findings for the patient.

Wadden, T. A., & Stunkard, A. J. (1993). Psychosocial consequences of obesity and dieting. In A. J. Stunkard & T. A. Wadden (Eds.), *Obesity: Theory and therapy* (pp. 163–177). New York: Raven Press. In this chapter the authors summarize findings concerning prejudice and discrimination toward overweight individuals, as well as the psychosocial consequences of dieting.

Yalom, I. (1989). *Love's executioner and other tales of psychotherapy.* New York: Basic Books. This book contains a chapter entitled the "The Fat Lady," in which the author describes his countertransference toward an overweight patient whom he treated in psychotherapy.

• 101 •

PREVENTION OF OBESITY

Albert J. Stunkard

Our current understanding of the prevention of obesity can summarized in one sentence: We have not been able to prevent obesity in the past, and we do not have the tools to do better in the future. Despite the epidemic of dieting, the proliferation of low-fat foods, the popularity of jogging, and the $30-billion weight reduction industry, the prevalence of obesity in the United States continues to rise. Today, when it is so popular to call for the prevention of disease, it is well to remember these facts and not to invest in currently inadequate measures designed to prevent obesity.

The appeal of prevention is clear. It can be quick, economical and very effective, and it can spare suffering and greatly reduce the cost of disease. Examples of the success of prevention inspire awe. In the 1850s, John Snow removed the handle of the Broad Street pump and stopped the cholera epidemic that was devastating an area of London. Two centuries ago, Jenner's crude vaccination helped to control smallpox; and today's more sophisticated vaccines have essentially wiped out poliomyelitis, the most dreaded infectious disease of its time.

Such heroic feats have fueled the hopes of those who call for the prevention of disease. But there is no parallel between the prevention of cholera and the prevention of obesity. Cholera was prevented by removal of the causative agent, the cholera vibrio; treatment became unnecessary. Even the modern success in lowering the rates of coronary heart disease has depended largely upon the control of the contributing causes, especially smoking and hypertension.

Far from removing the causes of obesity, efforts at prevention have been little more than watered-down versions of treatment, which has itself proven incapable of achieving long-term weight loss. Prevention and treatment share the same (behavioral) conceptual framework and, although efforts at prevention have been attempted to target groups (as Jeffery notes in Chapter 99), virtually all public health interventions for obesity have had an individual perspective.

By the criterion of group versus individual focus, the one program that might be considered a success of prevention was, in fact, a treatment program. Epstein's follow-up of a small, controlled trial of behavioral treatment showed that children who had received treatment 10 years before were less overweight than those who had not (see Chapter 91).

Such results of treatment may be considered "secondary prevention," that is, prevention of further worsening of a condition that is already established. It is, of course, possible that the vast treatment efforts of the American people have had this kind of secondary preventive effect; without all this treatment the prevalence of obesity might have increased more rapidly than it has. Unfortunately, we have no way of knowing whether this is the case.

EVALUATING PREVENTION EFFORTS

What measures of change would be the most effective assessment of the impact of prevention on groups of obese people? The most intuitively obvious measure appears to be a reduction in the prevalence of obesity. This measure has been used, but it presents problems.

The definition of obesity for epidemiological purposes is arbitrary, depending on nothing more than the selection of a particular cutting point in a continuous distribution. Just as estimates of the prevalence of obesity have varied at the whim of the most recent weight standards, so will estimates of the effectiveness of preventive measures vary with the criteria. Furthermore, estimates of prevalence will also be compromised by the relatively small numbers at the right tail of the distribution (see Chapter 68).

A more stable estimate of change is provided by measures of central tendency. Such estimates are highly correlated with the prevalence of obesity, since the relation between the mean and the tail of the distribution of body mass index (BMI) is an orderly one. Any shift in the mean is reflected in the tail, and the stability of measures of central tendency far exceeds that of the tail. Similar analyses of alcohol consumption have shown that the mean consumption in the population strongly predicts consumption in the tail, which consists, as does the tail of the BMI, of the clinically affected.

TYPES AND EFFECTS OF PREVENTION PROGRAMS

Using as a criterion the size of the target population, three types of programs may be considered to be preventive: work-site programs, school programs, and community programs. Enough research has been carried out with work-site programs to make it clear that they can reach large numbers of overweight persons at very low cost and that they are instrumental in helping a large percentage of them achieve modest weight reductions. Unfortunately it has also become clear that the maintenance of these weight losses is no better, and may be worse, than the disappointing results of clinical programs.

School-based programs may meet the criterion of a large target population. However, the seven chapters on obesity prevention in the recently published volume on the prevention and treatment of childhood obesity, which deal with much of what is known about the topic, contain no evidence that a school-based program has ever prevented obesity.

The most critical test of the ability to prevent obesity is provided by four well-funded, large-scale community programs of health promotion that have been carried out during the past 15 years. Since these attempts were multiple risk-factor intervention programs, it was possible to compare the impact of the programs on obesity with their impact on smoking, high blood pressure, and serum cholesterol levels. Such comparison showed that obesity is far harder to control than are other coronary risk factors.

It should be noted that the prevention of obesity was not the primary target of any of these programs. Yet each contained ambitious projects designed to control obesity that should have been facilitated by the overall efforts at health promotion. Neverthe-less, none slowed the powerful secular trend toward an increase in the prevalence of obesity (see Chapter 68), and none has provided the long-term evaluation that would be necessary to determine whether obesity had been prevented.

The Stanford Three-Community Study

This study was a 2-year attempt to reduce coronary risk factors in two small towns in California through a health promotion program that relied largely on an intensive media campaign. The program achieved a significant reduction in coronary risk factors other than obesity but had no effect on the secular increase in the prevalence of obesity, which occurred in the intervention and control communities alike. Reflecting the greater sensitivity of measures of central tendency noted above, however, there was a small difference in mean increase in body weight favoring the intervention community. Whereas body weight in the control community manifested the expected secular in-crease, although it was no more than a modest 0.45 kilogram, body weight in the intervention community showed no change. The statistical significance of the difference between the communities in this large study was no more than $p < .04$. By contrast, there were substantial decreases in each of the other coronary risk factors.

The Stanford Five-City Study

This study was an ambitious 5-year health promotion program in which the experience with the Stanford Three-Community Study was used to replicate and extend its findings. Changes in risk factors in two small cities with a total population of 123,000 were compared with those in two carefully selected control cities with a total population of 198,000. Only morbidity and mortality were measured in the fifth city. The intensive intervention program moved beyond the primary media emphasis of the earlier one to include extensive face-to-face contact, community organization, work-site treatment, and other organized community events.

Two types of samples were assessed: One was a cohort of persons followed across the entire period of the study; the other involved independent cross-sectional samples of the population. Once again several coronary risk factors were found to be significantly reduced—smoking, blood pressure, and serum cholesterol levels in the cohort sample, and blood pressure and serum cholesterol levels in the independent samples. Once again obesity fared badly. In the cohort sample there was a marked increase in the BMI of subjects in both intervention and control cities, with no difference between the two, while the increase in the prevalence of obesity (3.5%) in the *intervention* cities was even greater than that in the control cities (1.6%). The BMI showed a striking increase (from 2% to 5%) in both the intervention and the control cities, with no difference between the two.

In the comparison of the independent samples, results were more favorable in the intervention cities. Although all cities showed the secular increase in weight, that in the intervention cities (BMI of 0.57 kilograms) was slightly less than that in the control cities (BMI of 1.25 kilograms).

The North Karelia Study

This study was a 5-year health program in the Finnish province with the highest rate of coronary heart disease in Finland, which had, in turn, the highest rate of coronary heart disease in the world. The program succeeded in reducing coronary risk factors (22%, compared with a reduction of 12% in a control community). The only risk factor for which there was no change was obesity. The experimental and control communities differed in neither prevalence of obesity nor in weight gain.

The Minnesota Heart Health Program

This study was a 7-year multicomponent community health promotion program whose effects were compared in three sets of two communities each—one urban, one suburban, and one rural. The results of this program differed from those of the other three community studies in that the intervention had little more effect on the other risk factors than it had on obesity. During the course of the trial there were strong and favorable secular trends in the reduction of risk factors other than obesity and little evidence that the intervention programs accelerated these secular trends. By contrast, the secular trend in body weight was unfavorable, and a variety of highly imaginative weight reduction programs at work sites and in the community had no effect on the increase in BMI.

THE FUTURE

The striking increase in obesity and in mean weight levels in this country must be due to social forces (see Chapter 14). If social forces can produce these effects, it seems reasonable to believe that social forces can reverse them. We do not, however, know which social forces might reverse the increase in obesity, nor how to mobilize them. We do know that our interventions have been largely educational and focused on the individual. It seems reasonable to move beyond such measures to include efforts to effect broad changes in the environment. Jeffery suggests how environmental changes might help reduce the exposure of large populations to factors that promote obesity (see Chapter 99).

One environmental change would be to improve the quality of the food served in school lunch programs and factory cafeterias and to limit access to high-fat foods in all facilities supported by public funds. Other measures might include controlling the advertising of junk foods and labeling processed foods in an intelligible manner. Finally, we may consider the ultimate social reinforcer—subsidization of the production of healthy foods and taxation of the production of unhealthy foods.

Whether obesity is seen as a problem severe enough to persuade the American people to endorse such broad-ranging changes in policy is an open question. The answer to this question as well as to questions of the effectiveness of environmental measures to prevent obesity lies in further research.

FURTHER READING

Epstein, L. H., Valoski, A., Wing, R. R., & McCurley, J. (1990). Ten-year follow-up of behavioral, family-based treatment for obese children. *Journal of the American Medical Association, 264,* 2519–2523. A description of the only study to show an enduring effect of treatment for obesity.

Farquhar, J. W., Fortmann, S. P., Flora, J. A., Taylor, C. B., Haskell, W. L., Williams, P. T., Maccoby, N., & Wood, P. D. (1990). Effects of community-wide education on cardiovascular disease risk factors: The Stanford Five-City Project. *Journal of the American Medical Association, 264,* 359–365. Farquhar and his team followed up their first study with the very ambitious program described in this article.

Farquhar, J. W., Maccoby, N., & Wood, P. D. (1977). Community education for cardiovascular disease. *Lancet, i,* 1192–1195. The landmark report of health promotion at the community level (see Farquhar et al., 1990).

Jeffery, R. W., Folsom, A. R., Luepker, R. V., Jacobs, D. R., Gillum, R. F., Taylor, H. L., & Blackburn, H. (1984). Prevalence of overweight and weight loss behavior in a metropolitan adult population: The Minnesota Heart Survey experience. *American Journal of Public Health, 74,* 349–352. A description of the first, disappointing results of the large-scale Minnesota Heart Health Program.

Luepker, R. V., Murray, D. M., Jacobs, D. R., et al. (in press). Community education for cardiovascular disease prevention: Risk factor changes in the Minnesota Heart Health Program. *American Journal of Public Health.* Ten years after Jeffery's first report, Luepker et al. summarize the final, disappointing results of the Minnesota Study.

Puska, P., Salonen, J., Nissinen, A., et al. (1983). Change in risk factors for coronary heart disease during 10 years of community intervention programme: North Karelia Project. *British Medical Journal, 287,* 1840–1844. The definitive description of the pioneering Finnish study that had the greatest success in mobilizing the community for health.

Stunkard, A. J., Cohen, R. Y., & Felix, M. R. J. (1989). Weight loss competitions at the work site: How they work and how well. *Preventive Medicine, 18,* 460–474. A summary of the results of weight loss competition at the work site.

Taylor, C. B., & Stunkard, A. J. (1993). Public health approaches to weight control. In A. J. Stunkard & T. A. Wadden (Eds.), *Obesity: Theory and therapy* (pp. 335–353). New York: Raven Press. This chapter provides what may be the best overall description of public health approaches to weight control.

Williams, C. L., & Kimm, S. Y. S. (Eds.). (1993, October 29). Prevention and treatment of childhood obesity. *Annals of the New York Academy of Sciences, 699.* The authors of this volume, the most recent publication dealing with the prevention of childhood obesity, find no evidence that obesity can be prevented.

INDEX